OXFORD IB DIPLOMA PROGRAMME

2ND EDITION

PSYCHOLOGY

COURSE COMPANION

Alexey Popov
Lee Parker
Darren Seath

OXFORD
UNIVERSITY PRESS

Great Clarendon Street, Oxford, OX2 6DP, United Kingdom

Oxford University Press is a department of the University of Oxford. It furthers the University's objective of excellence in research, scholarship, and education by publishing worldwide. Oxford is a registered trade mark of Oxford University Press in the UK and in certain other countries

British Library Cataloguing in Publication Data
Data available

978-0-19-839811-0

10 9 8 7 6 5 4 3

Paper used in the production of this book is a natural, recyclable product made from wood grown in sustainable forests. The manufacturing process conforms to the environmental regulations of the country of origin.

Printed in United Kingdom by Bell and Bain Ltd, Glasgow

Acknowledgements

The author and publisher are grateful for permission to reprint extracts from the following copyright material:

Ajzen, Icek: 'The theory of planned behaviour is alive and well, and not ready to retire: a commentary on Sniehotta, Presseau, and Araújo-Soare' from Health Psychology Review, Vol. 9, Issue 2, published by Taylor & Francis, 2015, reprinted by permission.

Allport, Gordon W: The Nature of Prejudice, Copyright 1954 by Perseus Books Publishing L.L.C., reprinted by permission of Perseus Books, a member of the Perseus Books Group, permission conveyed through Copyright Clearance Center, Inc.

Baddeley, Alan: 'Exploring the central executive', in The Quarterly Journal of Experimental Psychology, 1996, Vol. 49A, (1), pp. 5-28, reprinted by permission of the publisher (Taylor & Francis Ltd., www.tandfonline.com).

Baron, Jonathan: Thinking and Deciding (fourth edition), Cambridge University Press, 2008.

Bower, GH, Black, JB and Turner, TJ: 'Scripts in memory for text', in Cognitive Psychology, 1979, Vol. 11, pp. 177-220, reprinted by permission of Elsevier.

Bransford, JD & Johnson, MK: p. 719, in Visual Information Processing, 1973, W G Chase, New York, Academic Press, reprinted by permission of Elsevier.

Burbank, V. K: 'Fighting Women. Anger and Aggression in Aboriginal Australia', Berkeley: University of California Press, (1994), reprinted by permission of University of California Press Books.

Center for Science in the Public Interest: report 'Carbonating the World – The Marketing and Health Impact of Sugar Drinks in Low- and Middle-income Countries', reprinted by permission.

Cutler, WB, Friedmann, E and McCoy, NL: 'Pheromonal influences on sociosexual behavior in men' by, in Archives of Sexual Behavior, 1998, Vol. 21, number 1, pp. 1–13, reprinted by permission of Springer.

Hamilton, M: 'A rating scale for depression', 1960, in Journal of Neurology, Neurosurgery, and Psychiatry, Vol. 23, pp. 56-62, reprinted by permission of BMJ Publishing Group Ltd.

Holmes, Thomas H and Rahe, Richard H: abridged version of table 'The Social Readjustment Rating Scale' in Journal of Psychosomatic Research, 1967, Vol. 11, Issue 2, pp. 213-218, Copyright 1967, reprinted by permission of Elsevier.

Johnson, D H and Johnson F P: Joining Together: Group Theory and Group Skills, 1st Ed., © 1975, reprinted by permission of Pearson Education, Inc., New York, New York.

International Baccalaureate Organization: various extracts from IB Diploma Programme Psychology Guide © International Baccalaureate Organization, 2017.

Kabat-Zinn, J: 'Some reflections on the origins of MBSR, skilful means, and the trouble with maps' in Contemporary Buddhism, 2011, Vol. 12, 1, pp. 281-306, reprinted by permission of the publisher (Taylor & Francis Ltd), http://www.tandfonline.com.

Kahneman, D and Tversky, A: 'The framing of decisions and the psychology of choice', in Science, Vol. 211, pp. 453–458, reprinted by permission of AAAS.

Selye, H: 'The General-Adaptation-Syndrome' in Annual Review of Medicine, 1951, Vol. 2, pp. 327-342, © by Annual Reviews, http://www.annualreviews.org, reprinted by permission of Annual Reviews.

Skinner, BF: ''Superstition' in the pigeon', in Journal of Experimental Psychology, 1948, Vol. 38 (2), pp. 168–172, this material is in the public domain.

Talarico, JM and Rubin, DC: 'Confidence, not consistency, characterizes flashbulb memories', 2003, in Psychological Science, Vol 14, 5, SAGE Journals.

World Health Organization: report 'World Health Statistics 2016'

http://www.who.int/gho/publications/world_health_statistics/2016/en/, copyright WHO 2016, reprinted by permission.

World Health Organization: 'Obesity and overweight' – Fact sheet N°311 - updated June 2016, http://www.who.int/mediacentre/factsheets/fs311/en/, copyright WHO 2016, reprinted by permission.

World Health Organization, Health Topics, Health Promotion, http://www.who.int/topics/health_promotion/en/, copyright WHO, reprinted by permission.

World Health Organization: 'Fiscal Policies for Diet and Prevention of Non-communicable Diseases', copyright WHO, 2016, reprinted by permission.

Although we have made every effort to trace and contact all copyright holders before publication, this has not been possible in all cases. If notified, the publisher will rectify any errors or omissions at the earliest opportunity.

Photo and artwork permissions are continued on the last page

Course Companion definition

The IB Diploma Programme Course Companions are resource materials designed to support students throughout their two-year Diploma Programme course of study in a particular subject. They will help students gain an understanding of what is expected from the study of an IB Diploma Programme subject while presenting content in a way that illustrates the purpose and aims of the IB. They reflect the philosophy and approach of the IB and encourage a deep understanding of each subject by making connections to wider issues and providing opportunities for critical thinking.

The books mirror the IB philosophy of viewing the curriculum in terms of a whole-course approach; the use of a wide range of resources; international-mindedness; the IB learner profile and the IB Diploma Programme core requirements; theory of knowledge; the extended essay; and creativity, action, service (CAS).

Each book can be used in conjunction with other materials and indeed, students of the IB are required and encouraged to draw conclusions from a variety of resources. Suggestions for additional and further reading are given in each book and suggestions for how to extend research are provided.

In addition, the Course Companions provide advice and guidance on the specific course assessment requirements and on academic honesty protocol. They are distinctive and authoritative without being prescriptive.

IB mission statement

The International Baccalaureate aims to develop inquiring, knowledgable and caring young people who help to create a better and more peaceful world through intercultural understanding and respect.

To this end the IB works with schools, governments and international organizations to develop challenging programmes of international education and rigorous assessment.

These programmes encourage students across the world to become active, compassionate, and lifelong learners who understand that other people, with their differences, can also be right.

The IB learner profile

The aim of all IB programmes is to develop internationally minded people who, recognizing their common humanity and shared guardianship of the planet, help to create a better and more peaceful world. IB learners strive to be:

Inquirers   They develop their natural curiosity. They acquire the skills necessary to conduct inquiry and research and show independence in learning. They actively enjoy learning and this love of learning will be sustained throughout their lives.

Knowledgable   They explore concepts, ideas, and issues that have local and global significance. In so doing, they acquire in-depth knowledge and develop understanding across a broad and balanced range of disciplines.

Thinkers   They exercise initiative in applying thinking skills critically and creatively to recognize and approach complex problems, and make reasoned, ethical decisions.

Communicators   They understand and express ideas and information confidently and creatively in more than one language and in a variety of modes of communication. They work effectively and willingly in collaboration with others.

Principled   They act with integrity and honesty, with a strong sense of fairness, justice, and respect for the dignity of the individual, groups, and communities. They take responsibility for their own actions and the consequences that accompany them.

Open-minded They understand and appreciate their own cultures and personal histories, and are open to the perspectives, values, and traditions of other individuals and communities. They are accustomed to seeking and evaluating a range of points of view, and are willing to grow from the experience.

Caring They show empathy, compassion, and respect towards the needs and feelings of others. They have a personal commitment to service, and act to make a positive difference to the lives of others and to the environment.

Risk-takers They approach unfamiliar situations and uncertainty with courage and forethought, and have the independence of spirit to explore new roles, ideas, and strategies. They are brave and articulate in defending their beliefs.

Balanced They understand the importance of intellectual, physical, and emotional balance to achieve personal well-being for themselves and others.

Reflective They give thoughtful consideration to their own learning and experience. They are able to assess and understand their strengths and limitations in order to support their learning and personal development.

A note on academic honesty

It is of vital importance to acknowledge and appropriately credit the owners of information when that information is used in your work. After all, owners of ideas (intellectual property) have property rights. To have an authentic piece of work, it must be based on your individual and original ideas with the work of others fully acknowledged. Therefore, all assignments, written or oral, completed for assessment must use your own language and expression. Where sources are used or referred to, whether in the form of direct quotation or paraphrase, such sources must be appropriately acknowledged.

How do I acknowledge the work of others?
The way that you acknowledge that you have used the ideas of other people is through the use of footnotes and bibliographies.

Footnotes (placed at the bottom of a page) or endnotes (placed at the end of a document) are to be provided when you quote or paraphrase from another document, or closely summarize the information provided in another document. You do not need to provide a footnote for information that is part of a 'body of knowledge'. That is, definitions do not need to be footnoted as they are part of the assumed knowledge.

Bibliographies should include a formal list of the resources that you used in your work. The listing should include all resources, including books, magazines, newspaper articles, Internet based resources, CDs and works of art. 'Formal' means that you should use one of the several accepted forms of presentation. You must provide full information as to how a reader or viewer of your work can find the same information. A bibliography is compulsory in the extended essay.

What constitutes misconduct?
Misconduct is behaviour that results in, or may result in, you or any student gaining an unfair advantage in one or more assessment component. Misconduct includes plagiarism and collusion.

Plagiarism is defined as the representation of the ideas or work of another person as your own. The following are some of the ways to avoid plagiarism:

- Words and ideas of another person used to support one's arguments must be acknowledged.

- Passages that are quoted verbatim must be enclosed within quotation marks and acknowledged.
- CD-ROMs, email messages, web sites on the Internet, and any other electronic media must be treated in the same way as books and journals.
- The sources of all photographs, maps, illustrations, computer programs, data, graphs, audio-visual, and similar material must be acknowledged if they are not your own work.
- Works of art, whether music, film, dance, theatre arts, or visual arts, and where the creative use of a part of a work takes place, must be acknowledged.

Collusion is defined as supporting malpractice by another student. This includes:

- allowing your work to be copied or submitted for assessment by another student

- duplicating work for different assessment components and/or diploma requirements.

Other forms of misconduct include any action that gives you an unfair advantage or affects the results of another student. Examples include, taking unauthorized material into an examination room, misconduct during an examination, and falsifying a CAS record.

Contents

Introduction

This book is a Course Companion for students of psychology in the International Baccalaureate Diploma Programme at higher and standard levels.

It is designed to be used extensively both in class and at home. We have tried to provide deep coverage of all topics in the syllabus, focusing on a variety of arguments supported by both classic and contemporary research. Your job is to study the material along with the discussions and activities that you have in class, take notes, make mind maps and use other techniques to "compress" the information and understand the topics. When you eat, you chew the food before swallowing it, which helps you digest the food better. This Course Companion is no different: if you want to digest it, you need to chew it (this is a metaphor, so please do not literally chew the book).

To help you, the book has a number of features that you can use to enhance your learning skills.

- Inquiry questions at the start of every section will encourage you to think about problems that do not have an easy solution. Take a stance, but be ready to change it as you discover new knowledge.

- Material provided in the text will equip you with a range of arguments and evaluation points to deepen the inquiry questions and uncover their hidden dimensions.

- These arguments will be supported with empirical research, because knowledge in psychology is procedural: in order to understand it fully, you need to know how it was obtained.

- "What you will learn in this section" boxes will help you summarize the key points.

- "This section also links to" will support you in making links between topics—this is an

important skill because human behaviour is complex and should be studied in all its aspects.

- "Psychology in real life" features will apply the concepts discussed in the text to some real-life scenarios, to help you see the vast practical applications.

- "ATL skills" will suggest a number of questions and activities for you and your classmates to develop your learning skills further, and help you become better researchers and communicators.

- TOK links will challenge you to see knowledge concepts behind key psychological terms, allowing you to compare psychology meaningfully to other disciplines.

- Exercises and links to external materials (such as videos and research papers) will take you beyond this book while at the same time staying focused on the topics relevant to the syllabus.

There are two overarching themes in everything that we are discussing in this book: research and ethics. Research is important because every claim in psychology has a history of discovery behind it. Ethics is important because the focus of research in psychology is living beings—human and non-human animals—so research needs to be done responsibly.

Your teacher will provide you with information from the IB psychology subject guide: aims of the course, list of topics that you need to know, assessment requirements and criteria. Remember to refer to this information so that you clearly understand what is expected of you at all times.

Psychology is a journey full of exciting discoveries—but no spoilers—you will see for yourself.

Alexey Popov, Lee Parker, Darren Seath

RESEARCH METHODOLOGY

Topics

Introduction

This unit deals with research methods used in psychology. In any discipline, knowledge of research methods greatly increases our ability to understand a topic. Psychology is not an exception. The ability to evaluate psychological knowledge critically on the basis of how it was obtained is essential to avoid misconceptions.

Speaking of misconceptions, there are plenty of them in this field. Psychology is a popular discipline which makes it vulnerable to numerous popular interpretations. So it is important to clearly understand what psychology is and what it is not.

Knowledge of methods also allows you to see the whole research process clearly, with all its strengths and limitations. When studying the material in this chapter, you will no longer take statements like "British psychologists have discovered …" at face value. You will read between the lines and understand what was done by the "British psychologists" and to what extent their inferences are justified.

Psychology is a special discipline. On the one hand, it is scientific, which means that psychologists, just like physicists or chemists, rigorously test hypotheses and eliminate competing explanations in an attempt to achieve objective knowledge. On the other hand, unlike natural sciences that study "nature", psychology studies humans, inherently subjective creatures. So psychology is an attempt to study the subjective (for example,

the mind) objectively. Not an easy task, if you think about it.

This unit may seem a little abstract to you but it builds an important foundation for the understanding of the material in all other units. Applying the knowledge and skills related to research methodology, you will be able to critically evaluate knowledge in specific areas of psychology and arrive at balanced conclusions, avoiding misconceptions and unjustified generalizations. We will keep referring you back to this unit so that you can apply and reinforce the concepts related to research methodology.

We start by discussing the definition of psychology, what it is and what it is not. Then we introduce two broad groups of research methods: quantitative and qualitative. These two groups of methods differ dramatically in their rationale and objectives, but at the same time can be combined to complement each other in a holistic investigation. Following this, we discuss four overarching concepts that apply to both quantitative and qualitative research: sampling, credibility, generalizability and bias. Next, we look at the application of these concepts separately in quantitative (experiments, correlational studies) and qualitative research. Finally, any discipline that involves research with living beings needs to adhere to the principles of ethics. We discuss ethical considerations in psychological research.

1

- What is scientific psychology?
- How can we tell if a research study is credible?
- How can we study subjective phenomena objectively?
- How is correlation different from causation?
- How is quantitative research different from qualitative research?

What you will learn in this section

- What is psychology?
  - Psychology is the scientific study of behaviour and mental processes
  - Science and non-science
  - Behaviour and mental processes
  - A study of non-human animals
  - What IB psychology is not

- Research methodology: quantitative and qualitative methods
  - Qualitative versus quantitative comparison
  - Types of quantitative research: experimental, correlational, descriptive
  - Types of qualitative research
- Sampling, credibility, generalizability and bias in research: an overview

What is psychology?

"Psychology is the scientific study of behaviour and mental processes." This is the definition we are going to use throughout this book. Although it is quite a short definition, there are a lot of implications in it. Let's try and uncover them one by one.

Psychology is the scientific study... This part of the definition excludes such areas as pop psychology, that is, simple and appealing explanations that are not backed up by empirical evidence. What makes a theory or a study scientific, or where is the line between science and non-science? This is largely a TOK question and you will return to it throughout the book, but here are some major points.

- It should be supported by empirical evidence and be based on this evidence.

- It should be falsifiable, that is, it should be possible for the theory or study to be proven wrong.

- There should be a history of independent attempts to test the theory or replicate the study.

Exercise

Look at the following research questions and pick one that you find interesting:

1. Do children who watch more violent TV shows become more violent?

2. Does extrasensory perception exist?

3. Are women attracted to men by the smell of their body?

4. Is abuse experienced differently in heterosexual and gay relationships?

5. Are breathing exercises effective for reducing test anxiety?

6. What emotions do people experience when watching horror movies in a cinema?

7. Are people in arranged marriages happier than people who married by choice?

If you were to conduct a research study to answer the question that you picked, how would you go about it? Think about details such as who your participants would be, what they would be required to do, how you would measure results and how you would ensure that the results are believable.

Das lesende und rechnende Pferd, mit seinem Lehrer HERRN von OSTEN (Berlin)

▲ Figure 1.1 Wilhelm von Osten and Clever Hans

In the early twentieth century, under the influence of Charles Darwin's theory of evolution, the public was very interested in animal intelligence: if humans evolved from animals, animals must be at least partially intelligent, so what exactly are they capable of? The case of Clever Hans sparked a lot of interest. Hans was a horse. Its owner Wilhelm von Osten, a mathematics teacher, claimed that he had taught Hans to solve arithmetic problems (addition, subtraction, multiplication, division, fractions), read, spell and understand some German. Questions could be asked verbally or in writing, and Hans would respond by tapping his hoof a certain number of times. Von Osten exhibited the horse frequently and gained a lot of public attention. A special committee was formed in Germany (called the Hans Commission). They ran a series of tests and concluded that the performance was not a fraud. So Hans's abilities were officially recognized as phenomenal!

However, another independent investigation carried out later by Oskar Pfungst, a psychologist, yielded different results. It demonstrated that Hans could not actually perform mental operations such as multiplication, but the horse was very responsive to clues that were provided by unsuspecting humans. To arrive at these conclusions, Pfungst successively tested a number of alternative hypotheses.

1. What if spectators give the horse hints or clues? He tested the horse and the questioner in the absence of spectators, but the horse continued to solve tasks correctly anyway.

2. What if von Osten himself gives the horse some clues? Another questioner was used during several trials, but the horse's performance did not worsen.

3. What if something in the questioner gives the correct answer away and the horse can feel that? Blinders were used to test this hypothesis. It turned out that when Hans was wearing blinders responses (the number of hoof taps) were incorrect most of the time. So, it was something in the questioner after all.

4. Did the questioners consciously let the horse know the correct answer, though? Additional trials were organized so that the questioner either knew or did not know the answer to the questions. It turned out that Clever Hans could only answer the questions correctly when the questioner knew the answer in advance.

This changed the focus of research from the horse to the questioner. When Pfungst carried out his observations, it was concluded that questioners who knew the answers had a tendency to become more tense as the hoof tapping approached the correct answer which would be reflected in their posture and facial expressions without them realizing it. This was probably the clue that the horse was using. This makes sense evolutionarily, as detection of small postural changes is important as a survival skill for horses in the wild. Clever Hans certainly was clever, but the nature of his abilities was not mathematical (Goodwin, 2010)!

ATL skills: Thinking

How does Pfungst's investigation illustrate the concepts of empirical evidence, falsification and replication?

Von Osten himself, however, was never convinced of Pfungst's findings and he continued to exhibit the horse throughout Germany, gaining as much popularity as before. Nonetheless, scientifically, this was one of the starting points for designing rigorous experimental methodology in psychology and other human sciences. It was recognized that experiments, if not carefully controlled, could produce **artifacts**—results that are associated with the effect of unforeseen factors. *not presented naturally*

This whole story shows how claims can and should be tested scientifically, that is, by conducting a systematic evidence-based investigation that puts forward one hypothesis after another and tests them in a rigorous fashion. Note also how the whole investigation attempted to falsify the existing theory rather than support it.

… study of behaviour and mental processes. A scientific investigation requires an empirical approach to research, that is, relying on observation as a means of data collection. On the other hand, psychology (which comes from the Greek *psyche* = soul and *logos* = study, "the study of the soul") concerns itself with a wealth of phenomena, many of which are not directly observable. The first step in solving this dilemma is to identify something that can be observed directly. That's **behaviour**. Behaviour is everything that can be registered by an independent observer: it includes overt actions as well as gestures, facial expressions, verbal responses, endocrine reactions and so on. What stays "behind the scene" are the **mental processes** such as attention, perception, memory and thinking. We cannot observe them directly (which led some psychologists to say that they represent a "black box" and cannot be studied

scientifically), but we can observe the indirect effects mental processes have on one's behaviour. So, we can infer something about the mental world as well.

ATL skills: Thinking

Brainstorm some behavioural indicators of the following:

- attention *eye contact*
- anxiety *darting eyes, restricted body language fixing = stay rooted*
- embarrassment. *flushed face, self-comforting body language - hand in wrong hands*

To what extent do you think is it possible to use behavioural indicators to infer these "internal" phenomena? Would the inference be reliable?

Throughout this book we will use the term "behaviour" to refer to external, observable manifestations while the term "mental processes" will be used to denote internal patterns of information processing. However, you need to be aware of the fact that the term "behaviour" is often used in a more general sense, as an umbrella term for everything psychological. So sometimes you will encounter references to mental processes as types of "behaviour". This is not exactly accurate, but acceptable.

Note that the definition of psychology does not specify human behaviour or mental processes. This is because research with non-human animals is also an integral part of psychology. Since humans are just a stage in the continuous process of evolution, the study of animals may inform our understanding of human behaviour (and mental processes).

IB psychology is an academic discipline with an emphasis on rigorous research and scientific knowledge, but psychology is broader than pure academics and research. When people think about psychology many imagine counsellors and psychotherapists, practitioners who work with individual clients. University workers in lab coats conducting research is not the first thing that comes to mind. However, IB psychology focuses on academic knowledge and scientific research rather than counselling skills. This is because thorough understanding of psychological concepts and being able to think critically about psychological phenomena is of paramount importance in all spheres of psychology, including counselling. It makes perfect sense to start with building these skills, much like the need to study aerodynamics before you are allowed to pilot an airplane.

Research methodology: quantitative and qualitative methods

All research methods used in psychology can be categorized as either quantitative or qualitative. Data in quantitative research comes in the form of numbers. The aim of quantitative research is usually to arrive at numerically expressed laws that characterize behaviour of large groups of individuals (that is, universal laws). This is much like the aim of the natural sciences in which it has been the ideal for a long time to have a set of simple rules that describe the behaviour of all material objects throughout the universe (think about laws of gravity in classic Newtonian physics, for example). In philosophy of science such orientation on deriving universal laws is called the **nomothetic approach**.

Quantitative research operates with **variables**. A variable ("something that can take on varying values") is any characteristic that is objectively registered and quantified. Since psychology deals with a lot of "internal" characteristics that are not directly observable, they need to be **operationalized** first. For this reason, there's an important distinction between **constructs** and **operationalizations**.

A construct is any theoretically defined variable, for example, violence, aggression, attraction, memory, attention, love, anxiety. To define a construct, you give it a definition which delineates it from other similar (and dissimilar) constructs. Such definitions are based on theories. As a rule constructs cannot be directly observed: they are called constructs for a reason—we have "constructed" them based on theory.

To enable research, constructs need to be operationalized. Operationalization of a construct means expressing it in terms of observable behaviour. For example, to operationalize verbal aggression you might look at "the number of insulting comments per hour" or "the number of swear words per 100 words in the most recent Facebook posts". To operationalize anxiety you

might look at a self-report score on an anxiety questionnaire, the level of cortisol (the stress hormone) in the bloodstream or weight loss. As you can see, there are usually multiple ways in which a construct may be operationalized; the researcher needs to use creativity in designing a good operationalization that captures the essence of the construct and yet is directly observable and reliably measurable. As you will see throughout examples in this book, it is often a creative operationalization that makes research in psychology outstanding.

> ### ATL skills: Research and communication
>
> In small groups think of operationalizations of the following constructs: belief in God, assertiveness, shyness, pain, love, friendship, prejudice, tolerance to uncertainty, intelligence, wisdom.
>
> Is it equally easy to operationalize them?
>
> Discuss each other's operationalizations and outline their strengths and limitations.

There are three types of quantitative research.

- **Experimental studies**. The experiment in its simplest form includes one **independent variable** (IV) and one **dependent variable** (DV), while the other potentially important variables are controlled. The IV is the one manipulated by the researcher. The DV is expected to change as the IV changes. For example, if you want to investigate the effect of psychotherapy on depression, you might randomly assign participants to two groups: the experimental group will receive psychotherapy while the control group will not. After a while you might measure the level of depression by conducting a standardized clinical interview (diagnosis) with each of them. In this case the IV is psychotherapy. You manipulate the IV by changing its value: yes or no. The DV is depression; it is operationalized through the standardized diagnostic procedure. If the DV is different in the two groups, you may conclude that a change in the IV "caused" a change in the DV. This is why the experiment is the only method that allows **cause-and-effect inferences**. conclusion via evidence & reasoning

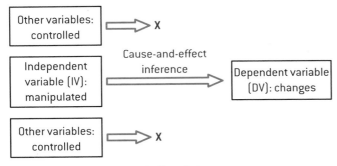

▲ Figure 1.2 Cause-and-effect inference

- **Correlational studies.** Correlational studies are different from experiments in that the researcher does not manipulate any variables (there are no IVs or DVs). Variables are measured and the relationship between them is quantified. For example, if you want to establish if there is any relationship between violent behaviour of adolescents and how much time they spend watching violent television shows, you may recruit a sample of adolescents and measure their violent behaviour (by self-report, by ratings from classmates or even by observation in a natural setting) and the average number of hours per day spent watching violent television shows. Then you can correlate these two variables using a formula. Suppose you obtained a large positive correlation. This means that there's a trend in the data: the more time an adolescent spends watching violent shows, the more violent he or she is. However, you cannot make cause-and-effect inferences from correlational studies. Since you did not manipulate one of the variables, you do not know the direction of influence. It could be the case that watching violence influences violent behaviour (this would probably be the most popular, intuitive assumption). However, it is also possible that adolescents who behave violently choose to watch violent television programmes. Or there could even be a third variable (for example, low self-esteem) that influences both violent behaviour and watching violence on television. What you observe "on the surface" is just that—"co-relation", the fact that one variable changes as the other one changes.

ATL skills: Communication and social

In small groups come up with results of fictitious studies that would demonstrate either correlation or causation. Here are two examples.

1. In a group of adults we measured their attitudes to horror films and the number of siblings they have. We found that the more siblings you have, the more you like horror films.

2. We told one group of astronauts that their mission would start in a month and the other group that the mission would start in a year. We measured anxiety and found that it was higher in the group of astronauts who expected the mission to start in a month.

As you go through your list of fictitious studies, the other groups will have to say whether the study shows correlation or causation.

- **Descriptive studies**. In descriptive studies relationships between variables are not investigated, and the variables are approached separately. An example of a descriptive quantitative study would be a public opinion survey. We ask questions (for example, "Do you support the current policies of the President?") and we are interested in the distribution of answers to this particular question. Descriptive studies are often used in sociology and they are sometimes used in psychology to conduct a broad investigation of a phenomenon before "delving deeper" into the specifics.

Qualitative research is different. Its main focus is an in-depth study of a particular phenomenon. "In-depth" entails going beyond what can be objectively measured and quantified into the realm of human experiences, interpretations and meanings. Qualitative research makes use of such data collection methods as interviews or observations. Data comes in the form of texts: interview transcripts, observational notes, and so on. Interpretation of data involves a degree of subjectivity, but analysis is deeper than we can usually achieve through quantitative approaches. In philosophy of science such orientation on an in-depth analysis of a particular case or phenomenon (without trying to derive universally applicable laws) is called the **idiographic approach**.

Parameter	Quantitative research	Qualitative research
Aim	Nomothetic approach: derive universally applicable laws	Idiographic approach: in-depth understanding of a particular case or phenomenon
Data	Numbers	Texts
Focus	Behavioural manifestations (operationalizations)	Human experiences, interpretations, meanings
Objectivity	More objective (the researcher is eliminated from the studied reality)	More subjective (the researcher is included in the studied reality)

▲ Table 1.1 Quantitative versus qualitative research

Qualitative research methods that we will discuss in this chapter are:

- observation
- interview
- focus group
- case study
- content analysis.

Sampling, credibility, generalizability and bias in research

Sampling, credibility, generalizability and bias are some of the characteristics used to describe a research study and make a judgment of its quality. These characteristics are universal for social sciences, but they can be approached very differently by quantitative and qualitative researchers, sometimes even with distinctly different sets of terms to express the same ideas. So it is important that you understand both these overarching concepts and the way they are broken down in quantitative as compared to qualitative research. Let's start with the overarching concepts. *all embracing*

A sample is the group of individuals taking part in the research study. **Sampling** is the process of finding and recruiting individuals for the study. There are different sampling techniques, and it is important to be aware of their strengths and limitations as sampling may affect the results of the study. For example, if the aim of your research is to see if anxiety correlates with aggression in teenagers (in general), but you only sample teenagers from one school in a criminal neighbourhood, your sampling technique will have important implications for the conclusions you will be able to make. Similarly, if you study political views of unemployed people and you recruit your sample by asking a small number of participants to bring their friends (and possibly friends of friends), you might end up with a limited sample because people of similar political views are more likely to be friends with each other.

Credibility refers to the degree to which the results of the study can be trusted to reflect the reality. It is closely linked to **bias**, because the results of the study do not reflect reality if there was some sort of bias in it. There are a lot of "traps" that a researcher can walk into. For example, in an interview, while the researcher believes the interviewee's responses to be true, participants may actually guess the aim of the study and respond in a way that they think the researcher is expecting them to. Or researchers themselves, being interested in confirming their hypothesis, may selectively notice supporting evidence and unintentionally ignore contradicting evidence. If there is indication that potential sources of bias were, to the best of our knowledge and abilities, controlled or eliminated, credibility of the research study is believed to be high. Quantitative and qualitative research approaches to credibility and bias are distinctly different, although they overlap in some aspects.

Generalizability refers to the extent to which the results of the study can be applied beyond the sample and the settings used in the study itself. Sometimes, especially in quantitative research, you want to generalize findings from the sample to a much wider group of people (called "population") because your aim is to discover universal laws of behaviour. Sometimes the research study is conducted in artificial settings (for example, a laboratory experiment), but you want to believe that people will behave the same way in their natural setting in daily life too. In any case, generalizability is an important aspect in the interpretation of findings. Again, the ways in which quantitative and qualitative research studies approach generalizability of findings is distinctly different.

The table below gives you an overview of the main concepts used to characterize sampling, generalizability, credibility and bias in experimental, correlational and qualitative research. As you read on, you will understand these concepts better. Refer to this table from time to time so that you place them clearly in the general framework.

Overview table:
Sampling, generalizability, credibility and bias in qualitative and quantitative research

Overarching concepts	Quantitative research		Qualitative research
	Experimental studies	**Correlational studies**	
Sampling	Random Stratified Self-selected Opportunity	Same	Quota sampling Purposive sampling Theoretical sampling Snowball sampling Convenience sampling
Generalizability	External validity: – Population validity – Ecological validity Construct validity	Population validity Construct validity	Sample-to-population generalization Case-to-case generalization Theoretical generalization
Credibility	Internal validity: to what extent is the DV influenced by the IV and not some other variable? Controlling confounding variables: eliminating or keeping constant in all conditions	No special term used: "validity" and "credibility" can be used interchangeably Credibility is high if no bias occurred	Credibility = trustworthiness. To what extent do the findings reflect the reality? Triangulation Establishing a rapport Iterative questioning Reflexivity Credibility checks Thick descriptions
Bias	Threats to internal validity: – Selection – History – Maturation – Testing effect – Instrumentation – Regression to the mean – Experimental mortality – Experimenter bias – Demand characteristics	On the level of measurement of variables: depends on the method of measurement On the level of interpretation of findings: – Curvilinear relationships – The third variable problem – Spurious correlations	Participant bias: – Acquiescence – Social desirability – Dominant respondent – Sensitivity Researcher bias: – Confirmation bias – Leading questions bias – Question order bias – Sampling bias – Biased reporting

▲ Table 1.2

Quantitative research: the experiment

Inquiry questions

- Why do experiments allow cause-and-effect inferences?

- How can bias in experimental research be prevented?

- How can findings from a small group of people be generalized to an entire population?

- How can experiments be designed?

What you will learn in this section

- Confounding variables
- Sampling in the experiment
  - Representativeness
  - Random sampling
  - Stratified sampling
  - Opportunity sampling
  - Self-selected sampling
- Experimental designs
  - Independent measures design
  - Matched pairs design; matching variable
  - Repeated measures design; order effects; counterbalancing
- Credibility and generalizability in the experiment: types of validity
  - Construct validity
  - Internal validity

- External validity: population and ecological
- Bias in experimental research: threats to internal validity
  - Selection
  - History
  - Maturation
  - Testing effect
  - Instrumentation
  - Regression to the mean
  - Mortality
  - Demand characteristics
  - Experimenter bias
- Quasi-experiments versus true experiments
- Natural experiments and field experiments

Confounding variables

As we mentioned, the experiment is the only method that allows researchers to make cause-and-effect inferences. This is achieved by defining the independent variable (IV) and the dependent variable (DV), manipulating the IV and observing how the DV changes in response to this manipulation.

Psychological reality is very complex and the trick is to isolate the IV so that when you manipulate it, nothing else changes. Imagine, for example, that you manipulate X and observe the resulting changes in Y. However, every time you manipulate

X, you also unintentionally change Z. In reality it is Z that causes a change in Y, but you incorrectly conclude that X (your IV) is the cause of Y, thus incorrectly confirming your hypothesis. If this sounds too abstract, think about the following example: X is sleep deprivation (which you manipulate by waking up one group of participants every 15 minutes when they sleep, while the control group sleeps normally) and Y is memory performance (which you measure by a simple memory test in the morning). Without realizing that this might be an important factor, you let the control group sleep at home while the experimental group sleeps in a laboratory being supervised by an experimenter. So there's another variable, variable Z: stress caused by the unfamiliar environment. It could be the case that in this experiment it was the unfamiliar environment (Z) that caused a reduction in memory performance (Y), rather than sleep deprivation (X).

Variables that can potentially distort the relationship between the IV and the DV (like Z in the example above) are called **confounding variables**. They contribute to bias. These variables need to be controlled, either by eliminating them or keeping them constant in all groups of participants so that they do not affect the comparison.

Discussion

How could the researchers have controlled the confounding variable in this example?

Sampling in the experiment

Being a truly nomothetic method, the experiment aims at discovering universal laws of behaviour applicable to large groups of people across a variety of situations. This makes relevant the distinction between the **sample** and the **target population**. The target population is the group of people to which the findings of the study are expected to be generalized. The sample is the group of people taking part in the experiment itself. How can we ensure that whatever results are obtained in the sample can be generalized to the target population? We do this through **representativeness**—the key property of a sample. A sample is said to be representative of the target population if it reflects all its essential characteristics.

Exercise

Imagine you are investigating the influence of praise on the school performance of teenagers. For this experiment you need to have a sample of participants that you would split into two groups (experimental and control). In the experimental group the teacher is instructed to praise every student three times a week while in the control group the teacher is told to only praise the students once every week. At the end of the research period performance grades in the two groups are compared.

Suppose that the participants in this experiment are high school students from one of the schools in your city. Will you be able to generalize the findings to the target population, that is, teenagers in general? This depends on how representative your sample is. For this you need to take into account your target population and the aim of the research.

- The aim of the research links to the **participant characteristics** that are essential. Whatever can theoretically influence the relationship between the IV and the DV is essential. For example, cultural background may be essential for how a teenager reacts to praise (depending on that teenager's cultural attitudes to adults, teachers and authority in general). Socio-economic background may be important as well: theoretically there may be a connection between the socio-economic status of a teenager's family and their value of education. The type of school is another potentially important factor: in top schools where students pursue quality education and prestigious college placements teachers' praise may be a point of pride, whereas in public schools in criminal neighbourhoods it may lead to bullying from classmates.

- If the sample is representative, it must reflect the essential characteristics of the target population. Is the sample of teenagers from one school in our example sufficient to reflect all these characteristics? No, because it does not represent the variation of cultural backgrounds, socio-economic backgrounds and types of schools found in the population.

- If the sample is not representative of the essential characteristics of the target population, there are two ways to fix it: either keep sampling or narrow down the target population and do not claim that the research findings are more generalizable than they really are.

Given the aim of the study, how would you increase representativeness of your sample?

There is no quantitative way to establish representativeness of a sample and it is always the expert decision of a researcher to say whether a particular characteristic is essential or not. This is done on the basis of prior knowledge from published theories and research studies. In any case the choice of the target population needs to be well justified and explicitly explained.

Several **sampling techniques** can be used in an experiment. The choice depends on the aim of the research, available resources and the nature of the target population.

- **Random sampling**. This is the ideal approach to make the sample representative. In random sampling every member of the target population has an equal chance of becoming part of the sample. With a sufficient sample size this means that you take into account all possible essential characteristics of the target population, even the ones you never suspected to play a role. Arguably, a random sample of sufficient size is a good representation of a population, making the results easily generalizable. However, random sampling is not always possible for practical reasons. If your target population is large, for example, all teenagers in the world, it is impossible to ensure that each member of this population gets an equal chance to enter your sample. Being based in Europe, you cannot just create a list of all teenagers in the world, randomly select a sample and then call Lynn from Fiji to come and join your experiment. In

this case you either believe that cross-cultural differences are not essential (for your hypothesis) or narrow down your target population. On the other hand, if your target population is students from your school, it is perfectly possible to create the full list of students and select your participants randomly from this list. An example of random sampling strategy is a pre-election telephone survey where participants are selected randomly from the telephone book (or a random selection of Facebook profiles). Even in this case, though, you have to admit that the target population is not all the citizens of a particular country; it is all the citizens of the country who own a telephone (or have a Facebook profile).

- **Stratified sampling**. This approach is more theory-driven. First you decide the essential characteristics the sample has to reflect. Then you study the distribution of these characteristics in the target population (for this you may use statistical data available from various agencies). Then you recruit your participants in a way that keeps the same proportions in the sample as is observed in the population. For example, imagine that your target population is all the students in your school. The characteristics you decide are important for the aim of the study are age (primary school, middle school, high school) and grade point average—GPA (low, average, high). You study school records and find out the distribution of students across these categories:

	Low GPA	Average GPA	High GPA	Total
Primary school	0%	10%	10%	20%
Middle school	5%	30%	15%	50%
High school	5%	20%	5%	30%
Total	10%	60%	30%	100%

▲ Table 1.3

For a stratified sample you need to ensure that your sample has the same proportions. For every cell of this table you can either sample randomly or use other approaches (see below). In any case, what makes stratified sampling special is that it is theory-driven and it ensures that theory-defined essential characteristics of the population are fairly and equally represented in the sample. This may be the ideal choice when you are certain about essential participant characteristics and when available sample sizes are not large.

- **Convenience (opportunity) sampling**. For this technique you recruit participants that are more easily available. For example, university students are a very popular choice because researchers are usually also university professors so it is easy for them to find samples there. Jokingly, psychology has been sometimes referred to as a study of "US college freshmen and white rats". There could be several reasons for choosing convenience sampling. First, it is the technique of choice when financial resources and time are limited. Second, there could be reasons to believe that people are not that different in terms of the phenomenon under study. For example, if you study the influence of caffeine on attention, there are reasons to believe that results will be similar cross-culturally, and it might be a waste of time to use a stratified or a random sample. Finally, convenience sampling is useful when wide generalization of findings is not the primary goal of your research, for example, if you are conducting an exploratory study and you are not sure the hypothesis will be supported by evidence. If the hypothesis will not "work" in a small sample, why waste time testing it in a representative sample? Or you are replicating someone else's research and your aim is to see if the universal law (that was discovered by this someone) will hold true in your specific sample, thus trying to falsify prior theory. The limitation of convenience sampling is, of course, lack of representativeness.

- **Self-selected sampling**. This refers to recruiting volunteers. An example of this approach is advertising the experiment in a newspaper and using the participants who respond to the advert. The strength of self-selected sampling is that it is a quick and relatively easy way to recruit individuals while at the same time having wide coverage (many different people read newspapers). The most essential limitation, again, is representativeness. People who volunteer to take part in experiments may be more motivated than the general population, or they may be looking for the incentives (in many studies participants are financially rewarded for their time).

Exercise

Now that you know what sampling strategies can be used in an experiment, how would you change your approach to recruiting a sample for the investigation of the influence of praise on school performance of teenagers?

Experimental designs

Experiments always involve manipulating some variables and measuring the change in others. But the specific ways in which this can be organized differ depending on the aims of the research. The organization of groups and conditions in an experiment is known as the experimental design, and there are three basic types of experimental design.

Independent measures design involves random allocation of participants into groups and a comparison between these groups. In its simplest form, you randomly allocate participants from your sample into the experimental group and the control group. Then you manipulate the experimental conditions so that they are the same in the two groups except for the independent variable. After the manipulation you compare the dependent variable in the two groups.

ATL skills: Research

Consider the difference between random sampling (selecting the sample from the target population) and random group allocation (dividing your sample into groups). It is possible to have random group allocation in non-random samples and vice versa.

The rationale behind random group allocation is that all potential confounding variables cancel each other out. If the groups are not equivalent at the start of the experiment, you will be comparing apples to oranges. Imagine that you are testing the hypothesis that praise at school improves students' performance and for this you take two existing groups of students, with one being rarely praised by their teachers and the other one often praised. Arguably, the groups might not be equivalent: they have different experiences with the teachers, different ingroup values and habits, and so on—but to account for all these potentially important factors is impossible.

Conversely, when the group sizes are sufficiently large and allocation is completely random, chances are that groups will be equivalent—the larger the sample, the higher the chance.

Of course, there could be more than two groups, depending on how many IVs you use and how many levels each variable has. In the above example, you could use more than one IV: the influence of praise and the allocation of homework on school performance. With two levels for each of these IVs you would need to randomly allocate participants into four groups:

	Homework given	Homework not given
Rarely praised	1	2
Frequently praised	3	4

▲ Table 1.4

This experimental design with two IVs, each with two levels, is quite frequently used in psychological experiments. It is known as a 2 × 2 experimental design. Of course you can think of other combinations: 2 × 3 (two IVs, three levels in each), 3 × 2 (three IVs, two levels in each), 4 × 4 (four IVs, four levels in each). The more cells you have in this table, the larger the sample you need, so at some point it becomes impractical to increase the number of groups.

To summarize, regardless of the number of IVs and their levels, an experiment follows an independent measures design when the IV is manipulated by randomly allocating participants into groups. This allows us to assume that the groups are equivalent from the start so whatever difference we observe at the end of the experiment must have been caused by our experimental manipulation.

Matched pairs design is similar to independent measures. The only difference is that instead of completely random allocation, researchers use matching to form the groups.

To illustrate matching, let's consider an example. Suppose you are conducting a study of the effect of sleep deprivation on memory. For this you need two groups of participants. One of the groups will sleep peacefully in the laboratory and the other group will be woken up every 15 minutes. In the morning you will give both groups a memory test and compare their performance. You suspect that there is one confounding variable that may influence the results: memory abilities. Some people generally have better memory than others, therefore it is important to you that the two groups at the start of the experiment are equivalent in their memory abilities. Random allocation will usually make that happen, but you only have 20 participants (10 in each group). With a small sample like this there is a chance that random allocation will not work. So you want to control the equivalence of memory abilities "manually" while leaving everything else to random chance. For this you test memory abilities in your participants prior to the experiment. Then you rank participants

according to their memory abilities (for example, from the highest to the lowest). Then you take the first two participants from the top of the list and randomly allocate one of them to the experimental group and the other one to the control group. You take the next two participants and repeat the procedure for the rest of the list. The two resulting groups are certainly equivalent in terms of memory abilities and probably (due to random chance) equivalent in all other characteristics.

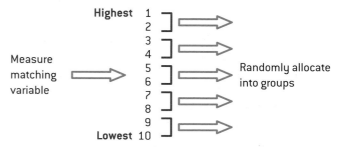

▲ Figure 1.3 Matched pairs design

The variable that is controlled (memory abilities in the example above) is called the **matching variable**. Matched pairs designs are preferred when:

- the researcher finds it particularly important that the groups are equivalent in a specific variable

- the sample size is not large, therefore there is a chance that random allocation into groups will not be sufficient to ensure group equivalence.

Repeated measures design is used when the goal is to compare conditions rather than groups of participants. The same group of participants is exposed to two (or more) conditions, and the conditions are compared. For example, imagine your aim is to investigate the effect of classical music on learning. You ask your participants to learn a list of trigrams (meaningless combinations of three letters such as HPX, LJW) for 10 minutes in silence and register the number of trigrams correctly recalled. Then you ask the same participants to learn a different list of trigrams for another 10 minutes, but this time with classical music playing in the background. You compare results from the first and the second trial.

The problem with repeated measures designs is that they are vulnerable to **order effects**: results may be different depending on which condition comes first (for example, silence then classical music or classical music then silence). Order effects may appear due to various reasons, such as the following.

- Practise: participants practise, improve their on-task concentration and become more comfortable with the experimental task during the first trial. Their performance in the second trial increases.

- Fatigue: participants get tired during the first trial, and their concentration decreases. Their performance in the second trial decreases.

To overcome order effects researchers use **counterbalancing**. Counterbalancing involves using other groups of participants where the order of the conditions is reversed. For our example, two groups could be used: one given the sequence "silence then music" and one given the sequence "music then silence". It is important to note that comparison will still be made between conditions, not between groups. Data from group 1 condition 1 will be collated with data from group 2 condition 2, and vice versa. These two collated data sets will be compared.

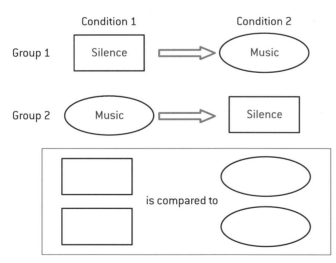

▲ Figure 1.4 Counterbalancing

An advantage of repeated measures designs is that people are essentially compared to themselves, which overcomes the influence of **participant variability** (differences between the groups before the experiment starts). It makes the comparison more reliable. Another advantage following from this is that smaller sample sizes are required.

Credibility and generalizability in the experiment: types of validity

As you have seen, credibility and generalizability are overarching terms that are used to characterize the quality of research studies. When it comes to experiments specifically, these terms are very rarely used. Instead the quality of experiments is characterized by their construct, internal and external validity.

Construct validity characterizes the quality of operationalizations. As you know, the phenomenon under study is first defined theoretically as a construct and then expressed in terms of observable behaviour (operationalization). Operationalization makes empirical research possible. At the same time when results are interpreted research findings are linked back to constructs. Moving from an operationalization to a construct is always a bit of a leap. Construct validity of an experiment is high if this leap is justified and if the operationalization provides sufficient coverage of the construct. For example, in some research studies anxiety was measured by a fidgetometer, a specially constructed chair that registers movements at various points and so calculates the amount of "fidgeting". Subjects would be invited to the laboratory and asked to wait in a chair, not suspecting that the experiment has already started. The rationale is that the more anxious you are, the more you fidget in the chair. Are the readings of a fidgetometer a good operationalization of anxiety? On the one hand, it is an objective measure. On the other hand, fidgeting may be a symptom of something other than anxiety. Also the relationship between anxiety and increased fidgeting first has to be demonstrated in empirical research.

Internal validity characterizes the methodological quality of the experiment. Internal validity is high when confounding variables have been controlled and we are quite certain that it was the change in the IV (not something else) that caused the change in the DV. In other words, internal validity links directly to bias: the less bias, the higher the internal validity of the experiment. Biases in the experiment (threats to internal validity) will be discussed below.

External validity characterizes generalizability of findings in the experiment. There are two types of external validity: population validity and ecological validity. **Population validity** refers to the extent to which findings can be generalized from the sample to the target population. Population validity is high when the sample is representative of the target population and an appropriate sampling technique is used. **Ecological validity** refers to the extent to which findings can be generalized from the experiment to other settings or situations. It links to the artificiality of experimental conditions. In highly controlled laboratory experiments subjects often find themselves in situations that do not resemble their daily life. For example, in memory experiments they are often asked to memorize long lists of trigrams. To what

extent can findings from such studies be applied to everyday learning situations?

There is an inverse relationship between internal validity and ecological validity. To avoid bias and control for confounding variables, you make the experimental procedures more standardized and artificial. This reduces ecological validity. Conversely, in an attempt to increase ecological validity you may allow more freedom in how people behave and what settings they choose, but this would mean that you are losing control over some potentially confounding variables.

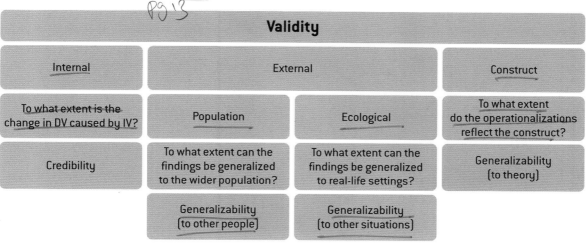

▲ Figure 1.5 Validity of experiments

Exercise

- Leaf through this book (consider the units on the biological, cognitive or sociocultural approach to behaviour), find a description of any experimental study and analyse its construct, internal and external validity. If you feel that you do not have enough detail, you could find more information on the study online, or even read the original article.

- Present the results of your analysis in class.

Bias in experimental research: threats to internal validity

Bias in experimental research comes in the form of confounding factors that may influence the cause-and-effect relationship between the IV and the DV, decreasing internal validity. Below you will find a description of several common sources of threat to internal validity, based on Campbell (1969).

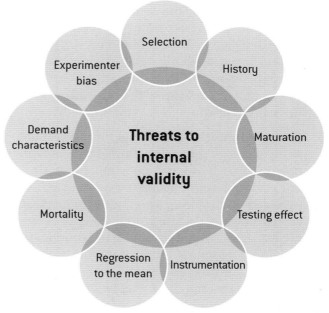

▲ Figure 1.6 Sources of threat to internal validity

1. **Selection**. This occurs if for some reason groups are not equivalent at the start of the experiment: apart from the planned IV-related difference, they differ in some other variable. As a result, we cannot be sure if the post-experiment differences between groups reflect the influence of the IV or this other variable. Selection occurs in independent measures and matched pairs designs in case group allocation was not completely random.

2. **History**. This refers to outside events that happen to participants in the course of the experiment. These outside events become a problem when they can potentially influence the DV or are not evenly distributed in the comparison groups. History is especially important in lengthy experiments where the DV is measured sometime after the onset of the study. For an example of history-related bias think of a memory experiment where participants are required to memorize long lists of words and the experiment is conducted in two groups (experimental and control) simultaneously in two different rooms on the opposite sides of a school. As the experiment begins, there is some noise coming from road construction outside. The control group is closer to the construction site so the noise in their room is louder. Since distracting noise can affect memory performance and levels of noise were not equal in the two groups, resulting differences in the DV may reflect the influence of the IV as well as the confounding variable (noise). To counteract history as a threat to internal validity such confounding variables should be either eliminated or kept constant in all comparison groups (for example, change the rooms so that they are both on the same side of the school building).

3. **Maturation**. In the course of the experiment participants go through natural developmental processes, such as fatigue or simply growth. For example, suppose you are piloting a psychological training programme to increase assertiveness in middle school students. You measure assertiveness at the start, conduct the training programme for several months and measure assertiveness again. The resulting increase of assertiveness may be due to either the IV (the training) or simply to the fact that the middle school students grew up a

little and naturally became more assertive. The counteracting strategy would be using a control group (the same time period, the same measurements but no training sessions).

4. **Testing effect**. The first measurement of the DV may affect the second (and subsequent) measurements. For example, suppose you are investigating the effectiveness of a video to reduce test anxiety in primary school children. For this your participants take an ability test preceded by a self-report anxiety measure at time A. They then watch your specially designed video and repeat the procedure (test and self-report anxiety measure) at time B. The difference in anxiety between time A and time B may be the result of both the video and the fact that it is their second time taking the test—they are more familiar with the format and therefore may be naturally less anxious. A solution to this is to use a control group where you show a neutral video of the same duration. Suppose you get the following results:

Group	Test anxiety (on a scale 0–100)	
	Before Test 1	Before Test 2
Experimental (specially designed video)	90	55
Control (neutral video)	90	70

▲ Table 1.5

Analysis of these results can reveal that a reduction of anxiety by 20 points is probably due to the testing effect; however, over and above that there is a 15-point anxiety effect of the specially designed video.

In repeated measures designs testing effect is a special case of order effects, and counterbalancing is used to control for it.

5. **Instrumentation**. This effect occurs when the instrument measuring the DV changes slightly between measurements. For psychology this becomes relevant when you consider that an "instrument of measurement" is often a human observer. Suppose you are investigating bullying on a school campus during breaks. You are looking at two groups of students who are exposed to different experimental conditions. If

you observe group 1 in the morning and group 2 in the afternoon, you might be more tired in the afternoon and miss some important behaviours. If you observe one of the groups during a short break and the other one during the lunch break, observations during the lunch break may be less accurate because it is more crowded. To avoid this researchers should try to standardize measurement conditions as much as possible across all comparison groups and all observers.

6. **Regression to the mean**. This is an interesting source of bias that becomes a concern when the initial score on the DV is extreme (either low or high). Extreme scores have a purely statistical tendency to become more average on subsequent trials. Suppose you have designed anxiety reduction training for students. To test its effectiveness, you administer an anxiety questionnaire in a group of students and select a sample of students who have the largest score (for example, 80–100 on a 100-point scale). With these students you then conduct your training session and measure their anxiety again. Even if we assume that testing effects are not an issue, we would expect extremely anxious students to naturally become less anxious even without the training session. To put it more precisely, the probability that extremely anxious students will become even more anxious is less than the probability that they will become less anxious. This means that statistically a reduction of anxiety should be expected. A counter-measure is a control group with the same starting average anxiety level and measurements at the same point of time, but without the intervention.

7. **Experimental mortality**. This refers to the fact that some participants drop out during an experiment, which may become a problem if dropouts are not random. Suppose you are investigating the influence of emotion on ethical decision-making. For this you give your participants a number of scenarios of the type "Would you kill 1 person to save 1000?" In the control group the description of this "one person" is neutral, but in the experimental group this is someone they know personally, so there is more emotional involvement. You hypothesize that people will be less likely to be utilitarian in their decision-making when they are personally involved (note that this research

would create distress among participants and so raises ethical issues; it is quite possible such a study would not be approved by the ethics committee). Suppose that several participants in the experimental group refuse to continue participation and drop out, more so than in the control group. Ethical issues aside, this presents a methodological issue as well: even if the two groups were equivalent at the start of the experiment, they may be non-equivalent now. There appears a confounding variable (sensitivity) which is disproportionally represented in the two groups. There is no reliable way to counteract experimental mortality other than designing experimental conditions in such a way that participants would not feel the need to drop out.

8. **Demand characteristics**. This refers to a situation in which participants understand the purpose of the experiment and change their behaviour subconsciously to fit that interpretation. In other words, they behave in ways that they think the experimenter expects. This can happen for various reasons, for example, participants may feel that they will somehow be evaluated and so behave in a socially desirable way. To avoid demand characteristics, deception may be used to conceal the true purpose of the study (however, deception raises ethical issues—see below). You can consider using post-experimental questionnaires to find out to what extent demand characteristics may have influenced the results (this strategy does not prevent demand characteristics but just estimates their impact). Note that in repeated measures designs demand characteristics are a larger threat because participants take part in more than one condition and so have greater opportunities to figure out or guess the aim of the study.

9. **Experimenter bias**. This refers to situations in which the researcher unintentionally exerts an influence on the results of the study, for example, the Clever Hans case discussed above. Existence of this bias was first rigorously supported by Rosenthal and Fode (1963). In this experiment rats were studied for their maze-running performance. Rats were split into two groups at random, but the laboratory assistants (psychology students) were told that one of the groups was "maze-bright" and

the other one was "maze-dull" and that this difference in ability was genetic. Laboratory assistants had to follow a rigorous and standardized experimental procedure in which rats were tested on their performance in learning the maze task. This was supposed to be an identical study conducted with identical rats, but results showed that the rats labelled "maze-dull" performed significantly worse than the ones labelled "maze-bright". It was concluded that the result was an artifact: it was caused by experimenter bias rather than any genuine differences between the groups of rats. Post-experiment investigations revealed that experimenter bias was not intentional or conscious. The results were induced by subtle differences in the way laboratory assistants handled the rats. For example, without realizing it, assistants handled "maze-bright" rats for slightly longer and so stress was more reduced for these rats than for "maze-dull" rats. A counter-measure against experimenter bias

is using so-called **double-blind designs** where information that could introduce bias is withheld both from the participants and from the people conducting the experiment. The study of Rosenthal and Fode would have been double-blind if the laboratory assistants had not been told which group of rats had which label.

Exercise

Once again leaf through this book and find a description of any experimental study.

- To what extent was this experimental study susceptible to one of the sources of threat to internal validity? What does it tell you about credibility of the study?

- If you do not have enough detail, find more information on the study online, or even read the original article.

- Present the results of your analysis in class.

ATL skills: Self-management

Athabasca University has a great learning resource on threats to internal validity. One tutorial consists of two parts, where part 1 is the theoretical background and definitions and part 2 is a practical exercise involving the analysis of 36 hypothetical experiments.

If you want to practise identifying potential sources of bias in experiments, you can access the tutorial here: https://psych.athabascau.ca/open/validity/index.php

Quasi-experiments versus true experiments

Quasi-experiments are different from "true" experiments in that the allocation into groups is not done randomly. Instead some pre-existing inter-group difference is used. "Quasi" is a prefix meaning "almost". The major limitation of a quasi-experimental design is that cause-and-effect inferences cannot be made. This is because we cannot be sure of the equivalence of comparison groups at the start of the study: pre-existing differences in one variable may be accompanied by a difference in unexpected confounding variables.

Suppose your hypothesis is that anxiety influences test performance. You have an opportunity sample of high school students. An intuitively obvious way to test this hypothesis would be to administer an anxiety questionnaire, divide the sample into two groups (anxious and non-anxious) based on

the results, and then model a testing situation and compare test performance. The IV in this study is anxiety (it has two levels) and the DV is test performance. However, the researcher does not really manipulate the IV in this study. Pre-existing differences in anxiety are used, so we cannot be sure that anxiety is the only variable that differs in the two groups. For example, it is possible that high school students with high levels of anxiety also tend to have unstable attention, and it is actually attention that influences test performance. The bottom line is that we will be able to conclude that "anxiety is linked to test performance", but strictly speaking we will not be able to say "anxiety influences test performance".

To test the "influence" hypothesis a true experiment would be required, so we would have to manipulate the IV. How can you manipulate anxiety? One example is splitting participants randomly into two groups and telling one of the groups that they should expect results of their college applications later today. Anticipation of these results would probably increase anxiety in the experimental group. Then the test can be given. (Note that such an experiment would have ethical issues since it involves major deception and creates distress among participants.)

Other examples of pre-existing differences are age, gender, cultural background and occupation. Formation of experimental groups based on these variables implies a quasi-experiment. Sometimes a "true" experiment cannot be conducted because it is impossible to manipulate the IV (for example, how do you manipulate age or gender?) so quasi-experiments are justified.

In the way they are designed (superficially) quasi-experiments resemble "true" experiments, but in terms of the possible inferences (essentially) they are more like correlational studies.

Field experiments and natural experiments

Field experiments are conducted in a real-life setting. The researcher manipulates the IV, but since participants are in their natural setting many extraneous variables cannot be controlled. The strength of field experiments is higher ecological validity as compared to experiments in a laboratory. The limitation is less control over potentially confounding variables so there is lower internal validity. An example of a field experiment is **Piliavin, Rodin and Piliavin's** (1969) subway study in which the researchers pretended to collapse on a subway train and observed if other passengers would come to help. To manipulate the IV, some researchers were carrying a cane (the cane condition) while others were carrying a bottle (the drunk condition).

Natural experiments, just like field experiments, are conducted in participants' natural environment, but here the researcher has no control over the IV—the IV occurred naturally. Ecological validity in natural experiments is an advantage and internal validity is a disadvantage owing to there being less control over confounding variables. Another advantage of natural experiments is that they can be used when it is unethical to manipulate the IV, for example, comparing rates of development in orphans that were adopted and in those who stayed in the orphanage. Since researchers do not manipulate the IV, all natural experiments are quasi-experiments.

Type of experiment	Independent variable	Settings	Can we infer causation?
True laboratory experiment	Manipulated by the researcher	Laboratory	Yes
True field experiment	Manipulated by the researcher	Real-life	Yes (but there may be confounding variables)
Natural experiment	Manipulated by the nature	Real-life	No
Quasi-experiment	Not manipulated; pre-existing difference	Laboratory or real-life	No

▲ Table 1.6

Exercise

Go online and find examples of quasi-experiments, natural experiments and field experiments in psychology.

Inquiry questions

- What does it mean for two variables to correlate with each other?

- What should be avoided when interpreting correlations?

- Can two correlating variables be unrelated in fact?

- Can correlations show curvilinear relationships?

What you will learn in this section

- What is a correlation?
  - Effect size
  - Statistical significance
- Limitations of correlational studies
  - Causation cannot be inferred
  - The third variable problem

- Curvilinear relationships
- Spurious correlations
- Sampling and generalizability in correlational studies
- Credibility and bias in correlational studies

What is a correlation?

Correlational studies are different from experiments in that no variable is manipulated by the researcher, so causation cannot be inferred. Two or more variables are measured and the relationship between them is mathematically quantified.

The way it is done can be illustrated graphically through scatter plots. Suppose

you are interested in investigating if there is a relationship between anxiety and aggressiveness in a group of students. For this you recruit a sample of students and measure anxiety with a self-report questionnaire and aggressiveness through observation during breaks. You get two scores for each participant: anxiety and aggressiveness. Suppose both scores can take values from 0 to 100. The whole sample can be graphically represented with a scatter plot.

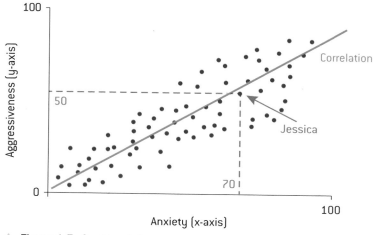

▲ Figure 1.7 Scatter plot

Each dot on the scatter plot represents one person. The coordinates of each dot give you the scores obtained for each of the variables. For example, Jessica's score on anxiety is 70 (the x-axis coordinate) and her score on aggressiveness is 50 (the y-axis coordinate). The whole scatter plot looks like a "cloud" of participants in the two-dimensional space of the two variables. A **correlation** is a measure of <u>linear relationship</u> between two variables. Graphically a correlation is a straight line that best approximates this "cloud" in the scatter plot.

In the example above, the correlation is positive because the cloud of participants is oblong and

there is a tendency: as X increases, Y increases, so if an individual got a high score on variable X, that person probably also got a high score on variable Y, and vice versa. This is where the name "correlation" comes from: the two variables "co-relate". Remember that correlation does not imply causation: we cannot say that X influences Y, nor can we say that Y influences X. All we know is that there is a link between them.

A correlation coefficient can vary from −1 to +1. The scatter plots below demonstrate some examples:

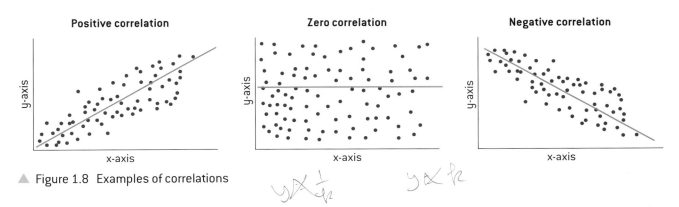

Figure 1.8 Examples of correlations

A positive correlation demonstrates the tendency for one variable to increase as the other variable increases. A negative correlation demonstrates the inverse tendency: when one variable increases the other variable decreases. The steeper the line, the stronger the relationship. A perfect correlation of 1 (or −1) is a straight line with the slope of 45 degrees: as one variable increases by one unit, the other variable increases (or decreases) by exactly one unit. A correlation close to zero is a flat line. It shows that there is no relationship between the two variables: the fact that a person scored high or low on variable X tells us nothing about his or her score on variable Y. Graphically such scatter plots are more like a circle or a rectangle.

Effect size and statistical significance

The absolute value of the correlation coefficient (the number from −1 to 1) is called the **effect size**. How do you know if a correlation is small or large? There are widely accepted guidelines based on **Cohen's** (1988) suggestions to interpret the effect size of correlations in social sciences.

Correlation coefficient effect size (r)	Interpretation
Less than 0.10	Negligible
0.10–0.29	Small
0.30–0.49	Medium
0.50 and larger	Large

Table 1.7 Effect sizes for correlation coefficients

The effect size is not the only parameter that is important when interpreting a correlation coefficient. Another is the level of **statistical significance**. Statistical significance shows the likelihood that a correlation of this size has been obtained by chance. In other words, what is the probability that you will replicate the study with a different sample and the correlation will turn to zero? It depends on the sample size: with small samples you cannot be sure that an obtained correlation, even if it is relatively large, has not been obtained due to random chance. With large samples correlation estimates are more reliable and you can be more confident that the correlation is not a product of random chance but a genuine reflection of a relationship between the two variables in the population. The probability that a correlation has been obtained due to random chance can be estimated. Again, there are conventional cut-off points when results are considered to be "statistically significant" or not.

The probability that the result is due to random chance	Notation	Interpretation
More than 5%	p = n.s.	Result is non-significant
Less than 5%	$p < .05$	Result is statistically significant (reliably different from zero)
Less than 1%	$p < .01$	Result is very significant
Less than 0.1%	$p < .001$	Result is highly significant

▲ Table 1.8

The conventional cut-off point for statistical significance is 5%. Whatever result you obtained, if the probability that this result is pure chance occurrence is less than 5%, we assume that the result is statistically significant, reliably different from zero and so would be replicated in at least 95 out of 100 independent samples drawn from the same target population.

TOK

As you see, the nature of knowledge in psychology, just like the other social sciences, is probabilistic. We only know something with a degree of certainty and there is a possibility this knowledge is a product of chance.

How does that compare to the nature of knowledge in other areas such as natural sciences (physics, chemistry, biology), ethics or indigenous knowledge systems?

What can we do to increase the degree of certainty in social sciences (for example, think about replication of studies)?

When interpreting correlations one needs to take into account both the effect size and the level of statistical significance. If a correlation is statistically significant, it does not mean that it is large, because in large samples even small correlations can be significant (reliably different from zero). So, scientists are looking for statistically significant correlations with large effect sizes.

ATL skills: Research

Correlations are denoted by the letter r. Below are some examples of results of fictitious correlational studies. See if you can interpret them using your knowledge of Cohen's effect size guidelines and levels of statistical significance:

$r = 0.14$, p = n.s.

$r = 0.10$, $p < .05$

$r = 0.34$, $p < .01$

$r = 0.61$, $p < .001$

Limitations of correlational studies

Correlational studies have several major limitations.

- As already mentioned, correlations **cannot be interpreted in terms of causation**.

- **"The third variable problem"**. There is always a possibility that a third variable exists that correlates both with X and Y and explains the correlation between them. For example, cities with a larger number of spa salons also tend to have more criminals. Is there a correlation between the number of criminals and the number of spa salons? Yes, but once you take into account the third variable, the size of the city, this correlation becomes meaningless.

- **Curvilinear relationships**. Sometimes variables are linked non-linearly. For example, a famous Yerkes-Dodson law in industrial psychology states that there is a relationship between arousal and performance: performance increases as arousal increases, but only up to a point. When levels of arousal surpass that point, performance begins to decrease.

Optimal performance is observed when levels of arousal are average. This can be seen in the scatter plot below.

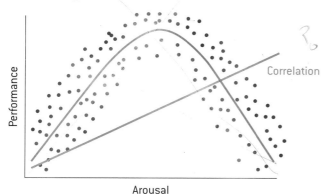

Figure 1.9 Arousal and performance

However, this relationship can only be captured by looking at the graph. Since correlation coefficients are linear, the best they could do is to find a straight line that fits best to the scatter plot. So, if we were using correlational methods to find a relationship between arousal and performance, we would probably end up obtaining a small to medium correlation coefficient. Psychological reality is complex and there are a lot of potentially curvilinear relationships between variables, but correlational methods reduce these relationships to linear, easily quantifiable patterns.

Spurious correlations. When a research study involves calculating multiple correlations between multiple variables, there is a possibility that some of the statistically significant correlations would be the result of random chance. Remember that a statistically significant correlation is the one that is different from zero with the probability of 95%. There is still a 5% chance that the correlation is an artifact and the relationship actually does not exist in reality. When we calculate 100 correlations and only pick the ones that turned out to be significant, this increases the chance that we have picked spurious correlations.

Sampling and generalizability in correlational studies

Sampling strategies in correlational research are the same as in experiments. First the target population is identified depending on the aims of the study and then a sample is drawn from the population using random, stratified, opportunity or self-selected sampling.

Generalizability of findings in correlational research is directly linked with sampling and depends on representativeness of the sample. Again, this is much like population validity in experiments.

Credibility and bias in correlational research

Bias in correlational research can occur on the level of variable measurement and on the level of interpretation of findings.

On the level of measurement of variables, various biases may occur and they are not specific to correlational research. For example, if observation is used to measure one of the variables, the researcher needs to be aware of all the biases inherent in observation. If questionnaires are used to measure variables, biases inherent in questionnaires become an issue. The list goes on.

On the level of interpretation of findings, the following considerations represent potential sources of bias.

- Curvilinear relationships between variables (see above). If this is suspected, researchers should generate and study scatter plots.

- "The third variable problem". Correlational research is more credible if the researcher considers potential "third variables" in advance and includes them in the research in order to explicitly study the links between X and Y and this third variable.

- Spurious correlations. To increase credibility, results of multiple comparisons should be interpreted with caution. Effect sizes need to be considered together with the level of statistical significance.

ATL skills: Self-management

Go back to the overview table (Table 1.2). Compare and contrast sampling, generalizability, credibility and bias in correlational research with those in experimental research.

- In what aspects are the approaches different?
- In what aspects are they the same?
- Are there any aspects where the ideas are similar but the terminology differs?

Inquiry questions

- To what extent can findings from qualitative research be generalized?

- How can credibility of qualitative research studies be ensured?

- What are the differences and similarities in how qualitative and quantitative research approaches sampling, credibility, generalizability and bias?

What you will learn in this section

- Credibility in qualitative research
  - Triangulation: method, data, researcher, theory
  - Rapport
  - Iterative questioning
  - Reflexivity: personal, epistemological
  - Credibility checks
  - Thick descriptions
- Bias in qualitative research
- Participant bias
  - Acquiescence bias
  - Social desirability bias
  - Dominant respondent bias
  - Sensitivity bias
- Researcher bias
  - Confirmation bias
  - Leading questions bias

- Question order bias
- Sampling bias
- Biased reporting
- Sampling in qualitative research
  - Quota sampling
  - Purposive sampling
  - Theoretical sampling
  - Snowball sampling
  - Convenience sampling
- Generalizability in qualitative research
  - Sample-to-population generalization
  - Theoretical generalization
  - Case-to-case generalization = transferability

Credibility in qualitative research

Credibility in qualitative research is an equivalent of internal validity in the experimental method. As you have seen, internal validity is a measure of the extent to which the experiment tests what it is intended to test. To ensure internal validity in experimental research we need to make sure that it is the IV, not anything else, that causes the change in the DV. To do this, we identify all the possible confounding variables and control them, either by eliminating them or by keeping them constant in all groups of participants.

In a similar fashion, credibility in qualitative research is related to the question, "To what extent do the findings reflect the reality?" If a true picture of the phenomenon under study is being presented, the study is credible.

The term "**trustworthiness**" is also used to denote credibility in qualitative research.

To ensure that what is presented in the findings of a qualitative study is true, several types of measures can be taken.

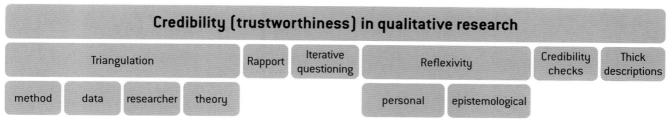

▲ Figure 1.10 Trustworthiness

- **Triangulation**. This refers to a combination of different approaches to collecting and interpreting data. There are several types of triangulation all of which can be used to enhance the credibility of a study.

  - Method triangulation. The use of different methods in combination can compensate for their individual limitations and reinforce their strengths. If the same results are obtained using various methods (for example, interviews and observations), credibility increases.

  - Data triangulation. This refers to using data from a variety of accessible sources. For example, if participants during an interview refer to certain documents, these documents may be studied in order to gain a clearer understanding of the participants' experiences. Observations may be supported by studying documented biographical data, and so on.

  - Researcher triangulation. As follows from the name, this refers to combining observations/interpretations of different researchers. Undoubtedly, if two people see

the same thing, this increases credibility of their findings.

  - Theory triangulation. This refers to using multiple perspectives or theories to interpret the data.

- **Establishing a rapport**. Researchers should ensure that participants are being honest. For example, the researcher should remind participants about voluntary participation and the right to withdraw so that responses are only obtained from participants who are willing to contribute. It should be made clear to participants that there are no right or wrong answers and in general a good rapport should be established with participants so that they alter their behaviour in the presence of the researcher as little as possible.

- **Iterative questioning**. In many research projects, especially those involving sensitive data, there is a risk that participants will distort data either intentionally (lying) or unintentionally to try to create a certain impression on the researcher. Spotting ambiguous answers and returning to the topic later while at the same time rephrasing the question might help researchers to gain a deeper insight into the sensitive phenomenon.

- **Reflexivity**. Researchers should reflect on the possibility that their own biases might have interfered with the observations or interpretations. Arguably, due to the nature of qualitative research that requires the involvement of the researcher in the studied reality, a certain degree of bias is unavoidable. However, researchers need to be able to identify the findings that might have been affected by these biases the most, and if they were affected, how. There are two types of reflexivity:

  - **epistemological reflexivity**, linked to knowledge of the strengths and limitations of the method used to collect data ("the following behaviours were observed … however, they should be interpreted with caution because participants were aware that they were being observed and hence might have modified their behaviour")

  - **personal reflexivity**, linked to the personal beliefs and expectations of the researcher ("I noticed that overcoming trauma was particularly emphasized in their conversations, however, since I myself have a history of overcoming childhood trauma, this observation could have been influenced by my personal beliefs and should be cross-checked by an independent interviewer").

- **Credibility checks**. This refers to checking accuracy of data by asking participants themselves to read transcripts of interviews or field notes of observations and confirm that the transcripts or notes are an accurate representation of what they said (meant) or did. This is often used in interviews with the interviewees receiving the transcripts or notes and being asked to correct any inaccuracies or provide clarifications.

- **"Thick descriptions"**. This refers to explaining not just the observed behaviour itself, but also the context in which it occurred so that the description becomes meaningful to an outsider who never observed the phenomenon first-hand. Essentially it boils down to describing the phenomenon in sufficient detail so that it can be understood holistically and in context. For example, imagine a stranger smiled at you.

This behaviour out of context can be reported "thinly", just stating the fact, or it can be placed in a context (who, where, in what circumstances), making it meaningful. To provide thick descriptions researchers should reflect anything that they observe and hear including their own interpretations, even if some of these details do not seem significant at the time. Thick descriptions are also referred to as "rich" descriptions; these terms are interchangeable.

ATL skills: Research

To what extent is this similar to the way internal validity is ensured in experimental research? What are the differences?

Bias in qualitative research

In quantitative research we deal with potential bias by trying to eliminate it completely or keeping the potentially confounding variables constant in all comparison groups. In qualitative research this approach is not possible, and bias is actually an integral part of the research process because the researcher is a tool through which data is collected. So, while some types of bias may be avoided, other types of bias are inevitable and need to be reflected on and accounted for.

Sources of bias in qualitative research may be associated both with the researcher and the participant. Let's look at the major sources of bias.

Participant bias

- **Acquiescence bias** is a tendency to give positive answers whatever the question. Some people are acquiescent by nature, and in some others acquiescence may be induced by the nature of the questions or the researcher's behaviour. To avoid this bias, researchers should be careful not to ask leading questions, making their questions open-ended, neutral and focused on the opinions of the participant.

- **Social desirability bias** is participants' tendency to respond or behave in a way that they think will make them liked or accepted. Participants may guess (or at least have a vague idea about) the aim of the study and try to look better than they really are. This may be done intentionally or unintentionally. Research into sensitive topics is especially vulnerable to social desirability. To reduce this bias, questions should be phrased in a non-judgmental way that suggests that any answer is acceptable. Another trick that researchers use is to ask questions about a third person (for example, what do your friends think about …?). This helps participants to disengage from the sensitive topics and provide more honest answers.

- **Dominant respondent bias** occurs in a group interview setting when one of the participants influences the behaviour and responses of the others. Dominant respondents may "hijack" talking time or intimidate others by demonstrating their assertiveness or superior knowledge of the subject. Researchers should be trained to keep dominant respondents in check and make sure that all participants are provided with equal opportunities to speak and are in a safe and comfortable environment to voice their opinions.

- **Sensitivity bias** is a tendency of participants to answer regular questions honestly, but distort their responses to questions on sensitive subjects. They may even give incorrect information to hide secrets. The solution to this problem is to build a good rapport with each participant and create trust between the participant and the researcher. To build trust, the researcher needs to behave professionally, make ethical guidelines regarding issues such as confidentiality absolutely clear to the participant and increase the sensitivity of the questions gradually while being responsive to the participant's concerns.

Researcher bias

- **Confirmation bias** occurs when the researcher has a prior belief and uses the research in an unintentional attempt to confirm that belief. Confirmation bias may influence the way questions are worded, the small nuances in the researcher's non-verbal behaviour, and selectivity of attention while observing behaviour or interpreting the data. Information that supports the prior belief is attended to, while information that contradicts it is disregarded. Reflexivity is the solution to confirmation bias. Confirmation bias is such a deeply grounded error in human information processing that it is largely unavoidable in qualitative research where data can only be

collected "through" a human observer. So rather than avoiding it, researchers should be trained to recognize it and take it into account. If the possibility of bias is recognized, research can then be repeated with another observer to corroborate the findings (or not).

- **Leading questions bias** occurs when respondents in an interview are inclined to answer in a certain way because the wording of the question encourages them to do so. Even if an interview is carefully planned in advance, researchers often ask additional follow-up or clarification questions, and these may potentially cause distortions in the responses. Interviewers should be rigorously trained in asking open-ended, neutral questions that do not suggest a particular answer. Also they should avoid paraphrasing the participant's response to make sure they understood it correctly. Questions should be worded in the participant's own language.

- **Question order bias** occurs when responses to one question influence the participant's responses to the following questions. This bias stems from the human tendency to be consistent in our beliefs and actions. For example, if the first question on the interview asked if you liked sports and you hesitated but said yes, you would probably be inclined later to give more positive answers about your attitudes to gym membership. To minimize this bias, general questions should be asked before more specific ones, positive questions before negative ones, and behaviour questions before attitude questions.

- **Sampling bias** occurs when the sample is not adequate for the aims of the research. For example, the selection of people who are not "the best fit" in terms of the research purposes may be the result of convenience sampling. Also there are "professional participants" who look for opportunities to take part in research that provides financial incentives for participation. Although they can be accessed quickly and recruited easily, samples consisting entirely of "professional participants" should be used with caution.

- **Biased reporting** occurs when some findings of the study are not equally represented in the research report. For example, the researcher might choose to only briefly mention pieces of evidence that do not "fit". Reflexivity, integrity and training of researchers are the means to counteract biased reporting.

Bias in qualitative research	
Participant bias	**Researcher bias**
• Acquiescence	• Confirmation bias
• Social desirability	• Leading questions bias
• Dominant respondent	• Question order bias
• Sensitivity	• Sampling bias
	• Biased reporting

▲ Figure 1.11 Types of bias in qualitative research

To sum up, some types of bias in qualitative research may be eliminated while some others need to be recognized and taken into account. Reflexivity and triangulation are the two most important instruments that allow the researcher to reduce the influence of bias in qualitative research.

With regards to researcher bias, special attention needs to be paid to incorporating all data in the report and acknowledging the limitations of the research study, as well as asking independent researchers to review the results and procedure followed. With regards to participant bias, it is important to ask carefully crafted, indirect and open-ended questions and maintain neutrality.

The presence of biases is directly linked to both credibility and generalizability of research findings.

ATL skills: Thinking and self-management

The sources of bias in experimental and qualitative research appear in the table below. See if you can find any overlaps and discuss in class.

Experimental research	Qualitative research
Selection	Acquiescence bias
History	Social desirability bias
Maturation	Dominant respondent bias
Testing effect	Sensitivity bias
Instrumentation	Researcher bias
Regression to the mean	Confirmation bias
Experimental mortality	Leading questions bias
Experimenter bias	Question order bias
Demand characteristics	Sampling bias
	Biased reporting

Sampling and generalizability in qualitative research

Generalization is a broad inference from particular observations. It is "an inference about the unobserved based on the observed" (Polit and Beck, 2010, Elsevier).

Traditionally generalizability has been the focus of debate between supporters of quantitative and qualitative methods. The main argument against generalizability in qualitative research is that samples are not statistically representative of the target population. As you know, representativeness in quantitative research is a necessary requirement for findings to be applied beyond the sample to the target population it represents. A "weak" counter-argument to that is to say that qualitative methods do not aim to apply research findings to a wider population, in other words, the purpose of qualitative methods is the study of a particular sample but not the population it "represents". However, some scholars make a stronger argument and claim that generalizability is in fact achievable, to a certain extent, in qualitative research.

There are other arguments too, less popular, but no less valid. Some scientists doubt that generalizability is possible in principle, even in quantitative studies. They argue that every research study is embedded in a certain context (sample, setting, time, and so on), and generalization of findings would always include a degree of unsubstantiated speculation. Some other scholars argue that qualitative research is in fact more generalizable. They claim that rich data obtained in qualitative studies allows us to gain a deeper understanding of the phenomenon and so make more accurate inferences about its nature.

Sampling

In quantitative research, representativeness of the sample (and therefore the ability to generalize results to a wider population) is ensured through random sampling. In random sampling each member of the target population has an equal chance of being included in the sample. In other words, random sampling is probabilistic. However, sampling in qualitative research is **non-probabilistic**. These are the most commonly used types of sampling in qualitative research.

- **Quota sampling**. In quota sampling it is decided prior to the start of research how many people to include in the sample and which characteristics they should have. This decision is driven by the research question—researchers look for people whose experiences would most likely provide an insight into the topic. Using various recruitment strategies, researchers then recruit participants until the quotas are met. Quota sampling is similar to stratified sampling in quantitative research in that both the important participant characteristics and the necessary sample proportions are pre-defined.

- **Purposive sampling**. This is similar to quota sampling in the sense that the main characteristics of participants are defined in advance and then researchers recruit participants who have these characteristics. However, the proportions and the sample size are not defined.

- **Theoretical sampling**. This is a special type of purposive sampling that stops when the point of data saturation is reached. **Data saturation** means that no new information is obtained from new participants added to the sample. Whether information is "new" or not is defined on the basis of a background theory: if no new evidence (or counterevidence) for the claims of the theory emerges, data saturation is reached. Generalization in this case is made from the data to the theory.

- **Snowball sampling**. In this approach a small number of participants are invited and asked to invite other people they know who also are of interest for the purposes of the research. This approach is mostly used in pilot research studies (when there are insufficient resources to carefully select participants) or in research with groups of people who are very difficult to reach (for example, drug users, youth gang members).

- **Convenience sampling**. The most superficial approach where you just use the sample that is easily available or accessible (for example, professors might conduct research with university students simply because it is time- and cost-efficient).

Generalizability of research findings in qualitative research may depend on the type of sampling used—studies using quota, purposive or theoretical sampling are more generalizable.

Types of generalizability

Firestone (1993) distinguished between three types of generalizability that provide a convenient framework for comparing quantitative and qualitative studies.

1. **Sample-to-population generalization**. The researcher starts by identifying the target population and then selects a sample that is representative of this population. The best approach to achieve this is to use random sampling. The concept that is used to describe sample-to-population generalizability in experiments is "population validity" (part of "external validity"). Due to the non-probabilistic nature of samples in qualitative research, this type of generalization is difficult.

2. **Theoretical generalization**. Generalization is made from particular observations to a broader theory. In quantitative research theoretical generalization takes the form of construct validity: it is the leap we make from directly observable operationalizations to the unobservable construct. In qualitative research theoretical generalization is achieved through rigorous analysis and interpretation of research findings: we can generalize to a wider theory if data saturation was achieved, thick descriptions provided, analysis was in-depth and free of biases, and so on. Theory plays a much greater role in qualitative research than in quantitative.

3. **Case-to-case generalization**, also known as **transferability**. Generalization is made to a different group of people or a different setting or context. In qualitative research transferability is the responsibility of both the researcher and the reader of the research report. The researcher's responsibility is to ensure that thick descriptions are provided so that the reader has sufficient information and details about the context of the study. The reader's responsibility is to decide whether or not the context described in

the report is similar to a new situation (Polit and Beck, 2010). A rough and pretty distant equivalent of transferability in quantitative research would probably be "ecological validity" (another part of "external validity").

ATL skills: Research and self-management

Compare the sampling techniques used in experiments and in qualitative research studies. Use any kind of visual representation to demonstrate the results of this comparison and present it in class.

How are the three types of generalizability approached in experiments and qualitative research studies? Which of these do you think are better achieved in qualitative research as compared to experimental research?

Go back to the overview table (Table 1.2) and see if it reflects your current knowledge of generalizability.

Qualitative research methods

Inquiry questions

- What is the range of qualitative methods used in psychology?

- How and why should one qualitative method be chosen over the others?

What you will learn in this section

- Observation

  - Reasons for choosing observation as the method

  - Reflexivity in observation

  - Types of observation: laboratory versus naturalistic; overt versus covert; structured versus unstructured; participant observation

- Interview

  - Reasons for choosing the interview

  - Interview transcripts and interview notes

  - Structured, semi-structured and unstructured interviews

- Focus group

  - Reasons for choosing the focus group

  - Limitations of the focus group method

- Content analysis

  - Five steps of inductive content analysis

  - Grounded theory

- Case study

  - Why are case studies referred to as a separate method?

  - Reasons for choosing the case study

  - Limitations of the case study method

Observation

There are several common reasons for choosing the method of observation.

- The focus of the research is on how people interact, interpret each other's behaviour and act upon these interpretations in a natural setting. For example, if you observe a group of primary school children in a typical enrichment class you may understand a lot about their everyday school life. Most other research methods are artificial in the sense that they place the participant in a specially constructed research context.

- The researcher believes that meaningful knowledge in the research area cannot be generated without observation, for example, because it cannot be articulated. For example, if you want to gain an insight into the behaviour of your classmates during a fire drill at your school, it will probably be more meaningful to observe an actual fire drill than to conduct an interview and analyse verbal responses.

- Observation allows the researcher to become immersed deeply into the studied phenomenon, sometimes even becoming part of it. Arguably, this is a strength because you gain almost first-hand experiences.

Observation is "experiential" and the researcher is strongly involved in the process of data generation. All generated data is the product of his or her selective attention and interpretations. This makes reflexivity especially important.

So, the main advantage of observation is the ability to generate diverse data about the behaviour of participants in a naturally occurring setting. The major limitation would be susceptibility to biases, so reflexivity and other methods of ensuring credibility and generalizability of qualitative research need to be used extensively.

There are several types of observation, and the particular type chosen will have broad implications in terms of credibility, reflexivity, generalizability and ethics.

- **Laboratory versus naturalistic observation.** Naturalistic observation is carried out in naturally occurring settings, that is, a place that has not been arranged for the purposes of the study. Sometimes naturalistic observation would be the only choice (for example, in situations where it is unethical to arrange settings for the behaviour of interest to occur). If you wanted to study inter-group discrimination and violence, it would be unethical to encourage violence in a research setting. However, you may observe naturally occurring violence. A drawback is that it may be time-consuming because the behaviour of interest only occurs at certain times.

- Observation may be overt or covert. **Overt observation** occurs when participants are aware of the fact that they are being observed. Clearly the ethics of this approach are a strength as participants give their informed consent, but there are methodological limitations—biases related to participant expectations. When people know that they are being observed, they can intentionally or unintentionally change their behaviour. In contrast, in **covert observation** the researcher does not inform the members of the group about the reasons for his or her presence. An advantage of covert observation is gaining access to groups that would not normally agree to participate in research (for example, socially isolated or violent groups). Another strength is the avoidance of participant bias—subjects do not know they are being observed, so they behave naturally. The ethics here are a disadvantage. Participants do not give their consent to take part in the study. One way to avoid this issue is to debrief participants after the observation session and

ask for their consent prior to using the data for research purposes.

- **Participant observation.** In this method the observer becomes part of the observed group. For example, many anthropologists spend time living among members of an indigenous society in order to study their culture "from the inside". For a great example of this, watch the BBC documentaries *Tribe* and *Amazon* with Bruce Parry. The advantage of participant observations is that they allow the researcher to gain first-hand experiences with the phenomenon of interest, gaining valuable insights. However, the drawbacks include the risk that the observer will lose objectivity as he or she becomes too involved with the studied group of individuals. This may happen because the researcher begins to identify himself or herself with the group. Of course, there is also the ethical issue: if participants do not realize that one of the members of their group is in fact an observer collecting information, this may be ethically questionable, especially in sensitive research topics.

- **Structured versus unstructured observation.** In structured observation information is recorded systematically and in a standardized way. For example, structured observation may be conducted with a checklist of behaviours of interest where the observer is required to note the occurrence of these specific behaviours in pre-defined time intervals. Rosen, Carrier and Cheever (2013) conducted structured observations of the use of technology among school students. Observers were equipped with a checklist of behaviours related to the use of technology (using a browser, using a telephone, and so on) and they had to fill out this checklist minute-by-minute. Unstructured observations do not have a pre-defined structure and observers simply register whatever behaviours they find noteworthy. Note that structured observation operates with numbers rather than text, which may be sufficient to say that structured observation is a quantitative research method. However, it is still idiographic rather than nomothetic (see Table 1.1).

Exercise

- Suppose your aim is to study ways in which destructive cults brainwash their new members, and observation is your method. What type of observation would you use and why?

- Describe how you would set up your research procedure both in terms of preparation and the actual observation process.

Interview

In-depth interviews are one of the most popular qualitative research methods for several reasons.

- This may be the only way to get an insight into the nature of subjective experiences and interpretations. Since attitudes, values, patterns of interpretation and other subjective phenomena are unobservable, the most straightforward way to study them is to rely on the participants' verbal reports.

- Interviews may be used to understand the meanings participants attach to certain events and their points of view. Again, this is not directly achievable by most other methods.

- In-depth individual interviews are useful when the topic is too sensitive for people to discuss in a group setting.

Interviews are a very personal form of research because there is direct contact between the interviewer and the interviewee. At the same time, interviews can, and often do, touch upon sensitive topics such as coping with a terminal illness, experiencing phobias, daily routines related to internet addiction and drug use.

Interviewing techniques are driven by the goal of learning as much as possible about the interviewee's opinions and experiences. The interviewer tries to build a rapport with the participant and then engage the person by asking neutral and carefully phrased questions, listening carefully to his or her responses and asking follow-up questions. The interviewer is the main research instrument. Tiny nuances in verbal and non-verbal behaviour of the interviewer may affect the interviewee's responses. For example, it is common in everyday conversations to ask leading questions, but interviewers must avoid doing it. This is why interviewers receive intensive training.

Interview data comes in the form of an audio or video recording which is subsequently converted to an **interview transcript**. Sometimes data also includes **interview notes**, accompanying observations about the participant and the interview context. Transcripts are later coded and analysed in line with the aims of the research.

There are three types of interview, depending on how fixed the list and the sequence of the questions is.

- **Structured interviews** include a fixed list of questions that need to be asked in a fixed order. It is most useful when the research project involves multiple interviewers and it is essential that they all conduct the sessions in a similar way. This allows many participants to be interviewed and some comparisons to be made (for example, comparing responses from male and female participants, across age groups, across cultures).

- **Semi-structured interviews** do not specify an order or a particular set of questions. They are somewhat like a checklist: the researcher knows that certain questions must be asked, but beyond that he or she can ask follow-up questions to get clarifications. If it better fits the natural flow of the conversation, the researcher can change the question order. Semi-structured interviews are better suited for smaller research projects, but they are also more effective in studying the unique experiences of each participant.

- **Unstructured interviews** are mostly participant-driven, and every next question is determined by the interviewee's answer to the previous one. Of course, the researcher still has to keep in mind the overall purpose of the research and stay focused on exploring a particular topic. However, two different interviewees may end up getting very different questions.

Suppose you are interested in studying the reasons why teenagers join criminal groups. You used snowball sampling techniques to recruit 10 participants. Would you use a structured, semi-structured or unstructured interview? Why?

What do you think are the factors that need to be considered in conducting an interview with teenage gang members?

Focus group

The focus group is a special type of semi-structured interview that is conducted simultaneously with a group of 6–10 people. The key factor is that participants are encouraged to interact with each other and the interviewer serves as a facilitator. Participants discuss responses to every question and react to each other's statements. This provides additional data because they use their own language, agree and disagree with each other, enrich each other's perspectives and demonstrate a variety of opinions. The focus group facilitator can observe group dynamics and make use of it by directing group members' interaction so that they stay focused on the research topic.

The advantages of a focus group include the following.

- It is a quick way to get information from several participants at the same time.

- It creates a more natural and comfortable environment than a face-to-face interview, ensuring less participant bias.

- It is easier to respond to sensitive questions when you are in a group.

- Multiple perspectives are discussed so a more holistic understanding of the topic is achieved.

However, there are several "new" limitations that come as a cost for including group dynamics into the research process.

- If one of the participants is especially dominant, this may distort the responses of the other participants (for example, if they feel a need to conform), and it is the facilitator's responsibility to ensure that each participant contributes freely to the conversation.

- It is more difficult to preserve anonymity and confidentiality.

- Focus groups are especially demanding in terms of sampling and creating interview transcripts.

Content analysis

Interview recordings need to be transcribed and then analysed—but how do you analyse a text in a systematic and rigorous way while minimizing researcher bias? The widely used approach to analysing texts produced by participants is known as **inductive content analysis**, or thematic analysis. The goal of inductive content analysis is to derive a set of recurring themes. When extracting the themes the researcher has to maintain a balance between description and interpretation in the sense that the text needs to be interpreted, but these interpretations must be backed up by evidence from the text.

TOK

What is the difference between induction and deduction? If you do not remember, look it up.

Inductive content analysis follows a series of steps (Elo and Kungäs, 2008).

1. Writing the transcript. There are two types of transcript: verbatim or post-modern. Verbatim transcripts are word-for-word accounts of everything the participant said. Post-modern transcripts include notes about the intonation, gestures and other non-verbal elements in the participant's behaviour.

2. Reading the raw material several times and identifying initial themes. This is done iteratively. Researchers start with low-level themes, trying to stay as close to the text as possible. When the first reading is done, a set of initial themes is identified and may be written on the margins. The second reading is done and the themes are confirmed (and revised); also new themes may be added. This is done several times. Sometimes independent coders are used to check the credibility of deriving low-level themes from the text.

3. Low-level themes are grouped into a smaller number of high-level themes. This grouping involves an element of interpretation on the

part of the researcher: they need to decide if X, Y and Z belong to category A. As a credibility check, other researchers may be involved in the process so that results of grouping can be compared across researchers. The result of this stage of analysis is a manageable set of high-level meaningful units that summarize the transcript.

4. A summary table of themes is prepared. The table lists all the high-level emergent themes, all the lower-level themes within them, and supporting quotations from the raw transcript. The structure of themes can also be revised slightly at this point to account for parts of the transcript that are still unexplained. Data saturation is reached when subsequent readings of the transcript do not lead to identifying any new themes.

5. Finally, conclusions are formulated based on the summary table. These conclusions link the emergent themes to the theory. As a credibility check, participants may be shown the results of the analysis and asked to confirm the emergent themes as well as the derived interpretations.

The resulting analysis may be accompanied by "**memos**" that explain to the reader how and why certain analysis decisions were made, increasing the "thickness" of descriptions (which, as you know, increases credibility).

Inductive content analysis can also be applied to observational data. In this case the raw material for analysis comes in the form of field notes describing a participant's behaviour rather than interview transcripts.

If a theory emerges from the data, it is referred to as a "**grounded theory**". The name suggests that grounded theory "grows out of" empirical data as opposed to prior beliefs.

Exercise

- Find an example in this book of a study that used the interview or the focus group as the primary research method. What type of interview or focus group was it? How was content analysis organized?

- What can you say about generalizability and credibility of the findings?

Case study

A case study is an in-depth investigation of an individual or a group. You might say that this is not a proper definition because other research methods can also be defined this way, and you would be right. In fact, case studies can involve a variety of other methods (observations, interviews, and so on), anything that deepens our understanding of an individual or a group of interest. There are several reasons why case studies are referred to as a separate research method, even though they are actually a combination of other methods.

- The individual or group that is the object of a case study is unique in some way. As a result, the purpose is to gain a deep understanding of this particular individual or group.

- Sampling is not an issue: you are interested in this particular case, not the population this case "represents".

- There is less focus on generalizability. Findings do get generalized, but this is a by-product of the in-depth description and explanation of the case (case-to-case and theoretical generalization).

- The case is studied thoroughly, using a combination of different methods, and often longitudinally. This is why we defined a case study as an "in-depth investigation".

What are the reasons for choosing a case study as the preferred method?

First, case studies are useful to investigate phenomena that could not be studied otherwise. For example, it is a group that is hard to get access to and you may only get a chance to study one individual (think about studying the personality of a serial killer).

Second, case studies can contradict established theories and help develop new theories. Why is this a good thing? According to the principle of falsification in science (Karl Popper), the proper way to test a theory is to find one case that contradicts it. If you cannot, the theory stands, but if you succeed, the theory needs to be rejected or modified, and this is how science develops. To test the theory that "all swans are white" you need to try and find one black swan. In a similar fashion, universal theories of memory in cognitive psychology can be tested by studying individuals with unusual or unique memory abilities. If in these individuals memory proves to function differently, then the universal theory of memory is not as universal as we thought. So, "boundary" cases are interesting, and since they are quite rare, we want to study them thoroughly.

Case studies have several limitations. Researcher bias can be a problem as, due to the longitudinal nature of the study, researchers might get too involved. Participant bias is also a potential problem for the same reason: the participant interacts with the researcher for a long period and it is easier for the participant to become susceptible to acquiescence, social desirability, and so on. The generalization of findings is especially problematic from a single case to other settings or to a wider population. Generalization depends on thickness of descriptions and triangulation (other researchers, other case studies, and so on).

Apart from the ethical considerations involved in qualitative research in general, case studies are especially demanding in terms of anonymity and confidentiality—it is difficult to preserve anonymity of unique cases. In case studies of patients with brain damage it may be difficult to obtain informed consent because they might not fully realize the terms of the document. It is debatable how "informed" this informed consent is exactly. In cases like this it is usually a parent or spouse who has overall responsibility for the patient and gives consent.

Ethics in psychological research

Inquiry questions

- Since psychology is a study of living beings, what ethical issues does it raise?
- How can we decide what is ethical and what is not in psychology?

What you will learn in this section

- Ethical considerations in conducting the study
  - Informed consent
  - Protection from harm
  - Anonymity and confidentiality
  - Withdrawal from participation
  - Deception
  - Debriefing
  - Cost-benefit analysis in ambiguous cases
- Ethics committees
- The Little Albert experiment

- Ethical considerations in reporting the results
  - Data fabrication
  - Plagiarism
  - Publication credit
  - Sharing research data for verification
  - Handling of sensitive personal information
  - Social implications of reporting scientific results
- The controversy around Cyril Burt

Ethics is an integral part of psychological research because it is research with living beings (humans and animals). This is one of the things that distinguishes the human sciences from the natural sciences—ethically, the study of human beings is not the same as the study of material objects.

All around the world the activities of psychologists are regulated by codes of ethics. These codes outline the ethical principles and procedures to be followed in all aspects of a psychologist's professional activities: counselling, testing and research. If a psychologist breaches the code, his or her professional license may be discontinued. Codes of ethics have been developed by international as well as national psychological associations, and there is a lot of overlap in their content as the ethical considerations in psychology are pretty much universal.

Exercise

Explore the Code of Ethics on the website of American Psychological Association (APA) and the Code of Human Research Ethics by British Psychological Society (BPS).

Compare the two codes and make a poster for your classroom highlighting the main similarities and differences:

APA: http://www.apa.org/ethics/code/.

Exercise (continued)

BPS:
http://beta.bps.org.uk/news-and-policy/bps-code-human-research-ethics-2nd-edition-2014

Since IB psychology is an academic subject (involving no counselling), we will only focus on ethical considerations related to research. We will also break them into two large groups:

- ethical considerations in conducting the study
- ethical considerations in reporting the results.

Ethical considerations in conducting the study

The following list outlines the main ethical considerations to be addressed when conducting a research study in psychology.

- **Informed consent**. Participation in a study must be voluntary, and participants must fully understand the nature of their involvement, including the aims of the study, what tasks they will be exposed to and how the data will be used. Researchers should provide as much information as possible and in the clearest possible way, hence the name "informed" consent. If the participant is a minor, consent should be obtained from parents or legal guardians.

- **Protection from harm**. At all times during the study participants must be protected from physical and mental harm. This includes possible negative long-term consequences of participating in a research study.

- **Anonymity and confidentiality**. These two terms are often used interchangeably, but they refer to slightly different things. Participation in a research study is confidential if there is someone (for example, the researcher) who can connect the results of the study to the identity of a particular participant, but terms of the agreement prevent this person from sharing the

data with anyone. So, the participant provides personal data, but the data stays confidential under the research agreement. Participation in a study is anonymous if no one can trace the results back to a participant's identity because no personal details have been provided. An example of anonymity would be filling out an online survey without providing your name.

- **Withdrawal from participation**. It must be made explicitly clear to participants that, since their participation is voluntary, they are free to withdraw from the study at any time they want. Researchers must not prevent participants from withdrawing or try to convince them to stay.

- **Deception**. In many cases the true aims of the study cannot be revealed to the participants because it would change their behaviour (for example, due to social desirability). So a degree of deception needs to be used. In some research methods deception is part of the process (for example, covert observation). Researchers must be careful and if deception is used, it must be kept to the necessary minimum.

- **Debriefing**. After the study participants must be fully informed about its nature, its true aims, how the data will be used and stored. They must be given an opportunity to review their results and withdraw the data if they want to. If deception was used, it must be revealed. Care must be taken to protect participants from any possible harm including long-term effects such as recurring uncomfortable thoughts. In some cases psychological help must be offered to monitor the psychological state of the participant for some time after the study (for example, in sleep deprivation studies).

ATL skills: Self-management

To memorize short lists, it is useful to use acrostics—phrases in which the first letter of each word stands for one of the elements on the list. For example, the ethical considerations in conducting a study may be combined in the following acrostic:

Can (consent)

Do (debriefing)

Cannot (confidentiality)

Do (deception)

ATL skills (continued)

With (withdrawal)

Participants (protection from harm)

Try making such acrostics of your own with other lists in this unit: threats to internal validity, types of bias in qualitative research, and so on.

Display the results in your classroom to share with others and gradually you will pick out the ones that are most easily memorized.

Very often ethical decisions prior to conducting a study are not easy, and a **cost-benefit analysis** needs to be conducted. For example, sometimes participants should not know the true aim of the study for their behaviour to be more natural. Sometimes it is difficult to preserve confidentiality (for example, in unique cases). Sometimes there is a risk that participants could get mentally or physically harmed. For example, in the famous Stanford Prison Experiment (Haney, Banks and Zimbardo, 1973) participants were led to believe that they were imprisoned and were kept in harsh conditions, being humiliated and dehumanized by other participants (who were randomly assigned the role of guards). Studies of such phenomena as obedience, conformity, compliance, violence and prejudice can rarely be designed so that they are harmless to the participants. So can we make the decision to relax some of the ethical standards for a particular study?

Such decisions can be made in some circumstances, including:

- if potentially the study can reveal scientific information that will benefit a lot of people

- if there is no way the study of a phenomenon can be conducted without relaxing an ethical standard.

In all countries professional bodies of psychologists have **ethics committees** that resolve ambiguous issues and approve research proposals. Research proposals with a full description of the aims, procedures and anticipated results are submitted to the committee and reviewed. In some cases, when research is potentially useful, ethically ambiguous research studies may get the "green light". Then the researchers will need to be extra careful in making sure that participant harm is minimized and long-term follow-up after the study is provided. Failure to cooperate with an ethics committee is itself a violation of ethics.

Psychology in real life

If you want to know more about the Stanford Prison Experiment, explore this website: http://www.prisonexp.org/.

You may also find Philip Zimbardo's TED Talk "The psychology of evil" interesting: https://www.ted.com/talks/philip_zimbardo_on_the_psychology_of_evil.

Research in focus: The Little Albert experiment

The Little Albert experiment was carried out by John B Watson (Watson and Rayner, 1920). The study provided evidence of classical conditioning in humans. Similar to Ivan Pavlov's experiments with his dogs (salivating at the sound of a bell), Watson was trying to form a certain reaction in response to a certain stimulus in a human baby. Watson observed that a baby's fearful reaction to loud noises was an innate, automatic response. When they hear a loud noise, little children always display behavioural signs of fear (tears, and so on). So he set out to form a fearful reaction to a neutral stimulus, furry objects, using the classic Pavlovian techniques.

Now he fears even Santa Claus

▲ Figure 1.12 Little Albert experiment

Their participant was a nine-month-old infant from a hospital who was referred to as "Albert" for the purposes of the experiment. During the baseline test Albert was exposed to a white rat, a rabbit, masks with hair, cotton, wool and other objects. Albert showed no fear in response to these objects. During the experiment a white laboratory rat was placed in front of Albert and he played with it. Every time the baby touched the rat, however, researchers hit a suspended steel bar behind his back with a hammer, producing a very loud sound. Naturally, the baby cried and showed fear. After pairing these two stimuli several times, the steel bar was taken away and Albert was only presented with the rat. In line with the Pavlovian theory, Albert would show signs of distress, cry and crawl away. So, the researcher "succeeded" in forming a fear of a rat in a baby. In further trials it was revealed that fear in Little Albert was actually generalized to other furry objects. He would show distress, cry and crawl away at the sight of a rabbit, a furry dog and even a Santa Claus mask with a beard.

As you can see, the study exposed the infant to severe distress and potential long-term detrimental consequences. To make things worse, Albert left the hospital (taken away by his mother who did not leave any contact details) shortly after the experiment, and although Watson had planned to carry out de-sensitization, he never had the opportunity. So Albert returned to his daily life with a set of newly formed phobias, and without ever realizing why he had them.

What are the major ethical issues in this study? How would you go about conducting the study in a more ethically appropriate way?

Ethical considerations in reporting the results

The following list gives the main ethical considerations to be addressed when reporting results.

- **Data fabrication**. This is a serious violation of ethical standards and psychologists may lose their license if they fabricate data. If an error is found in already published results, reasonable measures should be taken to correct it (for example, retraction of an article or publication of an erratum).

- **Plagiarism**. It is unethical to present parts of another's work or data as one's own.

- **Publication credit**. Authorship on a publication should accurately reflect the relative contributions of all the authors. For example, the APA Code of Ethics states specifically that if a publication is based primarily on a student's work, the student must be listed as the first author, even though his or her professors co-authored the publication.

- **Sharing research data for verification**. Researchers should not withhold the data used to derive conclusions presented in the publication. The journey from raw data (in the form of a matrix with numbers for quantitative research or a text/transcript for qualitative research) to inferences and conclusions is full of intermediate decisions, interpretations and inevitable omissions. It is healthy scientific curiosity to want to replicate the analysis, and any request from an independent researcher to share raw data should be satisfied, provided both parties use the data ethically and responsibly. This entails, for example, making the shared data set anonymous (deleting the names or other identifiers) and only using the shared data set for the stated purposes.

- **Handling of sensitive personal information**. This refers to how the results of the study are conveyed to individual participants.

  - **Handling of information obtained in genetic research**. Research into genetic influences on human behaviour, such as twin, adoption or family studies, can sometimes lead to revealing private information to one individual about other members of the person's family. Examples include misattributed parentage or health status. In twin studies one may discover that he or she has a twin that he or she has never met. Information of this sort may be disclosed accidentally during interviews, inferred by the participants in the debriefing session or in the report of results. All these considerations imply certain requirements in the way results should be relayed to participants. Such information must be handled with care and sensitivity, and if detrimental consequences are suspected, subjects should be monitored for some time after the end of the study, and psychological counselling may be offered.

○ **Handling of information related to mental disorders**. Some studies may result in revealing the presence of illness that was previously unknown (for example, a study of depressive symptoms in response to life stress requires carrying out a diagnosis of depression for all participants). This knowledge may have a lot of unwelcome consequences such as a change in self-esteem or a change in family perceptions and expectations for a child. On the other hand, research may reveal that some family members do not have the disease now, but they are at higher risk of

developing it in the future. People may not want to know that.

● **Social implications of reporting scientific results**. Researchers must keep in mind potential effects of the way research conclusions are formulated on the scientific community and society in general. For example, imagine you conducted a research study that supported the idea that homosexuality is inherited. Where should you publish the results? Should it be a narrowly specialized scientific journal or a more popular journal that targets a wider audience including non-scientists? Stating that homosexuality is inherited (and bluntly believing in this statement because it "came from the scientists") may have deep effects on society. At the same time, you can never be sure of the results of a single research study—there might have been bias; measurements might have been inaccurate; findings may later turn out to be false. Science is a very meticulous (and often inconclusive) process, and care must be taken to report results precisely and accurately, recognizing all potential limitations of the research study, especially if the findings are of social significance.

Research in focus: The controversy around Cyril Burt

There is much controversy about the work of Cyril Burt, a British psychologist who became famous for his contributions to intelligence testing. In 1942 he became president of the British Psychological Society. He was responsible for administration and interpretation of mental ability tests in London schools. In one of his most famous studies he conducted research with 42 identical twins reared apart. His results showed that the IQ scores of identical twins reared apart were much more similar than that of non-identical twins reared together. He concluded that genetic inheritance in intelligence plays a much greater role than environmental factors (such as education).

In 1956 Burt reported on another study, this time with 53 pairs of identical twins raised apart, where he found a high correlation (0.771) between the IQ scores of the twins. This was

exactly the same correlation (to the third decimal place) that he had reported in an earlier study with a smaller sample size. Burt's research was very influential in forming educational policies in the country, for example, the belief that intelligence is fixed and hereditary led to the practice of using standardized tests to measure intelligence in school children and allocate them to schools based on the results.

After his death in 1971 the British Psychological Society found him guilty of publishing a series of fraudulent articles and fabricating data to support the theory that intelligence is inherited. The case was built on several details that were considered to be highly suspicious.

● There was a very unlikely coincidence of the same correlation coefficient in the two studies.

Research in focus (continued)

- Some factors that should theoretically influence intelligence (such as mental illness or childhood influences) were suspiciously unimportant in Burt's data sets, almost a statistical impossibility.

- Identical twins reared apart is an extremely rare sample; there were only three other studies at that time using this kind of sample and none of them had more than 20 pairs of twins as participants.

- Burt's two female collaborators who worked for him collecting and processing data could not be found, their contact with Burt could not be traced and it was even suspected that these people never existed!

However, some scholars have recently re-examined the claims made earlier and found that evidence of Burt's fraud is not conclusive, or at least he deserved the benefit of doubt.

In any case, data sets and publications that raise questions regarding their credibility are in themselves an ethical concern, even if they are not falsified intentionally. This is especially true for settings where research findings are used to inform social (for example, educational) policies.

▲ Figure 1.13 Cyril Burt

Exercise

At the beginning of this unit you came up with a research proposal related to a research question. Go back and review that proposal. Now that you are equipped with more knowledge about research methodology in psychology, what would you change in your original proposal and why?

BIOLOGICAL APPROACH TO BEHAVIOUR

Topics

- Introduction
- The brain and behaviour
  - Localization
  - Neuroplasticity
  - Neurotransmitters and their effect on behaviour
  - Techniques used to study the brain in relation to behaviour
- Hormones and behaviour
  - Hormones and behaviour
  - Pheromones and behaviour
- Genetics and behaviour
  - Genes and behaviour, genetic similarities
  - Evolutionary explanations for behaviour
- The role of animal research in understanding human behaviour (HL only)

Introduction

Psychology in real life

Let's begin this journey with a thought experiment. Imagine you live in a society of knowledge, a city of dreams called Humanborough. It is a society of rational people who live to maximize their well-being and happiness and who value knowledge over most other things. The most prestigious career is that of a researcher. Crime is rare, and there are no wars. People are modest in their material needs. They would not buy a new phone if the old one still worked. The most popular pastime is learning (taking online courses, attending weekend schools, reading, and so on). Of course, this society faces all the regular human problems: illness and death, disabilities, interpersonal conflicts, jealousy, individuals' inability to always live up to their potential. Everything as usual, except people of Humanborough are ready to use knowledge as the basis to find a solution.

These people have elected you as their leader. They trust your judgment immensely. Your job is to manage research programmes and their applications to contribute to the well-being of this society. The slogan of your campaign was no less than "Make Humans Better". The question is, how?

While you are contemplating the scope of the task, note that elements of Humanborough can be seen in today's real-world popular culture. Here are some examples of films that were built around the idea of using scientific knowledge to "make humans better".

1. *Limitless* (2011) is a film based on the novel *The Dark Fields* by Alan Glynn. The main character discovers a pill that allows him to use 100% of his brain potential, becoming a meta-human with superb cognitive abilities.

2. *Lucy* (2014): after absorbing special drugs in her bloodstream the main character gains psychokinetic abilities and turns into an invincible warrior.

3. *Avatar* (2009): a special apparatus enables a physically disabled marine to control the body of his "avatar"—an alien life form exploring the planet Pandora.

4. *Robocop* (1987 and 2014) features a cyborg that is a blend of a human and a machine. A human brain controls the immense power of its mechanical body.

5. *The Island* (2005): a powerful corporation is growing clones of rich clients to be used for organ transplantation.

6. *Transcendence* (2014): the main character's consciousness is uploaded into a computer.

Can you recall any other films or fiction stories based on similar ideas? Share what you have watched with your classmates.

To what extent do you think these ideas are real?

If you were to decide on your first big project as a leader of Humanborough, what would it be? You may use the films to give you ideas, but you may also be creative. As you read this unit, you will explore more possibilities.

As you know from Unit 1 on research methodology, psychology is the scientific study of behaviour and mental processes, and science pursues four goals: description, explanation, prediction and control. Each subsequent goal supersedes the previous one: you need to describe in order to explain, you need to explain in order to predict, and you need to predict to be able to control.

When it comes to explanation, you need to identify a **cause** of a phenomenon. This is why researchers want to make cause-and-effect inferences and why experiments are so valued as a research method. Knowledge of causes allows you to predict and, in the long run, control the phenomenon under study.

Identifying causes in human sciences has some issues we have to consider. Human behaviour is complex and multi-determined. This means that at any given point of time behaviour is influenced by a whole system of various factors. Some of these factors influence behaviour directly, others indirectly. Some have immediate effects, and the effects of some others only manifest in the long term. So, to study behaviour **holistically** all these various factors need to be taken into account. However, as you remember, the experiment is the only method that allows cause-and-effect inferences, and the experiment requires that one variable is manipulated and all other variables are carefully controlled (eliminated or kept constant). The dilemma is: we understand that behaviour is influenced by multiple factors simultaneously, but to study it scientifically we have to isolate factors one by one. Research therefore inevitably becomes **reductionist**.

Holism 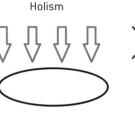   Reductionism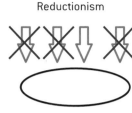

We know that behaviour is influenced by multiple factors

However, to study them scientifically, we have to isolate them one by one

▲ Figure 2.1 Holism versus reductionism

In theory of knowledge reductionism is an attempt to explain a complex phenomenon by its constituent parts. It may be understood as reducing the whole to its parts.

Holism is a methodological position that attempts to gain understanding of the whole in all its complexity. It claims that the whole is bigger than the sum of its parts.

You can probably think of a number of examples of holism and reductionism from various areas of knowledge.

IB psychology broadly divides all factors influencing human behaviour into three groups: biological, cognitive and sociocultural. For example, love is a psychological phenomenon—how do we explain it? Some scientists would claim that love is a chemical reaction of the brain. Others would say that love is a mental process, the product of information processing. Yet others would emphasize the influence of social and cultural norms. All of these claims are reductionist—they are reducing the complex phenomenon of love to its simple constituents. Clearly, the truth lies in combining all these claims. However, one needs to understand the parts before one understands the whole. Experimental research is often reductionist by necessity because it attempts to isolate the effect of one variable.

The biological approach to behaviour looks at behaviour as a product of evolution, genetic inheritance, brain structure or chemical processes in the body. It rests on the following **principles**.

1   **Behaviour is the product of physiology** (the structure and function of the nervous and endocrine systems). The structure is how a system is constructed; for example, brain damage is a structural problem. The function is how the system operates; for example, low activity in certain parts of the brain is a functional problem of the nervous system, while abnormal levels of hormones are a functional problem of the endocrine system.

2   **Behaviour can be genetically inherited**. The idea that characteristics such as eye colour are inherited raises no objection, but inheritance of behaviours such as perfectionism or preference in movie genres is not so obvious. However, this assumption is made in the biological approach: patterns of behaviour can be inherited as well as physical characteristics. This principle follows from principle 1, because the structure and function of the nervous and endocrine systems are to a large extent genetically determined.

3   **Animal research may inform our understanding of human behaviour**. This principle follows from principle 2: we share a large portion of the genotype with our animal ancestors, and since genotype determines behaviour, animal behaviour in some aspects may be very similar to that of humans. This justifies animal research in psychology.

Note that in the three principles above the term "behaviour" is used broadly and also includes mental processes.

Note also that a principle is a broad assumption that guides research in a certain area. What makes a principle different from all other assumptions is its breadth and its fundamental nature. It is fundamental in the sense that if this assumption was not true, research in the area would not make any sense. For example, if we did not assume behaviour to be the product of physiology, the biological approach to behaviour would be meaningless.

Can you name similar principles in some other areas of knowledge?

2 Localization

Inquiry questions

- Is every behaviour associated with a specific brain region?

- Is there a specialized centre for every psychological function in the brain?

- How can these brain centres be discovered?

- Are some psychological functions more localized than others?

What you will learn in this section

- Localization of function is the idea that every behaviour is associated with a specific brain region

- It rests on the first principle of the biological approach (behaviour may be the product of brain structure)

- Brain structure

  - Cortex

  - Cerebellum

  - Limbic system

  - Brain stem

  - Each of these structures and sub-structures is associated with certain functions, but the term "associated with" implies mild localization only

- Research supporting strict localization

  - Early studies showed that a person with damage to a very specific brain area may demonstrate a very specific malfunction in behaviour

  - Paul Broca (1861): the case study of "Tan"; Broca's area and Broca's aphasia—the loss of articulated speech

  - Carl Wernicke (1874): Wernicke's area, Wernicke's aphasia—a general impairment of language comprehension, while at the same time speech production is intact

  - Wilder Penfield used the method of neural stimulation in treating patients

with severe epilepsy; created a map of sensory and motor cortex known as the cortical homunculus

- Research opposing the idea of strict localization

  - Karl Lashley: the method of induced brain damage in experiments with rats in a maze; the principle of mass action (there is a correlation between learning abilities and the percentage of cortex removed, but not the location of removed cells), equipotentiality (one part of the cortex can take over the functions of another part); conclusion—memory is distributed rather than localized

- There needs to be a converging position; currently, neuroscience supports relative localization: it admits localization for some functions under some conditions, but it also clearly outlines limits of localization

- Relativity of localization: the split-brain study

  - Gazzaniga (1967) and Sperry (1968): research into lateralization—a special case of localization; language is mostly lateralized in the left hemisphere, but there are exceptions

    - The right hemisphere can comprehend simple words such as "pencil": the patient correctly picks a pencil from behind the screen with the left hand

- The right hemisphere can spell simple words such as "love", but this differs from person to person
- Visuospatial abilities are better controlled by the right hemisphere
- Emotional responses are not lateralized

- Conclusions

  - Some functions are localized, and brain damage will lead to a loss of function

  - Localization is limited in the following ways

    - Some functions are localized weakly, that is, several brain areas may be responsible for it but some areas are dominant

- Some functions are widely distributed
- Some components of a function may be localized while other components of the same function are distributed in the brain
- Localization is not static (neuroplasticity)

This section also links to:

- Sharot *et al* (2007) flashbulb memory (cognitive approach to behaviour)

- Saxe and Kanwisher (2003) theory of mind (developmental psychology)

- neuroplasticity, Maguire *et al* (2000).

The first principle of the biological approach to behaviour implies that behaviour may be the **product of brain structure**—but what exactly is the connection between patterns of behaviour and parts of the brain?

It is very tempting to assume that every behaviour (speech, attention, aggression, hunger, embarrassment, and so on) has its specific place in the brain and is associated with a certain brain area. This idea is known as **localization of function**. Of course, it would be handy if we discovered brain centres for nearly everything—a brain centre for hope, a brain centre for enjoyment, a brain centre for criminal behaviour. Partially this has been achieved, but only partially. Understanding some important limitations of localization theory is necessary.

We will first briefly consider the brain structure so that you have an idea about the major areas of the brain and the functions they have been associated with. Then we will look at several studies that support the idea of localization, but also show its limitations.

Brain structure

The nervous system is a system of **neurons**—cells that perform the function of communication in the body. The central nervous system consists of the spinal cord and **the brain**.

The major parts of the human brain are the:

- cortex
- cerebellum
- limbic system
- brain stem.

The **cortex** is the layer of neurons with a folded surface covering the brain on the outside. It is the largest part of the human brain associated with higher-order functions such as abstract thought or voluntary action. Evolutionarily, this part of the brain developed the latest. The cortex is divided into four sections called "lobes".

- The **frontal lobes** are associated with reasoning, planning, thinking and decision-making, voluntary action, complex emotions, and so on.

- The **parietal lobe** is associated with movement, orientation, perception and recognition.

- The **occipital lobe** is associated with visual processing.

- The **temporal lobes** are associated with processing auditory information, memory and speech.

Note that we say "associated with": this implies a mild form of localization; that is, the lobe has been demonstrated to be involved in a certain function, but it is not necessarily the only brain structure that influences the function. For example, although temporal lobes are involved in memory processes, a lot of other brain regions play their role in memory too.

There is a deep furrow along the cortex that divides it into the **left and right hemispheres**. A structure of neurons that connects these two hemispheres is known as the **corpus callosum**.

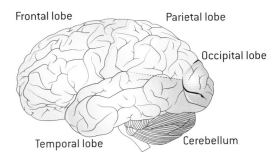

▲ Figure 2.2 Sections of the cortex

The cerebellum ("the little brain") got this name because it looks somewhat like the cortex: it has two hemispheres and a folded surface. It is associated with coordination of movement and balance.

The **limbic system** is an evolutionarily older subcortical structure. It is sometimes referred to as the "emotional brain". It includes several structures, some of which are as follows.

- The **thalamus** has mostly sensory functions. Nerves from almost all sensory organs reach the thalamus as a final "hub" before they are connected to the cortex.

- The **hypothalamus** is "below" the thalamus in the brain and it is involved in such functions as emotion, thirst and hunger.

- The **amygdala** is involved in memory, emotion and fear.

- The **hippocampus** is important for such functions as learning, memory and transferring short-term memory to a more permanent store, spatial orientation.

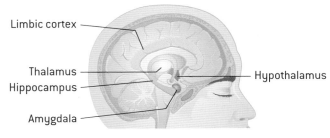

▲ Figure 2.3 The limbic system

The **brain stem** is underneath the limbic system and its main function is to regulate the basic vital processes such as breathing or heartbeat. It connects the brain to the spinal cord. This part of the human brain is very much like the entire brain found in lower animals such as reptiles.

How were all these connections between brain areas and psychological functions established? Does a certain brain area directly and exclusively correspond to a certain function? To understand all the hidden nuances of the theory of localization of function you need to look at how research is organized.

Research supporting strict localization

The first research studies that inspired psychologists to investigate the idea of strict localization of function were performed with patients with brain damage. Some of these studies showed that a person with damage to a very specific brain area may demonstrate a very specific malfunction in behaviour. One of the earliest discoveries in this sphere was the discovery of a speech centre by **Paul Broca (1861)** in the case study of "Tan".

Case study: Louis Leborgne ("Tan")

Louis Leborgne, now better known as "Tan", lost the ability to speak when he was 30. Later, Tan developed gangrene and was admitted for surgery which was to be performed by Paul Broca, a French physician who also specialized in language. By that time "tan" was the only syllable that Leborgne could pronounce. He typically repeated it twice ("tan-tan") and accompanied it with quite expressive hand gestures. His condition remained the same until his death. His inability to speak (or write) was the only malfunction: his intelligence was intact, he understood everything he was asked and tried to communicate back … he just couldn't utter anything other than "tan".

Broca carefully described Tan's condition, which is now known as **Broca's aphasia** (the loss of articulated speech). When Tan died, at the age of 51, an autopsy of his brain was carried out and it revealed a lesion in the frontal area of the left hemisphere, in particular a region in the posterior inferior frontal gyrus. This region is now known as **Broca's area**.

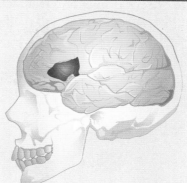

▲ Figure 2.4 Broca's area

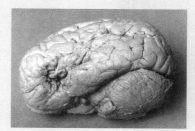

▲ Figure 2.5 Tan's brain

Broca was cautious about rushing to publish his conclusions. He described 25 additional patients with the same problem before finally asserting that speech articulation is controlled by the left frontal lobe.

However, the area responsible for articulate speech may be more complex than we would like to think.

Tan's brain (which was carefully preserved by Broca) was re-examined more than 100 years later with the use of modern technology, and it turned out that the lesion had actually been broader than documented by Broca. He did not notice this detail because he decided to preserve the brain intact rather than dissecting it.

ATL skills: Thinking and research

There are some details about Broca's research that may make you wonder about his methods.

- With a discovery of such significance for its time, why didn't Broca rush to publish the findings and assert the existence of a brain centre for speech articulation? Why was one case not enough? What do you think is the significance of corroborating your findings by additional research in human sciences, and how does that compare to natural sciences?

- Broca did not cut Tan's brain open, so did not notice some lesions inside it. If you were Broca, would you make the same decision and preserve the brain for later generations rather than dissecting it and studying it yourself?

Broca's finding was inspiring. It suggested that other functions can also be mapped onto specific brain areas. **Wernicke's area** was discovered by Carl Wernicke in 1874. It is an area located in the temporal lobe of the dominant hemisphere (which is the left hemisphere for most individuals). Wernicke's area is responsible for the comprehension of written and spoken language.

People with **Wernicke's aphasia** have a general impairment of language comprehension, while at the same time speech production is intact. As a result, when they speak they sound really fluent and natural, but what they say is in fact largely meaningless.

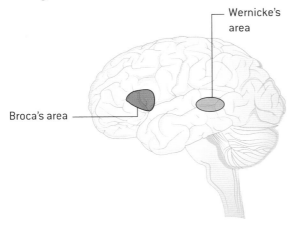

▲ Figure 2.6   Areas of the brain discovered by Broca and Wernicke

One commonality between research of Broca and Wernicke is the method they used: studying a patient with a naturally occurring brain lesion and conducting brain autopsy after the patient's death. This method has a number of drawbacks, including the following.

- A naturally occurring brain lesion is rarely neat or confined to a specific area.
- As cynical as this sounds, you have to wait until the patient dies.

ATL skills: Communication

In small groups, discuss the following question: what alternative methods can you suggest that would not involve waiting for the patient to die to conduct an autopsy?

Remember about ethics of research in psychology!

As a large group, discuss the relative pros and cons of the alternative methods you suggested.

See video

Patients with aphasias sometimes agree to be recorded. Videos of interviews with these patients can be found online, and these give you a good insight into the nature of the malfunction. Here are two examples that you may want to see. Note that aphasias differ in their severity.

Broca's aphasia: Sarah Scott developed Broca's aphasia after she suffered a stroke at age 18. https://www.youtube.com/watch?v=1aplTvEQ6ew. You can also search for videos that show her progress over the years as she attended

speech therapy.

Wernicke's aphasia: Byron Peterson, a stroke survivor, can be seen at:

https://www.youtube.com/watch?v=3oef68YabD0

Mapping of brain functions was done on a larger scale by **Wilder Penfield** (1891–1976), a Canadian neurosurgeon. He used the method of **neural stimulation**. As part of his work he was treating patients with severe epilepsy by destroying nerve cells that initiated the seizure. Before conducting the surgery, though, he would stimulate various parts of the brain while the patient was still conscious, and observe the effects this stimulation had on behaviour. This allowed him to create a map of the sensory and motor cortex known as **the cortical homunculus**. The cortical homunculus is an original model of the body within the brain: it shows the relative representation of various parts of the body in the sensory cortex. As you can see in Figure 2.7, such body parts as hands, tongue and lips are very widely represented in the cortex of the human brain.

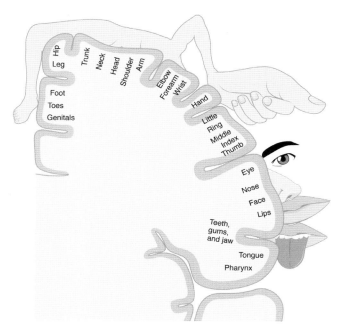

▲ Figure 2.7 2D representation of the cortical homunculus

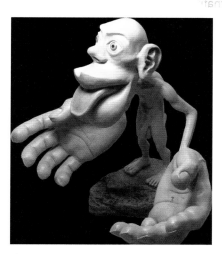

▲ Figure 2.8 3D representation of the cortical homunculus

All these discoveries (by Broca, Wernicke and Penfield) suggest that psychological functions have directly corresponding regions in the brain. We might want to conclude that psychological functions are strictly localized—but it is not that simple.

Research opposing the idea of strict localization

Karl Lashley (1890–1958) used the technique of measuring behaviour before and after a specific carefully controlled **induced brain damage** in the cortex of rats. In a typical study he would train a rat to run through a maze without errors in search of food. After learning occurred, he would remove an area from the cortex. Then he would place the rat back at the start of the maze and register the change in behaviour. He removed varying portions of the cortex in different rats, ranging from 10% to 50%. The idea was that if memory of the maze is localized somewhere, then by removing area after area you will finally be able to pinpoint the specific region in the cortex responsible for it. This search turned out to be a failure, so Lashley abandoned his own initial hypothesis. He concluded that memory was **distributed rather than localized**; a conclusion supported by the following observations.

- **The principle of mass action** based on a correlation observed between the percentage of cortex removed and learning abilities. The less cortex, the slower and more inefficient the learning. The key idea here is that performance deterioration depends on the percentage of cortex destroyed but not on the location of the destroyed cells.

- **Equipotentiality**—this refers to the ability of one part of the cortex to take over the functions of another part of the cortex.

These observations led Lashley to conclude that memory is widely distributed across the cortex. This conclusion is mostly supported today. However, it has been shown that memory is not as evenly (and uniformly) distributed in the cortex as Lashley thought.

ATL skills: Thinking

To what extent would you say Lashley's research was ethically justified? Induced brain damage is a very invasive technique and the research design required the use of many rats.

Conduct a cost-benefit analysis: list the costs as well as potential benefits of this research study. If you were a member of the ethics committee, would you approve it?

▲ Figure 2.9 Karl Lashley

To some extent the difference in the two extreme positions (the localizationism of Broca, Wernicke and Penfield versus the holism of Lashley) may be explained by the methods they used in their studies. Localizationists relied on aphasia resulting from brain damage. Holists investigated maze-running behaviour. However, learning to run through a maze is in itself a highly complex behaviour that involves motor and sensory functions, so it may not be suitable enough for the study of localization.

There needs to be a converging position that is a more accurate reflection of localization in the brain. Currently, neuroscience supports **relative localization**: it admits localization for some functions under some conditions, but it also clearly outlines limits of localization.

Before we formulate these limits let's look at another research study that demonstrates relativity of localization of function (that is, localization and distribution at the same time): split-brain research by Gazzaniga (1967) and Sperry (1968).

Relativity of localization: the split-brain research

It has to be noted that split-brain studies represent research into **lateralization**—the division of functions between the two hemispheres of the cortex. Lateralization is a special case of localization.

Research in this area was pioneered by **Roger Sperry**. Initially, the studies were conducted with animals, for example, cats.

An opportunity to replicate the studies with humans emerged when it was discovered that surgically cutting corpus callosum was an effective measure against severe epilepsy with uncontrollable seizures. Roger Sperry was joined by **Michael Gazzaniga**, and in 1967 Gazzaniga published results of the first research with human split-brain patients. Four of the ten patients who had undergone this surgical procedure by that time agreed to participate. The patients were examined thoroughly over a long time period with various tests.

The aims of the study were to test the theory of lateralization and to see if the two hemispheres have uniquely different functions.

ATL skills: Thinking and self-management

There is a lot of fun in trying to guess the results of a study. First, it recreates some of the thrill of scientific discovery that the researchers experienced. Second, some of the findings in psychology are counter-intuitive, as they go against what is expected based on common sense—but this makes these findings even more valuable because they uncover our own biases and misconceptions.

Try to guess what happens to a person's behaviour and mental processes when the link between hemispheres is severed.

Note that this is a useful exercise to be used throughout the book. When you encounter an interesting study and learn about its aims and procedure, close the book for a second and try to predict the findings. This will also help you remember material better.

Initial observations showed that patients seemed to be remarkably unaffected by the surgery. There was no change in their personality and intelligence, and one of the patients on awakening from the surgery joked that he had a "splitting headache" and recited a tongue-twister.

The authors devised a technique where the participant had to sit in front of a board and look at the dot in the middle of it. Visual stimuli would then be presented for one tenth of a second either to the left or the right visual field (the far left or far right on the board). Optic nerves from the left eye are connected in our brain to the right hemisphere, and vice versa. So, by presenting the stimulus to the left visual field the researcher "sends it" to the right hemisphere, and stimuli from the right visual field goes to the left hemisphere. Also, a variety of objects were placed behind the screen so that participants could feel them with their hands.

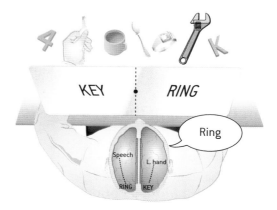

▲ Figure 2.10 The test used in Sperry and Gazzaniga's split-brain research

Here are some results obtained in a typical test with split-brain patients.

- When shown the **picture of a spoon** to the left visual field (connected to the right hemisphere) and asked to name or describe what they saw, the patients said nothing. However, when asked to pick a corresponding object from a group of objects behind the screen, they felt around and picked a spoon (with their left hand, because it is controlled by the right hemisphere). Patients could not explain why they picked the spoon. The right hemisphere saw the spoon and picked it from behind the screen using the left hand, but the centre of speech is in the left hemisphere so the patients were unable to explain what they saw and what they did. This supports lateralization of language in the left hemisphere.

▲ Figure 2.11 Visual test for split-brain patients

Source: Gazzaniga (1967, p 27)

- However, when a **simple word**, such as "pencil", was flashed to the right hemisphere, the patients were able to pick a pencil from a group of objects behind the screen with their left hand. This shows that the right hemisphere does have some amount of language comprehension and language is not exclusive to the left hemisphere. Language production, however, is confined to the left hemisphere.

- When **the word "heart"** was flashed on the screen so that "he" was presented in the left visual field and "art" in the right visual field, the patients said that they saw "art" but pointed (with their left hand) to the card with the word "he" on it. This corroborates the previous findings, but also shows that the two hemispheres process stimuli independently.

- Some patients were able to **spell simple words** with their left hand, although it differed from person to person. For example, when researchers

placed four plastic letters in a pile behind the screen, one patient was able to spell "love" with his left hand (the instruction was simply "spell a word"). Of course, after completing the task the patient was not able to say what word he had just spelled! This shows that the right hemisphere is even capable of language production, but only in the simplest form and only in some patients.

The four findings listed above demonstrate the dominance of the left hemisphere for language. The left hemisphere produces speech and makes a person consciously aware of something. However, this lateralization is not strict: some forms of language production and comprehension can be performed by the right hemisphere also. Moreover, it differs somewhat from person to person.

- The right hemisphere performs better in tasks that involve **visual construction**. A redrawn picture was a much closer match to the original when done by the left hand (controlled by the right hemisphere) than the right hand (controlled by the left hemisphere), even in right-handed people. So, if you think you cannot draw, do you think switching hands might help?

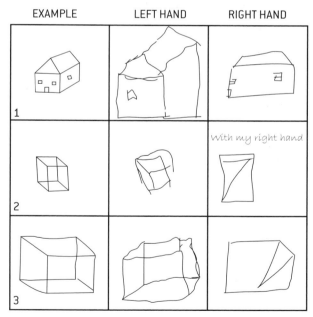

▲ Figure 2.12 Example drawings from the study

Source: Gazzaniga (1967, p 28)

- Both hemispheres independently are capable of forming an **emotional response**. In other words, emotions are not lateralized. In one series of tests, various objects were flashed on the screen and among them the picture of a nude woman. This immediately evoked an emotional response irrespective of where on the screen the picture was flashed. If it was flashed to the left hemisphere, the patient laughed and identified it. Whereas, the researchers reported of a female patient: "When it was later presented to the right hemisphere, she said in reply to a question that she saw nothing, but almost immediately a sly smile spread over her face and she began to chuckle. Asked what she was laughing at, she said: 'I don't know … nothing … oh – that funny machine'." (Gazzaniga, 1967, p 29).

ATL skills: Research and self-management

(A – M – P– R – C – E)

To fully understand a research study, you need to identify its key components: **a**im, **m**ethod, **p**rocedure, **r**esults and **c**onclusions. You also need to be able to **e**valuate a study by identifying its strengths and limitations.

Being able to identify and formulate these components is an important skill. As research studies are described throughout this book, these components will or will not be explicitly stated. When they are not, the expectation is that you can fill in the gaps yourself, on the basis of context and your prior knowledge.

Review what you know about Sperry and Gazzaniga's research with split-brain patients and discuss the following questions.

1. What research method (or methods) did they use?

2. What are the main results and the main conclusions? Note that it is essential to separate the two. Results are the findings obtained in the study; they are related to the measurement of the key variables. Conclusions are based on how these findings relate to the background theory or the aim of the study.

3. What are the main strengths and limitations? Review Unit 1 on research methodology if you find answering this question difficult. For example, if you decided that the study is an experiment, what threats to internal validity could have caused problems? How can you characterize sampling, credibility, generalizability and bias as applied to this research study?

"Filling in the gaps" is a very useful exercise as you are reading this book.

Exercise

To strengthen your knowledge of Sperry and Gazzaniga's procedure and findings, investigate this interactive online game from Nobelprize.org, the official website for the Nobel Prize: https://www.nobelprize.org/educational/medicine/split-brain/

See if you can predict all the findings and explain all the results.

Conclusions

Summarizing split-brain studies and other research accumulated over the years, does all this mean that localization of function is relative?

Some functions are indeed localized in very specific parts of the brain, and damage to this part will lead to loss of the function. Examples that have been discussed here include Broca's area for the production of articulate speech and Wernicke's area for language comprehension. As you read this book and read about the subject of psychology more widely, you will come across a lot of examples and research studies that support localization of some other functions. For example, **Sharot et al (2007)** demonstrated that selective activation of left amygdala is responsible for the formation of flashbulb memories—a special memory mechanism when situations that are unexpected and emotionally laden get "imprinted" in the brain with perceptual clarity (see Unit 3 on the cognitive approach to behaviour). **Saxe and Kanwisher (2003)** showed that understanding when another person's belief is false is localized in the tempo-parietal junction (see "Theory of mind" in Unit 8 on developmental psychology). **Maguire et al (2000)** found that spatial memory in London taxi drivers is localized in the hippocampus (see later in this unit). Most modern discoveries in this area are made with the use of non-invasive methods—brain imaging technology.

However, the quest for a complete map of localized functions has reached its limits. Here are the most prominent points.

- Some functions are **localized weakly**; that is, several brain areas may be responsible for a function but some areas are dominant. There were many examples of weakly localized (lateralized) functions in Sperry and Gazzaniga's research. Although the left hemisphere was consistently shown to be dominant for language, the right hemisphere was also shown to be capable of understanding some simple language. Scientists have been generally more successful in establishing strict localization for sensory and motor functions than for higher-order cognitive functions such as memory, thinking and learning.

- Some functions are **widely distributed**. An example from Sperry and Gazzaniga's research would be the ability of both the hemispheres to form an emotional reaction independently of each other. Karl Lashley demonstrated that maze-running memory was widely distributed in the cortex of the brain of rats.

- Some **components of a function** may be localized while other components of the same function are distributed in the brain. One example involves language: we cannot say that language (as a holistic function) is localized somewhere in the brain, but some specific components of language are (such as the production of articulate speech in Broca's area).

- Localization is **not static**. Functional areas move about. For example, people with damage to a functional brain area may learn to "re-specialize" other brain areas to perform this function. This is known as **neuroplasticity**: many neurons can potentially perform a variety of functions, and the brain can take over the functions from the damaged parts. Like localization, neuroplasticity is relative—there are limits. You will learn more about this in the next section.

These considerations outline the modern views on localization of function. Function mapping is far from being over, and a lot of amazing things are still out there to be discovered.

TOK

Some of the concepts you have encountered in this unit are used in other areas of knowledge too. Discuss how these concepts are used elsewhere and ask classmates whose subject choices are different from your own. Focus on the concepts of:

- function (for example, in mathematics, history, art)
- structure (for example, in physics, chemistry, TOK)
- localization (for example, in geography, astronomy)
- system (for example, in natural sciences, mathematics)
- the relative and absolute (for example, in physics)
- the weak and strong (for example, in religious knowledge systems)
- the static and dynamic (for example, in history, TOK).

Psychology in real life

Think about the potential practical applications of the idea of localization. How can it be used to improve the life of people in Humanborough? Now that you know that localization is relative and some functions are more localized than others, consider these questions.

- Would you fund a scientific programme to search for all strictly localized functions?
- Would you study the brains of children to determine their future abilities?
- Would you research the possibility to relocalize psychological functions in the brain?
- Localization of which psychological functions would you like to establish as a priority? Would it be aggression or attraction, for example? Would it be something else?
- Would you authorize animal research in this area?
- Which methods of research would you most invest in?

Give your reasoned arguments and present your vision in class.

Neuroplasticity

Inquiry questions

- If behaviour is a product of brain structure, to what extent can the brain itself be changed?

- For example, if a patient's Broca's area is damaged, would it be possible to re-grow this area in another region of the brain?

- Does the brain change itself in response to other environmental influences, for example, when we learn a new skill?

- If the brain does change itself, what are the potential practical applications of using this process?

What you will learn in this section

- Definitions

  - Neuroplasticity is the ability of the brain to change through the making and braking of synaptic connections between neurons; causing factors are both genetic and environmental

  - Different scales of neuroplasticity—from synaptic plasticity to cortical remapping

  - Synaptic plasticity depends on the activity of neurons

- Remapping of the sensory cortex

  - Merzenich et al (1984): cortical remapping of sensory inputs from the hand occurs within 62 days in owl monkeys—adjacent areas spread and occupy parts of the now unused area for the amputated digit

- Neuroplasticity as a mechanism of learning

  - Neuroplasticity occurs on a regular basis in our daily lives; when you learn your brain gradually reshapes itself

  - Example 1—Draganski et al (2004): learning a simple juggling routine increases the volume of grey matter in the mid-temporal area in both hemispheres; lack of practice makes this area shrink, but not to the original size

  - Example 2—Draganski et al (2006): learning large amounts of abstract material leads to an increase of grey matter in the parietal cortex and the posterior hippocampus

  - Example 3—Maguire et al (2000): neuroplasticity is observed in natural settings too; London taxi drivers, as compared to controls, have redistributed brain matter in the hippocampus: more in the posterior, less in the anterior

- Practical applications

  - Bach-y-Rita et al (1969): sense substitution

  - Human echolocation

  - Brain-machine interfaces

This section also links to:

- localization of function, brain scanning technology, the use of animal research

- cognitive processing in the digital world (cognitive approach to behaviour)

- brain development (developmental psychology).

Definitions

Neuroplasticity is the ability of the brain to change throughout the course of life. The change occurs through the making and breaking of synaptic connections between neurons. In this process neural networks in the brain literally change their shape. The reasons for such changes are both genetic (normal pre-programmed development of the brain) and environmental (for example, injury, brain damage or simply learning new skills).

Neuroplasticity can be observed on different scales. On the smallest scale, at the level of a single neuron, it takes the form of **synaptic plasticity**: the ability of the neuron to form new synaptic connections and break up the old ones. On the largest scale, neuroplasticity takes the form of **cortical remapping**: the phenomenon when brain area X assumes the functions of brain area Y, for example, due to injury.

Synaptic plasticity depends on **the activity of neurons**. If two nearby neurons are frequently activated at the same time, a synaptic connection between them may gradually form. Similarly, if two neurons are rarely activated together, the existing connection may gradually fall apart. This has been summarized like this: "neurons that fire together, wire together" (which was originally said by Carla Shatz and is quoted in Doidge, 2007) and "neurons that fire out of sync, fail to link" (Doidge, 2007, pp 63–64).

Remapping of the sensory cortex

One of the early studies of neuroplasticity on the level of cortical remapping was done by **Merzenich *et al* (1984)**. Researchers studied the cortical representation of the hand in eight adult owl monkeys. The procedure involved three steps.

1. Sensory inputs from all the hand digits (fingers) were mapped in the cortex. To do this, electrodes were inserted in the cortical area known to be responsible for sensation from the hand, then researchers stimulated various areas on all the fingers one by one and noted which electrode was responding to the stimulation. Monkeys were anesthetized before this procedure.

2. The third digit (the middle finger) on the monkey's hand was amputated.

3. Sixty-two days later a remapping was done to see how the cortical area responsible for sensitivity from the hand changed after amputation.

▲ Figure 2.13 Owl monkey

Results of the first mapping showed that there were five distinct areas in the brain, each responsible for one finger, and adjacent fingers were represented in adjacent areas in the cortex. What happens to the area responsible for the third finger after this finger is amputated? It was found that the adjacent areas (those responsible for sensitivity from digits 2 and 4) spread and occupied parts of the now unused area. The areas responsible for digits 2 and 4 became larger while the areas responsible for digits 1 and 5 stayed the same. It was concluded that cortical remapping of sensory inputs from the hand occurs within 62 days in owl monkeys.

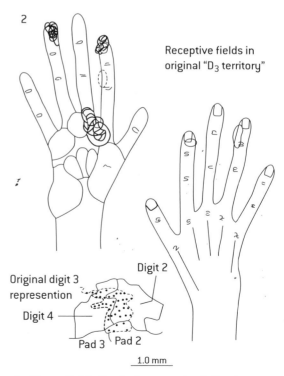

▲ Figure 2.14 Cortical remapping following digit amputation in adult owl monkeys

Source: Merzenich *et al* (1984, p 595)

Neuroplasticity as a mechanism of learning

Neuroplasticity is not confined to making up for damage. It occurs on a regular basis in our daily lives. For example, neuroplasticity is thought to be the **brain mechanism of learning**. When you learn, your brain gradually reshapes itself.

Draganski *et al* **(2004)** conducted a study to find out whether the human brain can really change structure in response to environmental demands. The researchers used a random sampling design and a self-selected sample—they randomly allocated a sample of volunteers into one of two groups: jugglers and non-jugglers. They made sure that both groups had no experience of juggling before the start of the experiment. The first brain scan was performed at this point. Participants in the juggler group subsequently spent three months learning a classic juggling routine with three balls. The second brain scan was performed. Then the participants spent another three months where they were instructed not to practise juggling. Finally, the third brain scan was performed after this non-practice period. The control group (the non-jugglers) just lived their daily lives and had their brains scanned three times on the same schedule as the jugglers.

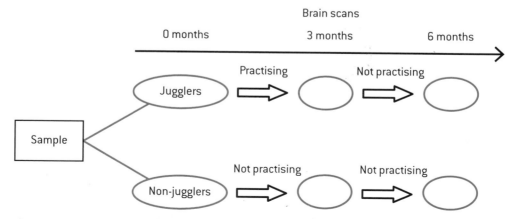

▲ Figure 2.15 The procedure followed in Draganski *et al* (2004)

Comparison of brain scans in the two groups prior to the start of the experiment showed no differences in brain structure. At the second scan, however, the juggler group had significantly more grey matter in some areas of the cortex, most notably the **mid-temporal area** in both hemispheres. These areas were known to be implicated in coordination of movement. At the time of the third scan these differences decreased, but the amount of grey matter in these areas in jugglers was still greater than at the time of the first scan. Also, there was a correlation between juggling performance and the amount of change: brain changes in participants who trained better were more pronounced. In other words, as you learn a simple juggling routine, certain areas of your brain grow. When you fail to practise, they shrink back significantly (perhaps not to the initial state, though).

ATL skills: Research

The study of Draganski *et al* (2004) is an example of how different research methods can be combined in a single study. Is this an experiment or a correlational study?

On the one hand, there is random allocation into groups (juggling versus non-juggling). On the other hand, the researchers computed a correlation between amount of juggling and grey matter growth.

In cases like this you need to determine the main research method and the supplementary methods. The main research method is the one used to test the hypothesis. In Draganski *et al* (2004) the aim was to see whether environmental demand (juggling) leads to a change in brain structure (grey matter volume). This implies causation. This hypothesis was tested in an experiment. When the researchers got their answer (which was yes), they additionally looked at the relationship between amount of learning and rate of grey matter growth. Correlation was therefore a supplementary method used to clarify the main finding.

Knowing what method was used, what can you say about the methodological quality of the study (sampling, credibility, generalizability and bias)?

Do you want to know what areas of your brain are growing as you are reading this book? We have some evidence for learning a large amount of abstract material in preparation for an examination in medicine and that is close enough. **Draganski et al (2006)** looked at 38 medical students and 12 control subjects matched for age and sex. The first scan was obtained three months before the examination, the second scan on the first or second day after the examination, and the third scan three months later (after the examination the students had a break). Results showed that, although there were no differences in regional grey matter at baseline, there were two major changes occurring in the brains of the medical students.

- There was an increase of grey matter in the parietal cortex in both hemispheres. The volume of grey matter in this region did not decrease by the time of the third scan. Studying for an examination in medicine has a more lasting impact on the brain than learning a juggling routine! The changes stay with you even after a study break.

- There was an increase of grey matter in the posterior hippocampus. The pattern was different here. Grey matter gradually increased from the first scan to the third; that is, grey matter in the hippocampus continued to grow even after the examination.

The results of the study were in line with prior knowledge that these areas were involved in the formation of new memories. However, the changes in posterior hippocampus after the examination were surprising. They contradicted the hypothesis because any increase in grey matter after the examination could not be induced by learning. Based on previously discovered properties of the hippocampus, the researchers suggest the following explanation. Stress is known to reduce grey matter volume in hippocampal regions. This may have resulted in two opposite effects on the

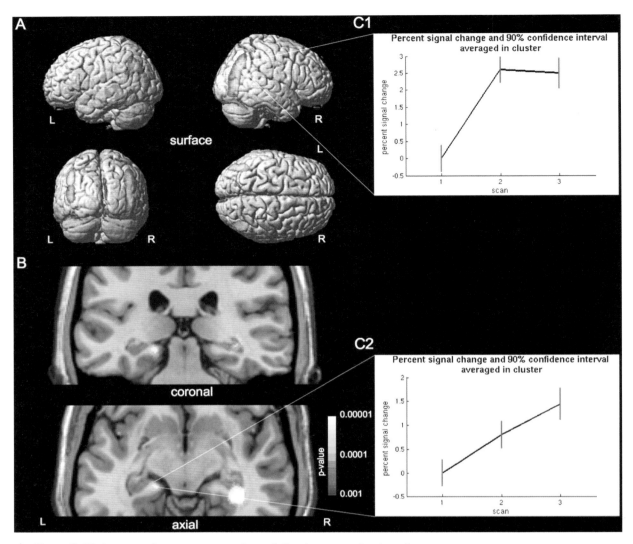

▲ Figure 2.16   Increase in grey matter volume following extensive learning

Source: Draganski *et al* (2006, p 6315)

hippocampus simultaneously between the first and the second scan: learning increased grey matter in the posterior hippocampus but examination stress decreased it. After the examination this negative influence of the examination stress was corrected and the lost hippocampal volume was restored, while the grey matter that was formed due to learning remained.

Exercise

A very useful exercise to develop critical thinking in psychology is coming up with alternative explanations. Review the results of Draganski *et al* (2006)—the researchers saw that grey matter increase in the parietal cortex was abrupt: it increased from the first measurement to the second and stayed on the same level by the third measurement; grey matter increase in the hippocampus was gradual from the first measurement to the third.

Go online and read more about the known functions of the hippocampus (for example, start with Wikipedia). What alternative explanations of Draganski *et al*'s (2006) findings can you think of? How plausible are they?

Another well-known study showing both localization of function and neuroplasticity for spatial memory is that of London taxi drivers. The value of this study is that it looks at human neuroplasticity in a natural setting.

Maguire *et al* (2000) investigated the brains of London taxi drivers, a group chosen for their extensive navigation experience. The researchers hypothesized that the structure of the hippocampus would be different because prior animal studies had shown the hippocampus to be involved in spatial abilities. Taxi drivers in London undergo an intensive training programme on how to navigate in the city, and have to pass a set of stringent examinations to be licensed. Participants in this study were 16 right-handed male licensed taxi drivers. Their average pre-licensing training time was 2 years and the average experience as a taxi driver was 14.3 years (with a range from 1.5 to 42 years of experience). All taxi drivers had healthy medical profiles.

Brain scans of control subjects were taken from the database of brain scans at the same unit where brain scans were performed with taxi drivers. The scans were obtained by magnetic resonance imaging (MRI). It was important to make the comparison groups as equivalent as possible in terms of potential confounding variables, so some exclusion criteria were applied to the control subjects. Subjects below 32 and above 62 years old were excluded, as well as subjects who were female, left-handed or had any health issues. This resulted in the selection of (brain scans of) 50 healthy right-handed male subjects who did not drive a taxi.

Results indicated an increased brain matter volume in the brains of taxi drivers as compared to control subjects in the posterior hippocampus. At the same time, control subjects had greater volumes of grey matter in the anterior hippocampus. This meant there was no difference between the groups in terms of the general volume of the hippocampus, but there was significant redistribution of grey matter from the anterior to posterior hippocampus in the brains of taxi drivers. Brain matter "shifted" from the front to the back.

However, this study is a quasi-experiment. The researchers did not randomly assign people to be either taxi drivers or controls. The results

obtained are therefore essentially correlational and cause-and-effect inferences cannot be made. It seems plausible to suggest that driving a taxi in London leads to redistribution of grey matter in the hippocampus, but we cannot be certain. One of the possible alternative explanations for this finding is that people with larger grey matter volumes in the posterior hippocampus (and lesser volumes in the anterior) are naturally predisposed to choose professions that depend on navigational skills. In other words, people become taxi drivers because they have a special brain, not the other way around.

To test this alternative explanation, Maguire *et al* examined the correlation between hippocampal volume and amount of time spent as a taxi driver. Grey matter volume in the posterior hippocampus correlated positively and significantly with experience as a taxi driver ($r = 0.6$, $p < 0.05$), and there was a reverse relationship with grey matter volume in the anterior hippocampus ($r = -0.6$, $p < 0.05$). Note that the effect size is exactly the same but with a different sign. This led researchers to conclude that, since grey matter volumes change as taxi drivers' experience increases, these differences are indeed the result of neuroplasticity.

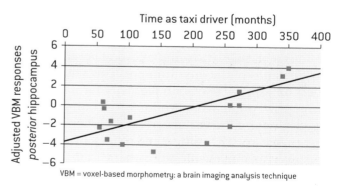

VBM = voxel-based morphometry: a brain imaging analysis technique

▲ Figure 2.17 Correlation between hippocampal volume and amount of time spent as a taxi driver

Source: Maguire *et al* (2000, p 4401)

Redistribution of grey matter in the hippocampus itself can be explained by attributing different functions to the two regions: it is now accepted that the posterior hippocampus is involved when previously learned spatial information is used, whereas the anterior hippocampus is responsible for learning new spatial information.

You might be wondering how many details of a study you need to remember for your examination. You should rely on understanding rather than memorization. Range the study details according to their relevance to the argument you are making.

In the context of our discussion, the main argument that is supported by Maguire *et al* (2000) is that neuroplasticity occurs in spatial memory in real-life settings. This is supported by the observation that experience driving a taxi in London correlates with grey matter volume in the hippocampus.

In light of this main thesis statement, some of the more relevant details would include: this was a quasi-experiment; however, the correlation between grey matter volume and experience makes cause–effect inferences more plausible; there was redistribution of grey matter between posterior and anterior hippocampus; researchers used MRI scans and the control group was carefully matched to the group of taxi drivers.

Some of the less relevant details would include: sample size, age and the exact value of the correlation.

If you understand the essential details of the study and how they are linked to the main argument or thesis statement, it will be easy to remember them. If you also remember small details, it will be a bonus but is not usually necessary.

In any case, make it a rule to separate essential details of every study from the additional details. A good exercise is to write down the key studies in the "A – M – P – R – C – E" form as concisely as you can.

If you have difficulty interpreting the expression ($r = 0.6$, $p < 0.05$), it is time to go back and review "Correlational studies" in Unit 1 on research methodology.

Practical applications

All the evidence discussed so far challenges the idea that the brain is "fixed" and that certain psychological functions are hard-wired in certain parts of the brain. At least to some extent, the brain is a plastic structure that can adapt itself to the demands of the environment. This raises the question: can we use brain plasticity for practical purposes? Potential applications are countless. Can we rewire the visual cortex of blind people so that they can "see" using some other senses? For a person with a mechanical prosthetic limb, can we implant electrodes into the motor cortex and train the brain to control the artificial limb?

The idea that other senses may be used to make up for the lost sense is known as **sense substitution**. One of the first neuroscientists to introduce this idea was **Paul Bach-y-Rita** (1934–2006). His pioneering work in sensory substitution started with the invention of a chair that allowed congenitally blind people to "see" (Bach-y-Rita *et al*, 1969). It was a chair with a large camera behind it. The camera scanned the area and converted the image to an electrical signal sent to 400 vibrating stimulators attached to the back of the chair. The blind subject sat in the chair and learned to recognize visual stimuli from the vibrating signals against his or her back. This way subjects gradually learned to recognize images: objects, shadows and faces. The brain interpreted tactile information and converted it into visual images, which requires neuroplasticity to change the visual cortex and other brain areas. As Bach-y-Rita said: "You see with your brain, not your eyes".

Paul Bach-y-Rita's research was inspired by his personal family history. In 1959 his father had a stroke that yielded massive damage to his brain leaving him mostly paralysed and resulting in loss of speech. At that time, psychological functions were still believed to be strictly localized and hard-wired into specific areas of the brain, so the paralysis and other impairments were believed to be permanent. However, Paul's brother George did not give up and devised his own rehabilitation programme for his father, turning daily routines into exercises. Over several years, his father restored most of the motor functions and regained speech, a recovery that was named unprecedented.

From the TOK point of view, this is an example of how personal knowledge can affect shared knowledge within a discipline.

Another application of neuroplasticity is **human echolocation**. Some blind people can acquire the ability to see around them with echoes: they produce clicking sounds with their mouth and analyse echoes as the sounds bounce off the objects in front of them. Studies have demonstrated that this auditory information in such people is processed in the visual rather than auditory cortex areas (Thaler, Arnot and Goodale 2011).

- Sonar
- Returning sound waves

▲ Figure 2.18 Echolocation

Yet another promising area is **brain-machine interfaces**. These include artificial sensory organs and bionic limbs that can be controlled by thought.

See video

Here are some TED Talks worth watching.

Michael Merzenich reviews modern evidence of neuroplasticity and talks about a range of potential practical applications in "Growing evidence of brain plasticity" (2004): https://www.ted.com/talks/michael_merzenich_on_the_elastic_brain

Daniel Kish was blind from the age of 13 months. He taught himself to use echolocation instead of vision. He demonstrates how he does it. "How I use sonar to navigate the world" (2015): https://www.ted.com/talks/daniel_kish_how_i_use_sonar_to_navigate_the_world

Tan Le demonstrates a brain-computer interface that allows you to control your computer with your mere thoughts in "A headset that reads your brainwaves" (2010): https://www.ted.com/talks/tan_le_a_headset_that_reads_your_brainwaves

▶ ❚❚ ◼

Psychology in real life

Now that you know the research behind neuroplasticity, how could you use it to "make humans better" in Humanborough? Does it give you any more ideas?

Think about one concrete idea that uses the ideas of neuroplasticity to solve a practical problem. This could be something similar to sense substitution, human echolocation or brain-machine interfaces, but you might also think of something completely different. Do not worry about how realistic it is. Present your idea in class and discuss with your classmates.

Neurotransmitters and behaviour

- Some aspects of human behaviour can be explained by chemistry—but can we use chemistry to control people's behaviour in constructive ways?

- For example, do you think we can invent a drug that will make people fall in love with each other?

- Can we invent a drug that will make people tell the truth?

- How can we study the effects of neurotransmitters on behaviour, given the large number of interacting factors and confounding variables?

What you will learn in this section

- Nervous system processes

  - The structure of a neuron

  - The nature of information transmission in the nervous system is partly electrical and partly chemical

  - Electrical processes: threshold of excitation, action potential

  - Chemical processes: neurotransmitters and how they function

  - Excitatory and inhibitory neurotransmitters

  - Agonists and antagonists

- Limitations in neurotransmitter research (increasing levels of neurotransmitter X results in a change in behaviour Z)

  - X may function as an agonist or antagonist for Y, which affects Z (indirect effect)

  - X may serve as a trigger for a long-lasting process of change (postponed effect)

  - X is usually not the only factor affecting Z (multi-determination)

  - X is never the only factor that changes (side effects)

- Effect of serotonin on prosocial behaviour

  - Serotonin reduces acceptability of personal harm and in this way promotes prosocial behaviour

  - Crockett et al (2010)—participants solved moral dilemmas after receiving a dose of either citalopram (an SSRI) or placebo

- Effect of dopamine on romantic love

  - Fisher, Aron and Brown (2005): looking at pictures of loved ones is associated with higher activity in the dopaminergic pathway—a system that generates and transmits dopamine and increases dopamine-related activity in the brain

- The role of dopamine in Parkinson's disease

  - Freed et al (2001): transplantation of dopamine-producing neurons in the putamen of patients with severe Parkinson's disease results in some clinical benefit in younger but not older patients

- The role of serotonin in depression

  - The serotonin hypothesis: low levels of serotonin in the brain play a causal role in developing depression

  - Typical study: if a drug that is known to affect serotonin (for example, an SSRI) leads to a reduction of symptoms in the experimental group, it is concluded that the level of serotonin is the cause of depression

○ Caspi *et al* (2003): a particular gene (the serotonin transporter gene 5-HTT) determines one's vulnerability to developing depression in response to stressful life events

This section also links to:

- etiology of depression, the serotonin hypothesis (abnormal psychology)

- formation of personal relationships (attraction, romantic love), prosocial behaviour (psychology of personal relationships)

- techniques used to study the brain.

Nervous system processes

The first principle of the biological approach to behaviour stated: behaviour is the product of physiology (the structure and function of the nervous and endocrine systems). So far, we have considered the **structure** of the nervous system—we have looked at localization of function and neuroplasticity as structural phenomena. Now let's consider the **function** of the nervous system: how does it work? What processes are used to transfer information in the nervous system? What are the behavioural correlates of these processes?

The nervous system is a system of **neurons**, the nervous cells. A neuron consists of three parts: **the body (soma)**, **dendrites** and **axon**. Dendrites and axon are filaments that extrude from the soma: typically multiple dendrites but always a single axon. The function of dendrites (and soma) is to receive signals from other neurons, while the function of the axon is to transmit signals further. Where the axon of one neuron approaches a dendrite or soma of another neuron, a **synapse** is formed. This means that a synapse (or a **synaptic gap**) is a structure that connects two neurons: the word "synapse" comes from the Greek *synapsis* meaning "conjunction". Each neuron on average has about 15,000 connections with other neurons, so it is a very elaborate network.

The nature of information transmission in the nervous system is partly electrical and partly chemical. Every neuron has a certain **threshold of excitation** received from the other neurons, and if the sum excitation exceeds this threshold, the neuron "fires"—generates a brief pulse called **action potential** that travels along the axon to other neurons, passing the excitation further. Note that the action potential is all-or-none: it either fires or not, and there is no such thing as "firing weakly" or "firing strongly". This might remind you of the coding languages used in computers: essentially, they all boil down to a sequence of 0s and 1s.

The pulse reaches the end of the axon and there, at the synaptic gap, the mechanism of transmission becomes chemical. This happens as follows. When the action potential reaches the end of the axon, a **neurotransmitter** is released from the **axon terminal** into the **synaptic gap**. Neurotransmitters are chemical messengers. They are constantly synthesized in the neuron and moved to the axon terminal to be stored there. A released neurotransmitter is available in the synaptic gap for a short period during which it may be destroyed (metabolized), pulled back into the pre-synaptic axon terminal through **reuptake**, or reach the **post-synaptic membrane** and bind to one of the receptors on its surface.

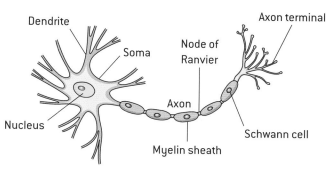

▲ Figure 2.19 A neuron

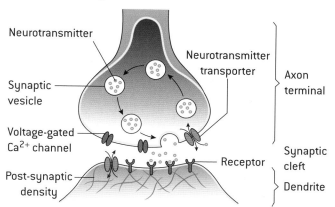

▲ Figure 2.20 Neurotransmission

If the neurotransmitter binds to a receptor in the post-synaptic membrane, this process changes the membrane potential and so contributes to activating an electric pulse in the post-synaptic neuron. Here the chemical mechanism becomes electrical again.

ATL skills: Thinking and self-management

This partially electrical and partially chemical process seems quite complicated. What do you think is the evolutionary rationale behind it? Why did it evolve in this way?

Try to visualize the whole process. If you cannot, view the example video given below or search for other "neurotransmission" videos online.

See video

A video showing the process is available at: https://www.youtube.com/watch?v= p5zFgT4aofA

There are many different neurotransmitters. Their exact number is unknown but more than 100 have been identified. All neurotransmitters are broadly divided into two groups: excitatory and inhibitory. **Excitatory neurotransmitters** allow the impulse to cross the synapse. They produce stimulating effects on the brain. **Inhibitory neurotransmitters** stop the impulse, preventing it from crossing the synapse. They produce calming effects on the brain. These neurotransmitters are always in a state of dynamic balance. When excitatory or inhibitory neurotransmitters are out of their optimal ranges in the brain, this may cause various behavioural malfunctions such as mental disorders.

Neurotransmitters themselves are affected by agonists and antagonists. **Agonists** are chemicals that enhance the action of a neurotransmitter. **Antagonists** are chemicals that counteract a neurotransmitter and so prevent a signal from being passed further.

Many drugs function as agonists or antagonists. For example, a class of drugs known as SSRIs (**selective serotonin reuptake inhibitors**) do exactly what their name suggests: selectively inhibit (block) the reuptake of the neurotransmitter serotonin from the synaptic gap. This increases the concentration of serotonin in the synapse. SSRIs have been shown to be effective against depression.

As you see, neurotransmission is a complex process determined simultaneously by multiple factors. Imagine we have artificially increased the level of neurotransmitter X in the brain and this resulted in a change of behaviour Z (for example, elevated mood). Can we say that neurotransmitter X influences elevated mood? Yes, to a certain extent, but with a lot of limitations to be kept in mind.

- X may function as an agonist for neurotransmitter Y, which in turn may affect behaviour Z. In other words, the effects of neurotransmitters may be indirect, sometimes with many links between the "cause" and the "effect".

- X may serve as a trigger for a long-lasting process of change in a system of interconnected variables. In other words, the effects of X on Z may be postponed.

- X is usually not the only factor affecting Z.

- X is never the only factor that changes. As you artificially increase the level of X, this may result in various side effects.

Research into the influence of neurotransmission on behaviour will therefore always be reductionist in the sense that we need to manipulate one variable (X) and assume that it is the only variable that changes. Nevertheless, with all the limitations in mind, research into the influence of neurotransmission on behaviour is highly intriguing, partly because it gives us a key to influencing human behaviour through intake of chemicals.

ATL skills: Thinking

To be able to demonstrate experimentally that X influences Z, we need to isolate the effects of X from all other potentially confounding variables by controlling them or keeping them constant in all conditions. You can see the tremendous difficulty of this task, especially in such a complex system of interconnected variables as a human being.

Here is a Nobel Prize question: can you think of any other method that will allow us to make cause–effect inferences and at the same time show a more complex picture of direct and indirect, immediate and postponed effects? Hint: think about the field of computer modelling.

Areas that have been shown to be affected by neurotransmitters have included mood, memory, sexual arousal and mental illness, among many others. Let's look at some of the effects of specific neurotransmitters.

Effect of serotonin on prosocial behaviour

Crockett *et al* **(2010)** investigated the effect of serotonin on prosocial behaviour. Serotonin is an inhibitory neurotransmitter that is involved in sustaining stable mood and regulating sleep cycles, for instance. This example has been selected intentionally to demonstrate that researchers attempt to establish links between seemingly distant variables. Effects of neurotransmission on something such as mood or fatigue are believable because these are rooted in biological processes, but prosocial behaviour seems to be a person's own choice or free will. How can a person's free will be affected by a biological factor?

TOK

Determinism versus free will

Determinism is the philosophical position that claims everything in the world has a preceding cause. It says that in order to understand the world we need to identify the causes. Modern sciences—especially the natural sciences—are largely deterministic.

An opposing position—known as **teleology** (from *"teleo"*, meaning "aim")—asserts that everything in the world has a purpose. To understand the world we need to understand where it is going. Religion is usually teleological.

When it comes to human beings, some philosophers assume strong determinism, saying that every action is determined by preceding potentially identifiable causes. However, others believe that humans, unlike everything else in the world, are able to choose their actions freely, often despite the factors that influence them.

What do you think?

A sample of volunteers was recruited for the study. It included 30 healthy subjects (mean age 26).

The experiment followed a repeated measures design with two conditions. In condition 1 participants were given a dose of citalopram. This drug is a highly selective serotonin reuptake inhibitor (SSRI): a chemical that blocks reuptake of serotonin from the synapse, in this way boosting its concentration and prolonging its effects. In condition 2 (the control) participants were given a **placebo** (a harmless substance with no active effect). The design was counter-balanced, and this was a double-blind study.

After taking the drug, participants were given a series of moral dilemmas that involved choosing between a utilitarian outcome (saving five lives) and aversive harmful actions (such as killing an innocent person). Aversive harmful actions in the scenarios were of two types: personal (for example, pushing a man off a bridge to stop a train and prevent it from hitting five people) and impersonal (for example, pressing a lever to divert a train off a track where it will hit five people to a track where it will hit one).

TOK

This kind of dilemma is known as "the trolley problem", and it is a popular discussion in relation to ethics.

In the **impersonal version** of the problem there is a runaway trolley moving along the tracks, and you see that there are five people on the tracks ahead and the trolley is about to hit them. You have a choice to press the lever and divert the trolley onto another track where it will hit and kill one person, or do nothing.

▲ Figure 2.21 "The trolley problem"

In the **personal version** there is only one track, but you are standing on a bridge above it and there is another man on the bridge. You have a choice to push the man off the bridge so that his body will stop the trolley and prevent it from hitting five people ahead. Logically, the outcome is the same as in the impersonal version but it feels different, doesn't it?

What do you think is the right thing to do in both the scenarios? What do you think most people choose to do?

Results showed that responses in the impersonal version were unaffected by citalopram. However, after receiving a dose of citalopram participants were less likely to push the man off the bridge in the personal scenario than participants in the placebo condition. Would you push a man off the bridge to stop the train and prevent it from hitting five other people? If you were an average participant in this study, you would probably say no, but after receiving a dose of citalopram you would be opposed to the idea even more strongly. Note that your judgment on the impersonal version (pressing a lever) would be unaffected.

Researchers concluded that serotonin reduces acceptability of personal harm and in this way promotes prosocial behaviour. It modulates reactions of the brain to emotionally salient situations so that inflicting harm on other people is judged as less acceptable.

A limitation of the study that the authors recognized is that citalopram intake induced slight nausea. This might mean that participants could work out what condition they were in on that trial. However, it is not possible to estimate the extent to which this might have influenced the results.

Effect of dopamine on romantic love

Fisher, Aron and Brown (2005) conducted a study of the neural mechanisms of romantic love. This study suggested the central role of dopamine in the brain response to loved ones. Dopamine is an excitatory neurotransmitter that is involved in our desire to get things done (motivation), in controlling the brain's reward and pleasure centres and in regulating emotional responses. Ten men and seven women who were currently "intensely in love" (but not with each other) were recruited for the study by word of mouth as well as through flyers. The mean age was 21 years and the mean reported duration of being in love was 7 months. All participants were placed in a functional magnetic resonance imaging (fMRI) scanner and engaged in a standardized procedure involving looking at photographs while their brains were being scanned. There were four stages.

1. For 30 seconds each participant viewed a photograph of his or her beloved person.

2. Participants were given a 40-second filler activity which was to count back from a given number.

3. For 30 more seconds participants viewed a photograph of an emotionally neutral acquaintance.

4. The final stage was another 20 seconds of counting back from a number.

These four steps were repeated six times, so the total procedure lasted for 720 seconds (12 minutes).

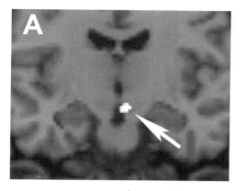 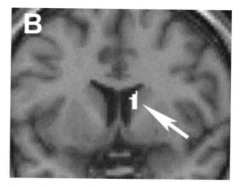

A: ventral tegmental area; B: caudate nucleus

▲ Figure 2.22 Pattern of activation in participants' brains in response to the photographs of their beloved persons

Source: Fisher, Aron and Brown (2005, p 59)

Results showed a specific pattern of activation in the brains of participants in response to the photographs of their loved ones: activation was observed in dopamine-rich neural systems, primarily the ventral tegmental area (VTA) and caudate nucleus. Both these regions are rich in dopamine and form the key part of the so-called **dopaminergic pathway**—a system that generates and transmits dopamine and increases dopamine-related activity in the brain. It is a reward system because dopaminergic activity is associated with motivation and feelings of pleasure. In this way, dopamine activity in the brain plays a role in romantic love.

ATL skills: Thinking

You will learn later in this unit that fMRI is based on the principle of measuring blood flow in specific parts of the brain. The assumption is that the more blood flow there is in a brain region, the more active the region is at this particular moment. So what was observed in Fisher, Aron and Brown's (2005) study is that when you are looking at a picture of a person you love, there is more blood flow in the regions of your brain that are known to produce dopamine.

From this the researchers inferred the role of dopamine in romantic love. To what extent do you think it is a substantiated conclusion? Or is it far-fetched?

Exercise

If you are interested to see how the authors themselves justified their conclusion, review the original article:

https://tinyurl.com/mk7hesj

Reading original research articles from time to time is useful to give you a deeper understanding of real-world psychological research.

Helen Fisher's website is also worth exploring: http://www.helenfisher.com/

It has a number of Helen Fisher's talks relating to the psychology of love.

The role of dopamine in Parkinson's disease

Freed *et al* (2001) studied the role of dopamine in Parkinson's disease. Parkinson's disease is a degenerative disorder that mainly affects the motor functions of the nervous system. The early symptoms of the disease are shaking, rigidity, and difficulty with movement and walking. Later in the development of the disease, thinking and behavioural problems also occur. Currently there is no cure for Parkinson's disease and the exact causes are unknown. In the study by Freed *et al*, the sample consisted of 40 patients who were 34–75 years old and had severe Parkinson's disease, with the mean duration of 14 years.

The sample was randomly divided into two groups: the experimental group received a transplant of nerve cells and the control group underwent sham surgery. In the transplant group, nerve tissue containing dopamine-producing neurons was taken from embryos aborted 7–8 weeks after conception and transplanted into the patients' **putamen**—a structure of the limbic system involved in movement regulation. All surgeries were performed with the patient awake. Local anesthesia was administered to the skin of the forehead and four holes were drilled through the frontal bone, after which the tissue was transplanted through long needles. In the sham surgery group, holes were drilled in the skull but the dura (a thick membrane that surrounds the brain) was not penetrated. Otherwise, the procedure was identical.

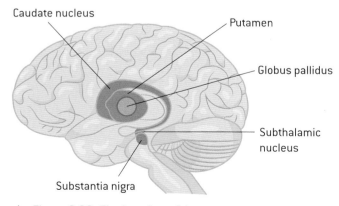
▲ Figure 2.23 The location of the putamen

The protocol of the study and the consent form describing the risks and potential benefits were approved by the ethics committee. A separate written informed consent form was used for the women who donated fetal tissue from abortions.

ATL skills: Thinking

We are dealing with an ethically sensitive study. It involved aborted embryos, nerve tissue transplants and a sham surgery. To what extent are these procedures ethically justified by the anticipated benefits of the study?

Discussion

Would you approve this study if you were a member of the ethics committee? State your position in class and discuss it with others.

A number of measures were taken both before and after the surgery. They included clinical observations and interviews, and brain scans—positron emission tomography (PET). All patients were followed up longitudinally for one year.

Results of the study indicated the following.

- Irrespective of the age group, PET scans revealed increased growth of dopamine-producing cells in the putamen.

- A reduction of symptoms by 28% was found in the patients in the transplant group, but only the younger ones (aged 60 or younger). No improvement was registered in the older sub-group of patients (aged over 60).

The overall conclusion was that transplantation of dopamine-producing neurons in the putamen of patients with severe Parkinson's disease results in some clinical benefit in younger but not older patients. Less response to treatment in the older patients despite successful growth of dopamine neurons may be attributed to lower neuroplasticity of the brain.

Transplantation of embryonic dopamine neurons

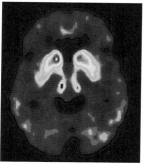 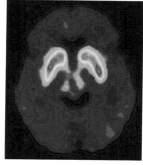

Before surgery   After surgery

Sham surgery

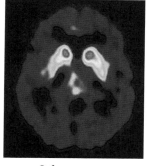 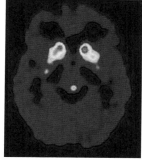

Before surgery   After surgery

▲ Figure 2.24 PET scans from the study

Source: Freed *et al* (2001, p 715)

The role of serotonin in depression

Serotonin has been shown to be involved in the symptoms of major depressive disorder. If you study abnormal psychology (see Unit 5) as an option you will learn a lot more about this topic. The serotonin hypothesis states that low levels of serotonin in the brain play a causal role in developing depression. Studies have mainly involved clinical trials with two groups of patients. The experimental group would be given a drug that affects levels of serotonin in the brain and the control group would be given a placebo (a harmless substance that the patient believes to be a drug), after which the symptoms of depression would be compared. If a drug that is known to affect serotonin (for example, an SSRI) leads to a reduction of symptoms in the experimental group, it is concluded that the level of serotonin is the cause of depression.

However, this logic has a number of limitations.

First, drugs affect neurotransmitters within minutes, but the behavioural effects do not manifest immediately. Sometimes it takes weeks. This suggests that the influence may be indirect or there

could exist a longer path where changing levels of serotonin is just one stage. For example, one theory suggests that increased stress can damage neurons in the hippocampus and so lead to depression, whereas SSRIs restore the damaged neurons gradually, alleviating the symptoms (Taupin, 2006).

Second, not all patients benefit from drugs. This suggests that the link between serotonin and depression is not universal (that is, not applicable to all people without exception).

Whether it is universal or not, direct or indirect, the presence of the link between serotonin and depression is not questioned. Recently, depression was also linked to a particular gene—the serotonin transporter gene 5-HTT—and it was shown that this gene determines one's vulnerability to developing depression in response to stressful life events (Caspi *et al*, 2003).

Exercise

Neurotransmission can explain drug addiction. Some scientists say that the mechanism of drug addiction is that a synthetic drug replaces the naturally produced neurotransmitter and the organism starts to depend on the intake of the drug to keep the neurotransmitter at its natural levels.

Review this article on neurotransmission and cocaine, then create a flowchart to visualize the development of drug addiction: https://tinyurl.com/l9jdghw

Psychology in real life

Imagine that Crockett, Fisher and Freed were leaders of three independent research teams that you previously funded in Humanborough. They have reported their findings to you.

What do you make of these findings as a policy-maker? What practical applications can be developed based on this research?

Prioritize these three research programmes based on their practical significance and suggest one concrete practical application for the one at the top of your list. For example, if you chose Crockett *et al* how can serotonin be used (ethically) to increase rates of prosocial behaviour in society?

Would you continue funding all three of them?

Techniques used to study the brain in relation to behaviour

Inquiry questions

- To what extent can we see inside the brain using modern technology?
- Is there a limit to what and when we can see?
- Can we observe mental processes as well as brain structure?
- What are the principles of brain imaging?

What you will learn in this section

- Neuroimaging techniques
  - Computerized axial tomography (CAT)
  - Magnetic resonance imaging (MRI)
  - Functional magnetic resonance imaging (fRMI)
  - Positron emission tomography (PET)
  - Electroencephalography (EEG)
- Relative strengths and limitations of each technique

- The use of neuroimaging in research studies

This section also links to:

- research studies using brain scanning technology (found in almost every unit)
- studies in the biological approach to behaviour: Draganski *et al* (2004), Draganski *et al* (2006), Freed *et al* (2001), Fisher, Aron and Brown (2005), Maguire *et al* (2000).

For a long time brain research was limited to studying victims of stroke or accident and using invasive methods such as autopsy to study their brains. Comparing behavioural deviations observed in these people after the accident and abnormalities in brain structure discovered after their death led to some insights about the functions of certain brain areas. This was how Broca's and Wernicke's areas were discovered, for example.

Obviously, it is an advantage to be able to use non-invasive methods, allowing us to study the brain without cutting the skull open. Such methods are widely used today. They are collectively known as **brain imaging techniques**, or **neuroimaging**.

Exam tip

You may wonder whether neuroimaging counts as a research method. It doesn't. Similar to a ruler being only a method of measuring length, neuroimaging is a method of measuring variables; it is not a research method in itself. Depending on the context of research, neuroimaging may be used in experiments, correlational studies, observations, case studies, and so on.

Five of the most commonly used brain imaging techniques are computerized axial tomography (CAT), positron emission tomography (PET), magnetic resonance imaging (MRI), functional magnetic resonance imaging (fMRI), and electroencephalography (EEG).

Computerized axial tomography

Computerized axial tomography (CAT) works on the principle of differential absorption of X-rays. The subject lies on a table that slides inside a cylindrical apparatus, where a moving source of X-rays scans the subject's head. After passing through the head the X-ray beam is picked up by a detector and analysed. Bone and hard tissue absorb X-rays better than soft tissue. As multiple X-ray beams go through the head it is possible to reveal the structural features of the brain.

The strength of this technique is that it is a quick non-invasive method of studying brain structure. It has an advantage over standard X-rays because CAT records images of hard and soft tissue as well as blood vessels simultaneously. Unlike some other techniques, CAT scans can be made for people who have implanted medical devices.

The limitation is that CAT scans involve some level of radiation exposure.

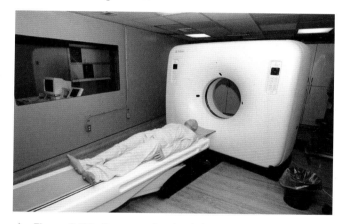

▲ Figure 2.25 Computerized axial tomography

Magnetic resonance imaging

Magnetic resonance imaging (MRI) is different from CAT in that it does not involve X-rays. In general, MRI is often compared to CAT because it has the same purpose—to produce a high-resolution three-dimensional image of brain structure. MRI is based on the principle that some atomic nuclei—in particular those of hydrogen atoms—can emit energy when placed in an external magnetic field. When these pulses of energy are detected by the scanner, the relative distribution of hydrogen atoms in the brain can be mapped. Hydrogen atoms exist naturally in the body, but their concentration in different types of tissue is different. For example, the highest concentration of hydrogen atoms is found in water (H_2O) and fat. Analysing the pattern of emission of energy in response to magnetic fields, we can see inside the brain. After excitation by the magnetic field each tissue returns to its equilibrium state—and the time required to do so

differs in different types of tissue. This information is also analysed. This is why it is necessary to rapidly change the parameters of the magnetic field and switch it on and off repeatedly. The result is the loud noise that is characteristic of any MRI scanner.

The advantages of MRI as compared to CAT include the following.

- It allows non-exposure to radiation and, as a consequence, less risk of radiation-induced cancer.

- MRI has better resolution. This makes it particularly useful for detecting abnormalities in soft tissue—such as the brain.

However, MRI does have disadvantages.

- People with metal in their body, for example, cardiac pacemakers or shrapnel, cannot undergo the procedure because metal will attract to the magnetic field (one can only imagine what happens). Several deaths have been reported in patients with undisclosed metallic implants who underwent the procedure.

- An MRI scan can be an issue for claustrophobic people because it requires being placed in a narrow tube. Also, longer scan times are required: in some cases people have to stay inside the tube for as long as 40 minutes. Specially constructed mirror glasses are sometimes used to create the illusion of openness of the space inside the scanner.

- Lying still for a long time may be problematic for young children, especially since the procedure is new and may be frightening (partly because MRI scanners are noisy). For this reason, children having MRI scans are often sedated. Some clinics try to turn MRI scans into a fun adventure, pretending that the MRI scanner is a pirate ship, for example.

- An MRI scan is more expensive than a CAT scan. However, the costs are falling.

- Interestingly, the high resolution and sensitivity of an MRI scan is a risk in itself due to incidental findings. Sometimes the scan will pick up slight abnormalities in the brain structure that are not actually related to the symptoms being investigated. This may create anxiety and cause patients to seek unnecessary treatment.

Discussion

How do you make small children patiently lie in the MRI scanner? You turn the diagnostic procedure into a play experience! Look at this article on how the MRI scanner was redesigned into a pirate ship: https://tinyurl.com/ofmoy4a

With this analogy, can you think of a way to perform brain scans on animals? Come up with ideas and discuss in class.

	CAT	MRI	fMRI	PET	EEG
Does it investigate structure or processes?	Structure	Structure	Processes	Processes	Processes
Spatial resolution	Up to 1–2 mm	Up to 1–2 mm	Up to 1–2 mm	4 mm	Very poor
Temporal resolution	NA	NA	1 second	30–40 seconds	Milliseconds
Major challenges	Radiation exposure	Up to 40 minutes spent without movement in a narrow noisy tube	Cancelling out random noise, a lot of trials required	Radiation exposure	Cancelling out random noise

▲ Table 2.1 Comparison of neuroimaging methods

ATL skills: Self-management

You can continue Table 2.1 by adding more rows to it. For example, you might add "Strengths". As you read this unit, expand the table and add new details to it.

Functional magnetic resonance imaging

Functional magnetic resonance imaging (fMRI) is called functional for a reason: the image obtained in the scan is dynamic. While MRI and CAT are only able to reveal the structural features of the brain, fMRI can also show the ongoing brain processes. In a typical fMRI study the subject is required to carry out some task in which periods of activity are alternated with periods of rest. The principle at work is that when a brain region is active during the performance of a task, the flow of oxygenated blood in that region increases. The response of blood to rapidly changing magnetic fields differs depending on the flow and the level of oxygenation. The signal that is analysed by the fMRI scanner to reconstruct brain activity is known as **BOLD (blood-oxygen-level dependent) signal**. There are other biomarkers as well, but BOLD is the most widely used. The flow of oxygenated blood directly correlates with the energy used by brain cells, and this directly corresponds to the level of activity in a specific brain region.

An fMRI scan, just like any other brain imaging technique, is characterized by spatial resolution and temporal resolution. **Spatial resolution** is the ability to discriminate between nearby locations: just as with the resolution of your computer screen, the lower it is, the more pixelated the picture and the less detail you can discern. Whereas resolution of your screen is measured in pixels, that of an fMRI scanner is measured in **voxels**. You can think of them as "volumetric pixels"—a cube of neurons. A voxel is the smallest "brain particle" that we are able to see through a scanner. Typically, the size of a voxel that an fMRI scanner is able to operate with ranges from 1 to 5 mm. Small voxels have less blood flow, so the signal is weaker and the required scanning time is longer. A voxel contains several million neurons and several billion synapses. This marks the limit of what can be achieved with brain imaging technology: we can only see a relatively crude picture of brain functioning.

Temporal resolution is the smallest time period in which changes in brain activity can be registered. Think about it as the rate at which snapshots of the brain are taken—"frames per second". Currently, the temporal resolution achieved in fMRI is about 1 second. This also marks a limitation: fMRI is well suited for studying processes that last at least for several seconds (memory, face recognition, thinking about alternatives of a choice and emotional reactions) but is not suited for studying instantaneous processes such as information travelling from the retina to the visual cortex (which takes milliseconds).

With the ability to capture brain processes comes the challenge of distinguishing the ones that interest you from **random noise**. Brain activity associated with the task that the subject is performing has to be separated from all sorts of background activity. Potential sources of noise are head movements in the scanner resulting from the subject fidgeting, pressing buttons (as required by the experimental procedure) or even simply breathing. A clear scan requires the subject's head to be motionless, but this is not realistic. Random thoughts and sensations also result in noise. A lot of noise can be accounted for if the number of trials is sufficient and powerful statistical techniques are used, but some sources of bias are impossible to eliminate.

These are the advantages of fMRI.

- It offers excellent spatial resolution (up to 1–2 mm).

- Unlike structural imaging techniques, it allows us to see brain processes.

There are some disadvantages.

- There is poor temporal resolution (about 1 second) when using fMRI as compared to electromagnetic techniques such as EEG (<1 millisecond).

- All the considerations that were relevant to MRI also apply to fMRI: claustrophobia, cost, lengthy procedure and inability to use it with medical implants.

▲ Figure 2.26   Functional magnetic resonance imaging

ATL skills: Thinking

Every technology, even the most modern, is prone to errors. The more sensitive the technology, the higher the probability of the so-called false positives—results that are not meaningful, but picked up due to the extreme sensitivity of the device. A typical fMRI scans across 130,000 voxels, which inflates the probability that one of them will be shown as "active" accidentally due to random chance.

Review this one-page report of a study that was intentionally designed to demonstrate this problem: Bennett *et al* (2009) https://tinyurl.com/yb27fq2

The sample of the study was one dead Atlantic salmon that was placed in an fMRI scanner and shown photographs of humans in various social situations. The salmon was "asked" to determine the emotions experienced by people in the photographs. The amazing thing is that comparison of the dead salmon's brain responses to pictures showing different social situations revealed some statistically significant results.

This study won the Ig Nobel Prize in neuroscience.

Positron emission tomography

Positron emission tomography (PET), like fMRI, uses blood flow as the indicator of brain activity. A radioactive tracer is used that binds itself to molecules naturally used in the brain, such as glucose. This radioactive tracer is administered into the subject's blood stream. It has a short half-life period (that is, it decays quickly). The scanner then registers radio frequencies emitted by the decaying tracer. Brain areas that are more active require more blood supply, so the distribution of the tracer in the brain will depend on what regions are mostly in use at the time of the scan.

PET has a decent spatial resolution of about 4 mm throughout the brain. However, its temporal resolution is only 30–40 seconds, so quick processes are not easily detected. The biggest advantage of PET scans is their good spatial resolution but they are used less and less these days given the existence of non-invasive alternatives (fMRI) which do not require administration of a radioactive chemical.

PET is useful for detecting tumours and metastases, as well as other diffuse brain diseases, so that it becomes clear what areas are affected by the spreading disease. It is often helpful in diagnosing causes of dementias.

Another advantage of PET is that scanners can be small—so small that a small PET scanner has been constructed that can be worn by a rat on its head like a hat. The device is called RatCAP (Schulz *et al*, 2011). The rat is conscious and fully mobile, it performs various tasks while its brain activity is being measured. This is very useful for research and potentially can lead to a lot of insights into brain functioning.

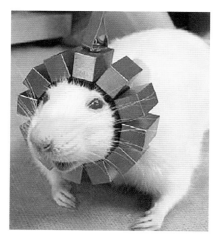

▲ Figure 2.27 The RatCAP

Electroencephalography

Electroencephalography (EEG) measures electric potentials generated by neural circuits. Neurons communicate with each other by sending electrical impulses along their axons. An impulse fired in an individual neuron is "invisible" to any device outside of the skull because the impulse is too tiny. However, when large groups of neurons fire synchronously, electric potentials generated by these impulses become detectable at the head surface. Electrodes are attached to the scalp in predetermined points and pick up the changes in the electric potential of the scalp areas. This information is used to generate an electroencephalogram.

EEG has a perfect temporal resolution. It is capable of detecting changes in brain activity within milliseconds. In this sense it outperforms other techniques such as fMRI. However, its spatial resolution is a weakness: in practice EEG is not used to establish the origin location of the electrical signal. EEG is good for measuring brain activity "on the whole".

As it makes visible changes in the overall patterns of brain activity (sometimes referred to as **brain waves**), EEG is commonly used to diagnose such conditions as epilepsy and sleep disorders.

These are the advantages of EEG.

- It is a low-cost technique.

- Unlike PET and fMRI, EEG measures neuronal activity directly.

- EEG can be offered as a mobile service because the apparatus can be manually transported. For comparison, the weight of an fMRI scanner is about 1 ton.

- EEG is silent, which is an advantage because responses to auditory stimuli can be studied. This is difficult with noisy fMRI scanners.

- EEG is completely non-invasive in comparison to most other neuroimaging techniques.

Using EEG also has disadvantages.

- EEG offers extremely low spatial resolution, so it only gives a very crude picture in terms of localization.

- EEG is good for measuring electric activity in the cortex, but not so good for detecting activity in subcortical areas. The farther away from the surface of the scalp, the weaker the signal.

- It takes considerable experience to interpret an encephalogram correctly because a number of artifacts contribute to noise in the data, and the signal–noise ratio is quite low. Some potential sources of noise are: heartbeat, muscle movements, eye movements and eye blinks, and poor grounding of the apparatus connection.

The use of neuroimaging in research studies

You have encountered some studies using neuroimaging techniques already and there will be many more throughout this book.

These are the examples we have discussed so far.

- Draganski *et al* (2004) used MRI to determine changes in brain structure in response to learning a simple juggling routine for three months.

- Draganski *et al* (2006) used MRI to see if brain structure changed as a result of revising for an examination in medicine.

- Maguire *et al* (2000) compared MRI scans between London taxi drivers and controls to see if hippocampus played a role in spatial memory.

- Freed *et al* (2001) used PET scans to study dopamine-producing cells in the brains of Parkinson's disease patients.

- Fisher, Aron and Brown (2005) used fMRI to study brain processes in response to looking at the picture of a loved person.

Brain imaging technology provided a useful and fruitful alternative to invasive methods such as post-mortem studies or neural stimulation by implanted electrodes.

Knowing relative strengths and limitations of specific brain scanning technologies, as well as major considerations involved in choosing between them, will automatically enable you to add evaluation points to research studies that used technology to scan brain structure or processes. The choice is based on a variety of factors including available technology, cost, ethics and aims of the study.

ATL skills: Self-management

As you continue reading this book, make a rule of noting research studies that used brain imaging technology. Analyse how and why the decision was made to use a particular scanning technique.

Psychology in real life

Look back at the research projects that you have proposed so far for the people of Humanborough and pick your top three. What techniques, if any, would you use in these projects? Would they be invasive or non-invasive? Would they investigate structure or processes? What factors would you need to consider to make the final choice?

Hormones and behaviour

Inquiry questions

- Do hormones influence behaviour?

- How far does this influence spread? For example, it might be easy to admit that hormones influence sleep-wake cycles, but do they also influence things such as moral choice?

- Can we say that hormones influence some behaviours negatively and some positively?

- What is the role of hormones in interpersonal relationships (for example, friendship or conflict)?

What you will learn in this section

- The function of hormones

  - Unlike neurotransmitters, hormones travel with blood, regulate long-term ongoing processes and allow for lesser voluntary control; the nervous system and the endocrine system are interdependent

  - Hormones do not influence behaviour directly; instead, they change the probability that a certain behaviour will occur in response to a certain environmental stimulus

- Oxytocin

  - It is produced in the hypothalamus and released into the blood by the pituitary gland

  - It plays a role in sexual reproduction, childbirth and social bonding

  - Romero *et al* (2014): oxytocin promotes social bonds in mammals in non-reproductive contexts

  - Oxytocin is also linked to such behaviours as interpersonal trust, fidelity or even intergroup conflict

- The role of oxytocin in interpersonal trust

  - Kosfeld *et al* (2005): oxytocin increases trust in humans

  - Experimental task: the game "Investor"

  - Alternative explanations

    - Oxytocin reduces risk aversion in general (eliminated because results were not replicated with computers instead of human partners)

    - Oxytocin specifically increases trust in other humans (accepted)

- The role of oxytocin in fidelity

  - Scheele *et al* (2012): by selectively influencing men in a relationship to keep greater distance from women strangers, oxytocin may promote fidelity

  - Experimental tasks: stop-distance paradigm and approach/avoidance task

  - Oxytocin selectively inhibits approach to certain stimuli—attractive women—in men who are in a stable relationship, but not in single men

  - This may play a role in maintaining the stability of monogamous bonds

- The role of oxytocin in inter-group conflict

  - De Dreu *et al* (2012): oxytocin promotes defence-motivated non-cooperation between groups

  - Experimental task: a modified version of the "Prisoner's dilemma"

  - Oxytocin-induced non-cooperation was motivated by the desire to protect vulnerable group members (and not so much by the desire to protect oneself)

- The role of oxytocin in human ethnocentrism

  o De Dreu *et al* (2011): oxytocin promotes human ethnocentrism

  o Experimental task: utilitarian moral dilemmas

  o Males under oxytocin were more likely to sacrifice an outgroup target than an ingroup target

  o This inter-group bias is created by increasing ingroup favouritism, but not outgroup derogation

This section also links to:

- neurotransmitters

- research methodology

- decision-making (cognitive approach to behaviour)

- social identity, enculturation, acculturation (sociocultural approach to behaviour)

- stress (health psychology)

- cooperation and competition, discrimination, prosocial behaviour, origins of conflict (psychology of human relationships).

The function of hormones

In their function hormones are similar to neurotransmitters: essentially both are chemical messengers. However, neural communication (neurotransmission) and hormonal communication differ in a number of ways.

- Hormones are released into the bloodstream and travel with blood to reach their destination. Conversely, neurotransmission is communication along nervous cells. The implication of this is that hormones can reach places that the nervous system does not cover, because the network of blood vessels is more elaborate.

- The nervous system regulates relatively rapid processes (movement, emotion, decisions, and so on), whereas hormones can regulate long-term ongoing processes such as growth, metabolism, digestion or reproduction.

- Generally speaking, the degree of voluntary control over neural regulation is higher than over hormonal regulation. For example, it is possible for you to control your emotions to a certain extent, whereas the degree of control you have over your growth is negligible.

- However, it should be noted that the nervous system and the endocrine system are interdependent. These two systems interact and to some extent can influence each other. Also, some chemicals may be both hormones and neurotransmitters, for example, adrenaline.

Hormones are released by **endocrine glands**: adrenal glands, hypothalamus, pineal gland, pituitary gland, thyroid, parathyroid, thymus, pancreas, testes and ovaries. Together, these form the endocrine system.

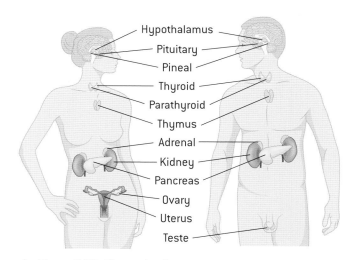

▲ Figure 2.28 The endocrine system

Hormones can only influence cells that have receptors for this particular hormone. Such cells are called **target cells**. When a hormone binds to a receptor it launches a sequence of changes, some of which are genomic: **gene activation** or **gene suppression**. Essentially, what this means is that hormones do not influence behaviour directly. Instead, they change the probability that a certain behaviour will occur in response to a certain environmental stimulus. This is like buying ice-cream on a hot day: hot weather itself does not cause you to buy ice-cream, but it certainly increases the probability that you will.

There is a variety of hormones produced in the body and they all have different functions. The most well-known hormones include adrenaline, noradrenaline, cortisol, oxytocin, insulin, testosterone and oestrogen. We will look at evidence that links hormones to behaviour using one specific example—**oxytocin**.

Oxytocin

Oxytocin is produced in the hypothalamus and released into the blood by the pituitary gland. It plays a role in sexual reproduction, childbirth and social bonding. It has been referred to as "the love hormone", "the bonding hormone" and "the cuddle chemical". For example, oxytocin is released from stimulation of nipples during breastfeeding and this helps to establish a stronger bond between the mother and the child. It is also released with every kiss or hug.

Romero *et al* (2014) demonstrated that oxytocin promotes social bonds in mammals in non-reproductive contexts. In their study 16 dogs were sprayed intra-nasally either with oxytocin or a placebo (in a repeated measures, double-blind counterbalanced design). They were placed with their owner and another dog in the same room and their behaviour was recorded by four cameras during one hour. The room was empty except for a chair on which the dog owner sat. The owner was instructed to move the chair in pre-designated positions every 10 minutes, but otherwise sit quietly and not actively interact with the dog.

Later the recordings were analysed using a checklist of dog behaviours. Results showed that dogs sprayed with oxytocin showed higher affiliation towards their owner. Affiliation was operationalized as sniffing, licking, gentle touching with the nose or paw, play bouts and body contact. They also spent significantly more time in close proximity to the owner. Similar results were observed for the dog partner (the other dog present in the room): affiliation and approach behaviours were more frequent in the oxytocin condition. Furthermore, the effect of oxytocin was found to be bidirectional: subsequent blood tests showed that the more often the dog interacted with the owner and the dog partner, the higher the levels of endogenous oxytocin it had. So oxytocin "triggers" social interaction, and social interaction affects the release of more oxytocin. The researchers concluded that oxytocin performs the function of maintaining close social bonds in mammals. In the "Acknowledgement" section of their article they did not forget to thank the dogs for participating.

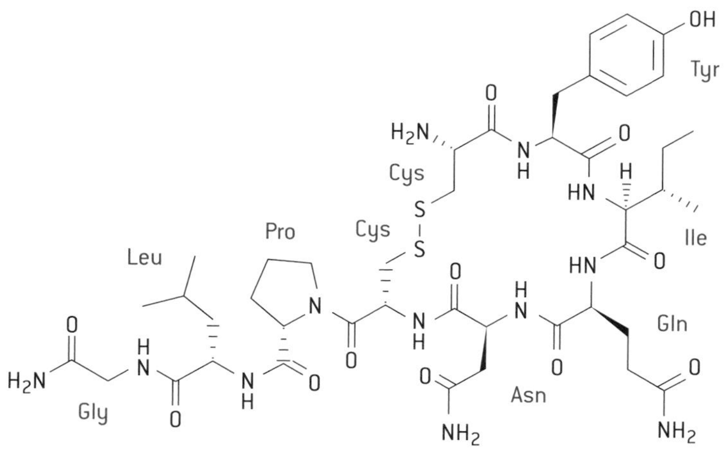

▲ Figure 2.29 Oxytocin

The role of oxytocin in instinctive behavioural sequences, such as attachment to a baby in response to nipple stimulation, is well understood and has been observed in animals as well as in humans. It would be more interesting to find out if there is a link between the hormone and seemingly unrelated behaviours such as interpersonal trust, fidelity or even inter-group conflict.

See video

There's yet another name for oxytocin that Paul Zak used in his TED Talk—the "moral molecule". Watch his talk "Trust, morality—and oxytocin?" (2011) and note what functions he ascribes to the hormone and what empirical research he uses as support for his arguments.

https://www.ted.com/talks/paul_zak_trust_morality_and_oxytocin

The role of oxytocin in interpersonal trust

Kosfeld *et al* (2005) claimed that oxytocin increases trust in humans. Participants were 128 healthy male students (mean age 22 years). Subjects were randomly allocated into either the oxytocin group or placebo group. Substances were administered via an intra-nasal spray.

For the purposes of the experiment the researchers designed a trust game with real monetary stakes. In this game subjects were paired anonymously and played the role of either an investor or a trustee. In game theory this game is known as "Investor". Each round of the game (each with a new partner) consists of three steps.

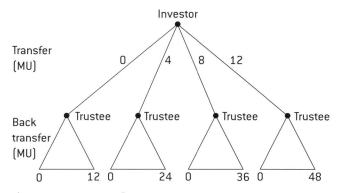

▲ Figure 2.30 The "Investor" game

As step 1, the experimenter gives both the investor and the trustee an endowment of 12 monetary units.

In step 2, the investor needs to decide how much of that to send to the trustee (there are four options: 0,

4, 8, 12). The experimenter triples whatever is sent to the trustee: if the investor sends 4 units, the trustee receives 12, if the investor sends 12 units the trustee receives 36, and so on. Remember that the trustees have their own endowment, which is added to their total. For example, if the investor sends 8, the trustee receives 24 and so has 24 + 12 = 36 monetary units.

In step 3, the trustee decides how much of the now available money to send back to the investor. The idea is that if I (the investor) completely trust you (the trustee), I will send you 12 monetary units, it will turn into 36, and I trust that you will send me back at least 18 and maybe more. Can I trust you, though? We only interact once during this experiment, so you have a temptation of keeping the whole sum with you. In order to trust you, I need to overcome aversion towards this risk.

Participants played the game four times in the same role, each time paired randomly with a new partner. At the end of the experiment the total earned monetary units were exchanged for real money.

ATL skills: Social

Before you read the results of the experiment, play the "Investor" game in class, to get a feel of the task that the participants were required to do. Do not use real money: this activity is for the sake of science, not gambling!

Note your thoughts as you are playing. If you are the investor, what factors do you consider when you are choosing the amount for the investment? If you are a trustee, what does the sum of your return depend on?

Results of the experiment showed that the level of trust in those participants who received a dose of oxytocin was higher than in the control group. The median transfer of investors was 10 in the oxytocin group and 8 in the control group. Forty-five percent of subjects in the oxytocin group showed the maximum trust level (12 monetary units), whereas only 21% in the placebo group showed the maximum trust level.

The authors suggested two alternative explanations for this finding.

- Oxytocin reduces risk aversion in general.
- Oxytocin increases people's trust in other humans.

In order to clarify, they designed a follow-up study in which an independent group of subjects played a similar trust game, but this time against a random mechanism (software). The algorithm in the software was modelled after decisions of real people (trustees) in the previous experiments, so the investors faced exactly the same risks as in the "human" experiment, only this time they knew they were playing against machines. No difference was observed in this experiment between the oxytocin and placebo groups. The median transfer was eight monetary units in both conditions.

The researchers concluded that oxytocin specifically affects trust in interpersonal interactions.

ATL skills: Thinking and research

Write the study in the "A – M – P – R – C – E" format. Be concise. When you evaluate, consider methodological aspects (sampling, generalizability, credibility, bias) and ethical aspects.

Note that the researchers suggested alternative explanations for their findings and then conducted follow-up studies to eliminate one of the alternatives. This shows how a whole research programme rather than a separate study is normally needed to test a hypothesis properly. Alternative explanations and their elimination is also a great exercise in critical thinking.

The role of oxytocin in fidelity

Scheele *et al* (2012) showed that oxytocin modulates social distance between men and women. The researchers studied 86 heterosexual men. Some of them were single and others were in a stable monogamous relationship. Using a double-blind independent measures design, a researcher administered either oxytocin or a placebo intranasally.

Subjects participated in two independent tasks. In the first task—"**stop-distance paradigm**"—subjects were positioned at one end of the room with their toes on the mark on the floor, while an attractive female experimenter was positioned on the other side of the room. The subject was then required to move slowly towards the female experimenter and stop at a distance that made him feel slightly uncomfortable (too close). Care was taken to assure that the experimenter maintained the same appearance over all the trials.

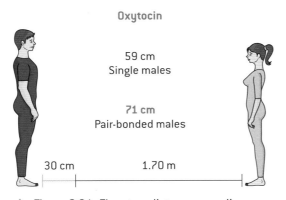
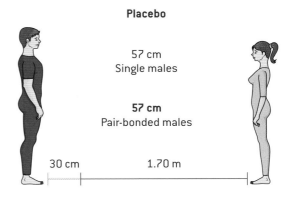

Oxytocin

59 cm
Single males

71 cm
Pair-bonded males

30 cm   1.70 m

Placebo

57 cm
Single males

57 cm
Pair-bonded males

30 cm   1.70 m

▲ Figure 2.31 The stop-distance paradigm

In the second task—"**approach/avoidance task**"—subjects viewed a series of pictures on a screen with their head positioned on a chin rest at the viewing distance of 50 cm. Pictures were flashed for two seconds each. There were four types of picture, shown in random order: positive social (attractive women), positive non-social (beautiful landscapes), negative social (mutilations) and negative non-social (dirt). All participants had a joystick, and if they liked the picture they were instructed to pull the joystick, which resulted in an increase in the picture's size. Conversely, if they did not like what they saw, they pushed the joystick and this reduced the picture's size. This way approach or avoidance was simulated.

Results of the experiment in the first task showed that oxytocin stimulated men in a monogamous relationship, but not single ones, to keep a greater distance between themselves and an attractive woman. It was concluded that oxytocin caused men in a relationship to "stay away from" an attractive woman who was not his partner.

Results of the experiment in the second task showed that the only group of pictures affected by oxytocin and relationship status was the positive social group (pictures of attractive women). Specifically, participants who received oxytocin had slower reaction time (that is, pulled the joystick more reluctantly) in response to these pictures, but only if they were in a relationship. It was concluded that oxytocin selectively inhibits approach to certain stimuli—attractive women—in men who are in a stable relationship, but not in single men.

From the results of these trials it is seen that by selectively influencing men in a relationship to keep greater distance from attractive women they do not know, oxytocin may promote fidelity.

The role of oxytocin in inter-group conflict

There are less obvious effects of oxytocin, too. For example, do you think it can play a role in prejudice, discrimination or maybe even conflict? It turns out it can, but these come as side effects of increased bonding with your own group. The following two studies will look at these seemingly surprising negative effects of oxytocin.

De Dreu *et al* **(2012)** looked at the role of oxytocin in inter-group conflict—more specifically, **defence-motivated non-cooperation**.

This was a double-blind experiment using the independent measures design. The sample consisted of 102 males and they self-administered either a dose of oxytocin or placebo through nasal spray. Participants were randomly assigned to three-person groups and told that they would need to compete against another group of three people.

Following this, each participant was paired with a member of another three-person group and played a modified version of the "Prisoner's dilemma".

TOK

"Prisoner's dilemma" is probably the most commonly mentioned problem of game theory. Game theory is an interesting interdisciplinary field that combines mathematics, decision theory, economics and other areas. It is a theory that models the behaviour of two or more rational agents whose actions and outcomes depend on each other. Things get even more interesting when you compare the rational predictions of the mathematical theory (game theory) to real-life behaviour of participants in these situations (behavioural game theory).

The standard "Prisoner's dilemma" is as follows. Two members of a criminal gang are arrested. Each prisoner is kept in an isolated chamber and they have no means of communicating with each other. They are interrogated independently and each of them has to choose one of two actions. They are also given the same deal, which is presented in the form of a matrix of outcomes, as shown in Figure 2.32.

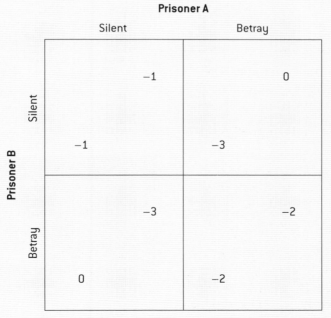

▲ Figure 2.32 Options for players of the "Prisoner's dilemma"

If A and B each choose to betray the partner and testify against that person, they are both given two years in prison. If A and B both remain silent, they only get one year each. If A chooses to testify against B, but B keeps silent, A will be free and B will get three years in prison (and vice versa).

TOK (continued)

It looks as if the most rational choice in this situation is to remain silent—this minimizes the total time spent in prison. However, the problem is that both A and B have a temptation to testify against the partner and be free, so there's a high chance that the outcome will actually be two years in prison for each of them.

What would you do if you were in the situation that is the "Prisoner's dilemma"?

What applications of game theory in various areas of knowledge can you think of?

Figure 2.33 shows an example of the game played by participants in the study.

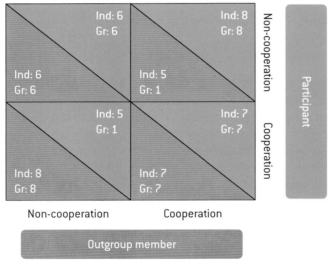

(Ind = individual; Gr = group)

▲ Figure 2.33 The modified version of the "Prisoner's dilemma" played in the study

Just as in the standard "Prisoner's dilemma", the two participants are asked to choose, simultaneously and independently, whether they want to cooperate or compete. Although the decision is made independently, both players see the pay-off matrix. They can see the following possible outcomes.

A If I (the participant) cooperate and he (the outgroup player) also cooperates, I win 7 points, the members of my group win 7, he wins 7 and the members of his group win 7. This is an attractive option: everyone wins quite a lot.

B If I compete and he competes, we only win 6— both I and my group members and he and his group members. This is less attractive than outcome A for all of us.

C If I cooperate but he competes, he and the members of his group win 8—the largest

possible pay-off. At the same time, I only win 5, and the members of my group only win 1. This means that I am vulnerable to my opponent's non-cooperation, but my group members are even more vulnerable.

D If he cooperates but I compete, outcome C is reversed.

What decision would you make if you were playing this game? Outcome A (cooperate-cooperate) seems to be the most rational choice, but the problem is that there always exists a temptation to switch from cooperating to competing because this will increase the pay-off from 7 to 8. You know this, and you can probably decide that 7 is almost as good as 8 and choose to cooperate. However, you also know that your opponent has the same temptation. Will he be reasonable and sacrifice 1 unit of profit for the common good? You hope so—but what if he doesn't, and goes for outcome C? In this case you will suffer (not too much), but your group will suffer a lot: its pay-off will be 7 times smaller. The main question is: how likely is it that, in order to prevent outcome C from happening, you will strike first and choose to compete rather than cooperate? That's what we call defence-motivated non-cooperation.

TOK

Sometimes a war begins when one country strikes another country pre-emptively, because it is afraid to become the victim if it doesn't strike first. To what extent do you find this reasoning rational?

In general, can negative social events be the result of positive, rational reasoning?

Participants were asked to make a choice between cooperation and non-cooperation five times. The numeric rewards were varied on these five trials. The pay-offs from the game were converted to real money and given to the participants.

Results of the study showed that a player's defence-motivated non-cooperation:

- is more likely if vulnerability of the player's group is high (for example, suppose we change 1 to 0 in the pay-off matrix)

- does not depend so much on the player's own vulnerability

- is more likely in the oxytocin condition.

The researchers concluded that oxytocin-induced non-cooperation is motivated by the desire to protect vulnerable group members (and not so much by the desire to protect oneself). This reinforces the role of oxytocin in creating bonds with the members of your ingroup, but also shows how oxytocin has a reverse, negative side—defensiveness and non-cooperation with others.

The role of oxytocin in human ethnocentrism

De Dreu *et al* **(2011)** found that oxytocin promotes human ethnocentrism, a type of inter-group bias where one's own ethnic group is perceived as more important than or superior to others. When exaggerated, ethnocentrism may lead to xenophobia. (This is not something that oxytocin—"the love hormone", "the bonding hormone", "the cuddle chemical"—has usually been associated with.) De Dreu *et al* (2011) conducted a series of experiments all of which used double-blind placebo-control independent measures designs. Participants in the studies were indigenous Dutch males. They self-administered either oxytocin or a placebo intra-nasally. Experiments involved exposing subjects to images of people belonging either to their ingroup (Dutch males) or outgroup (immigrants from the Middle East and German citizens).

Experiments used "moral-choice dilemma" tasks, such as the famous trolley problem we have already discussed (see "Neurotransmitters and behaviour"). Participants in the oxytocin and placebo groups were given a series of moral-choice dilemmas where decision had to be made as to whether one person should be killed in order to save five other people (for example,

hitting the switch that will divert the trolley to another track, killing one individual and saving five). In some of these tasks the target person (the one who had to be killed) was a member of participants' ingroup, and in other tasks a member of their outgroup. This was achieved by manipulating the name of the target person: either a typically Dutch name (Dirk or Peter, for example) or a typically Arab name (such as Ahmed or Youssef) or a typically German name (such as Markus or Helmut). The other five individuals were unnamed and so their identity or ethnic background was not indicated. The question was, in a task like this, would a Dutch person prefer to sacrifice a non-Dutch person, and how does this depend on oxytocin?

ATL skills: Self-management

The studies that have been discussed in this section link to various other topics in this book. It might be a good idea to keep track of the links and connections as you are reading the book. In your notes, think of a special sign that will show a link to another topic.

For now, look at the four studies mentioned in this section (Kosfeld *et al* 2005; Scheele *et al* 2012; De Dreu *et al* 2011; De Dreu *et al* 2012) and think how they can link to topics and concepts of:

- prejudice and discrimination
- interpersonal relationships (friendship, attraction)
- prosocial behaviour
- conflict
- acculturation.

Results showed that under oxytocin males were more likely to sacrifice an outgroup target than an ingroup target, while under the placebo there was no significant difference. There are two alternative explanations for this finding.

- Oxytocin promotes ingroup favouritism.
- Oxytocin promotes outgroup derogation.

Further analysis of the data revealed that, compared with males in the placebo (control) condition, males under oxytocin were less likely to sacrifice a member of their ingroup, but were not more likely to sacrifice a member of the outgroup (as shown in Table 2.2). Based on this, the first explanation has to be the preferred one.

Oxytocin creates inter-group bias by increasing ingroup favouritism. It does not promote outgroup derogation. This is good news … or is it?

	Oxytocin	Control
Frequency of sacrificing outgroup targets	Equal in oxytocin and control conditions	
Frequency of sacrificing ingroup targets	Less in oxytocin condition	
Are outgroup targets sacrificed more frequently than ingroup targets?	Yes	No

▲ Table 2.2 Findings of De Dreu *et al* (2011)

Psychology in real life

Now that you know about various effects that oxytocin has on human behaviour, how can you use this knowledge to inform policy-making in Humanborough?

Think about one concrete project that you would like to implement. List its potential risks and benefits.

Pheromones and behaviour

Inquiry questions

- Do human pheromones exist?
- If they do, what effects do they have on human behaviour?
- What are the major limitations of research into human pheromones?

What you will learn in this section

- Pheromones
  - Chemical communication among members of the same species
  - Although the role of pheromones in animal behaviour is not doubted, the effects of pheromones on human behaviour have been the subject of much debate
- Localization of processing pheromonal information in the brain
  - The vomeronasal organ (VNO) and accessory olfactory bulb
  - Human fetuses have the accessory olfactory bulb, but it regresses and disappears after birth. The VNO in people appears to be non-functional: there is no connection to the central nervous system.
- Search for a human sex pheromone: laboratory experiments
  - Lundstrom and Olsson (2005): androstadienone increases women's mood in the presence of a male experimenter and has no effect when the experimenter is female
  - If a chemical does not perform gender-signalling function, the chances are that it will not produce any other gender-related effects and so it is not a sex pheromone; Hare *et al* (2017): androstadienone and astratetraenol do not act as signals of gender or of attractiveness
  - Conclusion: some chemicals influence women's mood, but these same chemicals do not signal gender or affect mate perception, so we cannot classify them as a sex pheromone
- Search for a human sex pheromone: field experiments
  - Attempt to solve two problems: look at a broader range of behaviours and overcome artificiality of experimental tasks
  - Cutler, Friedmann and McCoy (1998): (male participants) a synthetic human pheromone did not just increase libido but increased the attractiveness of men to women
  - McCoy and Pitino (2002): (female participants) a synthesized pheromone increased sexual attraction of women to men
- Criticism of research into human pheromones
  - Limitations of a typical experiment (Verhaeghe, Gheysen and Enzlin, 2013)
    - Population validity—most studies used self-selected samples
    - Participant bias (demand characteristics)—there are hints that may lead participants to guess the true aims of the study
    - Ecological validity—a concentration solution of the pheromone much higher than that found in natural sweat is used
    - Internal validity—other smells act as confounding variables

- ◆ Experimenter bias—the gender, the looks and the behaviour of the experimenter might be significant
- ◆ Construct validity—even if the influence of a chemical substance or a scent on the behaviour of human subjects is demonstrated, this does not mean that the chemical substance is a pheromone
- ◆ Ethics
- ○ Further limitations
  - ◆ Publication bias—researchers who conduct human pheromone studies

are often commercially interested in the results

- ◆ Replicability—this has been an issue in the research with human pheromones; research remains inconclusive

This section also links to:

- hormones and behaviour
- localization of function
- research methodology
- formation of personal relationships, attraction (psychology of human relationships).

Pheromones

The word **pheromone** is derived from the Greek *phero* (I carry) and *hormon* (stimulating), so pheromones are chemicals that "carry stimulation". The term appeared when scientists observed termites and noticed that a chemical substance released by one termite affects the behaviour of other termites. It was suggested as an umbrella term for various forms of **chemical communication** among members of the same species. For some social insects (for example,

termites) chemical communication is the main form of communication. Pheromones have also been shown to play a role in the behaviour of mammals, mainly in mating behaviour. For example, if he cannot sense pheromones signalling fertility, a male rhesus monkey will ignore the romantic attention of a female (Herz, 2009).

Such findings are inspiring and of course they raise the question: do pheromones play a role in human attraction? The effects of pheromones on human behaviour have been the subject of much debate.

Psychology in real life

The Athena Institute, founded by Dr Winnifred Cutler, markets two brands of Athena pheromone: one for men and one for women. The one for women is a fragrance additive. You are supposed to add it to your regular alcohol-based perfume and "dab the mixture above upper lip, behind ears and elsewhere at least every other day". It is claimed that the product enhances your "sex appeal" and promotes your "sexual attractiveness". This is one of the customers' feedback published on the website:

Suzie: "Men are absolutely freaking out. I work as a bartender and men are flocking around me. I have told my girlfriends it must be the LOVE POTION. My girlfriends in the bar say they can almost feel the energy of the men's attraction to me".

Source: https://www.athenainstitute.com/1013.html

How do you evaluate the credibility of such products?

What evidence should be used to back up the claims made about such products?

Would you buy the Athena pheromone? (Note: at the time of this book's publication, the product costs around US$100 for a vial.)

Localization of processing pheromonal information in the brain

Although many pheromones have a smell, pheromonal information in the brains of animals is not processed in the same brain regions as

ordinary smells. The region of the brain responsible for processing smell is called the **main olfactory bulb**. However, pheromones are processed differently from regular smells. Mammals have a separate structure called **the vomeronasal organ**

(VNO) which is located in the anterior nasal cavity. Nerves from the VNO in animal brains connect to a special region called the **accessory olfactory bulb**. This region is adjacent to, but separate from, the main olfactory bulb (Herz, 2009).

A major difficulty with extrapolating animal research to human behaviour is linked to the fact that humans do not have either the VNO or the accessory olfactory bulb. On this point, though, we need to be accurate: human fetuses do have the accessory olfactory bulb, but it regresses and disappears after birth. Some people do have the VNO while some don't. Even in those who have the VNO, it appears to be non-functional: there is no connection to the central nervous system. If pheromonal information is indeed processed in the human brain, it must be processed somewhere else.

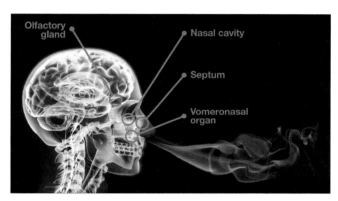

Olfactory gland
Nasal cavity
Septum
Vomeronasal organ

▲ Figure 2.34 The brain in relation to processing pheromones

Search for a human sex pheromone: laboratory experiments

Evidence for the influence of pheromones on human behaviour has been inconclusive. There are many intriguing findings, but there is always an alternative explanation or lack of clarity that prevents us from claiming pheromonal effects with certainty.

For example, **Lundstrom and Olsson (2005)** studied the effects of **androstadienone**—a derivative of testosterone and one of the chemical components of sweat. The study involved studying a woman's mood after being exposed to: either androstadienone or control solution; and in the presence of either a male or a female experimenter. Results showed that androstadienone increased women's mood in the presence of a male experimenter and had no effect when the experimenter was female. It is tempting

to conclude that androstadienone as a pheromone intensifies women's reactions to men, but the study has important limitations.

- The concentration of androstadienone used in the study was much higher than the normal amount found in male sweat—which is a common feature of pheromone studies.

- It is hard to separate the effects of the pheromone from the effects of the experimenter. For example, what if the male experimenter was simply particularly handsome? Additional research has to be done in this area.

ATL skills: Thinking and research

As a researcher, how would you overcome the two problems listed above? Can you decrease the pheromone concentration? Can you think of a way to quantify and control attractiveness of the male experimenter?

It is widely recognized that a basic function of a sex pheromone, whatever other additional functions it performs, is to signal gender. If a chemical does not perform gender-signalling function, the chances are that it will not produce any other gender-related effects and so it is not a sex pheromone. Therefore, to prove that androstadienone or any other chemical is a sex pheromone one needs to show that it signals gender.

Following this logic, **Hare *et al* (2017)** investigated whether androstadienone (AND) and **estratetraenol** (EST)—the best-known candidates for human sex pheromones—signal gender and affect mate perception. The experiment used a repeated measures design. Heterosexual participants completed two computer-based tasks twice on two consecutive days. While completing the task, on one of the days they were exposed to the putative pheromone (AND or EST) masked with clove oil, and on the other days they were exposed to a control scent (clove oil only). Substances were administered by a cotton ball taped under the nose throughout the task. The design was counterbalanced (some participants had the pheromone on the first day and the control substance on the second day, some vice versa). The first computer-based task involved showing the participants five "gender-neutral facial morphs", and participants had to indicate the gender (male or female). In the second task participants were shown opposite-sex photographs and asked to rate them for attractiveness on a scale from 1 to 10. The study was double-blinded. There were two experimenters—a male and a female—and they alternated for different sessions.

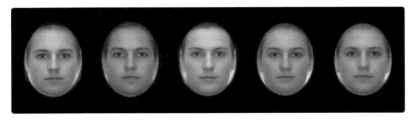

▲ Figure 2.35 Gender-neutral facial morphs

Source: Hare *et al* (2017)

Results of the first task revealed no difference in gender assigned to the morphed faces in the pheromone versus control condition. Similarly, results of the second task revealed no difference in the average attractiveness ratings of opposite-sex photographs. The authors concluded that AND and EST do not act as signals of gender or of attractiveness, which means that they do not qualify as sex pheromones. Incidentally, the gender of the experimenter had no effect on the results.

So far, we have two contradictory studies— but they are not as contradictory as it seems. If we assume that the methodological quality of both studies was high and the findings accurately reflect reality, we may admit that some chemicals such as androstadienone influence women's mood. However, these chemicals do not signal gender and they do not affect mate perception, so we cannot classify them as a sex pheromone. Of course there is always an alternative explanation, which is that one of the studies was biased in some way.

ATL skills: Communication

If you were to assume that the contradictory findings in these two studies were in fact due to the bias present in one of them, which one would you pick as the more biased study? Write a short statement explaining your point of view and giving reasons.

Maybe the problem is that both the studies concentrated on a very specific behaviour and in order to clarify the functions of a putative pheromone we need to look at a wider range of behaviours. Or maybe the problem is in the artificiality of the experimental tasks.

The following two research studies attempted to address both the problems—they were conducted in real-life settings and accounted for a wider range of behaviours.

ATL skills: Social

Before you go on, get into small groups and come up with some ideas for field experiments with putative human pheromones. If you had a substance that you believed was a candidate for the human sex pheromone and you had to conduct a field experiment to test this substance, what would you do?

Search for a human sex pheromone: field experiments

Cutler, Friedmann and McCoy (1998) investigated whether synthesized male pheromones increase sociosexual behaviour of men. Participants (38 men) were recruited through local press releases that invited volunteers to participate in an experiment with the aim to "test whether a male pheromone added to aftershave lotion would increase the romance in their lives" (Cutler, Friedmann and McCoy, 1998, p 4). There were a number of selection criteria: male, heterosexual, 25–42 years old, in good health, not taking any medication, with regular appearance ("neither unusually handsome nor unattractive"), shaving regularly and having adequate social skills with women. To ensure that participants fitted the selection criteria they were screened with personality questionnaires and anyone with personality traits too strongly deviating from the average was excluded.

"Since you started doing pheromone research you've become hideously ugly, yet I still find you irresistible."

Participants were randomly divided into two groups (in a double-blind manner). Each participant brought his aftershave lotion (which was examined by the researchers) and was asked to use it after every shave and at least three times a week throughout the study period. Participants were also given a behavioural calendar which they had to fill out daily indicating the incidence of six behaviours on that day. The behaviours were:

- petting, affection and/or kissing
- sleeping next to a romantic partner
- sexual intercourse
- informal dates (that is, dates not arranged before that day)
- formal dates (that is, dates that were pre-arranged)
- masturbation.

After a baseline period of two weeks, subjects returned to the laboratory and the technician (who was blinded to the conditions) added either ethanol or pheromone with ethanol to their aftershave lotion. The pheromone was a synthesized version of a pheromone naturally secreted by men. Participants went on to use their aftershave lotion for a six-week trial period (so the total study time was eight weeks).

ATL skills: Thinking

Why do you think the researchers used ethanol in both the conditions? You will find the answer later in this section.

Results showed that there were significantly more men in the pheromone group (as compared to the placebo group) who had an increase over the baseline in the first four behaviours (petting, affection and/or kissing; sleeping next to a partner; sexual intercourse; and informal dates). For example, 47% of men in the pheromone condition reported an increase in the frequency of sexual intercourse, as compared to 9.5% in the placebo group. Differences were not observed for the last two behaviours (formal dates and masturbation). Why? The researchers concluded that applying the synthetic pheromone resulted in an increase of sociosexual behaviours "in which the willingness of a female partner plays the major role" (Cutler, Friedman and McCoy, 1998, p 10). In contrast, behaviours like masturbation did not increase. The researchers took it as evidence that the synthetic human pheromone did not just increase libido but actually increased the attractiveness of men to women.

ATL skills: Communication

Referring to this study, how do you think can we explain the lack of increase in formal dates (that is, dates that are planned in advance)? Come up with a possible explanation and discuss with a partner.

McCoy and Pitino (2002) conducted a similar study with female subjects. Participants were 36 regularly menstruating women (mean age 28). Either the synthesized pheromone or a placebo was added to their perfume. Seven sociosexual behaviours were recorded weekly across three menstrual cycles—the same six as Cutler, Friedman and McCoy (1998) used plus an additional category of "male approaches". Similar to the previous study, a significant increase over the baseline was found in the pheromone group (as compared to the control group) in such behaviours as sexual intercourse; sleeping next to a partner; formal dates; and petting, affection and/or kissing. There was no increase in the other three behaviours (male approaches, informal dates and masturbation). The authors concluded that the synthesized pheromone increased sexual attraction of women to men.

These findings seem promising. However, the discovery of human pheromones has not been widely recognized by the scientific community.

The reason is the existence of multiple counter-arguments and important limitations in all typical research studies in this area.

Criticism of research into human pheromones

A typical experiment with putative human pheromones suffers from a number of methodological limitations (Verhaeghe, Gheysen and Enzlin, 2013).

- **Population validity.** The fact that most of the studies used self-selected samples (that is, volunteers who respond to posters or advertisements). This means that the majority of studies are performed with young, relatively educated participants.

- **Participant bias (demand characteristics).** In most studies, researchers try not to disclose the true nature of the study to participants. Mild deception is used and subjects are told that the study looks at effects of "odours". However, there are hints that may lead participants to guess the true aims of the study.

  ○ Many volunteers participate in more than one psychological experiment and they may know that researchers use deception when it comes to revealing the aims of the study.

  ○ Participants are aware of the exclusion criteria (for example, women using contraceptive pills are not included in the sample).

  ○ Study surveys or interviews include questions about participants' sexual orientation.

- **Ecological validity.** Studies typically use a concentration solution of the pheromone much higher than that found in natural sweat. As a result, some participants can identify the smell and report that the applied solution smells like "sweat", "urine" and "clothes". This artificially high concentration can distort participants' behaviour in ways that do not occur naturally. Researchers make efforts to mask the smell by adding a masking agent both to the pheromone and the control solution. This may partially solve the problem of demand characteristics, but not that of ecological validity.

- **Internal validity.** Other smells act as confounding variables, so it is important to control subjects' odourlessness, which is difficult.

- **Experimenter bias.** Since the study of pheromones focuses on participants' responses to other people, there are important sources of bias that are more crucial in pheromone research than anywhere else: the gender, the looks and the behaviour of the experimenter or the research assistant conducting the study. This is difficult to control or keep constant in all the groups.

- **Construct validity.** Even if the influence of a chemical substance or a scent on the behaviour of human subjects is demonstrated, this does not mean that the chemical substance is a pheromone. There are many smells and substances (such as those resulting from industrial pollution or naturally found in the environment) that can have an effect on human behaviour. To be a pheromone, the substance must perform the function of communication between two individuals.

- **Ethics.** There may be some ethical issues involved. For example, in one study women were required to wipe pads containing armpit sweat obtained from donors under their noses each day for three months.

ATL skills: Thinking and research

Review the studies discussed in this section and apply the seven listed limitations to them. Is it likely that these limitations were inherent in the studies? Which of the studies were most vulnerable to which limitations?

Apart from the methodological quality of a typical study, researchers who conduct human pheromone studies are often commercially interested in the results. So it is likely that publication bias will occur—with researchers publishing only supporting evidence and failing to publish "unsuccessful" research.

Development of knowledge

Science is a logical system, but it is also a social institution. So does science develop primarily according to the laws of logic or the laws of society?

There have been different perspectives on this in the philosophy of science. For example, Karl Popper (who proposed the principle of falsifiability as a criterion to differentiate between science and pseudo-science) asserted that science primarily is a logical system. If evidence that contradicts a theory is discovered, the theory needs to be refuted, and the whole process of scientific development is driven by a search for truth. Thomas Kuhn (who proposed the concepts of paradigm and paradigm shift) claimed that science is primarily a social institution, so the survival of theories will largely depend on who supports them.

Suppose a theory does not have rigorous scientific proof (yet), but it is commercially significant. Would commercial considerations interfere with establishing the truth, and in what ways?

Dr Winnifred Cutler (the author of a study discussed earlier) is the founder of a company that produces and sells a synthesized human pheromone. McCoy and Pitino are her colleagues, and their study used a pheromone produced by the same company. While this in itself does not imply that publication bias has occurred, more independent researchers without any commercial interest in the findings are needed to increase credibility.

The most straightforward way to establish credibility of an experiment is to replicate it. **Replicability** has been an issue in the research with human pheromones. Despite some promising findings, experiments discussed above are countered by other studies that fail to show an effect of pheromones on human behaviour. So, the effect is elusive and the research inconclusive (a statement that can apply to many studies in psychology).

See video

In his TED Talk "The smelly mystery of the human pheromone", Tristram Wyatt explains the fundamental flaws in current pheromone research.

Watch the talk and write down:

- arguments that are new

- arguments that have been discussed in this section.

https://www.ted.com/talks/tristram_wyatt_the_smelly_mystery_of_the_human_pheromone

▶ ❚❚ ■

Discussion

Now that you are familiar with more arguments in the quest for human sex pheromones, would you reconsider your opinions about Dr Cutler's commercial products (and hundreds of similar alternatives that exist on the market)?

You might want to visit the website again and look at it through the lens of ideas discussed in this section.

Here is a website of another company marketing pheromones, for comparison: http://pheromones.com/

Genes and behaviour; genetic similarities

Inquiry questions

- To what extent is our behaviour determined by genetic inheritance?
- Is intelligence genetically pre-determined?
- Can genetic and environmental influence interact?
- In what ways can genetic inheritance be modulated by environmental influences?
- How can we estimate heritability of a trait or behaviour?

What you will learn in this section

- Genotype and phenotype
    - DNA, chromosomes, genes, base pairs, alleles: sentence, lines, words, letters, spelling
    - gene—a unit of heredity
- Nature-nurture debate
    - The debate needs to be reformulated
        - What are the relative contributions of biological and environmental factors to a specific trait or behaviour?
        - How do biological and environmental influences interact?
- Methods of research
    - Methods based on the principle of genetic similarity
        - twin studies
        - family studies
        - adoption studies
    - Molecular genetics
- Genetic heritability: the Falconer model
    - The Falconer model assumes that phenotype comprises three types of influences: genetics, shared environment and individual environment, $1 = A + C + E$

- Genetic heritability (A) can be estimated by directly measuring the similarity (correlation) between monozygotic twins (rMZ) and dizygotic twins (rDZ)
- The influence of genetics on the environment: niche-picking
    - Genetic predisposition causes people to select certain environments which, in turn, start to affect their behaviour
    - This may explain why heritability coefficients change during life, typically becoming larger
- Heritability of intelligence: twin studies
    - Bouchard and McGue (1981): a review of 111 studies on IQ correlations between relatives; results show that intelligence is to a large extent genetically inherited
    - It is important to keep in mind the typical limitations inherent in any twin study (Joseph, 2015)
        - Many twin pairs were not separated immediately after birth
        - Many separated twins grew up in similar environments in terms of culture and socio-economic status (SES)
        - Twins share a common prenatal environment

- ◆ Findings might not be generalizable to a wider population
- ◆ The similar physical features might elicit similar responses from the environment
- ◆ Tests of intelligence have certain issues with validity and reliability

- Heritability of intelligence: adoption studies
  - ○ Most of the existing studies support the idea that IQ is increased by adoption into more prosperous families; at the same time the same studies demonstrate that adopted child–biological parent correlations are always higher that adopted child–adoptive parent correlations
  - ○ Kendler *et al* (2015): study of sibling pairs in which one of the siblings was home-reared and the other one was adopted away
    - ◆ Cognitive ability is environmentally malleable: there was a 5-point IQ increase on average by age 18
    - ◆ On the other hand, results also suggest heritability of intelligence: there was a correlation between the cognitive ability of adopted children and the educational level of biological parents
  - ○ Explanation: additive influence of environment and genetics
  - ○ Scarr and Weinberg (1983): the Transracial Adoption Study
    - ◆ Additive influence of environment and genetics (in line with previous studies)
      - ◇ Average intelligence increases: black children placed in white families increased their IQ scores substantially as compared to black children reared in their own homes
      - ◇ Correlation with biological parents is higher: biological parent–adopted child correlations were

higher than adoptive parent–adopted child correlations (0.43 versus 0.29)
    - ◆ Contradictory finding
      - ◇ Young siblings were very similar to each other, whether they were genetically related or not (correlations 0.42– 0.44); this finding can only be explained by the predominant influence of the rearing environment on the development of IQ
  - ○ This contradiction is reconciled in Scarr and Weinberg's (1983) second study: the Adolescent Adoption Study
    - ◆ IQ correlation of adopted children who were reared together for 18 years was zero
    - ◆ Explanation: niche-picking; biologically related children select similar environments, and genetic heritability of intelligence becomes higher with age

- The influence of environment on genetics: regulation of gene expression
  - ○ Gene expression: transcription and translation
  - ○ Regulation of gene expression; epigenetic changes
  - ○ Having a gene does not automatically mean that this gene will be manifested in the phenotype
  - ○ Methylation: the process when chemicals are added to the DNA molecule and repress gene transcription

- Behavioural epigenetics: regulating response to stress
  - ○ Weaver *et al* (2004): rats raised by mothers who were less nurturing were more sensitive to stress when they became adults; this was linked to the suppression of the glucocorticoid receptor gene, meaning a smaller number of glucocorticoid receptors in the brain and so increased production of stress hormones

- Research with humans is limited because brain tissue has to be obtained (through post-mortem examination); also, research is contradictory

  - Miller *et al* (2009): studying gene expression in people raised in poverty versus wealthy environments, the researchers expected to find suppression of the glucocorticoid receptor genes, but did not; however, they analysed blood cells and not brain cells

  - McGowan *et al* (2009): conducted post-mortem examinations of brains of 24 individuals who had committed suicide; people who had been abused as a child had more chemicals in their brain cells suppressing the expression of the glucocorticoid receptor gene

- Behavioural epigenetics: personality traits

  - Studies suggest that measurable environmental differences cannot explain all the discordance in identical twins' phenotypes; epigenetics can be a factor that explains this

- Kaminsky *et al* (2008): in a case study of a pair of identical twins the researchers ran epigenetic tests of DNA extracted from blood cells

- One of the twins was more risk-aversive and had a tendency to overreact to minor problems with a high degree of anxiety

- The DLX1 gene of this twin was significantly more methylated; this gene is involved in the production of neurons that form a part of the stress centre of the brain

This section also links to:

- research methodology

- biological explanations for depression (abnormal psychology)

  - Kendler *et al* (2006): twin studies

  - Silberg *et al* (1999): gene–environment interaction (G × E)

  - Caspi *et al* (2003), Chiao and Blizinsky (2010): molecular genetics

  - gene–environment correlation (rGE).

Exam tip

This section is longer than the others because it embraces two topics from the syllabus:

- genes and behaviour

- genetic similarities.

Genes and behaviour is a more general topic so whatever is covered in this section is relevant to it, with a focus on the nature-nurture debate. Genetic similarities is a more specific topic as it relates to the research methods (and studies) based on the idea of similarity between relatives and non-relatives: twin studies, family studies and adoption studies. In other words, the second topic is "embedded" in the first topic.

Genotype and phenotype

All cells in the human body that have a nucleus contain a set of **chromosomes** (from the Greek *chroma* meaning "colour" and *soma* meaning "body", which is due to their strong staining by certain dyes). A chromosome is a thread-like structure that contains a DNA molecule. The long DNA molecule is tightly coiled many times around supporting proteins, so a chromosome is a "package" that contains folded DNA.

DNA (deoxyribonucleic acid) stores information. It is a code made up of a long sequence of four chemical **bases** (A = adenine, G = guanine, C = cytosine, T = thymine). The bases are paired up, making a sequence of **base pairs**. The DNA has a characteristic structure of the double helix which looks a bit like a ladder where base pairs are the ladder's rungs (US National Library of Medicine, 2017). Information is coded in this sequence of bases like letters in a sentence (change the order of letters and you get a different sentence). This is an incredibly long sentence, though: human DNA consists of about 3 billion bases.

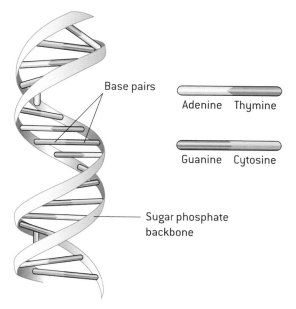

▲ Figure 2.36 DNA

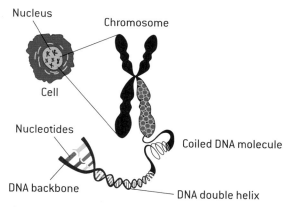

▲ Figure 2.37 A chromosome

As a long sentence will break into lines, this long sequence of chemical bases is broken up into 23 chromosomes, so each chromosome contains a part of the sequence. Each chromosome is present twice in each cell (except for sex cells). Humans have 23 pairs of chromosomes. One of the chromosomes in each pair is from your mother and the other one from your father. Both the chromosomes in the pair have a code for identical characteristics (height, eye colour, and so on), but the chromosomes themselves might not be identical.

If DNA is one extremely long sentence, and base pairs are letters, then genes are probably words. A **gene** is a unit of heredity, a region of DNA that encodes a specific trait or function. For example, there is a gene for eye colour, a gene for height, and so on. The total number of genes in the human organism is currently estimated to be around 20,000.

To summarize our metaphor, human DNA is a sentence that consists of 23 lines, 20,000 words and 3 billion letters. Each word is spelled twice, once by the father and once by the mother—and it may be spelled a little differently by each. The combination of these two spellings determines the trait or a function.

What we have referred to as "spelling" are components known as **alleles**. Alleles are different forms of the gene. They can be dominant or recessive. The trait controlled by the recessive

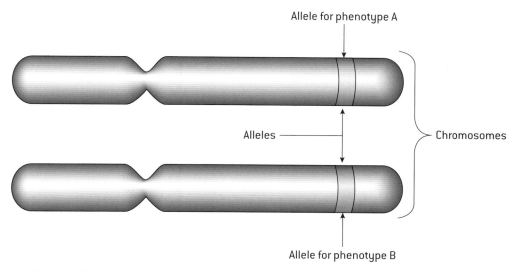

▲ Figure 2.38 Gene alleles

allele only develops if the allele is present in both chromosomes in the pair, whereas the trait controlled by the dominant allele will develop if at least one of the chromosomes in the pair contains it. For example, in the gene that codes for eye colour the allele for brown eyes is dominant and the allele for blue eyes is recessive. So you will have blue eyes only if both the alleles in your chromosome pair are recessive. In the other three combinations your eyes will be brown.

The set of traits as coded in an individual's DNA is called **genotype**. The set of traits that actually manifest in an individual's body, appearance or behaviour is called **phenotype**. Phenotype comprises observable characteristics (eye colour, height, and so on) and unobservable characteristics (blood type, immune system, and so on), as well as behaviour. Genotype is the "plan" and phenotype is its implementation.

The nature-nurture debate

Nature-nurture is the long-lasting debate in psychology and philosophy that attempts to establish whether human behaviour is determined primarily by biological factors such as genetics and brain structure (that is, nature) or environmental factors such as education and friends (that is, nurture).

Today it is widely recognized that the debate needs to be reformulated. There is little doubt that human behaviour is influenced by both nature and nurture. What is more interesting is to answer the following questions.

- What are the relative contributions of biological and environmental factors into a specific trait or behaviour? For example, what is the relative importance of biological factors as compared to the environment in developing intelligence? Can we quantify these relative contributions?

- How do biological and environmental influences interact? For example, can biological factors influence environmental factors and only then influence behaviour? Can environment influence biological factors such as genetics?

Methods of research

The main methods used to study the influence of genotype on behaviour are as follows.

- Twin studies. The main principle is estimating the similarity between identical (monozygotic—MZ) twins and comparing it to the similarity between fraternal (dizygotic—DZ) twins. MZ twins develop from the same egg and share 100% of genotype. DZ twins develop from different eggs and share 50% of genotype, just like regular siblings. If identical twins are more similar to each other than fraternal twins, we can attribute it to genetic influences.

- Family studies. This method also uses the principle of genetic relatedness, but compares relatives on a broader scale and across generations, for example, comparing children to parents, grandparents, siblings, cousins, and uncles and aunts.

- Adoption studies. These compare adopted children to their adoptive parents, biological parents, adoptive siblings and biological siblings. We can infer genetic influences if adopted children are more similar to their biological parents than to their adoptive parents.

- Molecular genetics. Studies of molecular genetics are based on using modern technology for genetic mapping and identifying the alleles of particular genes in a particular individual. Genetic variants are then correlated with observed behaviour. These methods are usually used to identify specific genes responsible for specific behaviour—the "gene of depression", "gene of aggression", and so on.

The first three methods involve the use of **genetic similarity** as the principle of research.

Genetic heritability: the Falconer model

Genetic heritability is the quantitative measure of the relative contribution of genetic factors into a trait or behaviour. Estimation of genetic heritability is performed in **twin studies** and is based on the so-called **Falconer model,** which assumes that phenotype is comprised of three types of influence. These are:

- genetics
- shared environment
- individual environment.

Shared environment is the part of environmental influences that is common to the two twins (such as similar schooling, and the same exposure to books and technology). Individual environment comprises environmental influences that are unique to each of the twins (different friends at school, different hobbies, and so on). This idea can be written in the following form:

$$1 = A + C + E$$

(where A = genetic inheritance, C = shared or common environment, E = individual environment).

In this formula, 1 means that the combination of these three influences theoretically can explain 100% of observed variation in phenotype. In other words, there exist no other factors that influence a certain trait or behaviour apart from these three. Heritability in this model equals A.

ATL skills: Research

The Falconer model

The challenge in the Falconer model is to estimate A—but how can we do that, given that we cannot directly observe any of the terms in this formula?

That is where twin studies help. We know that MZ (identical) twins share 100% of their genotype. We also know that DZ (fraternal) twins share on average 50% of their genotype, much like regular siblings. So, using the same logic, what contributes to the similarity between MZ twins? The answer is two things, their common genotype and their shared environment:

$$rMZ = A + C$$

(where rMZ is similarity between MZ twins).

What contributes to the similarity between DZ twins? The same two factors, but the contribution of genetics is twice smaller:

$$rDZ = \frac{1}{2}A + C$$

(where rDZ is similarity between DZ twins).

Since we can directly observe rMZ and rDZ (by collecting a sample of twins and measuring the similarity between them), we can estimate all other elements of the formula:

$$A = 2(rMZ - rDZ)$$

$$C = 2rDZ - rMZ$$

$$E = 1 - rMZ$$

You might want to try and derive these formulas yourself.

So to estimate heritability of a trait, for example, intelligence (A), using the Falconer model we take a representative sample of twins, measure IQ correlation between MZ twins and IQ correlation between DZ twins, then put these values into the formula above and arrive at an estimate.

The influence of genetics on the environment: niche-picking

Genes and environment are not completely independent: in many instances genes influence environment too. So we need to look at how the interaction between these two factors develops **dynamically**. One form of this dynamic development is **niche-picking**: the phenomenon when genetic predisposition causes individuals to select environments that, in turn, start to affect their behaviour. For example, a child predisposed to depression may intentionally seek out high-demanding environments where it is hard to succeed.

Niche-picking may explain one interesting property of heritability coefficients: they change during life, typically becoming larger. This means that if you use a sample of adolescent twins and the Falconer model to arrive at an estimate of heritability (A), this estimate will typically be smaller than if you use a sample of older twins. As you grow up, your genetic programme "unfolds" causing you to choose certain "niches" in the environment. In this way, in terms of their behaviour, MZ twins become more and more similar with age. This phenomenon cannot be explained by the Falconer model.

Exercise

What are the relative contributions of nature and nurture in a person's IQ? Do you think your intellectual abilities are mostly due to the genes you inherited from your parents, the environment around you or your own efforts? Give your reasons.

Heritability of intelligence: twin studies

Bouchard and McGue (1981) conducted a meta-analysis of 111 studies on IQ correlations between relatives.

The median correlations they obtained are shown in Table 2.3. Let's take a close look at the table. MZ twins share 100% of their genes because they develop from the same egg. DZ twins share 50% of genes, just like siblings and just like parents with their biological children; (children take roughly half of their genes from each of the parents). There is no genetic similarity between adopting parents and their adopted children.

Expected similarity	IQ correlation between	% of shared genes	Median correlation
1	MZ twins reared together	100	0.85
2	MZ twins reared apart	100	0.67
3	DZ twins reared together	50	0.58
3	Siblings reared together	50	0.45
3	Parent and offspring reared together	50	0.39
4	Siblings reared apart	50	0.24
4	Parent and offspring reared apart	50	0.22
5	Adopting parent and offspring	0	0.18

▲ Table 2.3

Source: based on Bouchard and McGue (1981, p 1056)

Imagine genes were the only thing causing IQ differences between people. In this case we should observe the following pattern: MZ twins have a perfect correlation of 1 (irrespective of whether they are reared together or apart), DZ twins, siblings and parents with their biological children have the second largest correlation, and adopting parents and offspring a correlation of zero.

However, environment also contributes to the variability of IQ, so MZ twins reared together are expected to have a higher correlation than MZ twins reared apart due to the exposure to a common environment. Taking this into account, the expected degree of similarity is given in the first column of Table 2.3. As you see, the median correlations obtained from the summary of 111 studies follow this predicted pattern.

Note the following points.

- Even MZ twins reared together do not have a perfect correlation of their IQ scores. This

probably shows the influence of individual environments on the development of IQ.

- At the same time, a correlation with an effect size 0.85 is large. (It would be a good idea to go back to Unit 1 on research methodology and review the boundaries of correlation coefficients.)

- If you put two of the values—correlation between MZ twins reared together and correlation between DZ twins reared together—into Falconer's formula (see above), you obtain the estimate of heritability of IQ:
  $2 \times (0.85 - 0.58) = 2 \times 0.27 = 54\%$
  In other words, intelligence (based on the results of this review and the Falconer model) is 54% inherited.

All in all, results of the study demonstrate that intelligence is to a large extent (54%) genetically inherited. However, one needs to keep in mind the typical limitations inherent in any twin study (Joseph, 2015).

- The assumption that similarity between MZ twins reared apart is solely due to genotype is limited, for these reasons.

  ○ Many twin pairs were not separated immediately after birth, so they experienced some formative months or years together.

  ○ Many twin pairs, even when separated, grew up in similar cultural and SES environments. They were not "randomly allocated" into different environments.

  ○ Twins share a common prenatal environment. Moreover, prenatal environment of MZ twins is more similar than that of DZ twins.

- Twin studies are usually small in sample size and rare due to the uniqueness of their target group. This implies fewer opportunities for replication.

- Twins might not be as representative of the general population as we would like them to be, so twin study findings might not be generalizable to a wider population.

- The similar physical features of the twins might elicit similar responses from the environment (for example, it is known that attractive people are treated better than average-looking people).

Heritability of intelligence: adoption studies

Adoption studies provide a direct test of environmental malleability of cognitive abilities. There are two aspects of adoption studies that may provide slightly different angles on the nature-nurture problem. These aspects are:

- computing the correlation between cognitive abilities of the adopted child and the adoptive parents and comparing it to the correlation between cognitive abilities of the adopted child and the biological parents

- comparing cognitive abilities of adopted children to those of their siblings who were not adopted but raised by their biological parents.

Interestingly, these two approaches yield contradictory results. In general, most of the existing studies support the idea that IQ is increased by adoption into more prosperous families. This is demonstrated by comparing the average IQ of children adopted into higher-SES families and the average IQ of their biological home-reared siblings. At the same time the same studies demonstrate that adopted child–biological parent correlations are always higher that adopted child–adoptive parent correlations, suggesting that the genetic component in cognitive abilities is strong. Together these two effects suggest the **additive influence** of genetics and environment on the development of intelligence: adopting into a higher-SES family results in an increase in IQ, but this increase will be higher or lower depending on the genetic inheritance of the child.

An example of a study that demonstrated this additive influence is **Kendler *et al* (2015)**. The researchers conducted a rigorously designed adoption study of a sample of sibling pairs in which one of the siblings was home-reared and the other one was adopted away.

The complete national Swedish register of male-male siblings was searched, initially identifying 436 male sibling sets where one of the members was reared by adoptive parents. IQ scores were taken from the Military Conscription Register (which includes cognitive assessment data for all 18-year-old men in Sweden). Available data also included the educational attainment of both biological and adoptive parents.

Demand for child adoption in Sweden was considerably larger than the number of children available for adoption, so potential adoptive parents were carefully screened. The mean educational level was significantly higher in the group of adoptive parents as compared to biological parents. There was a modest correlation (r = 0.18) between the educational levels of biological and adoptive parents, which may suggest some effects of **selective placement**.

Selective placement is the main limitation of adoption studies. It occurs because adoption agencies take special care to place children in environments that are similar to the biological parents' environment.

Why do you think do they do that?

To what extent do you think selective placement might have compromised the results of this study?

Results of the study are summarized in Table 2.4.

	Mean IQ at age 18	Correlation with	
		Education of biological parents	Education of adoptive parents
Adopted siblings	96.9	0.20	0.18
Home-reared siblings	92.0	0.34	–

▲ Table 2.4

Source: based on Kendler *et al* (2015, p 4613)

Interpretation of these findings suggests that cognitive ability is environmentally malleable: there was a 5-point IQ increase on average by age 18. The fact that there is a correlation between cognitive ability of adopted children and educational levels of adoptive parents supports this conclusion. On the other hand, results also suggest heritability of intelligence: this is evident from the correlation between cognitive ability of adopted children and the educational level of biological parents. Results seem to suggest an additive influence of environment and genetics: the largest IQ scores were observed in adopted children from well-educated biological families adopted into well-educated families.

Scarr and Weinberg (1983) reported on the results of two longitudinal studies launched in 1974, both of which investigated malleability of intelligence. One of the studies—**the Transracial Adoption Study**—was designed to see if black children reared by white families performed on tests of IQ and school achievement as well as other adoptees. The other study—**the Adolescent Adoption Study**—looked at how differences in cognitive ability accumulate over years till adolescence. Collectively these two studies are known as the **Minnesota Adoption Studies**.

The Transracial Adoption Study sampled 101 adoptive families who had biological children but who also adopted transracially. Some of the adopted children were black and some white; some children were adopted in the first year of life and some after 12 months of age. All children were assessed on IQ and school achievement tests.

Why would the authors of the study assume that adoption of black children into white families would result in cognitive benefits?

To understand the rationale behind the study, note the following background details.

- Back in 1974, random samples of black and white participants did not perform equally well on tests of intelligence and school achievement (the average IQ for white participants was around 100 while the average IQ for black participants was around 85–90). This could mostly be attributed to a lower SES status of black families, as well as stronger exposure of the white population to the culture of achievement, schools and tests.

- The black population of Minnesota was small in 1974 (around 1% of the total population). There were many black children available for adoption and few black families to adopt them.

- Typically, adoption agencies place children in well-off families with higher-than-average SES and non-abusive environments. All adoptive families that participated in the study could be classified as highly educated and above average in income.

- So a black child adopted into a white family at that time would typically end up in a richer environment. If intelligence is malleable, we can expect IQ scores of adopted children to be higher than the population baseline.

Group	Average IQ
White population	100
Mean IQ of adoptive parents	120
Natural children of the adoptive parents	119
Black children reared in their own homes	90
Adopted children (white)	111
Adopted children (black)	106
Black children adopted in the first 12 months of life	110

▲ Table 2.5

Source: based on Scarr and Weinberg (1976) and Scarr and Weinberg (1983)

Table 2.5 summarizes the main results of the study.

Overall, results of the study support the idea of additive influence of genetics and the environment to the development of IQ. In this sense it corroborated the findings of Kendler *et al* (2015).

On the one hand, adoption increased cognitive abilities of adopted children.

- Black children placed in white families increased their IQ scores substantially as compared to black children reared in their own homes (an increase of 16 IQ points).

- Early adoption resulted in higher IQ scores than late adoption. Black children adopted early scored 110 IQ points on average—almost as high as the average score of adopted white children.

On the other hand, just as in Kendler *et al*'s (2015) study, the correlation between the IQ of adoptive parents and adopted children was lower than the correlation between adopted children and their biological parents (0.29 and 0.43 respectively). From these data researchers estimated that 40–70% of IQ variance in the sample was due to genetic differences among the children (Scarr and Weinberg, 1983, pp 262–63).

The additive influence suggests that an increase in IQ occurs due to environmental factors, but also suggests that how responsive a particular child would be to environmental influences depends on the child's genetics. Children with "good" genetics placed in "good" environments get double advantage.

A contradictory finding from the same study, however, is that young siblings were very similar to each other, whether they were genetically related or not. The IQ correlations of adopted siblings were very nearly as high as those of the biological siblings reared together (0.44 and 0.42 respectively): there is the same amount of similarity between two adopted siblings as there is between two natural siblings. This finding can only be explained by the predominant influence of the rearing environment on the development of IQ.

This contradiction is reconciled in the second study—**the Adolescent Adoption Study**. In this study participants were adolescents who had been adopted early in the first year of life and spent an average of 18 years in their new families. Their adoptive parents, their biological parents and biological children of their adoptive parents also participated in the study. The IQ correlations of the biologically related siblings were similar to those in the Transracial Adoption Study: 0.35. However, the IQ correlation of adopted children who were reared together for 18 years was zero.

Researchers concluded that observed results may be due to **niche-picking**. Young children reared in the same family are similar to each other, no matter whether they are genetically related or not, because they share a similar rearing environment. On the other hand, older adolescents are similar only if they share genes. This may mean that they have escaped the influences of the family and are now free to select their own environment. The fact that biologically related children select similar environments (which may explain the observed correlation of 0.35) is an example of niche-picking.

In this way, genetically related people become more and more similar with age as the genetic programme "unfolds" and the child begins to pick his or her "niches" in the environment. This process can either strengthen or weaken the effects of the rearing environment.

Exercise

The Minnesota Center for Twin and Family Research (MCTFR) is currently heading five different projects, including two that added modern technology to twin research: the GEDI project has added the study of DNA and the MRI project has added MRI parameters. You can learn more about the projects here: http://mctfr.psych.umn.edu/aboutus/index.html

Write a short paragraph to answer the question: can DNA mapping and brain imaging lead to potential breakthroughs in the nature-nurture debate?

ATL skills: Self-management

Write down a summary of the findings of these three studies:

- Bouchard and McGue (1981)
- Kendler *et al* (2015)
- Scarr and Weinberg (1983).

For each study highlight the findings that are most essential in the context of the nature-nurture debate.

Compare the findings.

The influence of environment on genetics: regulation of gene expression

ATL skills: Thinking

We have seen how genetics can influence a trait either directly or indirectly through niche-picking.

Do you think the environment can influence genetics? How?

Biologically, genotype becomes manifested as phenotype through a process called **gene expression**. Each gene contains instructions for the synthesis of a **functional product**—in most cases a protein—a molecule which will then influence the chemical composition of the cells that determine the trait (eye colour, for example). For simplicity, from now on we will call all functional products **proteins**. Proteins usually are a chain of amino acids.

The process of constructing a protein based on the plan encoded in the DNA involves two major steps: **transcription** and **translation**. In transcription, the sequence of the gene is copied to make an **RNA (ribonucleic acid)** molecule. In translation, the RNA molecule is decoded into a sequence of amino acids in a protein. So transcription uses the same "language" of base pairs while translation uses a different language of amino acids in a protein. Transcription is like photocopying and translation is like reading aloud from the photocopy.

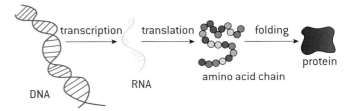

▲ Figure 2.39 Gene expression

In humans transcription takes place in the nucleus of a cell, and translation takes place in cell structures known as ribosomes. A ribosome latches onto the RNA molecule, finds its starting point (indicated by a special chemical) and rapidly moves along the RNA, synthesizing one amino acid at a time, building a protein that mirrors the RNA. Once the protein is finished, it is transported to its destination (either within the cell or not) and performs its job.

A wide range of sophisticated mechanisms can be used by the body to increase or decrease the production of proteins based on the genetic code. Collectively these mechanisms are known as **regulation of gene expression**. The important implication here is that having a gene does not automatically mean that this gene will be manifested in the phenotype. Any step of gene expression can be modulated, from the DNA–RNA transcription to modification of a protein after translation. Some genes can be suppressed completely. The process when chemicals are added to the DNA molecule, and so repress gene transcription, is known as **methylation**. Imagine your photocopying machine started to print certain words indistinctly, as if trying to refuse to print these words. That's what methylation can probably be compared to.

Regulation of gene expression results in **epigenetic changes** (from the Greek *epi* meaning "over" or "outside of")—deviation of phenotypes from the genetic code in the DNA sequence. Epigenetic changes can be attributed to environmental influences, and in this sense it is a study of how nurture influences nature.

If they ask you anything you don't know, just just say it's due to epigenetics.

Epigenetic changes can influence the growth of neurons in the developing brain of a child and influence brain activity in adults. Both processes result in a change of behaviour.

Behavioural epigenetics: regulating response to stress

Behavioural epigenetics was demonstrated in the pioneering research of **Weaver *et al* (2004)**. They found that the type of nurturing rats receive from their mothers in the young ones' early life affects the way their brain responds to stress later in life. More specifically, rats raised by mothers that were less nurturing (for example, licked and groomed their young less often) were more sensitive to stress when they became adults. For example, when their movements were restricted (by placing them in a narrow tube), their adrenal glands produced more stress hormones. This increased production of stress hormones was

linked to a fewer number of receptors for these hormones in the brain (specifically **glucocorticoid receptors**). In its turn, the smaller number of glucocorticoid receptors in the brain was linked to the suppression of the **glucocorticoid receptor gene**. The gene itself did not differ in the groups of rats receiving different nurturing, but rats raised by less-nurturing mothers had more chemicals that inhibited transcription of the glucocorticoid receptor gene. As a result, fewer receptors were produced; more stress hormones were released; and the organism suffered more consequences of stress.

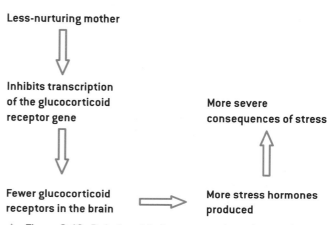

▲ Figure 2.40 Relationship between reduced nurturing when young and response to stress in rats

To confirm their findings, the researchers conducted studies where they gave rats substances that reversed the effects of transcription suppression for that particular gene, and this treatment normalized responses to stress even in less-nurtured rats (Miller, 2010).

Such research studies have far-reaching implications. If similar mechanisms are demonstrated in humans, then we can pinpoint specific causes for certain behavioural changes on the level of proteins. For example, there are well-researched and documented effects of poverty in early childhood on health and behavioural patterns later in life (see Unit 8 on developmental psychology). Children who experience poverty early in life undergo changes in cognitive abilities, social behaviour and other areas. The question is: can the mechanism of these changes be behavioural epigenetics? Imagine we found that the effects of extreme early poverty on cognitive development of children can be traced back to specific chemicals suppressing the expression of certain genes—then can we invent a drug that would suppress the effects of these chemicals and so reverse the influence of poverty?

While this area of research is intriguing, there is a major issue that slows down the development of our knowledge in this field. To study gene expression, human brain tissue needs to be obtained—and the only way to do it (ethically) is through post-mortem examination.

Evidence in this area is inconclusive. **Miller et al (2009)** studied gene expression in people raised in poverty versus wealthy environments. The researchers expected to find increased concentrations of chemicals that suppress the glucocorticoid receptor genes, as predicted by Weaver *et al*'s research with rodents, but they didn't. However, they measured these chemicals in white blood cells, and arguably epigenetic changes in brain and blood cells might not be the same. **McGowan et al (2009)** conducted post-mortem examinations of the brains of 24 individuals who had committed suicide. Half of these people had been abused in childhood. Examination revealed epigenetic changes in brain cells similar to those in the rodent study: people who had been abused as children had more chemicals in their brain cells suppressing the expression of the glucocorticoid receptor gene.

The work is still ongoing, and it is a burning topic, so any wide generalizations would at this point be premature (Miller, 2010).

Behavioural epigenetics: personality traits

MZ (identical) twins are 100% similar in terms of their DNA sequence. However, certain phenotypical differences between MZ twins are observed. Traditionally these differences have been attributed to individual environments. However, some recent studies suggest that measurable environmental differences cannot explain all the discordance in identical twins' phenotypes. There may exist other factors over and above what was suggested in the Falconer model. One such possible factor is epigenetics.

Kaminsky *et al* (2008) conducted an extensive case study of a pair of identical twins using cognitive and personality tests as well as genetic and epigenetic tests. Epigenetic testing was performed on DNA extracted from blood cells.

Participants were two 49-year-old female MZ twins, one of them a war journalist and the other an office manager in a law firm. When they were young they were very close to each other and their parents tried to raise them in the same way and ensure they were undistinguishable (for example, the parents dressed the girls the same). At age 17 the "war twin" left home, travelled a lot and ended up choosing the career of a war journalist working in multiple war zones in Africa, the Middle East and the Balkans. She was exposed to atrocities of war, saw people killed and lost close colleagues. She married in her forties and never had children. Occasionally she drank alcohol in excess. Her sister's life turned out to be quite different. She settled down early with a career in law, married young and soon had two children. She drank alcohol occasionally, but never in excess. Despite living far from each other, the "war twin" and the "law twin" remained emotionally close and met as often as they could.

Personality questionnaires showed a difference in that whereas the war twin's profile appeared normal, the law twin had a tendency to overreact to minor problems with a high degree of anxiety and tension. According to tests, the law twin also was more risk-aversive than the war twin.

Variations in gene expression were examined by comparing methylation pairwise in 12,192 DNA regions (genes). Results showed that one particular gene was differentially methylated in the war twin and in the law twin. This was the DLX1 gene. This gene is known to be involved in the production of neurons that form a part of the stress centre of the brain. The authors suggest that this discordance in DLX1 gene methylation can explain the reduced overall level of anxiety in the war twin as compared to the law twin.

Note that a cause–effect relationship in the study should be inferred with caution because differences in DLX1 methylation may themselves have been caused by the environment. The researchers also recognize that one twin pair is not enough to make definitive statements about the role of DLX1 methylation in the development of stress responses in MZ twins. Another important limitation of the study is that DNA was obtained from blood cells and, as you know, gene expression in blood and brain cells may be different.

ATL skills: Thinking and self-management

In this section we have looked at various aspects of genetic influences on behaviour. These are the key points.

- Different traits are influenced by genetic inheritance to different degrees.

- The traditional way to estimate this influence is through studies based on genetic similarity (twin, family and adoption studies).

- Using the example of intelligence, we have seen that these studies demonstrate additive influence of genetics and environment. On the one hand, adoption into more enriched environments results in an increase in average IQ scores. On the other hand, IQ of adopted children correlates more strongly with that of their biological parents. This suggests that biological influences add to environmental influences.

- Another finding is that genetic heritability increases with age. Similarity between related individuals increases as they grow older. This suggests niche-picking: biological factors can influence environmental factors.

- Environmental factors can influence biological factors through the process of regulation of gene expression. Genes can be switched on and off in response to environmental influences.

- We have therefore seen that there is a complex dynamic interaction between genetic and environmental factors, which makes the nature-nurture debate in its original form outdated.

Review the section and find the supporting arguments and evidence for each of these key points.

Psychology in real life

To what extent would it be possible—and acceptable—to use genetics in Humanborough in the following projects?

- Using knowledge of heritability of certain traits and genetic mapping, you set out to establish a dating agency that would match people based on the predicted qualities of their offspring.

- Your aim is to invent a drug that would reverse the effects of methylation of the glucocorticoid gene and market it as a drug that "reverses the effects of bad parenting".

- You want to enhance requirements for selective placement in adoption agencies.

Evolutionary explanations for behaviour

Inquiry questions

- Is the theory of evolution useful for explaining human behaviour?

- What is the explanatory power of evolutionary explanations for behaviour? Can they be used for all possible behaviours?

- If we are genetically similar to animals and genes affect behaviour, does it mean we are behaviourally similar to animals too?

What you will learn in this section

- The theory of evolution
  - The need to survive and reproduce
  - Differential fitness
  - Survival of the fittest
  - Natural selection
- A range of evolutionary explanations in psychology
  - Chiao and Blizinsky (2010): gene-culture co-evolution theory
  - Hamilton (1964), Madsen *et al* (2007): kin selection theory
  - LeDoux (1996): brain pathways of processing fear stimuli
  - Call and Tomasello (2008): theory of mind, animal research
  - Harlow (1958), Shaver and Hazan (1988): theory of attachment (from animal to human research)
- Evolutionary explanation for disgust
  - Curtis, Aunger and Rabie (2004): disgust evolved as a protection from risk of disease
  - Five specific hypotheses; a strong support for the evolutionary explanation is only expected if all the five hypotheses are backed up by evidence

- Criticism of evolutionary explanations in psychology
  - Massive modularity versus neuroplasticity
  - Speculations about the environment
  - Testability
  - Assumptions about linearity of development
  - Cultural variation
  - Adaptation versus other evolutionary mechanisms

This section also links to:

- emotional processing (cognitive approach to behaviour)
- biological explanations for depression (abnormal psychology)
- prosocial behaviour, altruism, formation of personal relationships (psychology of human relationships)
- theory of mind (developmental psychology)
- genetics and animal studies.

One major conclusion that can be drawn from research into genetic foundations of behaviour is that genes can code for behaviour as well as physical traits.

We know that physical traits are subject to evolutionary pressures. If genes code for behaviour as well as physical traits, does it mean that behaviour is subject to evolutionary pressures too? This seems to be a reasonable idea. This is why a variety of behaviours (more accurately, the origin of these behaviours) have been explained using evolutionary reasoning.

First we will briefly review the ideas of evolution, then review some major examples of evolutionary explanations in psychology, including the ones you will come across in other units, and then we will focus on one example—the emotion of disgust—to demonstrate typical reasoning of evolutionary psychologists. We will also discuss major flaws and limitations of evolutionary explanations for behaviour.

The theory of evolution

Evolution is the process by which organisms change from generation to generation as a result of a change in heritable characteristics. It is not just any random change; as suggested by Charles Darwin, there is deep logic to this process.

The modern **theory of evolution** (a combination of Darwin's theory with the discoveries of genetics) is based on the following premises.

- Biological organisms are driven by the **need to survive and reproduce**.

- There is considerable variation in the traits of individual organisms from the same population. Organisms having different traits are adapted to their environment to varying degrees—some better, some worse. This is called "**differential fitness**".

- Those organisms that are well adapted to the environment have higher chances of surviving and producing offspring. Organisms that are less adapted die out or are unable to produce offspring. This is called "**survival of the fittest**".

- Gradually as those organisms that are less adapted do not pass on their genes, those genes

disappear from the population gene pool. More adapted organisms produce more offspring, so their genes in the gene pool get stronger. This is called "**natural selection**".

As the environment changes, organisms need to adapt to this change. Scarce resources (such as food and mates) make organisms fight for survival.

The theory of evolution has a great explanatory power. It explains the variety of species and their modifications that we observe in the world by placing all these species into a developmental historical perspective. It also traces back common ancestors for all organisms, including humans.

Modern research has shown that in terms of their DNA humans are 99.5% similar to each other. As a species, we share 98% of genes with chimpanzees, 90% with cats, 69% with rats, and 60% with chickens and fruit flies. This hints at the possibility of using animals to get an insight into human behaviour and links to the principles of a biological approach to behaviour.

TOK

Can you name examples from various areas of knowledge (history, natural and human sciences, mathematics, arts, religious knowledge systems, indigenous knowledge systems, ethics) where evolutionary ideas have been influential?

ATL skills: Thinking

Review the principles of the biological approach to behaviour from the start of this unit. How are they linked to the idea that behaviour can have an evolutionary basis?

A range of evolutionary explanations in psychology

Evolutionary psychology attempts to explain psychological traits or behaviours as adaptations. Evolutionary explanations in psychology have been proposed for a wide range of phenomena. Here is just a brief overview of some popular explanations, some of which are discussed in greater detail elsewhere in this book.

Topic	Evolutionary explanation	Notes
Mental disorders	**Chiao and Blizinsky (2010)** proposed **gene-culture co-evolution theory** to explain the higher prevalence of genetic susceptibility to depression in collectivistic societies (where the prevalence of depression itself is lower). In their conclusions they synthesized three findings. ● Short alleles of 5-HTT, the serotonin transporter gene, make people more vulnerable to stressful life events. ● There is a higher frequency of short alleles of 5-HTT in people in countries with collectivistic values. ● In collectivistic societies people report depression more rarely. The researchers suggested that collectivistic values have evolved in these societies as a buffer against increased genetic susceptibility to depression.	See Unit 5 on abnormal psychology
Altruism (prosocial behaviour)	**Kin selection theory** explains altruistic behaviour observed both in animals and humans. Altruism does not fit well into the concept of natural selection because one organism helps another with no reward and even at some cost to itself. Kin selection theory suggests that the evolutionary meaning of altruism is the increase of survival of one's genes rather than an individual. For this reason it predicts that altruistic acts will be more frequent in close relatives than in distant relatives. The theory was proposed by **Hamilton (1964)** and tested in a number of experiments including with human subjects (such as **Madsen et al, 2007**).	See Unit 7 on the psychology of human relationships
The influence of emotion on cognition and behaviour	**LeDoux (1996)** described two physiological pathways of emotions; namely, processing fear stimuli. The fast pathway goes through thalamus and amygdala, whereas the slow pathway also involves the structures of the hippocampus and neocortex. The evolutionary meaning of this is that our brain is hard-wired to produce a quick automatic reaction to fear stimuli, but this reaction can also be "overriden" in exceptional circumstances. This may be linked to principles of natural selection because in limited time and dangerous situations it adds survival value to react quickly rather than deeply assess the situation. The same explanation can be extended to stereotypes and cognitive biases.	See Unit 3 on the cognitive approach to behaviour
Attachment	Research of attachment is closely linked with animal studies and animal models of behaviour. From the survival perspective, an organism maximizes its survival fitness if there is a balance between: ● staying close to the attachment figures in unfamiliar, potentially dangerous situations ● venturing outside and exploring the world to develop necessary life skills. **Harlow's (1958)** studies with monkeys demonstrate the existence of attachment styles and the importance of such behaviours as clinging and grooming. **Shaver and Hazan's (1988)** research shows parallels between attachment styles in childhood and later adult relationship patterns in humans.	See Unit 8 on developmental psychology

Topic	Evolutionary explanation	Notes
Theory of mind	**Theory of mind**, or the ability to recognize the beliefs and intentions of others, may be something that humans as a species have uniquely. However, a lot of insight into the nature of this ability was derived from animal studies. In some species, theory of mind exists in underdeveloped forms, and it is possible to trace the evolution of this ability if we compare performance of animals and humans in the same types of tasks (**Call and Tomasello, 2008**). The survival value of theory of mind may be linked to the complexity of the social world. As society becomes increasingly complex and survival depends on cooperation to a larger degree, it becomes important to understand the beliefs of others.	See Unit 8 on developmental psychology

▲ Table 2.6

Evolutionary explanation for disgust

To demonstrate typical reasoning of evolutionary psychologists, we will look at one specific example.

Curtis, Aunger and Rabie (2004) published a study suggesting that disgust evolved as a protection from risk of disease. Researchers reasoned that if this was true, then the following conditions have to be fulfilled.

- Disgust should be felt more strongly when faced with a disease-salient stimulus as opposed to a similar stimulus with less salience.

- Disgust should operate in a similar way across cultures.

- Disgust should be more pronounced in females since they have to protect their babies in addition to themselves.

- Disgust should become weaker as the individual's reproductive potential declines with age (there is less responsibility to care about offspring).

- Disgust should be stronger in contact with strangers than with close relatives because strangers potentially can carry novel pathogens.

Note that if any of these conditions were not fulfilled, this would present a challenge for the idea that disgust is a product of evolution. For example, if disgust was felt equally in response to disease-salient and less salient stimuli, then the proposed evolutionary explanation would fall apart: disgust would not be connected to risk of disease. Cross-cultural differences are also hardly compatible with the explanation: how can there be cross-cultural differences in something that is the product of evolution of humans as a species?

So, a strong support for the evolutionary explanation is only expected if all the five hypotheses are backed up by evidence. Evolutionary explanation in this case is a model, and we are trying to fit it into observational data. If it fits well, the evolutionary explanation is accepted (with caution), because it seems plausible. If it does not fit well, we change the model. The more observations we have that are consistent with the predictions of the model, the higher is our trust in the model itself.

ATL skills: Thinking

Can you name other examples where models are used in psychological research?

To test their hypotheses, Curtis, Aunger and Rabie (2004) used a survey placed on the BBC Science website. The survey was advertised in a BBC documentary. It was completed by over 77,000 people from 165 countries. However, after data cleaning, the final sample size was slightly less than 40,000. For example, all participants who had watched the BBC documentary were excluded because they could have been exposed to the hypothesis of the study.

First, respondents were asked a set of demographic questions on their age, sex, country, and so on. Then they were asked to rate 20 photographs (appearing one by one on separate screens) for disgust on a scale from 1 (not disgusting) to

5 (very disgusting). Of these photographs, 14 comprised 7 pairs of disease-salient versus less salient stimuli. For example, one photograph depicted a white towel with a blue stain on it, and the paired photograph showed the same towel with the stain depicted in reddish-yellow resembling blood and bodily secretions.

▲ Figure 2.41 Examples of photographs used in the study

Source: Curtis, Aunger and Rabie (2004, p 131)

Results showed support for all five hypotheses.

- First, disease-salient stimuli were rated as more disgusting than less salient ones. For example, the plate of organic-looking fluid was rated as 61% more disgusting than the plate of blue fluid that looked chemical (ratings were 1.6 versus 2.6). For the towel pictures, the organic-looking substance produced much higher ratings of disgust than the blue chemical (1.6 versus 3.9).

- Second, the results were consistent across cultures.

- Third, females rated the disease-salient pictures as more disgusting than men. This was true for all the disease-salient pictures used in the study.

- Fourth, as predicted, there was an age-based decline in the sensitivity to disease-salient stimuli.

- Finally, there was one question in the survey that asked participants to choose with whom they would be less likely to share a toothbrush. The average responses were ranged in the following order: postman (least likely), the boss, the weatherman, a sibling, a best friend, the spouse or partner. This shows that disgust is felt more strongly in contact with strangers than with relatives.

Therefore, all five tests supported the evolutionary explanation of disgust as a response that reduces risk of disease.

TOK

Now that many humans have constructed an artificial environment and no longer need to focus on physical survival to the same extent as before, do you think evolution is losing its power as an explanatory principle? Many people live in the world of business partners and competitors rather than physical dangers. While your economic status does affect your offspring, physical survival (in the developed countries) is no longer at stake. Does it mean that natural selection is not working anymore? If so, what was it replaced by?

Criticism of evolutionary explanations in psychology

Evolutionary psychology has a great explanatory power. In many instances evolutionary explanations fit nicely into our observations, tying them all together. However, some of the limitations that are commonly mentioned by critics are as follows.

- **Massive modularity versus neuroplasticity.** Researchers have attempted to expand the field and propose that mind on the whole is a product of evolutionary processes. If you suggest that mind is a product of evolution, though, you must also make one major assumption—modularity of mind (also known as "massive modularity"). It states that mind consists of modules that have evolved to perform certain fitness-related functions (Samuels, 1998). These modules must have a neurological basis. However, what we know about neuroplasticity contradicts this assumption. If the brain can change itself dramatically during the course of life, boundaries between modules are erased. This raises this question: how much neuroplasticity would be enough for us to challenge the assumption that the "modules" even existed in the first place? There have been advances that demonstrated that certain modules do exist. For example, macaques have been shown to have a specialized group of neurons that function as a snake-detection brain module. These neurons respond very quickly to images of snakes even if the macaque has never seen a snake before (Le *et al*, 2013). So, highly specialized modules such as snake detection cause little doubt, but it is massive modularity on the whole that is questionable.

- **Speculations about the environment**. Evolutionary adaptation is always adaptation to a certain environment. So to suggest an evolutionary explanation of a trait, you need to have knowledge about the environment in which this trait evolved. However, our knowledge of the environments in which homo sapiens evolved as a species is scarce. A lot of reasoning in this field, arguably, is speculative.

- **Testability**. Evolutionary explanations for behaviour are difficult—and in many cases impossible—to test. Critics of evolutionary psychology say that these explanations rest on a logical fallacy known as **ad hoc reasoning**. Ad hoc fallacy, also known as "a just-so story", takes a phenomenon as it exists and "cooks" an unverifiable story about how it came to be. Critics argue that such believable stories may be made up for just about anything: for example, you may explain altruism by survival of genes of relatives and egoism by survival of your own genes. Evolutionary psychologists respond that it is not exactly like that. For example, as you have seen, Curtis, Aunger and Rabie (2004) formulated a set of five predictions all of which, logically, had to be true if the evolutionary explanation was true. Then they tested these predictions. This is not exactly like "cooking a story".

- **Assumptions about linearity of development**. This is a related argument. Evolutionary explanations have no other choice but to assume that a trait has been gradually evolving to perform a certain function. However, it is possible that at some point in the past it actually evolved to perform some other function, different from the one it is (presumably) performing now. An example of this is **exaptation**—the situation when a trait evolves to perform one function but later starts performing a different function. Bird feathers are an exaptation: they originally evolved for temperature regulation but later re-specialized for flight.

- **Cultural variation**. Just as neuroplasticity is not entirely compatible with the idea of massive modularity of mind, existing cultural variations in traits are not entirely compatible with the idea that these traits developed as a universal adaptation to the universal challenges that humans faced as a species. Of course, one can always claim that different geographical groups of people faced different environmental challenges, but it weakens the evolutionary argument. This is why evolutionary psychologists prefer to study universal traits. For example, Curtis, Aunger and Rabie (2004) chose to study the emotion of disgust—one of the few universal, basic emotions experienced and interpreted similarly across cultures.

- **Adaptation versus other evolutionary mechanisms**. It may be hard to distinguish between genuine adaptation and other, more neutral processes. Examples of these include **genetic drift** (random variations in genotype that occur naturally) and **spandrels**. A spandrel is a by-product of evolution, a trait that developed as a result of the evolution of some other characteristic (Gould and Lewontin, 1979). An example of a spandrel is the short arms of tyrannosaurus rex. A common explanation would be to assume that these arms were developed to serve a purpose—such as raising the animal up after sleep—but Gould and Lewontin (1979) dismiss such explanations as ridiculous. Instead they suggest that the animal's tiny arms are simply a by-product of the rest of the body getting bigger and bigger. In other words, the arms did not change, the body did.

All limitations notwithstanding, evolutionary psychology remains a very promising field, mostly because it provides a theoretical framework that brings together multiple different observations and pieces of knowledge about human behaviour. No other theoretical framework with the same integrating potential exists so far. Modern psychology has been broken down into many research areas, but it lacks an overarching theory. Evolutionary psychology makes a good candidate for filling this gap.

See video

Robert Wright in his TED Talk "The evolution of compassion" (2009) looks at evolutionary roots of prosocial behaviour:
https://www.ted.com/talks/robert_wright_the_evolution_of_compassion

Lisa Nip in her TED Talk "How humans could evolve to survive in space" (2015) claims that humans have reached a stage when they can start controlling how evolution further develops, and so they can modify their own bodies in the desirable direction:
https://www.ted.com/talks/lisa_nip_how_humans_could_evolve_to_survive_in_space

▶ ❚❚ ■

Psychology in real life

To what extent can evolutionary explanations of behaviour be used in applied projects in Humanborough? Do they have any practical value at all?

For example, if you believe that disgust is an adaptation, you know what categories of people are more "resistant" to disgust (according to Curtis, Aunger and Rabie's study, it was elderly males). Can this knowledge be used for practical purposes?

Review evolutionary explanations briefly discussed in this section other than those relating to disgust. Try to come up with one concrete practical project that is based on ideas of evolutionary psychology.

The role of animal research in understanding human behaviour (HL only)

Inquiry questions

- Can animal studies provide an insight into human behaviour?
- Is psychological experimentation with animals ethical?

What you will learn in this section

- The value of animal models in psychology research

  - Purposes of animal research

  - An animal model is a concept that refers to using animal research to test a certain cause–effect hypothesis about a certain human behaviour

  - Types of experimental manipulation used in animal models

  - Using animal research to inform our understanding of human behaviour relies on the assumption that animal and human brains are similar; MacLean (1990): the theory of triune brain

  - Comparative neurobiology has discovered microscopic differences between animals and humans in certain brain areas; this suggests that the evolution of the brain might have been more complex than simply building newer structures upon older structures

  - Therefore, in addition to comparing brain structure, we need to compare psychological functions

  - Premack (2007): in order to prevent confusing similarities with equivalence, we need to focus on the areas of difference; examples are teaching and short-term memory

  - Summary of pros and cons of working with animal models

- Examples of animal research

  - Overview of the animal studies in this chapter

    - Lashley's experiments with rats; Merzenich *et al* (1984): brain and behaviour

    - Romero *et al* (2014): hormones and behaviour

    - Weaver *et al* (2004): genetics and behaviour

- Ethical considerations in animal research

  - Overview of ethical guidelines from APA Code of Ethics

This section also links to: any animal studies elsewhere in the book (see, for example, theory of mind in humans and animals in developmental psychology).

Throughout this unit we have discussed biological foundations of behaviour: the nervous system and the endocrine system, genetic inheritance, evolutionary considerations. We have looked at several animal studies and discussed the findings in the context of human behaviour. The third principle of biological approach to behaviour (see the introduction to this unit) stated: "Animal research may inform our understanding of human behaviour". In some sense this principle is a consequence of the first two principles: "Behaviour is the product of physiology" and "Behaviour can be genetically inherited". Human physiology and genetic set-up is similar to that of animals, which naturally suggests that animal research is to some extent generalizable to humans. The question is, what is this extent exactly?

This section summarizes some arguments related to the value of animal models in research in psychology. We will refer once again to animal studies covered in this unit, as these can be used to support the arguments. Finally, we will discuss ethical considerations in animal research.

The value of animal models in psychology research

The number of animals used in psychological research annually in the USA alone has been estimated to be 1.25–2.5 million, and about 7.5% of psychological research is animal-based (Shapiro, 1998). The most popular species to be used in psychological research are rats, mice, pigeons, cats, rabbits, hamsters, dogs, chimpanzees and baboons.

Research differs in terms of purposes for which animals are used. Researchers in the field of **comparative psychology** are interested in animal research as an end in itself. They either focus on a particular species or compare this species to humans. Another group of researchers advocates the study of animals as models of human beings and the expectation is that the findings will be universal and generalizable. A third group of researchers use animal studies to understand particular human conditions such as diseases.

An animal model is a concept that refers to using animal research to test a certain cause–effect hypothesis about a certain human behaviour. So an animal model is not just broadly "using animals to understand human behaviour". It is a specific model. For example, there are several animal models to explain depression: stress models (which explain the onset of depression by higher exposure to stressful situations), separation models (which explain depression by being separated from attachment figures), medical models (which explain depression by chemical imbalances in the brain), and more.

There are four major types of experimental manipulation used in animal models (Shapiro, 1998). These four types are:

- genetic manipulation (when animals are bred in a certain way)

- invasive manipulations with the nervous system (parts of the brain are stimulated with electrodes, lesioned or removed)

- invasive manipulations with other body parts (parts may be stimulated by substances or damaged)

- behavioural and environmental manipulations (such as electric shocks for rats depending on their performance in a maze-learning task).

Using animal research to inform our understanding of human behaviour relies on the assumption that animal and human brains are similar. Comparison of animal and human brains seemingly conveys a very consistent story of evolution: as species evolved, new structures were built on top of older structures; so the deeper we go into the brain, the more "primitive" structures we will find. There is a popular theory of **triune brain** proposed by **MacLean (1990)**. This theory divides the human brain into three parts: reptilian complex, paleomammalian complex (the limbic system), and neocortex. The idea is that the deeper brain structures can be found in animals as well; and the further down you go inside the brain, the further down you see in evolution. For example, the reptilian complex that you have in your brain should resemble the full brain of a reptile.

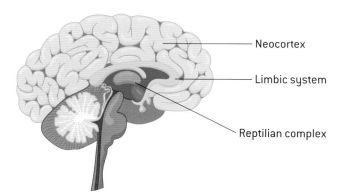

▲ Figure 2.42   Triune brain

However, some recent developments in the field of comparative neurobiology have led to the discovery of microscopic differences between animals and humans in certain brain areas. For example, some brain areas that both humans and primates have in common were found to be different in terms of how neurons are structured within them. This suggests that the evolution of the brain might have been more complex than simply building newer structures upon older structures.

These discoveries led some scientists to argue that comparison of brain differences might not give us full understanding of how animals are psychologically similar to humans, and that we need to compare **psychological functions** as well (that is, we also need to look at the problem from the cognitive and the social perspective).

Premack (2007) carried out such a comparison. Premack argued that in order to prevent confusing similarities with equivalence, we need to focus on the important areas of difference between humans and animals relevant to psychological research. Every time we find a similarity, we need to ask ourselves: what is the dissimilarity? Let's look at two examples.

One example is teaching. Some animals teach their young. For example, adult cats injure mice and bring them to their kittens so that the kittens can practise stalking and killing their victims. However, although this looks like some of the basic forms of teaching found in humans, human teaching is certainly more complex than that. For example, animals predominantly teach one thing—eating, while in humans the targets of teaching are very diverse (Premack, 2007).

Another example is short-term memory. A chimpanzee has the same limit for the number of units it can remember without rehearsing as a human being—about seven units. If you are told a sequence of seven numbers (for example, the numbers 8, 3, 6, 9, 1, 4, 2) and asked to repeat them (without rehearsing) several seconds later, you will be able to do so because your short-term memory can keep that much information. A chimpanzee would also be able to do this. There is a temptation to see a deep similarity between the species in terms of their short-term memory, but a closer examination shows that humans, unlike primates, are capable of **chunking**. For us the following sequence—54, 12, 47, 89, 71—is a sequence of 5 units, whereas for a chimpanzee it is a sequence of 10. It works even better if the units are letters and the "chunks" are words. It can be said that short-term memory in humans and chimpanzees is similar on some level, but not equivalent (Premack, 2007).

Here is a summary of some advantages and disadvantages of working with animal models.

These are some of the advantages.

- Humans and animals are identical in many ways, both in terms of brain structure and genetically.

- Studies with animal models do produce results: useful models of human behaviour and life-saving treatments have been developed based on animal experimentation. For example, insulin was discovered in an experiment where dogs had their pancreas removed.

- Animal studies allow researchers to embrace the full lifespan. While human subjects often outlive researchers themselves, laboratory mice live 2–3 years and this presents an opportunity to see their behaviour across their lifespan and even across generations. This is especially helpful in genetic research.

- Animal research may be highly controlled. For example, the "knockout" technique has been developed to selectively switch off one of the genes in the DNA sequence. All other things being equal, this technique provides great insight into the function of individual genes. The ability to better control confounding variables means higher internal validity of experiments.

- Animal subjects are relatively inexpensive and easily accessible, easy to handle and manage.

Some of the disadvantages are as follows.

- Animals and humans are never exactly the same, and we can never know the extent of the difference. This means that animal research, if successful, still needs to be replicated with humans in order to be sure that findings are generalizable.

- Even if humans and animals are similar in some aspect biologically, they can still differ psychologically (Premack, 2007).

- When scientists develop new biomedical treatments for mental disorders, they usually first test them with mouse models. However, results from mouse models are never directly applied to humans. Even if mouse models yield successful results, the drug needs to be tested on larger animals first. It is like a pyramid of generalization where mice are at the bottom and humans are at the top.

- Animals are tested in strictly controlled laboratory environments, so arguably they may be under stress. As a result, their reactions to experimental manipulations may not be quite the same as in their natural environments: there may be an issue with ecological validity.

- Although humans and animals are similar in many ways, they are still essentially different. For example, over 85 vaccines for HIV worked well in primates but all of them have failed in humans (Bailey, 2008). On the contrary, some results that are negative in animals can actually turn out to be positive in humans. For example, aspirin proved dangerous for animals but it is now one of the most widely used drugs for humans.

Discussion

Review the section of the PETA (People for the Ethical Treatment of Animals) website devoted to animals used for experimentation: http://www.peta.org/issues/animals-used-for-experimentation/

You are going to have a class debate for and against using animals for experimentation in psychology. Randomly split into two groups. One group will present the argument "for", the other "against". Both groups should first take time to prepare their arguments and possible rebuttals for the opposing group's claims.

Examples of animal research

Table 2.7 gives an overview of the animal studies you have looked at, together with the major findings.

Topic	Study	Findings
Brain and behaviour (localization)	Lashley's experiments with rats: removing varying portions of the cortex to see if memory of the maze disappears	Performance deterioration depends on the percentage of cortex destroyed but not on the location of the destroyed cells. This challenges the idea of localization of function for memory.
Brain and behaviour (neuroplasticity)	Merzenich et al (1984): cortical representations of the hand in adult owl monkeys	There was re-specialization of brain matter responsible for one digit so that it became responsible for other, adjacent digits.
Hormones and behaviour	Romero et al (2014): the role of oxytocin in promoting social bonds in mammals in non-reproductive contexts	Dogs were placed in a room with their owner and another dog. Dogs sprayed with oxytocin showed higher affiliation towards their owner. Similar results were observed for the other dog in the room: affiliation and approach behaviours were more frequent in the oxytocin condition.
Genetics and behaviour (epigenetics)	Weaver et al (2004): epigenetic research on how the type of nurturing rats receive from their mothers in early life affects the way their brain responds to stress in later life	Less nurturing in early life was linked to the suppression of the glucocorticoid receptor gene. The genetic sequences themselves did not differ. This study demonstrates the effects of gene suppression on behaviour.

▲ Table 2.7

To what extent can animal research in these examples provide an insight into human behaviour?

Karl Lashley's experiments with rats cannot be replicated with human subjects: systematic removal of parts of the cortex in large samples of people sounds horrifying! However, the study was insightful: we understand now that some complex psychological functions may be distributed rather than localized, and this may be used to explain other findings from human research (for example, controversial findings of Sperry and Gazzaniga regarding different degrees of lateralization for different functions). So the insight provided here is not in terms of direct generalization of results from animals to humans, but in terms of developing a better theory that would explain human behaviour.

Merzenich *et al*'s (1984) study of cortical representations of the hand in adult owl monkeys is important because it provides a direct test of neuroplasticity: brain scan—intentional damage—another brain scan. Can we repeat this with human subjects? No, that would not be ethical. However, the study provides support for a more general principle: the brain can modify itself in response to structural damage, and cortical areas can re-specialize. This general principle is very insightful in terms of research with human subjects and practical applications: sense substitution, artificial limbs and brain-machine interfaces (see "Neuroplasticity"). Again, in this case we are dealing with theoretical generalization of animal research rather than direct animal-to-human generalization.

Romero *et al* (2014) looked at the role of oxytocin in promoting social bonds in mammals (dogs). This research can be replicated with human subjects— and it has been (see "Hormones and behaviour"). Such research studies are insightful in a different way: we can compare results from human and animal studies and see to *what extent* human behaviour is like animal behaviour and why. This comparison, together with evolutionary theories of behaviour, can help us understand humans better. For example, oxytocin in the animal world has very straightforward effects: you can observe how the social behaviour of a dog visibly changes after a dose of the hormone. However, in human subjects the effects are subtle because humans' behaviour is also affected by a number of social norms (which in this context function as confounding variables).

Weaver *et al* (2004) looked at stress-related epigenetic changes in the brain of rats depending on the type of nurturing they received from their mothers. Potentially, understanding of epigenetics of stress can lead to a breakthrough in health psychology: if we understand the "chemistry" of bad parenting, maybe we can reverse its effects.

Promising results from Weaver *et al* (2004) encouraged researchers such as McGowan *et al* (2009) to look for possibilities to replicate it with humans. As you remember from "Genetics and behaviour", they conducted post-mortem examinations of brains of 24 individuals (with a different history of abuse in childhood) who had committed suicide. How do you come up with a research idea like this, unless it is informed by prior animal research? In this case, animal research provides an insight into human behaviour because it helps generate new hypotheses.

ATL skills: Self-management

There are also some useful examples that you will learn in other parts of the course. One of them is the extensive research of theory of mind in humans and animals (see "Theory of mind" in Unit 8 on developmental psychology).

Every time you encounter an animal study you should use the context to critically evaluate the value of animal models in that particular study. Use the advantages and disadvantages listed earlier in this section. The value of animal models links directly to whether or not animal research can provide insight into human behaviour.

Ethical considerations in animal research

Professional associations of psychologists in most countries publish guidelines for research with animals. For example, the American Psychological Association (APA) has a separate document for this purpose. The document outlines the main considerations that must be addressed at all stages of research involving animals. Here are just the most crucial of them (APA, 2012).

- Any animal study should be justified "with a clear scientific purpose". One of the following justifications may be used. The study will:
  - increase scientific knowledge of behaviour
  - increase our understanding of a particular species
  - give results that will benefit humans or other animals.

- If non-human animals are chosen for research, it has to be ensured that the chosen species is the best choice to address the research question, the minimum required number of non-human participants is used, and it should be assumed that whatever procedures cause pain in humans would cause pain in animals too.

- All animal research proposals must be submitted to the Ethics Committee prior to conducting the study.

- Psychologists and their assistants conducting the study must be familiar with the species-specific characteristics of normal behaviour so that they will be able to tell when the animal is stressed or unhealthy.

- Laboratory animals must be given humane care.

- Whenever possible, the experimental procedures should be designed in a way that minimizes discomfort of the animal. APA guidelines also advise researchers to first test the painful stimuli to be used with non-human animals on themselves, whenever reasonable.

- If a research animal is observed to be in distress or chronic pain and this is not necessary for the aims of the study, it should be euthanized.

- Animals reared in the laboratory must not be released into the wild.

Exercise

To learn more about ethical guidelines in research with non-human animals read the full APA guidelines:

https://tinyurl.com/jw3yca2

A useful exercise would also be to find guidelines published by British Psychological Society (BPS) and compare the two documents.

TOK

Ethics as an area of knowledge involves the use of thought experiments. Here is one possible thought experiment that has been used as an argument to say that animal experiments are ethically justified.

Imagine you see a small van with 500 mice in it rolling slowly towards the edge of a cliff. There is no driver in the van. In its way there's a stroller with a human baby in it. There are two possible outcomes.

- You push the stroller away and let the van roll slowly off the cliff, killing the mice.

- You do nothing and the stroller prevents the van from going over the cliff, but this kills the human baby.

Defenders of animal experimentation say that everyone would choose the first option because human life is more valuable than animal life. They also say that using animal studies to develop potentially life-saving medicine is equivalent to this thought experiment.

What do you think about this argument?

Psychology in real life

Review all the projects you have proposed for the people of Humanborough. What is the role of animal studies in these projects?

Exercise

Summarize all the Humanborough projects on one poster and have a "gallery walk" with your classmates or even present the poster in a session for the whole school.

Topics:

- Concepts and principles of the cognitive approach to behaviour

- Cognitive processing:

    - Models of memory (multi-store, working memory)

    - Schema theory

    - Thinking and decision-making

- Reliability of cognitive processes:

    - Reconstructive memory

    - Biases in thinking and decision-making

- Emotion and cognition: the influence of emotion on cognitive processes

- Cognitive processing in the digital world (HL only)

Introduction

Psychology in real life

Have you heard about subliminal tapes? These are auditory messages that contain embedded signals that are so weak that they do not reach conscious awareness, but that go straight into your subconscious mind. Calling them "tapes" is a tribute to history because the industry started when tape recorders were in use, but subliminal messages may be carried on digital media too.

Subliminal messages work miracles. They can enhance your learning. For example, there are recordings that help you learn languages or generally improve your memory. You can also use them for self-help purposes: weight loss, increasing work motivation, becoming more confident socially. The best thing about these recordings is that they do not require any conscious effort on your part, and you can even learn in your sleep.

Wouldn't it be nice to learn while you sleep?

Potentials Unlimited, one of the numerous companies who produce and market such subliminal recordings, offer recordings with a wide range of effects. Here are just some of them: memory improvement, faster reading, creative writing, better time management, as well as freedom from acne, removal of warts, and being better at table tennis! You can browse through their catalogue yourself: www.potentialsunlimited.com

Do these claims have an empirical basis? A lot of studies have been conducted in order to find out. In one of these studies Merikle and Skanes (1992) recruited a sample of females who were both overweight and believed in the effectiveness of subliminal messages. Participants were randomly allocated into three groups. One group listened to a weight-loss tape from an official manufacturer. The second group thought they listened to a weight-loss tape but actually they were given a tape to reduce fear of dentists (from the same manufacturer). Finally, the third group was waitlisted: they were told that the number of participants had reached its maximum and that the experiment would start for them later. All participants from all groups were weighed on a weekly basis for five weeks. The audible content in the auditory tapes used in the experiment was identical (classical music and sounds of nature). Results? Participants from the first group indeed lost some weight (although not much). However, participants from the second group lost exactly the same amount of weight—and so did participants from the third group who never even listened to the tapes. So weight reduction was equal in all three groups.

Researchers concluded that the effect may be explained by increased concentration on the problem: in this case, once they agree to participate in a study, people are more likely to pay more attention to their weight, which in itself has beneficial effects.

So subliminal messages and the idea that you can learn new skills while you sleep have been debunked.

But have they become less popular? No. Subliminal messaging companies continue to flourish and people continue to spend money on their products. This in itself is interesting: it looks as if people are prone to take shortcuts, save thinking energy, and make irrational decisions even when faced with contrasting evidence—but why?

The cognitive approach to behaviour focuses on mental (cognitive) processes, in other words, what happens in our mind when we process information. In the previous unit we looked at the brain and we recognized the fact that the brain is a basis for human behaviour and experiences. We also discussed the concept of reductionism and how it would be incorrect to reduce the mind to physiological processes.

However, there is one crucial difference between the brain and the mind in terms of research. The brain is a thing, and the mind is a construct. The mind cannot be observed directly. This poses a problem because it opens the door to all sorts of speculations, like the claim that listening to subliminal auditory messages in your sleep can improve your table tennis skills. How do we study something unobservable and yet stay within the limits of rigorous, testable science?

Answering this question requires taking a look at the history of research in this area. Concepts and principles of the cognitive approach to behaviour were shaped in the long and somewhat controversial process of development of cognitive psychology. In this process building and testing models has become an essential part of cognitive psychology. Specific examples of cognitive models include schema theory, models of memory and models of decision-making. It is also understood that cognitive processes can be biased. Studying biases in cognitive processing has become an independent area of research that is gaining increasing popularity. Another pertinent area of research is cognitive processing in the digital world; in other words, answering the question: how does digital technology affect cognition?

Note that the section that follows ("Concepts and principles of the cognitive approach to behaviour") does not directly correspond to a topic from the IB psychology subject guide. However, this section sets a conceptual background that will be later referred to throughout the unit, so it is important for your understanding of the essential building blocks of cognitive psychology.

3 Concepts and principles of the cognitive approach to behaviour

Inquiry questions

- How can mental processes, which are not directly observable, be scientifically studied?

- Can the human mind be compared to a computer?

- How reliable are human beings as information processors?

- Does cognition guide behaviour?

What you will learn in this section

- Four principles underlying the cognitive approach to behaviour

    o Mental processes can be studied scientifically

    o Mental representations guide behaviour

    o Cognitive processes do not function in isolation

    o Biases in cognitive processes can be systematic and predictable

- The origin and the essence of these principles with reference to the history of cognitive psychology

    o Introspectionism

    o Psychoanalysis

    o Behaviourism

    o Cognitive psychology

    o Behavioural economics

- The idea of the computer metaphor and its implications

- Models as a research tool in cognitive psychology

This section also links to:

- schema theory

- biases in thinking and decision-making

- reliability of memory

- emotion and cognition.

It can feel very natural for us to talk about "cognitive processes"; even without a rigorous definition we intuitively understand what they are: thoughts, emotions, memories, generally, the mind. However, cognitive processes have not always been accepted as part of scientific psychology. In fact, "the mind" as a concept was once dethroned and had to fight its way back.

In order to understand the key assumptions of the cognitive approach better, we will look at its history.

TOK

One of the five elements of the knowledge framework in TOK is the historical development of an area of knowledge. Historical development helps understand the current state better.

History of the cognitive approach

Step 1: introspectionism

As psychology parted from philosophy and became a separately recognized discipline, it needed a method of research. Why? If you have a method, you can claim to be an **empirical** science, as opposed to purely **metaphysical** areas of knowledge. The first method that psychology used was the method of **introspection**. Think about the parts of this word for a second and you'll understand what it means: intro = within, inside; spection = looking (compare to *inspection, retrospect, prospect, spectator, spectacles*).

The method of introspection literally involved "looking inside of oneself", that is, the subjective observation of one's own experiences. In the typical experiment the psychologist would expose you to a stimulus (for example, an oscillating pendulum or an optical illusion) and ask you to describe what you see or feel. You would then be asked to describe small elements of your experience, for example, what was your experience of colour? Motion? Shape?

Wilhelm Wundt started the first psychological laboratory in the University of Leipzig in 1876, which some people say is the year of birth of experimental psychology.

▲ Figure 3.1 Wilhelm Wundt

So, step 1 marked the transition from the metaphysical to the empirical. At the same time, with introspection as the method, the focus was on **conscious** subjective experiences.

TOK

Give examples of metaphysical disciplines or areas of knowledge. Is philosophy metaphysical? How about religion, ethics, geography, mathematics or the arts?

Empirical means "based on experience". Give examples of empirical sciences. Is psychology an empirical science? If so, does it mean that knowledge in psychology solely relies on observational data and that theories do not play an important role? What exactly is the role of theories in psychological research?

Step 2: psychoanalysis

Sigmund Freud (1856–1939), the father of **psychoanalysis**, revolutionized psychology, and indeed the culture, of that time in many ways. However, the cornerstone of his work is the introduction of "**the unconscious**". He claimed that conscious subjective experiences are just one insignificant part of human psyche, and not the main one. In psychoanalysis, the leading role in directing a person's experiences and behaviour is given to the unconscious **drives and desires** that we inherit from our ancestors. The role of the conscious mind is to control these primitive drives when they pose a threat to one's survival or well-

being. For example, we might experience a strong sexual drive towards someone, but stop ourselves from acting upon it, because, unlike animals, we need to obey some intricate laws of human society. However, for Freud, the unconscious drives are so strong that they will eventually find a way out, for example, in the form of dreams, misplaced affection or misplaced aggression.

The point here is that Freud claimed that people are essentially irrational, and that the "mind" is only part of a wider **"psyche"** that includes both conscious and unconscious components. This claim turned our attention to **irrationality** and **unconsciousness**. For this, psychoanalysis uses such methods as dream interpretation or analysis of associations.

ATL skills: Thinking

1. Do you agree that people are essentially irrational? Can you give examples of irrational behaviour that you have come across at some point in your life?

2. What prevents people from making rational choices?

3. Have you ever done something "unconsciously" (that is, without realizing why you are doing it)?

Step 3: behaviourism

As usually happens in the development of science, the next stage challenges the previous stage by rejecting one of its underlying principles and suggesting another principle instead.

TOK

1. Think of examples from other sciences when, in the process of development, the new approach rejected an underlying principle of the previous approach and suggested something different instead.

2. How does this relate to the idea of paradigm shift?

3. What is usually the relationship between the new theory and the old theory in such cases? Do they contradict each other? Or does the new theory subsume the old theory? Or do they just study different, unrelated aspects of reality?

4. Think about these examples:

   - Newtonian mechanics and Einstein's general theory of relativity, in particular the belief that light travels in a straight line and the belief that light can travel in a curved trajectory near large bodies of mass

With the rise of behaviourism, scientists claimed that "psychology of the mind" is not scientific, because the mind is not observable. This means that any inferences about the mind are not directly testable, therefore, "the mind" should be disposed of as a "**useless construct**".

If not the mind, what should psychology study instead? Whatever is directly observable, and that is **behaviour**, hence the name, behaviourism.

A word of caution here—it is often believed that behaviourists denied the existence of mind. That is not entirely accurate. They did not deny its existence. They said that since we cannot directly observe it, it is useless for the purposes of objective science, so if psychology is a science, it should ignore mind whether it exists or not.

This led behaviourists to the famous **"black box" metaphor**. Mind is a black box. We cannot see what happens inside it, but we can observe the inputs (stimuli) and outputs (reactions). As a matter of fact, systematic observation and experimentation with stimuli and reactions became the crux of behaviourism, a paradigm that dominated psychology in the first half of the 20th century.

▲ Figure 3.2 Black box metaphor

To get a better sense of behaviourism, we will focus on one of its central concepts, that of **operant conditioning**.

Operant conditioning theory was developed by **BF Skinner** in 1937. Operant conditioning is a process of shaping an organism's behaviour (be it that of an animal or a human being) by manipulating the consequences. The assumption is that, when left alone, an organism displays a variety of behaviours that are the result of a complex history of how this organism previously interacted with the environment (this is known as **operant behaviour**). For example, if you place a pigeon in a cage, it will sometimes flap its wings, sometimes walk around the cage, sometimes peck on the floor. All these behaviours are probably caused by some prior influences, but it's practically impossible to trace all those tiny influences back.

However, what happens if you want to shape the pigeon's behaviour and start reinforcing its behaviour in a specific desired direction? Suppose you wanted to teach the pigeon to continuously flap its right wing. You could wait for this behaviour to occur naturally (the pigeon flapping its right wing "spontaneously") and then reinforce it by rewarding the pigeon with a grain. In theory, the probability of this behaviour occurring again in the future has increased. You wait for the pigeon to flap the right wing again and reward it with a grain again. Every time, you reinforce the desirable behaviour.

▲ Figure 3.3 BF Skinner

Reinforcement is not the only way to manipulate the consequences of behaviour. There's also **punishment** (in most research studies, electric shock seems to be the favourite of psychologists). Operant conditioning is using punishment and reinforcement to shape an organism's behaviour by manipulating consequences of behaviour.

In fact, operant conditioning proved to be a highly efficient way of shaping behaviour and was widely used in psychological experiments to establish "**laws of behaviour**". If you have laws of behaviour, you can predict behaviour. If you can predict it, you can control it. This whole emerging new science of behaviour looked so promising—and so objective, just like the natural sciences—that Skinner went so far as to announce: "Give me a child and I'll shape him into anything".

On a smaller scale, this was empirically tested. Rumour has it that Skinner once challenged his scientific opponents to name one genuinely human behaviour that he could not bring up in his pigeons. They suggested that he should try and create superstition in pigeons. It is not possible to explain superstition without resorting to "mental", "unobservable" factors.

Skinner took up the challenge and in 1948 designed a study in which a group of hungry pigeons were put into an experimental cage for a few minutes each day. The cage had a mechanism that would feed the bird at regular intervals. The trick was that the food would come through the mechanism (for example, every 5 seconds) no matter what the bird was doing at that moment. The conditioning process is straightforward: if the bird happens to be executing some behaviour when the food arrives, there will be a tendency to repeat that behaviour as a result. As Skinner describes it, in six out of eight cases the resulting behaviours were so specific that different observers agreed "superstition" was a proper word to describe them. Skinner described it:

> "One bird was conditioned to turn counter-clockwise about the cage, making two or three turns between reinforcements. Another repeatedly thrust its head into one of the upper corners of the cage. A third developed a 'tossing' response, as if placing its head beneath an invisible bar and lifting it repeatedly.

Two birds developed a pendulum motion of the head and body, in which the head was extended forward and swung from right to left with a sharp movement followed by a somewhat slower return. The body generally followed the movement and a few steps might be taken when it was extensive. Another bird was conditioned to make incomplete pecking or brushing movements directed toward but not touching the floor." (Skinner, 1948, p 168)

One thing to note before we proceed to the next step is that learning, according to behaviourists, occurs through the process of **trial and error**. An organism tries out certain behaviours, and, depending on the consequences, some behaviours get reinforced and some get inhibited.

ATL skills: Communication

Explain behaviourism to a friend who does not study psychology. Use simple language to explain, but make sure you use all the following words:

behaviour, useless construct, black box, operant behaviour, operant conditioning, punishment, reinforcement, trial-and-error learning

Step 4: cognitive psychology

This notion of trial-and-error learning was first attacked by **EC Tolman** in a version of behaviourism known as "**teleological behaviourism**". In his article "Cognitive maps in rats and men" (1948) he described, among others, a study of spatial orientation in rats.

Research in focus: Cognitive maps in rats and men

Rats were first trained to run through a maze shown in the figure below.

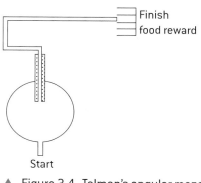

▲ Figure 3.4   Tolman's angular maze

In this maze, they had to run across a round table and into the entrance of a curved corridor that took several turns and finally led them to a food reward. The rats learned their way through the maze relatively quickly (in 12 trials on average). We say that a rat has learned to run through the maze when, after a number of trials, we place it at the start of the maze and it goes through the maze without errors. From the behaviourist perspective, we are looking at an example of operant learning in a series of trial-and-error attempts, where going in the right direction was rewarded by finding food and going in the wrong direction was punished by hitting a dead-end.

After that, the maze was suddenly changed to a "sunburst" pattern, like the one shown in Figure 3.5.

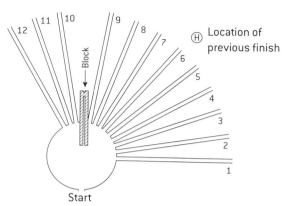

▲ Figure 3.5 Tolman's radial maze

As you can see, the pathway that the rats had been conditioned to choose was now blocked. Instead, they had 12 alternate paths.

There were two competing hypotheses:

- Hypothesis 1—operant conditioning and trial-and-error learning are accurate descriptions of reality, and rats should choose the paths closest to the original path, that is, paths 9 and 10.

- Hypothesis 2—trial-and-error learning is not an accurate model of learning as it occurs in reality, and rats will be able to form some internal mental representation of the first maze, hence they will choose the path that goes in the direction of the food reward according to their internal representation.

The results of the experiment showed that the significant majority of rats chose path 6 in the new maze.

What are the implications of this study?

- This result contradicts behaviourism. If we deny the importance of the black box, we will not be able to explain the behaviour of the rats that we observe in this study. We will have to admit that some "mental" variables hidden in the black box not only exist, but are important for scientific inquiry.

- Learning does not only take the trial-and-error form. At least in some cases learning is **latent** and relies on **mental representations** (mental maps) of the environment.

- Mental representations, although they cannot be observed, can be inferred **indirectly** through patterns of behaviour executed by an organism.

- Rather than being a chain of stimuli and responses, behaviour is actually **purposeful**, that is, organisms may be driven by an internal aim. This is where the name "teleological behaviourism" comes from. In philosophy, teleology is the study of aims or purposes. (The opposite of teleology is determinism, the study of causes.)

Classical behaviourism was very deterministic. By introducing a teleological aspect to it and finding empirical evidence for latent learning and mental representations, Tolman, among others, started the cognitive revolution in psychology.

Cognitive psychology gained popularity in the 1950s, 1960s and 1970s. Researchers recognized the importance of the black box and turned their attention to the study of internal, cognitive processes. How did they do that? They needed a method. There had to be an adequate response to the argument that cognitive processes are not directly observable, while not returning to introspectionism and preserving the values of rigorous experimentation to maintain a high scientific standard.

The solution came in the form of using **models** as a tool of scientific inquiry. Historically this coincided with the appearance of computers and information theory, so one overarching model that gained popularity in cognitive psychology was **the computer metaphor**.

1. To what extent are models useful as a tool of acquiring knowledge?

2. Name examples of models that are used in other disciplines, for example, geography, natural sciences, mathematics.

3. What are the common limitations of models? Think about the inevitable simplification.

4. If models simplify reality, why use them in the production of knowledge?

After you familiarize yourself with the computer metaphor in psychology, answer this question: why does the computer metaphor qualify as a model?

In the computer metaphor, the brain is the hardware and the mind is the software. The mind consists of some functional blocks, and these blocks work together to receive, encode, store, process and exchange information. Just as computers have different kinds of memory, for example, human memory in one of the models is postulated to have distinctly different "stores": sensory store, short-term memory store, long-term memory store. Models in cognitive psychology describe how information flows from one store to another and the nature of the interaction between different subsystems of this complex cognitive architecture. (We will come back to the computer metaphor in this unit and look at more specific examples of models in cognitive psychology.)

To sum up step 4, psychology turned attention back to the black box, but on a new level. Instead of introspection, which had been criticized heavily on the grounds of subjectivity, psychology now made use of models. A scientist suggests a model of a cognitive process and, based on this model, formulates a number of predictions. These predictions are experimentally tested; the model is fit to the observed data. If the model does not fit well enough, it is revised and the cycle repeats. It is similar to the process used in physics to study subatomic particles, which are also directly unobservable: we build models and predict how the particles will behave when they collide with each other; then we accelerate and collide the particles and compare the observed behaviour to the predictions.

Step 5: behavioural economics

The computer metaphor seems to fit so well with our understanding of how mind works. What could be wrong with it?

One thing that the computer metaphor does not account for is human irrationality. Think back to step 2. This is exactly what Freud did not accept about psychology of the mind. The computer metaphor operates on the assumption of rationality in information processing. No one would deny that people have biases and make mistakes, but under the computer metaphor in step 4 these were considered to be "bugs in the system", occasional deviations from the general rule.

The first major attack on this assumption was from the notion of **cognitive biases**. This notion was introduced in 1972 by **Amos Tversky** and **Daniel Kahneman**, the only psychologists so far to have won the Nobel Prize (there's no Nobel Prize for psychology, so they were awarded for economics). Essentially, cognitive biases are systematic deviations from rationality in judgment. What makes their discovery game-changing is the fact that they are **systematic**: as it turns out, many mistakes in judgments are not random, they are recurrent, predictable and very common for human decision-making. So, irrationality is not some occasional deviation from the norm; it is the norm in itself.

This area of research is rapidly gaining popularity. A lot of cognitive biases have been systematically studied and documented. For example, people have a tendency to overestimate small probabilities and underestimate large probabilities (as you might guess, this has been extensively used by insurance companies).

Behavioural economics emerged on the basis of cognitive biases as a whole new knowledge area. Behavioural economics studies economic decision-making and tries to include irrational variables into traditional economic models to better explain (and predict) people's choices, especially under uncertainty. The monetary gains from a thoughtful evidence-based application of psychological variables in economic models have been attractive. We will return to the discussion of cognitive biases in decision-making later in this unit.

See video

Dan Ariely (from Duke University) extensively popularizes research in the field of cognitive biases and behavioural economics. A good way to get a feel for this area of research is through his insightful TED Talks:

"Are we in control of our own decisions" (2008). www.ted.com/talks/dan_ariely_asks_are_we_in_control_of_our_own_decisions

"Our buggy moral code" (2009). www.ted.com/talks/dan_ariely_on_our_buggy_moral_code

He is also famous for his book *Predictably Irrational*, and his courses have been made available on the website *Coursera*. Check these out to get a glimpse of behavioural economics.

▶ ❚❚ ■

Overview

If you look back at the five steps in the development of the cognitive approach in psychology, you will see that they make a spiral pattern with each next step identifying an issue in the previous stage and suggesting an improvement. Note that the stages do not replace each other. For example, behavioural economics has not "replaced" cognitive psychology but rather formed its own independent areas of research.

In this unit, we will look more closely at steps 4 and 5. The cognitive approach in psychology deals with studying mental representations and cognitive processes. Some cognitive processes are: perception, memory, thinking, problem-solving, decision-making, imagination, language. For the purposes of this unit, we will mostly focus on memory, thinking and decision-making.

Step	Description	Key words
1. Introspectionism	Psychology should study the mind. The mind is rational and can therefore be studied by means of introspection.	Conscious, rational, introspection
2. Psychoanalysis	Rationality is but a small part of human life. The mind is mostly irrational and should therefore be studied by methods such as dream interpretation.	Unconscious, irrational, psychoanalysis
3. Behaviourism	Such methods are highly subjective and the mind is not directly observable. The mind is a black box, and psychology should study observable behaviour (inputs and outputs).	Observable, objective, trial and error, black box
4. Cognitive psychology	Doing so, however, does not allow us to understand a number of complex behaviours. The black box is an important component and should be returned to the realm of psychology. However, it should be studied objectively. This can be done by using models. We make predictions based on models, fit the predictions with observed data and choose the best-fitting model. The overarching model for cognitive psychology is the computer metaphor.	Latent, mental representation, model, computer metaphor, conscious, rational
5. Behavioural economics	People make mistakes in their judgments, and these mistakes are not just random deviations from the norm. Sometimes the biases are systematic and predictable. Irrational decisions are an important part of human behaviour, and irrationality in judgment and decision-making should be accounted for in the models of cognitive functioning.	Latent, mental representation, model, computer metaphor, unconscious, irrational

▲ Table 3.1

Principles of the cognitive approach to behaviour

From the history of the development of cognitive psychology we can formulate the basic principles that define the cognitive approach.

- Principle 1—mental processes can be studied scientifically (remember our discussion about testing predictions based on models, and how this is exactly what modern physics uses when studying unobservable particles).

- Principle 2—mental representations guide behaviour (remember Tolman's research and our discussion on the black box being an important moderator between stimuli and reactions).

- Principle 3—cognitive processes do not function in isolation.

- Principle 4—biases in cognitive processes can be systematic and predictable (remember step 5 and the ideas of behavioural economics).

These principles underlie research in the cognitive approach, and it is a good idea for you to keep them in mind at all times when considering the cognitive approach.

ATL skills: Self-management

The principles of the cognitive approach to behaviour are important assumptions made by cognitive psychologists. You need to clearly understand these principles and refer to them when relevant in answering examination questions.

Create a mind map or another visualization of the principles of the cognitive approach to behaviour. Include references to supporting research studies. Use mind map-building software so that you can add supporting studies to each principle later as you go through the material in this unit.

Exam tip

Please keep in mind that the section "Concepts and principles of the cognitive approach to behaviour" does not directly correspond to any topic from the IB psychology subject guide. This means that you will not be directly assessed on this section and there will be no examination questions related to the principles or the history of the cognitive approach.

However, it is important to understand the concepts presented here (such as mental representations or models) because these concepts will be used in other topics throughout the unit.

While you are not required to use this material in examination answers, you can use it, to the extent that it is relevant and you stay focused on the question.

Models of memory

Inquiry questions

- Does memory consist of separate stores?
- How many separate stores are there?
- What is the duration and capacity of human memory?

- Is rehearsal the best way to memorize information?
- How can we test hypotheses about the existence of separate stores in human memory?

What you will learn in this section

- Atkinson and Shiffrin (1968): the multi-store memory model

  - Sensory memory, short-term memory (STM), long-term memory (LTM)

  - Duration, capacity and transfer conditions

- Support for the model

  - Support for sensory memory: partial report technique (Sperling, 1960)

  - Support for STM and LTM being separate memory stores: serial position effect (Glanzer and Cunitz, 1966)

- Criticism of the model

  - Emphasis on structure over function

  - Rote rehearsal is the only mechanism of transfer; alternative model: levels of processing (Craik and Lockhart, 1972)

  - Only explains the flow of information in one direction, but bidirectional flow is necessary to explain the findings of the levels-of-processing model (Craik and Tulving, 1975)

  - LTM might not be a unitary store: procedural, episodic and semantic memory

  - There might be more components in short-term memory (working memory model)

- Baddeley and Hitch (1974): the working memory model

  - The dual task technique

  - The central executive, the visuospatial sketchpad and the phonological loop

- Support for the model

  - Memory for speech material uses a sound-based storage system (the phonological loop): phonological similarity effect discovered by Conrad and Hull (1964)

  - Effects of articulatory suppression on phonological similarity effect: Baddeley, Lewis and Vallar (1984); this supports separate stores for visual and auditory information

  - Support for the central executive: Baddeley (1996)

- Evaluation of the model

  - Good explanatory power

  - Hard to test empirically in all its entirety

This section also links to:

- principles of the cognitive approach to behaviour

- localization of function (biological approach to behaviour)

- models of thinking and decision-making.

Psychology in real life

Anterograde amnesia is a type of memory loss that affects the ability to form new memories but does not affect memories of the past. There are many well-documented cases of anterograde amnesia that can shed light on the nature of human memory.

Michelle Philpots suffered a head injury twice: once in a motorcycle accident in 1985 and again in a car accident five years later. These injuries triggered the development of epileptic seizures and loss of the ability to form new memories completely by 1994. Since that time Michelle's memory is wiped clean every time she goes to sleep. When she wakes up she believes it is still 1994. Her husband has to show her their wedding pictures every morning to remind her that they are married (they got married in 1997). She discovers every morning that she is much older than she thinks. Also she has no idea that she is suffering from memory loss—this is another discovery she makes on a daily basis. You could say that her memory span is 24 hours, but forgetting can occur in shorter time intervals, too. At some point she got fired from her office job after she photocopied the same single document over and over again multiple times. Her husband is grateful that she remembers him. He keeps a collection of photos handy and tells his wife the history of their life together every single time she wakes up. On the plus side, she never gets bored with good old jokes and TV programmes, and she gets to fall in love with her husband over and over again. This story became the basis of a popular Hollywood comedy, *50 First Dates*. https://tinyurl.com/m7mbg98

Clive Wearing's window of awareness is even shorter than that, somewhere between 7 and 30 seconds. He can forget the beginning of a sentence before you get to its end. In 1985 he was an acknowledged expert in music, at the height of his career. He suffered from encephalitis which resulted in extensive damage to the hippocampus. He has both retrograde amnesia (inability to recall the past) and anterograde amnesia. He remembers little of his life before 1985. Remarkably, however, he recalls how to play the piano and conduct the choir. Every 20–30 seconds he keeps waking up from the coma. He was encouraged to keep a journal of his thoughts, and he keeps writing, in sudden joyful insight, that he is finally awake and fully conscious … only to notice a couple of seconds later that the whole journal is filled with identical entries. He gets frustrated, he crosses out the previous entries and circles the new one, and it starts all over again. He is always glad to see his wife and he greets her every time he sees her as if it's the first time after a really long break, even if she just went to the bathroom for a couple of minutes. There is a documentary about Clive Wearing that is worth watching if you want to know more: https://tinyurl.com/kqxqdcu

The multi-store memory model

Memory is a cognitive process used to encode, store and retrieve information. The multi-store memory model was proposed by **Atkinson and Shiffrin** in 1968. In this model, human memory is said to consist of three separate components:

1. sensory memory
2. short-term memory store
3. long-term memory store.

Each of these components is characterized by a specific **duration** (for how long the store is able to hold information) and **capacity** (how many units of information it can hold). In order for information to move to the next memory store, certain **conditions** have to be met.

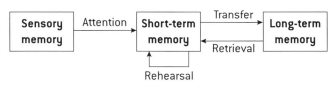

▲ Figure 3.6 Multi-store memory model

The **sensory memory store** (or the sensory register) does not process information. Its function is to detect information and hold it until it is either transferred further into the short-term memory store or lost. Sensory memory actually consists of several sub-components, one for each modality: visual information, auditory, olfactory, and so on. Most of the research, however, has focused on **iconic memory** (for visual inputs) and **echoic memory** (for auditory inputs).

The capacity of sensory memory is only limited by our perception, for example, iconic memory can keep everything that enters our visual field and echoic memory can hold everything that we acoustically perceive at any moment.

However, the duration of sensory memory is short. Traces in iconic memory decay after 1 second of inattention, while traces in echoic memory can decay after 2–5 seconds.

The condition that has to be met for information to transfer from sensory memory to short-term memory is **attention**. If a unit of information is attended to, it does not decay, but moves to the next memory store. Conversely, if it does not catch our attention, it fades away. So potentially sensory memory has unlimited capacity, but it is only transient, and we can only attend to a small subset of information stored in sensory memory.

TOK

The fact that we can only attend to a limited amount of information in our sensory memory at a given time links to the TOK concept of "selectivity of perception". Recall examples from various areas of knowledge that show how selectivity of perception affects our knowledge in a discipline. How does it work in history, for example?

As information enters the **short-term memory (STM)** store, it can undergo some primitive transformations. For example, if you see a word (visually), you can subvocally pronounce it and it will enter the short-term memory store acoustically. So the differences between modalities in short-term memory, to some extent, are erased.

The capacity of short-term memory has been extensively studied, and it has been established to be **7±2 chunks** of information. This number was empirically justified in GA Miller's article "The Magical Number Seven" in 1956. The trick is that a chunk is not only an individual unit, it can be a meaningful combination of individual units. For example, the sequence of symbols PCBMXBMWXBOXPS4 makes 15 units of information, which falls outside the capacity of short-term memory. If, however, you perform some grouping: PC – BMX – BMW – XBOX – PS4, it now becomes five chunks!

The duration of short-term memory is somewhat dependent on the modality, but is generally no longer than 30 seconds. If the information is left unattended, the trace fades away in this period of time.

The condition for increasing the duration of short-term memory and transferring information into the third store (long-term memory) is **rehearsal**. If we rehearse information (for example, repeat words over and over again or keep coming back to a mental image), it stays in the STM longer, and eventually the trace gets consolidated and the information enters the long-term memory store.

Long-term memory (LTM) is described as a place for storing large amounts of information for indefinite periods of time (Galotti, 2008, p 147).

The current estimate of the capacity of LTM is that it is potentially virtually unlimited. Psychologists have failed to quantify the capacity of LTM or at least provide an approximate estimate. You can probably remember times when you saw or heard something and never thought of it again, but then suddenly one day some contextual cue triggers those distant memories, and you suddenly remember something that you thought had been long forgotten. There are also well-known case studies of "memory champions". In some cases memory champions can recollect long strings of digits that they had memorized many years before, although they never rehearsed the digits since that time.

Exercise

Do some research and suggest your explanation for phenomenal memory (extraordinary memory powers). How is phenomenal memory possible? Can it be learned?

You may start exploring the issue with this story of Laurence Kim Peek (1951–2009), an American savant who became the inspiration for the movie *Rain Man*. He read countless books and instantly memorized them. Reportedly he could accurately recall the contents of at least 12,000 books. He could also carry out complex calculations in his mind without a need for a calculator.

https://tinyurl.com/kn3u27d

Although the capacity of LTM is potentially unlimited, not all information that is stored in LTM is easily retrievable. It is not storing but retrieving information from memory that may be problematic.

Similarly, the limit for the duration of long-term memory has not been established, and potentially it is longer than a lifetime.

As mentioned above, the condition for information to enter LTM is rehearsal. According to the classical multi-store memory model, rehearsal gradually consolidates the memory trace and so increases the probability of information permanently entering the LTM store.

ATL skills: Thinking

1. Why is Atkinson and Shiffrin's multi-store memory model a model?

2. List all the essential properties of models (irrespective of the area of knowledge) and discuss how these properties are manifested in the multi-store memory model.

Remember that Atkinson and Shiffrin's multi-store memory model is a model. It has a lot of components that require testing. It raises these questions.

1. Are the memory stores really distinct and separate? For example, is sensory memory really separate from STM?

2. Are there really three memory stores, not more, not less?

3. Are sensory modalities within sensory memory just modalities? Why not separate memory stores?

4. Is there a physiological basis for the memory stores or are they just constructs? In other words, do the separate stores exist objectively in the form of separate brain structures?

5. Is rehearsal necessary and sufficient for the transfer of information from STM to LTM? Can this transfer occur without rehearsal? Can the transfer fail to occur in the presence of rehearsal?

6. Does information really only flow in one direction (from sensory memory to LTM)? Can information flow backwards, for example, can LTM influence which pieces of data are selected from sensory memory and transferred into STM?

Exercise

1. Split into six groups.

2. Each group will take one of the six questions listed above and design an experiment to empirically answer the question.

3. When presenting your experiment to the larger group, demonstrate how exactly your experimental procedure will support (or refute) the hypothesis that is relevant to the question.

Think "out of the box". Don't worry if the suggestions seem absurd. Psychologists spend years carefully designing studies like that. The purpose of the exercise is just to try, (probably) fail and then laugh about it!

All these questions and predictions require a series of carefully controlled experiments. One reason for us studying this model in IB psychology is that it was one of the most successful and popular models of the time, in the sense that it stood up to trial by empirical data.

Support for the multi-store memory model

We will consider two research studies that aimed to test different aspects of the multi-store memory model.

In 1960 **Sperling** tested the existence of iconic memory (part of sensory memory). He used the so-called "partial-report technique". In the experiment participants were presented with a tachistoscopic image of a grid of alphanumeric characters, as shown in Figure 3.7.

7	I	V	F
X	L	5	3
B	4	W	7

▲ Figure 3.7 An example of a grid used in the study

The image was flashed up for only 50 milliseconds (ms: 1/20 of a second).

There were two conditions.

- In the **whole-report** condition, participants were given an empty grid and required to fill it out with all the alphanumeric characters in the appropriate positions. They were asked to guess when they were not certain. Participants were able to recall an average of 4 out of 12 characters (35%).

- In the **partial-report** condition, participants were presented with the stimulus as before, but were only required to recall one of the rows from the grid. The instruction indicating which row to recall was given in the form of a sound. The tone sounded approximately 50 ms *after* the visual presentation, so participants did not know until they heard the tone which of the rows was called for. Participants were instructed to recall the top row on hearing a high tone, the middle row on hearing a middle tone, and the bottom row on hearing a low tone. Participants were usually able to recall three or four characters from the row. As the row was selected at random, and after the presentation of the stimulus, we can conclude that 75–100% of the entire grid was accessible to the participant for a brief amount of time after the presentation of stimulus.

The interpretation of the findings, in line with the multi-store memory model, is that after we have been exposed to a visual stimulus, its trace stays in our memory for a short period of time. If attended to, some parts of this trace can be further consolidated and transferred into the STM. If not attended to, the information decays.

Glanzer and Cunitz (1966) are famous for their research on **serial position effect**, which serves as support for STM and LTM being separate memory stores. Serial position effect is the tendency to recall the first and the last items on a list better than items in the middle. Participants were required to memorize lists of words followed by a free-recall task (a free-recall task is when you are permitted to recall the words in any order).

There were two conditions.

- In the first condition, participants (240 army-enlisted men) were presented with recordings of 20-word lists consisting of common one-syllable nouns. Immediately after hearing the words they were required to do a free-recall task for two minutes. Results of these trials clearly demonstrated serial position effect in both its aspects: participants were better at remembering words at the start of the list (**primacy effect**) and at the end of the list (**recency effect**). This

did not depend on the number of repetitions of each word (see Figure 3.8).

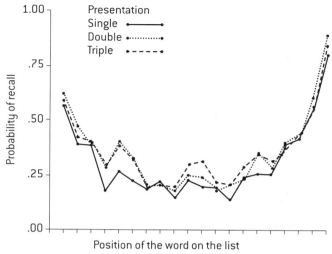

▲ Figure 3.8 Serial position effect

- In the second condition, researchers introduced a delay between the end of the list and the start of recall. During the delay, participants engaged in a filler task: counting backwards from a given number for 30 seconds. The filler task was meant to prevent rehearsal. The resulting data indicated that participants were still successful at recalling the words from the start of the list (primacy effect preserved), but were no longer able to recall the words from the end of the list (recency effect disappeared).

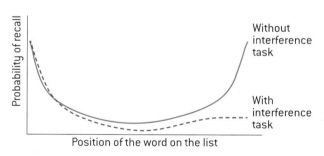

▲ Figure 3.9 Disappearance of recency effect after a filler task

Why does the recency effect disappear while the primacy effect stays? Glanzer and Cunitz explained that when people are hearing a list of words with the intention to memorize them, they tend to repeat the words to themselves. The first words on the list get repeated (rehearsed) more often and enter the long-term memory, which is unaffected by the delay and the filler task. However, the last words on the list are not rehearsed enough.

Without rehearsal, their trace in short-term memory decays in just 30 seconds, so the recency effect disappears after the filler task. Since one of the effects disappears and the other does not, it supports the idea that STM and LTM have **separate memory mechanisms** behind them.

Criticism of the multi-store memory model

There are some criticisms that are common for any model in cognitive psychology (for example, simplification, an inability to observe the components of the model, absence of a clear physiological basis), but the multi-store memory model has been criticized for a variety of more specific reasons.

First, a limitation of this model is that it focuses on structure rather than the process. Even the definition of memory as a cognitive process implies that to understand how information flows is more important than to see how many separate stores it goes through. This is not to say, of course, that structure is not important. However, structure in this model is emphasized.

Second, due to this lack of attention to memory as a process, the only mechanism that enables transfer of information from STM to LTM in the original multi-store memory model is rote rehearsal. This seems to be an oversimplification that ignores various strategies that may enhance memorization. To counter this, **Craik and Lockhart** (1972) proposed the **levels of processing (LOP)** model of memory. In this model recall is a function of depth of processing. According to Craik and Lockhart, information undergoes a series of levels of processing, shallow and deep, and the deeper information is processed, the stronger its trace in long-term memory. Shallow processing only takes into account superficial features of the stimulus, such as the physical properties (**structural processing**) or the acoustic properties (**phonetic processing**). This is exactly what happens in rote rehearsal: we either repeat something to ourselves (phonetic) or recreate the mental image of how something looks (structural). Deep processing, on the other hand, occurs in the form of **semantic processing** and involves building the stimulus into the structure of meaningful connections and associations, that is, linking it to prior knowledge.

One of the research studies that tested this model was conducted by Craik and Tulving.

Research in focus: Craik and Tulving (1975)

This experiment followed a repeated measures design. Using a tachistoscope, participants were shown words for 200 milliseconds. Before seeing each word, they were asked one of three types of yes-or-no questions, each relating to a different level of processing. These are examples of the questions.

- Is the word in capital letters? (structural processing)

- Does the word rhyme with "weight"? (phonetic processing)

- Is the word a type of fish? (semantic processing)

- Would the word fit the sentence "He met a ____ in the street"? (semantic processing)

After participants were asked the question, the word was revealed and they were required to press one of the buttons (yes or no) to indicate their response. After completing the whole list, they were given either a free-recall task ("recall all the words you can in any order") or a recognition task (where they were given a longer list of words and required to pick out the ones that they had seen earlier).

Both for recall and for recognition, memory performance was significantly better for those words that were preceded by a "semantic" question. For example, for a recognition task, the average percentage of words correctly recognized was:

- 16% for structural processing

- 57% for phonetic processing

- 83% for semantic processing. (Craik and Tulving, 1975, p 273).

The study supports the idea that consolidation of memory traces in LTM is not only due to rote rehearsal, and long-term memory is a function of *how* the information was processed at the stage of encoding.

Third, the multi-store memory model has been criticized for the fact that it only explains the flow of information in one direction, from sensory memory to the LTM. However, it can be argued that the opposite flow of information also takes place. For example, how can chunking (Miller, 1956) occur without using information that is already stored in the LTM? We perform chunking based on prior knowledge, and this has to require some access to the LTM. On the other hand, semantic processing at the stage of encoding (Craik and Tulving, 1975) also cannot occur without access to categories stored in the LTM. To know the answer to the question, "Is this word a type of fish?", I need to access my knowledge of different kinds of fish. If this influences the early stages of encoding (as was demonstrated in the levels of processing model), then we have to admit that there is **bidirectional flow of information** between memory stores.

Fourth, it has been argued that LTM is not a unitary store, and there are differences in the way different types of information are stored. At least three types of memory might be stored differently: **episodic** (memory of events), **procedural** (how-to memory, for example, memory of how to tie your laces or how to ride a bike) and **semantic** (general knowledge). One source of evidence for these claims is from case studies of amnesia where some memories were lost while others stayed intact.

Fifth, in a similar fashion, it has been argued that the unitary view of short-term memory is too simplistic, and there are more subcomponents in the STM. A much more sophisticated approach to STM was proposed by Baddeley and Hitch in 1974 (see below).

Working memory model

Research revealed some phenomena that did not fit well with the view of STM as a unitary system. These "uncomfortable" results came from research studies that utilized the **dual-task technique**. In this technique, the participant is required to perform two memory operations simultaneously, for example, listen to a list of words (auditory stimulus) and memorize a series of geometrical shapes (visual stimulus). If STM really is a unitary store, the two sets of stimuli should interfere with each other, so memory will be limited by 7±2 units of whatever modality. However, it was discovered that in some cases performing a simultaneous task does *not* interfere with memory performance. For example, drawing something does not interfere

with memorizing an auditory sequence of digits. To explain these conflicting findings, **Baddeley and Hitch** (1974) developed the working memory model. This model focuses on the structure of STM.

In the original model, working memory consists of a **central executive** that coordinates two subsystems: the **visuospatial sketchpad** and the **phonological loop**.

- The visuospatial sketchpad ("the inner eye") holds visual and spatial information.

- The phonological loop holds sound information and is further subdivided into the phonological store ("the inner ear") and the articulatory rehearsal component ("the inner voice"). The inner ear holds sound in a passive manner, for example, it holds someone's speech as we hear it. The inner voice, on the other hand, performs the following important functions.

  First, it turns visual stimuli into sounds. For example, if we are shown a list of written words, we may subvocally pronounce these words, changing the modality from visual to auditory, and the words will enter our STM through the auditory channel.

  Second, it allows the rehearsal of information held in the inner ear. By constantly repeating the words, we are increasing the duration of working memory and increasing the chances of transferring the information further into long-term memory storage.

- The central executive is a system that allocates resources between the visuospatial sketchpad and the phonological loop. In this sense, it is the "manager" for the other two systems.

In 2000 Baddeley and Hitch also added the fourth component, the **episodic buffer**, as a component that integrates information from the other components and also links this information to long-term memory structures.

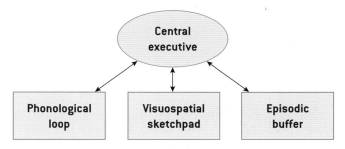

▲ Figure 3.10 Working memory model

Support for the working memory model

One of the starting principles of this model (that requires empirical testing) is the division of the unitary STM into three independent subcomponents: the central executive, the visuospatial sketchpad and the phonological loop. This has found support in a variety of studies using the dual-task technique. In some trials, both tasks used the same modality. The model predicts that in this case the two tasks will interfere with each other and the performance will be hindered. In other trials, the tasks used different modalities. The model predicts that the performance of the tasks will not be significantly hindered in this case.

Conrad and Hull (1964) demonstrated the **phonological similarity effect**. In their study participants were required to recall lists of letters. Some lists of letters were phonologically similar (for example, B, D, C, G, P) while others were not (for example, F, H, P, R, X). They found that rhyming lists were more difficult to remember. This is because the traces of similarly sounding letters (if they are encoded acoustically) are easier to confuse with each other. This supported the idea that memory for speech material uses a sound-based storage system, which we now know as the phonological store.

Baddeley, Lewis and Vallar (1984) explored the effects of **articulatory suppression** on the phonological similarity effect. Articulatory suppression is a method of blocking the "inner voice" (articulatory rehearsal component). In an experimental situation, articulatory suppression is simply asking your participants to repeat a sequence of sounds (for example, the-the-the or one-two-three-one-two-three) over and over again while at the same time performing the experimental task. In doing this, the capacity of the "inner voice" is filled up. What happens in this situation, according to the predictions of the working memory model? (Think back to the two functions of the "inner voice" discussed earlier.)

First, visual inputs cannot be recoded into sounds and hence cannot enter the phonological store.

Second, auditory inputs can enter the phonological store, but their rehearsal will be impossible.

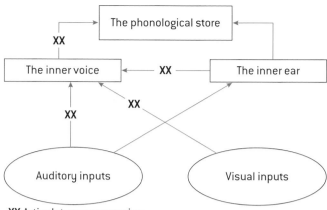

XX Articulatory suppression

▲ Figure 3.11 Effects of articulatory suppression

Baddeley, Lewis and Vallar used four conditions:

	Spoken mode of presentation	Written mode of presentation
Rhyming words	1	3
Non-rhyming words	2	4

▲ Table 3.2 Conditions in Baddeley, Lewis and Vallar (1984)

The results indicated that there was a phonological similarity effect between conditions 1 and 2 (that is, rhyming words were significantly harder to recall than non-rhyming words), but there was no phonological similarity effect between conditions 3 and 4 (for written material, rate of recall for both rhyming and non-rhyming words was the same).

When articulatory rehearsal is inhibited, spoken information can still enter the phonological store (the "inner ear") directly. Since rhyming words sound similar and create similar traces, these traces are easier to confuse so we observe the phonological similarity effect. Written information can also enter working memory, but it does not get recoded into sounds. Presumably it enters the visuospatial sketchpad. As the information is coded visually, the traces are not that easy to confuse, and the phonological similarity effect is not observed.

ATL skills: Thinking

1. Evaluate the extent to which this study supports the working memory model.

2. Are there alternative explanations that would fit equally well into the observed data?

For the central executive, one of the studies that provided supporting evidence was conducted by **Alan Baddeley** (1996). The starting point of his reasoning was that since the theoretical function of the central executive is to distribute and switch attention, it should be inhibited by tasks that require attentional switches, and at the same time it should not be inhibited by tasks that do not require attentional switches.

In the study, participants were required to produce random sequences of digits by pressing keyboard keys at the rate of one per second, determined by a metronome. To produce a random sequence of digits, you have to use your attentional resources because you need to take into account the previous digits that you have selected. So the dependent variable in this experiment was the **randomness** of the digit sequence (participants were required to produce sequences of 100

digits overall). The more random the sequence, the better the central executive performed at controlling this cognitive task.

Simultaneously, participants were required to engage in one of three tasks, at the same rate of one unit per second.

1. Recite the alphabet (A, B, C and so on).

2. Count (1, 2, 3 and so on).

3. Alternate between letters and numbers (A, 1, B, 2, C, 3 and so on).

The results showed that "whereas neither counting nor reciting the alphabet had a detectable effect on the randomness of keypressing, the concurrent alternation task markedly reduced randomness" (Baddeley, 1996, p 18). So it was concluded that this constant switching of retrieval plans is performed by a separate memory system (the central executive).

ATL skills: Research

Do you remember research methodology? Experiments are characterized by validity, and there are three broad types of validity: internal, external and construct.

Evaluate the construct validity of Baddeley's (1996) study. To what extent is randomness of a string of digits a good operationalization of the function of the central executive?

Evaluation of the working memory model

Overall, the strength of the working memory model is that it is more sophisticated than the multi-store memory model and allows us to explain a wider range of phenomena (for example, participants' performance in the dual-task technique or observable effects of articulatory suppression). The model can integrate a large number of findings from work on short-term memory. Subsequent research has also shown that there are physiological correlates to some of the separate components of the model. For example, distinctly different brain parts "light up" in brain scanning images when the task activates either the phonological loop or the visuospatial sketchpad. Finally, on the plus side, the working memory model does not overemphasize the role of rehearsal.

However, it should be noted that models of this degree of complexity are harder to test empirically.

You must have noticed that all the experiments, however complicated, are only designed to test one specific aspect of the model (for example, the central executive). For complex models, it becomes increasingly difficult to design well-controlled studies that would test the model in its entirety. This means that the model is difficult to falsify. Maybe as a consequence of this, and due to the existence of multiple potential explanations of the same experimental result, the exact role of some of the components of the model (the central executive and especially the episodic buffer) remains unclear. Similarly, it has been argued that the visuospatial sketchpad should be further divided into two separate components, one for visual information and one for spatial information. Finally, working memory only involves STM and does not take into account other memory structures, such as LTM and sensory memory.

Psychology in real life

Do cases of amnesia support the idea of separate memory stores? Yes, they do. If brain injury destroys one memory process but does not destroy the others, it really is supporting evidence. However, sometimes memory impairment occurs without any visible brain injury.

Patient WO, known as William, can remember everything in his life clearly until 1.40 p.m. on 14 March 2005. This was the moment he was injected with a local anesthetic before a routine procedure at the dentist. Since then he can only store memories for 90 minutes. What baffles psychologists is that there was no brain injury involved in this case of anterograde amnesia—so what is the physiological basis? Since then, every day WO has woken up thinking it's the date of his dentist appointment. Before the appointment, his health was perfectly normal and there seemed to be nothing wrong with his brain. Now he relies completely on his electronic journal that lists the things he has done, has to remember, and has to do. WO is indeed caught in a 90-minute window of the present. Time goes past and takes all memories with it. The single new episode his memory was able to retain was the knowledge of the death of his father—not how it happened or when, but the very fact. https://tinyurl.com/k7aeevv

How can this case of amnesia be explained? Search online for some of the current hypotheses.

Schema theory

- How does prior knowledge influence processing of new information?

- How does context influence comprehension?

- What is the utility of perceiving things through the "lens" of prior knowledge and expectations?

- How do we make sense of the ocean of data around us?

What you will learn in this section

- Concepts of schema theory
  - Cognitive schemas—mental representations that organize our knowledge, beliefs and expectations
  - Schemas are derived from prior experience
  - Schemas may be studied through the effects that they have on more observable processes, for example, memory
  - Schemas influence memory at all stages: encoding, storage and retrieval
- Schemas influence encoding
  - Bransford and Johnson (1972): the effect of context on comprehension and memory of text passages
- Schemas influence retrieval
  - Anderson and Pichert (1978): a change of perspective at the stage of retrieval leads to recall of an additional 7.1% of information relevant to the new perspective
- Types of schemas: social schemas, self-schemas, scripts
  - Social schemas influence our interpretation of others: Darley and Gross (1983)

- Scripts help us make sense of sequential data: Bower, Black and Turner (1979)
  - Self-schemas are an integral part of Aaron Beck's theory of depression
- Top-down and bottom-up processing
  - The Rat Man of Bugelski and Alampay (1961)
  - Schematic processing might be biased but it saves energy
  - Pattern recognition and effort after meaning

This section also links to:

- principles of the cognitive approach—mental representations guide behaviour

- concepts of the cognitive approach to behaviour (behaviourism and cognitive psychology)

- models of memory (memory processes)

- reliability of memory (see further in this chapter)

- stereotypes (sociocultural approach to behaviour)

- Aaron Beck's depression theory (abnormal psychology)

- biases in thinking and decision-making (confirmation bias).

Concepts of schema theory

Remember those rats from EC Tolman's study? Very few things can compare to the excitement that a scientist feels observing something that might potentially become a groundbreaking discovery. Imagine Tolman's feelings as, at a time dominated by behaviourism (with its trial-and-error learning), he was observing his rats pick the pathway that was leading in the direction of the food reward. He must have thought that it looked like they were guided by some sort of an internal representation, a map of the maze. Trial after trial, his rats confirmed his interpretations, and he must have had difficulty falling asleep that night, thinking about all the exciting implications of this discovery.

It is not only rats who create internal maps of their surroundings. If you search your memory for a minute, you will find many other examples. Taxi drivers do not find themselves to be helpless if the road they have been taking for years is blocked. They quickly recalculate their route and use other roads, taking shortcuts and getting successfully to the destination. Basketball players always know where the basket is and always know exactly what force they should apply to the ball to send it to the target. Even as you are reading this, you are trying to fit this new information into your "internal map" of psychology, in which towns are the concepts and highways are the connections between them.

Cognitive schemas (or schemata) is an umbrella term for all such phenomena. Cognitive schemas are defined as mental representations that organize our knowledge, beliefs and expectations. **Mental representation** is a pretty broad concept. It can be applied to practically anything in the black box. Notice how this links to the principles underlying the cognitive approach to behaviour, especially the second principle: mental representations guide behaviour. So are cognitive schemas all mental representations or just a subset of them? In fact they are a subset, just those mental representations that organize our knowledge, beliefs and expectations.

To do so, these mental representations need to be quite stable, deeply rooted and organized. Schemas are derived from prior experience. If your potential business partner tells you that his favourite month is August, it will probably not influence your expectations and how you prepare for your first meeting. However, if he tells you that he is a 60-year-old Colombian, it might influence you. This is because, due to your experience, you

have some deeply-rooted age and cultural schemas (what 60 year olds are like, what Colombians are like), but most likely you do not have a schema for people who prefer different months of the year.

Since schemas cannot be observed directly, how do we go about studying them? One way of doing so is to look at the effects that schemas have on more directly observable processes such as memory. Research has shown that schemas influence memory processes at all stages—encoding, storage and retrieval. We will discuss two studies that support this claim.

ATL skills: Thinking and research

Before you read about the studies, try to think of an experiment that you might conduct to test the following theoretical hypotheses:

- Schemas influence encoding of material in memory.
- Schemas influence retrieval of material from memory.

What will be your independent variable (IV)?
What will be the dependent variable (DV)?
How would you operationalize them? What will your experimental procedure be like?

TOK

What is the role of prior experience in gaining new knowledge? Is it a tool for acquiring new knowledge or rather an obstacle?

One of the tests for truth in theory of knowledge, the coherence test, claims that something is true if it fits well into what you already know. What are the possible criticisms of this test for truth?

Schemas influence encoding

Bransford and Johnson (1972) carried out an experiment in which they investigated the effect of context on comprehension and memory of text passages. It followed an independent measures design, and used five groups of participants.

Irrespective of the group, all the participants heard the following tape-recorded passage:

> "If the balloons popped, the sound wouldn't be able to carry since everything would be too far away from the correct floor. A closed window would also prevent the sound from carrying, since most buildings tend to be well insulated. Since the whole operation depends on a steady flow of electricity, a break in the middle of the wire

would also cause problems. Of course, the fellow could shout, but the human voice is not loud enough to carry that far. An additional problem is that a string could break on the instrument. Then there could be no accompaniment to the message. It is clear that the best situation would involve less distance. Then there would be fewer potential problems. With face to face contact, the least number of things could go wrong". (Bransford and Johnson, 1972, p 719)

ATL skills: Research

Now that you have read the passage, try closing the book and repeating its main ideas.

Overall, there are 14 idea units in this passage. How many can you remember? (It is not necessary to remember word for word.)

Participants were instructed, after hearing the passage, to recall it as accurately as they could, and if they could not remember it word for word, to write down as many ideas as possible. They were given seven minutes to do that.

The five conditions were as follows.

1. No context (1): participants simply heard the passage.

2. No context (2): participants heard the passage twice.

3. Context before: prior to hearing the passage participants were provided with a context picture (see Figure 3.12) and given 30 seconds to study it.

4. Context after: the same picture was shown, but after participants heard the passage.

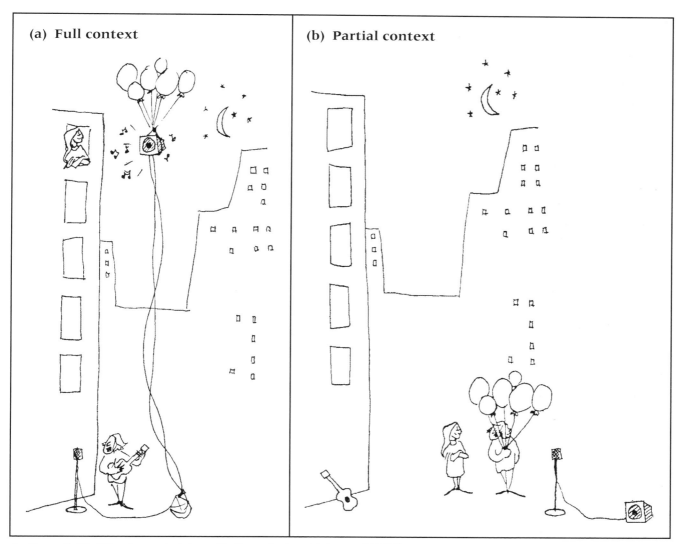

(a) **Full context**   (b) **Partial context**

▲ Figure 3.12 Stimulus material used in Bransford and Johnson (1972)

5. Partial context: a context picture was provided before the passage. This picture contained all the objects, but the objects were rearranged (see Figure 3.12).

Out of the 14 idea units contained in the passage, this is how many, on average, participants were able to recall:

1. No context (1): 3.6 idea units

2. No context (2): 3.8 idea units

3. Context before: 8.0 idea units

4. Context after: 3.6 idea units

5. Partial context: 4.0 idea units

Clearly, the "context before" condition made a difference. Hearing the same passage twice makes almost no difference in terms of comprehension and memory; presenting the context after the passage is no good; and a partial context (which shows the objects but not relations between them) is only marginally better than no context at all.

Using the schema theory, this finding can be interpreted by referring to a "mental representation" that the full context picture creates prior to hearing the text passage. After the schema has been created (or activated), it influences the organization of our knowledge. Arguably, the idea units from the text passage are more effectively encoded because, in the process of encoding, they are linked with the schema.

Exercise

We use the example of Bransford and Johnson's (1972) study extensively in Unit 9 of this book ("Internal assessment"). It would be useful to know details about the study and familiarize yourself with the original paper published in the *Journal of Verbal Learning and Verbal Behaviour*.

The paper can be accessed here: https://tinyurl.com/kp479dh Read the paper and find out what confounding variables the authors controlled and how.

Think about all the possible implications of this finding. The takeaway message might be that if you want to understand and remember things better, make sure that you clearly know the context *before* you start studying the new material. For example, before studying schema theory, it is important to understand that schema theory is a consequence of one of the principles that define the cognitive approach to behaviour (mental representations guide behaviour), that schema is an umbrella term for a large number of mental representations, and that mental representations are the building blocks of the black box that cognitive psychologists studied to prove wrong the trial-and-error approach of classical behaviourism. If you know the context, everything makes much more sense.

Schemas influence retrieval

Anderson and Pichert (1978) demonstrated that schemas not only influence the memory process of encoding (transferring information to LTM), but also have an influence at the stage of retrieval (retrieving information from LTM).

Imagine you are a participant in their study. You are an introductory educational psychology student who is participating in the study in order to fulfill a course requirement. You are invited for a briefing and told that the study concerns "how people think about and remember stories". Being a psychology student and hearing such a vague explanation of the aim of the study, you might start to suspect that the experimenters are using mild deception and are not telling you the complete truth about the actual aim of the experiment.

ATL skills: Communication

Is deception justified in this study? Why? Explain it in no more than two sentences.

After this, there's a series of tasks that you are required to perform.

1. You are assigned either the homebuyer or the burglar perspective ("Imagine you are a homebuyer", "Imagine you are a burglar").

2. You are asked to read a text passage (373 words) about what two boys did at the home of one of the boys when they were skipping school. The passage contains a number of points of interest to a burglar or real estate agent, a total of 73 ideas. For example, the story includes such details as: "Tall hedges hid the house from the road", "They went in the side door, Mark explaining that it was always open in case his younger sisters got home earlier than his mother", "The basement had been damp and musty ever since the new plumbing was installed".

3. You are given two minutes to read the passage.

4. There is a filler verbal task (for 12 minutes you are solving problems on a vocabulary test).

5. Following this, you are given two blank pages and asked to reproduce the story in as much detail as possible.

6. There is another five-minute filler task.

7. Next, the instructions require you either to keep the same initial perspective (homebuyer or burglar) or to change it.

8. You are required to recall the text for a second time (without reading it again).

In all there were four groups of participants:

	Same perspective	Change in perspective
Homebuyer	1	3
Burglar	2	4

▲ Table 3.3 Conditions in Anderson and Pichert (1978)

Results revealed the following pattern.

- For the first recall, the group that had the burglar perspective recalled more burglar information whereas the group that had the homebuyer perspective recalled more homebuyer information.

- The people who changed perspective recalled more information important to the second perspective but unimportant to the first. Subjects who changed perspective (groups 3 and 4) recalled an additional 7.1% of the now important information (note that they did not recall these details during the first recall). On the other hand, subjects who did not change perspective (groups 1 and 2) recalled 2.9% less of the still unimportant information.

Exercise

Evaluate the following aspects of the study.

- Internal validity: what are the potential confounding variables? How well were they controlled?

- External validity: are there any issues with generalizing the findings to a wider population?

- Construct validity: what are the independent variable and dependent variable and how were they operationalized? Does the operationalization capture the essence of the theoretical constructs?

- Replicability

- Theoretical and practical implications

Do not forget that evaluation implies a balanced approach, considering both strengths and limitations.

If you identified limitations, how could you modify the study to overcome them?

Imagine you are replicating this study for your internal assessment. It is too complex but how can you simplify the procedure to fit the IA requirements?

Schemas organize knowledge that is stored in our memory. Any new information that we acquire does not just get passively registered; it is actively perceived through the lens of existing schemas. They start acting at the stage of encoding and they continue acting as we store information in our LTM, and even as we retrieve it from there. The study of Anderson and Pichert (1978) supports the idea that schemas influence retrieval of information from memory as well as encoding. Although the effect is not large (7.1% of information relevant to the new perspective), it is significant.

We have just compared schemas to a lens through which we perceive reality. How clean is this lens, though? Can it distort information? Apparently, it can, and it gives rise to a number of **biases** and **memory confabulation** (these will be further discussed later in the section "Reliability of memory").

What practical applications of these findings can you think of? For example, how can our knowledge of the effect of schemas on memory be used in education?

Types of schemas

There are many special cases and types of schemas, depending on the particular aspect of human experience that is influenced by mental representations. For example, the following types of schemas have been proposed:

- social schemas—mental representations about various groups of people, for example, a stereotype

- scripts—schemas about sequences of events, for example, going to a restaurant or making coffee

- self-schemas—mental representations about ourselves.

One example that illustrates the effect of social schemas on our perception and interpretations is **Darley and Gross (1983)**. In this study, one group of participants was led to believe that a child (a girl) came from a high socio-economic status (SES) background and the other group was told that the child came from a low-SES background. Both groups then watched the same video of the child taking an academic test. They were required to judge the academic performance of the girl. In accordance with the predictions of social schema theory, participants who thought that the child came from a high-SES environment gave considerably higher ratings for the academic performance of the girl in the video. This showed that pre-stored schemas (about what it means to be rich and what it means to be poor) were used as a lens through which the ambiguous information was perceived, and participants' interpretations were changed accordingly.

A study by **Bower, Black and Turner (1979)** showed how scripts stored in our memory help us make sense of sequential data. The aim of the study was to see if in recalling a text, subjects will use the underlying script to fill in gaps of actions not explicitly mentioned in the text. The

idea behind the study is as follows. Suppose an underlying abstract script exists for the following sequence of events: a, b, c, d, e, f, g. Now suppose there is a text that includes sentences corresponding to events a, c, e, g. If you present this text to a group of participants and ask them (after a series of filler tasks) to recall the text, they will probably "fill in the gaps", that is, remember events b, d, f even though they were not originally in the text. This rests on the idea that we encode the text based on the underlying script, that is, we remember the generalized idea behind a text rather than the text itself.

Here is an example of two texts that served as manifestations of the same underlying script:

> The doctor. John was feeling bad today so he decided to go see a family doctor. He checked in with the doctor's receptionist, and then looked through several medical magazines that were on the table by his chair. Finally the nurse came and asked him to take off his clothes. The doctor was very nice to him. He eventually prescribed some pills for John. Then John left the doctor's office and headed home.

> The dentist. Bill had a bad toothache. It seemed like forever before he finally arrived at the dentist's office. Bill looked around at the various dental posters on the wall. Finally the dental hygienist checked and x-rayed his teeth. He wondered what the dentist was doing. The dentist said that Bill had a lot of cavities. As soon as he'd made another appointment, he left the dentist's office.

> (Bower, Black and Turner, 1979, p 190)

Note how in these two stories the only similar ideas are the opening statement and the closing statement. Technically, the stories are completely different in all other aspects.

As predicted, after reading both the stories (and carrying out a 20-minute filler task) participants were prone to insert gap fillers, for example, recalling "checking in with the receptionist" for the dentist story.

The concept of self-schemas is used extensively in **Aaron Beck's theory of depression**. The negative self-schema that depressed people develop about themselves, and the corresponding automatic thinking patterns are, in this theory, the driving force of depression. You will learn more about Aaron Beck's cognitive theory of depression later (see Unit 5 on abnormal psychology).

Exercise

To what extent can depression be explained by cognitive factors? Look through Unit 5 on abnormal psychology to see how the cognitive theory of depression is supported by empirical research.

Bottom-up and top-down processing

The concept of schemas raises an important issue that goes far beyond the realm of psychology. Generally speaking, there are two broad types of information processing: bottom-up processing and top-down processing.

- Bottom-up information processing occurs when the cognitive process is data-driven; perception is not biased by prior knowledge or expectations. It is a case of "pure" information processing based on the reality as it is.

- Top-down processing occurs when your prior knowledge or expectations (schemas) act as a lens or a filter for the information that you receive and process.

A classic example that can help to visualize top-down processing is the **Rat Man of Bugelski and Alampay (1961)**. Participants in this study saw an ambiguous picture (see Figure 3.13) after being exposed to a series of drawings of either animals (condition 1) or faces (condition 2). In the first condition, participants were more likely to interpret the ambiguous stimulus as a rat; in the second condition they were more likely to see a man wearing glasses. After viewing a series of drawings they had an implicit expectation which influenced their perception of reality.

▲ Figure 3.13 The Rat Man

One might think, intuitively, that top-down processing is a bad thing, because it can potentially lead to a variety of biases. However, it is actually very necessary. In sciences, arguably, it's simply impossible to "perceive data" without the background of a theory. Theory tells the scientist what to look for and how to look for it. Otherwise real-life data is too fuzzy. Without the guiding theory this data does not make sense. In a similar fashion, if we didn't have some (simplified) expectations about the world, sequences of events, ourselves and other people, we would find it extremely difficult to make day-to-day decisions. Schematic processing might, indeed, be simplified and biased, and it can lead to stereotypes, but it saves energy.

Using schematic processing, we see patterns in otherwise unstructured stimuli (**pattern recognition**) and find meaning in those patterns (**effort after meaning**). In one of his TED Talks entitled "Why people believe weird things", Michael Shermer, the founding publisher of *Sceptic* magazine and editor of Sceptic.com, calls humans "pattern-seeking animals".

Arguably, evolution has predisposed us to see certain patterns even when the stimulus is not clear or is vague, because these patterns might be potentially important to us. That might explain, for example, the buzz around the "Face on Mars", the famous photograph of the Mars surface taken by NASA's Viking spacecraft in 1971. Back then, the resolution was low and the image was not particularly clear, but there have been claims that this picture proves the existence of artificial objects on Mars and, potentially, an extraterrestrial civilization. However, this was debunked in 2001 when a high-resolution picture was taken of the same surface object, revealing that it was nothing more than a rock formation. People have a schema of a face because recognizing faces is an important aspect of survival. Pattern recognition as a part of top-down processing driven by this schema leads us to perceive faces readily even when the data is fuzzy. (If you are not convinced, search for "Charlie Chaplin illusion" on YouTube.)

See video

The Charlie Chaplin illusion: https://www.youtube.com/watch?v=QbKw0_v2clo

Michael Shermer, "Why people believe weird things": https://www.ted.com/talks/michael_shermer_on_believing_strange_things

▶ ❚❚ ■ ────────────────

Similarly, we seem to have a drive for finding meaning in these patterns. This might explain conspiracy theories that flourished around the "Face on Mars".

▲ Figure 3.14 "Face on Mars" photograph

Psychology in real life

Gillian Gibbons, a UK national who worked as a teacher in a private school in Sudan, asked her 7-year-old students to decide on a name for a classroom teddy bear as part of a larger project on studying animals. The children voted for "Muhammad". As part of their assignment later they needed to take pictures of the teddy bear and write diary entries about it which the teacher collected in a single workbook entitled "My name is Muhammad". What seemed like a harmless class assignment turned out to be a cultural shock for Ms Gibbons. When some parents saw the workbook, they complained to the Ministry of Education claiming that Ms Gibbons had offended Islam by allowing an animal to be named after Prophet Muhammad. Insulting the Prophet is a grave offence in Sudan.

Ms Gibbons was arrested at her home on 25 November 2007. This 54-year-old teacher was facing a charge of up

to 1 year in jail, a fine and 40 lashes with a whip. The case gained wide coverage and there were demonstrations with people demanding a more severe punishment. She was finally found guilty and sentenced to 15 days in jail with subsequent deportation from Sudan. She was pardoned after nine days (which caused some protests in the public) and returned to England immediately after release.

This shows how a cultural misunderstanding, a difference in "cultural schemas", can have severe consequences. https://tinyurl.com/lnx6a3x

Thinking and decision-making

Inquiry questions

- Do people make rational decisions?
- Are human errors in thinking and decision-making predictable?
- Do intentions affect behaviour?

- How can we test a model of thinking empirically and in a quantifiable way?
- How can we research the process of thinking rather than its outcomes?

What you will learn in this section

- Normative models and descriptive models
  - Normative models describe the way that thinking should be; they assume unlimited time and resources, examples: formal logic, theory of probability, utility theory
  - Descriptive models describe thinking as it actually occurs in real life
- Macro-level decision-making models: the theory of reasoned action Fishbein, 1967) and the theory of planned behaviour (Ajzen, 1985)
  - Ajzen and Fishbein (1973): meta-analysis shows a 0.63 correlation between intention and behaviour
  - Albarracin et al (2001): meta-analysis of condom use; correlation between intention and behaviour 0.51; Intention-intention-behaviour relationship is weaker for behaviours assessed prospectively
  - Predictive validity of the models is high, but direction of causality is inferred because research is essentially correlational
- Micro-level decision-making model: the adaptive decision maker framework (Payne, Bettman and Johnson, 1993)
  - Multiattribute choice problems

- Alternative-based strategies: weighted additive strategy (WADD), satisficing strategy (SAT)
- Attribute-based strategies: lexicographic strategy (LEX), elimination by aspects (EBA)
- Strategy selection is guided by four meta-goals: maximizing decision accuracy, minimizing the cognitive effort, minimizing the experience of negative emotion, maximizing the ease of justification of a decision
- Supporting study: Luce, Bettman and Payne (1997), minimizing experience of negative emotions occurred through avoiding emotionally difficult trade-offs between options
- More research methods used in the cognitive approach to behaviour:
  - Self-report measures (behavioural and attitudinal)
    - Data matrix, correlation analysis
    - Predictive validity of a model
  - Meta-analysis
  - Computer simulation
  - Verbal protocols
  - Monitored information search
  - Neuroimaging techniques

This section also links to:

- concepts of the cognitive approach to behaviour (the role of models)
- principles of the cognitive approach—mental processes can be studied scientifically; cognitive processes do not function in isolation

- research methodology
- biases in thinking and decision-making
- emotion and cognition
- brain structure, localization of function (biological approach to behaviour).

Thinking and decision-making: normative models and descriptive models

In the computer metaphor different cognitive processes are responsible for processing information at different stages. For example, the function of perception (as a cognitive process) is to register information, while the function of memory is to encode, store and retrieve it. The function of **thinking** is to modify this information: we break down information into lesser parts (analysis), bring different pieces of information together (synthesis), relate certain pieces of information to certain categories (categorization), make conclusions and inferences, and so on. Unlike other cognitive processes, thinking produces new information. Using thinking, we combine and restructure existing knowledge to generate new knowledge. Thinking has been defined in many ways, including "going beyond the information given" (Bruner, 1957) and "searching through a problem-space" (Newell and Simon, 1972).

Decision-making is a cognitive process that involves selecting one of the possible beliefs or actions, that is, making a choice between some alternatives. It is closely linked to thinking because before we can choose, we have to analyse. So thinking is an integral prerequisite of any act of decision-making.

Thinking and decision-making are complex higher-order cognitive processes, which may be the reason why this field of research is so interdisciplinary. Thinking and decision-making are studied by psychologists, philosophers, economists, neuroscientists, computer scientists, linguists (because abstract thinking involves language) and anthropologists among others. Much like memory, thinking and decision-making are

implicit processes that cannot be directly observed. They also involve interaction between a large number of factors. For this reason, the scientific study of thinking and decision-making is not possible without **models**. So how do we approach making a model of thinking? It seems like an immense task.

As a starting point, it is necessary to distinguish between two broad groups of models (Baron, 2008).

ATL skills: Communication

Imagine a 12-year-old asks you why it is important to make a "model of thinking". Explain it to him or her.

Normative models

Normative models describe the way that thinking should be. They assume that unlimited time and resources are available to make a decision. They define what is right and wrong, correct and incorrect, effective and ineffective.

One example of a normative model of thinking is **formal logic**, as developed by Aristotle. The building block of the system of formal logic is a deductive syllogism: a combination of two premises and a conclusion (which follows from these premises). There is a set of rules that describes when syllogisms are valid and when they are not. For example:

(Premise 1) All men are mortal.

(Premise 2) All Greeks are men.

(Conclusion) Hence, all Greeks are mortal.

This example is valid. Formal logic explains why. In fact, there is even a name for this type of syllogism: Barbara. "A" stands for a general affirmative statement ("All men are mortal" is affirmative because it asserts something, and general because it refers to all men). Since all three statements in the syllogism are of the same type, it gives us triple A, hence the name (bArbArA).

Another example of a normative economic model is the **theory of probability**. When we make investment decisions, we might go with our intuition, but the "normative" thing to do is to analyse the success or failure frequencies in the past for similar enterprises under similar circumstances, and then make decisions based on the likely outcomes projected from this analysis.

Utility theory is the normative model for decisions involving uncertainty and trade-offs between alternatives. According to this theory, the rational decision-maker should calculate the expected utility (the degree to which it helps us achieve our goals) for each option and then choose the option that maximizes this utility.

The important thing to understand is that normative models give us a standard against which real-life thinking and decision-making may be compared. Why do we even need other models? Because normative models are unrealistic. Nobody actually thinks in syllogisms in real life. And nobody has access to a large amount of statistical data for every possible decision. We need to take shortcuts.

TOK

In what areas of knowledge have people been more successful in using the "ideal" normative models of thinking and decision-making? How did they manage?

Descriptive models

Descriptive models show what people actually do when they think and make decisions. They focus on an accurate description of real-life thinking patterns and the main measure of effectiveness for such models is how closely the model fits observed data from various samples of participants. Descriptive models will be the main focus of our discussion in this section, because this is what interests a psychologist. However, descriptive models acquire much deeper meaning when we compare them to normative models, as we study how human thinking processes deviate from the predictions of the normative model and try to explain (and predict) these deviations.

ATL skills: Thinking

You are about to discover some things about how people make decisions. Before you read on, can you make some predictions on the basis of your common knowledge and interpersonal experience? Answer these questions and give your reasons.

1. Are people mostly rational beings?
2. If there are errors in our judgments, are these errors predictable?
3. Can people control the rationality of their decisions?
4. What factors are most important when making a choice between several alternatives?
5. What are the goals that people generally pursue when they make decisions?

Multiple descriptive models have been proposed to describe the real-life processes of human thinking and decision-making. We will consider several examples: the theory of reasoned action, the theory of planned behaviour, and the adaptive decision-maker framework.

The theory of reasoned action and the theory of planned behaviour

The theory of reasoned action (TRA) aims to explain the relationship between attitudes and behaviours when making choices. This theory was proposed by **Martin Fishbein** in 1967. The main idea of the theory is that an individual's choice of a particular behaviour is based on the expected outcomes of that behaviour. If we believe that a particular behaviour will lead to a particular (desired) outcome, this creates a predisposition known as the **behavioural intention**. The stronger the behavioural intention, the stronger the effort we put into implementing the plan and hence the higher the probability that this behaviour will actually be executed.

There are two factors that determine behavioural intention: **attitudes** and **subjective norms**. An attitude describes your individual perception of the behaviour (whether this behaviour is positive or negative) while the subjective norm describes the perceived social pressure regarding this behaviour (if it is socially acceptable or desirable to do it). Depending on the situation, attitudes and subjective norms might have varying degrees of importance in determining the intention.

In 1985 the theory was extended and became what is known as the **theory of planned behaviour (TPB)**. This theory introduced the third factor that influences behavioural intentions: **perceived behavioural control**. This was added to account for situations in which the attitude is positive, and the subjective norms do not prevent you from performing the behaviour; however, you do not think you are able to carry out the action.

The theory of reasoned action and the theory of planned behaviour have seen extensive applications in an attempt to explain a range of specific behaviours. We will consider several examples that demonstrate the nature of this research and the methods that are usually applied in it.

Research in focus: Methods of research for macro-level cognitive models

The majority of research studies in this area use self-report behavioural and attitudinal measures. The items on questionnaires and surveys are framed differently to refer to different components of the model. For example:

- Behaviour—"I always use available discount coupons when I make purchases online": True or false

- Intention—"I intend to use available discount coupons next time I buy something expensive": Likely or unlikely

- Attitude—"Spending time to collect coupons and plan their use is…": Good/bad; pleasant/unpleasant

- Perceived norms—"Most of my friends would not approve of me collecting discount coupons": Agree or disagree

- Perceived behavioural control—"I am sure I can save a considerable amount of money by collecting discount coupons": Agree or disagree

After this information is collected, you have a large **data matrix** in which each row corresponds to an individual participant and each column corresponds to a question on the survey (or a group of questions all related to a particular attitude or an aspect of behaviour). You also have a theoretical model, for example, for the theory of planned behaviour:

Using **correlation analysis** (and its more sophisticated extensions) you then estimate the extent to which this model fits the observed data (that is, the data matrix). For example, in order to conclude that the model is a good fit to the data, the following trends should be observed.

- There **should** be a large and significant correlation between: attitude and intention; perceived norms and intention; perceived control and intention; intention and future behaviour.

- There **should not** be a large correlation between norms and future behaviour; attitudes and future behaviour, and so on. If one of these correlations exists, you have to refute the model as it means that one of these components is linked to behaviour directly, which contradicts the very idea of the theory of planned behaviour.

Collectively, the four variables should be able to explain a significant portion of variance in the responses to the target variable (future behaviour). In other words, using the data it should be possible to build a mathematical formula that predicts future behaviour from the other four variables with a high degree of probability. This measure of probability is also referred to as **the predictive validity of the model**.

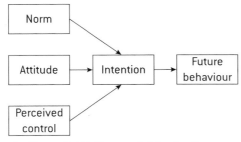

▲ Figure 3.15 The model for the theory of planned behaviour

Take a minute to recall what you know about correlation (see "Research methodology"). To test your knowledge, answer these questions.

- What is the "third variable"?
- What does it mean when someone says that a correlation is "statistically significant"?
- What is the range of values of the correlation coefficient?
- What does a negative correlation mean?
- What does a zero correlation mean?
- What is the difference between effect size and statistical significance?
- What does this mean: $r = 0.56$, $p < 0.05$?

Research studies have shown that the predictive validity of TPB for a range of specific activities is quite impressive. **Ajzen and Fishbein (1973)**, as a result of their own meta-analysis of published research, report a 0.63 correlation between intentions and behaviour.

ATL skills: Self-management

Is this correlation small or large? Review Unit 1 on research methodology.

Albarracin *et al* (2001) conducted a meta-analysis of TRA and TPB as models of condom use. The practical significance of the study lies in the fact that identification of important attitudinal or behavioural predictors of the frequency of condom use can help greatly in the prevention of HIV and STD epidemics. This is why it is important to understand why people choose to use or not to use condoms.

ATL skills: Research

Discuss the relative strengths and limitations of meta-analysis as a research method. How does meta-analysis relate to the problem of replicability in science?

The meta-analysis comprised 42 published and unpublished articles and a total of 96 data sets (which were brought together in one combined data matrix). Fitting the models of TRA and TPB into this data set and estimating the predictive validity of the models, they arrived at the following conclusions.

- Both the TRA and TPB are successful predictors of condom use. The average correlation between intention and behaviour in these models is 0.51. Notice that it is a weaker intention–behaviour association than that reported by Ajzen and Fishbein (1973). One possible explanation is that people generally have less control over condom use than other behaviours in some other domains.

- It makes a difference whether behaviour is assessed **retrospectively or prospectively**. In the former case, assessments of intentions and behaviour are carried out at the same time. In the latter case, intentions and behaviour are assessed at different time periods. Naturally, the intention–behaviour relationship is weaker for behaviours assessed prospectively (0.45) than for behaviours assessed retrospectively (0.57). However, even 0.45 is sufficient enough to say that the predictive validity of the model is high.

- "Thus, people are more likely to use condoms if they have previously formed the corresponding intentions. These intentions to use condoms appear to derive from attitudes, subjective norms, and perceived behavioural control" (Albarracin *et al*, 2001).

It should be noted, however, that this study relies on the assumption that self-reported condom use is an accurate reflection of the participants' actual everyday behaviour. Another important limitation is that although studies like this are based on complex models and they quantitatively estimate the fit of the theoretical model to the observed data, they are still correlational. This means that the direction of causality, although plausible, is still just **inferred**. Is it possible, for example, that behaviour influences intentions rather than the other way around? Longitudinal studies in which intentions and behaviours are assessed at different points in time can provide valuable insights into the direction of causality in decision-making models.

Finally, it should be noted that the study had a lot of potential implications for HIV prevention efforts.

Can you think of a way to test the predictions of the theory of planned behaviour in an experimental, rather than correlational, design? Suggest some ideas.

The adaptive decision-maker framework

There is an increasing recognition of the fact that **emotions** may influence our thinking and decision-making. The consequences of decisions result in experiencing certain emotions. The memory of such emotions, and the anticipation of them, may then become one of the driving factors in decision-making. One of the models that includes emotions in the process of decision-making is known as the adaptive decision-maker framework. Let's have a closer look at it.

In the classical information-processing approach which was dominated by normative models, the decision-maker was assumed to be completely **rational**, with complete knowledge and unlimited computational capacity. This was later doubted, first by acknowledging that human computational capacity is not unlimited, therefore descriptive models should account for "bounded human rationality" (Simon, 1955). We do not have the mental capacity to consider all aspects and nuances of a complex situation, evaluate and compare all the attributes of all the possible options, and accurately calculate risks and expected outcomes, especially under time constraints. So we should be using simpler decision-making strategies that use less cognitive resources.

The next step in the same direction was to say that apart from exhibiting bounded rationality, people actually don't always try to make rational choices—accuracy of decisions is not the only driving force behind human choices. One example of an alternative goal is minimizing the cost or effort involved in the decision (people are not only looking for the best decisions; they sometimes opt for the easiest).

The adaptive decision-maker framework **(Payne, Bettman and Johnson, 1993)** postulates that people possess a toolbox of strategies that may be used in thinking and decision-making tasks, so they may use different strategies in different situations. Some strategies for use when making a choice (considering a set of options or alternatives and picking the best one) are as follows.

- **Weighted additive strategy (WADD).** This strategy is considered to be normative for multi-attribute choice problems (choice problems involving multiple alternatives compared against multiple attributes). This is a maximizing strategy: for every alternative you multiply the value of every attribute by the importance (weight) of the attribute, then calculate the **weighted sum**, after which you choose the alternative where the weighted sum is the largest. In normative decision-making models (that mathematically justify the most rational choices) this is also known as calculating the "utility" of a choice (hence the name for the normative model, utility theory (see above)). This strategy requires a lot of effort.

- **Lexicographic strategy (LEX).** Choose the most important attribute and then the option that has the best value for that attribute. Undoubtedly, this strategy is not optimal (in that it simply ignores a number of attributes), but it has been shown that in a variety of situations this strategy is actually reasonable: under some circumstances it does not lead to a significant reduction in accuracy, yet does lead to a significant reduction in effort.

- **Satisficing strategy (SAT).** Determine a specific cut-off point for every attribute. Then consider the first option. For every attribute of this option, compare the value of that attribute to the cut-off point. If at least one of the attributes is lower than the cut-off point, reject the option and consider the next one. Stop when you reach an option that exceeds all the cut-off points. If no option passes the test, the cut-off points are relaxed and the process is repeated.

- **Elimination by aspects (EBA).** Choose the most important attribute and eliminate all the options that do not meet your requirements for this attribute. Then select the second most important attribute and eliminate more options. Continue until only one option remains.

Let's consider a hypothetical example. Imagine you are planning to meet some friends (some of whom are bringing children) at a restaurant and you are choosing from five options and against five attributes (quality of food, price, and so on). Each attribute may have one of three possible values: "bad", "average" and "good".

		Attributes			
		Quality of food	Price	Distance from home	Catering to a variety of dietary needs	Playroom for children
Alternatives	"Southern Sun"	Good	Average	Good	Bad	Bad
	"Northern Wind"	Bad	Good	Average	Average	Bad
	"Western Traditional"	Average	Bad	Bad	Bad	Good
	"Eastern Delicacy"	Average	Good	Average	Good	Bad
	"Global Junction"	Good	Average	Bad	Bad	Average

▲ Table 3.4 Hypothetical example for decision strategies

If you are using the WADD strategy, assign numerical values to attributes (for example, bad = 1, average = 2, good = 3) and then calculate the weighted sum of attributes for each of the alternatives. The score you get for "Southern Sun" is 3 + 2 + 3 + 1 + 1 = 10. The restaurant that will score the highest is "Eastern Delicacy" (2 + 3 + 2 + 3 + 1 = 11). So this is the one you will choose.

If you are using the LEX strategy, first decide which of the attributes is most important to you (say, playroom for children) and then pick the best alternative for that attribute (in our case, "Western Traditional").

In SAT, decide on a cut-off score (for example, you decide that all attributes in the best choice should be at least average) and look for the option that satisfies this condition. If no such option is found (as is the case in the current example, since each of the alternatives scores "bad" for at least one of the attributes), relax the condition. For example, you might decide that the attribute playroom for children does not necessarily have to be good or average, and now "Eastern Delicacy" would satisfy your new condition and be the restaurant of choice.

In EBA, your thinking might be like this. Important attributes should be at least "average". The most important attribute is "quality of food". So you eliminate "Northern Wind". The second most important attribute is "catering to a variety of diets". So you eliminate three more restaurants. Only "Eastern Delicacy" is left, and this is the restaurant you choose.

Strategies like WADD and SAT are called **alternative-based**, because you are considering different attributes for the same alternative. Strategies like LEX and EBA are **attribute-based**, because you select an important attribute and compare different alternatives against this attribute. This will be important later in this section when we

consider the role of emotion in decision-making, since "alternative-based" strategies potentially involve more emotionally uncomfortable trade-offs (for example, in "Southern Sun" there's really great food, but there isn't a playroom for children).

Exercise

Think of some real-life examples in which:

- you predominantly use each of the four strategies

- some strategies are more emotionally uncomfortable than others

- trade-offs created by alternative-based strategies cause a negative emotional experience.

Of course, in real-life decision-making we do not consistently use one of the clear-cut strategies. In fact, we use a variety of strategies that might combine the four discussed above. What is important for the adaptive decision-maker framework is that people have a toolbox of strategies that they may or may not use depending on the situation.

So if people have all the strategies at their disposal (in the "toolbox"), how and why do they choose between them in a particular situation? Here is where emotions and other "irrational" factors come into play. According to the adaptive decision-maker framework, **strategy selection is guided by goals**. There are **four meta-goals** proposed in the framework.

- **Maximizing decision accuracy.** This is the only goal assumed in normative choice models. Making a choice between the four strategies outlined above, an individual who focuses on maximizing the accuracy of the decision would prefer the WADD strategy, making an attempt to quantify all attributes and consider all possible attributes for all possible options.

- **Minimizing the cognitive effort.** Of the above-mentioned strategies, LEX is probably the most energy-saving, since it only involves two quick steps.

- **Minimizing the experience of negative emotion.** In real-life decision-making, some attributes or options can be emotion-laden. For example, you are choosing a car and you have ruled out one of the brands because its name creates unpleasant associations in your language. (This was the case with the Russian car brand "Zhiguli" which had to be renamed because to the European ear it sounded like "gigolo", dramatically decreasing sales.) In another example you are choosing a house and you see one that exceeds your expectations, but you are not going to buy it because a violent crime happened in it several years ago. How can negative emotions impact decision-making? There are two competing hypotheses.

  - Hypothesis A—the negative emotion will interfere with the decision, compromising both the speed and accuracy of the decision. In this hypothesis emotion is not part of a decision-making model. Rather it is an external factor that has a negative impact on the process.

  - Hypothesis B—decision-making will directly adapt to the negative emotion. In this case, emotion should be included in decision-making models as an integral part, since accounting for emotions would help us better understand and predict choice outcomes. As will be shown later, hypothesis B gained empirical support in research studies.

- **Maximizing the ease of justification of a decision** (to others or to oneself). The authors

of the adaptive decision-maker framework argue that inclusion of this meta-goal explains a number of effects that had been established in research but could not be explained by existing thinking and decision-making models. One example is the so-called asymmetric dominance effect which you will learn about later in this unit (see "Biases in thinking and decision-making").

ATL skills: Thinking

How does this model link to the principles of cognitive approach to behaviour? In particular, how does the model relate to principle 3 (cognitive processes do not function in isolation)?

There's one important difference between the adaptive decision-maker framework and the theory of reasoned action. The theory of reasoned action is an example of a **macro-level decision-making model**. It focuses on the choice outcomes (for example, condom use) and relatively stable characteristics (such as attitudes, perceived norms) that might predict these outcomes. In other words, the theory deals with results of decisions on a large scale. On the other hand, the adaptive decision-maker framework is an example of a **micro-level model**. It focuses on the process of making a decision, the strategies being used when processing available information, and so on. Such models zoom in on decision processes on a smaller scale.

Undoubtedly, micro-level models attempt to describe processes that are more **situation-dependent, fluid and complex**. With such complex and transient objects of research, collecting self-report measures and analysing correlation patterns is no longer a valid method. There should be other methods that allow a deeper insight into the nature of separate acts of decision-making, an insight into the process rather than the outcomes of this process.

Research in focus: Methods of research for micro-level cognitive models

These methods allow a deeper insight into the nature of separate acts of decision-making, an insight into the process rather than the outcomes of this process.

- **Computer simulations:** these can be performed **without human subjects**

(which is simultaneously an advantage and a disadvantage). In computer simulations various hypothetical decision-making scenarios are typically programmed and then various decision strategies (for example, WADD, SAT, EBA) are compared

Research in focus (continued)

in terms of decision accuracy. To compare the performance of different strategies, a normative model is used as a point of reference (in this case WADD can be taken as the normative model since it provides the most comprehensive analysis of alternatives). This allows the researcher to quickly (and without the need to actually involve human subjects) change the starting parameters of the situation (for example, the number of attributes and alternatives) and run multiple comparisons. It makes possible such conclusions as: "In decision sets with little trade-off between attributes and a small number of alternatives WADD and LEX perform equally well". The researcher can also make these computer models more complicated by adding hypothetical variables that model genuine human behaviour. For example, they may introduce a hypothetical "tendency to avoid emotion-laden decisions" or computational constraints (for example, no more than 7±2 units of information). This is done on the basis of prior research. Of course, conclusions and inferences derived from such simulations are only hypothetical, but they provide a lot of insights for subsequent experiments that may involve human subjects and compare their behaviour to that predicted by the computer model.

- **Verbal protocols:** another name for this technique is "think-aloud protocols". Subjects are asked to give continuous verbal reports while performing a task, that is, to think aloud. For example, you may be given a mathematical problem and asked to solve it, but at the same time never stop verbalizing everything that is going on in your mind. Transcripts of such think-aloud sessions are then analysed with the aim of deriving some clear-cut stages or strategies in the decision-making process.

- **Monitored information search:** in this method the process of information acquisition by the participant is monitored and recorded. The assumption is that this "trajectory" of information acquisition will reflect your decision-making processes: you will look at those bits of information that are most important to you at this moment while making the choice. Typically researchers will register what information is sought, in what order, and for how long each piece of information is processed (reaction time). This can take the form of software that records the movements and clicks of a mouse cursor, or sophisticated techniques such as eye-movement tracking.

- Of course, **neuroimaging techniques** are also used to shed light on the neuronal mechanisms of decision-making.

We will consider one example of a study that used **monitored information search** to test the prediction that decision-making directly adapts to negative emotions ("hypothesis B" above).

Luce, Bettman and Payne (1997) hypothesized that task-related negative emotion will encourage decision-makers to process information more extensively (because they attach more importance to the accuracy of decision) and at the same time in a way that avoids emotionally difficult trade-offs between options.

Twenty-seven undergraduate students were asked to imagine they were members of a charity that provides children with financial support. Their task was to choose one child from a group of five children described in terms of five attributes (see the table below):

Child	Willingness to learn	Age	Personality	Family size	Living conditions
Sang	Poor	Prefer	Good	6 people	Bad
Rene	Very good	Prefer	Average	3 people	Adequate
Zivae	Very good	Prefer	Very poor	6 people	Adequate
Kito	Very poor	Indifferent	Very good	4 people	Very bad
Jaime	Very poor	Don't prefer	Poor	7 people	Very bad

▲ Table 3.5 Based on Luce, Bettman and Payne (1997, p 391)

The importance of the attributes was explained in the following way.

- Willingness to learn and personality are important because children who score better on these attributes would be more likely to help others in their community.

- Age is important because a relationship will have to be established with the child through correspondence which requires a certain maturity.

- Family size is important because the entire family benefits from the charity.

- Living conditions are important because the charity should target children living in relatively worse conditions.

You will see that the attribute values conflict with each other—there is no dominant alternative, that is, an alternative that would be best across all the attributes. The task was performed by using the "Mouselab" computer program. In this software the choice was presented to the subjects in the form of a matrix (much like Table 3.5), but all information in the cells was hidden behind boxes that could be opened by a mouse click. The software recorded the order in which boxes were opened, the time spent in each box, and the final choice. The order in which boxes were opened was observed through counting the number of times subjects used two patterns:

- after opening box A, opening a box for the same alternative but a different attribute (alternative-based transitions)

- after opening box A, opening a box for the same attribute but a different alternative (attribute-based transitions).

Attribute-based transitions involve fewer trade-offs and so theoretically they help you to avoid making emotion-laden choices. For example, if you open the box saying that Kito's personality is "very good", it could be emotionally difficult for you to find out that Kito's willingness to learn is "very poor", since it creates a trade-off and poses a difficult dilemma. However, it is emotionally easier to avoid such trade-offs and open "personality" boxes for other children.

In order to manipulate negative emotion, participants were split into two groups.

- In the higher-emotion group participants were provided with a more specific and extensive background text describing the children's situation. They were also told that the four eliminated children were not likely to receive support anywhere else. This was meant to enhance the perception of the choice as high-stakes.

- In the lower-emotion group the background texts were more superficial and participants were told that the four remaining children were likely to receive support elsewhere.

Results of the study supported the pattern that was predicted by the adaptive decision-maker framework.

- Participants in the higher-emotion group opened a larger number of boxes and spent more time on the task (which shows that they were processing information more extensively, probably due to more importance attached to the accuracy of decisions).

- Participants in the higher-emotion group engaged more frequently in attribute-based transitions (which shows that they were avoiding emotionally difficult trade-offs between options).

Exercise

Make a schematic representation of this study outlining its main elements and results.

Do not forget to include:

- aim
- hypothesis
- independent variable (IV), dependent variable (DV)
- operationalization of IV and DV
- procedure
- result
- conclusion (link results back to the hypothesis).

Psychology in real life

On 24 April 2013 an eight-storey commercial building named Rana Plaza collapsed in Dhaka, Bangladesh. It is now considered the deadliest accidental structural failure in modern history. Approximately 2,500 people were rescued from the building alive, while the search for the dead lasted three weeks with a total death toll of 1,129. The building housed multiple garment factories, several shops and a bank. On 23 April reporters found cracks in the foundation of the building, the footage of which appeared in the news on a television channel. Immediately after that the building was evacuated, and the shops and the bank on the lower floors were closed. However, later that day the owner of the building made an announcement to the media saying that the building was safe and the workers should return to their workplace tomorrow. Workers were also threatened with loss of monthly salary if they failed to return to the factories. On the morning of the following day there was a power outage in the buildings, and back-up generators were started to keep the factories running. The building collapsed at 8.57am.

Thirty-eight people were charged with murder, and the building owner was caught trying to flee across the border to India.

Apart from the decision to force workers to return to their workplace, charges were filed on the basis of numerous violations in the construction of the building itself: it was built on a filled-in pond, it was converted from commercial to industrial use, and three floors were added above the original permit.

Apart from numerous legal and moral issues, all this raises a lot of questions regarding how people make their decisions and why these decisions can turn out to be so irrational.

https://tinyurl.com/hpg5l25

Reliability of cognitive processes: reconstructive memory

Inquiry questions

- Is memory passive retrieval of information from the long-term store, or rather active reconstruction of information from the past?

- Does external information influence the way we remember things?

- Can memory of an event change with the course of time?

- How are false memories created?

What you will learn in this section

- Unreliability of memory

  - Schema influences what is encoded and what is retrieved

  - Memories can be distorted

- The theory of reconstructive memory: post-event information may alter the memory of an event

  - Loftus and Palmer (1974) experiment 1: eyewitness testimony, two competing explanations: response bias and genuine memory change

  - Loftus and Palmer (1974) experiment 2: support for the genuine memory change explanation.

- Verbal post-event information can interfere with visual information obtained originally; this alters not only recall but also visual recognition

  - Support: Loftus, Miller and Burns (1978)

- However, when misleading information is not an option on the test, the effect disappears; this takes us back to the alternative explanation: response bias

  - Support: McCloskey and Zaragoza (1985)

- Meta-analysis as a way to resolve contradictory research

  - Payne, Toglia and Anastasi (1994): showed that genuine memory change occurs even when misleading information is not an option on the test; however, the effect is small

- Research in naturalistic settings contradicts the theory of reconstructive memory, but may be explained by another memory mechanism: flashbulb memory

  - Yuille and Cutshall (1986)

This section also links to:

- schema theory (memory may be changed during storage, processing and retrieval)

- flashbulb memory

- principles of the cognitive approach to behaviour—biases in cognitive processes can be systematic and predictable

- research methodology.

Unreliability of memory

We have already considered the way that schemas may influence memory processes at all stages of information processing, including encoding and retrieval. Studies like Anderson and Pichert (1978) show that schemas can determine what you do and do not remember even after the information has been coded and stored in the long-term memory. Depending on the schema you are using, you will find it easier to recall some details. This shows one of the limitations to reliability of memory: retrieval of information from LTM may depend on whether or not you are using a particular schema. This is why we sometimes find it difficult to recall things, but then they "jump back" to us when the context changes and something in the new context triggers those memories.

However, the fact that retrieval (or non-retrieval) of information depends on schemas in use is only one dimension of unreliability of memory. Another dimension is the tendency of memory to be **distorted**. Is it possible that we recall something, but it never actually happened? Or it did, but not quite the way we remember?

The theory of reconstructive memory and eyewitness testimony

There's a theory that proposes that memory, rather than being the passive retrieval of information from the long-term storage, is an **active process** that involves the reconstruction of information, the theory of **reconstructive memory**. Reconstruction literally means that you construct the memory again.

ATL skills: Self-management

Think about one of your early childhood memories, something that happened to you when you were very young. How clearly do you remember this episode? Some details are probably more accessible to you than others, and you remember those clearly. Some details are a bit vague. Some details or contextual information is not available, there are gaps.

Now imagine you were to tell this childhood memory to someone else. To make the story more coherent, you might want to fill in some gaps with details that seem logical to you, for example, if this happened in the morning and you were on your way somewhere, you were probably on your way to school. The next time you retell this story, you will be more likely to mention that you were on your way to school, and what's more, you will think you are **remembering** it. Interestingly, the more often you recollect (reconstruct) your childhood memories, the less accurate they can become!

In order to see the extent to which memories can be altered by irrelevant external influences, **Loftus and Palmer (1974)** conducted their famous study on **eyewitness testimony**. It is important to note that the study actually consisted of two parts—experiment 1 and experiment 2—because there were two competing hypotheses.

In **experiment 1**, 45 students were split into 5 groups and shown film recordings of traffic accidents (each participant was shown 7 films). The order in which the films were shown was different for each participant. Following each film, participants were given a questionnaire asking them to answer a series of questions about the accident. Most of the questions on the questionnaire were just meant as distracters, but there was one critical question that asked about the speed of the vehicles involved in the collision. This question varied among the five groups of participants: one group was asked "About how fast were the cars going when they hit each other?", and for the other groups the word "hit" was changed for "smashed", "collided", "bumped" or "contacted". Results showed that the mean speed estimates varied significantly for the five groups:

Verb	Mean speed estimate (mph)
Smashed	40.5
Collided	39.3
Bumped	38.1
Hit	34.0
Contacted	31.8

▲ Table 3.6 Findings from Loftus and Palmer (1974)

The accuracy of estimates here does not really matter: numerous studies had previously shown that people in general are not very good at judging how fast a vehicle is travelling. The crucial point, however, is that all participants watched the same films, and yet they gave significantly different mean speed estimates.

Loftus and Palmer suggested that this finding could be interpreted in two possible ways.

- **Response bias**: for example, a subject might be uncertain whether to say 30 mph or 40 mph, and a verb of a higher intensity (such as "smashed") biases the response to a higher estimate. Memory of the event in this case does not change.

- **Memory change**: the question causes a change in the subject's memory representation of the accident. For example, the verb "smashed" actually alters the memory so that the subject remembers the accident as having been more severe than it actually was.

To choose between the two competing explanations, Loftus and Palmer conducted **experiment 2**. The rationale behind the second study was that if memory actually undergoes a change, the subject should be more likely to "remember" other details (that did not actually occur, but fit well into the newly constructed memory).

Discussion

Before you read about experiment 2, can you devise your own experiments? How would you design an experiment to choose between the two competing hypotheses?

Split into groups and then discuss each other's ideas.

In **experiment 2**, 150 students participated. They were shown a film depicting a multiple-car accident. Following the film, they were given a questionnaire that included a number of distracter questions and one critical question. This time participants were only split into three groups: "smashed into each other", "hit each other" and a control group (that was not asked the critical question). One week later the subjects were given a questionnaire again (without watching the film). The questionnaire consisted of 10 questions, and the critical yes/no question was "Did you see any broken glass?" There had not been any broken glass in the video. Results showed that the probability of saying "yes" to the question about broken glass was 32% when the verb "smashed" was used, and only 14% when the word "hit" was used (which was almost the same as the 12% in the control group). So, a higher-intensity verb led both to a higher speed estimate and a higher probability of recollecting an event that had never actually occurred.

Based on this result, the authors concluded that the second explanation for experiment 1 should be preferred: an actual change in memory, not just response bias!

In line with the theory of reconstructive memory, Loftus and Palmer suggest that memory for some complex event is based on **two kinds of information**: information obtained during the perception of the event and external post-event information. Over time, information from these two sources is integrated in such a way that we are unable to tell them apart. Applied to the study, this means that subjects who were given the question with the verb "smashed into" used this verb as post-event information suggesting that the accident had been severe. This post-event information was integrated into their memory of the original event, and since broken glass is commensurate with a severe accident, these subjects were more likely to think that they had seen broken glass in the film.

These findings can also be interpreted from the perspective of schema theory: the high-intensity verb "smashed" used in the leading question activates a schema for severe car accidents. Memory is then reconstructed through the lens of this schema.

ATL skills: Communication

The theory of reconstructive memory and research into the reliability of eyewitness testimony has triggered many social and even political campaigns related to legal practices. These revolved around cases where accusations were made based on eyewitness testimony alone, as well as the phenomenon of false memories.

Go online and find out more about the scope of this problem and changes that have been implemented in some countries.

Prepare a short presentation based on the results of your search.

Misleading information, recognition and visual memory

In Loftus and Palmer (1974) post-event information was verbal and the response to the experimental task (answering a question about broken glass) was also verbal. Some critics pointed to this as a limitation of the study, because visual and verbal information might be stored separately, and the leading question might have interfered with the verbal storage but not the visual one. So, it remained to be seen whether or not verbal post-event information could be integrated with visual information obtained originally at the time of the event.

Another argument against applicability of these results to natural conditions is that real-life eyewitness testimony often involves **recognition** (recognizing a stimulus as something you had already seen) rather than **recall** (in the absence of a stimulus). Eyewitness testimony is often required in recognizing individuals suspected of committing a crime. Also in the previous example we saw that leading questions (with verbs of varying emotional intensity) may provide post-event information that contributes to reconstructive memory. In real-life situations, however, post-event information might take more aggressive forms, for example, providing a person with **misleading information**. This might happen in police interrogations or in the presence of other conflicting testimonies.

How reliable is (reconstructive) memory in the event of recognition and in the presence of misleading information? Also, can verbal post-event information interfere with visual information obtained originally?

Loftus, Miller and Burns (1978) carried out an experiment with the aim of investigating how verbal information supplied after an event influences a witness's visual memory for that event. In the recognition procedure, 195 students from the University of Washington were shown a series of 30 colour slides depicting successive stages in a car–pedestrian accident. The slides featured a red Datsun travelling along a side street toward an intersection with either **a stop sign** (for half the subjects) or **a yield sign** (for the other half). These two critical slides are shown below.

▲ Figure 3.16 Critical slides from the recognition task

In the remaining slides, the Datsun turned right and knocked down a pedestrian who was crossing at the crosswalk. After viewing the slides, the subjects answered a series of 20 questions. Question 17 on the list was either "Did another car pass the red Datsun while it was stopped at the stop sign?" for half the subjects or the same question with the words "stop sign" replaced by "yield sign" for the other half. This resulted in a **2-by-2 experimental design**:

	Sign in the question	
Sign in the slides:	**Stop**	**Yield**
Stop	Group 1 (consistent information)	Group 2 (inconsistent information)
Yield	Group 3 (inconsistent information)	Group 4 (consistent information)

▲ Table 3.7 Groups in Loftus, Miller and Burns (1978)

ATL skills: Research

What is a 2-by-2 experimental design? If you cannot recall, review Unit 1 on research methodology.

Note that in order to test the hypothesis in this experiment groups 1 and 4 (combined) were compared to groups 2 and 3 (combined).

As you can see, half the subjects received consistent post-event information while for the other half this information was inconsistent with their actual visual memories. After a filler activity, a **forced-choice recognition test** was administered in which subjects were required to pick the slide they had actually seen from a pair of slides.

Results indicated that subjects who received misleading post-event information were able to correctly recognize the slide actually seen in 41% of the cases, whereas subjects who received consistent post-event information made a correct choice in 75% of the cases.

In a variation of this experiment, both the questionnaire and the recognition task were administered not immediately but a week later. Correct recognition of the slide in the inconsistent-information group in this case was even less likely.

In other words, misleading post-event verbal information was integrated with visual information from before, which resulted in reconstructive memory. The more time passes from the moment of the original event, the stronger effect misleading information has on our visual memory. This finding answered the visual–verbal controversy from before: verbal post-event information actually can integrate with visual information and alter it.

Exercise

Compare the two studies (Loftus and Palmer, 1974; Loftus, Miller and Burns, 1978) in terms of their:

- independent variable (IV)
- dependent variable (DV)
- operationalization of IV and DV
- conclusions.

Make a table and formulate these elements for both studies using full sentences. Be careful with terminology.

Back to alternative explanations: response bias

However, even the results of this study can be doubted. **McCloskey and Zaragoza (1985)** suggested an alternative explanation and claimed that the results might have been obtained due to response bias, not an actual change in memory (back to the conflicting hypothesis in Loftus and Palmer's experiment 1). McCloskey and Zaragoza used the same slide-recognition procedure but introduced one crucial change. In one of their studies, subjects (undergraduate students) were presented with a series of 79 colour slides depicting a maintenance man entering an office, repairing a chair, finding and stealing $20 and a calculator, and leaving. The slide sequence included four critical slides. For each of these slides there were three different versions. For example, in one of the critical slides the tool picked up by the maintenance man was different: a hammer, a wrench or a screwdriver. After this, the subjects were required to read a narrative giving a detailed description of the incident. Some information in the narrative was misleading. For example, half of the subjects who saw a hammer in the slides received a narrative referring to it simply as a tool (control condition), whereas the other half received a narrative mentioning either a wrench or a screwdriver (misled condition).

Up to this point, the procedure is essentially similar to that of Loftus, Miller and Burns. However, the crucial difference was in the way the forced-choice recognition test was designed. In this test, some of the misled participants were given the misleading option along with the original one, whereas others were given the original option and a third option. For example, a group of participants saw a hammer in the slides and then later read about a wrench in the narrative (misleading information). In the forced-choice test, some of these participants would be asked to choose between a hammer and a wrench and others would be asked to choose between a hammer and a screwdriver. Note that for these participants the screwdriver appeared neither in the slides nor in the narrative.

To outline the key comparison that was the focus of the study, let's look at the example in the table below:

Group	Saw in the slides:	Narrative referred to:	Forced choice between	% correct
1 (control)	Hammer	Tool	Hammer and either wrench or screwdriver (randomly)	69
2	Hammer	Wrench	Hammer and wrench	40
3	Hammer	Wrench	Hammer and screwdriver	66

▲ Table 3.8 Findings from McCloskey and Zaragoza (1985)

In the control group, the object from the slides was correctly recognized by 69% of participants. This is higher than you would expect by chance if you assume that subjects do not remember, so they are guessing (50%).

In the second group (which followed the logic of the previous studies) the correct object was chosen by 40% of participants, lower than you would expect by chance. According to the classical interpretation (Loftus, Miller and Burns), this would mean that misleading information integrated with the prior visual information and distorted it (at least in some participants).

In the third group, however, the percentage of correct responses was 66, practically no different from the control condition.

On the basis of these findings McCloskey and Zaragoza claimed that the presentation of misleading information (wrench) did not have an effect on the original memory. They argued that the lower number of correct responses in group 2 might be explained by the fact that some participants forgot the details from the slides, and the narrative simply filled in that gap (but it did not change their memory). When given the test later, they might have shown response bias, that is, they were more likely to report having seen a wrench even though they did not remember seeing it. However, when the misleading information is not an option on the test, participants perform just as well as those in the control group, which seems to indicate that their original memory was not modified or distorted in any way.

Discussion

Memory change or response bias? Organize a debate.

Split into two groups. Each group adopts one of the two positions. Take your time to study the empirical evidence and come up with arguments in support of your position, as well as potential counter-arguments for the opponents' standpoint.

Do not forget to back up your arguments with empirical evidence.

Meta-analysis

We have looked at three eyewitness testimony studies and we have seen how these studies represent a history of **contradictory** research. This is not surprising at all. In fact, finding flaws with previous research is a driving force of scientific discovery, not only in psychology. In crucial topics like this, multiple research studies that seem to contradict each other is a common occurrence. A common way to resolve such contradictions is to conduct a **meta-analysis**.

TOK

1. How is contradictory research resolved in other areas of knowledge?

2. How does this relate to the concept of paradigm shifts?

3. Are meta-analyses possible in other areas of knowledge? What are the limitations of meta-analyses?

Payne, Toglia and Anastasi (1994) conducted a meta-analysis of 44 research studies that used the "modified recognition test", the same procedure that was used in McCloskey and Zaragoza (1985), when the misleading information was not an option on the test. When all the studies were combined, the average recognition level in the misled condition was lower than the average recognition level in the control condition (71.7% versus 75.8%). This is a small difference, but it was **statistically significant**. The authors concluded that the misinformation effect exists even in the "modified recognition test", although this effect is not robust across all the studies. The data from the meta-analysis were also used to see whether there is a relationship between the misinformation effect and the length of the retention interval. Results showed that the longer the retention interval, the more likely the misinformation effect.

ATL skills: Research

"This is a small difference, but it was statistically significant".

What does this mean exactly? Can you name other examples from psychology where results were "weak" but "significant"?

Refer back to Unit 1 on research methodology and make sure that you remember the meaning of the concepts "effect size" and "statistical significance".

Research in naturalistic settings

Another common point of criticism of this whole area of research is its artificiality and the resulting lack of ecological validity. There are a number of research studies that looked at eyewitness testimony in **naturalistic settings**. Having the advantage of higher ecological validity, these studies tend to lack internal validity: when you observe your subjects in real-life settings, you inevitably lose control of a number of potentially confounding variables.

ATL skills: Research

"There's a trade-off between internal and external validity of an experiment".

Explain why. Refer back to Unit 1 on research methodology.

One example of such research is **Yuille and Cutshall (1986).** Participants in this study were eyewitnesses to a real crime in Vancouver. A thief entered a gun, shop, tied up the owner, stole money and guns, and left. The owner managed to free himself, get a revolver and go outside. Gunshots followed, resulting in the thief being killed and the store owner injured. The shooting was witnessed by 21 people from various viewpoints. They were all interviewed by the police. Thirteen of them agreed to participate in scientific research approximately four months after the incident. Interviews were used to collect data, but experimental elements were also used (half the participants were asked leading questions whereas the other half were not). Results of the study showed that the misleading questions had very little effect on recall. Generally, participants correctly recalled a large number of accurate details. The accuracy of eyewitness accounts was carefully established by comparing them to the official police records.

However, the authors admit that this field study might have tapped into a separate and independent memory mechanism: **flashbulb memory**. This occurs when an incident is accompanied by a strong emotional reaction on the part of the viewer. Flashbulb memory will be the focus of discussion later on in this unit (see "Flashbulb memory").

Overall, eyewitness testimony research has sparked a lot of debate. The practice of using eyewitness evidence in courts has been attacked by psychologists and forensic specialists who claimed that memories can be unreliable and manipulated. This has influenced the legal systems and juridical practices in many countries around the world. Research into the reliability of eyewitness testimony sheds light both on a number of flaws in court practices and on reliability of memory as a cognitive process.

Psychology in real life

Paul Ingram was an active Christian, well-known and respected in his community in Washington State. He was a deputy sheriff and Chairman of the local Republican party. It all changed in 1988 when his two daughters accused him of sexual abuse. After months of interrogation Paul confessed and pleaded guilty without trial. He provided many vivid descriptions of his crimes.

When Paul was interrogated by the police, he said at first that he had no memories of the abuse. At the same time, he said that he didn't raise his daughters to lie. Investigators and court-appointed experts told him that it was common for child abusers to be in a state of denial and suppress memories of their crimes. Paul's pastor conducted an exorcism ritual and confirmed that Paul had an evil side. He advised Paul to pray to the Lord for his memories to return. As Paul prayed, he began to see images of him abusing Ericka and Julie when they were little. The police asked for details, and details followed, very vivid, including the set-up of the room and the time on the clock.

Then the girls' claims grew stronger. They said they had been victims of more than 800 satanic rituals that involved more than 30 members of the sheriff's department, and that they were impregnated several times and given abortions by their father. They claimed they had many scars from the violent rituals. They also drew maps to show where on Ingram property the satanic rituals had been taking place. They said they had witnessed more than 30 murders and burial of the bodies.

Despite a very extensive search, none of these claims could be supported by evidence, such as medical examination and even excavation of Ingram properties.

Psychology in real life (continued)

Finally, Dr Richard Ofshe, an expert in "cult behaviour", was hired to investigate the case. He conducted extensive interviews with both Paul and his daughters and became convinced that the daughters were not telling the truth and Paul had been manipulated into developing false memories. To test this, he met with Paul and told him that Ericka and Julie described an episode when Paul forced incest between one of them and one of their brothers while he was watching. In fact, Ofshe had made this episode up. Paul told Ofshe he could not remember the incident. Ofshe asked Paul to return to his cell and pray about it in the same way that he used to recover his other memories. What followed several months later was a detailed written confession to an incident that only existed in Paul's mind. However, this "experiment" was not taken by the court seriously. Paul was sentenced to 20 years in prison. He remained in jail until 2003.

https://tinyurl.com/kamdcjv

Biases in thinking and decision-making

Inquiry questions

- Do people tend to take shortcuts when thinking and making decisions?

- What kind of simplified decisions strategies do they use?

- Do these strategies lead to biased or irrational decisions?

- Are these biases predictable?

What you will learn in this section

- System 1 and system 2 thinking

  ○ Heuristics are cognitive shortcuts or simplified strategies; heuristics lead to cognitive biases which may be identified by comparing the decision to a normative model

  ○ System 1: immediate automatic responses; system 2: rational deliberate thinking (Daniel Kahneman)

- Common causes of intuitive thinking

- The tendency to focus on a limited amount of available information

  ○ This tendency is the result of selective attention and schemas

  ○ Asymmetric dominance (Huber, Payne and Puto, 1982)

    • Explanations of asymmetric dominance: selective attention and a desire to justify one's choice

  ○ Framing effect (Tversky and Kahneman, 1981)

    • Prospect theory: individuals think about utilities as changes from a reference point

    • Violation of the normative expected-utility theory

    • "Avoid risks, but take risks to avoid losses"

- The tendency to seek out information that confirms pre-existing beliefs

  ○ Confirmation bias. Wason's four-card problem (Wason, 1968)

  ○ Congruence bias (Tschirgi, 1980; Wason, 1960): people are trying to obtain positive results rather than useful information

  ○ Illusory correlation and implicit personality theories (Chapman and Chapman, 1969): illusory correlations based on prior beliefs are stable and resistant to change

- The tendency to avoid the mental stress of holding inconsistent cognitions

  ○ The theory of cognitive dissonance

    • Belief disconfirmation paradigm (Festinger, 1956)

    • Induced-compliance paradigm (Freedman and Fraser, 1966)

This section also links to:

- principles of the cognitive approach to behaviour—cognitive processes do not function in isolation; biases in cognitive processes can be systematic and predictable

- thinking and decision-making (normative and descriptive models; limited computational capacity, the influence of emotion on thinking, meta-goals of decision-making)

- stereotypes (sociocultural approach to behaviour).

Psychology in real life

An interesting case of friendly competition between humans and machines is the Supreme Court Forecasting Project 2002: http://wusct.wustl.edu/

It compared the accuracy of two different ways to predict outcomes of the Supreme Court cases in the USA: informed opinions of 83 legal experts versus a computer algorithm. They were predicting in advance the votes of each of the nine individual justices for every case in the Supreme Court in 2002. The same algorithm was used to predict outcomes of all cases, but legal experts were only predicting the cases that were within their area of expertise.

The computer algorithm seemed very reductionist. It only took into account six simple factors such as the issue area

of the case or whether or not the petitioner argued that a law or practice is unconstitutional.

Both predictions were posted publicly on a website prior to the announcement of each of the Court's decisions. There was a lot of suspense.

The experts lost the game: the computer correctly predicted 75% of the Supreme Court decisions, while the experts collectively made only 59.1% of correct predictions. Note that all the decisions were binary (affirm/reverse), so the experts did only 9.1% better than what could be achieved by a toss of a coin.

Why can human experts who have access to detailed information about a case turn out to be such bad predictors? What is it about human decision-making that allows a simple computer algorithm to outperform collective wisdom of people with years of education and experience behind them? If human decisions are biased, can these biases be fixed?

System 1 and system 2 thinking

We have already discussed the important distinction between **normative models** (for example, logic, theory of probability, utility theory) and **descriptive models** of thinking and decision-making. Attractive as they are in leading us to the most rational choice, normative decision theories are unrealistic when it comes to making decisions in real life. As already discussed, they do not account for:

- limited computational capacity

- the influence of emotion on thinking

- other goals that the decision-maker might have, for example, justifying the choice to others, confirming one's own belief or supporting self-esteem.

So, naturally, people use shortcuts and incomplete, simplified strategies which are known as **heuristics**. Heuristics may also be expressed as rules, which makes them an exciting area of research. If we identify and describe a set of common heuristics and prove that people actually use them in real-life decision-making scenarios, we will be able to predict what people are likely to think or do in certain situations. Moreover, we might be able to design computer intelligence that mimics human intelligence.

TOK

1. According to some philosophers, science has four functions: to describe, to explain, to predict and to control.

   To what extent can we describe, explain, predict and control human decisions?

2. Do you believe that artificial intelligence can be developed to the level where it can mimic human decisions, that is, predict what decisions humans will make in a particular situation?

Using heuristics leads to **cognitive biases** (which can be described effectively if you compare heuristics to the normative model for a particular situation). However, heuristics are useful. First, they save energy; we don't have to meticulously analyse all the aspects of the situation every time we are faced with a choice. Second, heuristics are often based on experience, which means that you used them before and it worked reasonably well. Of course the rule saying "if it worked before, it will work now" is not perfect, but it is reasonable enough for a variety of everyday situations.

Daniel Kahneman in 2003 proposed an extension to the information-processing approach by differentiating between **two independent systems**, system 1 and system 2.

This differentiation has become the core of his bestselling book *Thinking, Fast and Slow* (2011), which is a must-read if you have an interest in cognitive biases and behavioural economics. According to the theory, **system 1** thinking is fast, instinctive, emotional, automatic and relatively unconscious, whereas **system 2** thinking is slower, more analytical, logical, rule-based and conscious. System 1 is commonly referred to as "intuition".

Exercise

Go online and search for "behavioural economics". What is it? What are the main landmarks of research in this area?

Present your findings briefly in class.

It has been argued that system 1 developed as an adaptive reasoning mechanism which is based on prior experience (and survival goals) and enables us to make fast and reasonably accurate decisions that have proved to be sufficiently successful in the past. System 2 evolved later with the development of language and abstract reasoning, and this enables us to overcome some of our immediate automatic responses and analyse the situation in greater depth.

Due to this legacy, we use system 1 in the majority of common situations, but we switch to system 2 when the situation is unusual and complex or when we encounter difficulties with our intuitive response. By this reasoning, our thinking works **sequentially**: first, there is a fast and automatic system 1 response, and then this response is (or is not) corrected by the more conscious cognitive efforts of system 2.

System 1 works better in "predictable" environments. Arguably, in today's world with its high degree of complexity, tremendous rates of the production of new knowledge and rapidly changing circumstances, individuals need to be much more flexible and adapt more quickly. So the cognitive demands placed on system 2 processing seem to be increasing. This makes the study of heuristics and biases associated with system 1, as well as the way in which descriptive models of thinking deviate from normative models, even more pertinent.

Common causes of intuitive thinking

There have been numerous attempts to identify the common heuristics and cognitive biases, starting in the 1970s and, as the area gained more and more popularity, continuing in the three decades that followed. This has given rise to attempts at classification and a search for common causes of intuitive (automatic) thinking.

There is no universally accepted classification of heuristics or the common causes underlying them. However, we will focus on several major factors as examples to take a peek into the sheer variety:

- the tendency to focus on a limited amount of available information (asymmetric dominance, framing effect)
- the tendency to seek out information that confirms pre-existing beliefs (confirmation bias, congruence bias, illusory correlations and implicit personality theories)
- the tendency to avoid the mental stress of holding inconsistent cognitions (cognitive dissonance).

The tendency to focus on a limited amount of available information

ATL skills: Self-management

Before you read on, remember four meta-goals in the adaptive decision-maker framework discussed earlier in this chapter. If you find it difficult, go back and review the section "Thinking and decision-making".

As you continue reading, think about which of the four meta-goals can explain the tendency to focus on a limited amount of available information. You will find an answer later in the text.

Remember what you know about sensory memory and how it gets transferred into short-term memory (STM). Sensory memory has a high capacity, but a very limited duration. In order for information to reach STM, this information has to be attended to. However, we cannot pay attention to many chunks of information at the same time. From the sea of stimuli around us we have to single out one stimulus that we focus on and process further. This is known as **selective attention**.

Remember what you know about schemas (top-down processing), and you will realize that selective attention is mediated by our existing preconceptions and expectations—while travelling from sensory memory to STM, information passes through a "lens" of schemas. This may distort information or, at the very least, filter out certain aspects or details, however important they may be from the point of view of a normative model.

Let's look at several examples of cognitive biases that are rooted in this inherent tendency to focus on a limited amount of available information: asymmetric dominance and framing effect.

Asymmetric dominance

Huber, Payne and Puto (1982) studied decisions involving an **asymmetrically dominated decoy**. An example will make it clear what this is.

Suppose you are choosing between two alternatives, A and B, and you are basing your decision on two dimensions. For example, you are choosing between two holiday destinations (A = Swiss Alps and B = Goa), and there are two parameters that are important to you, affordability (you prefer cheaper) and ski opportunities (you like skiing more than swimming in the sea). In Graph A on the right, neither the target nor the competitor dominate the other, because one is better on one dimension and the other is better on the other dimension. You would prefer Goa because it is cheaper, but at the same time you would prefer the Swiss Alps because there is a skiing opportunity. Now what if we introduce the third option, a decoy? Imagine your third choice is C = Seychelles (see Graph B). For the sake of this example, let's say that having a holiday in the Seychelles is slightly more affordable than in the Swiss Alps, at the same time skiing is not a possibility, just as in Goa. This alternative (the Seychelles) is said to be an asymmetrically dominated decoy, because it is dominated by Goa (the same skiing opportunities, however more affordable), but not dominated by Swiss Alps (better skiing opportunities, but less affordable).

Note how the decoy is not a desirable choice. Of the three options, why would you choose it? If you attach more importance to skiing opportunities, you would choose the Alps, if you attach more importance to affordability, you would go for Goa. So why is it important?

It turns out that adding an asymmetrically dominated decoy in the choice set increases the probability of choosing the option that dominates the decoy. In our example, it means that people

who are given options A, B and C would be more likely to choose B, compared with people who are given only two options, A and B. Note that nobody chooses C, but the mere presence of C in the choice set increases the probability of the choice of B.

Similarly, if we wanted more people to choose the Swiss Alps, we might have manipulated the choice set differently. In the choice set A, B, D (see Graph C below) D is the northern part of the Ural Mountains in Central Russia. For the sake of this example, let's say this destination is as expensive as the Swiss Alps (given the remoteness of the place), and there are plenty of skiing opportunities, but the skiing facilities are not as modern as in the Alps. In this new choice set, D is the asymmetrically dominated decoy (which people will not choose). It is dominated by the Swiss Alps (better facilities, the same in terms of affordability) but it is not dominated by Goa (better affordability, but less skiing opportunities). So, the theory predicts that in this choice set people would be more likely to prefer the Alps.

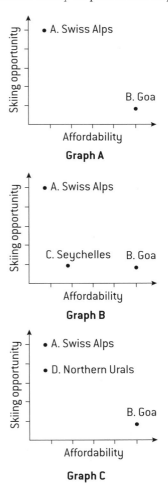

Graph A

Graph B

Graph C

▲ Figure 3.17 Asymmetrically dominated decoys

Huber, Payne and Puto confirmed this prediction in a sample of 153 students who were required to make choices in six categories: cars, restaurants, beers, lotteries, films and television sets. Just as in our examples, the decision environments included two or three alternatives, with each alternative defined on two attributes. Overall, the predicted choice reversals were not large (3–9% of participants **switched their choice** in the predicted direction when the decoy was added to the choice set), but statistically significant.

Note that asymmetric dominance violates the normative model of rational choice, as there is no logical reason why the decoy can change your preferences. How can this result be explained?

- First, there's an explanation in terms of selective attention. We **selectively attend to one of the attributes** (for example, affordability) and ignore the other. We seem to be incapable of processing both the attributes simultaneously and look for an "excuse" to simplify the problem and process only one.

- Second, one might explain the observed data by the desire of the decision-maker to justify his or her choice. Arguably, the decoy gives you one more reason to say, "I have chosen X, because …".

At this point you might remember our discussion of the adaptive decision-maker framework in which maximizing the ease of justification of a decision is one of the four meta-goals of decision-making.

A difference of 3–9% may become hugely important in large corporations looking for a competitive edge. Huber, Payne and Puto give the following example of a practical application of asymmetric dominance effect. A store owner has two camel hair jackets priced at $100 and $150 and finds that the more expensive jacket is not selling. A new camel hair jacket is added and displayed for $250; the new jacket does not sell, but sales of the $150 jacket increase. Think about more practical implications, for example, the choice of burgers at your local McDonalds. Potentially using the asymmetric dominance effect in marketing can bring millions in profit, and it does.

ATL skills: Social

Get into small groups and think of other practical applications of this cognitive bias. Use your knowledge from other subjects, such as history or business management.

Framing effect

The most influential normative model of choice under uncertainty is **expected utility theory**. In this theory you multiply the utility of an outcome by the probability of that outcome, and choose the outcome that yields the highest number. For example, suppose you were choosing between two gambles: if you choose option A, you get $10 for certain; if you choose option B, you get $200 with 6% probability. According to the normative theory, it is more rational to take a risk: the expected utility of option A is 10 * 1 = $10, whereas the expected utility of option B is 200 * 0.06 = $12.

However, numerous studies have demonstrated that in their real-life choices people do not always adhere to the predictions of the normative model. They seem to be too eager to take risk in some situations and too avoidant of risks in others, depending on seemingly irrelevant factors.

In 1979 Daniel Kahneman and Amos Tversky proposed a descriptive theory of decision-making under risk that is known as **prospect theory**. The idea behind the theory was to take the normative expected utility model and to modify it as little as possible to explain the observed deviations from the normative model. They were successful, and prospect theory quickly gained popularity as a descriptive model of choice.

Prospect theory claims that **individuals think about utilities as changes from a reference point** (and the reference point may be easily changed by the way the problem is formulated).

In one of their famous experiments, **Tversky and Kahneman (1981)** gave their subjects the following problem.

Imagine that the USA is preparing for an outbreak of an unusual Asian disease, which is expected to kill 600 people. Two alternative programs to combat the disease have been proposed. Assume that the exact scientific estimate of the consequences of the program are as follows:

(and the options were different for two independent groups of subjects)

Group 1	Group 2:
Program A: 200 people will be saved.	**Program A:** 400 people will die.
Program B: there is 1/3 probability that 600 people will be saved, and 2/3 probability that no people will be saved.	**Program B:** there is 1/3 probability that nobody will die, and 2/3 probability that 600 people will die.

▲ Table 3.9 Response options for the two groups in Tversky and Kahneman (1981)

Note that both choice sets are identical. The only difference is in how the situation is described, either in terms of **potential gains** ("will be saved") or in terms of **potential losses** ("will die"). Having said that, it is interesting that participants' choices in these two groups were reversed. Here is the percentage of individuals who chose each of the two programs in the two groups:

	Group 1	Group 2
Program A	72%	22%
Program B	28%	78%

▲ Table 3.10 Findings from Tversky and Kahneman (1981)

Since nothing changed in the problem from the rational point of view, this reversal of choices cannot be explained by the normative (expected utility) model. The expected utilities of the two programs are the same. So how can we explain the deviation from the normative model?

Presumably most individuals in group 1 choose program A because they are trying to avoid the risk of not saving anyone at all (2/3 probability). Whereas in group 2 individuals seemed to be more willing to take the risk: 400 deaths seems almost as bad as 600 deaths, so why not take a chance?

Tversky and Kahneman explain this finding in terms of a **shift in the reference point**. In the first version the reference point is the future state (600 people dead), so the options are perceived as potential **gains** (how many people can I save?). In the second version the reference is shifted to the present state (no one has died yet), so the options are perceived as potential **losses** (how many people can we lose?).

So, depending on whether outcomes are described ("framed") as gains or losses, subjects give different judgments: they are more willing to take risks to avoid losses and have a tendency to avoid risk

associated with gains. In other words, "Avoid risks, but take risks to avoid losses" (Baron, 2008, p 270). This is known as **the framing effect**.

The prospect theory proposes a mathematical way to describe such deviations from the normative model. Schematically it is shown in Figure 3.18. In terms of the normative model, it does not matter where the reference point is: the value function should be a straight line. However, people assign less (positive) value to gains and more (negative) value to losses. We selectively redistribute our attention to the potential outcomes based on how the problem is framed.

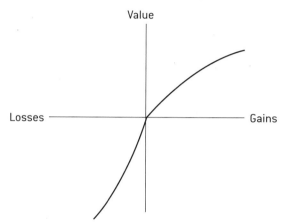

▲ Figure 3.18 Value function in prospect theory

ATL skills: Communication

How can using the framing effect be translated into monetary gains?

Think about how insurance agents frame their offers ("If you buy this insurance package you may avoid losing …").

Can you identify other examples (commercials, business offers, job vacancies)? Think of some and share with the group.

The tendency to seek out information that confirms pre-existing beliefs
Confirmation bias

TOK

What do you know about confirmation bias from TOK classes? How does it create an obstacle in the production of knowledge?

Another common source of heuristics is the tendency to seek out information that confirms pre-existing beliefs. You might have discussed the role of confirmation bias in your theory of knowledge classes. Let's look at the psychological research behind this phenomenon.

A good illustration of confirmation bias as a logical heuristic (that is, a heuristic that violates logic as the normative model) is **Wason's four-card problem (1968)**.

Suppose you have the following four cards and you know that each card has a letter on one side and a number on the other side. You are also given the following rule: "If a card has a vowel on one side, then it has an even number on the other side". Your task is to "name those cards, and only those cards, that need to be turned over in order to determine whether the rule is true or false".

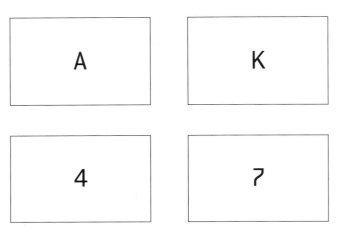

▲ Figure 3.19 Wason's four-card problem

Which cards will you turn over? And why?

The most popular answers in Wason's study were either "A only" or "A and 4". To see what the correct answer is, follow this logic.

- If you turn over the first card and there is an even number on the other side, it will support the rule. If there's an odd number on the other side, it will refute the rule.

- If you turn over the second card and there is an even number on the other side, it tells you nothing about the rule. Neither does an odd number. Since the letter is a consonant, any result will neither support nor refute the rule that you are testing.

- If you turn over the third card and there is a vowel on the other side, it will support the rule.

However, if there is a consonant, it will not tell you anything about the rule (the rule does not say that consonants must be coupled with odd numbers). So, turning over the third card can potentially support your rule, but cannot refute it.

- This is not the case with the fourth card. If the letter on the other side is a consonant, it tells you nothing about the rule. If it is a vowel, though, that would refute the rule.

So the two options that can potentially refute the rule are A and 7. Only in this combination of trials are we actually testing ("falsifying") the hypothesis. It goes in line with the logic of hypothesis testing widely accepted in science. Why do individuals normally give a different pattern of responses? Presumably people are much more attentive to information that can potentially support their expectations and at the same time they tend to ignore information that can potentially contradict their expectations. This preference for potentially supporting evidence is known as confirmation bias.

TOK

What do you know about the falsification principle (Popper, 1959)? What does it mean for a theory to be "falsifiable"? What is the role of falsification in sciences compared to other areas of knowledge?

Congruence bias

Some authors argue that the term "confirmation bias" does not accurately describe these decision-making patterns and offer the term "congruence bias" instead, stressing that the cause of the heuristic is the subject's failure to come up with alternative hypotheses. In other words, the essential thinking behind the congruence heuristic is as follows: "To test a hypothesis, think of a result that would be found if the hypothesis were true and then look for that result (and do not worry about other hypotheses that might yield the same result" (Baron, 2008, p 173).

Congruence bias makes subjects act as if they were trying to obtain positive results (supporting evidence) rather than useful information. This is seen in **Tschirgi (1980)** who gave subjects problems like the following.

John decided to make a cake. When he ran out of some ingredients, this is what he did.

- He used margarine instead of butter for the shortening.

- He used honey instead of sugar for the sweetening.

- He used brown wholewheat flour instead of regular white flour.

The cake turned out great; it was so moist. John thought the reason the cake was so great was the honey. He thought that the type of shortening (butter or margarine) or the type of flour really didn't matter. What should he do to prove his point when he makes the next cake?

Subjects were required to choose from the following options.

A. Use sugar instead of honey

B. Keep the honey, but change everything else

C. Change everythin.

Most subjects chose to keep the honey, but change everything else (option B). Is this the "correct" response? Let's think logically. If John's hypothesis is true, option A will ruin the cake, but support the hypothesis (that is, provide valuable information). Option B in this case will not ruin the cake, but will provide equally valuable information. Option C is a distractor. So it seems like both option A and B potentially are valuable in terms of hypothesis-testing. Interestingly, subjects demonstrated a preference for option B.

In another condition in the study, the description and the options were the same, but subjects were told that: "The cake turned out just terrible. It was so runny". Again, John thought that the reason the cake was so terrible was the honey.

In this condition subjects demonstrated a preference for option A, use sugar instead of honey.

Again, both options A and B are potentially informative in terms of hypothesis-testing, but this time option B ruins the cake, whereas option A does not.

Researchers concluded that subjects in the experiment were pursuing the goal of obtaining a result that would be **"positive" rather than "informative"**.

There seems to be nothing wrong with trying to test a hypothesis and cook a great cake at the same time. We will compare this to another study done by **Wason (1960)** but first do the exercise to try the study for yourself.

Exercise

Ask your friend to read about Wason's experiment below and then construct his or her own experiment by analogy.

Let your friend lead your participation. It will only take five minutes.

Were you able to identify the correct rule?

In this study subjects were given a sequence of numbers (for example, 2, 4, 6) and told that the sequence followed a rule. The task was to discover the rule. To do that, participants could generate additional three-number sequences, and the experimenter told them whether these new sequences followed the rule or not. Usually the subjects would assume that the rule was "numbers ascending by 2", which was reflected in the testing sequences that they produced: 1, 3, 5; 8, 10, 12; 50, 52, 54, and so on. Every time they got positive feedback from the researcher ("yes, this sequence follows the same rule"). The crucial observation here was that subjects rarely questioned their favoured hypothesis and after several trials they usually claimed to have discovered the rule.

ATL skills: Thinking

In what ways does Wason's (1960) rule discovery task resemble Tschirgi's (1980) cake task? Is this essentially the same task?

However, other hypotheses can fit the sequence 2, 4, 6 equally well. In fact, the correct rule in this study was "any ascending numbers". In order to find it out, a typical participant of this study, just like a typical real-world scientist, had to generate alternative hypotheses (for example, 1, 2, 3 or 6, 4, 2), which rarely happened, due to congruence bias. Subjects are looking for positive results that favour their initial expectation rather than informative results. This may be really detrimental when it comes to real science! Unlike making a cake, science requires you to seek out informative results, not positive ones.

Illusory correlations and implicit personality theories

The tendency to seek out information that confirms pre-existing beliefs is also seen in illusory correlations and implicit personality theories. An illusory correlation is a belief that two phenomena are connected when in fact they are not. You will come across illusory correlations in the sociocultural approach to behaviour when you study stereotypes, because illusory correlations are often believed to be the mechanism of stereotype formation.

Implicit personality theories are sets of beliefs that you have about the behaviour of others; you predict their behaviour on the basis of those beliefs. For example, you may implicitly believe that all muscular, bald men are dangerous (based on the history of your interactions with them in the past or maybe a number of movies that you have watched), and so you would avoid bald, well-built males in a variety of situations due to your (stereotyped) implicit personality theory.

Discussion

Find out more about the history of using the Rorschach ink-blot test. Present your findings in class.

What do you think about projective tests in general?

What is the role of confirming pre-existing beliefs in the formation of illusory correlations and implicit personality theories? **Chapman and Chapman (1969)** demonstrated this in a sample of practising psychodiagnosticians (N = 32) who used the Rorschach ink-blot test in their practice. They concentrated specifically on diagnosing male homosexuality. Prior research had revealed some Rorschach signs that are statistically associated with male homosexuality and some that are not. Two signs that had

been shown to be clinically valid signs of male homosexuality are:

- response on Card IV of "human or animal – contorted, monstrous, or threatening"; examples would be "a horrid beast" or "a giant with shrunken arms"

- response on Card V of an "animalized human or humanized animal"; examples would be "pigeon wearing mittens" or "a woman, dressed as a bat".

However, when asked to recollect their clinical experience and name the Rorschach signs that they had found to be most diagnostic of homosexuality, clinicians failed to mention these two signs and named other signs instead, for example, feminine clothing ("a woman's bra" in Card III), humans with confused or uncertain sex, male or female genitalia.

▲ Figure 3.20 Rorschach Card IV

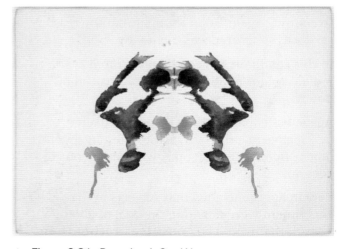

▲ Figure 3.21 Rorschach Card V

▲ Figure 3.22 Rorschach Card III

All these signs had a strong verbal associative connection to homosexuality. When asked to rate the associative similarity of a sign with homosexuality, clinicians rated the similarity as high for the popular (and invalid) signs and low for the valid (and unpopular) ones. For example, contrary to statistical evidence, they said that seeing "a woman's bra" in Card III was a sign of homosexuality, and at the same time they failed to recognize seeing "a horrid beast" in Card V as one.

Chapman and Chapman (1969) also studied whether naive observers would make the same errors as the clinicians did. Participants were students in an introductory psychology course. The fabricated clinical materials consisted of 30 Rorschach cards, on each of which there was one response about the ink blot and two statements about the patient who (allegedly) gave this response. For example, the typical card would show an ink blot and three statements:

- Response: "A pigeon wearing mittens"

- Statement: A man who said he has sexual feelings towards other men

- Statement: A man who said he feels sad and depressed much of the time.

The response was taken either from a valid diagnostic category (for example, "A giant with shrunken arms" for Card IV) or an invalid one (for example, "a woman's bra" for Card III). The two statements were taken from a pool of four symptoms—homosexuality (in 1969 when the study was conducted homosexuality was still considered to be a mental disorder), depression, paranoia, inferiority complex. The combinations of responses and statements were manipulated to be completely random, that is, there was no statistical relation between homosexuality and the frequency of any of the responses. However, when asked to formulate a rule after being exposed to all 30 cards (what kind of responses are most common for homosexuals?) participants readily named the invalid ones (for example, seeing "a woman's bra" in Card III). So, naive participants arrived at the same results, and used the same justifications, as experienced clinicians, and yet in neither of the groups were the results valid! Participants seemed to have a set of prior beliefs (probably based on common sense) and they were selectively interpreting available data to support, but not contradict, those beliefs.

Even more strikingly, when in follow-up experiments Chapman and Chapman manipulated the valid signs to **actually correlate** with homosexuality (in most of the cases mentioning homosexuality on the card was coupled with a valid sign such as seeing a "horrid beast" in Card IV), this had practically **no effect** on the subjects' conclusions. They still failed to see the connection between homosexuality and the valid signs, and continued to see a connection with the invalid ones (such as seeing a "woman's bra" in Card III). Illusory correlations based on prior beliefs turn out to be quite stable and resistant to change even in the presence of counterevidence.

ATL skills: Communication

Do you think illusory correlations and implicit personality theories can affect psychological and medical practices on a wider scale? Would you go as far as saying that they are inevitable?

The tendency to avoid the mental stress of holding inconsistent cognitions

Another source of cognitive biases and system I thinking is the tendency to avoid the mental stress of holding inconsistent cognitions.

This was extensively demonstrated by **Leon Festinger** in his **theory of cognitive dissonance** as well as in supporting research. Cognitive dissonance is the mental stress caused by the inconsistency between:

- two (or more) contradictory beliefs or ideas
- one's action and one's belief
- new information and existing beliefs.

According to the theory, an individual who experiences such inconsistency ("dissonance") feels stressed and uncomfortable, and is driven by a desire to **reduce dissonance**. In the action versus belief example, there are only two logical ways to reduce dissonance: change your behaviour or change your belief. It would be logical to assume, from the common sense perspective, that "beliefs drive behaviour". However, many research studies have actually shown that "behaviour drives beliefs" to a much larger extent.

One way to empirically test the predictions of the theory of cognitive dissonance is through observation of groups of people who strongly believe in something but new evidence runs contrary to their beliefs. This research framework is known as the "**belief disconfirmation paradigm**". A well-known example, and the birth of the theory of cognitive dissonance, is Leon Festinger's book *When Prophecy Fails* (1956). In this he describes a small UFO cult in Chicago called the Seekers, who believed in an imminent apocalypse and took strong actions to support their belief. The leader of the cult, a self-proclaimed prophet, "received messages" that the world would end at midnight on 21 December 1954. They also believed that they were selected to be the survivors and start a new civilization, and for this, a spacecraft was coming to pick them up and they had to prepare for departure. As part of the preparation they had given up their jobs, spouses and possessions, which shows how committed they were to the belief. Festinger infiltrated the group to conduct participant observations and collected valuable information on what happens if such strong beliefs are disconfirmed by evidence.

After the prophecy proved to be false (the space shuttle did not pick them up at midnight) the group spent several hours in a state of tension which is very well conveyed in Festinger's detailed observation report. At 4.45am the leader went to a separate room and received another

"message" which said that the apocalypse had been called off because the members of the religious group saved the Earth by their pure thoughts and efforts: "The little group, sitting all night long, had spread so much light that God had saved the world from destruction" (Festinger, Riecken and Schachter, 1956, p 169, *When Prophecy Fails: A Social and Psychological Study of a Modern Group that Predicted the Destruction of the World*). Interestingly, although the group had been notoriously closed to the world outside and had never given interviews, on the morning of the following day they began a campaign to spread the message as far as possible, calling newspapers and setting up interviews.

This shows how, when new information disconfirms existing beliefs, **the belief itself may be twisted**, and social support may be sought to further support this new belief; if many people start sharing the belief, then it becomes more justified. This also shows how people change their beliefs when it is impossible to change (take back) their behaviour.

Another research framework that is often used to test the theory of cognitive dissonance is known as the **induced-compliance paradigm**. An example is the study of **Freedman and Fraser (1966)** in which participants from the experimental group were asked to sign a petition on the issue of safe driving (participants from the control group were not asked to do anything). Two weeks later, all participants were asked to put a large sign on their front lawn saying "Drive Carefully" (a larger, more substantial request). Results showed that fewer than 20% of the control group agreed to put the large sign on their lawn, while over 55% of subjects in the experimental group agreed to this larger request.

This shows how once a behaviour is demonstrated ("I signed a petition for safe driving"), a behaviour–belief discrepancy may occur ("If I don't want to put this large sign on my lawn, why did I sign the petition two weeks ago?"). To avoid psychological discomfort caused by this dissonance, subjects would try to adjust their initial beliefs ("Maybe I feel strongly about safe driving, after all, and I support their cause").

Many effective persuasion techniques are based on the principles of cognitive dissonance.

Exercise

Explore some other well-known heuristics and biases, as well as a range of their potential practical applications:

Dan Ariely's book *Predictably Irrational*: https://tinyurl.com/k683ou4

Daniel Kahneman's book *Thinking, Fast and Slow*: https://tinyurl.com/hx6w569

Laurie Santos's TED Talk "A monkey economy as irrational as ours" (in which she compares economic decisions in humans and monkeys and finds some striking similarities): https://www.ted.com/talks/laurie_santos

Make a list of the most commonly mentioned cognitive biases and make it a rule for the next week to observe and take a note of real-life examples of heuristics and cognitive biases in people's decisions.

Emotion and cognition

Inquiry questions

- Do emotions depend primarily on physiological or cognitive factors?

- Does flashbulb memory exist as a special type of memory?

- Are flashbulb memories both vivid and accurate?

- Can retelling the event to other people change the original memory of the event?

What you will learn in this section

- Theories of emotion: a gradual shift of emphasis from bodily responses to cognitive factors

    - Darwin (1872): Emotions are vestigial patterns of action

    - James–Lange (1884): theory of emotion

    - Cannon–Bard (1927): theory of emotion

    - Schachter and Singer (1962): two-factor theory of emotion

    - Lazarus (1982): initial cognitive appraisal

    - LeDoux (1996): two physiological pathways

- The influence of emotion on cognition: linking back to what you already know (biases in thinking and decision-making, eyewitness testimony)

- The theory of flashbulb memory

- Brown and Kulik (1977): study of factors leading to flashbulb memories, the mechanism of formation and the mechanism of rehearsal

- Three contradictory questions:

    - What is the neural basis of flashbulb memory?

    - Is vividness of flashbulb memories determined by the event itself or by subsequent rehearsal?

    - How accurate are flashbulb memories?

- What is the neural basis of flashbulb memory?

    - Sharot et al (2007): a study of personal recollections of the 9/11 terrorist attacks in New York City

    - Sharot et al (2004): a study of remembering emotional stimuli

    - Flashbulb memory does have a neural basis (selective activation of the amygdala), but could be a special case of a deeper mechanism—processing emotionally laden stimuli

- Is vividness of flashbulb memories the result of photographic encoding or subsequent rehearsal?

    - Neisser et al (1996): a study on flashbulb memories of the 1989 Loma Prieta earthquake

    - Bohannon (1988): a study of flashbulb memories for the Challenger Space Shuttle disaster

- How accurate are flashbulb memories?

    - Neisser and Harsch (1992): Challenger Space Shuttle study, flashbulb memories are only special in their perceived accuracy

    - Talarico and Rubin (2003): 9/11 attack study

This section also links to:

- eyewitness testimony: flashbulb memory as an explanation of the discrepancy between laboratory experiments and field studies

- localization of function (biological approach to behaviour)

- schema theory

- principles of the cognitive approach—cognitive processes do not function in isolation

- research methodology.

What is emotion? Is it a cognitive process? Is it a special mental representation that is independent of cognition? Are emotional information and semantic information processed in different brain areas, or is there mutual influence or overlap? The answer to these questions is not easy. As a matter of fact, there are several theoretical perspectives on the nature of emotion.

Etymologically the word "emotion" has the same root as the word "motivation". They both come from the Latin *movere* meaning "to move". The prefix "e" in "emotion" is an assimilated form of "ex" meaning "out". Motivation is something that "inwardly moves a person" whereas emotion is something that "moves a person in response to an external stimulus". This has two implications, both of which were reflected in later theories of emotion.

- Emotional response is **caused by a stimulus**.

- Emotional response **results in behaviour**.

Apparently the stimulus has personal significance on our well-being, so the brain reacts to the stimulus with a special mechanism that encourages certain action.

Theories of emotion

In 1872 **Charles Darwin** published the book *The Expression of the Emotions in Man and Animals* in which he claimed that emotions have an evolutionary meaning (either communication or survival) and can actually be nothing else but vestigial **patterns of action**. This goes well with the etymology of the word emotion (from "move"). For example, one of the current evolutionary explanations of the sweaty palms that we get when we experience a sudden fear is that sweat on the palms makes them softer and therefore enhances the grip on the bark when climbing up a tree. We might have inherited sweaty palms from our monkey ancestors who rushed to trees and climbed up in a moment of danger. Arguably, if emotions have an evolutionary basis and developed as certain adaptive actions, emotions

should be expressed **similarly across cultures**. This idea has found support in a number of studies and observations. For example, Darwin himself gives the example of blushing: blushing is characteristic of people of all cultures and all ages. Interestingly, blushing covers a larger area of the body in populations who habitually expose more skin (such as primitive tribes) but is mainly confined to the face and the neck in modern societies.

Discussion

1. What are the common limitations of evolutionary explanations of behaviour?

2. What other evolutionary explanations of behaviour have you studied so far? Do the same limitations apply to them?

3. What is an "ad hoc explanation" and what is its role in various areas of knowledge?

Not surprisingly, theories of emotion that followed were mainly concerned with bodily responses to external stimuli. Step by step, later theories shifted the focus to the role of **cognitive factors** in processing emotional information.

The **James–Lange theory of emotion** (proposed simultaneously by William James and Carl Lange in 1884) claimed that external stimuli cause a physiological change and the interpretation of this change is emotion. In other words, first you see a snake, then it produces certain physiological changes in your body (release of adrenaline, increased heart rate and so on) and then your mind interprets these changes as an emotion. You are afraid because your heart is beating fast; you feel happy because you smile; you feel sad because you cry. This theory seems somewhat counter-intuitive, if not primitive, but modern neuroscientific evidence actually supports some of its claims, especially the fact that feedback from bodily changes may play its role in modification of emotional responses.

The **Cannon–Bard theory of emotion (1927)** was based on a number of animal studies that showed that sensory events could not directly cause a physiological change without simultaneously triggering cognitive processing. It was proposed that emotional stimuli cause two parallel processes at the same time: a physiological response and a conscious experience of emotion. In other words, your conscious experience of emotion is not a result of the bodily change—it is a process that **accompanies** it.

Schachter and Singer (1962) claimed that emotions were a result of **two-stage processing**: first physiological response, then cognitive interpretation. For example, you see a potentially threatening stimulus (a snake) and it produces a physiological response (pounding heart). After this your brain quickly scans the environment looking for the possible explanation of this heart pounding. Noticing the snake, the brain cognitively interprets the heart pounding as fear and that is when fear is experienced as a conscious emotion. An advantage of this theory is that it provides an explanation for the fact that we may feel different emotions in the same physiological circumstances, such as tears of sadness and tears of joy.

Further elaboration of the role of cognitive interpretation in emotion was done in the work of **Richard Lazarus (1982)**. In his **theory of appraisal**, Lazarus shifted cognitive interpretation to the first stage of emotional processing, claiming that initial cognitive appraisal precedes physiological changes. The theory asserts that the quality and intensity of emotions are controlled though this process of the initial cognitive appraisal.

ATL skills: Thinking

Based on your everyday experience, which seems more plausible to you?

- First your body reacts, then your mind experiences this reaction as an emotion (James–Lange).

- Your body and your mind react at the same time, so emotion is caused directly by the stimulus (Cannon–Bard).

- First your body reacts, then your mind interprets this reaction based on environmental clues, then you feel an emotion (Schachter and Singer).

- First your mind assesses the situation, then your body reacts, then your mind interferes again (Lazarus).

Much light on the nature of emotions was shed by research into their **biological underpinnings**. **Joseph LeDoux (1996)** studied fear conditioning in rodents and looked at the sequence of stages the brain goes through when processing fear stimuli. The amygdala performs a key function in fear processing. LeDoux describes two pathways, or sensory roads, to the amygdala.

- **The fast pathway** leads from perceiving the stimulus (sensory input) to thalamus and then amygdala, producing an emotional response.

- **The slow pathway** leads from the stimulus to thalamus, then primary sensory cortex, association cortex, hippocampus, amygdala, and the response. In other words, in the slow pathway information travels additionally via the neocortex and hippocampus.

The idea of this theory is that our brain simultaneously produces a quick, direct emotional reaction and triggers a more sophisticated process of cognitive interpretation. Arguably, this allows us to be flexible in our reactions. On the one hand, the quick pathway prepares us for possible danger. On the other hand, the long pathway may process information more deeply and modify the initial emotional response. For example, if you walk along the street and suddenly see an aggressive dog barking at you, your heart rate will increase, your adrenal glands will release adrenaline into the blood stream, and your body will quickly enter a state of alertness. However, when you notice a second later that the dog is behind a tall fence, you will relax and the initial bodily changes will gradually fade away.

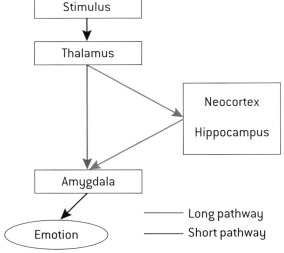

▲ Figure 3.23 Pathways of emotion (LeDoux, 1996)

The influence of emotion on cognition

We have seen how interrelated emotion and cognition are. Cognitive appraisal can be a mediator between physiological arousal and the subsequent emotional response (Schachter and Singer, 1962). Some initial cognitive appraisal can even precede the physiological response (Lazarus, 1982). Even biologically the two pathways of emotional response (LeDoux, 1996) have considerable intersections; they converge and diverge again. Apparently, the interaction between cognition and emotion in behaviour is **bidirectional**.

In the examples above we have seen how cognition influences (mediates) emotion. Let us now focus on **how emotion influences cognition**.

Think back to our discussion of biases in thinking and decision-making. Many of these biases are caused by emotional variables. For example:

- the meta-goal of minimizing the experience of negative emotion in the adaptive decision-maker framework

- the tendency to avoid potential losses in the framing effect

- cognitive dissonance—avoiding an unpleasant feeling of dissonance by introducing bias in one's beliefs.

However, in this section we will look at a more basic cognitive process, that of **memory**. Do emotions influence memory processes? If they do, what exactly is the extent and the mechanism of such influence? This will be discussed through the example of a special memory mechanism known as **flashbulb memory**. We have already mentioned flashbulb memory as an alternative explanation that can explain the discrepancy between laboratory experiments (for example, Loftus and Palmer, 1974) and field studies (for example, Yuille and Cutshall, 1986) of eyewitness testimony. One important difference between these two types of studies that can potentially explain the different results is that in field studies emotions are "real" whereas in laboratory experiments in which participants watch car accidents on pre-recorded videos emotional reactions are not triggered.

The theory of flashbulb memory

The theory of flashbulb memory was proposed by **Roger Brown and James Kulik** in 1977. According to them, flashbulb memories are vivid memories of the circumstances in which one first learned of a surprising and emotionally arousing event. They are like a "snapshot" of a significant event. An example that these authors used as a starting point in their investigation was the assassination of John F Kennedy in 1963. They observed that people generally had very vivid memories about the circumstances of first receiving the news about the assassination; they seemed to clearly remember where they were when they heard the news, what they were doing, who told them, what was the immediate aftermath, the weather, the smells in the air.

To further research the determinants of this phenomenon they gave 40 Caucasian and 40 African Americans ranging from 20 to 60 years old a questionnaire asking them about other assassinations as well as other socially and personally significant events. Answers were submitted in the form of free recall of unlimited length. It was found that a lot of other events also created vivid flashbulb memories. However, there were two variables that had to attain sufficiently high levels in order for flashbulb memory to occur: **surprise** and a high level of **personal consequentiality** (which causes emotional arousal). If these variables reach a sufficient level, this triggers a maintenance mechanism: **overt and covert rehearsal** which reinforces the degree of elaboration of the event in memory.

So the theory posits two separate, but related mechanisms of flashbulb memories: formation and maintenance.

The mechanism of formation is a photographic representation of events that are surprising and personally consequential and therefore emotionally arousing. Brown and Kulik used evolutionary arguments to explain the existence of such a mechanism: personally consequential events have high survival value so humans could have developed a special memory process to deal with them.

The mechanism of maintenance includes overt rehearsal (conversations with other people in which the event is reconstructed) and covert rehearsal (replaying the event in one's memory). Naturally, rehearsal consolidates memory traces and the memory is experienced as very vivid even years after the event.

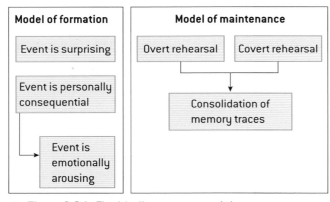

▲ Figure 3.24 Flashbulb memory model

The theory raised several contradictory questions that sparked a lot of additional research in this area.

- If flashbulb memory is a special type of memory, there has to exist a **unique neural mechanism**. So what is the physiological basis of flashbulb memory?

- The characteristic that distinguishes flashbulb memories from other memories is their **vividness**. According to the theory, vividness of such memories is determined by properties of the event (the level of surprise and personal consequentiality). But could it be due to

subsequent rehearsal rather than the event itself? In other words, people keep recreating emotional and personally significant events in their memory, and this might explain vividness without the necessity to postulate a "separate memory mechanism".

- Flashbulb memories are vivid and detailed. How **accurate** are they, though? We know from research on reconstructive memory that post-event information can alter an individual's memories. Discussing the event with other people (overt rehearsal), we may be exposed to leading questions or misleading information. Does it affect flashbulb memory? Brown and Kulik focused their research on vividness, but they never assessed the accuracy of flashbulb memories.

ATL skills: Research

1. For each of the three questions that follow formulate a hypothesis and design an experimental procedure that would allow you to test it. If you cannot think of an appropriate experiment, consider using other research methods.

2. What are the ethical considerations involved in the study of flashbulb memories? Participants are asked to reconstruct emotionally intensive events. Does that have any implications in terms of protecting participants from harm?

What is the neural basis of flashbulb memory?

Sharot *et al* **(2007)** conducted a study of personal recollections of the terrorist attacks in New York City in 2001, often referred to as the 9/11 attacks. Three years after the attacks 24 participants were asked to retrieve memories of that day as well as memories of personally selected control events from 2001. Researchers took into account the geographical position of the participant at the time of the attack: some had been in Downtown Manhattan, close to the World Trade Center, and some had been in Midtown, a few miles away.

Participants were placed in a functional MRI (fMRI) scanner and asked to retrieve 60 autobiographical memories related to a word cue presented on a screen, either "summer" or "September". These indicated whether the autobiographical memory should be of an event that occurred on 9/11 or during the preceding summer (June–August 2001).

The results of the study showed the following.

- The Downtown Manhattan participants exhibited **selective activation of the amygdala** as they recalled events from 9/11, but not while they recalled control events: 83% of participants in this group showed higher activation in the left amygdala during 9/11 trials than summer trials.

- This was not the same for the Midtown participants: only 40% of subjects exhibited selective activation of the left amygdala.

- During the 9/11 trials the Downtown Manhattan group showed higher amygdala activation than the Midtown group.

- There was no difference across groups for summer trials.

- Selective activation of the left amygdala correlated with the proximity of the participants to the World Trade Center during the attacks (r = 0.45, p < 0.05).

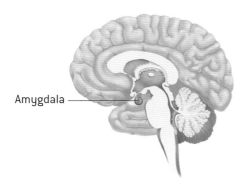

Amygdala

▲ Figure 3.25 Location of the amygdala in the human brain

Taken together, these results suggest supporting evidence for the idea that flashbulb memories **have a unique neural basis**. However, this is only true for individuals who personally experienced the event. Just having heard about an event does not seem to trigger this neural mechanism. Sharot *et al* conclude that it is **close personal experience** that is critical in engaging the neural mechanism that underlies flashbulb memories. In a sense, this narrows down the definition of flashbulb memories.

Furthermore, in another study **Sharot *et al* (2004)** demonstrated that selective activation of the amygdala is also observed while subjects are remembering negatively arousing photographs. In this study subjects were placed in an fMRI scanner and shown neutral and negatively arousing photographs, some new and some old (that they had seen an hour before). Activation of the amygdala was observed when subjects were looking at "old" emotionally arousing photographs but not the "new" ones. Hence amygdala is involved in **remembering emotional stimuli**. The pictures in this study were neither "surprising" nor "personally consequential", and yet the same neural mechanism was observed. This suggests that flashbulb memories (subjective experiences of memories as vivid and detailed) may be **a special case of a more basic underlying neural mechanism** linked to processing emotionally laden experiences.

ATL skills: Communication

Formulate in one sentence the conclusion that can be drawn from the two studies by Sharot and her colleagues.

Is vividness of flashbulb memories the result of photographic encoding or subsequent rehearsal?

Neisser *et al* (1996) conducted a study on flashbulb memories of the 1989 Loma Prieta earthquake in northern California shortly after the event and again 18 months later. Some informants were from California (close to the earthquake) and some from Atlanta, in the state of Georgia on the opposite coast of the USA (far from the earthquake). It was reported that the Californians' recollections of the earthquake were nearly perfect. At the same time, Atlantans who had relatives in the affected area remembered significantly more than those who did not. However, stress/arousal ratings were not significantly correlated with recall. In fact, many participants from California reported low levels of emotional arousal during the event. On the other hand, evidence suggested that repeated narrative rehearsals, the fact that some participants discussed the event more often with other people, may have played an important role.

Similarly **Bohannon (1988)** examined recollection of flashbulb memories for the Challenger Space

Shuttle disaster on 28 January 1986 in which the space shuttle broke apart 73 seconds after take-off, resulting in the deaths of the seven crew members. The accident received extensive media coverage and 17% of Americans witnessed the launch live. One group of participants was interviewed two weeks after the explosion and another group eight months after the incident. In a number of self-report measures participants were also asked to estimate both their emotional arousal and the number of times they discussed the incident with other people (overt rehearsal). Higher self-reported emotional reactions to the incident correlated significantly with greater vividness of recall after eight months, but so did rehearsal.

Overall, studies seem to demonstrate that rehearsal after the event makes an important contribution to the vividness of flashbulb memories. It is hard to tell whether it is rehearsal or emotion experienced at the time of the incident that is the main factor contributing to memory, because in correlational studies it is impossible to separate these two variables. However, we can at least say that emotional arousal is not the only factor that explains the outstanding vividness of flashbulb memories.

How accurate are flashbulb memories?

As mentioned earlier, while discussing an event with other people we may be exposed to leading questions or misleading information, which theoretically may affect flashbulb memory. At the same time many of the research studies discussed so far focused on vividness, but they never assessed accuracy of flashbulb memories.

Neisser and Harsch (1992) examined participants' memories of the Challenger Space Shuttle explosion. A questionnaire was given to 106 participants the day after the incident asking them about the circumstances surrounding receiving the news (where they were when they heard the news, what they were doing, and so on). The same questionnaire was then sent to the same participants three years later. Findings demonstrated that consistency of the responses was very low. On average, participants correctly answered only 2.95 questions out of 7 (42%). At the same time, they were very confident about the correctness of their memory: the mean self-reported rating of confidence was 83%. Participants were confident that they remembered the event

correctly both times and were very surprised to see their original responses to the questionnaire. When asked to explain the discrepancies between the first and second accounts, they couldn't do it.

Talarico and Rubin (2003) started their study the day after the 9/11 attack (12 September 2001). They asked 54 students to record their memory of first hearing about the terrorist attack and of a recent everyday event. The same students were tested again 1, 6 or 32 weeks later. For both the flashbulb and the everyday memory students also self-rated their emotional response to the news, vividness of memory and belief in its accuracy. The results showed the following.

- Accuracy for the flashbulb and everyday memories did not differ; both declined over time.

- Ratings of vividness and belief in the accuracy of memory declined only for everyday memories.

- Emotional response to the news correlated with later belief in the accuracy of memory.

- Emotional response to the news did not correlate with accuracy of memory.

The authors conclude that flashbulb memories are **only special in their perceived accuracy**. They say that the true mystery "is not why flashbulb memories are so accurate for so long, as Brown and Kulik (1977) thought, but why people are so confident for so long in the accuracy of their flashbulb memories" (Talarico and Rubin, 2003, p 460).

Overall, flashbulb memory is an interesting memory phenomenon, but its status is still being clarified. The special-mechanism hypothesis has been challenged as well as accuracy. The distinctiveness of subjective experiences about flashbulb memories still remains to be explained. One also has to recognize the inherent limitations of research: most research studies in this area tend to focus on public events accompanied by negative emotional experiences. The experience of such an event is hard to manipulate, which explains the predominance of correlational studies. An alternative approach would be to focus on personal events such as trauma or accidents, but this would mean lack of standardization in research conditions. With these limitations in mind, the exact definition of flashbulb memory (as a concept) still needs to be clarified.

Psychology in real life

Brian Williams, the well-known *Nightly News* anchor at NBC, was aboard a military helicopter in Iraq in 2003 when it was hit by a rocket-propelled grenade (RPG) and forced to come down. This incident, covered in the news later, contributed to his image as a fearless war reporter who faced the dangers of the war to bring the news to the world.

However, it turned out years later that there is a problem with this incident: the helicopter with Brian Williams on board was never hit by an RPG. It was another helicopter that took the hit, and Williams's helicopter just ended up landing near it an hour after. It was uncovered later in interviews with the helicopter pilot and other witnesses. Williams was accused of misrepresenting the Iraq incident, and lost credibility as a reporter. This led to a scandal, and in 2015 he was suspended from *Nightly News*.

Williams publicly apologized, admitting that his story of coming under fire in Iraq was false. He said: "I made a mistake in recalling the events of 12 years ago ... I don't know what screwed up in my mind that caused me to conflate one aircraft with another".

Could it be true? Could his memory of this highly traumatic event genuinely be distorted to this extent? Was he trying to fake a story to boost his reputation, or was he a victim of regular biases in human memory?

You can read (and watch) the full story in this *Washington Post* article: https://tinyurl.com/n4dlfe5

Inquiry questions

- Should we limit the amount of time that students spend on the internet or using technology?
- Is the internet changing how we think?
- Is digital technology making us less empathetic?
- How can technology be used to produce positive effects on both cognitive skills and human emotion?

- Background: neuroplasticity, interaction with digital technology, and cognitive processes
- Digital technology and cognitive skills
  - Interaction with digital technology has the potential to improve cognitive skills; Rosser *et al* (2007), study of laparoscopic surgeons who played video games
  - However, excessive exposure to digital technology results in negative long-term effects, Small and Vorgan (2008)
  - Some effects seem to be harmful, some beneficial
  - To some extent the benefits of digital technology can carry further and transfer to other skills; Sanchez (2012), effects of video games on science learning
  - Maybe interaction with some types of digital technology is beneficial, whereas interaction with other types is not; Fery and Ponserre (2001), the effects of training on a computer simulator on golf-playing skills
- Induced media multi-tasking
  - Moreno *et al* (2012): experience sampling method
  - Rosen, Carrier and Cheever (2013): young people have a strong need to constantly check on their updates; constant task-switching is detrimental to attention and focus

- What can be done to compensate for these negative effects? Rosen *et al* (2011), metacognitive strategies as a solution
- Loh and Kanai (2014): neurological correlates of media multi-tasking
- Digital technology and empathy in human interaction
  - Decline in empathy scores for the latest generations of people
  - Carrier *et al* (2015): investigation of the different uses of social networks (to support existing relationships or not)
  - Howard-Jones (2011): explanation of the conflicting evidence in research studies
- Digital technology and ADHD
  - Swing *et al* (2010)
- Methods used to study the interaction between digital technology and cognitive processes

This section also links to:

- research methodology
- localization of function (biological approach to behaviour)
- empathy, altruism (psychology of human relationships)
- cognitive development of adolescents, theory of mind (developmental psychology).

Psychology in real life

In 2015 Kaspersky Lab, a provider of digital security software, commissioned researchers to conduct an international survey to better understand how the use of digital technology affects the way people recall and use information. The researchers discovered a phenomenon that they called Digital Amnesia: forgetting information that you trust a digital device to remember for you.

Here are some of the more specific findings.

- More than half of adult participants could remember the telephone number of the house they lived in at age 10, but could not remember their children's numbers without looking them up.

- When asked a question, a third of participants would conduct an internet search before trying to remember.

- One quarter of participants would forget an online fact shortly after using it.

- Digital Amnesia was equally present in all age groups.

Digital technologies, the researchers conclude, change the way we think, learn, behave and remember.

Here is the full text of the report: https://tinyurl.com/o5vlnr6

What questions do you have after reading this report?

With the discovery of neuroplasticity it is common understanding that experience shapes neuronal connections and influences the physiology of the brain. Interaction with a certain stimulus or environment over time can strengthen cognitive functions that are utilized more often and weaken ones that are rarely used: "the neurons that fire together, wire together" (Groff, 2010, p 277). The more you interact with a stimulus, the more the neuronal connections in your brain adapt to these interactions.

In today's world, the stimuli with which we interact change at an incredible rate. We are surrounded by digital technology, and children in some societies learn how to use tablets even before they learn to speak. One third of smartphone owners check their messages before getting out of bed in the morning (Dokoupil, 2012).

So how does interaction with the new digital technologies (video games, internet, telecommunication, computers and gadgets) affect our cognitive processes?

- Is our mnemonic ability improving (because for every new piece of information we can now follow hyperlinks and so include it in a larger number of meaningful connections, enhancing semantic processing)?

- Is it deteriorating (because we rely too much on technology and hence underuse our own mental capacities)?

- Can the skills that we acquire in interaction with digital technology (for example, browsing through Wikipedia pages) be easily transferred to other situations (for example, working with conventional "paper" books)?

These are questions that require research and have potentially important implications. This is particularly relevant to the understanding of developing minds (children and adolescents), because neuroplasticity is most obvious at a young age.

Research studies to date are somewhat contradictory, which probably means that interaction between cognitive processing and digital technology is complex and multiple factors must be taken into consideration.

Discussion

Read this article on internet addiction from *The Guardian*: https://tinyurl.com/jzr4q8h

What strategies can we put in place to reduce the likelihood of a child developing an internet addiction?

Digital technology and cognitive skills

Some research studies show that interaction with digital technology has the potential to improve cognitive processing skills. For example, **Rosser** *et al* (2007) showed that laparoscopic surgeons who played video games for more than three hours a week made 37% fewer errors in surgery, and performed surgery 27% faster than their non-playing colleagues.

Surgery performance (errors and time) was not measured in real surgery situations. The researchers used a highly standardized set of simulations and drills that were part of the training that the surgeons received. For example, during one of the drills subjects were required to lift and move five triangular objects from one designated point to another by placing a needle through a loop on top of each triangle, using the non-dominant hand.

Playing video games was assessed in two ways. First, the researchers measured video game experience with a self-report questionnaire (length of time playing, types of games, and so on). Second, they measured video game mastery by asking participants to play three games (*Super Monkey Ball 2, Star Wars Racer Revenge, Silent Scope*) for 25 minutes and using the total score obtained in the games as an indicator of mastery. The overall video game skill was highly correlated with less time and fewer errors in performing the surgery drills (r = 0.63, p < 0.001). An explanation of this finding is the improvement of fine motor skills, reaction time and attention (in a game) and further transfer of these skills to a different situation (surgery).

▲ Figure 3.26 Video games in Rosser *et al's* (2007) study

Exercise

This is a condensed description of the Rosser *et al* study, but you need to be able to "unpack" it using your knowledge from other areas of the psychology course. Test your understanding by answering and discussing the following questions.

1. What kind of study is this (for example, experimental, correlational)?

2. What were the variables in this study? How many?

3. How were these variables operationalized?

4. What does r = 0.63 mean? Is it a tangible result? What does p < 0.001 mean?

5. Does the study show a cause–effect relationship between variables?

6. Are there any alternative explanations? For example, is it possible that surgery skill influences video game mastery and not the other way around?

7. To what extent are the results generalizable?

8. Are there any ethical considerations involved in the study?

If you need to, refer back to Unit 1 on research methodology.

However, **Small and Vorgan (2008)** summarize other research and show that excessive exposure to digital technology results in negative long-term effects, including addiction to the technology (for example, video game addiction), reduced judgment and decision-making abilities, and diminished capacity for delay of gratification. Correlations have been found between video game play and lower grades at school, as well as aggressiveness and decreased prosocial behaviour (Gentile *et al*, 2004).

A possible explanation for this contrasting evidence is that digital technology has a number of effects, some of them positive, some negative. For example, studies have demonstrated positive effects of video game play on experimental tasks involving:

- hand–eye coordination

- reaction time

- spatial visualization
- mental rotation.

However, can the benefits of digital technology such as video games carry further and transfer to skills that people require for everyday situations? It seems they can, at least to some extent.

Sanchez (2012) aimed to study whether there were positive effects of video games on science learning. It had been established already that some visuospatial games (like *Tetris* or first-person shooters) improve performance on visuospatial ability tests. However, these tests are not that much different from the video games themselves, for example, a typical item on a visuospatial test would ask you to mentally rotate or fold a figure. Sanchez wanted to see if this skill is transferable to a wider domain of science learning. It seems reasonable to assume that science learning requires visuospatial skills (among others), but can these very skills be enhanced by playing certain video games?

Sixty university students were randomly divided into two groups: the spatial training group who played a first-person shooter, *Halo: Combat Evolved*, and the non-spatial training group who played *Word Whomp*, a game that involves making words out of a group of six random letters to earn points. After playing the game, participants read a complex text about plate tectonics that contained 3,500 words with no illustrations. The text described a model of volcanic eruptions. After reading, participants were required to apply the learned concepts in a novel situation by writing an essay entitled "What caused Mt St Helens to erupt?" Independent scorers assessed the extent to which the essay demonstrated understanding of the important concepts of plate tectonics. As a result, participants from the spatial training group (the ones that played *Halo*) scored better on the essay. It was concluded that spatial training with the use of video games potentially can improve understanding of spatial relations. However, it should be noted that the study only demonstrated a short-term effect (the essay was written almost immediately after the game was played), and it is unclear if this effect endures in the long term.

Exercise

What other limitations and strengths of this study can you identify?

TOK

Cognitive processes are increasingly influenced by digital technology. But does this change the definition of knowledge?

Eli Pariser in his 2011 TED Talk "Beware online 'filter bubbles'" describes how we get trapped in a bubble of information pre-filtered to better fit our personal tastes. Today's search engines analyse our behaviour on the web and filter search information, pushing forward the results we would probably prefer.

In a group, use your personal laptops to search individually for an identical query (for example, "great music for a car ride") in a search engine and compare the outputs. To what extent are they similar?

Since we rely on search engines to make sense of the ocean of information, do we need to include information search algorithms in the definition of knowledge?

Eli Pariser's talk is available at https://www.ted.com/talks/eli_pariser_beware_online_filter_bubbles.

Another argument to bear in mind is that digital technology is very diverse. Some types of digital technology can be more beneficial to human cognitive processes than others. An interesting example of an "intentionally beneficial" use of digital technology is **virtual reality simulation**. The effects of using computer simulators with the aim of training new cognitive skills have been researched for such tasks as driving, flying airplanes, performing surgery and military operations.

One unusual study looked at the effects of training with a computer simulator on golf-playing skills. **Fery and Ponserre (2001)** studied 62 right-handed men with no prior golf experience. One group of participants engaged with the simulation with the intent to improve golf putting (the learning group), one group played the simulation to simply enjoy the game (the entertainment group), and one was a control group. Results showed that golf putting improved in both the entertainment and the learning group; however, improvement in the learning group was most significant. It was concluded that the usefulness of video game simulations on actual golf-putting skills depended on two conditions.

- The video game simulation must provide reliable demonstrations of actual putts (credibility).

- The user must want to use the game to make progress in actual putting (motivation).

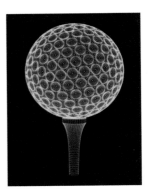

Induced media multi-tasking

An important dimension of digital technology is induced multi-tasking. Interacting with the modern digital environment, we carry out many more tasks simultaneously than we used to. There is always an urge to check new messages on social media (and a wealth of social media platforms, too). There are multiple tabs open on our laptops as personal computers have become increasingly multifunctional. There is easier accessibility to a variety of functions and online platforms through the use of smartphones.

Using the "experience sampling method", **Moreno *et al* (2012)** sent six text messages at random times every day to 189 university students with the aim of getting a statistical "snapshot" of their everyday activities. They found that more than half the time when the students were using the internet, they were multi-tasking, and the most popular off-task was social networking. This shows the scale of multi-tasking in naturalistic academic settings in the modern digital world.

How does this increased multi-tasking affect our cognitive processes? **Rosen, Carrier and Cheever (2013)** observed 263 students studying for 15 minutes in their homes (natural learning environments). They noted technologies present and computer windows open in the learning environment prior to studying and conducted a minute-by-minute assessment of on-task behaviour and off-task technology use. The study made use of trained student observers (N = 128) who were given an observation form that consisted of two parts. Part 1 included pre-observation data (studying location within the house, technologies present in the learning environment, windows open on a computer). After the relevant elements of the pre-observation sections were "ticked", observers used a minute-by-minute checklist (part 2) that included the following: email, Facebook, instant messaging, texting, talking on the telephone, television on, music on, music ear buds in ear, reading a book, reading a website, writing on paper, writing on the computer, eating or drinking, stretching/walking around. Also at each minute observers noted the number of windows open on the computer. After the observation participants were given a number of questionnaires assessing their attitude to technology. They were also required to indicate their current grade point average (GPA), a US scoring system that measures student performance.

Each trained student observer chose one to three participants to observe. They selected participants who they knew personally which ensured that the participants would be comfortable during the observation period. Researchers obtained informed consent from all participants and their parents in cases where participants were younger than 18. Approval for the study was also obtained from the ethics committee. The observer sat in the background in a position that was mutually determined to be the most unobtrusive to the participant. Participants were told to select a study environment where they typically study.

There were numerous results in the study, but in the context of our current discussion it is interesting to pinpoint several of them.

- On average participants were only capable of maintaining on-task behaviour for a short time (approximately 6 minutes) before switching to off-task behaviour. They also averaged only around 10 minutes on-task in total.

- Four variables predicted reduced on-task behaviour: technology available at the start of studying, stretching/walking, texting and Facebook use.

- Those students who accessed Facebook at least once during the 15-minute study period had lower GPAs.

Why does Facebook use hinder on-task behaviour and correlate negatively with GPA? The authors suggest that the switch from studying to Facebook may be caused by the **emotional gratification** that students receive from reading posts from friends, commenting on photographs, and so on. Another reason may be the similarity between the academic task and distractions from additional websites. These two reasons may drive our multi-tasking behaviour.

This being a correlational study, however, it is not possible to say conclusively whether it was preference for multi-tasking that caused students to create technologically abundant environments or vice versa, the technological environment created this preference for multi-tasking. It is a bit of a chicken-and-egg problem. Regardless, an interesting observation in the study revealed that students did not demonstrate a significant reduction in the amount of task-switching, even when they were preparing for an examination. This suggests that they had an intention to task switch, which is why they saturated their environments with easily distracting technologies.

ATL skills: Research

This study combines quantitative and qualitative elements. Recall what you know about interviews and observations as qualitative research methods (if necessary, refer to Unit 1 on research methodology) and answer the following questions.

1. What are the important considerations that need to be addressed before, during and after an interview? Were they addressed in this study?

2. What are the potential methodological limitations of observation? What are the types of observation? To what extent does this study control for potential methodological limitations?

3. To what extent can qualitative and quantitative data be combined in a single study? Was it done effectively in this case?

4. Discuss ethical considerations involved in this study.

Given these two premises, that modern young people have a strong need to constantly check their updates and that this constant task-switching is detrimental to attention and focus while studying, what can be done to compensate for these negative effects of technology? **Rosen et al (2011)** suggest **metacognitive strategies** as a solution. Metacognition ("meta" meaning "after" or "beyond") is the ability to consciously monitor and regulate your cognitive processes. In a study that supports this view, Rosen *et al* aimed to experimentally examine the impact of text-message interruptions on memory recall in a classroom environment. In this experiment students were viewing a videotaped lecture and received, depending on the condition, a small, medium or large number of text messages during the lecture. All these messages required a response. The dependent variable in the study was performance on the test after viewing the lecture. The findings showed a predictable pattern: the more text messages, the worse the test performance. However, this was mediated by **response delay**: students who replied to the texts immediately (no matter when they were received) scored significantly worse than those who chose to read and respond some time later (up to 5 minutes).

In other words, you can **consciously counterbalance** this automatic tendency to get distracted by regulating the time of the response. You can choose to stay focused on the lecture and only read the text message when the lecture gets more relaxed or when there is a break. This metacognitive strategy, however, requires a lot of conscious effort. You need to be a mature learner to regulate your automatic responses like that.

ATL skills: Self-management

To what extent are you capable of regulating these automatic responses in yourself? Before you answer, consider the evidence! Remember that people are naturally susceptible to quick automatic reactions, such as system I thinking in Kahneman's theory (see "Biases in thinking and decision-making") or instant checking of messages. Do you usually read messages immediately after receiving them? How hard would it be for you to delay this reaction?

Loh and Kanai (2014) investigated **neurological correlates** of media multi-tasking. They correlated scores on the media multi-tasking index (MMI), a self-report measure, with fMRI data from 75 healthy adults. Results showed that MMI scores were negatively correlated with grey matter density in the **anterior cingulated cortex (ACC)**, that is, individuals who reported higher amounts of media multi-tasking had smaller grey matter density in the ACC.

ATL skills: Thinking

How does this study link to the idea of "relative localization" of function in the human brain?

The ACC is known to be involved in cognitive control. For example, ACC activations have been observed in the Stroop task and selective attention tasks. This suggests that people who engage in heavy media multi-tasking demonstrate poorer cognitive control abilities.

The ACC region is also linked with another function: motivation and emotion processing. Reduced ACC volumes have been reported in people suffering from obsessive-compulsive disorder, post-traumatic stress disorder, depression and various addictions. This suggests a reduced ability in emotional and motivational regulation.

The authors of the study recognize two important limitations.

- Since this study is correlational, the direction of causality cannot be determined. Individuals with smaller ACC may be more susceptible to media multi-tasking, or engagement in media multi-tasking may affect the volume of ACC through neuroplasticity. Both explanations are equally plausible, and to choose between them one probably needs to conduct a longitudinal study.

- Generalizability of findings may be an issue since the sample consisted of educated individuals who were well exposed to technology. It is theoretically possible, however, that media consumption and multi-tasking patterns are different in different subpopulations.

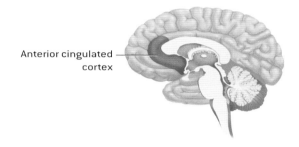

Anterior cingulated cortex

▲ Figure 3.27 Location of the anterior cingulated cortex (ACC) in the human brain

Digital technology and empathy in human interaction

Yet another dimension of cognitive functioning in the digital world is the way in which digital technology affects processing of emotional information. Are we becoming less emotionally sensitive now that we have the internet? Do we still have the ability to understand what other people feel now that we rely on emojis as a source of emotional information? Processing of emotional information is closely linked to the concept of **empathy:** empathy has both cognitive and emotional components. The cognitive component of empathy is our ability to take perspectives and understand what others feel, and the emotional component is "feeling along" with them. Naturally, empathic abilities affect human interactions.

Intuitively it seems plausible that since individuals displace face-to-face time by online interactions, empathic abilities should decrease. After all, our brain is shaped by our experience, and this change in experiences has to leave a trace. On the other hand, what if online interaction is not that different from face-to-face interaction, at least in terms of developing empathy? We can still process emotional information about a person's tragedy, even if this "person" is a story on our social media feed, can't we?

Research has shown a **decline in empathy scores** for the latest generations of people. For example, contemporary college students were shown to score significantly lower on standardized empathy questionnaires in comparison to college students 30 years before. So people seem to be becoming generally less empathetic, and it coincides with the onset of the digital era—but is this reason enough to conclude that digital technology influences cognitive abilities?

TOK

Does online interaction really displace face-to-face communication? How can we tell?

If two events coincide in history, can we conclude that they are connected, that is, that one event is the cause of the other? How does history as an area of knowledge establish causation in historical events?

Carrier *et al* (2015) set up an anonymous online questionnaire and collected information on daily media usage, real-world empathy, virtual empathy and social support. The sample included 1,726 participants, all born in the digital era (after 1980).

After analysing the correlation patterns between responses to individual questions, researchers obtained the following results.

- There appeared to be two mechanisms of the connection between online activity and cognitive real-life empathy. In one, online activity that leads to face-to-face communication increased empathy. In the other, online activity that does not lead to face-to-face communication reduced empathy.

- Activities that predicted increased amounts of face-to-face communication were: social networking sites, browsing websites, using email, using a computer for purposes other than being online.

- Video gaming reduced real-world empathy, irrespective of how much time was spent in face-to-face communication.

- Virtual empathy was positively correlated with real-world empathy.

- However, virtual empathy scores were lower than real-world empathy scores.

Why are the scores for virtual empathy lower than the scores for real-life empathy? One possible explanation is **lack of non-verbal clues** when you are communicating online. Texts lack additional emotional information—gestures, touch, facial expressions. However, according to the results of the study, we cannot say that spending time online actually "displaces" face-to-face communication. Carrier *et al* conclude that the negative effects of digital technology on empathy (observed in many previous studies) should be attributed to specific activities that are not associated with increased face-to-face communication (such as video games) rather than engaging with digital technology in general.

The authors recognize three inherent limitations of the study: convenience sampling (which does not guarantee generalizability of results), using self-report measures and the correlational nature of the study. Being a correlational study, it does not establish the direction of causality, and it is possible, theoretically, that a "third variable" existed (for example, extraversion) which explained both going online and the increased face-to-face communication.

It is generally believed, as a summary of research that has been conducted in this area, that online communication for **supporting existing friendships** produces positive effects. Issues arise when the use of the internet is excessive or inappropriate.

When the digital world was establishing its dominant position in the first half of the 1990s, several influential research studies demonstrated that teenagers who used the internet more often experienced more problems with social connectedness and well-being (Nie, 2001).

However, an important point is made by **Howard-Jones (2011)**: at that time the internet was not yet very popular, so it was difficult to maintain existing social networks online. So communication through the internet was probably used to establish new friendships and relationships rather than supporting existing ones. Now, with everyone online, the situation has been reversed. This might explain why reports from research studies have become more positive. However, even these results show that online communication only has positive effects when it is used to maintain existing relationships, whereas using the internet to make new friends is associated with lower empathy.

Discussion

How do you use social networks? Give examples of instances when you used online platforms to support your existing relationships. Give examples when your activity on social networks was not associated with face-to-face communication. Do you feel that these types of activities have different effects on how you feel about others?

Digital technology and attention deficit hyperactivity disorder

It has been suggested in the work of some researchers that the rise of digital technology might be responsible for increased rates of attention deficit hyperactivity disorder (ADHD) witnessed in the last several decades. Does digital technology affect attention? It seems plausible: television and computer games involve rapid changes in stimuli and seem not to prepare children to work with "less exciting" materials such as long and boring academic texts.

Swing *et al* (2010) showed a relationship between gaming and reduced classroom attention in a sample of students of 6–12 years old. It was a longitudinal study involving 4 measurements over a 13-month period. Attention problem data came from the observations of teachers who reported incidences of staying off-task, interrupting others, not paying attention, and so on. The study showed that playing games (at the beginning of this period) was associated with an increase in

attention problems over the course of the study. Those who exceeded two hours of daily screen entertainment time (television and computer games combined) were more likely to have attention problems later.

However, most research in this area is not longitudinal and therefore much more inconclusive. The direction of causality is still not clear enough. It could be the case that people who experience problems in attention develop gaming and watching habits involving longer screen time.

Methods used to study the interaction between digital technology and cognitive processes

As you know, knowledge in empirical sciences is procedural: to evaluate knowledge you need to be aware of the method that was used to obtain it.

As outlined in the *Psychology guide*, the topic "Cognitive processing in the digital world" includes three sub-topics, and one of them focuses on methods that may be used in this area of research. You may be asked to discuss, contrast or evaluate methods used to study the influence of digital technology on cognitive processes.

You are equipped already for answering these questions. Review Unit 1 on research methodology for a broad understanding of essential advantages and disadvantages of particular research methods (experimental, correlational and qualitative). Note that in this section we have selected research studies to demonstrate a variety of methods (review the ATL skills box that gives an overview of studies). Look once again at the arguments regarding positive and negative influences of technology in cognition. You will realize there are plenty of aspects you could talk about, depending on the exact wording of the actual examination question.

Nonetheless, here are some of the points that you might want to consider.

- We are surrounded by various forms of digital technology so, to approximate the reality of our everyday life, research studies should be conducted in real-life settings. This is achieved by using such methods as surveys, structured naturalistic observations or the experience sampling method.

- However, these methods have inherent limitations: it is impossible to make cause-effect inferences, they rely on self-report, and it is hard to isolate effects of specific variables.

- For this reason, such research should be supplemented by experiments. In an experiment, the researcher manipulates the independent variable and observes its effect on the dependent variable while carefully controlling all the other (confounding) variables. This allows researchers to make cause-effect inferences. An example is Rosser *et al*'s (2007) study of laparoscopic surgeons or Fery and Ponserre's (2001) study of golf-playing skills.

- However, controlling confounding variables inevitably makes research more artificial and more reductionist. As a result, such studies are usually specific to narrow populations (such as laparoscopic surgeons), concrete skills (such as golf-putting skills) or concrete forms of technology (such as first-person shooter video games).

- To bring in more variables and so make our understanding of the relationship between technology and cognitive processes more holistic, correlational research may be used. A subset of this is the investigation of neurological correlates with the help of brain imaging methods.

- To summarize, we can only fully understand the effects of digital technology on cognitive processes if we combine diverse sources of evidence: cause-effect data from experiments, patterns of correlations between multiple variables in surveys, rich descriptive data from observations and interviews, brain imaging. Ideally, data needs to be longitudinal because, as we have seen in the studies of social networks and empathy, the way technology affects our cognitive processes may change with the course of time.

ATL skills: Thinking and research

The research studies discussed in this section utilized a variety of research methods to study the interaction between digital technology and cognitive processes.

Link the studies to the methods. Remember that one study could have used a combination of different methods. Also note that the research methods listed below are not mutually exclusive: some methods can be special cases of others.

Rosser *et al* (2007)	1	a	Observation
Sanchez (2012)	2	b	Interview
Fery and Ponserre (2001)	3	c	Survey/questionnaire
Moreno *et al* (2012)	4	d	Correlational study
Rosen, Carrier and Cheever (2013)	5	e	Experiment
Rosen *et al* (2011)	6	f	Neuroimaging technology
Loh and Kanai (2014)	7	g	Experience sampling method
Carrier *et al* (2015)	8	h	Longitudinal study
Swing *et al* (2010)	9	i	Minute-by-minute assessment of behaviour

Discuss the relative strengths and limitations of each method for studying the interaction between digital technology and cognitive processes.

What are the ethical considerations, if any, associated with the use of each of these methods?

197

Exam tip

"Cognitive processing in the digital world" is an extension for HL students. The Diploma Programme *Psychology guide* specifies three aspects of this topic that may be applied in three areas. Here is how material in this section can be used to explicitly address the combination of these aspects and areas.

	Cognitive processing	Reliability of cognitive processes	Emotion and cognition
The positive and negative effects of modern technology on cognitive processes	**Positive influence** Visuospatial skills: Rosser *et al* (2007); transfer to science learning: Sanchez (2012); specific professional skills: Fery and Ponserre (2001) **Negative influence** Induced media multitasking: Rosen, Carrier and Cheever (2013), Loh and Kanai (2014). ADHD: Swing *et al* (2010)	Induced media multitasking reduces attention and focus: Rosen, Carrier and Cheever (2013), Loh and Kanai (2014) However, this can be counterbalanced by metacognitive strategies: Rosen *et al* (2011) Hypothetically excessive use of digital technology is linked to ADHD: Swing *et al* (2010)	Empathy and processing of emotional interpersonal information Decline in cognitive scores coincides with the onset of the digital year (Konrath, O'Brien and Hsing, 2010) But this is only true for online activities that do not enhance face-to-face communication (Carrier *et al*, 2015) With the course of time the number of online activities that enhance empathy is becoming larger (Howard-Jones, 2011)
Methods used to study the interaction between digital technology and cognitive processes	Observation Survey/questionnaire Correlational study Experiment Neuroimaging Minute-by-minute assessment of behaviour	Observation Interview Correlational study Experiment Neuroimaging Experience sampling method Longitudinal study Minute-by-minute assessment of behaviour	Survey/questionnaire Correlational study

Review this table in conjunction with the supporting evidence and see if you agree with the proposed distribution in material. You can and should be flexible in your approach, and you are invited to change some arguments and/or supporting studies.

SOCIOCULTURAL APPROACH TO BEHAVIOUR

Topics

- Introduction
- Cultural influences on individual attitudes, identities and behaviour—culture and cultural norms
  - Origins and definitions of culture
  - Cultural norms
  - Enculturation and cultural transmission
  - Culture of honour
- Cultural origins of behaviour and cognition—cultural dimensions
  - Individualism versus collectivism
  - Power distance index (PDI)
  - Personality traits and cultural dimensions
- Becoming oneself—socialization and social cognition

- Socialization
- Social cognitive theory
- Us and them—how we understand others
  - Social cognition
  - Attribution theories
  - Errors in attribution
  - The development and effect of stereotypes should be addressed with reference to one or more examples
  - Effects of stereotypes
  - Social identity theory
  - Acculturation
- HL only: The influence of globalization on individual behaviour

Introduction

Social psychology in a global context

The world is becoming increasingly interconnected. Electronically, culturally, linguistically—in fact in almost every imaginable way. The process through which this happened over the past 100 years or so is called globalization.

Globalization is seen by some as a threatening force to cultures, languages, religions and ways of life. The radicalization of groups around the world is one of the potential reactions to globalization and perceived westernization. Radical groups often believe that actions such as violent terrorist attacks are the only defence they have against what they perceive as an attack on their way of life and their identity. Groups of people around the world are seemingly willing to engage in extremes of violence to guard against globalization. This dichotomy is often described as nationalism versus globalism.

As people come into contact with greater numbers of more diverse individuals, it is important that we gain an understanding of why others may hold different, and sometimes opposing, views to our own. This exploration should begin with trying to understand others through the established norms under and through which they choose to live—in short, their socialization.

There are several assumptions made by social psychologists that rest at the heart of the field of social psychology. These assumptions are sometimes called principles. For example, it is assumed by social psychologists that people are social animals who have a deep need to foster and nurture social connections with others. It is also assumed that social and cultural groups influence behaviour. A third assumption is that people have a social identity (or identities) as well as a personal identity. Finally, it is assumed that the perspectives and worldviews that people hold are resistant to change.

People are shaped by their social environment; they then in turn help shape that social environment. Social psychology is the scientific examination of this bidirectional relationship (or **reciprocal determinism**). In other words, it is the study of the influence of human behaviours, beliefs, cognitions and attitudes on social groups and of the influence of the group on its members. Definitions vary but, at its core, social psychology attempts to explain how relationships with others influence how we think and behave.

Of course, thinking about social influence is nothing new. **Farr (1991)** distinguishes between the long past of social psychology and its short history. The long past of social psychology refers to an era when it was a point of interest for the western intellectual tradition, while the short history refers to the era since 1935 when social psychology has been treated as an experimental science. It is primarily the short history of social psychology as an experimental science that is the foundation upon which social psychology is built.

Psychology in real life

One current challenge of peaceful democracies is to find ways to absorb an increasing stream of ethnic, religious and cultural diversity. The most successful societies have shown openness and flexibility. If differing social groups see each other as positive, contributing members to a communal whole, there is less likelihood of conflict. Governments must find a way to bring in large numbers of migrants and refugees in a way that is supportive and understanding of the concerns and needs of both newcomers and citizens of the host country. Psychologists can help with this. Social psychologists are particularly well-suited to handle this very difficult and pressing problem. Psychology is not only about understanding how biology and cognition interrelate, it is just as much about examining issues that go beyond the individual. Social psychologists specialize in how people relate to one another, and particularly how social groups of people interact with other social groups; that is, inter-group interactions. This is the very concept that is at the heart of today's refugee and migration crisis.

Of course, every refugee is a feeling, thinking person who deserves respect and humanity. Too often, the media speaks of refugees as a faceless horde of ragged, dirty and desperate individuals. This faceless representation of an outgroup does not encourage feelings of empathy or compassion. Sometimes it takes an emotionally potent image or story to gain compassion for members of an outgroup. This was the case when the dead body of 3-year-old refugee Alan Kurdi was found on a beach in Turkey. This event immediately changed perceptions of millions of parents around the world from viewing refugees as faceless others to viewing them as parents and families. The tragedy of a single boy from one family was more moving than the cold reality of the thousands of deaths reported in the news media. We *understand* the numbers of lives lost but we *feel* the loss of a single life.

Adapted from: https://thepsychologist.bps.org.uk/migration-crisis-psychological-perspectives

Recent trends in the national politics of many western nations is a reaction to the current refugee and migrant crisis. President Trump was elected on a policy of "America First"; Geert Wilders in Holland, Marine Le Pen in

France and Nigel Farage, one of the leaders of the Brexit movement that sought to withdraw the UK from the European Union (EU), have to varying extents been involved in politics based on close control of immigration. Some people in many western nations are interpreting the current refugee and migrant crisis as a threat to their way of life. However, examples of welcoming policies can be seen in Germany and Canada, where many thousands of immigrants have been received with open arms and offers of help. Why is there this difference?

Psychological theories such as **realistic conflict theory** can help explain why so many are against welcoming migrants and refugees. Realistic conflict theory explains inter-group conflict (prejudice and discrimination) as arising from a competition for limited resources. Arguments often include comments like "Refugees will take our jobs", or "Why should we help them when we have our own homeless who need our help?" These are examples of perceived conflict over jobs or national social services. It would appear, according to realistic conflict theory, that the citizens of Canada and Germany do not feel that they are in conflict with incoming migrants. The challenge to western democracies, as well as to the hopeful migrants and refugees, is to develop a belief in all members of both groups that change and acceptance will benefit all involved.

Perhaps the beginning of understanding and acceptance comes from a social identity. If exclusion and walls are seen as solutions to challenges faced by globalization then it seems inevitable that we will see more conflict, war and suffering.

The Prime Minister of Canada, Justin Trudeau, described what he calls Canada's strength as follows in 2016: "Canadians understand that diversity is our strength. We know that Canada has succeeded—culturally, politically, economically—because of our diversity, not in spite of it" (http://pm.gc.ca/eng/news/2015/11/26/diversity-canadas-strength).

In the following pages, you will learn how social psychology can help us navigate our complicated, evermore integrated and globalizing world.

▲ Figure 4.1 Donald Trump

▲ Figure 4.2 Geert Wilders

▲ Figure 4.3 Nigel Farage

What you will learn in this section

- Culture

  ○ Origins of culture: we form social groups to protect ourselves and better enable us to survive in a given environment

  ○ Definitions of culture: Hofstede and Matsumoto

- Cultural norms: the unique set of attitudes, beliefs and behaviours that are specific to a particular culture

- Enculturation and cultural transmission

  ○ Lewin's gatekeeper theory: a psychology and communication theory related to who controls access to information and ideas in a social group

- Culture of honour

  ○ Cohen *et al* (1996): US southern culture of honour

○ Acculturation: a process of psychological and cultural change as a result of contact and interaction between cultures

This section also links to:

- stereotype formation

- evolutionary explanations for behaviour (biological approach to behaviour)

- origin of conflict; culture of honour (psychology of human relationships)

- gender identity and social roles (developmental psychology)

- the influence of globalization on individual behaviour.

Origins and definitions of culture

Culture is complex and difficult to define. Generally, culture is what we refer to when we talk about the behaviours, attitudes and identities that are common among a group of people who claim some form of unity with each other. It is something universally recognized, it affects each of us personally, and yet when pressed for a definition we seem unable to achieve consensus.

The origins of culture seem an appropriate place to begin looking for a definition. If we can explain its origins, perhaps we can define culture. Social psychologists hold the common assumption that humans, as social animals, have a basic need to belong. We form social groups to protect ourselves and better enable us to survive in a given environment.

According to Matsumoto (2007), "Culture is a solution to the problem of how to survive, given the problems in the environment, the physical and social needs that must be addressed, and the tools available". Although not really a definition, this is a great description of why culture is around in the first place. Culture is the response of a group of people to their environment and this should explain why so many different cultures exist around the world and why those in the more distinct environments will have more distinct cultures.

Cultures are different from one another because of differences in where the culture evolved. Different groups of people were responding to different environments, resources and social makeups such as sizes of families and communities. Differences in cultures can usually be split into two categories: **surface culture** and **deep culture**, as shown in Figure 4.4.

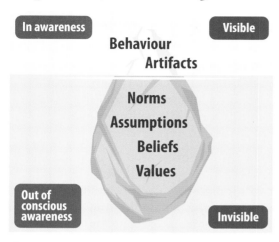

▲ Figure 4.4 The iceberg model: surface and deep culture

Surface culture refers to aspects such as the behaviours, customs, traditions and architecture of a culture that can be easily observed. Deep culture refers to the more cognitive elements of a culture such as gender roles, respect for authority and rules and concepts of social identity and the self. In short, deep culture is easily accessible to members of that culture but may be inaccessible or more difficult to understand by non-members. Social and cultural psychologists are interested in deep culture and how it influences behaviour both within and between groups. With the wave of **globalization** in the past century, different cultural groups around the world have become more interconnected and interrelated. Understanding other cultures and the potential areas for misunderstanding are key focuses of **cross-cultural psychologists** such as David Matsumoto, Geert Hofstede and Shalom Schwartz, among many others.

Here are two definitions of culture.

- **Hofstede** defines culture as "the collective programming of the mind distinguishing the members of one group or category of people from another" (Geert Hofstede, n.d.). It guides a group of people in their daily interactions and distinguishes them from other groups of people.

- **Matsumoto (2007)**: culture is a unique meaning and information system, shared by a group and transmitted across generations, that allows the group to:

  - meet basic needs of survival
  - coordinate socially to achieve a viable existence
  - transmit social behaviour
  - pursue happiness and well-being
  - derive meaning from life.

ATL skills: Thinking

Environmental context can influence culture. Cross-cultural research seems to show that factors such as a group's wealth, population density and the climate all shape culture. Using the two imaginary but realistic contexts below, create a profile (short description) of the deep cultures of the societies that evolved in each of these contexts.

Context 1: this culture evolved in an environmental context with high population density, harsh climate, few resources and isolation from outside influence because the area is surrounded by near impassable mountain ranges.

Context 2: this culture evolved in an environmental context with low population density, mild climate, many resources and constant contact with other cultures due to the area's central position on steppe land covering thousands of square kilometres.

What characteristics of each of these two cultures would enable people to meet basic needs of survival, coordinate socially to achieve a viable existence, transmit social behaviour, pursue happiness and well-being and derive meaning from life?

The different solutions to these challenges should be a profile of two distinct cultures.

To add to your ideas on environmental context and challenges in different cultures, investigate this further reading:

- *Cultural DNA: The Psychology of Globalization* by Gurnek Bains, published by Wiley, New Jersey, USA

- *The Culture Map: Decoding How People Think, Lead, and Get Things Done Across Cultures* by Erin Meyer, published by Public Affairs, New York, USA.

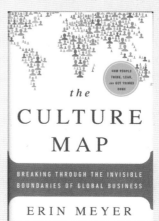

Cultural norms

Cultural norms and culture are similar concepts but they are not the same thing. Culture is a generic term given to the use of certain tools, practices and beliefs that groups use to survive and thrive in their environment (see the definitions above). **Cultural norms** are the unique set of attitudes, beliefs and behaviours specific to a particular culture. Given a specific environmental context, certain expectations of appropriate and inappropriate attitudes, beliefs and behaviours will arise. These constitute cultural norms.

All groups have culture and they are all the same in purpose but different in means. The term "culture" refers to the purpose while "cultural norm" refers to how to achieve the purpose. Different cultural groups have different cultural norms.

Culture	Cultural norms
A response by a group of people to the challenges of environmental context for the survival of a group of people	Who decides who will marry whom? How much personal space is normal? What is more important, the needs of the individual or the group? How important is hierarchy and authority? Are there specific gender roles? What are they? Who determines them?

▲ Table 4.1

Enculturation and cultural transmission

Cultures are dynamic in that they change over time to adjust to the changing demands of their environmental contexts, but they do remain largely stable as generations come and go. This continuity is important for the survival of cultures. Their survival relies on attitudes, behaviours and beliefs being passed from one generation to the next. This process is often referred to as **cultural transmission**.

Enculturation is the process by which individuals learn their culture. This could be via observation, formal instruction or direct personal experience. We learn a culture's rituals and traditions in order to function successfully within it.

Cultural transmission is accomplished through the process of **enculturation** and **social cognition**.

Cultural transmission is a theory of learning whereby individuals acquire a significant amount of information simply by interacting within their culture. Enculturation refers to the process of receiving this same information. In other words, cultural transmission and enculturation are two sides of the same coin.

Culture and cultural norms are in a bidirectional relationship with the individuals who make up particular cultural groups. Cultures and their norms grow out of the behaviour of individuals but individuals' behaviour is shaped by culture and norms (see "Social cognitive theory"), This should raise an important question: who decides what norms will be established and passed on?

Kurt Lewin (1890–1947) developed **gatekeeper theory**—a psychology and communication theory related to who controls access to information and ideas in a social group. Gatekeeper theory is simple but important. Gatekeepers are those people in society who decide what information is shared to groups and other individuals. Examples of gatekeepers are politicians, religious or spiritual leaders, news editors, teachers and university professors. Through a filtering process, these individuals decide what information is unwanted, controversial, corrupting or otherwise harmful to society and remove that information from circulation. The gatekeeper role normally starts in the home with parents controlling which messages their children need and which should be avoided.

An example: the culture of honour

A culture of honour exists in societies where individuals (normally men) place a high value on strength and social reputation and where any insult to someone's reputation, family or property is met with a violent response (Brown, Osterman and Barnes, 2009). Some examples of cultures of honour include the southern USA, some inner-city neighbourhoods in major US cities, and parts of the Middle East, India and Pakistan. What each of these cultures honours most varies; some value female chastity and devotion, others aggression towards outsiders or personal reputation. What they all share is a violent (or threat of a violent) response to perceived insults or challenges.

TOK

Are "alternative facts" really facts or are they lies?

Traditionally, the news media played an important role in social groups by deciding what events were important enough to be shared with their readers or viewers. Not only did the news media decide what information was important but they decided how that information should be delivered. In the past, there was an attempt to remain impartial when reporting on current events. It feels sometimes as if this attempt has been abandoned for one-sided and often heavily biased news reporting.

Recently, there has been an increase in what is called "fake news" and public figures stating what are falsifiable statements. Kellyanne Conway, a spokeswoman for President Trump, has defended untrue statements made by the Trump administration by calling them "alternative facts".

For more information, read the following article.

CNN "'Alternative facts': Why the Trump team is planting a flag in war on media": http://money.cnn.com/2017/01/22/media/alternative-facts-donald-trump/index.html

When societies need to make decisions about important things such as climate change, going to war or national budgets they need actual facts. These facts must be "real": they must accurately represent the world around us. What does it mean for gatekeepers and citizens if we accept the idea that there is such a thing as "alternative facts"?

To what extent has the internet and social media changed the relationship between society and gatekeepers?

To what extent do you agree with the statement: "alternative facts are not facts, they are falsehoods" (CNN, 2017)?

TOK

Natural and human sciences

"Memetics" and cultural transmission

In 1976, Richard Dawkins coined the term "meme" in his book *The Selfish Gene*. A meme is a "unit of culture" (an idea, belief or behaviour). In his book, Dawkins likens the cultural transmission of ideas to the biological transmission of genes—so memetics is the cultural equivalent of genetics in biology. In Dawkins' words, "Just as genes propagate themselves in the gene pool by leaping from body to body via sperms or eggs, so memes propagate themselves in the meme pool by leaping from brain to brain via a process which, in the broad sense, can be called imitation" [or learning] (Dawkins, 2006, p 192).

The interesting part about memes is that it does not matter whether the ideas or beliefs are true, a meme simply has to be beneficial to its host culture. According to Dawkins, one of the most successful memes is what he calls the God meme or religious practices. It does not matter whether God is real or whether any single religion has monopoly on the truth because the idea of God and religion have great psychological advantages to the members of a group whether or not it is true. In this way, the God meme has survived for millennia. Memetics is very controversial and is considered a pseudoscience by its detractors (Kantorovich, 2014).

Do you accept this analogy between genetics and memetics? What makes you say that?

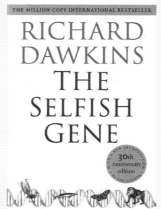

In terms of origin, cultures of honour may have formed in areas without a clear authority or rule of law. In this type of environment, protecting yourself, your possessions and your family may have required an aggressive defence against insult which could have served as a test to your ability to defend yourself. Social influence to take action against insult or challenge can be as simple as verbal encouragement to respond (for example, "Are you going to let him talk to you that way?" or "Are you just going to sit there and let him insult you? Be a man!") Children who are exposed to adults responding to threats or insults with violence along with accompanying positive reinforcements become **socialized** to engage in that behaviour as well. In short, children learn these behaviours simply by being a part of the culture.

ATL skills: Thinking

Think about social science as an area of knowledge. Do you think the experimental method can be used to gain knowledge in the social sciences? Can we trust the validity and reliability of the findings? To add to your ideas, read:

"Science's reproducibility problem: 100 psych studies were tested and only half held up", an article by Jessica Firger:

http://www.newsweek.com/reproducibility-science-psychology-studies-366744

Research in focus: Cultural origin and transmission

Dov Cohen, at the University of Illinois, led researchers in a quasi-experimental study to test his theory that southern white males in the USA responded differently to threats and insults than northern white males. Researchers set up three conditions to test for difference between northerners and southerners.

The US term "honor states" typically refers to the states in the southern USA.

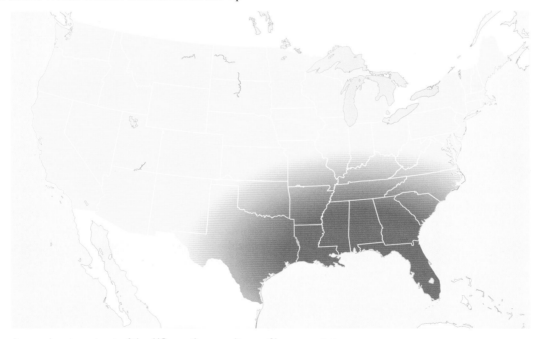

Approximate extent of the US southern culture of honour states

Participants were male University of Michigan students who either grew up in the south or the north of the USA. In three different conditions, a **confederate** bumped into the participant and then insulted him by calling him by a derogatory name. The northerners were relatively unaffected by the insult but southerners (comparative to northerners) were found to:

Research in focus (continued)

- think their masculine reputation was threatened

- be more upset (showing elevated levels of cortisol—a hormone associated with stress and arousal)

- be more physically primed for aggression (showing elevated levels of testosterone—a hormone associated with aggression and dominance)

- be more cognitively primed for aggression (completing artificial scenarios with more violent endings)

- be more likely to engage in aggressive and dominant behaviour.

Northerners were only half as likely as southerners to become more angry about than amused by an insult (35% versus 85%). Cohen and his team say this highlights the southern culture of honour in the insult-aggression cycle where insults diminish a man's reputation. This then results in an attempt to restore the lost reputation through aggression and violence (Cohen *et al*, 1996).

Additional research undertaken by Ryan Brown and colleagues at the University of Oklahoma found that US states with a culture of honour had higher incidences of high school violence. Students in culture of honour states were more likely to have brought a weapon to school in the past month than students from states with no culture of honour. In addition, the researchers found that over a 20-year period culture of honour states had more than double the number of school shootings per capita than states with no culture of honour (Brown, Osterman and Barnes, 2009). In separate research it has also been shown that culture of honour states have a higher level of major depression and both male and female suicide rates (Osterman and Brown, 2011).

The research by Cohen *et al* (1996) illustrates an important issue in relation to cross-cultural research. Although not explicitly about **acculturation** (see definition below), this research raises the question: what happens when members of a culture of honour are asked to live in a culture that does not include an insult-aggression cycle? Anticipated behaviours within a culture are part of the social fabric that hold groups together. When members of a group cannot anticipate the actions of others, mistrust and apprehension can seep into relationships and seed conflict.

Acculturation is a process of psychological and cultural change as a result of contact and interaction between cultures. This can result in changes to all (or both) cultures, not only the non-dominant culture (Berry, 2005).

In the distant past, this would not have caused concern or merited discussion because diverse cultural groups did not meet or influence each other significantly. Cultural conflict is a growing concern in our world as diverse cultural groups are increasingly living side by side with potentially incompatible attitudes, beliefs and behaviours.

ATL skills: Thinking

Why do you think some people are reluctant to accept immigrants or refugees from other cultures?

What challenges do you think would be faced by an incoming immigrant or refugee?

How do you think social psychologists could help to ease the challenges presented by the movement of people between cultures?

Cultural origins of behaviour and cognition—cultural dimensions

- How does culture influence behaviour?
- Are cultures comparable?

What you will learn in this section

- Hofstede's dimensions of culture
  - Individualism versus collectivism
  - Power distance index (PDI)
  - Gladwell: cockpit culture theory
  - Meeuwesen, van den Brink-Muinen and Hofstede (2009): patient–doctor communication
- Schwartz: theory of basic values
- Individual personality traits and cultural dimensions

This section also links to:

- culture syndromes and the role of culture in treatment (abnormal psychology)
- social responsibility—cooperation (psychology of human relationships)
- doctor–patient relations (health psychology)
- developing identity (developmental psychology)
- HL only: The influence of globalization on individual behaviour

Studying cultures from an outside perspective looking in is taking an **etic approach** to research. That means that cultural practices and beliefs are examined as if from above or outside the culture. This approach allows for cross-cultural study and analysis and is the basis of the research of Hofstede and Schwartz, among others. Typically, anthropologists are interested in **emic research** approaches—they prioritize trying to understand a culture from within. Emic research seeks to understand only culture-specific behaviour such as **cultural syndromes**. An example of emic research is that of Margaret Mead in the 1930s. Mead was interested in how three different cultures defined their gender roles. She was not interested in comparing them against each other, only in understanding the particular uniqueness of each one. Modern cross-cultural psychologists use an etic approach. (See discussion of Mead's study in Unit 8 on developmental psychology.)

Cross-cultural analysis of cultures can be complicated by the fact that cultures are each unique and inherently difficult to compare. In an attempt to simplify and standardize cross-cultural analysis, **Geert Hofstede** undertook research covering more than 70 countries. He used the 40 largest of these countries to come up with 5 dimensions of culture that can help explain patterns of human behaviour across cultures. By 2010, scores from 76 countries and regions were included.

Hofstede founded the personnel research department for IBM Europe in 1965. He soon undertook his massive study of the values of IBM employees across 40 countries in which IBM had subsidiaries. Hofstede distributed questionnaires to over 117,000 employees, asking about their values and behaviours. In 1973, he completed his initial study and the findings of his research suggested that certain trends emerged in the analysis of his data. He called these trends dimensions and originally identified four: individualism versus collectivism; the power distance index (PDI); masculinity versus femininity; and uncertainty avoidance (Hofstede, 1980). In further research, he added another two dimensions: long-term versus short-term orientation and indulgence versus restraint

(Hofstede 1991, 2011). The dimensions Hofstede identified are summarized below.

- **Individualism versus collectivism (1980).** In individualistic cultures, members define their identity according to personal characteristics. Personal identity is understood as a choice while people are viewed as unique; and personal autonomy, competitiveness and self-sufficiency are highly valued. In collectivist cultures, identity is more often connected to a social group, with the characteristics of the group influencing personal identity. Self-sufficiency, competitiveness and personal achievements are not as important as someone's responsibilities and relationship to the group.

- **Power distance index (PDI) (1980).** This dimension is a measure of the extent to which the less-powerful members of a group accept and expect that power will be distributed unevenly. This is very tightly related to how societies understand and tolerate inequality between members. Cultures with high PDI scores are tolerant of inequalities and tend to be hierarchical by nature. Cultures with low PDI scores do not tolerate inequalities without justification and members normally prefer an equal distribution of power and influence.

- **Masculinity versus femininity (1980).** In this dimension, "masculine" values include achievement, autonomy and competitiveness while "feminine" values include caring, cooperation and compassion. Hofstede rated cultures on the extent to which the dominant values of a culture were masculine or feminine—as he defined them.

- **Uncertainty avoidance index (1980).** This dimension measures the extent to which a culture is comfortable with ambiguity and uncertainty. Cultures with a strong (high) ratings on this index exhibit intolerance for ideas and behaviour that are unconventional and they avoid risk-taking behaviour. Weak-rating (low-scoring) cultures show more tolerance for behaviour outside the norm and are more likely to take risks.

- **Long-term versus short-term orientation (1991).** This dimension is based on the idea that cultures do not experience time in the same way. A low score on this dimension shows that a culture honours traditions

and norms while eyeing social change with suspicion—this culture is conservative in nature and looks to the past for guidance. A high score shows a culture that is pragmatic and favours anticipation of future needs as a driving force for change and innovation.

- **Indulgence versus restraint (2010).** This dimension measures the extent to which a culture allows relatively open access to the enjoyment of natural human drives. A high score reflects a culture with open access to indulgence while a low score reflects a more restrained, conservative culture in terms of personal gratification.

ATL skills: Research

Go to:
https://www.geert-hofstede.com/national-culture.html

Pick one national culture and examine its scores for each of the cultural dimensions.

Can you see any correlations between any of the dimensions (for example, does high Individualism correlate with masculinity)?

Choose another country and contrast the two countries' scores on Hofstede's cultural dimensions.

Don't forget to read the "What About" sections for each national culture. These can be found beneath the charts for each national culture's dimensions.

None of the dimensions act in isolation and national cultures are complex. Each dimension is expressed differently in each culture. Triandis (2001) points out that each collectivist or individualist culture is unique. For example, Korean collectivism is not the same as Kenyan or Chinese collectivism. One important way to distinguish between them is the degree to which they tolerate inequality, but there are many other ways—and cultures need to be measured along more than one dimension at a time. **Triandis (2001)** identified four categories of individualism versus collectivism.

- **Horizontal individualism**: members are unique and mostly of the same status.

- **Vertical individualism**: members are unique but it is possible to distinguish yourself and enjoy a higher status in a social hierarchy.

- **Horizontal collectivism**: members merge themselves with the ingroup and enjoy largely the same status.

- **Vertical collectivism**: members merge themselves with the ingroup and submit themselves to an authority in that ingroup.

In addition, there are correlations between the dimensions. In a sample of 10 European cultures,

Meeuwesen, van den Brink-Muinen and Hofstede (2009) found that a strong PDI was related to strong scores on collectivism and uncertainty avoidance, and less wealth (GDP); likewise, individualism was related to higher wealth and to weaker scores on PDI and uncertainty avoidance. It is worth noting that this is a small sample of relatively similar national cultures; however, it does show that dimensions of national culture do not exist in isolation from each other and that correlations are commonplace.

Individualism versus collectivism

Individualism (high score)	All cultures exist on a spectrum between either of these two extremes	Collectivism (low score)
Cultures characterized by: • loose ties between individuals; all individuals are expected to look after themselves, a sense of "I" or of the self is very strong • "others" being classified as individuals, not necessarily as outgroup members (**universalism**).		Cultures characterized by: • tight ties between members of strong ingroups; the sense of "we" is stronger than the sense of "I" or self • "others" being members of outgroups, so collectivists are inherently exclusive.

Nations/cultures (score out of 100)		Nations/cultures (score out of 100)	
USA	91	Russia	39
Australia	90	Kenya	25
UK	89	China	20
Germany	67	Ecuador	8

▲ Table 4.2

Source: https://www.geert-hofstede.com/national-culture.html

See video

10 minutes with Geert Hofstede on individualism versus collectivism

https://www.youtube.com/watch?v=zQj1VPNPHlI

▶ ❚❚ ■

Research in focus: Berry and Katz (1967)

John Berry is one of the most important cross-cultural researchers in the past 50 years. He conducted an early and very important cross-cultural study on individualism and collectivism across cultures including Scottish people, the

Tenme people of Sierra Leone and the Inuit (he called them Eskimo) people from Baffin Island in Northern Canada. The Tenme and Eskimo people are both subsistence cultures. Berry noted that these subsistence cultures are different from each other. Eskimo culture is a hunting and fishing society that allows individualism to develop fully among the children, resulting in a highly individualistic low food-accumulating society. The Tenme are rice farmers who harvest one crop a year and must share out the harvest among the group until the next harvest, representing a collectivist high food-accumulating society.

Berry and Katz were interested in research to see if the difference of these two cultures' individualism scores would correlate with their conformity. Berry hypothesized that the Eskimo would conform less often than the collectivist Tenme because the socialization of the Tenme depended on tight social relations and unity of the group to social norms.

The researchers used the Asch paradigm to measure conformity, where a series of lines of varying length are presented to participants. One target line is given on top of a page and eight lines of varying lengths are printed below the target line. The participants are asked to identify which of the other lines is of equal length to the target line. The participants are then given a "hint" identifying one line (incorrectly) as the line that "most" (Scottish, Tenme or Eskimo) people choose as being the correct one. Findings showed that the Tenme had a highly significant tendency to accept the suggestion of the cultural norm while the Eskimo group almost disregarded it entirely. As one Tenme participant stated, "When Tenme people choose a thing, we must all agree with the decision–this is what we call cooperation" (Berry, Katz 1967, p 417). It was concluded that the different results for the Tenme and Eskimo people are due to the different degree of conformity required by the contrasting social and environmental conditions of their cultures. These findings seem to support Hofstede's belief that the degree of individualism of a culture will affect group member behaviour (in this case, conformity).

Individualism and volunteering

The individualism of a culture has been shown in research to impact beliefs, attitudes, identities and behaviours. Researchers Parboteeah, Cullen and Lim collected data on over 38,000 individuals in 21 countries. They found that collectivism (along with religiosity, national wealth, liberal democratic values and education) has a positive relationship with formal volunteering (Parboteeah, Cullen, Lim 2004). Given collectivist characteristics of tight social connections and strong group identities, this seems to align with Hofstede's conception of collectivism.

Think about your knowledge of social norms and role identity.

Why do you think religiosity and liberal democratic values positively correlate with formal volunteering?

Kemmelmeier, Jambor and Letner (2006) sought to examine the relationship between individualism and voluntary, prosocial behaviour— the reasons for stranger-on-stranger giving.

The researchers differentiate their study from Parboteeah, Cullen and Lim's because they reject the claim that religiosity is a basis for prosocial behaviour. They argue that the dimension of individualism versus collectivism is unrelated to religious giving because giving in religious situations is often not a matter of personal choice but of social obligation (that is, having to pay a tithe).

Data was collected via telephone interviews from 2,553 participants from 40 US states. Researchers found that individualistic cultures were active in voluntary prosocial behaviour for causes they deemed to be in line with individualistic values such as self-determination, self-promotion or self-actualization (Kemmelmeier, Jambo, Letner 2006). Researchers found individualism was positively related to charitable giving and volunteerism and that both were more likely to occur in more individualist states.

An important point to consider about this research is that it focused on levels of giving and volunteering among strangers. **Lyengar et al (1999)** make the point that collectivist cultures tend to discriminate in favour of their ingroup. As a result, stranger-on-stranger helping may be less common among collectivist cultures than individualist ones. (see discussion of the role of oxytocin as a trigger for ingroup favouritism in Unit 2 on the biological approach to behaviour).

Additional research **(Finkelstein 2010)** examined the influence of culture on volunteer behaviour. Specifically, Finkelstein was interested in identifying if there were different *reasons why* individualists and collectivists engaged in voluntary, prosocial behaviour.

Finkelstein theorized that people volunteered for two reasons; motivation (to help) and role identity (someone who self-identifies as a volunteer will continue to volunteer to maintain his or her self-image). A study was carried out in which 194 undergraduates at a US university participated in exchange for extra course credit (perhaps there is a touch of irony in that they did not volunteer). Participants were asked to fill out online questionnaires. Interestingly, findings showed that both individualist and collectivist cultures were motivated to volunteer for career-related reasons. However, within individualist cultures career-related reasons were the strongest motivating factor. Collectivism was more closely associated with other-oriented motives and the development of a volunteer role identity (Finkelstein, 2010).

Given the research surrounding volunteerism and giving in individualist and collectivist cultures, it may be that although both culture types engage in voluntary, prosocial behaviour, the reasons why they do so may differ. Collectivist emphasis on the ingroup may make them more likely to give to ingroup members while individualists are more likely to give to strangers if the giving is in line with their individualistic values such as self-determination, self-promotion or self-actualization.

Cultural dimensions and acculturation

If you are studying the HL extension, "The influence of globalization on individual behaviour", see "How globalization influences behaviour" for more on this topic.

A recent study examining the cultural values promoted in Chinese and US advertising was conducted to test the hypothesis that a value shift from collectivist to individualist values would be evident since China opened its doors to trade in 1979. This is an interesting investigation into the acculturation of societal values related to advertising and consumer culture because of the variation between US and Chinese scores on the individualism versus collectivism dimension (91 and 20 respectively). Since television and its advertisements reflect social values, you would expect that Chinese advertisements would promote collectivist values. This study gives an interesting example of the acculturation process fuelled by globalization and the spread of consumer culture.

Hsu and Barker (2013) conducted a content analysis of 566 television advertisements, rating for individualism or collectivism and the prominence of traditional and modern themes. The researchers found that advertisements aimed at younger Chinese viewers scored higher on individualism than collectivism.

Looking at advertisements as a reflection of culture is important because marketing theory tells us that advertisers must reflect the values of their clients if they wish to create a market for their products. This, in turn, suggests that as China opened its doors to trade it also opened its doors to cultural influence from outside. This research is supported by earlier studies (Lin, 2001; Tsai and Lee, 2006) that suggest the trend in what Lin calls the westernization of Chinese advertisements began over a decade before Hsu and Barker's study.

Audience group	N	Individualism	Collectivisim	Modernity	Tradition
American younger	182	0.85	0.26	0.83	0.07
American older	134	0.82	0.34	0.8	0.09
Chinese younger	136	0.51	0.43	0.37	0.21
Chinese older	114	0.20	0.36	0.30	0.30

▲ Table 4.3 Means for individualism, collectivism, modernity and tradition in the television advertisements

Source: Hsu and Barker (2013)

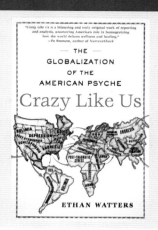
The PDI

High PDI (high score)	All cultures exist on a spectrum between either of these two extremes	Low PDI (low score)
Cultures characterized by: • strict social hierarchy • acceptance of inequality among members of an ingroup • deference to elders and superiors		Cultures characterized by: • a relatively flat social structure • low tolerance for inequality among members of an ingroup • willingness to question authority
Nations/cultures (score out of 100)		**Nations/cultures (score out of 100)**
Russia 93		USA 40
China 80		Australia 36
Ecuador 78		UK 35
Kenya 70		Germany 35

▲ Table 4.4

Source: https://www.geert-hofstede.com/national-culture.html

See video

10 minutes with Geert Hofstede on power distance

https://www.youtube.com/watch?v=DqAJclwfyCw

▶ ❚❚ ■ ────────

How does position on the PDI influence behaviour?

Obedience and authority are social elements learned early in the family and are inherent in the relationship between children and parents. This is an example of how culture is passed from one generation to the next. Children develop a clear sense of power relationships first in the home, then towards a broader group of older people and finally to the power structures of society itself. A society with low power distance will exhibit this low power distance in the home, in schools, in workplaces and up to the broadest aspects of society.

Meeuwesen, van den Brink-Muinen and Hofstede (2009) were interested in whether Hofstede's dimensions could predict cross-national differences in patient–doctor communication. The researchers collected data from 10 diverse

European countries including the following (shown here with their PDI scores): Estonia (40), Belgium (65), Sweden (31), Poland (68), Romania (90) and Great Britain (35). A total of 307 doctors (general practitioners) and 5,807 patients participated in the study. Participants filled out questionnaires and had their medical communications videotaped and analysed. The researchers found that the higher the nation's PDI score, the less unexpected information was shared and the shorter the consultation. This implies a more one-sided communication with the doctor primarily speaking to the patient. In countries with low PDI scores, doctors conveyed more information to their patients through more flexible communication styles and consultations lasted significantly longer (Meeuwesen, van den Brink-Muinen, Hofstede 2009).

The PDI is also very important to multinational organizations and businesses. Business psychology handles topics such as team dynamics and leadership. Knowing what strategies to use as a manager is very important when managing a multinational team, or teams in different national cultures. International business managers would be well served by reading the literature on power distance.

Eylon and Au (1999) researched power distance and empowerment in the workplace and found that the amount of supervision and management required to maximize work performance is culturally dependent. Using 135 participants who were MBA students from a Canadian university, the researchers examined the effects of empowerment on work satisfaction and performance. Participants were divided into high power distance and low power distance groups based on language and country of origin. Overall, the two groups were similar in work experience and demographics. Members of the two groups were then each put through three conditions; empowered, disempowered and a control.

Results showed that all participants were more satisfied when empowered than when not empowered, regardless of score on the PDI. However, differences were seen in work performance. There was no difference in work performance for participants from the low power distance cultures but the high power distance participants did significantly less well in the empowered condition. Eylon and Au's study (1999) therefore suggests that high and low power distance groups react differently to being empowered in the workplace. It seems to follow from these findings that high power distance groups may perform better while disempowered. Disempowered situations are characterized by more structured tasks, where information is more limited and responsibilities are explicit and few.

Similar research was undertaken to examine whether a desire to have a voice in decision-making processes varied across cultures. In the USA, it has long been established that people react poorly when they are not given a voice in decision-making. If this is untrue for other national cultures, it would inform leaders of multinational teams in how best to involve team members in decision-making processes.

Three separate studies were conducted by **Brockner et al in 2001**. All three studies found that there is a tendency for people in low power distance cultures (specifically, the USA and Germany) to respond less favourably (with lower commitment to the organization) to lower levels of voice—participation in decision-making—than people in high power distance cultures (specifically, China, Mexico and Hong Kong). Importantly, Brockner et al (2001) found that it is not the lack of participation in decision-making to which people object. It is when the lack of participation violates cultural norms that people are unhappy. This again points to the need for managers to understand the cultural differences in their teams and team members in order to maximize work satisfaction and performance.

Psychology in real life

Malcolm Gladwell—a cockpit culture theory of plane crashes

Early in the morning on 6 August 1997, a Korean Air 747 with 254 people on board slammed into a mountainside on the island of Guam, killing 228 people. Almost immediately, the National Transportation Safety Board

(NTSB) began its Aircraft Accident Report. The crew was well trained, very experienced and professional, yet poor communication between the flight crew in the cockpit was identified as a contributing factor in the tragedy. How could a very experienced captain and flight crew get things so wrong?

Psychology in real life (continued)

It turns out that this was not an isolated incident. Between 1970 and 1999, Korean Airlines experienced an unusually high crash rate, losing 16 aircraft in a string of unfortunate disasters and giving the company one of the worst flight safety records of any major airline at the time. In fact, the loss rate for Korean Air was 17 times higher than for similar airlines, such as United Airlines in the USA, between 1988 and 1998. What was going on in Korean Air to cause these kinds of systematic failures? Malcolm Gladwell, in his book *Outliers*, points to an unlikely and often invisible culprit—elements of Korean culture itself.

Gladwell focuses on Korea's relatively high PDI score (60) and the resultant communication problems between flight crew. Subsequent research into the culture of the cockpit found that in 17 out of 19 participating cultures, flight crews had a significantly higher PDI score than Hofstede's original research showed for their respective cultures (Merritt, 2000). In other words, the culture of flight crew seemed to exaggerate the original scores found on Hofstede's original PDI. This may be due to the fact that many airlines hire ex-military flight crews. The military, by its very nature, is strictly hierarchical with extreme power distance scores.

Earl Weener, former chief safety engineer for Boeing, makes the point that the cockpit of the 747 is designed for two equals working in close cooperation—there should be no hierarchy in the culture of the cockpit (Gladwell, 2008). A former Delta Airlines employee, David Greenberg, was brought in to improve Korean Air's safety record. He quickly surmised that Korean Air flight crew were, "trapped in roles dictated by the heavy weight of their country's cultural legacy. They needed an opportunity to step outside those roles when they sat in the cockpit" (Gladwell, 2008, p 246).

Once the connection between power distance and cockpit culture was identified, Greenberg and Korean Air removed Korean Air cockpits from Korean culture and re-normed the culture of the cockpit to reflect a much lower power distance. In this way, they eliminated the hierarchy that prevented flight crews from cooperating effectively.

Since 1999, Korean Air has improved its safety record to be in line with other major carriers. This is a remarkable turnaround that can at least partially be attributed to the re-norming of Korean Air cockpit culture.

▲ Figure 4.5 View of the wreckage from Korean Air flight 801

ATL skills: Thinking

Is it is ever acceptable to obey without question? As we have seen, the extent to which someone will do this may be culturally dependent.

One subculture within all cultures that shows extremely high PDI scores is in military organizations (and to a lesser extent police forces). These subgroups are normally made up of willing young men and women who have volunteered to be a part of a rigid and hierarchical culture.

Alfred Tennyson's 1889 poem *The Charge of the Light Brigade*, declared that "Theirs not to make reply, Theirs not to reason why, Theirs but to do and die". Tennyson was writing about the common soldier who was to obey orders no matter what the consequences. Even in western nations, now exhibiting a low PDI score, it was once considered noble and courageous to go blindly to your death if ordered to do so by a superior. This drastically different subculture is why the military and police communities are very interesting to social psychologists.

What personality traits do you consider ideal for military service? Do you believe soldiers are born or made?

How are new recruits socialized into the military culture?

Alternative or extended models of cross-cultural studies

Schwartz's theory of basic values

There is more than one model in cross-cultural psychology and it is always worth examining more than one way of explaining behaviour. Schwartz has offered a theory that he considers is an extension of Hofstede's dimensions. This theory features 10 basic values and their overarching higher-order groups.

Openness to change

1. **Self-direction**—independent thought and action; choosing, creating, exploring

2. **Stimulation**—excitement, novelty and challenge in life

Self-enhancement

3. **Hedonism**—pleasure and sensuous gratification for oneself

4. **Achievement**—personal success through demonstrating competence according to social standards

5. **Power**—social status and prestige, control or dominance over people and resources

Conservation

6. **Security**—safety, harmony and stability of society, of relationships and of self

7. **Conformity**—restraint of actions, inclinations and impulses likely to upset or harm others and violate social expectations or norms

8. **Tradition**—respect, commitment and acceptance of the customs and ideas that traditional culture or religion provide the self

Self-transcendence

9. **Benevolence**—preserving and enhancing the welfare of those with whom one is in frequent personal contact (the ingroup)

10. **Universalism**—understanding, appreciation, tolerance and protection for the welfare of all people and for nature (Schwartz, 2006).

Schwartz's theory of basic values not only claims to describe the basic values of all cultures but explains how they influence and interact with each other.

In an effort to show this visually, Schwartz created a circular chart that shows the relationship of the basic values (see Figure 4.6). For example: security, conformity and tradition have similar motivations and are fundamentally opposed to self-direction and stimulation; similarly, values of universalism and benevolence are offset to power and achievement. Values such as hedonism and stimulation are quite closely related to each other and therefore appear next to each other on the chart.

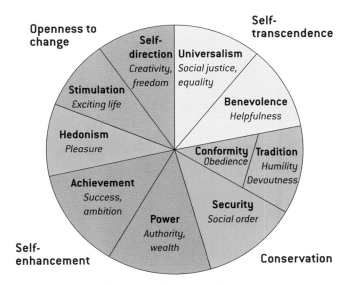

▲ Figure 4.6 Relationship of the 10 basic values in Schwartz's theory (Schwartz, 2006)

Placement on this matrix is determined by a questionnaire called the Schwartz Value Survey (SVS). The SVS has been taken by over 60,000 respondents in over 60 nations. (Fischer and Schwartz, 2011). The questionnaire measures the 10 basic principles on a scale of importance from −1 to 7. The higher the number, the more important that value is to the participant. The scale is:

- 7 (supreme importance)
- 6 (very important)
- 5, 4 (unlabelled)
- 3 (important)
- 2, 1 (unlabelled)
- 0 (not important)
- −1 (opposed to my values).

ATL skills: Thinking and self-management

There are many websites online where you can take the SVS. Take the survey and see if you can identify what your dominant values are.

Contrast Schwartz's model with Hofstede's dimensions of culture.

Is one model better than the other? What makes you say that?

Personality traits and cultural dimensions

▲ Figure 4.7 Völkertafel—17th-century stereotypes

The birth of the modern nation state in the 17th and 18th centuries led to the need to develop a national and cultural "we" that was different from all of the "others" that existed in other states. Eighteenth-century philosophers spent a lot of time and effort distinguishing between what they called the various "national characters" of Europe. One of the earliest attempts to collate these can be seen in the Völkertafel stereotypes (shown in Figure 4.7 and Table 4.5). This is an obvious early example of stereotyping that resembles what we would today call racism. This list of stereotypes is an important document as it represents an early attempt to define the relationship between cultures and personalities.

This dichotomy remains today. Hofstede and Schwartz do not claim to be describing the personalities within cultures but the characteristics of cultures overall. Studying personality requires the comparison of individuals while studying cultures requires comparing societies. As Hofstede and McCrae state, "individuals are to societies as trees are to forests" Hofstede and Macrae, 2004, p 65). Studying forests is not like studying trees. Forests are far more complex and require an analysis of an entire ecosystem, not a single organism. You would be guilty of committing an **ecological fallacy** (inferring information about individuals using information from a group to which they belong) if you used dimensions (designed for cultures) to

Names	Spaniard	Frenchman	Italian	German	Englishman	Swede	Pole	Hungarian	Russian	Turk
Customs	Lordly	Careless	Sneaky	Candid	Shapely	Strong and tall	Rustic	Disloyal	Wicked	Inconsistent
Character	Miracolous	Open minded, talkative	Jealously	Kind	Good mannered	Gruesome	Wild	Most gruesome	"gutungarisch" (?)	Young devil
Mind	Wise	Careful	Careful	Sharp minded	Graceful	Persistent	Not paying attention	Even less than a Pole	Non-existent	Strange
Traits	Manly	Childish	Adaptable	Follower	Feminine	Unrecognizable	Mediocre	Sanguinary	Infinitely rough	Tender
Science	Literate	Warfare	Ecclesiastical law (biblical science)	Secular law (natural science)	Philosophy	Sea related	Foreign languages	Latin	Greek	Wrong political (?)
Fashion	Honorable	Changeable	Worshipful	Adapting	French	Leather	Long skirts	Colourful	Furry	Feminine
Bad habits	Arrogant	Sneaky	Stingy	Extravagant	Anxious	Superstitious	Boastful	Traitor	Suspicious	Even more treacherous
They love	Honor	War	Gold	Drinking	Lust	Dining	Nobility	Riots	Beating people	Themselves
Typical diseases	Constipation	Syphilis	Bad plagues	Gout	Tuberculosis	Anasarca	Fractures	Polio (?)	Whooping cough	Impotence
Their land	Fertile	Well made	Pretty	Good	Fertile	Mountains	Forests	Fertile and gold-rich	Icy	Lovely
War virtues	Nobly	Maliciously	Careful	Invincible	Hero on the sea	Undaunted	Impetuous	Rebellious	Burdensome	Sneaky
Divine service	The best	Good	Better	Reverent	Variable	Zealous	Lonely believers	Indifferent	Apostate	Apostate too
Reigned by	Monarch	King	Patriarch	Emperor	Changing every day	Free lordship	An elected person	Doesn't matter	A volunteer	Tyrant
Plenty of	Fruits	Wares	Wine	Grain	Cattle	Ore	Fur	Everything	Bees	Soft things
Amusement	Gambling	Cheating	Babbling	Drinking	Working	Eating	Arguing	Doing nothing	Sleeping	Be ailing
Animal comparison	Elephant	Fox	Lynx	Lion	Horse	Ox	Bear	Wolf	Donkey	Cat
Death	In a boat	In war	In a monastery	In wine	In water	On the earth	In a stable	By the sword	In the snow	By betrayal

▲ Table 4.5 Völkertafel's stereotypes (17th century)

Source: http://imgur.com/gallery/gKbLD

compare individuals within those cultures. You would be equally guilty for using personality traits to compare cultures. So how can we get around this ecological fallacy?

Hofstede's cultural dimensions are a common way to measure and compare cultures. A widely used model for measuring and comparing personality is the five-factor model of personality (Macrae, John 1992). **Hofstede and McCrae (2004)** found that mean personality scores from 33 different countries significantly correlated with cultural dimension scores.

Macrae and John's (1992) model consists of the following factors. (This is sometimes referred to as the O–C–E–A–N model).

1. **Neuroticism**—tendency toward unstable emotions; tendency to frequently experience negative emotions such as anger, frustration, worry and sadness while appearing insensitive to others

2. **Extraversion**—tendency toward talkativeness, sociability and enjoyment of others; tendency to have a dominant style of behaviour

3. **Openness** to experience—tendency to appreciate new ideas, values, ideas and behaviours

4. **Agreeableness**—tendency to agree to go along with others; tendency to avoid asserting your own values, opinions or choices

5. **Conscientiousness**—tendency to be cautious, punctual, hardworking and a rule-follower.

Hofstede and McCrae (2004) found that:

- individualism correlated with extraversion

- uncertainty avoidance correlated with neuroticism and tended to score higher on openness to experience

- high power distance correlated with conscientiousness and extraversion

- masculinity correlated with neuroticism and cultures rating high in masculinity tended to rate themselves more open to experience than feminine cultures.

ATL skills: Thinking and research

Can science and psychological research give us accurate, data-based generalizations about individual personality traits within cultures?

Find out Hofstede's dimension scores for your country. Align those dimensions with the personality traits from the five-factor model.

Do you see any relationship between what the data tells you and who you think you are?

The individual and the group—social cognitive theory

Inquiry questions

- What determines your identity?
- Is violence a learned behaviour?

- How does culture influence health behaviour?

What you will learn in this section

- Socialization

  - Primary and secondary socialization: the process of becoming a member of a social group

- Social cognitive theory

  - Bandura's bobo doll experiments (1961, 1963, 1965) learning aggression through models

  - Social cognitive theory and prosocial behaviour

This section also links to:

- doctor–patient relations (health psychology)

- Bandura—origins of conflict (psychology of human relationships)

- developing identity (developmental psychology)

- the influence of globalization on individual behaviour

- cognitive processing in the digital world (cognitive approach to learning).

Socialization—how do we become who we are?

No child is born a nationalist, a racist, a sexist or a chauvinist—people must *become* these things. The process of becoming a member of a social group is called **socialization.** This begins at the most basic level in the family. This incredibly important stage in childhood development where a child learns the basic rules and norms of living in his or her group is called **primary socialization**. In short, primary socialization is the initial stage where **social norms** are passed between group members. There are many theories of socialization. Two examples are **gender socialization**, where children learn the attitudes and behaviours considered appropriate for their gender; and **cultural socialization**, where children are taught about their racial, cultural or ethnic heritage.

Primary socialization forces partially determine the prosocial or antisocial behaviours of a developing child. The most important primary socialization forces are the family, school peers and later peer groups. Families are the first point of social contact for babies. It is in these social relationships where babies first learn to bond, create and nurture relationships, mediate disputes and navigate the ethical conventions of a social group. The term "primary" refers to the distance from the target of the socialization forces, not the order in which they occur. Primary socialization forces bond directly with youths and transmit behavioural and attitudinal norms (Oetting, 1999). It is these forces that both monitor and correct behaviour to conform with norms. Some examples of this include parents coaxing a "please" or "thank you" from their children or encouraging children to share and treat other people with respect. Conversely, if a child witnesses a parent or role model expressing racist or derogatory opinions about a minority group, the child may think that behaviour is acceptable and continue to hold that derogatory opinion about the minority group.

Secondary socialization includes elements such as the larger community, extended family and (perhaps most notoriously) the media. Secondary socialization forces tend to influence adherence to or deviance from norms indirectly. That is, they influence behaviour and attitude by affecting the primary forces. They can influence the forces themselves or serve to reinforce or interfere with the transmissions of norms from primary forces. Children's television shows that model positive norms such as good manners and sharing are examples of "reinforcing secondary socialization", while media modelling antisocial violent behaviour or the mistreatment of others would be "detracting secondary socialization".

Secondary socialization forces are important because they play an important role in forming individual beliefs, behaviours, identities and attitudes beyond the family and close friends. Important questions arise, and beg study, when individuals do not receive input from their primary socialization forces. Youths subjected to racism, abuse (both physical and mental), poor or dangerous schools, or abandonment must seek alternative forms of socialization and can turn to secondary sources such as peer groups and the media (Garcia, 1999).

Group socialization is a form of secondary socialization where it is an individual's peer group, not the person's parental figures, that influences personality and behaviour.

Censorship

Governments often attempt to manage or manipulate cultural norms by controlling the sources and topics of information passed through the media (both social media and mass media). Some form of government censorship is practised in most countries around the world. Freedom House's 2017 report of press freedom claims that 45% of the world's population live in countries where the media (a key secondary socializing force) is not free. Perhaps more interesting is the fact that 2016 saw the lowest levels of media freedom in 13 years. The Freedom House report (2017) states that this is due mainly to "unprecedented threats to journalists and media outlets in major democracies".

ATL skills: Thinking

Media censorship is a hotly debated topic. The most common forms of media censorship are related to violence, hate speech and pornography but also often extend to political ideology and criticisms. Create a table of the pros and cons of media censorship, then answer the following questions.

- Who determines the norms of society?
- Who should be more responsible for the socialization of youths, parents and guardians or governments?
- Why do societies punish deviation from group norms?
- Do some societies punish deviance more severely? Which ones, and why?

Social cognitive theory

The fact that culture is learned from primary and secondary socialization is an important aspect of understanding how cultural norms are maintained or changed. The next step is to examine how these norms, behaviours, attitudes and identities are transmitted between group members. To this end, Albert Bandura developed his **social cognitive theory** (originally social learning theory).

Learning can be done both directly and indirectly. In other words, we can learn by performing an action or behaviour and experiencing the consequences ourselves (**direct**) or by observing the consequences of another person's actions or behaviour (**indirect**). Social cognitive theory is an attempt to explain how we learn from others.

Social cognitive theory began in the 1960s as social learning theory. **Social learning theory** is based upon a behaviourist approach to learning which uses **classical** and **operant conditioning** to describe how social learning occurs. The behaviourists believed that learning was simply a matter of conditioning a response from a stimulus.

Classical conditioning was famously studied by Ivan Pavlov and his dogs. In classical conditioning, an **unconditioned stimulus** (food) is paired with a **neutral stimulus** (a bell ringing). Over time, the neutral stimulus will become the **conditioned stimulus** which brings about the **conditioned response** (salivating dogs). In Pavlov's case, consistently pairing a ringing bell with food resulted in his dogs salivating at the sound of the bell. Pavlov received a Nobel Prize for his work in this area in 1904.

Operant conditioning is another form of learning studied by BF Skinner, considered one of the most important behavioural psychologists of the 20th century. In operant conditioning, a desired behaviour is followed by either punishment or reward to either strengthen the behaviour or weaken it. Learners or observers are more likely to engage in the behaviour for which they are rewarded.

The **behaviourist approach** to learning places an emphasis on observable behaviour (as opposed to cognition) and assumes that most behaviour is learned from the environment. In this approach, a stimulus is given from the environment and a response is measured in terms of a given behaviour, everything in between those two observable events is not considered. See Unit 3 for more on the behaviourist approach.

The behaviourist approach to learning seems to suggest that in order to learn something, individuals must observe it then try it. **Bandura (2005)** felt this trial-and-error type of learning could not explain how people learned language, customs or educational, religious and political practices. In short, Bandura felt that the complex process of socialization did not occur through trial and error.

TOK

Aristotle argued that people are born as a blank slate (*tabula rasa*) and begin to fill their mind as they grow older and acquire their behaviours and attitudes from their life experiences. Modern psychology has used adoption studies and twin studies to explore this claim. Steven Pinker in *The Blank Slate* makes the claim that humans are pre-programmed to develop certain traits (IQ, gender identity and alcoholism). Pinker is specifically interested in language and argues that people are born with innate dispositions toward spoken language (2016). Pinker is not referring to any specific language but simply language as the more general ability to understand and apply grammar and vocabulary to explain our world. This characterizes the classic debate between innatism (or nativism) and the concept of *tabula rasa*.

Where does language come from? Is it innate or learned?

Bandura understood behaviour, society and cognition as all mutually interrelated. He believed the behaviourists were too simplistic in explaining human behaviour as being a one-way relationship between the environment and behaviour. Bandura proposed a model of behaviour based upon **reciprocal**

determinism (or **triadic reciprocal determinism**). This is a model of the mutual influence of three sets of factors; personal (cognition, biology and mood), behavioural and environmental (see Figure 4.8). It works on the assumption that all three of these things are responsible for the way we behave.

For example, if you are in a bad mood and unhappy then you may affect the mood of those around you and the way they treat you. Others may choose to avoid contact with you or adopt your bad mood and unhappiness while interacting with you. This may, in turn, reinforce your bad mood and influence your behaviour in unhelpful ways when dealing with people around you. Conversely, imagine you are in a great mood and you are able to change your environment by improving the moods of the people around. In this way you can create a friendly, stimulating and supportive environment that will then influence how you interact with or behave with people in that environment.

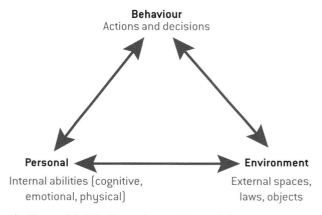

▲ Figure 4.8 Triadic reciprocal determinism

In relation to the topics discussed in this section, you may also wish to look at health belief models (see Unit 6 on health psychology) and thinking and decision-making (see Unit 3 on the cognitive approach to behaviour).

Exercise

Create your own example of a situation showing reciprocal determinism in the form of a cartoon strip. Make each image part of a timeline of an event where behaviour, personal characteristics and environment are interacting with, and influencing, each other. Try to be original but realistic.

In response to a perceived shortcoming of the behaviourists' explanation, Bandura adopted a cognitive approach to studying learning. In his book *Social Foundations of Thought and Action: A Social Cognitive Theory,* published in 1986, he refers to his theory of learning as social cognitive theory as opposed to social learning theory. **Bandura (1986)** adopted the assumption that the mind could be studied scientifically and therefore attempted to shed light into the "black box" of the mind. Although on the surface this may seem like a simple change, when he focused his theory of learning on human cognition, the theory became far more complex and better able to explain learning processes.

Behaviourist model

Cognitive model

▲ Figure 4.9 Bandura's social cognitive theory

Source: https://www.simplypsychology.org/bandura.html

Instead of simply stimulus–behaviour, Bandura's theory encourages researchers to examine the complex thought processes that occur between observation and behaviour: stimulus–*cognition*–behaviour. Bandura calls this an **agentic approach** to studying learning. To be an agent means to:

- have control over behaviour

- develop intentions and forethought—be able to visualize future behaviours

- regulate behaviour—do things that give satisfaction and reward while avoiding things that result in negative outcomes

- reflect on capabilities and goals—be self-aware and think about self-efficacy and the soundness of behaviour (Bandura, 2001).

Together, these factors describe the cognitive part of Bandura's cognitive theory of learning. In other words, human beings are agents in their own lives; we do not simply react to the world around us (behaviourist model). We pay attention to the people and events around us, interpret their behaviour (including rewards and punishments), design a plan considering our abilities and goals, and behave in a way that will bring about a desired outcome. It is in this way that we can learn from the mistakes and success of others (**vicarious learning**) as well as the reinforcements experienced by others (**vicarious reinforcement**). In evaluating the actions and consequences of behaviour performed by other people, individuals are able to learn without the need to perform an observed behaviour themselves.

Bandura broke down his social cognitive theory into four components; attention, retention, reproduction and motivation. Each one of these can be seen as a cognitive process.

Attention (observation)

In *Social Learning Theory* (1977), Bandura argues that instead of learning by trial and error, people learn their ways of thinking and behaving by paying attention to how others think and behave. He called this **observational learning**: learning that takes place by observing others. The stimuli that serve to expose learners (or observers) to particular behaviours are the models in the social environment. The people with whom an individual normally associates will determine, to a large extent, the types of modelling the individual is exposed to. A child born into an abusive family in a dangerous neighbourhood is more likely to be exposed to aggressive and violent models and so to aggressive and violent behaviours. Conversely, a child who is exposed only to pacifist and non-violent models will likely engage in pacifist and non-violent behaviour.

Bandura is most well known for a series of experiments carried out in the 1960s, starting with the key study **Bandura, Ross and Ross (1961)**. These experiments used a large inflatable doll as the object of aggression for a model while children observed model acting aggressively towards the doll. Collectively, these are known as the **bobo doll experiments.**

Aggression has long been the focus of social cognitive theory. In 1961, Bandura and colleagues

223

tested his social cognitive theory on 72 children (36 girls and 36 boys) between the ages of 3 and 6 enrolled at Stanford University's Nursery School (Bandura, Ross and Ross, 1961). The children were first split up into three groups (see Figure 4.10). One group was exposed to an adult aggressively playing with a bobo doll, a second group was exposed to an adult engaged in non-aggressive play and a third group was not given a model to observe. The children were rated on their aggressiveness by their nursery school teachers prior to the experiment to control for equal amounts of pre-exposure aggressiveness in each group.

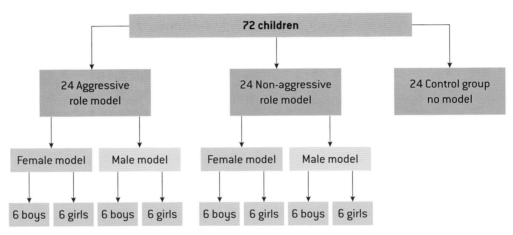

▲ Figure 4.10 Method for Bandura, Ross and Ross (1961) bobo doll experiment

Source: https://www.simplypsychology.org/bobo-doll.html

In both the aggressive and the non-aggressive conditions, a child was seated in one corner of a room while a model was escorted by the experimenter to another corner. The child was given prints and stickers to play with. The model's corner contained a Tinkertoy set, a mallet and a 1.5-metre tall bobo doll. (A bobo doll is an inflatable doll with a weight in the bottom so that the doll will right itself after being hit.) Once the model and the child were seated and playing, the experimenter left the room.

In the non-aggressive condition, the model ignored the doll and played quietly with the toys. In the aggressive condition, the model played briefly with the toys before turning to the bobo doll and "aggressing toward it" both verbally and physically for the rest of the time. The model hit the bobo doll in unique and novel ways so that "imitation" could be identified as opposed to unrelated but also aggressive play. After 10 minutes, the child was taken by the experimenter to another room.

At this point each of the children underwent an "instigation to aggression" stage where the child was given time to engage with attractive toys but separated from these toys once he or she became interested and began playing with them. At this point the child was told that he or she could play with toys in the adjoining room. This was the experimental room containing several toys similar to the first room, including a 1-metre tall bobo doll. The experimenter at this point remained in the room but worked quietly at a desk in the corner for the 20-minute session.

| Response category | Experimental groups | | | | Control groups |
| | Aggressive | | Non-aggressive | | |
	F Model	M Model	F Model	M Model	
Imitative physical aggression					
Female subjects	5.5	7.2	2.5	0.0	1.2
Male subjects	12.4	25.8	0.2	1.5	2.0
Imitative verbal aggression					
Female subjects	13.7	2.0	0.3	0.0	0.7
Male subjects	4.3	12.7	1.1	0.0	1.7
Mallet aggression					
Female subjects	17.2	18.7	0.5	0.5	13.1
Male subjects	15.5	28.8	18.7	6.7	13.5
Punches bobo doll					
Female subjects	6.3	16.5	5.8	4.3	11.7
Male subjects	18.9	11.9	15.6	14.8	15.7
Non-imitative aggression					
Female subjects	21.3	8.4	7.2	1.4	6.1
Male subjects	16.2	36.7	26.1	22.3	24.6
Aggressive gun play					
Female subjects	1.8	4.5	2.6	2.5	3.7
Male subjects	7.3	15.9	8.9	16.7	14.3

▲ Table 4.6 Mean aggression scores for experimental and control subjects

Source: Bandura, Ross and Ross (1961)

Results for this experiment supported the hypothesis that exposure of children to aggressive models would increase aggressiveness among the children (see Table 4.6). According to the researchers, this was clear confirmation of observational learning.

In addition, the researchers discovered that boys were more likely to imitate physical aggression while girls were more likely to imitate verbal aggression. Boys were also more aggressive than girls in all groups.

See video

Watch this video on social cognitive learning: https://www.youtube.com/watch?v=128Ts5r9NRE

Simply exposing someone to a model is not enough for learning to take place. The observer has to **pay attention** to the model and recognize a specific behaviour upon which to focus attention. Without due attention, observers will not learn behaviour. Related to this is the idea that some models command more attention than others and therefore interpersonal attraction is a component of modelling. For example, a child is more likely to model the behaviour of a close family member or of a particularly close peer over more distant relatives or an unfriendly peer. One exception noted by Bandura is televised models, who seem to hold attention despite the lack of social cohesion between model and observer (Bandura, 2005).

In 1963, Bandura partially replicated the 1961 bobo doll experiment. He used mediated violence (in the form of aggressive adult models on film, rather than live) and found that observing children exhibited the same learned aggression toward the doll. This has important ramifications for the effect of mediated violence on children.

For more on this see Unit 3 on the cognitive approach to behaviour, HL extension "Cognitive processing in the digital world".

Retention, reproduction, motivation (cognitions)

Related to the concept of attention is **retention**—Bandura stated, perhaps obviously, that observers have to remember what behaviour was observed in order to repeat it. This is important in instances when imitation of the learned behaviour is delayed.

Reproduction of a task is affected by self-efficacy. Self-efficacy is the belief that you are able to accomplish a task. High self-efficacy means you are optimistic and confident that you will be able to accomplish a task successfully; low self-efficacy or low confidence is the opposite (see Unit 6 on health psychology for more on this). People tend not to try something if they expect failure, so a belief that you are capable of successfully reproducing an observed behaviour is an important component of social cognitive/learning theory.

Bandura (2012) identified four sources of self-efficacy.

- **Mastery experiences**—past success reinforces the belief that further success is possible but failure (especially if it occurs before efficacy is achieved) reduces belief in a successful outcome.

- **Vicarious experiences**—this is where models are so important because seeing others, similar to themselves, succeed by sustained effort will raise observers' beliefs in their ability to carry out an action or behaviour successfully.

- **Social persuasion**—people who are convinced by others that they possess the ability to succeed at a given action or behaviour are likely to make a greater effort and to sustain it longer than those who receive either negative social reinforcement or none at all.

- **Emotional and physical states**—positive mood improves perceived self-efficacy and hopeless or sad moods can diminish it (Bandura, 1994).

TOK

Research on the impact of visualization and imagery training (using your imagination to picture yourself performing a task) has shown that imagination can be as effective as practising a skill physically (Jones *et al*, 2002). Researchers examined the effect of imagery script on a group of novice rock climbers.

Novice climbers were randomly assigned to either a control group who took part in a light exercise programme, or an experimental group who were exposed to a scripted imagery training programme. After the participants went through their respective training, they climbed a 5.1-metre high wall following a designated route. Levels of self-efficacy and stress were measured before and during the climb. There was no significant difference in climbing performance, but the experimental group reported lower levels of perceived stress and higher levels of self-efficacy as compared to the control group.

This study shows that imagining practising a task can reduce stress and improve self-efficacy, adding another source of self-efficacy to the list generated by Bandura in 1994. Do you think this research supports the concept of imagination as a way of knowing? What makes you say that?

Motivation to perform an action or demonstrate behaviour has a lot to do with **reinforcement**. If people perform an action and are rewarded for it, they are likely to be motivated to repeat the action. Similarly, if they are punished, they are not likely to repeat the action. So reinforcement (through **rewards or punishments**) can influence a person's motivation to act.

Similar to learning, reinforcement can be effective both directly and indirectly. We can learn through reinforcement of our own actions or through observing the reinforcement of others.

In a 1965 partial replication of Bandura and his colleagues' 1961 and 1963 studies, researchers sought to examine the role of reinforcement in the social learning of aggression. In this version, children watched a film where an adult model was acting aggressively toward a bobo doll. The children were separated into three conditions.

1. **Control:** the children witnessed the aggression without reward or punishment.

2. **Reward:** the children witnessed the aggression followed by the model being rewarded for the aggressive acts with candies and a soft drink.

3. **Punishment:** the children witnessed the aggression followed by the model being punished for the aggressive acts with a scolding and spanking.

After viewing the film, the children were observed in a playroom with toys similar to the ones used by the adult model in the film. It was found that the children in condition 3 performed significantly fewer aggressive acts than children in conditions 1 and 2 (Bandura, 1965).

Further support for Bandura's theory

Bandura's theory has been tested beyond the strict conditions of experimentation: it has been used to explain behaviour in the real world. Social cognitive theory has been effective in explaining marital violence. Violence is a learned behaviour and it has been accepted for many years that there is an intergenerational transmission of violence. **Mihalic and Elliott (1997)**. found that males and females who endured more physical violence as children had higher rates of marital violence as adults. Social cognitive theory is able to explain why this is. During childhood, observing how parents and other models behave in relationships provides an initial learning of behaviours that are "appropriate" for these relationships. Implicit in the act of violence is an understanding of that behaviour as socially acceptable, especially when the behaviour is rewarded with the achievement of a goal.

Other research, examining the cognitive determinants of aggressive behaviour in school children, found that perceived self-efficacy and reinforcement (punishment or reward) were both key in determining behaviour. In one study by **Perry, Perry and Rasmussen (1986)**, 160 children were sampled and categorized as either aggressive or not aggressive. Children were given two questionnaires, one measuring perceptions of self-efficacy in avoiding aggressive actions and the other measuring **outcome expectations** (that is, whether the children expected reward or punishment following the action). It was found that "aggressive children" found it easier

to engage in aggressive behaviour and more difficult to inhibit aggressive impulses. "Aggressive children" were also more confident that aggressive behaviour would produce rewards rather than punishments.

Interestingly, the researchers found that there were very few differences between the sexes on the perceived self-efficacy questionnaire but large differences on the outcome expectations questionnaire. Girls were more likely to expect that aggression would cause suffering in the victim and that the aggression would be punished more severely by peers. Conclusions from this study point toward the importance of self-efficacy and perceived reinforcement (rewards or punishments) as cognitive determinants of social learning in relation to the antisocial behaviour of aggression.

Social cognitive theory can also be used to explain the learning of prosocial behaviours. Using a sample of 647 kindergarteners (325 boys, 322 girls), **Sheridan et al (2011)** examined the perceived effectiveness of social cognitive theory in teaching children four skills: listening, following directions, problem-solving and knowing when to tell. A widely recognized programme called "Skillstream", developed by McGinnis and Goldstein, was used. This programme uses modelling, role-playing, performance feedback and generalization to encourage prosocial behaviour. In Sheridan et al (2011) results showed significant improvements in all skills. Additionally, classroom teachers as well as mental health staff reported overall improved sociability among the students. Conclusions from this study suggest that learning prosocial skills can be explained through social cognitive theory.

ATL skills: Thinking

Bandura's bobo doll studies were experiments undertaken in a laboratory with strictly controlled variables—arguably a very unnatural environment.

Can a social phenomenon that normally takes place within a complex set of social relationships ever be studied in such a contrived and controlled situation? In other words, do experiments on social learning lack ecological validity?

Digital technology and social learning

McLuhan believed that electronic media serve to extend humanities senses; for example, radio extended our ears and television our eyes. He also argued that it is not the content of a medium that affects human behaviour but the form of the medium itself. This, now famous, idea is summed up perfectly in McLuhan's quip that "the medium is the message" (McLuhan, 1964). In other words, it is not what is on the radio, television or the internet that is of interest, but the form and function of the medium that will change individuals and societies. The content of a medium is just "the juicy piece of meat carried by the burglar to distract the watchdog of the mind" (McLuhan, 1964, cited in Carr, 2011).

If we examine this effect through the lens of international cultural products, we see that from a receiver's perspective this could be seen as an insidious threat to national culture. Not only is the content of most western television culturally skewed toward western values, but the actual delivery system of the values also represents those foreign cultural components of consumerism, mass communications and all of the myriad gatekeepers who go along with it.

More recently, Carr (2011) wrote about this idea. Using some of the greatest minds in history, starting with Plato, Carr argues that the internet encourages scanning and skimming at the cost of concentration, contemplation and reflection. Essentially, he argues that the combination of neuroplasticity and repetitive interactions online are reshaping our brains.

For more on this see Unit 3 on the cognitive approach to behaviour, HL extension "Cognitive processing in the digital world".

The individual and the group—social identity theory and stereotyping

Inquiry questions

- What happens when cultures collide?
- Why do some people find it difficult to welcome those fleeing war or persecution?
- What kinds of challenges are faced by refugees or migrants once they arrive in their new culture?
- How do we come to understand others?

What you will learn in this section

- Social cognition
  - Principles of social cognition
- Attribution theories
  - Correspondent inference theory
  - Covariation model
  - Causal schemata model
- Errors in attribution
  - Fundamental attribution error
  - Ultimate attribution error
  - Taylor and Jaggi (1974): ethnocentrism and causal attribution
- The development and effect of stereotypes
  - Social schemas
  - Theories of stereotype formation
  - Self-fulfilling prophecy
  - Stereotype threat
- Social identity theory
  - Tajfel and Turner (1979): theory of inter-group conflict

- Sherif (1954): realistic conflict theory
- Acculturation: a process of psychological and cultural change as a result of contact and interaction between cultures
  - Why do cultures change?
  - Assimilation, integration, separation and marginalization
- Acculturative stress: biopsychosocial difficulties when adapting to a new cultural context

This section also links to:

- schema theory, thinking and decision-making, biases in thinking and decision-making (cognitive approach to behaviour)
- acculturative stress, obesity (health psychology)
- developmental psychology
- the influence of globalization on individual behaviour.

Social cognition

What is social cognition?

Social cognition is the study of how people understand their social world: their thinking, their actions and the environment in which their behaviour occurs. In order to make sense of the world we are required to engage in three cognitive processes. According to **Baron and Byrne (1997)** we must first *interpret* the information that we receive about other people by examining it within its social context and giving it meaning alongside our previous knowledge of the person or situation. We must then *analyse* the initial appraisal and modify it accordingly. For example, your first impression of a new teacher may not be favourable but as you become more familiar with the teacher you may adjust your perception of that person and maybe of yourself. Finally, you must be able to *recall* previous knowledge and experiences at the appropriate time. Our memory plays a crucial role in helping us make sense of our world.

We can all to some extent be considered social psychologists attempting to understand ourselves and others (Nisbett and Ross, 1980). We create our own theories of human behaviour and apply them to those we meet. We are what **Heider (1958)** terms "naive scientists", individuals who try to link observable behaviours to unobservable causes. We interpret the meaning of the behaviour based upon these causes rather than the behaviour itself. More formally, psychologists studying social cognition investigate areas such as impression formation, impression management, attribution and attribution bias, stereotype formation, prejudice and discrimination within the laboratory and in a more naturalistic setting.

The principles of social cognition

Gross (2001) and Fiske and Taylor (1991) claim that when studying social cognition researchers have made a number of assumptions about the thinking person, including the following.

- **People are cognitive misers** (Fiske and Taylor, 1991): humans are limited in their ability and capacity to process information. Accuracy may be sacrificed in favour of making a quick decision.

- **Humans engage in both automatic and controlled thinking:** when faced with a familiar or repetitive situation, such as entering a restaurant, people often rely on automatic thinking processes as this requires less time and effort; however, spontaneous thinking can often result in making mistakes. (links to Tversky and Kahneman, biases in thinking and decision-making.)

- **Humans seek consistency in behaviour:** this is best illustrated by Festinger's cognitive dissonance theory. When individuals hold two conflicting thoughts or cognitions they experience a level of discomfort or dissonance. For example, the two thoughts might be: "I like eating cake" and "Cake makes me fat". To reduce or eliminate the discomfort the individuals need to make their behaviour consistent with their cognition by discarding, self-justifying or modifying the inconsistent cognition.

- **Self-esteem guides human behaviour:** people with a high level of self-esteem will often view themselves in a more positive light and this may

improve their performance on cognitive tasks or in social situations. People with low self-esteem can often have a negative view of themselves and, as a result, they underperform on cognitive tasks and lack the motivation to engage in social situations. We will explore this further when discussing the formation of stereotypes and discrimination between ingroups and outgroups.

Attribution theories

At the most basic level, when interpreting the behaviour of others we tend to attribute the cause of the action to **personal (dispositional)** and **situational (external)** factors. We look for consistency, intentionality and the most simple or accessible explanation. This can explain the way in which many stereotypes are formed as we generalize an individual's behaviour to a whole population based on a false or erroneous attribution. Before discussing how attribution errors can contribute to the formation and maintenance of stereotypes, we will first provide some context by exploring attribution theories.

Note: it is important to bear in mind that attribution theory will not be tested in the examination and has been included only to extend understanding of the area of social cognition. Understanding attribution theory will facilitate understanding of errors in attribution discussed later in this section.

Heider's commonsense psychology inspired a number of psychologists to develop their own more structured theories that aimed to make sense of how we interpret the world. These are known as attribution theories.

Correspondent inference theory

Imagine that you wake up late one morning and your usual news programme has already started. The current report is discussing an attack involving a suicide bomber who has killed himself and 30 others in a shopping mall. If your initial thought is that the man is an evil murderer then you have made what **Jones and Davis (1965)** called a correspondent inference. The personality characteristic that you have given this man corresponds to the behaviour itself (murder is evil). Should you have been so quick to judge, though? After all, you missed the beginning of the news report. What if the bomber was forced to wear a suicide vest against his will? Would that have changed the disposition that you attributed to him? Jones and Davis (1965) claim that we will only make a dispositional attribution when we are 100% certain that an action was intentional.

Jones and Davis (1965) argue that the following factors will affect the likelihood of making dispositional attributions.

- **Hedonic relevance**—the behaviour positively or negatively affects the person making the attribution.

- **Free choice**—if the person chose to act out of his or her own free will then we are more likely to make a dispositional attribution.

- **Social desirability**—most of us aim to act in ways that are considered socially desirable. As desirable behaviour can be considered the norm, it doesn't tell us very much about a person. Undesirable behaviour, however, can give us a lot more information as it may be unexpected and it may shock us.

The covariation model

A more widely applicable model is the covariation model as it takes both dispositional (internal) and situational (external) factors into account. The covariation model makes use of our prior knowledge of an individual and how the person has acted in similar situations (see Figure 4.11).

Kelley (1967) claims that we utilize three types of information when making attributions.

- Consensus—the extent to which other people respond in the same way to a stimulus or situation.

- Consistency—the extent to which people respond in the same or similar manner to a given situation.

- Distinctiveness—the extent to which the behaviour varies in typical responses to similar stimuli.

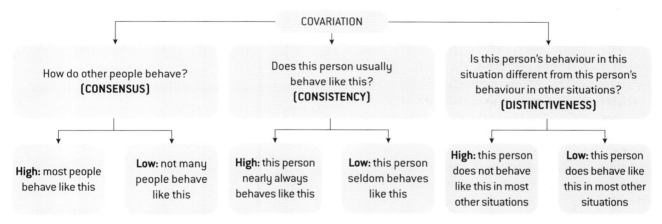

▲ Figure 4.11 The covariation model

We attribute high or low value to each type of information and consider the causal relationship by examining a behaviour over time. According to Kelley (1967), we make attributions with a combination of consensus, consistency and distinctiveness information.

This is best illustrated with an example, as attributions about behaviour depend on the extent to which they covary with each of the types of information outlined above. Anders is an IB psychology student seeking help with one of his essays. He approaches his teacher during his break to seek advice and discuss his concerns about the assignment. If Anders has sought advice during his breaks before then consistency is high, if this is the first time then consistency is low. Consensus is assessed by looking at whether other students also seek help from the teacher. If they do then consensus is high. Finally, does Anders also seek help in mathematics and science, or is it just in psychology? If he seeks help in all subjects then distinctiveness is low and there is nothing out of the ordinary about Anders' behaviour.

ATL skills: Thinking

Consider other combinations of information in this scenario. What would a combination of low consistency, high consensus and high distinctiveness reveal about Anders' behaviour?

Consider the above example. Thinking about Anders' behaviour required engagement in a conscious thought process in order to make a causal attribution. Not all of the information may be available in certain situations. It has been claimed that we are most likely to be exposed to all three types of information when we experience an unexpected or negative event (Baron and Byrne, 1997). The example above also required comparing Anders' behaviour to previous situations and to that of other students. The model is therefore less useful when considering a single or novel event.

Causal schemata model

When we are making causal attributions about people that we do not know, we will not be able to utilize the three types of information outlined in the covariation model (see Figure 4.11). Kelley claimed that in these situations we rely upon our "causal schemata" when making attributions. Causal schemata are our preconceived ideas or theories about the causes of an event or behaviour, based on past or similar experience. As cognitive misers, we tend to generalize a behaviour from one situation into another in order to save time and effort in making sense of it.

Using causal schemata allows quick attributions to be made when there is a lack of relevant information. Causal schemata can, however, reflect the views held by our society and culture at a given point in time. This may influence our own stereotypical views of an individual or group of people and therefore be incorrect. There are many factors that influence the attribution process: the amount of information that we have about an individual, our culture and our desire to cut corners as cognitive misers. It is not surprising, therefore, that our attributions are often biased or erroneous, and one way that psychologists have attempted to study the accuracy of attribution models is to investigate the extent to which individuals conform to any given model.

Errors in attribution

The fundamental attribution error (FAE)

Think back to the imaginary news report introduced earlier about the suicide bomber. As we all agree that killing innocent civilians in a shopping mall is an evil act, we may be quick to label this attacker an evil man and allocate many negative dispositional qualities or attributions. We have ignored any situational factors that may have led up to and/or caused this terrible event. This error in attribution may lead to a false judgment or stereotype being developed and generalized about an individual or group of people. Errors in attribution can, therefore, be considered one explanation of stereotype formation.

By focusing solely on the dispositional characteristics of this person and ignoring or excluding possible situational (external) factors, we have committed the **fundamental attribution error (FAE)**. The FAE refers to the tendency to overestimate the importance of dispositional factors and underestimate the importance of external or situational factors when attempting to explain the behaviour of others (Ross and Nisbett, 1991). This error has been demonstrated in multiple laboratory experiments that highlight the range of situations in which people may make this error.

Jones and Harris (1967) conducted three experiments in which participants had to try to estimate the "true attitude" of a person in relation to a controversial topic. Participants either read or listened to a speech concerning the rule of Cuba by Fidel Castro. The authors of the speeches had been allocated to either a pro-Castro condition, anti-Castro condition or "free choice" condition. Despite being well aware that authors had been allocated to each condition by the researchers, listeners and readers inferred a correspondence between the author's private views and the anti-Castro views expressed in the speech. This showed how they overestimated the importance of dispositional factors.

Another example of the FAE can be seen in an often-cited study conducted by Ross, Amabile and Steinmetz (1977). Participants played a quiz game and were assigned roles of "questioner" and "contestant". Questioners were allowed to create their own questions, drawing on their own personal knowledge. When asked to rate levels of general knowledge at the end of the study, participants rated the questioners as having higher levels of general knowledge than the contestants. Both uninvolved observers and the contestants themselves made this dispositional attribution.

Pettigrew (1979) highlights three common elements in these experimental displays of FAE.

- Powerful situational forces were minimized (with the experimenters' instructions and the quiz game format).

- Internal, dispositional characteristics of the salient person (the communicator and the questioner) are magnified.

- Role requirements (being an experimental subject or a quiz contestant) are not fully adjusted for in the final attribution.

Jones and Nisbett (1971) explained the FAE by highlighting that we have different information available to us when we are trying to explain our own behaviour over that of someone else. As we may not know what someone else is thinking, or the person's previous actions in similar scenarios, we focus on what we can see—the person's behaviour. It is clear that we view our own worlds and behaviour differently from that of others; therefore, our attributions reflect this.

Cross-cultural research has, however, made the important discovery that the FAE is not universal (Fletcher and Ward, 1988) and that in cultures such as in India, where family ties are strong and individuals' social position may be controlled, people may in fact be more likely to make situational attributions (Miller, 1984).

The ultimate attribution error (UAE)

"We live in a social environment which is in constant flux. Much of what happens to us is related to the activities of groups to which we do or do not belong; and the changing relations between these groups require constant readjustments of our understanding of what happens and constant causal attributions about the why and the how of the changing conditions of our life."

(Tajfel, 1969)

There is a plethora of research on attribution theory and errors on an individual level, but a limited amount concerning attribution on the intergroup level. Pettigrew's (1979) **ultimate attribution error (UAE)** is considered an extension of the FAE (Heider, 1958; Ross, 1977) involving the tendency to underestimate situational factors and overestimate personal factors as causes of a behaviour at a group level. Pettigrew claimed that the UAE served as to defend a negative stereotype of a perceived outgroup by attributing negative attributions for the behaviour of outgroup members. The UAE may therefore serve as a more appropriate account for how stereotypes are formed and maintained at an intergroup level where contact is less frequent and the stereotypes are often negative. When an outgroup member is seen to perform a negative act that is consistent with the observers' negative view, there is an increased tendency to attribute internal or dispositional attributions—and so maintain or reinforce the negative stereotype. A problem arises when an outgroup member is seen acting in a positive manner that doesn't conform to the existing negative stereotype (Hewstone, 1990). Pettigrew claimed that in these cases the positive acts are considered to be exceptions to the norm or a product of luck or chance. Subsequently, the negative stereotype is maintained.

Pettigrew claimed that prejudiced individuals are most likely to make this error, and increasingly so when they are aware of their own group's behaviours. Groups that have negative histories or conflict with each other are more likely to display the UAE. This seems observable in the daily news when we observe intergroup conflicts between Arabs and Israelis, Indians and Pakistanis in Kashmir or race relations in the USA.

Research in focus: (Taylor and Jaggi, 1974)

Taylor and Jaggi (1974) conducted the first study on inter-group casual attribution, using Hindu people in southern India. There is a history of conflict between the Hindu and Muslim population in the area, which provided the inter-group context for the research.

The researchers formed these hypotheses.

- Hindu participants would attribute positive behaviours of the ingroup to internal factors and attribute positive behaviours of the outgroups to external factors.

Research in focus (continued)

- Hindu participants would attribute positive behaviours of the ingroup to external factors and attribute negative behaviours of the outgroup to internal factors.

In stage 1 of the study, participants were asked to give an initial rating for the concept "Hindu" (self-judgment) and "Muslim" on 12 evaluative characteristics. They then read 16 one-paragraph descriptions.

In stage 2, participants imagined a story in which they were in either socially desirable or socially undesirable situations with either another Hindu (ingroup) or Muslim (outgroup). Participants had to then explain the behaviour of the individual from a choice of an internal (dispositional) or external (situational) attribution.

In all cases, Hindu participants were increasingly likely to attribute positive behaviours associated to their ingroup to internal factors than they were to attribute socially undesirable behaviour to internal factors. However, when participants were rating the behaviour of the outgroup they attributed socially desirable behaviour to internal factors 50% of the time.

The researchers concluded that there were great differences in how causal attributions were made between groups. Internal attribution for socially desirable behaviours was higher for ingroup actors in the stories. For socially undesirable behaviour, internal attribution was lower for ingroup actors than for outgroup actors in the stories.

Discussion

The results from Taylor and Jaggi (1974) seem to be closely related to Tajfel's social identity theory and the self-serving bias whereby achieving and maintaining self-esteem is very important.

Do you think UAE can be understood as a group-based self-serving bias? What makes you think that?

Hewstone (1990) reviews 19 articles on the UAE and claims that, while there is some support for the claims made by Pettigrew, the evidence is in fact limited. Hewstone therefore prefers to label the UAE as an "inter-group attributional bias".

The work on the ultimate attribution error has been heavily influenced by the research of Heider, Ross and Tajfel. Later in this unit Tajfel's research will be discussed in more depth.

Duncan (1976) conducted what is considered a more ecologically valid study. White American college students viewed a video recording of a violent interaction where one participant pushed the other. The researchers manipulated the race of the "protagonist" and the "victim". Participants were required to attribute the violent behaviour to either: (1) situational factors, (2) dispositional factors, (3) related specifically to the topic under discussion or (4) a combination of all these factors. Results highlighted a strong inter-group effect.

When the protagonist was black his behaviour was attributed more to dispositional factors than was the case for a white protagonist. The conclusion was that in the black protagonist condition more dispositional than situational attributions were made. The reverse was true in the white protagonist condition. The results therefore provide limited support for the UEA.

ATL skills: Research

Locate the following articles. These are often cited and given details of what is considered classic research in the field of impression formation and implicit personality theory.

- Asch. SE. 1946. "Forming impressions of personality". *Journal of Abnormal & Social Psychology*. Vol 41. Pp 258–290.
- Kelley, HH. 1950. "The warm-cold variable in first impressions of people". *Journal of Personality*. Vol 18. Pp 431–439.
- Luchin, AS. 1957. "Primacy-recency in impression formation" in C Hovland (ed.) *The Order of Presentation in Persuasion*. New Haven, Connecticut, USA. Yale University Press.

What are the main conclusions of this research?

How does this research develop our understanding of the individual and the group?

Stereotypes

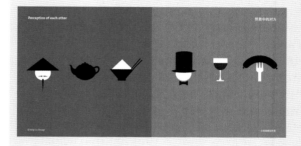

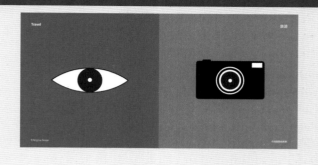
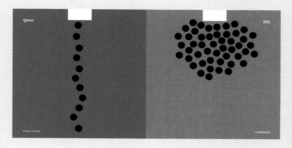
Discussion

Do you agree with Yang Liu's interpretation of these eastern and western cultures? What makes you say that? Discuss your views with a partner.

The term "stereotype" was first used in a psychological sense by Lippmann (1922) who defined stereotypes as "little pictures in our heads that help us interpret what we see". Aronson (2008) claims that when we stereotype we allow these pictures to dominate our thinking, causing us to assign identical characteristics to any person in a group, regardless of the variation among members of that group.

We all have images in our heads or cultural stereotypes of people that we think encapsulates their cultural identity and therefore individual behaviour. For example, if I asked you to imagine and draw a Frenchman, you may picture something like the image opposite, despite never having seen a Frenchman wearing this outfit.

So, where do these stereotypes come from and why do we use them? After all, it is clear that social stereotypes are grossly over-simplified and generalized abstractions that people share about their own group and another group (Oakes, Haslam and Turner 1994; Hogg and Vaughan, 1995).

▲ Figure 4.12 A common stereotype of a Frenchman

235

The fact is that stereotyping is inevitable and should not necessarily be considered a bad thing. We learn to assign characteristics to other groups from a very young age as it helps us to organize and make sense of the world around us. (See schema theory in Unit 3 on the cognitive approach to behaviour for more on this.)

Assigning stereotypes often takes place unconsciously and automatically. We place people into categories based upon our previous experiences with similar people using our existing **schemas**. Jean Piaget pioneered research in childhood development of schemas.

Using our schemas can allow us to respond to novel or unexpected situations more quickly. More commonly however, we consider stereotyping to be a negative process as it can cause us to ignore differences between individual members of a group, and can lead to biased or unfair treatment in the form of prejudice and discrimination.

In 2016, Donald Trump famously referred to a negative stereotype of Mexican people as part of his political campaign. See http://time.com/4473972/donald-trump-mexico-meeting-insult/ for some of Trump's comments. Similarly, the UK's Brexit campaign portrayed a negative impression of many immigrants and refugees, linking them to loss of jobs and a threat to national identity. As a result, the world was exposed to a very negative view of these specific demographics, which in turn resulted in an increase in reported hate crimes and overt prejudice.

This highlights that our schemas can be affected and subsequently updated by exposure to new first-hand personal experiences and information gathered from watching the news, movies and television shows. For example, popular television shows such as *Homeland* and *House of Cards* expose us to a very stereotypical view of Islam. This type of influence highlights the important role of **gatekeepers** in schema formation. Having recently been exposed to a new or alternative experience, your newly updated schema will be more easily accessible than those that have not been accessed for a while. **Accessibility** refers to the ease with which you can use your schema due to the fact that the memories have been retrieved recently. Schemas that relate to repeated personal experience, those that relate to a current goal or those that have recently been primed are all likely to be easily accessible. **Priming** refers to the process by which your recent personal experience increases the accessibility of a schema. For example, watching Donald Trump talk about Mexicans is likely to increase your accessibility to your own schema about Mexican people.

ATL skills: Research

Joel Parés, a former US Marine who became a photographer, created a series of photographs to present us with characters symbolic of the prejudices suffered by various groups based on their ethnicity, socio-economic status or sexual preference.

Do these images challenge your existing stereotypes? What makes you say that?

Parés told PetaPixel:

Many of us judge incorrectly by someone's ethnicity, by their profession, and by their sexual interest. The purpose of this series is to open our eyes and make us think twice before judging someone, because we all judge even if we try not to.

Where do stereotypes come from?

One idea about where stereotypes originate is the **grain of truth hypothesis.** Think back to the infographics by Yang Liu that you saw earlier. Whether you agreed with them or not is likely to have been affected by your own personal experience. For example, you may have accessed a memory of a holiday when you saw a Chinese tourist taking lots of pictures, or a German drinking beer, and this will have influenced your viewpoint. If you shared your view of these images with one of your friends, you will have shaped their view of a group of people by sharing your personal experiences with them. The discussion and subsequent stereotype therefore started with a small "grain of truth" (Allport, 1954). By communicating your experiences, you may have in essence helped to create and spread a new stereotype. The reality is, however, that a single experience of one person from a particular demographic is not enough to make a sweeping generalization to the entire group. We still we do it, though. Trump may have met one Mexican drug dealer (although that is unlikely), but he cannot and should not generalize to a large population.

Another factor is the formation of **illusory correlations**. It is common for people to see two variables as related when they are not. This is known as an illusory correlation. Common examples of illusory correlations include:

- a student believing that all Asians are good at mathematics because he sits next to a very able Asian mathematics student

- a woman believing that all pit bull dogs are dangerous because she has read one article on an aggressive pit bull

- a footballer putting his left boot on first before every match because he scored a goal the first time he did this.

Illusory correlations are relevant to stereotyping because group stereotypes can become viewed as perceived correlations between the group and a trait and/or behaviour—the correlations are illusory because they are falsely being understood as actual correlations.

For example, an individual may perceive a minority group as more likely to engage in a negative behaviour than a majority group, and therefore implicitly perceive a correlation between that individual's group membership and behaviour. It has been discovered that when we view another group's behaviour we pay attention to the most distinctive form of information. This is likely to be because this is the information that is most accessible to us and will therefore be the most likely form of information to influence the illusory correlation. We are rarely exposed to behaviours that do not conform to our society's norms or expectations and so it is not surprising that when we do experience a negative behaviour, we may associate it with a minority group. This may result in an unfairly negative stereotype of a minority group being formed. For example, a white boy may see a black boy screaming and shouting in public and correlate this violent verbal behaviour to the shouting boy's ethnicity. The white boy may then generalize this behaviour to the group and create the stereotype that all black people are violent.

A classic study conducted by **Hamilton and Gifford (1976)** researched how our expectations of events can distort how we process the information. Participants had to read descriptions of various people from two imaginary groups: group A and group B. Group A was considerably larger than group B. The readings contained descriptions of the individual's group membership and a specific behaviour. The behaviours were either helpful or harmful. For example, a teacher called John, a member of group B, screams at his students. Nick, a member of group A, helps at his local church. When asked to give their impressions of a typical group member, participants considered the behaviour of group B members (the minority) to be considerably less desirable than members of group A. There was no actual correlation between group membership and desirability and so participants were making an illusory correlation.

Schaller (1991) conducted a similar experiment with 141 US university students. Participants were told that the experiment was investigating how people perceive information about others. They again read sentences about members of two distinct groups, groups A and B. They were informed that there were fewer members of group B and so they would be reading fewer descriptions of group B members. Participants were then assigned group membership to either group A or group B. There was a control condition where no group membership was assigned. Participants were asked to read individual statements that contained information about the group membership of an individual and a specific desirable or undesirable behaviour. After reading all the statements, they were given questionnaires to answer that would assess the extent to which they perceived a relationship between group membership and behaviour. The findings clearly supported the hypothesis that being placed into a group would influence the processing of information and that participants would display positive discrimination in favour of their own ingroup. This social categorization effect is central to the understanding of social identity theory and can help explain how we form stereotypes and discriminate against others.

Social cognitive theory provides an explanation for the formation of stereotypes as a learned behaviour. This theory also relies upon gatekeeper theory to explain from whom the stereotype formation is learned.

Effects of stereotypes
Self-fulfilling prophecy

Schemas and stereotypes can cause people to change the way that they think about themselves and influence their behaviour. In some instances people can unconsciously change their behaviour, causing the schema to become true. This is called the self-fulfilling prophecy. People have a perception about how others will behave and as such treat them differently. The way in which they treat individuals causes those individuals to change their behaviour in such a way that the original expectation becomes true.

Rosenthal and Jacobson (1968) conducted a classic study that demonstrated the self-fulfilling prophecy. Teachers in an elementary school were told by researchers that certain students were likely to be "growth spurters" or academic "bloomers" in the next academic year based upon results of an academic test. The test did not actually exist and the students predicted to be "bloomers" were chosen at random. Any difference between students was therefore in how they were now perceived by their teachers. The researchers observed the classroom dynamics throughout the year and at the end of the year the students were given an IQ test. Students that were labelled as "bloomers" demonstrated an increase in IQ,

gaining higher scores than their peers. It appears that the teachers' perceptions of the students' ability affected the way that the teachers interacted with the students, making the predictions of students' ability become true. Later studies have discovered that teachers create a warmer learning environment for "bloomers", allowing them more time to answer questions. They also give "bloomers" more and better feedback on their completed assignments (Brophy, 1983; Snyder, 1984).

When looking at this research we must consider what happens if we apply a label to a group of people on the societal level. If we consider women less able at mathematics or African Americans less able at science it may affect their future life chances. Few opportunities in these areas may be offered to them and this may affect future job prospects and earning potential. With fewer women and African Americans pursuing jobs in the areas utilizing these skills, the label may be seen to carry some level of credibility, in this way reinforcing the label and creating a self-fulfilling prophecy.

> ## See video
>
> Watch this TED Talk by Thandie Newton: "Embracing otherness, embracing myself":
>
> https://www.ted.com/talks/ thandie_newton_embracing_ otherness_embracing_myself
>
>

Stereotype threat

Statistics have shown that there is a difference in the academic test performance between different groups of people. This has led to some common stereotypes. Two common stereotypes have been the subject of much research and discussion— the stereotypes that Anglo-Americans tend to outperform African Americans on academic testing; and the commonly held stereotype that women are less able than men at mathematics. These stereotypes were studied in relation to what Steele, Spencer and Aronson (2002) call **stereotype threat**.

Stereotype threat refers to the anxiety and apprehension experienced by an individual or members of a particular group when they believe that their behaviour in a specific situation may confirm and reinforce an existing negative group stereotype. There are many explanations as to why someone may underperform on a mathematics or science test, such as fatigue or lack of resources, but Steele and his colleagues claim that group stereotypes cause an individual to re-evaluate his or her behaviour in relation to the stereotype, often leading to underperformance. The researchers argue that our social identities—old, young, male, female, white man, female teacher, and so on—become more significant when we are in specific situations.

In turn, our social identity may affect the factors that we have to deal with in specific situations. Steele and his colleagues call these factors identity contingencies. They claim that identity contingencies are the circumstances that we must deal with in order to get the desired outcomes from a situation.

For example, a woman about to sit a mathematics test may be aware of the commonly held negative stereotype of the link between women and poor mathematics performance. In turn, the anxiety that she feels as a result of this stereotype may affect her subsequent performance on the test. This may manifest itself in a variety of ways, including poor concentration and increased heart rate, which will result in inferior performance.

Steele and Aronson (1995) studied the effect of stereotype threat on the intellectual test performance of African-American students. The researchers hypothesized that when African-American students sit an academic test they face the threat of confirming or being judged by a negative societal stereotype. This suspicion causes a fear of confirming the stereotype, with the result that students self-evaluate and underperform in academic situations.

The procedure involved administering a 30-minute test with items taken from the Graduate Record Examination (GRE). The test was of sufficient difficulty to stretch participants and cause frustration.

There were three experimental conditions.

- Condition 1—the **stereotype threat condition**: in this condition the test was described as being a measure of intellectual ability. This would cause the negative racial stereotype to become relevant to the black participants and establish stereotype threat.

- Condition 2—the **non-stereotype threat condition**: the test was merely described as a problem-solving task that was unrelated to intellectual ability. This should have not established any stereotype threat.

- Condition 3—the **challenge condition**: this was a second non-diagnostic condition. It described the difficult test as posing a challenge in the hope of raising motivation for the task.

It was predicted that white students would outperform black students on the diagnostic condition but not on the two non-diagnostic conditions. Results showed that black students in the diagnostic condition performed significantly worse than black participants in either of the two non-diagnostic conditions, as well as significantly worse than white participants in the diagnostic condition.

This experiment was seen by the researchers as evidence of stereotype threat and sits alongside over 300 studies that demonstrate the effect of stereotype threat on test performance (Aronson, 2010; Steele, 2010; cited in Aronson *et al*, 2014).

ATL skills: Research and thinking

As we have seen, Steele and Aronson (1995) investigated the effect of stereotype threat on academic performance when it links to negative racial stereotypes. To add to your learning, read this article by Claude Steele on stereotype threat and academic performance:

https://www.theatlantic.com/magazine/archive/1999/08/thin-ice-stereotype-threat-and-black-college-students/304663/

For further reading, turn to Claude Steele's book: *Whistling Vivaldi* (2010) published by W W Norton & Company, New York.

Another key area of focus has been the investigation of stereotype threat on female performance in mathematic tests. Find the following study on this topic:

Spencer, SJ, Steele, CM and Quinn, D. 1999. "Stereotype threat and women's math performance". *Journal of Experimental Social Psychology*. Vol 35. Pp 4–28.

Summarize this study.

How does this study contribute to our understanding of stereotype threat on academic performance?

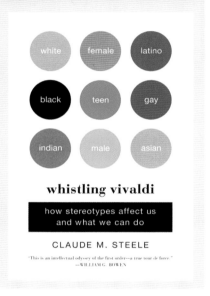

whistling vivaldi

how stereotypes affect us and what we can do

CLAUDE M. STEELE

Discussion

Discuss with a partner the use of the experimental method in developing our understanding of stereotypes and stereotype threat.

See video

As related viewing, watch Paul Bloom's TED Talk "Can prejudice ever be a good thing?"

https://www.ted.com/talks/paul_bloom_can_prejudice_ever_be_a_good_thing

Case study: Jane Elliott—"A class divided"

After the assassination of Martin Luther King Junior in 1968, a third-grade teacher in Iowa called Jane Elliott decided that she wanted to teach her students some important lessons on prejudice and discrimination. In order to do this she divided her class into groups based upon eye colour. Brown-eyed or blue-eyed students were clearly labelled by wearing collars around their necks. On the first day, she told the blue-eyed students that they were more well behaved and more intelligent than the brown-eyed students (and so gave them a positive stereotype). She offered them preferential treatment by allowing them to sit at the front of the class and to have first choice of materials and resources in lessons. The brown-eyed students suffered a great blow to their self-esteem. They became withdrawn and turned to each other for support.

On the second day, she reversed the assigned labels and offered the preferential treatment to the brown-eyed students. The brown-eyed students now became more engaged in class and even improved their performance on classroom activities. This simple experiment seems to highlight the importance of children's social identity and social contingencies within the classroom upon their academic ability.

See video

http://www.pbs.org/wgbh/frontline/film/class-divided/

▶ ❙❙ ■

Social identity theory

In 1979, Tajfel and Turner proposed a theory of inter-group conflict. Social identity theory has since become a prominent theory in social psychology and increased our understanding of social phenomena such as social identity, prejudice, discrimination and stereotyping. It is important to note that although a key part of the theory focuses on social categorization (membership to social groups), self-categorization theory was later developed as an extension of this earlier work.

As social identity theorists, Tajfel and Turner acknowledge the existence of two different types of self. Our **social identity**, which is of most relevance here, refers to the self in terms of our group membership such as our gender or ethnicity. Our **personal identity** refers to our self on a more individual, private and interpersonal level.

Elements of your personal identity may only be known by a loved one, or even only to yourself. It is possible to have multiple social and personal identities as we are all members of multiple social groups and are involved in many interpersonal relationships (Hogg and Vaughan, 2014).

Social identity theory is based upon the following three assumptions.

- Individuals strive to maintain or enhance their **self-esteem**. This will support having a positive **self-concept**.

- Membership to social groups can have both positive and negative associations. An individual's identity will therefore be viewed in light of the collective value or **salience** of the groups to which the person belongs.

- An individual will assess the value of his or her own **ingroup (us)** membership via a process of **social comparison** with an **out-group (them)**. When an individual perceives his or her ingroup more favourably than the outgroup this will result in more value being placed upon membership to the ingroup and a more positive social identity.

When individuals are unhappy with their group membership they may seek to leave the existing group and move to another with a more positive group identity. This factor is known as **permeability**, the ability to move between groups due to flexibility of group boundaries. Alternatively, when individuals must remain within their group as the group boundaries are **impermeable**, they may try to make their existing group appear more positive by displaying favouritism towards the ingroup. This will serve to increase their self-esteem and may result in discrimination against the outgroup.

Tajfel *et al* (1971) aimed to demonstrate that when individuals are allocated to groups based upon minimal characteristics—merely belonging to an ingroup or an outgroup—it is possible to create discrimination despite there being no existing prejudice. The study involved 64 boys, between 14 and 15 years old, from a school in Bristol, UK. They were allocated to groups based upon minimal characteristics; that is, they were assigned to groups based upon arbitrary and minimal criteria.

In the first study, boys were placed into groups based upon their estimates of the number of dots on a screen in a visual judgment task. They were then placed into groups labelled "overestimator" or "underestimator" based upon their estimates in the task. The allocation to the groups was in fact arbitrary and was designed to categorize the boys.

The boys were then told that they were going to be involved in a task that involved giving rewards and penalties to others in the form of real money. The boys would not know the identities of those to whom they allocated these rewards or penalties and none of their decisions would benefit or punish themselves. At the end of the experiment each boy would receive the amount that he had been awarded, although this was an insignificant amount (around 50p).

The boys were placed into cubicles and were given specially designed booklets that contained matrices like the one shown at the top of Table 4.7. Participants were required to circle one column and told that this would equate to rewarding or penalizing another participant. The booklet contained matrices that enabled ingroup choices, outgroup choices or intergroup choices.

For study 1														
Underestimator		−20	−17	−14	−11	−8	−5	−2	1	2	3	4	5	7	
Overestimator		7	6	5	4	3	2	1	−2	−5	−8	−11	−14	−17	−20
For study 2														
	Booklet for group preferring artist Klee													
These numbers are rewards for boy no. 70 from the Klee group	26	24	22	20	18	16	14	12	10	8	6	4	2	
These numbers are rewards for boy no. 20 of the Kandinsky group	20	19	18	17	16	15	14	13	12	11	10	9	8	

▲ Table 4.7 Example matrices

The findings from the first study highlighted that when the boys were required to make an intergroup choice (that is, either allocate rewards or penalties to one of their own group or a member of the outgroup) they displayed ingroup favouritism and allocated more rewards to members of their own group. When faced with allocating rewards or penalties to two members of the same group, ingroup or outgroup, the boys opted for a decision that would ensure maximum fairness. These results support the claims made by Tajfel that discrimination can be created by merely being allocated to a group. In short, when we are aware that an outgroup exists we will discriminate in favour of the ingroup.

In the second study, a different group of boys were arbitrarily categorized into groups based upon artistic preference. These participants were shown pictures of paintings by the artists Paul Klee and Wassily Kandinsky.

The second study was similar to the first, in that the boys would allocate rewards and penalties to other participants. The matrices in the second study were slightly different, though (see Table 4.7). In this study the matrices encouraged the boys to make one of three decisions.

- **Maximum joint profit:** boys could allocate the largest amount to both boys in the matrix.

- **Maximum ingroup profit:** boys could allocate the largest amount to members of their ingroup.

- **Maximum difference:** this decision maximized the amount given to the boys in their ingroup and minimized the amount given to members of the outgroup.

In the second study the findings showed that the boys would rather maximize the difference in the scores allocated between the ingroup and the outgroup, even at the expense of gaining a higher score and obtaining more money. When making a decision concerning two members of the ingroup, boys would opt for a choice of maximum fairness, demonstrating clear ingroup favouritism. This study highlights that discrimination can take place even when no previous prejudice or competition exists.

ATL skills: Research and thinking

Social identity theory provides one explanation of intergroup behaviour and discrimination. Musafer Sherif (1954) provided an alternative explanation in the form of **realistic conflict theory**.

Using your research skills, locate articles that summarize the main assumptions of realistic conflict theory.

Contrast realistic conflict theory with social identity theory.

For a detailed summary of both theories you may want to consult the original publication by Tajfel and Turner. You can find it here:

https://tinyurl.com/ya7ssaws

In 2001, researchers Alex Haslam and Steve Reicher conducted the BBC Prison Study which examined how people respond to being placed into groups of unequal power, either prison guards or prisoners.

Explore the study website: http://www.bbcprisonstudy.org/index.php

To what extent can the research findings be explained by:

- social identity theory
- realistic conflict theory?

Discussion

Take the points you identified when contrasting realistic conflict theory with social identity theory. Discuss your findings with a partner.

Acculturation

Why do cultures change?

Cultures are not static. They change over time, just as people change. They can change as a result of modernization, affluence, migration, education and a myriad of other reasons. Acculturation is one type of cultural change. **Acculturation** is a process of psychological and cultural change as a result of contact and interaction between cultures. This can result in change to all (or both) cultures not only the non-dominant culture (Berry, 2008). It is also important to note that change is both psychological (individual) and cultural (social); it affects individuals and society at large. Acculturation is often discussed as a process that takes place between dominant and non-dominant cultures.

It should not be surprising, therefore, that accelerating globalization is driving acculturation. The total number of international migrants (people living in a different country from the one in which they were born) reached 244 million in 2015. That represents a 40% increase from 2000 and includes 20 million refugees (United Nations, 2016). Interestingly, this *does not* mean that we are headed toward a single homogenized global culture. Contact with other cultures may be inevitable but the responses to contact range from total acceptance to total rejection.

Examples of resistance cultures that have survived and maintained their cultural identity are everywhere. First Nations (or Aboriginal) cultures in Canada, the USA, Australia and elsewhere have survived centuries of contact with other cultures. This contact was not always peaceful. Many First Nations cultures have been subjected to forced assimilation policies such as the introduction of residential schools which were designed to "kill the Indian and save the man". At these government-run or church-run schools, First Nations children were removed from their families, punished for speaking their native languages and forced to adopt European ways of life. Despite this, and over a century of contact with more dominant cultures, many distinct and vibrant First Nations cultures exist around the world. Indeed, many of these cultures are currently experiencing a resurgence, perhaps working in the opposite direction of assimilation as more and more First Nations youths are exposed to, and proud of, their cultural past. These are examples of cultural resistance and revitalization in the face of cultural domination.

See video

Watch this related TED Talk on pop culture in the Arab world:

https://www.ted.com/talks/ shereen_el_feki_pop_culture_ in_the_arab_world

▶ ❚❚ ■

Acculturation studies

Studies into acculturation are most interested in how cultures change as a result of migration and the resulting contact with other cultures. As a result of globalization, closing yourself off from contact with members outside your cultural group is no longer a viable option. It has become more important to study the strategies of dealing with acculturation rather than the willingness (or not) to accept change within your culture. In short, the world has become far too interrelated for cultural isolation. **Berry (2008)** argues that individuals can adopt four strategies for cultural change.

- **Assimilation**: when individuals are open to change and are unconcerned about any loss of their original culture. In this strategy, individuals openly seek interaction with cultures other than their own and are willing to adjust their behaviour, attitudes and beliefs.

- **Integration**: when individuals want to hold onto traditional values and beliefs but at the same time desire daily interactions with other cultures. This option can only be pursued by non-dominant groups when the dominant society is open and accommodating toward cultural change.

- **Separation**: when individuals value their original culture and are averse to losing touch with the values and traditions of their past. These individuals actively seek to avoid contact with other cultures.

- **Marginalization**: when individuals have little interest in maintaining their original culture but at the same time little interest in opening relations with other cultures.

The preferred strategy depends upon whether or not you are a member of the dominant or minority culture and what the cultural values are among both cultures. For example, assimilation is often sought by dominant groups reluctant to change and will result in a "melting pot" (for example, the US attitude towards immigration); when separation is forced, it is called segregation (for example, apartheid

South Africa). Multiculturalism is the result of an openness on the part of all cultures widely accepting of diversity (for example, the official immigration policy in Canada). Marginalization is the result of individual decisions to remain isolated and of social policies that limit or at least discourage cultural contributions from minority groups. Figure 4.13 illustrates Berry's (2008) research.

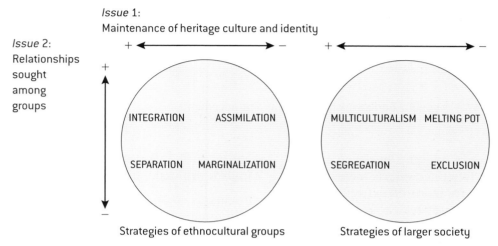

▲ Figure 4.13   Values of intercultural studies in ethnocultural groups and in the larger society

Source: Berry (2008)

How are acculturation studies designed?

Acculturation is a process that happens over time at both a group cultural level and at an individual level. It is therefore important that longitudinal studies take place that look at change over time. In addition, studies should look at changes in both (or all) cultures, not just the non-dominant one. Studies should also look at changes in individual psychology as well as changes in greater society (culture). Research often employs questionnaires and surveys so findings are often reliant on self-reported data. Finally, as with any psychological research, attaining results from multiple samples in multiple societies is very important. Findings from only one or two cultures is insufficient in explaining acculturation and its impact on identities, attitudes and beliefs.

How does acculturation impact behaviour?

Acculturation happens through contact and exchange between cultures. Communication is a very important determinant of acculturation. Strong communication and involvement on the part of immigrants with their original culture can help the acculturation process in the beginning (social support from the original culture before it is available from the new culture may be important here). Over the long term though, strong communication and involvement with original cultural groups may retard acculturation as this prevents effective communication and involvement with the new, adopted culture (Lakey, 2003).

When examining the impact of acculturation on behaviour, a significant limitation appears. First, most migration occurs from poorer, less-developed countries to richer, more-developed countries. As a result, research is biased toward a study of acculturation in one direction. There is very little opportunity to study the effects of acculturation in the other direction; that is, from rich countries to poorer ones. Acculturation studies look mostly at the movement of peoples from more traditionalist, poorer cultures to more liberal and richer cultures. This makes generalization problematic.

ATL skills: Thinking and research

Do you think the findings of acculturation studies are valid, considering they are the product of self-assessment? What makes you say that?

What changes would you propose to the research methodology of acculturation studies to make them less reliant on self-reporting?

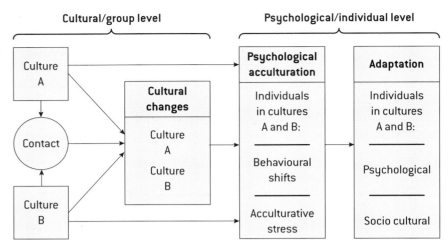

▲ Figure 4.14 A general framework for understanding acculturation

Source: Berry (2005)

The health behaviour of migrants has been extensively studied. Two main effects have been noticed. The **healthy migrant effect** refers to the concept that recent migrants tend to be healthier than their native born counterparts. The second effect, **the negative acculturation effect**, refers to the apparent diminishing difference between migrants and their native born counterparts over time. That is, the healthy migrant effect diminishes with great acculturation into unhealthy host country habits. The healthy migrant effect has not been theoretically founded and seems to run counter to the well-established connection between low socio-economic status and poor health. It has been largely explained by the fact that most host countries select for healthy migrants and that the food environments of migrant origin cultures are often healthier than those of first-world receiving cultures. (see "Clinical bias in diagnosis and the role of culture in treatment" in Unit 5 on abnormal psychology)

ATL skills: Thinking and research

A lot of research in psychology is accused of being W-E-I-R-D (**W**estern, **E**ducated, from **I**ndustrialized, **R**ich, and **D**emocratic countries). As a result, much psychological research is done in a very particular context that may bias findings. Acculturation studies are no exception.

Do you think the healthy immigrant effect and the negative acculturation effect may be two examples of this type of bias? What makes you say that?

Shah *et al* **(2015)** found a positive association between obesity and acculturation among 1,375 mainly South Asian (Indian, Pakistani and Bangladeshi) male migrant workers in the UAE.

Participants completed a health and lifestyle questionnaire between January and June 2012. Over half of those surveyed had lived in the UAE for more than six years and the most common occupations were drivers (23%), labourers and agricultural workers (17% each) and construction workers (12.5%). Findings showed that these migrant workers in the UAE had significantly higher body mass index (BMI) than men of the same age in their cultures of origin. The longer the migrants stay in the UAE, the greater the difference between their BMI and that of men in their culture of origin. The mean BMI among participants was higher than for working men aged 20–59 years in India (31.5 kg/m² versus 23.1 kg/m²) and Bangladesh (26.2 kg/m² versus 19.7 kg/m²). Prevalence of being overweight and of obesity in male Pakistani migrants was more than double than for Pakistani men in their origin culture. In addition, the prevalence of obesity and being overweight in the study sample (63.4%) was also higher than in Emirati men (58.6%). These findings seems to show that acculturation may contribute to obesity and being overweight.

Delavario *et al* **(2013)** found that there was a relationship between acculturation and obesity among Hispanic migrants in the USA. A literature review of nine studies conducted on migrants to the USA from eight different cultures of origin have found mixed results between men and women. Six studies found a positive association between higher acculturation and BMI, while three found that higher acculturation was associated with lower BMI mainly among women. The increase in BMI among men may be because migrants are moving into a culture that promotes unhealthy weight gain more than their culture of origin. Contrary findings for women have been explained by the western ideal of a slim female body and a resultant higher emphasis placed on physical activity and fitness, which would counter the positive association between acculturation and obesity.

Another study, also undertaken in the USA, supports the relationship between acculturation and obesity. This research looked at what researchers call unhealthy assimilation among Asian migrants. Unhealthy assimilation refers to convergence of the health of migrants to a less healthy new-culture standard. Ishizawa and Jones (2016) did find that second- and third-generation migrants had a higher likelihood of obesity than first-generation migrants or individuals from their origin culture, but the researchers did identify moderating factors. They found that neighbourhoods with a high migrant density and those households that retained their original language acted as buffers against obesity **(Ishizawa and Jones, 2016)**.

Length of stay has been found to be a contributing factor to obesity in a study of migrants in Portugal conducted by **Da Costa, Dias and Martins (2017)**. A study of over 31,000 people (of whom 4.6% were migrants) was conducted between 2007 and 2008. Findings showed that the prevalence of overweight was higher for native Portuguese than new migrants but that length of residence of migrants (more than 15 years) was positively associated with prevalence of overweight (Da Costa, Dias and Martins, 2017). In this case, it seems that the acculturative process included a change in diet or lifestyle that caused the migrants to mirror the obesity and overweight prevalence rates of native Portuguese.

There are other researchers who challenge the assumption that acculturation and obesity are necessarily correlated. These researchers imply that it is not the acculturative process itself that results in obesity but the culture to which one is acculturating that matters. A study of over 3,100 Spanish adolescents conducted by **Esteban-Gonzalo et al (2015)** found no significant difference in overweight risk between Spanish and immigrant adolescents. Findings did show that short-term immigrants (with less than six years' residence) had a higher overweight risk than longer-term immigrants and native Spanish people, but that the difference disappeared within six years.

Acculturative stress

Acculturation can be stressful. Obesity, substance abuse and cardiovascular disease are correlated with heightened levels of chronic stress (see Unit 6 on health psychology). Acculturative stress can be defined as biopsychosocial difficulties when adapting to a new cultural context. The term has been used as a synonym for culture shock and psychic shock. Another way to think of it is as the stress experienced by people who are coping with conflicting cultural norms (Sullivan, 2009).

Many people experience acculturation without the associated stress. Protective factors and determinants of acculturative stress include (but are not limited to) affluence, social support and the degree of similarity or difference in cultural contexts. These mirror the protective factors and risk factors of stress discussed in Unit 6 on health psychology.

Acculturative stress can arise when there is conflict between the various acculturation strategies and it can be a difficult challenge to individuals interacting with multiple cultures. This issue can become very problematic when members of the same non-dominant group have conflicting opinions on acculturative strategies. An example of this can be found with the Shafia so called "honour killings" in Canada outlined in "Psychology in real life" below.

According to Berry (2005), integration strategies result in the lowest levels of stress. This may be because individuals are not required to give up social identification with their original culture when they adopt and adapt some identification with their new culture. Assimilation and separation result in intermediate levels of stress while marginalization results in the highest levels of acculturative stress. If we examine these results using social identity theory, it seems that the more connected an individual feels to a group (whether that is the new culture, the old one or both), the less stress is experienced. This may be due to the protective factor of social support—those with connections to both cultures will have access to more social support than others.

Migration and acculturation have also been found to have an impact on mental health in children and adolescents. Batista-Pinto Wiese (2010) argues that migration and acculturative stress can have severe implications for young children and adolescents because migration can be understood as a life trauma. She points out that younger children can develop insecure, ambivalent or disorganized attachment while adolescents may show increased aggressive behaviour along with anxiety and depressive behaviour related to acculturation.

Discussion

Read "Psychology in real life" below, then answer these questions.

- Do you think acculturative stress played a role in the deaths of the Shafia girls?
- Why do you think it was difficult for these girls' parents to adapt to the cultural norms of life in Canada?
- To what extent should cultures be accepting and understanding of the norms and values of immigrants?
- Do you believe that immigrants and refugees should assimilate to the culture of their new homes?

Psychology in real life

Globalization has resulted in the mixing of cultures around the world. These cultures often hold conflicting values and in some cases these conflicts can have serious consequences. Take, for instance, the example of honour killing. Honour killing is not condoned by any major religion nor any nation state but some subcultures of conservative, traditional people believe honour killing is an acceptable, often necessary social practice.

An honour (or shame) killing is the murder of a family member due to the perpetrators' belief that the victim brought shame on the family or community and that the only way to erase the shame is to kill the victim. Honour killing is different from other forms of domestic violence for three reasons: honour killings are planned in advance, they can include multiple family members planning and committing the murder, and perpetrators often do not face negative stigma in their families or communities (Government of Canada, 2016).

In January 2012, three daughters and a first wife of Mohammed Shafia were found dead at the bottom of a canal in Kingston, Canada. In the coming months, it became clear that the Shafia family had killed the three girls, and the woman the girls knew as their aunt, for shaming the family. It would seem that the Shafia daughters' desired acculturative strategy was at odds with their parents' strategy.

The girls were caught between a conservative, traditional culture and a liberal, modern one. Their punishment for choosing the latter was death.

Ontario Superior Court Justice Robert Maranger presided over this case, which shocked the nation. Four family members were dead with three family members guilty of their murder. Michael Friscolanti tells the whole story of what happened.

> "The evidence, utterly heartbreaking, left no real doubt about the truth. Before they died, the Shafia sisters were caught in the ultimate culture clash, living in Canada but not allowed to be Canadian. They were expected to behave like good Muslim daughters, to wear the hijab and marry a fellow Afghan. And when they rebelled against their father's "traditions" and "customs"—covertly at first, then for all the community to see—the shame became too much to bear. Only a mass execution (staged to look like a foolish wrong turn) could wash away the stain of their secret boyfriends and revealing clothes."

(Friscolanti, 2017): http://www.macleans.ca/news/canada/inside-the-shafia-killings-that-shocked-a-nation/

If you are studying the HL extension, "The influence of globalization on individual behaviour", see "How globalization influences individual behaviour" for more information. You may wish to review the section "Origins of violence" in Unit 6 on human relationships if you are studying that option.

Exercise

Take the perspective of one of the murdered Shafia girls before this tragedy. Write a letter to your parents explaining how you feel about being split between two cultures. What are your motivations for acting the way you do?

Now take the perspective of one of the Shafia parents or the brother. Write a letter to one of your daughters (or sisters) explaining why you feel the way you do about how the person is acting. What reasons might your daughter (or sister) give for her emotions?

Studies into the psychological effects of acculturation are themselves culturally dependent. It is not necessarily the process of acculturation itself that is the cause of certain behaviour but the interplay of the cultures in contact that determine behaviour. In this sense, obesity may not be a result of acculturation. Instead it may be the result of the acculturation of non-western and western, industrialized cultures. The latter are often characterized by poor food environments with cheap foods weak in nutrients and high in added sugars and fats, along with sedentary lifestyles (as described in Unit 6 on health psychology). In order to understand acculturation, you must first understand the nature of the cultures in play. Only then will you be able to understand how the elements of those cultures have intermingled in their own unique acculturative process.

Inquiry questions

- Does globalization mean there will be a new global social identity (GSI)?
- Will globalization unite or divide us?
- To what extent can social psychology successfully address the issue of globalization and prevent conflict?

What you will learn in this section

- Globalization's influence on behaviour
  - Acculturation and social identity
- Effect of the interaction of local and global influences on behaviour
- Methods used to study the influence of globalization on behaviour
  - Hofstede and Schwartz: cross-cultural studies—values studies

How globalization influences behaviour

In this unit we have focused on the influence that social and cultural groups have on behaviour. Globalization plays an important role in this respect. As Scholte (2005) explains the process, "people become more able—physically, legally, culturally and psychologically—to engage with each other in 'one world'". Increasing interdependence and communication raises the question of whether we are headed for one global social identity (GSI). **Giddens (1991)** referred to this potential global identity that would socialize a "cosmopolitan" individual for whom humankind becomes a "we" and there are no "others". Research has shown that a GSI is possible and that it can foster global cooperation for an all-inclusive ingroup encompassing humanity as a whole.

Buchan *et al* **(2011)** wanted to see if identification with a global culture could motivate cooperation in the context of a global collective. Using samples from the USA, Italy, Russia, Argentina, South Africa and Iran, the researchers sampled a total of 1,122 participants. Two items were measured, social identity (either local, national or worldwide) and concern for global affairs (on global warming; the spread of pandemics; empowering the

International Court of Justice; and the world gap between rich and poor).

In addition, participants allocated funds to either a personal, national or global investment. Global accounts paid back the contribution multiplied by 3, national investments paid the contribution multiplied by 2 and personal investments paid back the contribution amount. In other words, participants could be guaranteed a small payout if they deposited into their personal accounts but maximum benefit would occur if all participants paid into the global account and then shared out the return. This requires a shared identity with global partners as well as trust in those partners.

Correlational results showed that social identification with a global community can affect sharing behaviour with regard to global public good and this occurred without an expectation regarding how much other participants were contributing. Findings published by **Hamburger Kolleg (2015)** claim three related findings.

- Participation in global networks will contribute to increased identification with a global community.
- GSI is a useful psychological construct. Generally, individuals with a high GSI tend to

look favourably on global flows of goods and people and are more aware of global issues than those with lower GSI scores. Women, the elderly and more educated people tend to have higher GSI scores while GSI score is negatively correlated with income. Perhaps this can be explained by **realistic conflict theory**.

- GSI is correlated with a willingness to cooperate at the global level.

These findings were supported in later research undertaken in Norway (Türken and Rudmin, 2013).

In contrast to this rosy view of the future of humanity as a single social ingroup, **Rosenmann, Reese and Cameron (2015)** point out that not everyone is pleased with a global cultural ingroup. The researchers call the typically western **values and cultural content** that is spreading through the world "globalized western culture". They also point out that this culture is a very (although not exclusively) US-English speaking and English speaking culture that is at odds with the values, traditions and beliefs of many cultures around the world. Globalized western cultures must therefore still be considered as exclusive of millions of individuals in scores or hundreds of social groups around the world.

People have always been members of overlapping, sometimes conflicting social groups, so this is nothing new. However, the challenges overlapping social identities present to the attitudes, values and identities of individuals cannot be ignored. Some people will be pressured to acculturate to a global ingroup more than others. At the heart of this issue is the question: does a globalized social ingroup require a single culture or can it survive the multiple social groups under a larger umbrella of social cohesion?

Discussion

If a GSI is to be established, it will require its own set of social norms for ingroup members. Create a list of cultural norms that you believe all members of the human race can agree upon.

What problems come to mind when you try to do this?

Can you create a GSI without a set of global social norms?

Perhaps the answer lies in diversity. In what appears to be an echo of Canadian Prime Minister Trudeau's statement about diversity (quoted in the introduction to this unit), Yi Wang of the Harbin Engineering University in China argues that globalization alongside unique cultural identities can form fruitful interactions (Yi, 2007).

Cultures do not homogenize as if they were paint poured into a bucket. As Berry points out, they react to influence and may prove remarkably resilient in the face of dominant cultures. Active strategies of integration and separation can defend cultural identities seemingly without limit. If strength does lie in diversity, assimilation should not be the goal of globalization. At some level, a centrally important cultural norm of a GSI will have to be acceptance of diversity under one flag. This would look like a culture of cultures that shares certain common values as universal human values.

The effect of the interaction of local and global influences on behaviour

This unit has dealt with the effect of local and global influences on behaviour. The acculturation studies discussed in this unit refer to this interaction. The theories and studies discussed in this unit can be applied to this extension.

Particularly applicable is the concept of acculturative stress. Acculturative stress refers to the biopsychosocial difficulties associated with adapting to a new cultural context. As cultures become increasingly interconnected and mutually aware, acculturative stress is likely to increase simply because the number of individuals experiencing the pull of competing cultural norms is increasing. As Berry suggests, the acculturative strategy chosen (integration, assimilation, separation or marginalization) can impact the level of stress experienced by individuals.

Young people growing up with traditionalist parents but living in a progressive, liberal society often experience challenges related to social identity and belonging in their social networks. People are members of multiple social groups at any given time but when those groups hold fundamentally conflicting values and beliefs, this can cause individual and social stressors. Resolving these conflicts involves a resetting of social identities that can fuel conflict within families.

At the heart of the issue lie some of the central theories of social psychology: social identity theory, socialization and enculturation, stereotyping and attribution theories. Human behaviour is tied tightly to our social groups so when our social groups are in conflict, so are our behaviours.

See video

In this TED Talk Alexander Betts examines issues related to the UK's 2016 vote to leave the EU: "Why Brexit happened—and what to do next"

https://www.ted.com/talks/alexander_betts_why_brexit_happened_and_what_to_do_next

---

Methods used to study the influence of globalization on behaviour

Cross-cultural studies (and therefore influences of globalization on behaviour) are dependent upon the extent to which we use constructs that identify common metric across cultures. Two constructs we have examined in this unit are Hofstede's cultural dimensions and Schwartz's theory of basic values. These measurements can be applied to all cultures and are used to measure relative differences between cultures. They are in turn used to measure changes to cultures over time as they acculturate due to interaction in a globalizing world.

One weakness of these studies is that cultural scores are based upon data collected from individuals, often in the form of self-reported questionnaires and surveys. As we have seen, this can be a problem because self-reporting is not always an accurate assessment of real-world behaviours and beliefs. Additionally, we have learned that although correlations exist between personality scores and cultural dimensions, these are different things. Extrapolating individual data to cultural dimensions is a tricky business and requires very large data pools that can never reach anything more than an approximation of group values.

Another challenge to studying cultures and globalization's influence on behaviour is the fact that cultures are dynamic and constantly in a state of adaptation and change. How can researchers identify which changes in behaviour are due to natural change within a culture and which are the result of globalization? It is a complicated business that requires a deep and nuanced understanding (and measurement) of all the cultures in interaction.

However, just because something is difficult does not mean that it cannot be done. Hofstede and Schwartz have both developed meaningful measurements that can be used to approximate the relative differences among cultures and these have been the basis for studies on globalization.

ATL skills: Thinking

In his 1964 book *Understanding Media: The Extensions of Man*, Canadian researcher Marshall McLuhan described the emergence of a "global village". He did not claim that this village would be a peaceful utopia. In fact, he understood the village to be an inherently tribal, mistrustful, vicious and violent place (Carr, 2017). Internet use has increased sevenfold in the 15 years between 2000 and 2015 and continued growth seems beyond doubt (Davidson, 2016). From a social psychological perspective it seems very important for us to understand how our increasingly interconnected world will impact the behaviours, attitudes and identities of its global citizens.

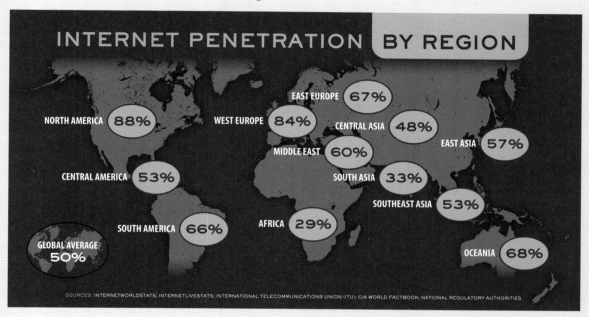

In addition to this growing online interconnectedness, the migration of people around the world has also increased a lot in recent years.

Do you think the growing interconnectedness made possible by the internet will result in greater understanding and improved conflict resolution—or do you think we will see increasing conflict and violence as we are drawn closer together in McLuhan's global village?

ABNORMAL PSYCHOLOGY

Topics

- Factors influencing diagnosis
  - Normality versus abnormality
  - Classification systems
  - Validity and reliability of diagnosis
  - The role of clinical biases in diagnosis
- Etiology of abnormal psychology
  - Prevalence rates and disorders
  - Explanations for disorders

- Biological explanations for depression
- Cognitive and sociocultural explanations for depression
- Treatment of disorders
  - Assessing the effectiveness of treatment
  - Biological treatment of depression
  - Psychological treatment of depression
  - The role of culture in treatment

Introduction

Abnormal psychology is a study of patterns of behaviour that deviate from the accepted norm. Although a lot of behaviours may be classified as such, abnormal psychology usually investigates behaviour in a clinical context and thus concerns itself mainly with diagnosis and treatment of **mental disorders**.

The fundamental task of abnormal psychology and a starting point for all further research is to establish **criteria of normality and abnormality** in human behaviour and experience. What is normal? Where is the threshold that needs to be crossed in order for behaviour to become abnormal? Is there one major criterion of abnormality or a set of criteria? Is abnormality a black-and-white concept or does it make sense to speak of "degrees of abnormality"?

Suppose we have established criteria of abnormality. A further issue that needs to be tackled is that of **diagnosis**. How do we diagnose a mental disorder? How can we be sure that the diagnosis matches the disorder correctly? To what extent is it possible to eliminate the chances of misdiagnosis? Will two clinicians observing the same patient arrive at the same diagnosis? These questions are related to the concept of **clinical bias** in diagnosis. It is important to know the extent to which clinical biases may affect diagnosis of disorders, as well as the potential sources of these biases. For

example, understanding of cultural differences may be crucial in differentiating abnormality from culturally specific behaviour.

Several diagnostic **classification systems** have been created to standardize diagnostic practices. These classification systems have become the major tool of diagnosing mental disorders. Classification systems are revised periodically, reflecting the ongoing changes in our understanding of mental health, its criteria and its determining factors.

Again, suppose for a second that we have established a reliable method of diagnosis. We know a mental disorder when we see one, and opinions of different clinicians converge. We now need to learn how to treat the disorder. For that, we need to understand what caused it in the first place.

The set of factors causing a disorder is referred to as "**etiology**". Usually etiology of a disorder comprises multiple factors—biological, cognitive and sociocultural. It is reasonable to aim at a holistic view of etiology that takes into account these multiple factors.

Knowledge of the predominant etiology is paramount for the selection of effective **treatment**. If one believes that the etiology of a disorder is mainly biological, biological treatments (for example, drugs) are the obvious choice. Conversely, if it is believed that a disorder is mainly caused by cognitive or social factors, psychological treatment may be the preferred option. Psychological treatment can target a person's cognitive processes (for example, beliefs and expectations) or the social support network. In any case, it is important to assess the **effectiveness of treatment**, and that is a task in itself.

We have just introduced such important key terms as: mental disorder, criteria of abnormality, diagnosis, classification system, etiology and treatment. These concepts will be used throughout the unit. It might be a good idea for you to draw a flowchart or other visual representing the relationship between these terms. You can then refer to this visual representation as you are studying the unit.

There is a great variety of recognized mental disorders included in the classification systems. To make our discussion more focused, we will concentrate on one example: **major depressive disorder (MDD)**. It belongs to the group of **affective disorders** because its main symptoms represent changes in a patient's mood.

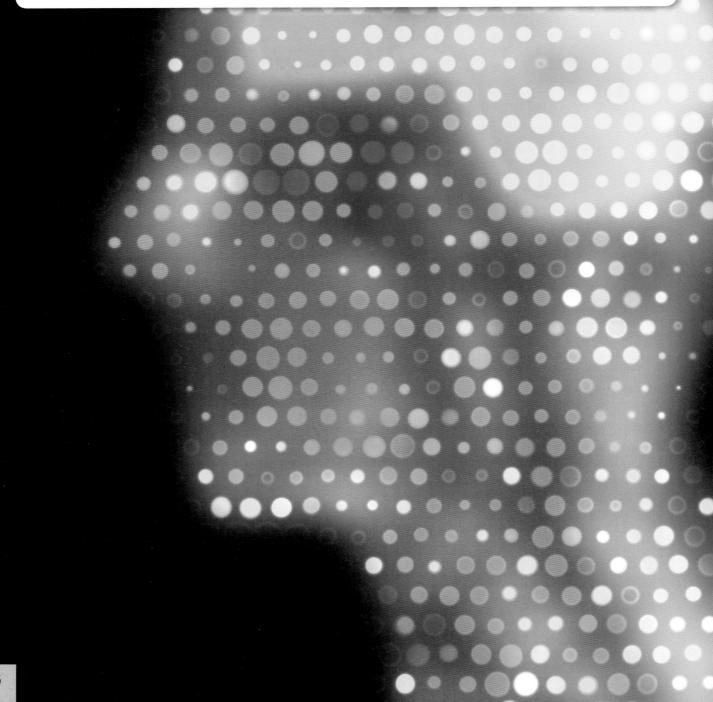

5 Normality versus abnormality

Inquiry questions

- What are the ethical considerations related to labeling a person as "abnormal"?

- Given that such labels influence people's lives, what can we do to ensure that the labels are used with caution?

- How can we design a definition of abnormality that would clearly distinguish normal behaviour from abnormal behaviour?

What you will learn in this section

- Approaches to defining abnormality

  - Abnormality as a deviation from social norms

  - Abnormality as inadequate functioning: Rosenhan and Seligman (1989)

  - Abnormality as a deviation from ideal mental health: Jahoda (1958)

  - Abnormality as statistical infrequency

  - The medical model of abnormality

- Strengths and limitations of each of the approaches

In the history of abnormal psychology, there have been multiple perspectives on the nature of abnormality. This means that multiple approaches to defining normality and abnormality could have co-existed during the same time period. The following broad approaches to defining abnormality have been most influential:

- abnormality as a deviation from social norms

- abnormality as inadequate functioning

- abnormality as a deviation from ideal mental health

- abnormality as statistical infrequency

- the medical model of abnormality.

Abnormality as a deviation from social norms

In a very general and intuitive way we usually define abnormality as something that falls outside the boundaries of what is accepted in society. In other words, abnormality is a deviation from social norms. However, even this initial definition raises a number of problems.

First, if abnormality is defined in relation to a society, how do we account for the fact that societies themselves are different and changeable? Norms and rules regulating people's behaviour are different from culture to culture. Even within the same culture, what was considered normal 100 years ago may be considered abnormal now, and vice versa.

Second, the fact that society gets to decide what behaviours are acceptable opens the door to using abnormality as a means of social control. If individuals do not behave in a way that serves a group's interests, the group can label those people as abnormal and lock them out. This extreme position has given rise to a whole movement of "anti-psychiatry". Thomas Szasz, one of the famous anti-psychiatrists, believed that "mental disorders" are nothing more than "problems in living", a temporary inability to find one's place within a given society. He believed that there is nothing wrong with individuals labeled "mentally ill" apart from the label itself.

Third, some patterns of behaviour may be socially acceptable, but potentially harmful to the individual. For example, one could claim that there is nothing unacceptable about a person who is afraid to walk out of his house. However, the inability to leave the house due to irrational fears may interfere greatly with that person's life.

Finally, abnormality must be evaluated in a context. For example, the way you behave in school and the way you behave at a party would be completely different, but acceptable in the given context.

Case study: Anoushka

Anoushka is a 27 year-old Indian married female. She comes from an upper-class family and works for a multinational corporation. Her job is to manage a team of web developers for software solutions in the field of logistics. When something goes wrong with the software it creates large-scale confusion and large financial losses, and she has to make sure that the team of coders respond to emergencies effectively while at the same time continuing to improve the software. It is a well-paid, but highly demanding and stressful, job.

She has always been an achiever. She topped her class in school and graduated from college with honours. Her education was expensive, and her parents always pointed out to her that they were spending most of their savings just to give her a good start in life. So she has learned to have high standards for herself.

Her extended family, although westernized to a large extent, is still traditionally Indian and Hindu (by religion). Her marriage was not arranged, but the opinion of both the families was extremely important and was carefully considered by both herself and her future husband before their decision to marry was announced. They would not have gone forward without the blessing from both sides.

Her husband values traditional Indian culture, but he allows her to be independent and pursue her career. He has a small business in hospitality. They have two children, one aged 7 and one

aged 5. Although they have a babysitter, her husband expects Anoushka to spend more time with the children. He believes that his job is to earn enough money to give them a good education. He spends little time with his family because he is constantly at work, and Anoushka tries her best to combine her career with looking after the kids.

Lately she has not been able to perform as well as she used to. For the past several weeks it was difficult for her to concentrate at work, which resulted in a series of mistakes and further deepened her feelings of "being a failure". Her colleagues also noticed that she is more fatigued than usual. She has developed insomnia. When asked how she feels, however, she says that everything is fine and that she is just a bit tired. She says it will pass once she has a couple of days off.

1. Is Anoushka depressed? We can sometimes use the word "depressed" loosely to refer to any intense sadness; however, can we say that she is depressed clinically?

2. What other information do we need in order to establish if Anoushka has a mental health issue?

3. If you were Anoushka's relative, would you advise her to see a mental health professional?

4. Does her cultural background have anything to do with her mental health?

ATL skills: Thinking

1. We have identified four major limitations in the definition of abnormality as deviation from social norms. Can you suggest any other approaches that would overcome these limitations?

2. In Anoushka's case described above, is there a deviation from social norms?

TOK

Who establishes social norms? Is the creation of social norms a rational and purposeful process or is it spontaneous?

To what extent are social norms a reliable source of knowledge about acceptable behaviour?

If social norms are a form of shared knowledge, to what extent should they be enforced upon personal knowledge? Is that the same as imposing social norms on the behaviour of a particular individual?

Abnormality as inadequate functioning

The definition of abnormality as inadequate functioning is based on the ideas of **Rosenhan and Seligman (1989)** who proposed seven criteria that can be used to establish abnormality:

- suffering—subjective experience of one's state as wrong

- maladaptiveness—inability to achieve major life goals, for example, inability to establish positive interpersonal relationships

- unconventional behaviour—behaviour that stands out and differs substantially from that of most people

- unpredictability/loss of control—lack of consistency in actions

- irrationality—others cannot understand why the person behaves in this way

- observer discomfort—it makes other people uncomfortable to witness this behaviour

- violation of moral standards—behaviour goes against the common moral norms established in the society.

A limitation of this approach is that it does not account for cases when abnormal behaviour may actually be adaptive. For example, irrational fear that prevents a woman from leaving her house may serve the purpose of failure avoidance. Moreover, some behaviours may be harmful but we do not classify them as abnormal, for example, extreme sports. Some behaviours may be uncomfortable to observers, but not cause any subjective suffering, for example, public displays of affection. Probably to account for this, Rosenhan and Seligman claimed that there exist **degrees of abnormality** based on how many criteria of abnormal behaviour are met.

They also argued that each individual criterion might not be significant on its own, but when several criteria are present abnormality may be inferred.

TOK

Think about the idea of using degrees of abnormality rather than a rigid distinction between normality and abnormality. The idea seems attractive, but does it always work?

Look up the terms "dichotomous" and "continuous". For example, there are dichotomous and continuous variables in empirical human sciences. What is the difference between the two?

What is the value of using dichotomous thresholds instead of continuous variables?

ATL skills: Research

In Unit 1 on research methodology we discussed the concept of statistical significance of a correlation. You know that statistical significance is a continuous parameter, but after a certain threshold ($p < 0.05$) we say that the result becomes "statistically significant". Should we use a similar logic with abnormal behaviour?

Abnormality as a deviation from ideal mental health

Ideal mental health as a criterion of normality was proposed by humanistic psychologists in the 1950s. Humanistic psychologists were known for their belief that psychology should focus on positive aspects of human experiences (health, happiness, self-realization, and so on) rather than negative things such as mental illness. They claimed that the excessive focus on the negative side of human existence predominant at that time was limited and did not allow researchers to see bigger issues lying behind problems, hence their interest in the idea of mental health (as opposed to mental disorders).

Marie Jahoda (1958) identified six characteristics of ideal mental health:

- efficient self-perception

- realistic self-esteem

- voluntary control of behaviour

- accurate perception of the world

- positive relationships

- self-direction and productivity.

A strength of this approach is that mental health is defined positively, through what a person needs to achieve. It also outlines the main dimensions of mental health in a balanced way: it embraces interpersonal relationships, self-perception, perception of the world, and so on. A weakness of the approach is feasibility of mental health: it may be impossible to fully achieve all six parameters of mental health, so most people would probably be classified as abnormal according to this framework. Another weakness is the fact that the parameters are difficult to measure or quantify. Finally, terms such as "efficient", "realistic" and "accurate" require further operationalization.

Abnormality as statistical infrequency

Statistical infrequency has also been used as a criterion of abnormality. In this approach a characteristic of behaviour or a trait of personality is classified as abnormal if it statistically unusual. For example, intelligence quotient (IQ), the scale most often used to measure intelligence, has the mean score 100 and a standard deviation of 15. Statistically this means that approximately 68% of individuals lie in the 85–115 range, 95% of individuals in the 70–130 range, and 99% of individuals in the 55–145 range. So what is "statistically rare"?

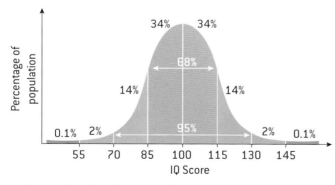

▲ Figure 5.1 Distribution of IQ scores

There are thresholds established in statistical research traditionally to gauge "norms". The first threshold is 95%. If an individual is different from 95% of the rest of the population (for example, he scored less than 70 or more than 130), he falls outside of the statistical norm. The second threshold, a more stringent one, is 99%. The third and the most stringent threshold is 99.9%. In the framework of defining abnormality in terms of statistical infrequency, an individual falling

outside of the 99.9% range could be considered as "severely abnormal".

ATL skills: Research

From your studies in the field of mathematics you will see links with what you already know about the properties of the normal distribution. What do you know about the properties of these ranges?

- Mean ± σ
- Mean ± 2σ
- Mean ± 3σ

If you think back to Unit 1 on research methodology and the concept of levels of statistical significance, you will also find links with the following:

- $p < 0.05$
- $p < 0.01$
- $p < 0.001$

This approach has limitations as well.

First, statistical norms change. For example, the average IQ in the world increases at the rate of approximately 3 IQ points every 10 years (the so-called **Flynn effect**). The norms of intelligence tests are periodically renewed, and a person who scores 100 on a modern IQ test is actually a bit smarter than a person who scored 100 on an earlier version of the same test several decades ago.

Second, statistically infrequent behaviour can sometimes be desirable. People with an extremely high IQ are valued in society; they are not discriminated against because of it.

At the same time, an obvious strength of this approach is that, unlike all the other approaches, it suggests a way to quantify abnormality.

To sum up these approaches

As you see, none of the approaches to defining abnormality is free of controversy. What should we do though? Some people clearly exhibit patterns of behaviour that threaten the society in which they live or cause distress to themselves. These individuals require help, and we need a common language for establishing the exact type of the problem. Without it we would not be able to determine a treatment strategy.

Suggest possible solutions to problems associated with defining abnormality. Discuss advantages and disadvantages of solutions that seem the most promising.

The medical model of abnormality

An alternative approach, rather than trying to formulate a common definition to fit all the possible types of mental disorders, is to look at each disorder separately and establish a set of **symptoms** that define it. In a way, this approach calls for a whole book as a definition, instead of one sentence. It becomes a dynamic effort of generations of clinicians rather than the work of a single scientist. Defining each disorder on the basis of its symptoms is known as the medical model of abnormality. This model assumes that disorders have a cause, but since the cause is not directly observable, it can only be inferred on the basis of more observable symptoms. For this reason, a medical classification of abnormal behaviour implies recognizable patterns of behaviour in every disorder.

ATL skills: Thinking

We have already come across the idea that something can be directly unobservable but nevertheless can be inferred on the basis of more observable manifestations. If you find it difficult to remember, go back to the section "Concepts and principles of the cognitive approach to behaviour" in Unit 3 and review the debate between behaviourists with their concept of "black box" and cognitive psychologists. In that unit we concluded that models can be used to scientifically study mental phenomena in psychology. Interestingly, this last approach to defining abnormality is also a "model".

What makes the medical model a "model"?

A strength of the medical model is its flexibility. It allows for various perspectives concerning mental illness, because it allows illness to be diagnosed regardless of your views about its causes. For example, one clinician might believe that depression is caused by a chemical imbalance in the brain, and another might believe that depression is caused by environmental factors creating excessive levels of stress. In any case, an identifiable set of symptoms allows them to reach a consensus regarding the presence of depression, that is, the medical model theoretically makes it possible for diagnosis to be independent of a clinician's theoretical orientations.

A major limitation of the medical model is that it is much more difficult to apply to mental illness than to physical disease. Symptoms of mental illness are not as obvious or observable as physical symptoms, for example, how do we establish a significant change in mood without relying on self-reports? Another difficulty in applying the medical model to abnormal behaviour is the need to decide which symptoms are related to which disorders. One symptom may be an indicator of multiple disorders, and it is only a combination of symptoms that can delineate between disorders. Using combinations of symptoms, however, raises further questions. Which symptoms must be present to establish a particular disorder and which symptoms are secondary? How many symptoms should be present and for what period of time?

Classification systems, on which the medical model of abnormality is based, are designed to tackle all these issues.

See video

Watch this TED Talk by Jon Ronson "Strange answers to the psychopath test":
https://tinyurl.com/o4t9bdb

▶ ❚❚ ■

The driving question behind this talk is: is there a definitive line that divides the crazy from the sane? How would you answer this question after watching the video? How can you characterize the "grey area" between normality and abnormality?

Psychology in real life

Think back to Anoushka's case. Apply the several approaches to defining abnormality discussed in this unit to her case. Does her behaviour fall under the category of abnormality? In what approaches?

What additional information could be helpful to delineate between normality and abnormality in Anoushka's case?

Classification systems

Inquiry questions

- How do we decide what symptoms to include in a diagnosis?

- How do we define the threshold between the presence and the absence of a disorder?

- What should be done to enable early diagnosis and prevention of mental disorders?

- Would you prefer to overdiagnose or underdiagnose?

What you will learn in this section

- The history of DSM: from DSM-I to DSM-5

- Other classification systems: ICD-10, CCMD-3

- Major challenges

  - Explanation versus description

  - Validity of diagnosis and its reliability

  - Delineation between categories

  - Changing social norms

  - Degrees of abnormality

  - Cross-cultural applicability

  - Medicalization

This section also links to:

- behaviourism, introspection, the concept of black box (cognitive approach to behaviour)

- research methodology

- social norms (sociocultural approach to behaviour).

As noted above, classification systems provide the basis of the medical model of abnormality.

Several classification systems are widely used today. In the western world the most well-known classification system is published as a manual by the American Psychiatric Association and is referred to as the **Diagnostic and Statistical Manual** (DSM). Using the DSM, clinicians arrive at a diagnosis by matching the individual's behaviour with the symptoms that define particular disorders (Ramsden, 2013). Currently the DSM is in its fifth edition.

History of the DSM

Looking at the brief history of the development of the DSM will help you to understand how views on mental illness have changed in the western world over the last 65 years.

DSM-I was published by the American Psychiatric Association in 1952 and included several categories of "personality disturbance". For example, homosexuality was listed as a mental disorder. It remained in the DSM until 1974. DSM-I was

heavily grounded in psychoanalytic traditions. This caused clinicians to look for origins of abnormal behaviour in childhood traumas. Homosexuality, for example, was explained by a fear of the opposite sex caused by traumatic relationships with the parents.

Exercise

Psychoanalytic traditions are based on a clinician's **interpretation** of the patient's behaviour and experiences. If you want to know more about psychoanalysis you can start by exploring this website: https://tinyurl.com/8a59dnq

Make an A4 poster explaining psychoanalysis to non-psychologists.

DSM-II was published in 1968. It was the result of a strong attack on both the psychiatric practices and the concept of mental illness itself. First, behaviourists criticized the use of unobservable constructs such as "trauma" or "motivation". Second, the anti-psychiatry movement emerged, with figures such as Thomas Szasz pointing out that psychiatry may well be just another way to label non-conformists and establish social control. However, change does not happen rapidly. DSM-II was quite similar to DSM-I. It largely retained its psychoanalytical orientation. It was explanatory rather than descriptive, referring to possible origins of disorders. At first homosexuality was retained as a disorder, but under the pressure of gay rights activists it was removed from DSM-II in one of its reprints.

▲ Figure 5.2 Thomas Szasz

DSM-III was published in 1980. It listed 265 diagnostic categories organized in five groups (axes)—the so-called multi-axial system. This new edition was a response to increasing criticism from some scholars such as David Rosenhan (see below). Doubts had been raised about various aspects of diagnosing mental illness. In a number of cases psychiatrists had been shown to be unable to discriminate between mental health and mental illness; some studies had attacked consistency of diagnosis; and some studies had questioned cross-cultural applicability of the DSM. The main change was the abandonment of psychoanalytic interpretations and a general shift from explaining disorders to describing them. The idea was that a focus on description and a set of observable symptoms would increase agreement between psychiatrists—less interpretation would be involved, so there would be less subjectivity. One criticism that followed was overmedicalization of population: too many people met the criteria of mental illness.

DSM-IV was published in 1994. It was the result of a very substantial revision process; a lot of experts were invited, split into groups, and each group conducted an extensive literature review, requested data from researchers and consulted clinical practitioners. The major change was the **clinical significance criterion**: from now on to be diagnosed with a disorder an individual had to exhibit symptoms that created clinically significant distress or impairment of daily functioning. This was meant to reduce overmedicalization.

The DSM-IV described each diagnosis in terms of five dimensions (axes) highlighting different aspects of the disorder.

1. Clinical disorders. This axis included patterns of behaviour that impair functioning. Examples include schizophrenia or depression.

2. Personality disorders. These involve rigid patterns of maladaptive behaviour (that have become part of a person's personality). Examples include antisocial, paranoid or narcissistic disorders.

3. General medical conditions.

4. Psychosocial and environmental problems contributing to the disorder, such as job loss, divorce, death of a close relative.

5. Global assessment of functioning (GAF) on a scale from 1 to 100. The clinician was to use this scale to evaluate the current need for treatment.

Together these five axes were meant to provide a broad range of information about the patient's mental state, not just a diagnosis (Nevid, Rathus and Greene, 2014). An example of a diagnosis in the multiaxial system is given below.

Example of a diagnosis in the multi-axial DSM system	
Axis I	Major depressive disorder, recurrent, moderate
Axis II	Dependent personality disorder
Axis III	Diabetes
Axis IV	Unemployment
Axis V	GAF = 59

▲ Table 5.1

ATL skills: Social

At first sight using a multi-axial system seems to be a good idea because it supports a more holistic approach to diagnosis. However, there are potential difficulties with applying this system. Suggest what these difficulties might be in a small group.

DSM-5 was published in 2013. The Roman numeral in the title was changed to Arabic as the plan was to update the DSM more frequently in future, with future editions reflecting both minor changes (using 5.1, 5.2, 5.3 and so on) and major changes (6, 7, 8). A major change in the DSM-5 was that the multi-axial system was eliminated. This was a response to critics who said that the axial distinctions were artificial and that in many cases similar disorders were artificially brought apart. We will return to DSM-5 diagnoses later in this unit when we consider diagnostic criteria for major depressive disorder. Problems with artificiality of axial distinctions will be discussed in more detail in the context of validity and reliability of diagnosis.

ATL skills: Thinking and self-management

Draw a timeline of the DSM. Reflect the main landmarks in its development and the main changes that were made in the process.

Other classification systems

The DSM is not the only classification system that has been widely used. The **International Classification of Diseases (ICD)** is maintained by the World Health Organization (WHO). This classification system is for all diseases including medical; behavioural abnormality is only part of it. It is in its tenth edition—ICD-10. ICD-10 is more widely used in European countries, while the DSM is in wider use in the USA.

China uses a system called the **Chinese Classification of Mental Disorders**, currently in its third edition (**CCMD-3**). It is intentionally similar to the DSM and the ICD, both in terms of its structure and its diagnostic categories. However, some diagnoses are modified to better reflect the cultural realities. Also it includes around 40 unique culturally related diagnoses.

▶ Figure 5.3

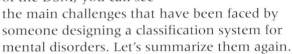

Major challenges in designing a classification system for mental disorders

Now that we have looked at the main stages in the development of the DSM, you can see the main challenges that have been faced by someone designing a classification system for mental disorders. Let's summarize them again.

- **Explanation** versus **description**. The DSM has been moving progressively towards less explanation and more description in an attempt to make diagnosis more consistent between clinicians using the manual.

- A related controversy is that between **validity** of diagnosis and its **reliability** (see below). In a nutshell, a shift to description allows clinicians to be more consistent in their diagnosis (higher reliability). However, at the same time a descriptive approach leaves less room for interpretation of individual circumstances, so diagnosis may become less accurate (that is, less valid).

- **Delineation** between categories. Disorders are diagnosed on the basis of a set of symptoms. These sets overlap. Deciding if a particular pattern of behaviour belongs to one category or another is not an easy task sometimes. It would be useful to have a clear set of diagnostic categories that place observable patterns of behaviour within one and only one category, but it is practically impossible for such a system to capture the complexities of real-life human behaviour.

- **Changing social norms**. Think back to the case of homosexuality in the DSM.

- The idea of "**degrees of abnormality**" was not widely accepted at the beginning. Disorders were viewed as something either present or absent. It is not surprising, because

establishing the severity of a symptom is more difficult than simply establishing its presence.

- **Cross-cultural applicability**. A good diagnostic system needs to be equally applicable to people of different cultural backgrounds. Is this even possible? We will discuss this in more detail later when we look at clinical biases in diagnosis and culture-bound syndromes.

- **Medicalization** of population. The way we define categories of mental illness has a direct influence on the percentage of the population that can be categorized as mentally ill. The situation where too many people can potentially be diagnosed with a mental disorder is not desirable.

ATL skills: Thinking and self-management

Go back to your timeline of the development of the DSM. How are the seven challenges reflected in the history of the DSM?

If you think that you don't have enough information to answer these questions, formulate exactly what extra knowledge you need. After you have done that, continue to look for answers as you read the rest of this unit.

See video

Watch the TED Talk by Elyn Saks "A tale of mental illness – from the inside" (2012). She tells the story of her schizophrenia: https://tinyurl.com/n8pynzq

What is it like to be mentally ill? Can you think of any artistic ways to express the main ideas in this talk?

▶ ❚❚ ■ ────────────

Discussion

Suggest some possible CAS projects related to raising awareness about mentally ill individuals and their experiences.

Inquiry questions

- What are the symptoms of clinical depression?
- How many people in the population are clinically depressed?
- How can this be estimated?

What you will learn in this section

- Diagnosis of depression: DSM-5

    ○ Symptoms and criteria of major depressive disorder (MDD)

    ○ The bereavement exclusion

- Prevalence rates of major depressive disorder

    ○ Point prevalence

    ○ Period prevalence (12-month, lifetime)

    ○ Onset age

    ○ Prevalence rates and age of onset of major depressive disorder: cultural and gender differences

- Factors influencing prevalence rate estimates

    ○ Classification systems

    ○ Clinical biases in diagnosis

This section also links to:

- clinical biases in diagnosis
- explanations for disorders—gene-culture coevolution theory
- treatment of disorders—culturally sensitive treatment
- cultural factors in the DSM.

Diagnosis of depression

DSM-5 formulates nine groups of symptoms of major depressive disorder (MDD):

- depressed mood
- diminished interest or pleasure in daily activities
- significant weight change, either loss or gain (more that 5% of body mass in a month)
- insomnia or hypersomnia
- psychomotor agitation or retardation (movement activity too fast or too slow)
- fatigue
- feelings of worthlessness or guilt
- diminished ability to think or concentrate
- recurrent suicidal thoughts.

Apart from that, there are several criteria for the diagnosis of MDD.

- Five or more of the listed symptoms have been present for two weeks.
- These symptoms represent a change from previous functioning.
- At least one of the symptoms is either depressed mood or loss of interest or pleasure.
- The symptoms cause significant distress or malfunctioning.
- The symptoms are not attributable to (or better explained by) other conditions and disorders.

A grey area in diagnosis is the so-called "bereavement exclusion"—depression-like symptoms that may accompany a significant loss, such as the death of a close person. In DSM-IV depression could not be diagnosed if symptoms occurred less than two weeks after the significant loss, because such symptoms were considered to be appropriate to the bereavement period. DSM-5, however, allows such diagnosis to be made. It states that the presence of depression in addition to the normal response should be carefully considered, based on the patient's individual history and cultural norms related to the expression of distress in the event of a significant loss.

This makes diagnosis of depression in DSM-5 more inclusive than it used to be in DSM-IV: a larger number of people can now be diagnosed with depression in the bereavement period.

> **ATL skills: Thinking and communication**
>
> To what extent is this a positive (or a negative) trend? Discuss methodological and ethical implications of this change in the diagnostic criteria.

Prevalence rates of major depressive disorder

The main parameters used in epidemiology to characterize the spread of a disorder are prevalence rate (point prevalence and period prevalence) and onset age.

- **Point prevalence rate** is the proportion of people in the population currently diagnosed with the disorder.

- **Period prevalence** is the proportion of a population that has the disorder at some time during a given period. For example, to study 12-month period prevalence you take a representative sample of people and count the number of people who have depression currently or develop it at any time during the subsequent 12-month period. Likewise, lifetime period prevalence is the proportion of a population who had depression at least once in their life. Thus, lifetime prevalence is always greater than 12-month prevalence, and 12-month prevalence is always greater than point prevalence.

- **Onset age** is the average age when individuals in a given population first develop the disorder.

According to the WHO forecast, depression will be the second leading cause of disability in the world by 2020 (currently ranked the fourth).

Prevalence rates of MDD have been found to vary considerably across cultures. A cross-national comparison in 2003 found lifetime prevalence of MDD that ranged from 1% (Czech Republic) to 16.9% (USA) (Kessler and Bromet, 2013). Lifetime prevalence of MDD is generally higher in high-income countries than in low-income countries. These differences may be the result of several possible factors, for example, severity threshold for reporting depression: how severe should the symptoms be before a typical representative of a given culture decides to report a mental health issue?

In 2015 the National Survey on Drug Use and Health in the USA estimated 12-month prevalence of MDD among adults (aged 18 or older). The average 12-month prevalence was found to be 6.7%, with women at 8.5% and men at 4.7% (NIMH, 2015). The risk of MDD for women has been consistently found to be roughly twice as much as for men. This has been explained by a variety of factors including hormones, work-related stressors, home responsibilities, caring for children, abuse and relationship strains.

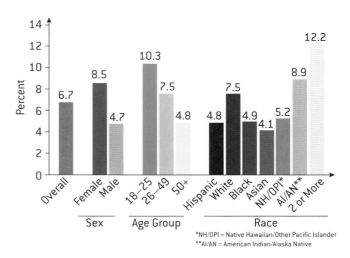

▲ Figure 5.4 12-month prevalence of MDD among US adults (NIMH, 2015)

Cross-cultural differences in the age of onset have also been found to be greater than for many other mental disorders. It ranges from adolescence to the early forties, but the median age of onset is in the mid-20s (Kessler and Bromet, 2013).

Depression has a tendency to be a recurrent disorder. A depressive episode typically lasts for 3–4 months and 80% of people experience at least one subsequent episode. In about 12% of cases, depression becomes a chronic disorder with symptoms lasting for two years or more.

Factors influencing prevalence rate estimates

Determining prevalence of disorders is not an easy task. Here are some of the factors that need to be taken into account when discussing this topic.

> ## Exam tip
>
> The topic "Prevalence rates and disorders" is closely linked to two other sections: "Classification systems" and "The role of clinical biases in diagnosis". You can use material from all three sections in response to the examination questions, but remember to stay focused on the requirements of the question and the command verb.

Classification system. As you know, diagnosis is made on the basis of a list of symptoms and diagnostic criteria. These may be subject to change with every subsequent edition of the diagnostic manual (for example, the bereavement exclusion for MDD was removed from DSM-5, thus resulting potentially in higher estimates of prevalence rates). It needs to be understood that there is no such thing as prevalence rates independent of a classification system.

Clinical biases in diagnosis. Let's conduct a thought experiment and imagine that a single classification system is used all around the globe. Even in this scenario, estimating prevalence of disorders may still be subject to bias. A lot would depend on how consistently this classification system would be applied across psychiatrists and across populations. What could go wrong?

Some populations may experience depressive symptoms, but be reluctant to report them. This is known as reporting bias. In some societies (such as China or India) it may be "shameful" to have depression, especially among traditional groups and older people. It needs to be understood that prevalence rate estimates are based on the number of people who sought psychological help and were diagnosed with a disorder, but societies differ considerably in terms of the amount of people who are likely to seek psychological help in the first place. For an example, see **Furnham and Malik (1994)** below (in "The role of clinical biases in diagnosis")—a study that attempted to explain why British Asians were rarely diagnosed with depression.

For now, let's continue the thought experiment and assume that all populations are equally willing to report depression. Even so, we can still face the problem of cultural, gender and age variations in the **expression of symptoms**. For example, **Payne (2012)** demonstrated that African-American and Caucasian clients would often express their symptoms differently, but clinicians tend to be insensitive to these cultural differences, which results in bias and misdiagnosis (see "The role of clinical biases in diagnosis"). A related problem is somatization—expressing psychological disturbance in the form of physical symptoms (see the section below for a more detailed discussion of this).

Given all the difficulties mentioned above, it is probably true that prevalence rate estimates on a national level are more accurate than cross-cultural comparison of prevalence rates. At the same time, group differences in prevalence rates (such as 8.5% versus 4.7% prevalence of depression in women and men, respectively) may probably be attributed to one of two factors: either genuine differences in the prevalence of a disorder, or differences in the way the disorder is presented or reported. It is not always easy to say which of the factors contributes more, so estimates of prevalence rates remain just that—estimates.

Validity and reliability of diagnosis

What you will learn in this section

- Reliability and validity of diagnosis

  - Inter-rater reliability and two ways to establish it: audio-/video-recordings and test-retest method

  - Kappa coefficient of inter-rater reliability

  - Validity: the concept; predictive validity

- Relationship between validity and reliability of diagnosis

- Reliability of the DSM

  - Alarmingly low in the earlier editions of the DSM: Beck *et al* (1962), agreement between two psychiatrists only 54%; Kendall (1974), unreliable re-diagnosis of schizophrenia and depression

  - Between DSM-II and DSM-III an initiative to make diagnostic categories observable and scientific: Carl Hempel

  - The increase in reliability in DSM-III was not universal: Di Nardo *et al* (1993), excellent reliability for some disorders, low reliability for others; the Structured Clinical Interview further improved reliability of the DSM; Williams *et al* (1992), DSM-III and SCID, kappa coefficients from 0.47 to 0.84

  - DSM-IV and DSM-5: average reliability estimates even lower than before, but this can be attributed to a more rigorous application of the scientific method; field trials for DSM-5 used exclusively the test-retest method; Chmielewski *et al* (2015), DSM-IV, mean kappa for the recording method 0.80, mean kappa for the test-retest method 0.47

  - Reliability of DSM-5 had mixed results: Regier *et al* (2013), the DSM has achieved the task of increasing reliability but it still varies considerably from one diagnostic category to another

- Validity of diagnosis: key problems

  - Heterogeneity of clinical presentation

  - Classification is based on symptomology rather than etiology

  - Where to draw boundaries between disorders? The issue of comorbidity

  - Stability of symptoms

  - Cut-off point between "clinically significant" and "clinically insignificant" symptoms

  - What treatment to choose?: lithium therapy is effective for depression but not schizophrenia; Cooper (1972), schizophrenia and depression in the USA and Great Britain

- Research of validity of diagnosis: two approaches

  o Establishing systematic biases in clinical judgment

  o Assessing the ability of psychiatrists to detect the disorder when the disorder is objectively known: Rosenhan (1973), being sane in insane places

This section also links to:

  o prevalence of disorders

  o the role of clinical biases in diagnosis

  o schema theory (cognitive approach to behaviour)

  o research methods (experiments, validity).

Reliability and validity of diagnosis: the concepts

Diagnosis literally means differentiating ("dia") knowledge ("gnosis"), or telling something apart from everything else. Diagnosis in abnormal behaviour refers to relating a pattern of behaviour to a certain category. Diagnosis is made on the basis of symptoms. Two essential characteristics that define the quality of diagnosis are its **validity** and **reliability**.

Diagnosis is considered reliable if it is consistent across clinicians—different clinicians using the same classification system should arrive at the same diagnosis for the same patient. This is referred to as **inter-rater reliability**. There are two ways to establish inter-rater reliability of diagnosis.

In the first, one clinician conducts the clinical interview with a patient and this interview gets recorded (**audio-/video-recording method**). This recording is then used by another clinician to arrive at a diagnosis independently. A strength of this approach is that the two clinicians use exactly the same stimulus: the same questions and the same reactions from the patient. However, at the same time this is a limitation because if the second clinician had to conduct an independent interview (which is exactly what happens in real-life diagnostic scenarios), the questions would be slightly different as well as the patient's behaviour and responses. So the audio-/video-recording method brings some artificiality in establishing inter-rater reliability of diagnosis.

In the second way, two clinicians conduct interviews with the same patient independently. This overcomes the artificiality issue outlined above, but raises a different issue: time. With the course of time the patient's symptoms may change naturally, so the difference in diagnosis can reflect either genuine changes in the disorder or

inconsistency between the two clinicians, and it is impossible to separate these two sources of error. Note also that the longer the time span between the two interviews, the higher the chance that the inconsistencies between clinicians will reflect genuine changes in the symptoms. This approach to establishing reliability of diagnosis is referred to as "**test-retest reliability**". Test-retest reliability is not opposite to but is rather a special type of inter-rater reliability. In both cases different clinicians make a diagnosis. It is the recording of a clinical interview that makes the difference.

Note that in some studies of test-retest reliability (usually those involving a structured clinical interview) the same clinician diagnoses the same patient twice with the same interview. Such designs are rare because they are open to bias: the clinician will most likely remember the initial diagnosis.

Reliability of diagnosis is quantifiable—we can express consistency of diagnosis across clinicians as a number. The statistic that is most commonly used for this is the kappa coefficient. Kappa can range from 0 to 1. Zero on this scale represents the amount of agreement that can be expected due to random chance. One represents perfect agreement between raters. There's no straightforward way to translate kappa to something more intuitive like "percentage of agreement between clinicians", but the table below presents the commonly used boundaries.

Value of kappa	Level of agreement
0–0.2	Minimal
0.21–0.39	Weak
0.40–0.59	Moderate
0.60–0.79	Strong
0.80–0.90	Almost perfect
Above 0.90	Perfect

▲ Table 5.2 Based on Cohen (1960)

Validity of diagnosis relates to its accuracy—the degree to which a diagnostic system measures the behaviours that it purports to measure. In other words, diagnosis is valid if it corresponds to the actual disorder. A special form of validity is **predictive validity**—the ability to predict how the disorder will respond to treatment. For example, if you have been prescribed antidepressants based on your diagnosis, and the drugs actually help and lead to a reduction of symptoms, your diagnosis is said to have high predictive validity.

Relationship between validity and reliability of diagnosis

The metaphor of shooting at a target is often used to illustrate the ideas of validity and reliability. In this metaphor, accuracy is determined by whether or not you hit the centre of the target. Consistency is determined by the spread—how likely you are to hit the same place on the target on the subsequent trials. Consider the four possible scenarios in the figure below.

Unreliable and invalid

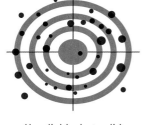
Unreliable, but valid

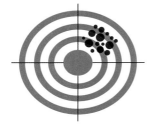
Reliable, not valid

Both reliable and valid

▲ Figure 5.5 The target metaphor for validity and reliability of diagnosis

In diagnosis you want to always hit the bull's eye, whether that is in different trials of the same clinician or different clinicians "shooting at the same target". However, this is hardly ever possible. A reliable but invalid diagnosis is dangerous because the consensus between clinicians inspires trust in their judgment, but misdiagnosis will result in both ethical issues (such as stigmatization) and treatment issues (ineffective treatment). An unreliable but valid diagnosis is a logical paradox, because what is not consistent (over time and across clinicians) cannot be valid by definition. Note that a valid measurement is reliable by definition, but the opposite is not necessarily true.

Interestingly, there is an **inverse relationship** (trade-off) between validity and reliability of diagnosis. Think about it. To diagnose a disorder accurately you need to take into account multiple factors such as a person's subjective interpretations of the events. For this you need to take one step beyond just registering the patient's observable behaviour and try to interpret this behaviour, making inferences about the patient's subjective experiences. Interpreting the patient's behaviour and experience, you understand the nature of the disorder more fully (increasing validity), but this opens the door to subjectivity and disagreement between yourself and other clinicians (decreasing reliability). On the other hand, if you want to increase reliability, you might want to make diagnostic criteria as standardized and observable as possible, which will make clinicians more consistent in applying the criteria, but the diagnosis itself more superficial (invalid).

ATL skills: Thinking and communication

Think back to the history of the DSM, especially the switch of the philosophy from interpretation to description that occurred at some point. Now that you understand the inverse relationship between validity and reliability of diagnosis, discuss the following.

1. Why did this switch occur?

2. Does a focus on description (as opposed to interpretation) increase validity of diagnosis?

Here's a highly debatable question: Given the trade-off between reliability and validity of diagnosis, is it better to increase validity or reliability? Discuss this dilemma from the ethical point of view.

TOK

Reliability of diagnosis links to the concept of replication. If research findings fail to be replicated in independent research, does it always means that the findings were not true?

Before you discuss this, review major results of Brian Nosek's "Reproducibility Project": https://tinyurl.com/jedsaxh and https://tinyurl.com/hyyhzg9

Reliability of the DSM

So how reliable are the classification systems used to diagnose mental disorders? Let's consider the example of the DSM and link this question to the main stages in its development.

Research into earlier editions of the DSM showed its reliability to be alarmingly low. For example, **Beck *et al* (1962)** found that agreement on specific diagnosis for 153 patients between two psychiatrists was only 54%. This means that in half the cases psychiatrists arrived at different diagnoses for the same patient. Note that this study was conducted when DSM-I was in use, with its orientation towards explanation and its reliance on the psychoanalytic traditions.

Similarly, **Kendall (1974)** studied almost 2,000 patients who were admitted to hospital from 1964 and then readmitted after 1969. It was found that schizophrenia was more often re-diagnosed as a form of depression than the other way around. The study shows that diagnosis was not very consistent over time. Of course, two interpretations are possible.

- The patients changed the pattern of their abnormal behaviour.

- Psychiatrists were not applying diagnostic criteria in a standardized and consistent way.

The first explanation is far less plausible because depression and schizophrenia are two separate and very different disorders caused by different factors.

After the criticism that ensued, the American Psychiatric Association started an initiative to make DSM categories more "scientific". **Carl Hempel**, a philosopher of science, was especially influential in suggesting that the criteria should be made observational. Hempel provided the impulse to start shifting the focus of DSM from explanation to observation.

ATL skills: Thinking

Would you have made a similar decision if you were in Carl Hempel's position? Given what you know about the relation between validity and reliability, what effects do you think it would have on validity of diagnosis?

This effort was fruitful, and diagnosis using the DSM-III categories was generally shown to be more reliable. Also many more research studies into the reliability of psychiatric diagnosis were conducted.

However, an increase in reliability in DSM-III was not universal: it depended on the disorder in the sense that for some disorders diagnosis was shown to be more reliable than for others. For example, **Di Nardo** *et al* **(1993)** using DSM-III found "excellent" inter-rater reliability for such disorders as simple phobia and obsessive-compulsive disorders (OCD) but quite low reliability for generalized anxiety disorder (GAD). Note that these are all anxiety disorders, so these differences exist even within one broad category of disorders.

Reliability of DSM-III was further improved when the **Structured Clinical Interview for DSM (SCID)** was published. This was a diagnostic interview that included a standardized set of questions that clinicians were supposed to ask, restricting improvisation. This facilitated consistency in the application of diagnostic criteria across clinicians—but the discrepancy between different disorders remained.

Exercise

Review this website that provides additional information about the SCID: http://www.scid4.org/

Role-play a dialogue between a patient and a clinician using the SCID.

Psychology in real life

Go back to Anoushka's case and draft a clinical interview you might use with her.

For example, **Williams** *et al* **(1992)** using DSM-III and SCID conducted a large test-retest reliability study of 592 patients (with a 1–3 week test-retest interval) and obtained the following results: 0.84 for bipolar disorder and substance abuse, 0.64 for MDD and only 0.47 for social phobia. This shows how reliability coefficients for different disorders vary even within the same diagnostic manual, with disorders that have more obvious behavioural manifestations being easier to diagnose consistently.

Of course, there were also attempts to estimate the "average" reliability coefficient of the DSM, but the practical value of such estimates is questionable.

From DSM-III to DSM-5 diagnostic categories were further refined and new, more standardized versions of SCID developed, in an attempt to increase consistency further. Surprisingly, some recent studies have shown lower reliability for DSM-5 compared to DSM-IV, even for the diagnostic categories that stayed unchanged (such as MDD). **Chmielewski** *et al* **(2015)** suggest an explanation for this: they claim that reliability to a large extent depends on the method with which it was established (their article is entitled "Method matters"). They point out that prior to DSM-5 the overwhelming majority of research studies that investigated inter-rater reliability used the audio-/video-recording method. In this method one clinician conducts the interview and arrives at a diagnosis, and another clinician watches (or listens to) the recording of the interview and gives his or her diagnosis independently. Reliability estimates using this method were typically high. This is not surprising given the fact that the information obtained by clinicians is identical. If these interviews were conducted by the clinicians independently, both the questions that they ask and the responses that the patient gives would be somewhat different.

The test-retest method of establishing reliability seems more natural. In this method two different clinicians conduct interviews with the patients independently. It is important to keep the test-retest interval sufficiently short so that the true changes in symptoms do not contaminate the results of the study. Short-term stability of symptoms is expected in most mental disorders.

Chmielewski *et al* reviewed past studies and concluded that most of the field trials to establish reliability of DSM-III were conducted using a combination of audio-/video-recording and test-retest methods, most of the field trials for DSM-IV used recordings, while field trials for DSM-5 used exclusively the test-retest method. They claim that the differences in reliability estimates might be a reflection of these different methods.

In their own study they recruited 339 patients and compared reliability estimates for DSM-IV categories using both methods. First, participants were interviewed using the SCID. The interview was recorded. These audio tapes were later assessed independently by a second interviewer. One week later, the participants were invited back and interviewed by a different clinician. Results confirmed the initial expectations. The mean kappa coefficient across all the disorders for the audio-recording method was 0.80, considered "almost perfect". The mean kappa coefficient for the test-retest method was 0.47, considered only "moderate". To ensure that the disagreement between clinicians over the one-week interval was not due to the true changes in the patients' symptoms, researchers compared these results to self-reports. Patients' self-reports of their symptoms indicated very little change over this short time period. So it was concluded that lower consistency of diagnosis in the test-retest condition is the result of the method used, not actual changes that patients underwent between the two interviews.

So where does DSM-5 stand now in terms of its reliability? **Regier *et al* (2013)** summarized the results of field trials of the DSM-5 in the USA and Canada for 23 diagnostic categories. All the field trials used the test-retest method. Two clinicians independently interviewed the same patient on different occasions in a clinical setting. Of the 23 diagnoses, 5 were in the strong range (kappa = 0.6–0.8), 9 in the moderate range (0.4–0.6), 6 in the weak range (0.2–0.4) and 3 diagnoses were in the unacceptable range (<0.2). MDD yielded the reliability estimate of 0.28 (weak), while reliability of PTSD was classified as very strong (0.67). "Mixed anxiety-depressive disorder" showed an unacceptable reliability of 0.05.

ATL skills: Thinking

What reasons can you suggest for this discrepancy in the estimates?

Researchers refer to the results of DSM-5 field studies as "mixed". On the one hand, more than half of the diagnostic categories ranked in the top bands of "strong" or "moderate" reliability. On the other hand, some results such as those for MDD (a widely diagnosed category) were alarming. However, to say that reliability of diagnosis for these disorders decreased would be incorrect, because field trials for DSM-5 used more realistic estimates—

ATL skills: Research

The section above about reliability of the DSM was rather complex, especially since it was presented from a historical perspective. However, it reflects real-life scientific processes. Researchers struggle to get "pure" estimates of reliability, but it is not easy at all, with all the changes in the manual and the overall approach to diagnosis.

To make sense of all these studies, try a couple of exercises that will help you structure information better.

1. Without mentioning any names or research studies summarize the main ideas of this section, starting as follows. Reliability of the DSM initially was low, but then …

2. Draw a flowchart of the main landmarks in the attempt to increase reliability of diagnosis in the DSM.

3. Complete the table (if you don't have enough information, you might want to do some research online).

Researcher	DSM edition	Method of establishing inter-rater reliability, audio-/video-recording or test-retest	One major finding (state in one sentence)
Beck *et al* (1962)			
Kendall (1974)			
Di Nardo *et al* (1993)			
Williams *et al* (1992)			
Chmielewski *et al* (2015)			
Regier *et al* (2013)			

test-retest designs and random samples of patients. Arguably, previous field studies for DSM-IV and DSM-III could have yielded biased results due to the use of the audio-/video-recording method and carefully trained clinicians—samples and interview situations did not reflect real-life settings.

The general consensus, however, is that the DSM has achieved the task of increasing reliability of diagnosis, although it still varies considerably from one diagnostic category to another.

Exam tip

Remember that you do not have to use all research studies in your responses. Understanding is more important. A good strategy while studying is to ensure that you are familiar and comfortable with the flow of argumentation first; you can add factual details later when you revise.

Validity of diagnosis: key problems

Reliability sets the stage for validity in the sense that valid diagnosis is a logical impossibility if reliability is low. We know that reliability is established by quantifying the consistency of diagnosis between two (or more) psychiatrists. How is validity of diagnosis established?

TOK

How do you know if your diagnosis "corresponds to reality", given that the only way to "see" the reality is through diagnosis itself? There's a similar circle in one of the definitions of knowledge in TOK. Knowledge is sometimes defined as a justified true belief, but the truth can only be established "to the best of our knowledge". How do you think this issue should be solved in TOK?

There are several key problems related to validity of diagnosis.

1. **Heterogeneity of clinical presentation**. This means that one and the same disorder can presumably manifest itself differently in different patients. To account for this, while at the same time preserving sufficient reliability, diagnostic manuals made the diagnostic criteria somewhat flexible. For example, to

be diagnosed with MDD based on DSM-IV the patient needs to exhibit five symptoms of the listed nine. Essentially, this means that the clinical presentation in two patients may only overlap in one symptom and they would still receive the same diagnosis. Given such different clinical presentations, how do we know that both are suffering from depression?

2. Classification is based on **symptomology rather than etiology**. When we classify physical disease we rely on the causes (etiology) of the problem, for example, the infectious agent or a genetic mutation. Since our knowledge of what causes mental disorders is currently very ambiguous and inconclusive, we have to rely on more superficial characteristics—symptoms. This will inevitably lead to overlap in diagnoses, because two disorders with separate causes might have the same symptoms, similar to medicine in which there are a lot of diseases that manifest themselves with flu-like symptoms (for example, malaria).

3. Where do we draw **boundaries** between disorders? This relates to the issue of **comorbidity**—co-occurrence of diagnoses. For example, generalized anxiety disorder frequently co-occurs with depression. Comorbidity is quite extensive among DSM diagnoses, and it raises questions about the validity of the classification. If two disorders frequently co-occur, could they be manifestations of the same underlying cause? Should they be combined in one category? Do we observe different disorders or just different symptoms? Comorbidity, if present, poses a threat to validity of psychiatric diagnosis.

4. **Stability** of symptoms. For diagnosis to be valid, it needs to be proven that the inferred disorder is stable over time, to exclude the possibility that the observed symptoms were a one-time occurrence due to chance or other factors.

5. **Cut-off point** between "clinically significant" and "clinically insignificant" symptoms (Hyman, 2010).

6. Finally, **selecting treatment**. The type of treatment depends on the type of disorder,

so it is important to identify the problem correctly. For example, lithium therapy was shown to be effective for severe depression but not for schizophrenia. **Cooper (1972)** asked American and British psychiatrists to diagnose patients by watching a number of videotaped clinical interviews. They found that schizophrenia was diagnosed twice as often in the USA than in Britain, and the reverse was true for depression. They used DSM-II diagnostic criteria. This study caused a lot of speculation about cultural differences in human behaviour. However, when the study was replicated later using DSM-III, the differences disappeared. In DSM-II schizophrenia was diagnosed both for acute and chronic manifestations of the disorder, whereas in DSM-III this was narrowed down to chronic symptoms only, which was more like the British approach to diagnosis. The results of the

study therefore have nothing to do with cross-cultural differences in behaviour. It is a study of diagnostic criteria and how changeable they are. When a certain set of symptoms is being relabelled, it affects the prescribed treatment. We want diagnosis to be valid because we want treatment to target the real cause.

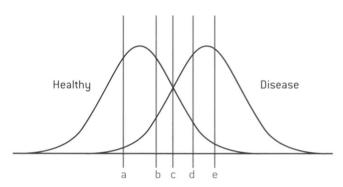

▲ Figure 5.6 Cut-off points

ATL skills: Social and communication

For the first three problems related to validity of diagnosis, split into two groups and have a debate, with each group taking one of the opposing perspectives. The idea is to come up with relevant arguments in favour of each extreme:

Clinical presentation of disorders is heterogeneous. At the same time we rely on a description of observed behaviour when we make a diagnosis. For this reason, diagnosis cannot be valid.	versus	Despite heterogeneous presentation of disorders we can still infer the correct cause if we take into account the context. In chemistry, for example, chemical reactions will manifest themselves differently in different conditions (for example, temperature), but we can still correctly recognize the chemical reaction.
Classification is based on symptomology rather than etiology. Different disorders may have the same symptoms. Therefore we will not be able to make a valid diagnosis of mental illnesses until we discover a way to diagnose their etiology directly, for example, until we find measurable biological markers of mental disorders.	versus	Diagnosis based on symptomology may not be as straightforward, but it can still be valid. Even in medical diseases symptoms are often enough to arrive at a diagnosis and knowledge of etiology (blood tests and so on) is often used only to support the initial diagnosis.
Comorbidity makes diagnosis impossible.	versus	Comorbidity is a common occurrence; it makes diagnosis more difficult but certainly not impossible.

Research of validity of diagnosis: two approaches

Validity of diagnosis, unlike reliability, cannot be quantified.

However, we can assess validity indirectly by intentionally attempting to discover lack of validity—targeting our research at the identification

of potential **biases** that compromise diagnosis. If we show that a systematic bias exists, that is, diagnosis is influenced by factors not related to the patient's actual disorder, we can infer that diagnosis lacks validity.

There are two broad approaches to how research in this area may be organized.

The first approach is establishing **systematic biases in clinical judgment**. In this approach we compare two sets of diagnoses that should not differ if diagnosis is valid. For example, we can compare diagnoses (given to the same patients using the same clinical interview) of two groups of clinicians with different theoretical orientations (for example, psychoanalysts versus behaviourists). If a diagnostic system is valid, the clinician's theoretical orientation should not affect the resulting diagnosis. If it does affect diagnosis, we have established a systematic threat to validity. Another example is comparing diagnoses of clinicians who belong to different cultural backgrounds. Such clinical biases will be discussed in detail later (see "The role of clinical biases in diagnosis").

The second approach is assessing the ability of psychiatrists to detect the disorder when the disorder is **objectively known** (but not disclosed to the psychiatrist). The famous example of this approach is the study of David Rosenhan (1973) entitled "Being sane in insane places".

▲ Figure 5.7   David Rosenhan

Rosenhan (1973)

The aim of this field study was to investigate if psychiatrists could tell the difference between sane and insane people. In this study eight mentally healthy subjects (including Rosenhan himself) volunteered to serve as pseudo-patients and seek admission to psychiatric hospitals. They were to present themselves for admission to 12 hospitals in 5 different US states. Following the same standardized instructions, the pseudo-patients called the hospital, made an appointment and on arrival complained of hearing voices that said "empty",

"hollow" and "thud". This was the only symptom that they made up. If asked, they were instructed to say that the voice was unfamiliar, the same sex as themselves and often unclear except for the three words. Other than this they were instructed to act normally and provide the interviewer with truthful information about themselves (however, they changed their names and occupation to protect their future employment records). They were also told that they would have to get out by their own means, by convincing the staff of their sanity.

Upon admission to the psychiatric ward, the pseudo-patients ceased simulating any symptoms. Rosenhan does note that the pseudo-patients were nervous at first, mainly due to the novelty of the situation and to the fear of being exposed and embarrassed, but this nervousness abated rapidly. Apart from this, pseudo-patients behaved normally. When asked by the staff how they were feeling, they said they were fine and no longer experienced any symptoms. In the hospital records their behaviour was described as friendly and cooperative. All instructions were followed, but medication was not swallowed. At the same time participants discreetly wrote down their observations of the ward, patients and the staff. Almost immediately after admission they sought to be discharged from the hospital.

All but one pseudo-patient was admitted to hospital with a diagnosis of schizophrenia. Each was discharged with a diagnosis of "schizophrenia in remission". The length of hospital stay varied between 7 and 52 days with an average of 19 days at the hospital. Not one of the pseudo-patients was detected by anyone on the hospital staff. This was an unexpected and in many ways stunning result.

Some accompanying observations render the result even more surprising.

First, although members of the staff failed to detect the pseudo-patients, the other patients were more observant. Many of them voiced suspicions and made comments like, "You're not crazy. You're a journalist or a professor. You're checking up on the hospital!"

Second, the normal behaviour of the pseudo-patients was often misinterpreted by the staff as symptoms of their illness. Examination of nursing records revealed that taking notes was called "engaging in writing behaviour", waiting outside the cafeteria before lunchtime was interpreted as "oral-acquisitive syndrome".

Third, the pseudo-patients after admission were largely ignored by the staff. One of the tests performed by the pseudo-patients was to approach members of the staff (nurses and psychiatrists) with innocent questions such as, "When am I likely to be discharged?" Somewhat shockingly, most of the responses were minimal. For example, psychiatrists moved on and ignored the question in 71% of the cases, and stopped and talked only 4% of the time. The nurses stayed in ward offices 90% of the time, and the amount of time spent by members of the staff with each patient was on average under seven minutes per day.

A follow-up study was conducted with the staff of a hospital that was aware (and sceptical) of the results of the first study. They were informed that during the next three months pseudo-patients could try to seek admission to the hospital. Staff members were asked to use a 10-point scale with each new patient to rate the likelihood of them being a pseudo-patient. Results showed that out of 193 patients judged during this period, 41 were confidently rated as a pseudo-patient by at least one staff member, and 19 patients were "detected" by both the psychiatrist and one other staff member. In fact, cunning Rosenhan did not send any pseudo-patients to the hospital.

Rosenhan concluded that psychiatrists could not reliably distinguish normal people from the mentally ill. Attempting to explain the reasons behind this, Rosenhan pointed at the "stickiness of a diagnostic label". According to him, once a person is labelled as a schizophrenic, this label sticks and everything the person does is perceived through that prism. You could probably link labelling to the formation of a schema: diagnostic labels are powerful schema-creators. Rosenhan also asserted that labels can have a self-confirming effect: if everyone around consistently expects you to behave in a certain way, you might actually start behaving that way. This may be linked to the phenomenon of "stereotype threat" (see Unit 4).

ATL skills: Thinking and communication

Identify the research method used by Rosenhan. Write down a brief summary of the research study in the following format: Aim, Method, Procedure, Results, Conclusion.

Which of the results of the study are linked to methodological considerations in diagnosis (validity) and which results link to ethical considerations?

Review the concept of schema and state how exactly it links to the results of Rosenhan's study.

How would you evaluate the ethical aspect of Rosenhan's study itself? Think about deception that was involved in conducting the study, pseudo-patients' distress and the reputation of hospitals. If you were a member of the ethics committee reviewing the proposal for the study, would you approve it?

Discussion

What ethical considerations related to diagnosis are raised in this study? Rosenhan used such terms as "depersonalization", "institutionalization", "stigmatization". All these concepts are linked to the concept of labelling. Discuss what consequences it might have in your culture to be labelled as mentally ill.

TOK

Labelling something and then interpreting all subsequent information through the lens of this label is not only characteristic of mental health. The same pattern can be observed in other areas of knowledge.

Can you name examples of labelling in the natural sciences, history, the arts, religious knowledge and indigenous knowledge systems?

Rosenhan's study sparked a lot of controversy among both scientists and practitioners. For example, Spitzer (1976) doubted that admission of pseudo-patients to hospitals can be interpreted as indicating lack of validity in psychiatric diagnosis. After all, they were admitted because they sought admission, a sort of behaviour that is not common in real-life scenarios. Other points of criticism voiced in relation to Rosenhan's study were as follows.

- At the time of the study DSM-II was in use. Much has improved since that time. For example, in DSM-IV hearing voices must be experienced for over a month before a diagnosis of schizophrenia can be made.

- Experiences of pseudo-patients differed from those of the real patients (who knew that their symptoms were true). In this way participant observations may be somewhat biased.

- The study did not take into account a cost-benefit analysis: when a real patient is let out of hospital and gets in trouble, there is always an outcry and hospitals are blamed. However cynical this may sound, admitting a healthy person into hospital may be "safer" than discharging a mentally ill person into the world.

- Finally, there was major deception involved in the study (hospital staff of several major hospitals were deceived). This raises serious ethical considerations.

Of course, simply discarding psychiatry on the basis of Rosenhan's findings would be too premature, far-fetched and even dangerous. What does a scientist need to do in response to emerging claims that diagnosis is invalid? Begin a careful and systematic exploration of clinical biases—what exactly can cause this discrepancy between diagnosis and reality? Can such biases be identified, explained, predicted and prevented? Post-Rosenhan research has accumulated some evidence in this area. This brings us to a discussion of the role of clinical biases in diagnosis.

Exercise

Explore Dr Stephen Ginn's blog post on Rosenhan's study: https://tinyurl.com/kr6scqv

Summarize the details that this blog post adds to what you already know.

Psychology in real life

Review the section on validity and reliability of diagnosis and discuss what additional dimensions it raises in relation to Anoushka's case. Do you now require more knowledge to decide whether Anoushka is depressed or not? If you think you do, decide precisely what knowledge you are lacking right now.

See if this gap has been filled after studying the following sections.

The role of clinical biases in diagnosis

Inquiry questions

- Since clinical diagnosis is essentially a human judgment, is it affected by the biases inherent in human thinking and decision-making?

- What can we do to minimize bias in diagnosis?

- Since the purpose of diagnosis is to understand a person's experiences deeply and this is only possible with a subjective approach, do we even need to eliminate bias?

What you will learn in this section

- Clinician variables in diagnosis

  - Clinician's attitudes and beliefs: Langwieler and Linden (1993), four psychiatrists with different theoretical backgrounds arrived at four different diagnoses

  - Clinician's abilities

  - Clinician's cognitive biases: confirmation bias and illusory correlation, Chapman and Chapman (1969)

- Patient variables in diagnosis

  - Reporting bias—certain symptoms exist in the population but they go unreported: Furnham and Malik (1994), cultural perceptions of depression are different in middle-aged, but not young British Asians

  - Somatization—expressing psychological disorders in the form of physical symptoms: Kleinman (1982), somatization may serve as a coping mechanism to avoid being stigmatized in the society; Lin, Carter and Kleinman (1985), refugees are more prone to somatization than immigrants "by choice"; acculturation involves high levels of stress coupled with low levels of social support

  - Expression of symptoms—altered behaviour of the patient in a clinical context: Payne (2012), African American and Caucasian patients express their symptoms differently, but clinicians are insensitive to such cultural differences (which results in bias)

- Cultural factors in the DSM

  - Cultural formulation interview

  - Alarcon (2009): a list of factors about which information must be gathered

  - Cultural syndromes: Ataque de nervios, Shenjing shuairuo, Taijin kyofusho, Dhat syndrome

This section also links to:

  - validity of diagnosis

  - cognitive biases in decision-making (cognitive approach to behaviour)

  - stereotypes, acculturation, globalization (sociocultural approach to behaviour).

Clinical biases in diagnosis may be associated with several groups of factors. The first broad group of factors relates to characteristics of the clinician—the so-called "clinician variables". The second group consists of "patient variables"—overdiagnosis or underdiagnosis of certain groups based on their age, gender, race/ethnicity. The third group, which partially overlaps with the first two, consists of cultural factors in diagnosis.

Clinician variables in diagnosis

Sources of clinician variables may include the following (Poland and Caplan, 2004).

1. The clinician's **attitudes and beliefs** about certain groups of individuals or disorders, for example, the psychiatrist's professional background or theoretical orientation. **Langwieler and Linden (1993)** analysed the influence of clinician variables on the diagnosis and treatment of depression by presenting a trained pseudo-patient to four clinicians, each with a different professional background. They thought that they were treating a real patient during regular working hours. Despite similar information about the case, four different diagnoses and four different treatments were chosen. When tape recordings of the patient's visit were analysed, it was noticed that it took no longer than three minutes for the initial diagnostic concept to emerge. This concept was then further refined and "clarified" in the clinical interview and led to the final diagnostic conclusion. Researchers concluded that diagnosis can be related to the professional background and personal attitudes of the clinician, which delineates one of the major sources of clinical bias.

2. The clinician's **abilities**, such as perspective-taking, self-reflection, tolerance for uncertainty, tolerance for difference.

3. The clinician's **cognitive biases**. Two examples of cognitive biases you already know (see Unit 3) that may be crucial in a clinical context are confirmation bias (the tendency to seek out information that confirms previously held beliefs) and illusory correlation (the tendency to see a relationship where it does not exist). Recall, for example, the study of **Chapman and Chapman (1969)** who investigated the ability of psychiatrists to use Rorschach's ink blots to diagnose homosexuality.

Psychology in real life

A patient reports to the clinic with symptoms suggestive of schizophrenia (hearing voices, illogical flow of thoughts, inability to interpret social situations correctly). He is 64 years old, seems detached and is highly religious. He has a rural Ugandan background, but he moved to the USA 15 years ago.

The psychiatrist is a Caucasian male coming from an upper middle-class family. He recently graduated from a medical school.

What factors can potentially cause biases in this interview? In a group list all potential biases you can think of. Then eliminate all sources of bias that do not belong to clinician variables. Group the remaining sources of bias into three categories: clinician's attitudes and beliefs, clinician's abilities, clinician's cognitive biases.

Patient variables in diagnosis

Sources of patient variables may include the fact that different groups of people behave differently in a clinical interview. Some groups may experience symptoms differently. Moreover, some groups may be reluctant to report psychological distress. Patient variables link to such phenomena as expression of symptoms, reporting bias, and somatization.

Reporting bias

You only seek professional help for mental illness if you believe you have one. What happens if you have it but refuse to accept it? The result is reporting bias—certain symptoms exist in the population, but they go unreported, so statistically it looks like a certain disorder is not prevalent in this population group. Kleinman (1977) made a distinction between disease (a biological malfunction) and illness (one's personal reaction to the disease). Unlike disease, illness is heavily influenced by culture.

ATL skills: Self-management

Reflect on your own reporting bias. For example, you have toothache but you don't report it to the dentist, although you know early intervention is important. Or you have insomnia but don't think it necessary to see a doctor about it.

What illnesses would you personally be reluctant to report to a professional? What illnesses go unreported most often in your culture?

For example, how "normal" is it to see a psychologist regarding marital problems in your society? How many of your friends are currently seeing a psychologist?

Furnham and Malik (1994) investigated cross-cultural beliefs about depression. They were trying to find an explanation for an earlier observation that British Asians (from Bangladesh, India and Pakistan) were rarely diagnosed with depression. They recognized several potential explanations for this.

- Depression is a western phenomenon and British Asians are genuinely healthier.

- British Asians do experience depression, but they underutilize mental health institutions despite their increased stress due to migration.

- British Asians present psychological problems somatically so they get diagnosed with physical disease instead.

The second explanation here is known as reporting bias. Of course, reporting bias is caused by a culturally mediated perception of a disorder (illness). So, a study of cross-cultural differences in these perceptions may potentially reveal the hidden mechanisms of reporting bias.

One hundred and fifty-two female subjects from middle-class backgrounds participated in the study, a group of middle-aged women (aged 35–62) and a group of younger women (17–28 years). Half of the participants were classified as Native British (born and educated in Britain); the other half were of Asian origin (India, Pakistan or Bangladesh) and had received education in their countries of origin.

All participants filled out questionnaires that targeted both their symptoms of mental illness and their beliefs about depression and anti-depressive behaviours.

The results showed that perception of depression differed among Asian and British participants. For example, Asian (but not British) women tended to agree with the following statements.

- "Having a job outside the home helps keep women from getting depressed."

- "When feeling depressed, it is more helpful to talk it over with a family member than with a friend."

- "Feeling depressed is no different from feeling depressed about something."

Interestingly, the differences were less pronounced in the group of younger women. This shows how globalization gradually influences younger representatives of traditional cultures.

Finally, Asian middle-aged women reported being depressed significantly less often than the other three samples. This could be attributed to their (culturally influenced) perceptions of depression. The authors of the study explained this cross-cultural difference by the underlying individualist-collectivist dimension, with the increased role of the extended family in the east and a tendency to explain distress by lack of fit into society (for example, lack of job).

ATL skills: Research

There are two independent variables in Furnham and Malik's study with two levels each: culture (British versus Asian) and age (middle-aged versus young). This means that the study followed a 2x2 design. Note, however, that the study is quasi-experimental: researchers did not randomly allocate participants to the groups, which limits our ability to make cause-and-effect inferences from the study findings.

1. Name the dependent variables and how they were operationalized.

2. Describe the interaction between two independent variables. Use this format: "A report less depression and use more collectivistic explanations of the illness than B, but only if A are ___ (younger/older)".

3. Which of the three potential explanations for the fact that British Asians are rarely diagnosed with depression is best supported by the results of Furnham and Malik's study? Why?

Discussion

Reporting bias exists. Discuss what ethical considerations this connects to. In today's globalized world should we (as a global community) educate people from collectivistic societies about the importance of reporting depression? Or should we respect the existing cultural norms and support them in ways of coping with depression that they already use (for example, keeping busy with household chores, spending more time with relatives, and so on)?

"The police called, we're taking you out of the clinical trial and putting you in a criminal trial."

▲ Figure 5.8

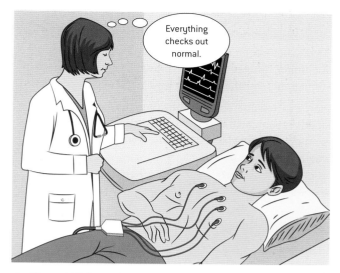

▲ Figure 5.9 Somatization

Somatization

Somatization refers to expressing psychological disturbance in the form of physical symptoms. Somatization is linked to reporting bias, because in social groups where somatization is prevalent potential patients could report their illness to physicians rather than mental health professionals. Some researchers point to somatization as an example of a culturally different manifestation of mental illness.

Kleinman (1982) found that Chinese patients expressed depression and other psychological problems mainly through somatic symptoms (for example, "I have a headache" instead of "I am sad"). He explains this tendency to "transform" psychological distress into physical symptoms by severe stigma attached to mental illness in Chinese and many other Asian cultures. In these societies somatization serves as a coping mechanism because it allows you to get support from your social network and provides a temporary relief from everyday responsibilities.

People in transition (cultural or geographical) were also shown to be prone to somatization. Certain groups of migrants, for example, have been forced to move because of war in their home countries, but their traditional society discourages them from displaying signs of weakness. This means that acculturation for these people involves high levels of stress coupled with low levels of social support.

Lin, Carter and Kleinman (1985) reviewed the clinical records of Chinese, Filipino, Vietnamese and Laotian patients in US primary care to determine the presence of somatization. A distinction was made between refugees and immigrants. About half of the patients had been born and raised in Vietnam and had been forced to migrate as refugees due to the war. A second group of patients had lived in China, Taiwan or Hong Kong, and it was their conscious choice to emigrate to the USA.

Somatization was defined as vague somatic symptoms such as headache, abdominal pain, dizziness and insomnia in the absence of a clear etiology. Somatization was diagnosed in 35% of patients. Refugees were more likely to have somatization than immigrants. Patients with somatization were more likely than patients with physical disorders to have a large household size and lower levels of education. Both these variables (household and school) point to how "traditional" the cultural background of the patient is. They were also more likely to be less proficient in English (this probably relates to lack of social support in the new country).

The authors concluded that somatization was one of the most important clinical problems in Asian refugees and immigrants. The more "traditional" their society was, the more they seemed to be prone to somatization. Refugee status also seems to be an important contributor to somatization.

283

Expression of symptoms

It has been firmly established that diagnosed rates of mental illness differ across cultural groups. For example, Hispanics are diagnosed with schizophrenia 1.5 times more often than Caucasians. African Americans, compared to Caucasians, are diagnosed more frequently with schizophrenia, substance abuse and dementia (DelBello *et al*, 2001). As you know, these observed differences could be due to multiple factors: genuinely existing differences, biased judgment of the clinician or altered behaviour of the patient in the clinical context. If altered behaviour is the case, we talk about cross-cultural differences in the expression of symptoms, for example, in the study of Steele and Aronson (1995) on "**stereotype threat**" in IQ testing. As you have seen, the testing situation itself activated stereotypical expectations, causing African-American subjects to unintentionally modify their behaviour so that the test score was lower (and in accordance with the stereotype). Something similar may be happening in psychiatric diagnosis, especially when the patient and the clinician have different cultural backgrounds: the patient might modify his or her behaviour unintentionally, trying to better fit into the clinician's schemas.

Payne (2012) showed 239 clinical workers and therapists four specially designed clinical videos and asked them to make diagnostic judgments. In two videos an actor played the role of a depressed man with classic symptoms of MDD. In the other two videos the actor "displayed" culturally expressed African-American symptoms of depression. The latter were established on the basis of prior studies that identified the key differences in the symptoms of depressed African-American patients compared with depressed Caucasian patients. Finally, the actor was either African American or Caucasian. The two actors were of similar age and physical appearance and they were dressed identically. Other confounding variables were also standardized as much as possible.

Broadly speaking, racial differences in clinical diagnosis may be the result of two factors: either the clinician's racial bias or genuine differences in the prevalence and expression of disorders. It is important to keep in mind these potential explanations, as when making an inference about clinician racial bias it has to be confirmed that the alternative explanation (genuine differences) has been excluded.

As applied to Payne's study, the **clinician bias hypothesis** would suggest that African-American and Caucasian patients exhibit similar depression symptoms but clinicians mistakenly judge these symptoms differently because of personal prejudices, cultural ignorance, and so on. Conversely, the **cultural variance hypothesis** would suggest that African-American and Caucasian clients express their symptoms differently, but clinicians are insensitive to such cultural differences (which results in bias). Note that both explanations assume that the client actually has the disorder (depression); it is only the way symptoms are expressed that differs.

	How often were patients misdiagnosed?	
	Classic symptoms	**Culturally expressed symptoms**
African-American patient	Group 1: not often	Group 3: often
Caucasian patient	Group 2: not often	Group 4: often

▲ Table 5.3 Results from Payne (2012)

The study did not directly support the clinician racial bias hypothesis, as no significant differences were found between clients of either race if they presented the same symptoms (for example, African-American clients presenting classic depressive symptoms were not misdiagnosed more often than Caucasian clients presenting the same symptoms). However, clinicians misdiagnosed depression more often when culturally expressed depressive symptoms were presented by clients of either race (see Table 5.3). The study lends support to the cultural variation hypothesis but not to the clinician racial bias hypothesis. It was concluded that it is not race itself that produces bias in diagnosis, but culturally specific expression of symptoms (which clinicians seem to be unaware of). This is good news: racial bias in diagnosis exists, but at least it is not caused by overt racism. The study suggests that clinicians can be better trained to recognize culturally specific expression of symptoms, which will potentially decrease bias and increase validity of diagnosis.

▲ Figure 5.10 Screen shots from Payne's study (2012)

Exercise

If you want to do additional research and make a presentation in class, review this article: "Expression and treatment of depression among Haitian immigrant women in the United States: Clinical observations" (Guerda *et al*, 2007) published in *American Journal of Psychotherapy*: https://tinyurl.com/grpboog

Based on the case studies outlined in the article, make a visual to compare three types of culturally specific presentations of depression: Douleur de Corps (pain in the body), Soulagement par Dieu (relief through God) and Lutte sans Victoire (fighting a winless battle).

Cultural factors in the DSM

As you have seen, prior to the publication of DSM-III attention of the psychiatric community was focused on increasing reliability of diagnostic categories, often at the expense of validity. As a result, DSM-III was criticized for lack of inclusion of cultural factors—disorder classifications were viewed as largely universal. DSM-IV represented some progress in terms of acceptance of cultural dimensions. Arguably, this progress could not be called considerable: it boiled down to including a "cultural formulation interview" in an appendix in the manual, and listing an incomplete glossary of "culture-bound syndromes". In DSM-5 cultural considerations were incorporated at a much deeper level. The cultural formulation interview also was refined and updated.

Psychology in real life

Review information on the cultural formulation interview in DSM-5: https://www.multiculturalmentalhealth.ca/clinical-tools/cultural-formulation/

When you drafted the questions to be used in an interview with Anoushka, to what extent did you incorporate cultural considerations in your interview? Go back to your initial draft, review it and consider adding questions in line with the cultural formulation interview.

Alarcon (2009) argues that cultural dimensions of diagnosis have often been incorporated in real-life psychiatric practices through vague declarations of the importance of cultural factors, but rarely given genuine and deep consideration. He suggests a list of factors about which information must be gathered in a well-structured clinical interview.

- Cultural variables: language, religion and spirituality, traditions and beliefs, migration history and level of acculturation. These should all be covered in the initial stage of the clinical interview, setting the stage for further investigation.

- Family data: he suggests that family is in itself a cultural (or micro-cultural) variable. This includes areas such as how the patient was raised, social interactions and community celebrations.

- Environmental influences in the culture: media, political structures, rules of public behaviour, rituals, schooling norms, and so on.

- Explanatory models: how the patient and the relatives explain the origin and the evolution of the symptoms. To know how the patients themselves explain their disorder may be crucial in seeing this disorder from the perspective of the reality in which it emerged.

- Patient's self-reported strengths and weaknesses: this information is also cultural since it is a product of self-observation, so it reflects culturally determined views of the patient about the possible coping resources.

TOK

Suppose you have gained knowledge of the five groups of cultural factors listed above. Will this allow you to better understand your patient who has a different cultural background? Undoubtedly it will improve your understanding to some extent, but will this improvement be large enough to make the qualitative "leap" from non-understanding to understanding?

Discuss the difference between knowledge and understanding. Does it require something else, in addition to a knowledge of cultural context, to understand your client's mental problem? If it does, what is required exactly?

It could be useful to conduct research online to explore the difference between two theories: epistemology (theory of knowledge) and hermeneutics (theory of understanding). How are they different?

Cultural syndromes

A culture-bound syndrome is a set of symptoms that are only recognized as illness in a specific culture. The term was included in DSM-IV, which listed the most common culture-bound conditions in Appendix I. Culture-bound syndromes were defined in the DSM-IV as recurrent, locality-specific patterns of aberrant behaviour and troubling experience that may or may not be linked to a particular diagnostic category. In DSM-5 the notion of "culture-bound syndromes" was replaced by "cultural syndromes".

The following examples of cultural syndromes are currently listed in DSM-5.

Ataque de nervios (translated from Spanish as "attack of nerves")—this is a syndrome found predominantly in Hispanic people as well as in the Philippines. Symptoms include uncontrollable screaming, trembling, sensation of heat in the chest and head, partial loss of consciousness and impulsive acts. Often individuals who experience an episode of Ataque do not subsequently remember it. Some scholars argue that this syndrome is a culturally acceptable reaction to stress within the Hispanic community (Steinberg, 1990).

Shenjing shuairuo (neurasthenia)—this condition may be metaphorically referred to as "weakness of the nerves" and includes symptoms of fatigue, anxiety, headache, weakness and generally depressed mood. In DSM-IV the diagnosis was shifted from the main section of the manual to the culture-bound syndromes appendix. The condition is thought to be specific to Asia. Shenjing shuairuo (which translates from Chinese as a "nervous breakdown") might be a culturally acceptable diagnosis that avoids being associated with a stigma of a mental disorder (stigmatization is stronger in traditional eastern societies). Traditional Chinese medicine describes this syndrome as a depletion of qi (vital energy).

Taijin kyofusho—fear of interpersonal relationships, a syndrome thought to be specific to the Japanese and the Korean culture. The syndrome includes being embarrassed about yourself or having a fear that others will not be pleased with one's appearance or body odour. The set of symptoms boils down to trying to avoid embarrassing others with one's presence. As a result of this extreme self-consciousness, sufferers' heart rate increases in the presence of others, they may have irrational beliefs about their body, face or bodily functions, and they may have panic attacks when around people, among other symptoms. The syndrome is believed to stem from emotional trauma and is more prevalent in men.

Dhat syndrome—this is found in male patients in the cultures of the Indian subcontinent. Patients complain about premature ejaculation or impotence and believe that they are passing semen in their urine, which has no objective medical signs. This syndrome has been related to traditional Hindu beliefs that view semen is a "vital fluid", and an excessive loss of semen may be associated with the loss of life energy.

Exercise

Find out more and make short presentations in class about other cultural syndromes currently included in DSM-5: Khyal cap, Ghost sickness, Kufungisisa, Maladi moun, Susto.

Do you think Anoushka's case might be a cultural syndrome?

Explanations for disorders—biological explanations for depression

Inquiry questions

- Although it is understood that human behaviour is caused by multiple interacting factors (biological, cognitive and sociocultural), how can we establish the major cause of a disorder?

- How do we untangle this complex knot of interacting variables?

- Should an effective treatment target the cause rather than the symptoms?

- How would you design the research programme to establish the primary cause of depression?

What you will learn in this section

- The concept of etiology

- Genetic heritability: the Falconer model

    - $1 = A + C + E$, estimating A

    - Sullivan, Neale and Kendler (2000): a meta-analysis of twin studies using the Falconer model; heritability of major depression

    - Kendler *et al* (2006): heritability of MDD higher in women than in men

- Genetic heritability: gene-environment interaction (GxE)

    - Occurs when two different genotypes respond to the same environmental stimuli in different ways

    - Silberg *et al* (1999): genetic predisposition causes adolescent girls to be more vulnerable to negative or stressful life events

    - Molecular genetics: can we pinpoint a specific gene that is responsible for this vulnerability?

    - Caspi *et al* (2003): a functional polymorphism in a serotonin transporter gene (5-HTT) moderates the influence of stressful life events on depression

    - Chiao and Blizinsky (2010): cultural values of collectivism buffer genetically susceptible populations (with a higher frequency of short alleles of 5-HTT) from increased vulnerability to stressful life events

- Genetic heritability: gene-environment correlation (rGE)—passive rGE, evocative rGE, active rGE

- The role of neurotransmitters

    - The "serotonin hypothesis" based on two types of serendipitous findings

    - Limitation of such studies: "treatment etiology fallacy"

    - Antidepressants do not produce effects immediately—this suggests the existence of a longer pathway

        - SSRIs influence the way the brain appraises emotional information (Harmer, Goodwin and Cohen, 2009).

        - SSRIs repair hippocampus neurons damaged by cortisol (Taupin, 2006).

This section also links to:

- neurotransmission; genetic influences on behaviour; twin studies, family studies, adoption studies (biological approach to behaviour)

- stress (health psychology)

- clinical bias in diagnosis

- research methodology.

The concept of etiology

Science in general pursues four goals: description, explanation, prediction and control. Description in abnormal psychology is now achieved by classification systems like ICD-10 or DSM-5. This allows us to reliably diagnose the problem. However, to move further and design a treatment we need to accurately establish a cause, that is, explain the illness. Having an explanation will allow us to predict the course of the disease and the patient's response to our interventions. This, in turn, will enable us to control the disorder—to treat it. So explanation is important as it opens the door to prediction and control.

Explanation of a disorder requires knowledge of its **etiology**—a set of causes of a disease or condition. Depending on our approach to understanding behaviour, we may distinguish between biological, cognitive and sociocultural etiologies of a disorder. Using the example of MDD, we will look at the existing explanations.

TOK

Think of other examples from various areas of knowledge where some of the four goals are achieved while some others are not. Take astrology as an example. What area of knowledge does it belong to? Does it achieve description, explanation, prediction and control? What about quantum mechanics? Or indigenous knowledge systems?

Biological explanations for depression embrace neurochemical factors (neurotransmitters and hormones) and genetic predisposition. Of course, these explanations are connected because abnormal levels of neurochemicals may be determined by a person's genetic set-up.

Genetic heritability: the Falconer model

As you have seen in Unit 2, there are three major methods used to establish heritability of traits: twin studies, family studies and adoption studies. Currently converging evidence from twin studies suggests a 40–50% heritability of depression, whereas family studies indicate that first-degree relatives of depressed patients are two to three times more likely to have depression than the general population (Lohoff, 2011).

Estimation of genetic heritability in twin studies is based on the so-called **Falconer model** which assumes that **phenotype** (observed characteristics such as the presence of symptoms of MDD) is comprised of three types of influences: genetics, shared environment and individual environment. This idea can be written in the following form:

$$1 = A + C + E$$

(where A = genetic inheritance, C = shared/common environment, E = individual environment)

ATL skills: Self-management

The Falconer model has been discussed at length in Unit 2 in the context of using twin studies to estimate heritability of intelligence.

What is the general idea behind estimating "A" in the Falconer model from rMZ and rDZ? What is the formula?

If you find it difficult to answer this question, review the relevant section of Unit 2.

In a recent meta-analysis of twin studies using this model, **Sullivan, Neale and Kendler (2000)** established the estimate of heritability of major depression at A = 37%, with a minimal contribution of shared environment (C = 0%) and a substantial contribution of unique/individual environmental factors (E = 63%). The authors concluded that major depression is a complex disorder that does not result from either genetic or environmental influences alone but is a combination of both.

Kendler et al (2006) conducted the Swedish national twin study of major depression. The aims of the study were to compare genetic effects on MDD first in males and females and second across different generations. Depression was assessed in 42,000 twins by DSM-IV criteria in a computer-assisted telephone interview. All twins were found in the Swedish Twin Registry. Results showed that the heritability of MDD was significantly higher in women (A = 42%) than men (A = 29%). No evidence was found for differences in the roles of genetic and environmental factors across generations spanning almost 60 years. So, the results of the study were in line with the previous estimates of heritability, but it showed a significant difference between men and women in terms of genetic predisposition to depression.

One of the hypotheses in Kendler *et al*'s study (2006) was that in different generations the role of genetic inheritance (relative to the role of environmental factors) would be different. This hypothesis was not supported empirically. What do you think was the theoretical rationale of this prediction?

If you want to find out for sure, review the original article and see if you were right: https://tinyurl.com/z8shmzx

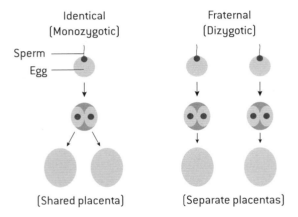

▲ Figure 5.11 Zygoticity of twins

Genetic heritability: gene-environment interaction (GxE)

One common limitation of research studies based on the Falconer model is that they ignore complex gene-environment interaction. The influence of genes on depression might not be as straightforward as such studies seem to suggest. Theoretically genes can create a certain susceptibility to environmental influences, but environment would still be the triggering factor. So research studies that try to bring together different types of influences and look at the dynamics of development of depression over years are especially valuable, and especially hard to conduct.

Gene-environment interaction (GxE) occurs when two different genotypes respond to the same environment in different ways.

Silberg *et al* (1999), to further understand the reasons for different heritability of depression in males and females, investigated the trajectories of depressive symptoms among boys and girls from childhood to adolescence. The study was inspired by previous observations that had shown that the rates of depression are similar in pre-adolescent boys and girls, but by mid-adolescence and later the dominance of depression in girls is firmly established.

The authors investigated the link between susceptibility to depression and environmental factors (stressful life events). They used data from more than 1,400 male and female juvenile twin pairs that were followed longitudinally from age 8 to age 16. Depressive symptoms were assessed using the Child and Adolescent Psychiatric Interview, and ratings of past-year life events were obtained in interviews with the mothers. The list of potentially stressful life events included such events as failing a grade or losing a close friend through arguments.

Results of the longitudinal analysis showed that the effect of negative life events on depressive symptoms in adolescent girls was stronger, suggesting that genetic predisposition causes girls at this age to be more vulnerable to negative or stressful life events. In other words, girls demonstrated a "genetic predisposition to experiencing particular stressful life events" (Silberg *et al*, 1999, p 230). This exemplifies one of the ways in which genes may interact with the environment: environmental factors serve as necessary mediators or triggers for genetic predisposition.

▲ Figure 5.12 Genetic and environmental influences

Molecular genetics is also promising in this field of research because it allows us to identify specific genes influencing complex psychological disorders, whereas in twin, family and adoption studies where genes are not "measured" directly we can only talk about some broad, latent, unspecified genetic predisposition. So, instead of talking about a broad genetic predisposition that makes you vulnerable to stressful events, can we pinpoint a specific gene that is responsible for this vulnerability?

Caspi *et al* (2003) found that a functional polymorphism in a serotonin transporter gene (5-HTT) moderated the influence of stressful life events on depression. This gene is involved in the reuptake of serotonin at brain synapses. In this study a representative birth cohort of more than 1,000 children from New Zealand were followed longitudinally. The sample was divided into three groups:

- both short alleles of 5-HTT
- one short allele and one long allele
- both long alleles.

Stressful life events occurring after the 21st birthday and before the 26th birthday were assessed with a "life-history calendar" which focused on 14 major stressful events in such fields as employment, finance, housing, health and relationships.

There were no differences between the three groups in the number of stressful life events they experienced; however, individuals who had the short allele of 5-HTT exhibited more depressive symptoms in relation to stressful life events. More specifically, individuals who carried a short allele whose life events occurred after their 21st birthday experienced increases in their depressive symptoms from the age of 21 to 26 years, whereas individuals carrying the long/long alleles did not (even though they experienced the same events at the same time). Among participants suffering four or more stressful life events, 33% of individuals with a short allele of 5-HTT developed depression, compared to 17% of those having the long/long variant.

Therefore, just as in Silberg *et al*, the study demonstrated that genetic set-up can moderate a person's sensitivity to adverse environmental effects (life stress). However, this study allowed researchers to pinpoint the specific alleles responsible for this increased vulnerability to stressful events.

Chiao and Blizinsky (2010) went further and included cultural variables in gene-environment interaction. They proposed a "**culture-gene coevolution theory**" which posits that cultural values buffer genetically susceptible populations from increased prevalence of affective and mood disorders. Using data from 50,000 individuals living in 29 countries, they examined the association between cultural values of individualism–collectivism and the frequency of allele variations of the serotonin transporter gene 5-HTT, relating it at the same time to the global variation in the prevalence of affective disorders. Data were taken from existing publications. For example, the average country indices on the scale of individualism–collectivism were taken from prior published research by Hoefstede. Depression prevalence data were taken from published medical research, and so on. The unit of analysis in this study was a nation—in a sense, they had 29 "participants".

They demonstrated that collectivistic cultures were significantly more likely to carry the short allele of 5-HTT. Interestingly, the other cultural dimensions (power distance, uncertainty avoidance, masculinity–femininity, and long-term/short-term orientation) did not correlate with the frequency of the short allele in the population. Additionally, nations with a higher frequency of short allele carriers showed a lower prevalence of depression. Sophisticated statistical techniques showed that collectivistic cultural values were a mediator between population frequency of short allele individuals and decreased prevalence of depression. The authors argue that cultural values of collectivism evolved as a means of encouraging

giving social support to others to protect genetically susceptible individuals from life stress.

ATL skills: Research

Chiao and Blizinsky (2010) suggest that some populations initially had a higher risk of depression (because they carried more short alleles of 5-HTT), and that these populations gradually developed collectivistic values to protect them against the dangers of depression. Interestingly, observed prevalence rates of depression in collectivistic cultures are lower. However, this may be due to somatization and reporting bias (see "The role of clinical biases in diagnosis").

Can you identify the research method used in this study? Based on this, what are the strengths and limitations of the study? To what extent do you think "culture-gene coevolution theory" is justified by the empirical data?

The authors acknowledge a possible limitation of the study: published cross-national estimates of prevalence of mental disorders may be vulnerable to response bias. There is more stigma associated with mental illness in collectivistic nations due to increased cultural pressures to conform to social norms. This may lead some individuals to fail to report their symptoms or seek psychological help, distorting cross-national estimates of prevalence.

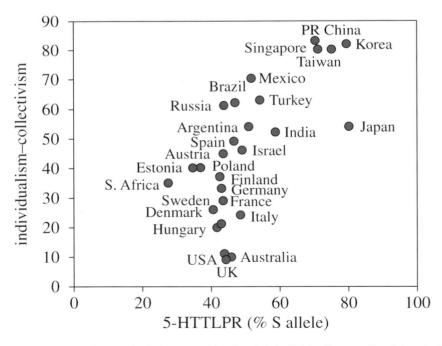

▲ Figure 5.13 Results from correlation analysis between Hoefstede's individualism–collectivism index and frequency of short allele carriers of the 5-HTT (Chiao and Blizinsky, 2010, p 532)

Genetic heritability: gene-environment correlation (rGE)

Gene-environment interaction is getting more and more attention recently because it has been recognized that both genes and environment are important in determining the development of a mental disorder. What is more interesting, however, is that genes and environment are not completely independent—in many instances genes influence environment too. So we need to look at how the interaction between these two factors is developing dynamically. This phenomenon is known as "gene-environment correlation", and there are three ways in which genes may influence the environment (Plomin, DeFries and Loehlin, 1977; Dick, 2011).

- Passive gene-environment correlation (passive rGE). Parents provide not only genotype, but also a rearing environment. In this sense genes and environment are correlated. For example, parents might pass on to their child a genetic predisposition to depression as well as a certain high-demanding, perfectionist rearing environment in which the child is likely to feel stressed.

- Evocative gene-environment correlation (evocative rGE). Your genotype influences the responses you receive from others. For example, a child who is predisposed to shyness and tears will receive more negative attention (or less attention) from others as compared to a child who is predisposed to be extroverted and outgoing. Similarly, having a genetic predisposition to depressive behaviour may influence a person to "evoke" certain environmental responses.

- Active gene-environment correlation (active rGE). An individual may actively select certain environments. For example, a child predisposed to depression may intentionally seek out high-demanding environments in which it is hard to succeed. This is also known as niche-picking.

The important point here is that sometimes what we think to be environmental influence actually has a genetic component in it. This genetic component only becomes evident if we look at gene-environment interaction dynamically.

TOK

Dynamic gene-environment correlation (rGE) may explain one interesting property of heritability coefficients: they change during life. They typically become larger!

This means that if you use a sample of adolescent twins and the Falconer model to arrive at an estimate of heritability (A), this estimate will typically be smaller than if you use a sample of older twins. In other words, the relative contribution of genetics to the similarity between twins (established in your research study) will be higher in older twins compared to younger twin samples.

Potentially this could be explained by niche-picking and other types of gene-environment correlation. As you grow up, your genetic programme "unfolds", causing you to choose certain "niches" in the environment. When they were younger, the twins were exposed to quite different environments but as they age, the twins pick the same niches. So, in terms of their behaviour, monozygotic twins become more and more similar with age.

This phenomenon cannot be explained by the Falconer model.

There are several popular Hollywood movies (for example, *Divergent*, *Insurgent*, *The Giver*, *The Mortal Instruments*, *The Hunger Games*) that capitalize on the idea of life pre-destination: young people are destined to become specific individuals, and they need to choose wisely to stay true to their pre-destination. To what extent do you think this idea is supported? Is your future "recorded" in your genes, gradually unfolding and creating the illusion that your choices are free?

The role of neurotransmitters

Genetic explanations are not the only biological explanations for depression (and mental disorders in general). Other areas of research focus included evolutionary explanations, the role of neurotransmitters and the role of hormones.

Let's look more closely at the role of neurotransmitters. We have already discussed the study of Caspi *et al* (2003) that links depression to 5-HTT, a serotonin transporter gene (and serotonin, as you remember, is a neurotransmitter). As a matter of fact, serotonin has been the most widely discussed neurotransmitter in the context of depression studies. The "**serotonin hypothesis**" of clinical depression is about 50 years old. This hypothesis states that low levels of serotonin in the brain play a causal role in developing MDD. Mostly this hypothesis has been based on two types of finding.

- Certain drugs (prescribed for completely different purposes) that were known to deplete levels of serotonin in the brain were also found to have depression-inducing side effects.

- Certain drugs such as monoamine oxidase inhibitors (MAO inhibitors) were found to be effective against symptoms of depression. Such findings were mostly due to chance, but later in carefully controlled animal studies MAO inhibitors were also shown to enhance effects of serotonin at the synapse (Cowen and Browning, 2015). Another class of drugs that was discovered later is selective serotonin reuptake inhibitors (SSRIs). As the name suggests, these chemicals inhibit the reuptake of excess serotonin in the synapse, increasing synaptic concentration of serotonin. SSRIs were also shown to be effective against symptoms of depression.

You might think that this pattern of findings is convincing evidence of the causal effect of serotonin in depression, but it's not that simple. Essentially, the findings are based on what is known as "**treatment etiology fallacy**": treatment X (which targets chemical Y) reduces symptoms of depression, therefore, chemical Y causes depression. This might not be entirely true for several reasons.

- Not all patients benefit from drugs. In some patients antidepressants do not produce any effect, and in a small number of patients the effects are negative. This means that the link between the level of a certain neurotransmitter and depressive symptoms is not direct; it is probably mediated by other variables.

- Even following recovery from depression levels of serotonin in many patients tend to remain low.

- Drugs increase levels of neurotransmitters within minutes, but the effects on mood are not that fast. It may take weeks for a drug to take effect.

The fact that antidepressants do not take effect immediately suggests that the influence of serotonin on depression might be indirect, or there might exist a longer pathway in which the administration of the antidepressant is just the first step.

For example, it has been shown that SSRIs influence the way the brain appraises emotional information, making automatic emotional responses somewhat more positive (Harmer *et al*, 2009). Of course, starting to see small things and transient situations in a more positive light does not rid you of depression, but these effects may gradually build up and, provided you have a proper supporting environment, eventually affect the symptoms.

Another theory suggests that stress hormones (such as cortisol) can damage neurons in the hippocampus leading to behavioural changes, and SSRIs gradually increase the growth of neurons in the hippocampus, repairing the damage (Taupin, 2006).

See video

Watch Rebecca Brachman's TED Talk, "Could a drug prevent depression and PTSD?" (2016): https://tinyurl.com/zbf9vsv

Discussion

This video gives an example of a serendipitous discovery that can potentially provide a breakthrough in the treatment of depression. What does it tell you about the way biological causes of depression are established? Could you suggest a better, more systematic way?

Explanations for disorders—cognitive and sociocultural explanations for depression

Inquiry questions

- How do biological factors of depression interact with other factors (cognitive and sociocultural)?

- How can patterns of information processing influence the development of depression?

- Are patterns of information processing (cognitive factors) an independent group of factors or are they the result of some sort of interaction between biological predisposition and environmental stimuli?

- How can culture and society influence the development of mental disorders? Which sociocultural variables influence depression the most?

What you will learn in this section

Cognitive explanations for depression

- Beck (1967): Cognitive theory of depression

    - The cognitive triad

    - Negative self-schemata

    - Faulty thinking patterns: arbitrary inference, selective abstraction, overgeneralization, personalization, dichotomous thinking

- Research support

    - Negative cognitive styles predict the development of depression, Alloy, Abramson and Francis (1999)—longitudinal study

    - Individuals with MDD exhibit negative attention biases, Caseras *et al* (2007)—eye-tracking study

    - Individuals with depression make more logical errors, Hammen and Krantz (1976)

- Strengths and limitations of cognitive explanations for depression

Sociocultural explanations for depression

- Social factors may be responsible for the development of depression

    - Brown and Harris (1978): a model of four "vulnerability factors"

    - Patten (1991): summarized the quantitative results of replications; concluded lack of intimate relationships increases the risk of developing depression 3.7 times; this increase of risk is comparable to smoking as a risk factor for atherosclerosis

- Mental disorder symptoms may spread from person to person along the network of interpersonal relationships (much like an infectious disease)

    - Rosenquist, Fowler and Christakis (2011): research using data from Framingham Heart Study—depression in one person causes depression in their friends: correlation in depressive symptoms between people up to three degrees of separation; changes in social ties predicted changes in depressive symptoms, but changes in depressive symptoms did not predict changes in social ties; directionality of friendship also important

This section also links to:

- schema theory; cognitive biases (cognitive approach to behaviour)

- cultural dimensions of behaviour, Hofstede (sociocultural approach to behaviour)
- stress (health psychology)
- treatment of depression, cognitive behavioural therapy (CBT)
- research methodology.

Cognitive explanations for depression

Aaron Beck's (1967) cognitive theory of depression is perhaps the most influential and empirically supported explanation of depression that views cognitive factors (thoughts and beliefs) as the major cause of depressive behaviour. Beck noticed the importance of so-called "**automatic thoughts**"—sub-vocal semi-conscious narrative that accompanies everything you do. Imagine someone asks you right now: "What have you been thinking about for the past five minutes?" You will probably realize that:

- you have been having a number of automatic thoughts without fully registering them on a conscious level
- these thoughts are characteristic of how you normally process your experience.

For many researchers those automatic thoughts were a by-product of other phenomena (behaviour, attitudes, and so on), but Beck saw a causal relationship and suggested that a change in automatic thoughts can lead to a change in behaviour. He noticed that automatic thoughts of patients with depression were often dark, exaggerated and irrational, for example, a person would automatically think, "Here we go again, I am such a loser" after every minor setback. So, cognitive theory of depression concentrates on the negative appraisal of events.

▲ Figure 5.14 Aaron Beck

Beck's cognitive theory identifies three elements of depression.

1. The cognitive triad. It includes deeply grounded beliefs about three aspects of reality.

   a) the self ("I am worthless", "I wish I wasn't the way I am")

   b) the world ("no one notices me", "people do not take me seriously")

   c) the future ("things can only get worse", "my efforts will be fruitless").

   The cognitive triad interferes with automatic thoughts, making them unrealistically pessimistic.

2. Negative self-schemata. Beck suggested that negative self-schemata can be a result of traumatic childhood experiences, such as excessive criticism, abuse in the family or bullying.

3. Faulty thinking patterns. The negative beliefs outlined above lead to a number of cognitive biases that people with depression often resort to when they interpret their daily experiences. Some of the faulty thinking patterns common for depression are:

   a) arbitrary inference (drawing far-fetched conclusions from insufficient evidence)

   b) selective abstraction (noticing one aspect of the experience and ignoring the others)

   c) overgeneralization (making conclusions on the basis of a single event)

   d) personalization (blaming oneself for everything)

   e) dichotomous thinking (black-and-white attitudes, "I am either a success or a total failure").

ATL skills: Self-management

What have you been thinking about for the past five minutes? Reflect.

According to Beck, the thinking of depressed people is full of irrational elements and biases. Becoming aware of these irrational elements and replacing them with more logical thinking is a way to overcome these negative thinking habits, which forms the basis of **cognitive behavioural therapy (CBT)**.

Discussion

To what extent do you think it is possible for people to change their behaviour by altering their automatic thinking patterns? Split into two teams and brainstorm arguments either for or against this theory. Have a brief debate where each team in turn presents one of the arguments and the other team asks questions.

The idea that depression is linked to irrational thinking patterns is supported by research.

First, it has been shown that **negative cognitive styles** predict the development of depression. **Alloy et al (1999)** claimed that the way people cognitively interpret their experiences (their "cognitive style") influences their vulnerability to depression. At the start of their study a sample of healthy college freshmen was split into two groups (high risk versus low risk) based on the presence of negative cognitive styles. Follow-up assessments (self-report questionnaires and semi-structured interviews) were conducted on a regular basis for 5.5 years after that. Results showed that 17% of the high-risk freshmen developed MDD during the first 2.5 years of follow-up, versus only 1% of the low-risk group.

Second, individuals with MDD have been shown to exhibit **negative attention biases**. This was supported in the study of **Caseras et al (2007)**. Participants in this study were shown a series of picture pairs with negative, positive and neutral scenes. Each picture pair was demonstrated for three seconds. Using eye-tracking technology researchers investigated two components of visual attention:

- biases in initial orienting, that is, which of the two pictures from the pair the participant looks at first

- maintenance of attention, that is, the duration of gaze on the picture that was initially fixated on.

They compared participants with depressive symptoms to participants who did not have these symptoms. Results showed that participants with depressive symptoms demonstrated a visible bias in maintenance of attention to negative pictures— their gaze stayed longer on negative scenes once it was fixated on them, as compared to neutral and positive scenes. No differences were found in initial orienting though. So, if you are experiencing depressive symptoms, you will not prefer to look at negative scenes initially, but once you see them it will take you much longer to disengage from them. You get "stuck".

ATL skills: Research

Recall other research studies you know that used eye-tracking technology. Look through this book and review the types of research studies that can be conducted using this method. What other uses of eye-tracking technology in the research of depression can you suggest? You might want to conduct some research and read about recent applications of this technology, then make a short report to the class.

Third, individuals with depression have been shown to make more logical errors. **Hammen and Krantz (1976)** asked depressed and non-depressed female participants to read stories describing situations in which women were encountering stressful experiences. After reading the stories they were asked to provide their interpretations of the women's experiences. It was found that participants suffering from depression made significantly more logical errors in their interpretations.

Cognitive explanations for depression have many strengths, including strong empirical support and the fact that patients in cognitive behavioural therapy are viewed as individuals who are responsible for their problems and have the power to solve them. A number of successful therapies have been built on the cognitive approach. Some criticisms of these explanations have focused on the correlational nature of most of the research studies. It is difficult to differentiate between thinking which causes depression and thinking that is caused by depression. For example, in the study of Alloy, Abramson and Francis (1999) the negative thinking style of one group of participants might have been determined by their predisposition to depression in the first place.

Discussion

Think of other strengths and limitations of cognitive explanations of behaviour and share your ideas in class.

A discussion of biological and cognitive explanations for depression also links closely to research into the effectiveness of drug therapy and cognitive behavioural therapy (see below). Any study that shows the effectiveness of a treatment provides support for the idea that the disorder is caused by a certain factor, but you need to remember treatment etiology fallacy and therefore interpret findings from such studies with caution.

Sociocultural explanations for depression

Brown and Harris (1978) proposed a model of depression which outlines how "vulnerability factors" may interact with triggering stressors to increase the risk of depression. They reported results of a community study of 458 women from London who were surveyed on the history of life events and depressive episodes. Semi-structured interviews were used to gather in-depth information. The overall finding was that four vulnerability factors, when combined with acute or chronic social stressors, were likely to provoke depression in women:

- three or more children under the age of 14

- lack of an intimate relationship with a husband or boyfriend

- lack of employment

- loss of mother before the age of 11 years.

The study demonstrated that it is not only personal factors that are involved in the development of depression, but social factors as well. Of course, the gender-biased sample makes it impossible to generalize the findings to men. The study was replicated several times and the results broadly supported the notion that the four vulnerability social factors are indeed associated with the development of depressive episodes. In particular, **Patten (1991)** summarized the quantitative results of replications and

concluded that the lack of an intimate relationship increases the risk of developing depression 3.7 times, whereas each of the other three factors "only" doubles the risk. This increase of risk is comparable, for example, to smoking as a risk factor for atherosclerosis (Patten, 1991).

ATL skills: Thinking

The limited sample composition in Brown and Harris's study is a clear limitation. Why do you think the researchers made the decision to limit their sample to working-class women from London?

A more recent development in this area is examining the structure of an individual's social network. There have been claims that some mental disorder symptoms may spread from person to person along the network of interpersonal relationships (much like an infectious disease).

Rosenquist, Fowler and Christakis (2011) investigated the possibility of person-to-person spread of depressive symptoms. Of course, just showing that people who are friends are more likely to jointly have depression would not be sufficient. It would be possible to explain such a result in at least three ways.

1. Depression in one person causes depression in their friends.

2. Depressed individuals notice each other and become friends.

3. Friends experience similar social and economic environments which explains their similar symptoms.

Isolating one of these explanations requires longitudinal data. Data for this research was obtained from Framingham Heart Study (FHS), a population-based longitudinal study of 12,067 individuals investigating risk factors for heart disease. To keep track of participants, FHS interviewers documented information on the participants' friends (based on their self-reports), neighbours (based on their address), co-workers (based on their job) and relatives. This information was collected longitudinally. Additionally, due to the fact that Framingham was a small town, many of the contacts were themselves participants in this study. Rosenquist, Fowler and Christakis (2011) computerized these records and obtained longitudinal information on the development of social network structure. To assess symptoms of depression, a standardized depression scale was administered three times between 1983 and 2001.

Results showed that there was a significant correlation in depressive symptoms between people up to three degrees of separation (a person's depression depends on the depression of his friend, his friend's friend, and his friend's friend's friend). Participants were 93% more likely to be depressed if a person they were directly connected to was also depressed. Participants were 43% more likely to be depressed if depression was observed in the friend of their friend (two degrees of separation), and 37% for the third degree of separation.

Changes in social ties predicted changes in depressive symptoms, but changes in depressive symptoms did not predict changes in social ties. In other words, new friends can influence you to become depressed, but becoming depressed does not come with acquiring new friends. This suggests that explanation (1) in the list above should be preferred to explanation (2).

Interestingly, directionality of friendship also appeared to be important. For example, in a couple where A nominated B as a friend but not vice versa (A → B), if B becomes depressed it doubles the chances of A also becoming depressed in the near future. If A becomes depressed, it has no effect on B. In contrast, in a mutual friendship (A ← → B), when B becomes depressed it increases the chances of A becoming depressed by 359%. This result suggests that explanation (1) should be preferred to explanation (3).

▲ Figure 5.15   Social network

ATL skills: Research

Rosenquist, Fowler and Christakis (2011) conducted a correlational study (they did not randomly allocate people to be friends). As we know, this means that cause-and-effect inferences cannot be made. However, their study was longitudinal and they looked at how the variables were changing dynamically. For example, they looked at how acquiring a new friend today correlates with developing depressive symptoms several years later. Does this change anything in terms of our ability to make cause-and-effect inferences?

Finally, on a cultural level, cultural perceptions (for example, cultural stigma) play an important role both in development and presentation of depressive symptoms (see sections "The role of clinical biases in diagnosis" and "The role of culture in treatment"). Refer also to the "culture-gene co-evolution theory" of Chiao and Blizinsky (2010).

Discussion

At the beginning of this unit you designed a research programme to establish the leading causes of depression. Now that you know the results of various research studies, does it change your approach? What other factors should you take into account and how do you want to modify your research proposal?

Assessing the effectiveness of treatment

Inquiry questions

- How can we assess the effectiveness of treatment?
- Is it quantifiable?
- Can we account for placebo effects and assess "pure" effectiveness?
- What methods of research are most suitable for this purpose?

What you will learn in this section

- Challenges in assessing the effectiveness of treatment

    o Severity of the disorder

    o Which treatment outcome to use

    o How to measure the selected treatment outcome

    o How to identify the exact mechanism of change

    o How to account for the placebo effect

- Approaches to assessing the effectiveness of treatment

    o Randomized control trials (RCTs)

    o Qualitative research studies

    o Meta-analyses

- Effectiveness of psychotherapy in general

    o Eysenck (1952): psychotherapy does not work; 67% of outpatients "spontaneously" recovered in two years without treatment; limitation: meta-analysis as a research method did not exist

    o Smith and Glass (1977): psychotherapy works; meta-analysis of 375 studies; the typical therapy client was better off than 75% of untreated individuals

    o Wampold (2007): effectiveness of psychotherapy is comparable to some established medical practices

- Specific and non-specific factors in the effectiveness of treatment

    o Eysenck (1952) and Smith and Glass (1977): very little difference between approaches to psychotherapy

    o Are there any specific factors that make psychotherapy effective? Jacobson *et al* (1996), in a "dismantling design" for cognitive-behavioural therapy "incomplete" treatments were shown to be as effective as the full treatment; Lambert (2013), sudden gains—a substantial number of patients respond to treatment much sooner than theory would predict

    o These puzzling results may potentially be explained by the effect of "common factors" (Wampold, 2007): client's willingness to trust the therapist to provide an explanation that will help the client; formation of working alliance with the client; placebo effects

- Summary: psychotherapy in general is effective, but common factors play a larger role than specific therapeutic techniques; however, it should be kept in mind that research excluded medication treatment and the nature of a meta-analysis is that it is not necessarily applicable to all individual cases

This section also links to:

- research methodology (meta-analysis)
- biological and psychological treatments for depression.

Challenges in assessing the effectiveness of treatment

Why we need to assess the effectiveness of treatment requires no explanation—it is important because therapy needs to be evidence-based. The question is **how**.

Any effort to assess treatment effectiveness needs to take into consideration many aspects of the problem, such as the following.

- **Severity of the disorder.** One treatment may be effective under one condition while another treatment may be effective under a different condition. For example, some treatments would work better in treating mild depression, while other treatments would be preferable for severe cases.

- **Treatment outcomes.** Assessing effectiveness depends on what outcomes we explore. Is it a reduction in the (observable) symptoms? General improvement of quality of life (as reported by the patient's relatives and friends)? Subjective feelings of improvement and satisfaction? Objective medical parameters? Short-term improvement or long-term improvement? Treatments may be effective for some outcomes but not others. For example, taking antidepressant drugs has been shown to lead quickly to a short-term reduction of symptoms, but some other non-medical approaches to the treatment of depression have been shown to have more long-lasting and enduring effects, although they do not take effect as quickly.

- A related problem is **measuring the therapy outcome**. Observable changes in behaviour are more easily registered and more reliable than self-reported improvement in subjective well-being. So when judging results on the effectiveness of a certain therapeutic approach, correction should be made for unreliability of measurement for some therapy outcomes.

- A special question of interest is the **exact mechanism of change**. If therapy produces desirable effects, what therapeutic elements exactly are responsible for that? Is it the client-therapist relationship (for example, rapport, trust), the specific techniques used in the therapeutic sessions, the length of the therapy or something else?

- In addition, there is the **placebo effect**. To demonstrate that a therapeutic approach to the treatment of a disorder is effective (for specific therapy outcomes, under specified conditions), it needs to be shown that this approach outperforms placebo.

Approaches to assessing the effectiveness of treatment

There are three major approaches to assessing the effectiveness of treatment.

Randomized control trials (RCTs)

As the name suggests, these are experiments following an independent measures design, with random allocation of participants into groups and careful control over potential confounding variables. RCTs are the primary method for establishing effectiveness of drugs in medicine, so it is not surprising that abnormal psychology inherited the method. Of course, it is easier to control confounding variables when it comes to drugs (for example, the double-blind method) than when it comes to therapy sessions. For example, it is impossible to use a double-blind method when you are comparing the effectiveness of drugs to the effectiveness of group therapy. Patients will know that they have been allocated to the group therapy condition because they are spending time discussing their symptoms with a group of other patients! Still, the RCT is considered the most basic and standard, even desirable, method for establishing treatment effectiveness. RCTs are subject to the usual types of experimental threats to validity—selection bias, mortality, regression to the mean, and so on.

Qualitative research studies

These studies tap into the subjective experiences of the patients, their interpretations of the treatment and the changes they are going through, something that cannot be captured by quantitative methods. This is in line with the constructivist approach on which qualitative research methodology rests: reality of the therapeutic session between a therapist and a client is co-constructed and subjective and, arguably, subjective methods should be used to understand subjective realities. Qualitative studies (interviews, focus groups, observations) of patients going through a certain type of treatment may be heuristic for generating a theory and subsequently testing that theory with the use of quantitative methods.

Meta-analyses

As you know, a meta-analysis is a statistical analysis of a combination of results published in a large number of research studies. "Participants" in a meta-analysis are research articles and other academic publications. Meta-analyses are especially important in the study of treatment effectiveness. This is because the number of confounding variables is tremendous, and it is not possible to consider them all in a standalone research project. For example, some studies of antidepressant therapy will be conducted with teenagers, some with grown-ups; some studies will be done in Europe and some in

Asia; in some studies the therapist will be more experienced and in some studies less. All these differences may be explored if you combine a large amount of research studies. It will give you an insight into the nature of these confounding variables and the extent to which they influence therapy outcomes. It will also help you arrive at a more balanced estimate of treatment effectiveness.

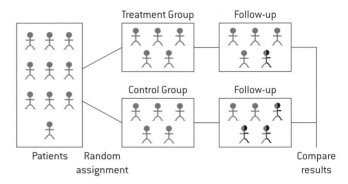

▲ Figure 5.16 Randomized control trial

Effectiveness of psychotherapy in general

Due to their integrative nature, meta-analyses allow us to answer such general questions as: does psychotherapy work in general? Which psychotherapeutic approach is better than the others?

Eysenck (1952) collected data available at that time and published a review in which he claimed, simply, that psychotherapy does not work. His analysis showed that 67% of outpatients "spontaneously" recovered in two years without treatment—a result quite comparable with what psychotherapy could achieve in the same time frame. This landmark publication resulted in much controversy and rigorous attempts to improve the approach to assessing the effectiveness of psychotherapy. It needs to be noted that at the time of Eysenck's review, randomized controlled trials were not widely recognized as the "golden standard" in psychotherapy research, so existing studies did not randomly assign patients to treatment versus no-treatment conditions. In other words, existing data was poor in quality. Meta-analysis as a research method also did not exist. It was developed later in response to these early anti-psychotherapy claims.

After all these developments in research had been implemented, **Smith and Glass (1977)** conducted a meta-analysis of 375 studies (and a total of 833 effect sizes reported there) of psychotherapy and counselling. They found that the typical therapy client was better off than 75% of untreated individuals (which means that therapy works; if it didn't, the result would be 50% due to random chance). So, their findings contradicted those of Eysenck.

A lot changed after that. First, more data was generated from a variety of carefully controlled experiments. Second, new evidence-based approaches to psychotherapy emerged, such as cognitive behavioural therapy (which did not exist when Eysenck was writing his first review). Third, meta-analysis provided a way to achieve more reliable estimates.

Wampold (2007) compared psychotherapy with medicine. Reviewed evidence suggested that psychotherapy, while clearly not effective with every single patient, is quite comparable to some established medical practices. In fact, his analysis showed that psychotherapy is more effective than widely used and evidence-based practices such as medical interventions in cardiology (for example, beta-blockers, angioplasty), asthma (for example, budesonide), influenza vaccine and cataract surgery. A number of research studies also suggest that psychotherapy is typically as effective as pharmacological treatments for mental disorders and at the same time has more long-lasting effects (Wampold, 2007). So, converging evidence does suggest that psychotherapy in general is effective.

This raises a question—how? What elements exactly explain the effectiveness of psychotherapy? One way to approach answering this question is to compare different approaches to psychotherapy in terms of their effectiveness.

Interestingly, both Eysenck and Smith and Glass observed very little difference in approaches to psychotherapy. For example, Smith and Glass used 10 approaches to psychotherapy in the meta-analysis (psychodynamic, client-centred, rational-emotive, behaviour modification, and so on). The type of therapy accounted only for about 10% in the outcome measures.

The finding that there is little difference between psychotherapeutic approaches if you combine data from a large variety of studies was replicated in several other meta-analyses. Coupled with the finding that psychotherapy in general is effective for the treatment of mental disorders, this raised the question of **specific and non-specific factors of psychotherapy**.

Non-specific factors are therapeutic influences associated with a wide range of approaches. For example, a trusting relationship and rapport in client-therapist interaction is a non-specific factor because it is supposed to be established in a variety of approaches. The same concerns **catharsis**—a release of strong or repressed emotions which often occurs in the safe psychotherapeutic setting and brings relief.

Specific factors are the ones associated with a concrete approach, that is, the specific techniques used in psychotherapy. An example would be re-evaluation of automatic thoughts in cognitive behavioural therapy or dream interpretation in psychoanalysis.

So what are the exact factors of effectiveness of psychotherapy? Are they specific or non-specific?

Specific and non-specific factors in the effectiveness of treatment

Studies by Eysenck and by Smith and Glass, although they arrived at diametrically opposite conclusions regarding the effectiveness of psychotherapy, shared the finding that there was little difference between specific psychotherapeutic approaches. Later meta-analyses corroborated this finding. This was surprising. Given that the variety of approaches is so diverse, why is there little difference? What is the mysterious component that makes psychotherapy effective?

An experimental design that can be used to establish specificity is the so-called "**dismantling design**" in which hypothesized "active ingredients" are removed from the standardized treatment programme and the result is subsequently compared to the "full" treatment (Wampold, 2007).

Jacobson *et al* (1996) used this design for cognitive behavioural therapy of depression. They randomly assigned 150 outpatients with major depression to one of three conditions:

1.   treatment focused exclusively on the behavioural activation component of CBT (home assignments to rehearse certain patterns of behaviour, and so on)

2.   treatment that combined behavioural activation and the teaching of skills to modify automatic thoughts

3.   the full CBT treatment including a focus on the modification of the core schema.

There was no evidence that the complete treatment produced better outcomes than any of the two "incomplete" treatments either right after the therapy or at a six-month follow-up. Moreover, both the "incomplete" treatments were shown to be as effective as the full treatment in terms of altering the patients' negative thinking patterns, although clearly these thinking patterns were targeted to a very different extent in the three approaches!

Another challenge in research into the effectiveness of treatment is to design a theory that would accurately explain the change processes occurring in a patient. It is not easy, and many observations that have been replicated in multiple studies just do not fit into the theoretical predictions of change processes. One such phenomenon that remains largely unexplained is **sudden gains**. Sudden gains are early dramatic treatment responses in psychotherapy that occur earlier than predicted. It has been shown that a substantial number of patients (17–40%) respond to treatment much sooner and more substantially than theory would predict (Lambert, 2013). Sudden gains occur in a variety of treatments (and disorders), and they comprise a substantial part of recovered patients, influencing the statistics that are later used to assess the effectiveness of the treatment programme.

ATL skills: Thinking and communication

The results of Jacobson *et al*'s (1996) research study, as well as the phenomenon of sudden gains, are somewhat counterintuitive and require an explanation. Can you suggest one?

Discuss in small groups. List several explanations first and then select the one your group thinks is the most plausible.

Present this explanation to the rest of the class and be ready to respond to their doubts and counter-arguments.

As you can see, some of the findings in this area have been puzzling. One of the areas of research that promises to connect all the dots is research into the so-called common psychotherapy factors.

Wampold (2007) suggests that three common factors of the effectiveness of psychotherapy are especially important.

1.   **Client's willingness to trust** the therapist to provide an explanation that will help. There is evidence to suggest that even in clinical trials where therapists are carefully selected, trained and monitored to deliver the standardized treatment procedure, there is great variation among therapists in one and the same condition, and this variation is often greater than that between experimental conditions. In other words, therapist variables may be more important than treatment variables.

2.   Formation of **working alliance** with the client. Some emerging evidence seems to suggest that it is not the treatment as such that is effective, but the way it is delivered—not the what, but the how. A working alliance entails readiness of the client to work collaboratively with the therapist to develop (and accept) an explanation for the client's problems.

3.   **Placebo effects**. As you will see later with the example of depression, a number of studies demonstrated a considerable advantage of depression treatment over a placebo whereas a number of studies failed to do so. In any case, the placebo effect is an inevitable part of any real-life treatment. It is a good idea to isolate this effect in research (in order to find out whether or not our treatment is more effective than placebo alone), but it also makes sense to accept placebo effect and use it in real-life therapeutic practice.

To summarize, current evidence suggests that psychotherapy in general is effective (or at least its effectiveness is comparable to medical treatments), but common (non-specific) factors play a larger role than specific therapeutic techniques. Remember, however, that this conclusion is not applicable to all treatments and all circumstances.

- All the meta-analyses discussed above dealt with psychological treatment and excluded medication treatment (such as antidepressants) from the analysis. The effectiveness of drug treatment, both general and in comparison to psychotherapy, will be discussed later in this unit.

- The nature of a meta-analysis is that it provides an overall result, but it does not necessarily mean that for any specific mental issue any treatment will be equally effective. For example, these same meta-analyses showed that systematic desensitization (a behavioural technique) was clearly more effective than other approaches when dealing with specific phobias. Later in this unit we will compare the effectiveness of drug, individual and group therapy in the treatment of depression.

ATL skills: Thinking

How can you use the idea of non-specific factors in psychotherapy to explain such puzzling findings as the effectiveness of incomplete treatments (Jacobson *et al*, 1996) and the phenomenon of sudden gains (Lambert, 2013)?

Biological treatment of depression

Inquiry questions

- Are antidepressants an effective treatment?

- Do they outperform other treatment methods?

- Do all antidepressants have the same clinical effect?

- Are antidepressants equally effective when it comes to response rates, remission rates and relapse rates?

What you will learn in this section

- Antidepressants

  - Tricyclic antidepressants (TCAs)

  - MAO (monoamine oxidase) inhibitors

  - Selective serotonin reuptake inhibitors (SSRIs)

- Effectiveness indicators

  - Response rates

  - Remission rates

  - Relapse rates

- Effectiveness of SSRIs

  - Treatment of adolescents with depression study (TADS): all three active treatments of depression (cognitive behavioural therapy—CBT, drug, combination) outperform placebo, combination treatment outperforms the other treatments in the short term; CBT gradually "catches up" with medication; no therapy effective for 100% of patients

  - Results support the chemical imbalance theory: depressive symptoms are caused by neurotransmitter imbalances in the brain and restoring balance will lead to a reduction in symptoms

- Current criticisms of biological treatments: publication bias and enhanced placebo effect

  - Kirsch *et al* (2002): meta-analysis of published and unpublished data; 82% of the effect of antidepressants was duplicated by placebo; mean difference between drug and placebo was only 1.8 on the HAM-D scale—statistically significant, but clinically insignificant

  - Kirsch (2014): all antidepressants show the same clinical effect irrespective of their physiological mechanism; this may be explained by the "enhanced placebo effect"

- Counter-arguments to the criticism: severity of depression needs to be taken into account

  - Hollon *et al* (2002): as initial depression scores increase, the difference between drugs and placebo becomes larger; at some point (HAM-D scores of 28) it reaches clinical significance

  - Elkin *et al* (1989): drugs were shown to be superior to placebo and faster and more effective than psychological treatment for severe depression

- Concluding remarks

  - A weaker claim: antidepressants are effective in a variety of situations (most notably severe symptoms that must be reduced urgently), but the decision regarding treatment and its duration should be made after a careful cost-benefit analysis

  - Attacks on the effectiveness of antidepressants continue: Bockting *et al* (2008), the effects of prolonged antidepressant treatment may reverse their course at some point of time because the brain presumably "pushes back" against drugs

This section also links to:

- biological explanations for disorders

- research methodology (effect size, statistical significance)

- neurotransmission (biological approach to behaviour)

- cognitive treatments of depression

- assessing effectiveness of treatment.

Psychology in real life

Your friend has been diagnosed with an episode of MDD. She is 17 years old, very quiet and shy. She is the only child in the family. As it turns out, she has been having suicidal thoughts lately, although to an outside observer everything in her life seems to be perfectly normal—regular problems of an average teenager. The doctor has prescribed her Fluoxetine. She has started to take it but it has resulted in severe headaches.

Of course it is up to the doctor to decide, but do you think it is recommended for her to continue medication and for how long? What information do you think is necessary to make this decision?

Antidepressants

Biological treatment of depression is based on the assumption of chemical imbalances in the brain as the major factor of the development of depression. Think back to our discussion of biological etiology (in particular, the role of neurotransmitters such as serotonin in producing depressive symptoms). This leads to the idea that if we restore the balance of neurotransmitters in the brain, depression symptoms will be reduced. The class of drugs that target key neurotransmitters involved in depression is known as antidepressants.

Tricyclic antidepressants (TCAs) were named this because their chemical structure contains three rings of atoms. The depression-reducing effect of these drugs was discovered accidentally. The mechanism of the action of these drugs is the inhibition of reuptake of certain neurotransmitters (such as serotonin and norepinephrine) after they had been released in the synaptic gap. This increases the concentration of neurotransmitters available in the synaptic gap. TCAs were shown to be effective, but later on they were largely replaced by other drugs because their side effects were sometimes quite severe (they included weight gain and dizziness, and an overdose could be fatal).

Note that epinephrine and norepinephrine are also referred to as adrenaline and noradrenaline.

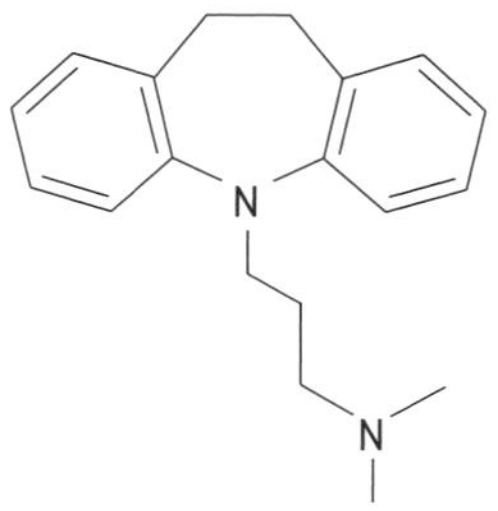

▲ Figure 5.17 Tricyclic antidepressant

MAO (monoamine oxidase) inhibitors are another well-known class of antidepressants. Monoamine oxidase is a chemical that breaks down monoamine neurotransmitters (such as serotonin, dopamine and norepinephrine). So, inhibiting monoamine oxidase leads, again, to an increase in the concentration of monoamines in the brain. This class of drugs has been shown to be particularly effective in treating atypical depression. However, some serious side effects were also reported.

Selective serotonin reuptake inhibitors (SSRIs), probably the most widely used class of antidepressants, function, as their name suggests, by selectively inhibiting reuptake of serotonin. This is the best thing about them—they block reuptake of serotonin only, not anything else. This means the number of potential side effects is smaller. In a sense, they are also "better" for scientific research—since we are only manipulating one independent variable (serotonin), it is easier to clearly attribute the observed reduction of symptoms to a certain cause. Perhaps the most popular chemical in this category is Fluoxetine. The most popular trade name for Fluoxetine is Prozac.

Exercise

Tricyclics, MAO inhibitors and SSRIs are classes of antidepressants. Within each class there are several chemicals. Each chemical may have one or more brand names. Search online and create a diagram showing a few examples of specific chemicals and brand names for each of the three classes of antidepressants.

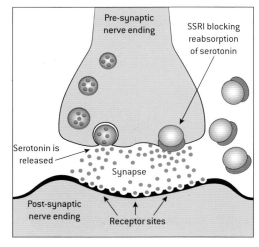

▲ Figure 5.18 Selective serotonin reuptake inhibitor

Effectiveness of SSRIs

What exactly is the effectiveness of selective serotonin reuptake inhibitors (SSRIs)? As you have seen, the answer to this question would typically depend on several factors including the outcome variable (for example, short-term or long-term), age of the patients, severity of disorder, and so on.

Treatment of adolescents with depression study (TADS) was a multi-site clinical research study funded by the NIMH (National Institute of Mental Health). It examined the short-term and long-term effectiveness of drug treatment, psychotherapy or a combination of the two for treating depression in adolescents aged 12–17. Thirteen clinics in the USA were involved in this trial and the whole project cost $17 million. The sample included 439 participants from all over the country diagnosed with major depression. The study was conducted in three stages.

- Stage 1 (the first 12 weeks), acute treatment—participants were randomly assigned to one of four groups: (a) Fluoxetine alone, (b) placebo + clinical management, (c) cognitive behavioural therapy (CBT) alone, (d) combination of Fluoxetine and CBT. Clinical management is a mode of treatment where clients and therapists meet and talk, but no specific psychotherapeutic technique is used. It was used here so that participants could not easily work out that they were in the placebo group. At the end of the 12-week period, participants who were taking the placebo were informed about it. If they showed no improvement during the study period, they were allowed to choose any of the other three modes of treatment (but they did not participate in the study any more).

- Stage 2, consolidation treatment—participants from the three active treatment groups (Fluoxetine, CBT and the combination) continued with their treatment for six more weeks.

- Stage 3, continuation treatment—participants who improved earlier were observed for another 18 weeks. So, the study lasted 36 weeks in total (March *et al*, 2007).

Three indicators are typically used in research to characterize effectiveness of a treatment in terms of reductions of symptoms of a disorder.

- Response rate: a 50% decrease in scores on a standardized depression scale, such as the Hamilton Depression Rating Scale (HAM-D).

- Remission rate: few or no symptoms of depression. An HAM-D score of less than 7 is sometimes used as an indicator of remission.

- Relapse rate: recurrence of a past condition (developing symptoms of depression again after the treatment was discontinued).

The main indicator used in this study to measure the effectiveness of treatment was **response rates**. Results are summarized in Table 5.4. For more information on this research visit the TADS page on the NIMH website https://www.nimh.nih.gov/funding/clinical-research/practical/tads/questions-and-answers-about-the-nimh-treatment-for-adolescents-with-depression-study-tads.shtml.

Response rates →	12 weeks	18 weeks	36 weeks
Placebo	35%	Discontinued	Discontinued
Fluoxetine	61%	69%	81%
CBT	44%	65%	81%
Fluoxetine + CBT	71%	85%	86%

▲ Table 5.4 Based on information available on the TADS website

ATL skills: Thinking and communication

Discuss the pros and cons of using each of the three indicators of effectiveness: response rates, remission rates and relapse rates. Why do you think it was decided to use response rates in the TADS project?

What conclusions can we derive from these results?

First, all three active treatments of depression outperform placebo. Combination treatment outperforms the other treatments in the short term.

Second, CBT gradually "catches up" with medication and even with a combination treatment. Given this finding, one may be tempted to ask if drugs should even be used—they may have unpleasant side effects and they do not allow the patient to learn new behaviours. However, in many cases what is needed is quick action, especially if depression at the initial stages is severe.

Combination treatment seems to be the best choice in a variety of situations. Cognitive treatment also depends a lot on the patient's involvement and motivation, something that depressed patients may not have especially at the initial stages.

Third, no therapy is effective for 100% of patients. Note that one in every five adolescents did not demonstrate response to treatment even after 36 weeks of continued medication.

However, the overall result of the study suggests that antidepressants (either alone or in combination with cognitive therapy) are effective for the treatment of depression both in the short term and in the long term. This seems to support the **chemical imbalance theory**—the proposition that depressive symptoms are caused by neurotransmitter imbalances in the brain and that restoring balance will lead to a reduction in symptoms.

Exercise

Biological treatments of depression (chemical imbalance theory) are based on the biological explanations for depression. Recall what you know about biological explanations for disorders and formulate several postulates (statements) that function as assumptions of biological treatment.

For example: assume that symptoms are caused by an imbalance of neurotransmitters in the synapse, hence we believe that restoring neurotransmitter balance in the symptoms will reduce symptoms.

Continue this list with two or three other statements.

Current criticisms of biological treatments: publication bias and enhanced placebo effect

Kirsch (2014) strongly opposed both the chemical imbalance theory and, more specifically, the serotonin theory. His analysis of both the published data and the unpublished data showed that the observed effectiveness of antidepressants can mostly be attributed to the placebo effect. He points out that all antidepressants show the same clinical effect irrespective of their physiological mechanism—some of them increase the level of serotonin, some decrease it and yet others do not change the level of serotonin at all.

He also points at the possibility of an "enhanced placebo effect" linked to the fact that in many clinical blind trials both clinicians and patients can sometimes work out what condition they are assigned to, demonstrating experimenter bias and demand characteristics. He goes as far as saying that antidepressants may, instead of curing depression, interfere with the brain's natural self-regulation processes, making a person even more vulnerable to depression in the future.

The first meta-analysis by Kirsch and Sapirstein (1998), in which they demonstrated that 75% of the improvement in the medication condition also occurred in the placebo condition, caused havoc in academic circles. Critics claimed that their selection of publications had not been representative. As a reaction to this **Kirsch et al (2002)** replicated the meta-analysis with a different set of clinical trials. For these purposes they used the Freedom of Information Act to ask the Food and Drug Administration (FDA) to send them data sets that had been submitted by pharmaceutical companies when obtaining approval for antidepressants. These data sets have one important advantage—the FDA funds clinical trials and requires companies to send in results of all funded trials, so they included both published and unpublished data. Another advantage is that all of them used one and the same measure of depression, the Hamilton Depression Rating Scale (HAM-D), making all the research studies directly comparable.

Almost half of the clinical trials sponsored by pharmaceutical companies were not published. With these extensive data sets the researchers found that 82% of the effect of antidepressants was duplicated by placebo. In terms of antidepressant effectiveness, there was very little difference between the drugs. The mean difference between the drug and the placebo conditions was not large. The HAM-D scale is scored from 0 to 53. Some natural fluctuations are expected: for example, a six-point difference can be obtained just by changes in sleep patterns. The mean difference between drug and placebo was only 1.8. The researchers concluded that when published and unpublished data are combined they fail to demonstrate clinically significant effectiveness of antidepressants.

The interpretation of HAM-D scores is as follows:

HAM-D score	Severity of symptoms
0–7	Normal
8–13	Mild depression
14–18	Moderate depression
19–22	Severe depression
≥ 23	Very severe depression

▲ Table 5.5

Hamilton, M: A rating scale for depression, *Journal of Neurology, Neurosurgery, and Psychiatry* 23:56-62, 1960, by permission of BMJ Publishing Group Ltd.

TOK

Discuss potential problems that can be caused by publication bias in other areas of knowledge. For example, to what extent is it possible that publication bias impacts our current state of knowledge in the natural sciences, history or religious knowledge systems?

ATL skills: Thinking

What are the ethical considerations linked to publication bias? Should you always publish your results in open sources, irrespective of the conclusions and the methodological quality of the study? Is it different in different research areas? For example, if you conducted a twin study and found that there is a strong genetic predisposition to depression, but later realized that there might have been sampling bias in your study, should the results be published? Should you openly warn the readers about the potential sampling bias?

Kirsch (2014) also points to the essential difference between **statistical significance** and **clinical significance**: with large sample sizes typically used in meta-analyses, even tiny effects may prove to be statistically significant, that is, reliably different from zero. This does not mean, however, that the effect will be clinically significant.

ATL skills: Research

If you don't remember what statistical significance is, review Unit 1 on research methodology. What is the difference between statistical significance and the effect size?

With large sample sizes even small effects can be statistically significant. This tells us that they are definitely larger than zero, but this does not mean that they are large. Does it pose a problem for experimental research in psychology on the whole? To maintain high population validity, we want large samples. But with large samples even tiny differences between the experimental and the control group may be found to be statistically significant.

What would be your solution to this problem?

▲ Figure 5.19 Publication bias

To summarize, drugs do not differ much from each other, but they outperform placebo. The degree of this advantage over placebo has been questioned in terms of its clinical but not statistical significance. Kirsch (2014) raises a further question: what is the common characteristic that all drugs have leading them to this slight advantage over placebo effects? Further debunking "the serotonin myth", he suggests that this common factor is "enhanced placebo effect". "Good" clinical trials of antidepressants are double blind. However, to what extent could such studies be blinded? Antidepressants have side effects, and you are usually warned about them (for ethical reasons). So what are the chances that you do not realize that you are in the drug group once the side effects kick in? Once you do, wouldn't you have the enhanced effects of positive expectations?

Counter-arguments to the criticism: severity of depression needs to be taken into account

The results of research that used collated published and unpublished clinical trial data cast a shadow of doubt on the effectiveness of antidepressants. However, we must keep in mind the limitations of meta-analyses: first, they arrive at average estimates across the whole body of available studies; second, they are only as good as the research studies comprising them.

One of the existing responses to Kirsch's criticism is that effectiveness of medical treatment may depend on the severity of the disorder.

For example, **Hollon et al (2002)** argued that most research studies in this area included patients who were not severely depressed. Indeed, one of the observed trends in meta-analytic data was that as initial depression scores increased, the difference

between drugs and placebo became larger, and at some point (initial HAM-D scores of 28 or above) reached clinical significance.

Elkin et al (1989) conducted a study in which 28 clinicians worked with 250 patients randomly assigned to one of four 16-week treatment conditions:

- interpersonal psychotherapy
- cognitive behavioural therapy
- antidepressant medication and clinical management
- placebo and clinical management.

Patients in all treatment groups showed a significant reduction in symptoms over this 16-week period. The consistent pattern of findings in terms of therapy effectiveness showed that placebo performed the worst, medication and clinical management performed the best, and the other two conditions (interpersonal psychotherapy and CBT) were only slightly less effective than medication. When severity of illness was taken into account, it was observed that the three treatment groups did not differ significantly in their effectiveness for mild or moderate depression, but there was a clearer advantage of medication in cases of severe depression.

So, drugs were shown to be superior to placebo and faster and more effective than psychological treatment for severe depression, at least in the 16-week treatment interval.

Concluding remarks

As you have seen, the history of research of biomedical treatments of depression has seen a number of changes, from a number of serendipitous discoveries to the "chemical imbalance" theory to further challenging this theory on the basis of research artifacts (publication bias, enhanced placebo effect). The idea that antidepressants are effective against the disorder has been refined and compartmentalized. A weaker and more precise claim is being made now—antidepressants are effective in a variety of situations (most notably severe symptoms that must be reduced urgently), but the decision regarding antidepressant treatment and its duration should be made on a case-to-case basis after a careful cost-benefit analysis.

Attacks on the effectiveness of antidepressant treatment continue to come from various directions. For example, one of the recent attacks came in the form of the argument that the brain "pushes back" against the initial symptom-reducing effects. Patients can initially respond to antidepressant treatment, but relapse later. **Bockting *et al* (2008)** found that 68% of patients who initially met remission criteria and continued medication relapsed in the course of two years. This indicates that the effects of prolonged antidepressant treatment may reverse their course at some point in time.

Psychology in real life

At the beginning of this section you considered whether or not continuation of antidepressant treatment should be recommended to your friend.

What other factors affecting the decision have you discovered while reading this section? Now that you know more, how would you modify your initial recommendation and why?

What aspects of the situation do you think people tend to ignore when they decide to take antidepressants?

See video

Watch Russ Altman's TED Talk "What really happens when you mix medications?": https://tinyurl.com/jeftz2c

▶ ❙❙ ◼ ─────────────────

Discussion

Why is there ambiguity regarding possible effects of drug interaction? To what extent is using search engine queries a reliable method of research in this area?

Can you think of any other innovative solutions to this problem?

Psychological treatment of depression

Inquiry questions

- Is psychological treatment better than medication?

- Should cognitive behavioural therapy (CBT) for depression be recommended to people from collectivistic cultures?

- Is group therapy better than individual therapy?

- What are the factors that need to be considered before CBT is recommended to a client?

- Would CBT be a good choice for Anoushka?

What you will learn in this section

- Cognitive behavioural therapy (CBT)

  o Cognitive restructuring and behavioural activation

  o CBT techniques: socratic questioning, behavioural experiments, thought records, situation exposure hierarchies, pleasant activity scheduling

- Effectiveness of CBT: response and remission

  o DeRubeis *et al* (2005): cognitive therapy can be as effective as medication for the treatment of moderate to severe depression, but the exact degree of effectiveness depends on therapist skill and experience

  o This result goes contrary to the idea that severely depressed patients automatically need drug treatment (compare with Hollon *et al* and Elkin *et al* from the previous section)

- Effectiveness of cognitive therapy could depend on which symptoms are targeted

  o Fournier *et al* (2013): medication is more effective in reducing cognitive/suicide symptoms, cognitive therapy is superior in terms of reducing vegetative symptoms; the future of treatment lies in targeting interventions to specific clusters of symptoms

- Effectiveness of CBT: relapse

  o CBT seems to be effective in the short term, but is this an enduring effect?

  o Hollon *et al* (2005): CBT has an enduring effect that extends beyond the end of the treatment

- Brain changes caused by CBT

  o If CBT is effective and the effects are enduring, what exactly is the mechanism of change that it triggers?

  o Goldapple *et al* (2004): similar effects in CBT and antidepressant treatment are achieved by distinctly different physiological pathways

- Cultural aspects of CBT

  o Doubts have been raised regarding applicability of CBT in the context of collectivistic cultures

  o Hodges and Oei (2007): although individual therapy may appear inappropriate for collectivistic cultures, it can actually be more effective, because clients will follow the directions of the therapist more readily

- Individual and group CBT

  o Toseland and Siporin (1986): group treatment is more effective than individual treatment in 25% of the studies

o McRoberts, Burlingame and Hoag (1998): difference between the effectiveness of the average individual and the average group treatment is close to zero, however, there is a trend that favours individual therapy for depression disorders

This section also links to:

- assessing effectiveness of treatment
- cognitive explanations for depression
- brain scanning technology (biological approach to behaviour)
- cultural dimensions of behaviour (individualism–collectivism) (sociocultural approach to behaviour).

Cognitive behavioural therapy

Cognitive behavioural therapy (CBT) is currently used for a number of other mental conditions as well, although originally it was developed to treat depression (see Beck's cognitive theory of depression). CBT is based on the assumption that the underlying cause of depression is maladaptive automatic thoughts that lead to irrational behaviour. As the name suggests, CBT targets both the automatic thoughts, to replace them with more reality-congruent information processing, and the behaviour, in an attempt to make it more rational and adjusted to the environment.

There are several features of CBT that make it different from many other forms of therapy.

- It has two major goals: **cognitive restructuring** and **behavioural activation** (change the way you think and start acting accordingly).
- It focuses on specific, well-defined problems.
- Patients are expected to be active, for example, they are given home assignments that are subsequently discussed or even graded.

Specific techniques used in a regular CBT session include the following.

Socratic questioning

Essentially, the therapist uses a series of questions that gradually lead the client to the realization that their beliefs are not rational nor are they supported by evidence. For example, the therapist might ask: "You claim that your colleagues think that you are useless. Name all the things that happened yesterday that support this claim."

Behavioural experiments

This technique is designed to counteract maladaptive beliefs. For example, if the client believes that it would be awkward and

embarrassing to speak in class, the therapist might ask her to try different behaviours on different days. On particular days she would have to speak and participate in class and register her feelings and thoughts, much like scientists do when they observe their participants. On other days she would have to be reserved, sit at the back of the class and answer vaguely and superficially. Results of these observations are further discussed and compared.

Thought records

This technique is also designed to challenge dysfunctional, irrational or unrealistic automatic thoughts. The client and the therapist identify a belief they want to explore and the client receives the assignment to keep systematic records of both the thoughts and the situations relevant to this belief. For example, if the client believes that colleagues at work don't respect her, she might be asked to keep a record of all relevant situations, for example, someone at work asked her for advice, someone offered her help, someone initiated a conversation. Looking at this systematically collected evidence, the client begins to realize that she has been ignoring evidence contradicting her dysfunctional belief.

Situation exposure hierarchies

In this technique the client makes a list of what she finds to be the most stressful situations or behaviours. For example, examinations may be very stressful for a depressed patient (because it involves a potential threat to already low self-esteem). The client makes a list of examination-related scenarios and arranges them on a continuum from 1 (least stressful, such as playing chess with a friend) to 10 (most stressful, such as taking a course online and having a high-stakes examination at the end of the course). After that the client is encouraged to try out behaviours from the bottom of the list until they become less stressful, and in this manner gradually makes her progress closer to the top of the list.

Pleasant activity scheduling

The client agrees (as part of her homework) that she will do one pleasant activity every day—something that she does not normally do, but something that brings her positive emotions or a sense of competence or mastery. This could be something very simple and quick like practising playing the guitar for 10 minutes or going outside to read a short chapter in a detective book.

ATL skills: Self-management

You don't need to be mentally ill to benefit from using these techniques. Select any negative belief about yourself or something that worries you in your own self-image or everyday behaviour. Take a notebook and set a goal for yourself. Formulate the goal positively and mention the time.

Over the course of several weeks use thought records, situation exposure hierarchies, behavioural experiments and scheduling of pleasant activities. See what happens.

Remember that this is a joking, amateur exercise. Therapists go through extensive training and they can apply these techniques professionally. However, even this amateur attempt to modify your own behaviour and thought patterns may help you get a feel of what happens in a CBT session.

Mental health professionals who practise CBT are rigorously trained to follow a special manual to make treatment as standardized as possible. The typical session lasts 50 minutes to an hour and includes the following series of steps.

1. checking on the patient's mood and symptoms
2. setting a clear agenda for the meeting
3. reviewing and evaluating the homework assignment
4. discussing the issues on the agenda (a variety of techniques such as Socratic questioning can be used here)
5. setting new homework.

CBT typically lasts 14 to 16 weeks. In this it is different from many other approaches where treatment is "open-ended". CBT specialists believe that realization of the fact that therapy is not infinite urges clients to take responsibility for their own improvement.

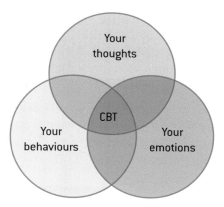

▲ Figure 5.20 Cognitive behavioural therapy

See video

There is an abundance of instructional videos on CBT on YouTube. You could use the following key words for your search: "cognitive behavioural therapy session", "cognitive behavioural session example". You might also want to find interviews with the founder of CBT, Aaron Beck.

Watch some of these videos. Make sure you see a couple of examples of CBT "in action".

What do you think of this approach to treatment? Do you believe it can be effective for the treatment of depression?

Effectiveness of CBT: response and remission

Some research studies have demonstrated that in many situations CBT can be as effective as medication.

For example, **DeRubeis *et al* (2005)** randomly assigned 240 patients with moderate to severe MDD to one of three conditions:

- 16 weeks of medication
- 16 weeks of individual CBT
- 8 weeks of placebo.

Scores on the Hamilton Depression Rating Scale served as the dependent variable. Results showed that at eight weeks medication had a response rate of 50%, CBT had a response rate of 43%, and they both outperformed placebo (25%). At 16 weeks response rates were 58% both for medication and CBT. Remission rates were 46% for medication and 40% for CBT.

When researchers analysed these results by research site they found that the trends were not uniform. At one site in particular medication turned out to be more effective than CBT. The researchers

attributed this to therapist skill. The conclusion was that CBT can be as effective as medication for the treatment of moderate to severe depression, but the exact degree of effectiveness depends on a therapist's skill and experience.

This result goes contrary to the idea that severely depressed patients automatically need drug treatment (compare with Hollon *et al* (2002) and Elkin *et al* (1989) from the previous section).

	8 weeks	16 weeks	
	Response rate	Response rate	Remission rate
Medication	50%	58%	46%
CBT	43%	58%	40%
Placebo	25%	-	-

▲ Table 5.6 Findings from DeRubeis *et al* (2005)

ATL skills: Self-management

Based on your knowledge of techniques used to study effectiveness of treatment, you should be able to answer the following questions.

- Why are remission rates at 16 weeks lower than response rates?

- Why was placebo discontinued after eight weeks?

- Why does response rate increase with time?

- Why is the increase of response rate faster for CBT than for medication?

If you find it difficult to answer these questions, go back and review the sections "Assessing the effectiveness of treatment" and "Biological treatment of depression".

It has been suggested that effectiveness of cognitive therapy could depend on which symptoms are targeted. Some symptoms could be reduced more effectively in response to CBT, while others may be better targeted by medication.

With this prediction in mind, **Fournier *et al* (2013)** looked at the effects of medication and cognitive therapy on specific depressive symptoms (rather than "depression" on the whole). Their sample consisted of 231 depressed outpatients randomly assigned to cognitive therapy, medication or placebo. There were several dependent variables—specific clusters of depressive symptoms: mood, cognitive/suicide, anxiety and vegetative symptoms. Results showed that at four weeks medication was more effective in reducing cognitive/suicide

symptoms than both CBT and placebo. By eight weeks, however, CBT "caught up" with medication in reducing this group of symptoms. Cognitive therapy was superior to the other groups in terms of reducing vegetative symptoms (such as insomnia). The researchers concluded that medication and CBT targeted slightly different clusters of symptoms. One might say that the future of treatment lies in targeting interventions to specific clusters of symptoms that a particular patient demonstrates.

Effectiveness of CBT: relapse

Another consideration in assessing the effectiveness of treatment is the duration of the treatment effect. CBT seems to be effective in the short term, but is this an enduring effect? Does it last when the therapy is discontinued? In other words, we need to look at relapse rates.

Hollon *et al* (2005) reviewed some background research and concluded that antidepressants prevent the return of symptoms, but only if treatment is continued. Their aim was to determine if cognitive therapy has a more enduring effect. The study was a randomized control trial and it had three groups of moderate-to-severe depression patients:

- patients who responded positively to cognitive therapy and were withdrawn from treatment for 12 months

- patients who responded to medication and continued medication

- patients who responded to medication and continued to receive a placebo.

Results showed that patients withdrawn from cognitive treatment were less likely to relapse than patients withdrawn from medication (31% compared to 76%) during the first 12-month period and even slightly less likely to relapse than the group that continued to take medication (47%). The study has two implications.

- CBT has an enduring effect that extends beyond the end of the treatment.

- Drugs, unlike CBT, seem to be good at reducing the symptoms, but they do not target the cause of the disorder.

Group	Relapse rate in 12 months
Responded to CBT, withdrawn from treatment	31%
Responded to medication, continued medication	47%
Responded to medication, continued placebo	76%

▲ Table 5.7 Findings from Hollon *et al* (2005)

Brain changes caused by CBT

If CBT is effective and the effects are enduring, what exactly is the mechanism of change that it triggers?

Goldapple *et al* **(2004)** used PET scans to examine brain changes underlying the response to CBT compared to antidepressant treatment. Seventeen unmedicated depressed patients with a mean HAM-D score of 20 were scanned before and after a course of CBT. Their average HAM-D score after treatment was 6.7. They were also compared to an independent group of 13 patients who had been treated and responded to an antidepressant—this group had a similar HAM-D score at the start of therapy and similar reduction of the score by the end of therapy.

Results showed that CBT was causing significant metabolic changes in the brain and the pattern of these changes was distinct from that seen in patients who responded to medication treatment. More specifically, CBT was associated with more "top-down" changes, that is, mostly in the cortex, whereas antidepressant treatment was associated

with "bottom-up" changes, that is, in limbic and subcortical regions (such as the brainstem). There were also brain changes common to the two groups, mostly in the cortical-limbic pathways—structures that connect the cortex to the limbic system. The authors concluded that similar effects in CBT and antidepressant treatment (modulation of cortical-limbic pathways) are achieved by distinctly different physiological pathways.

At the same time, a limitation of this study was that depressed patients seeking treatment were not randomly allocated to one of the two conditions. Patients who chose CBT were compared to patients who chose medication. If these two groups were not equivalent from the start of the experiment, this could have resulted in selection bias.

ATL skills: Social and communication

To what extent can the results of this study support the following concepts and principles from the biological approach to behaviour?

- The principle that behaviour has a physiological basis

- The principle that patterns of behaviour can be genetically inherited

- Evolutionary explanations of behaviour

- Localization of function

- Neuroplasticity

Discuss in a small group and share your ideas with the whole class.

Cultural aspects of CBT

It is also important to remember that there could be cultural aspects in the use of CBT. Doubts have been raised, for example, regarding applicability of CBT in the context of collectivistic cultures. After all, it may go against collectivistic values to take ownership for one's mental health issues in a one-on-one conversation with a stranger.

Hodges and Oei (2007) explored the conceptual compatibility between CBT and the common values of Chinese culture. They concluded that many typical CBT processes (such as teaching of skills, emphasis on homework, rational re-analysis of thoughts) go well with traditional Chinese values (such as respect for authority and hard work). This indicates that although individual therapy may appear inappropriate for collectivistic cultures, it can actually be even more effective there because clients will follow the directions of the therapist more readily. However, one has to remember that such a directive therapist–client relationship was not emphasized in the original CBT approach (where it is important that the client takes responsibility for his or her actions and thoughts and does not simply follow the directions of the therapist). CBT should not be excessively directive, but including certain directive elements in it (for example, following up on homework) can make it more suited to Chinese culture.

Discussion

To what extent would it be ethical to tweak the original philosophy of CBT (its focus on personal responsibility) to better fit into the context of collectivistic societies? Should clients with collectivistic values still be encouraged to follow the classic procedures (although it would not be as effective), or should we modify CBT to be more therapist-directed, since that is in line with the cultural expectation?

Individual and group CBT

Cognitive behavioural therapy may take the form of either individual or group sessions. Group therapy has its advantages and limitations. These are some of the obvious advantages.

- The cost is lower (more affordable).

- The therapist can directly observe the client's behaviour in a group (gives more information).

- Seeing others improve may be an additional stimulus for recovery.

- It gives an opportunity to test new behaviours with the other group members.

Some commonly mentioned disadvantages include the fact that some clients may be less comfortable

speaking in a group. There is also a possibility that group dynamics will actually be harmful to a client (for example, excessively harsh feedback from other group members).

Many studies support the idea that group therapy is as effective as individual therapy in a variety of situations. For example, **Toseland and Siporin (1986)** reviewed the clinical and the research literature and found that group treatment was more effective than individual treatment in 25% of the studies (and equally effective in 75%). However, it has been pointed out that the studies included in meta-analyses often investigate either individual or group treatment but not both. As a result the individual–group comparison is often between-study, not within-study. This adds many potentially confounding variables. After all, patients were not randomly allocated to one of the two conditions (individual versus group).

To remedy the situation, **McRoberts, Burlingame and Hoag (1998)** conducted a meta-analysis of primary studies that compared individual and group therapy directly within one study. Only 23 studies satisfied these selection criteria. Results indicated that the overall difference between the effectiveness of the average individual and the average group treatment is close to zero so there is no advantage for either of the treatment modalities. When the effectiveness of the two modalities was compared for specific diagnoses, differences were insignificant. However, there was a trend that favoured individual therapy for depression disorders.

It seems that group therapy for depression may be almost as effective as individual therapy. Apparently the choice needs to be made depending on individual circumstances.

TOK

CBT changes your thinking patterns by making them more realistic and reducing biases. To what extent is this similar to what scientists do?

Is there any similarity between techniques of CBT and methods of research used in the natural sciences, human sciences or the arts?

The role of culture in treatment

- Will people with different cultural backgrounds respond to treatment differently?

- What can be done to compensate for these differences in effectiveness?

- How different should the approach to treatment be in Anoushka's case, compared with an average western patient?

- If you were Anoushka's therapist, what measures would you implement to ensure that she responds to treatment?

What you will learn in this section

- Cultural factors influence compliance with treatment

  - Cultural background of the patient affects their responsiveness to antidepressant medication

  - Kinzie *et al* (1987): TCA blood levels in Southeast Asian patients

- Clinical negotiation may improve response to treatment in culturally diverse settings

  - Kirmayer (2001): emphasizes the importance of an open and active partnership between the patient and the clinician

- Internal model of illness needs to be taken into consideration

  - Internal model of illness is a culturally determined schematic representation of a mental disorder

  - Naeem *et al* (2012): a culturally sensitive CBT programme in Pakistan

  - Any therapist in this culture would have to deal with patients who continue their daily routine irrespective of their mental state.

  - Four main themes emerged in the interviews: patient's perceptions of depression; patient's model of causes of depression; modes of referral for help; patient's knowledge concerning treatment of depression

- Culturally sensitive treatment

  - Top-down adaptations and bottom-up adaptations

  - Ecological Validity Framework (Bernal, Bonilla and Bellido, 1995): language, persons, metaphors, content, concepts, goals, method, context

- Effectiveness of culturally sensitive treatment

  - Griner and Smith (2006): meta-analysis—moderately strong benefit of culturally adapted interventions; cultural adaptations carried out for specific sub-populations may be more effective than just making treatments more culturally flexible in general; acculturation is also an important factor in determining the effectiveness of culturally adapted treatment

  - Which specific elements of the treatment are responsible for this increased effectiveness?

  - Kalibatseva and Leong (2014): meta-analysis—accommodating for culture-specific values related to interpersonal relationships, family, and spirituality; exploration of the client's illness beliefs; destigmatization of depression as an illness

This section also links to:

- classification systems
- the role of clinical biases in diagnosis
- assessing the effectiveness of treatment
- research methodology

- schema theory (cognitive approach to behaviour)
- cultural dimensions of behaviour; cultural norms and values (sociocultural approach to behaviour).

Cultural factors influence compliance with treatment

As we have seen, there are extensive cross-cultural differences in how symptoms of mental disorders are experienced, presented and perceived. This may influence how effective the treatment is. There is evidence that treatment may be ineffective for many patients because the patient and the clinician perceive the treatment process differently. For example, it has been observed that the rate of patient compliance with treatment is much lower in intercultural settings, presumably because of differences in cultural expectations of treatment.

Another illustration of this argument is the following research study in which the cultural background of patients were shown to have an influence on how responsive they would be to antidepressant medication.

Kinzie *et al* **(1987)** examined 41 depressed Southeast Asian patients who underwent long-term treatment of depression with tricyclic antidepressants (TCA) in US clinics. Their TCA blood levels were examined and no detectable medicine level was found in 61% of the patients, while a therapeutic level of medicine was only found in six patients (15%)—there was high incidence of non-compliance with the treatment. Apparently, patients were not conscientious enough about following the prescription. There were some interesting inter group differences as well. For example, compliance with treatment was significantly higher in Cambodian patients than in Vietnamese patients.

Reasons for low levels of medication in the blood may include patients' reluctance to take medication if it is perceived as too strong, increased sensitivity to side effects and social stigma associated with taking psychiatric medicine. However, cultural

attitudes towards authority may lead such patients to maintain the appearance of strictly following the clinician's guidelines. This may be done in an effort not to offend the clinician.

After a discussion of the problems and benefits of antidepressant treatments was held with the patients, however, rates of compliance improved (among the Cambodians too). The researchers concluded that cultural and educational factors may influence compliance with the treatment of depression. They claim that TCA blood levels should be determined in Asian patients shortly after the start of the therapy. If non-compliance with treatment is detected (low TCA blood levels), a doctor-patient discussion should be held about beliefs surrounding medication and its effects.

See video

Watch Sebastian Junger's TED Talk "Our lonely society makes it hard to come home from war": https://tinyurl.com/zm6op97

Although it is not directly related to depression, it links to the idea that treatment of mental health problems is embedded in a cultural context.

▶ ❙❙ ■ ——————————————

Discussion

If culture makes it difficult to recover, to what extent is it possible to create a "micro-culture" in the therapist's office that would counteract the effects of this "bigger" culture?

Clinical negotiation may improve response to treatment in culturally diverse settings

Summarizing research studies on the differences in the clinical presentation of depression among various cultural groups, **Kirmayer (2001)** concludes that, since the cultural background of a person may lead them to interpret his or her symptoms differently and even reject psychological treatment, there must exist some form of a **clinical negotiation** between the clinician and the patient. The aim of this negotiation is to establish a common interpretation of the set of symptoms and frame it in culturally appropriate and acceptable terms.

Kirmayer pointed out that patients should be encouraged to take responsibility for understanding their illness and seeking out forms of treatment that make sense to them personally, which emphasizes the importance of an open and active partnership between the patient and the clinician rather than the directive or prescriptive approach. The role of the clinician in this process is to gain understanding of patients' cultural background and make communication as clear and as culturally appropriate as possible. The clinician also needs to make sure that patients are not afraid to speak up and voice their points of view or concerns about the course of the treatment.

Internal model of illness needs to be taken into consideration

A patient's beliefs about treatment are heavily influenced by the person's beliefs about the disorder itself, by the way the patient internally represents his or her illness. This is known as the patient's **internal model of illness**. Internal model of illness as a concept is closely linked to the concept of schema. Essentially, this is a culturally determined schematic representation of a mental disorder.

Naeem *et al* (2012) conducted a study which aimed to develop a culturally sensitive CBT programme and assess its effectiveness in the developing world (using Pakistan as an example). Extensive interviews were conducted with depressed patients in which participants were asked for their thoughts about the illness, its causes and treatments, as well as their views on psychotherapy. The interview data were collated with field notes from the author during his clinical field practice. A qualitative research method was chosen because such methods are particularly useful when very little is known about a population, as was the case. Additionally, the focus was on meanings and subjective interpretations in a social context, and quantitative methods are not suitable for that.

All patients attended a psychiatric outpatient clinic in Pakistan. All interviews were conducted in the Urdu language and tape recorded. Nine patients participated.

ATL skills: Thinking and research

Apply your knowledge of research methodology.

- In what situations are qualitative research methods preferable to quantitative methods?

- What is inductive content analysis? How is it conducted? For what purpose?

- What can be done to ensure credibility of a qualitative research study?

- What is the role of reflexivity in qualitative research? How was reflexivity used in Naeem *et al*'s (2012) study?

- What ethical considerations are important for an interview?

After all the data were transcribed and analysed (inductive content analysis), four main themes emerged.

- Patient's **perceptions of depression**. In general, physical symptoms were mentioned much more often. Headache was the most common complaint; sadness was also mentioned, but not emphasized. When asked what kind of illness they had, patients did not use any specific label and used expressions such as "weakness of brain", "physical illness", "illness of poor sleep" and "tension". When asked if they knew anything about depression, none of them recognized it as an illness. However, when given a forced choice, "Do you have a physical illness or a mental illness?", most patients recognized their illness as mental.

- Patient's **model of causes** of depression. When patients were asked about their knowledge of mental illnesses in general, they attributed these illnesses to "tensions and trauma", "problems in the environment", "thinking too much" and "worries". Patients never mentioned any names of mental illness. In fact, all but one had never heard the term "depression" and were not aware of the existence of types of mental illnesses.

- **Modes of referral for help**. Some patients referred themselves to the clinic, but the majority were referred by relatives.

- Patient's **knowledge and experience concerning treatment of depression**. Most patients believed that they could be cured by "good quality medicine". When asked about their experience with non-medical healers (for example, religious healers, magicians), only one patient admitted to it, but it is possible that they did not want to disclose their contact with local healers. It was observed that patients became particularly guarded and careful when talking about non-medical treatments.

The study helped the authors to develop CBT for local use. They gained an insight into the language used by patients to describe their experiences (for example, "tension") and so were able to better adapt CBT practices to the local needs. They also focused on reinterpretation of certain somatic symptoms as signs of depression (especially headache). Another important dimension that was identified as crucial for adapting CBT practices was the fact that although the "tension" interfered with the patients' daily activities, none of the patients stopped performing them. They carried on with their routine chores and ways of living, as well as their family roles. Some patients reported increased religious activities. Any therapist in this culture would have to deal with patients who continued their daily routine irrespective of their mental state. Patients would be looking for medication that would help them quickly, making them fully operational again in their daily activities.

TOK

In some instances, in Naeem *et al*'s (2012) study it looked like patients did not have any appropriate words for their experiences and they were using the closest equivalents that corresponded to their cultural schemas (for example, "tension").

To what extent do you think cultural differences in the perception of depression are influenced by language? Review the Sapir-Whorf hypothesis of linguistic relativity.

If language does influence perception of illness, would bilingual interviews with the patients be beneficial?

Imagine you are treating a depressed patient in Pakistan, his English proficiency is low, and both of you speak good Urdu. Would you still choose to conduct therapy sessions in English?

If you are interested, use a search engine to look for supporting and contradicting evidence for the Sapir-Whorf hypothesis. Note that it should be empirical evidence, preferably from controlled experimental studies.

Culturally sensitive treatment

Understanding that culture is an important variable that mediates the patient's response to treatment has triggered a lot of research and practical programmes in the field of designing culturally sensitive treatments for depression. How do you design a culturally sensitive approach to treatment?

You start with an evidence-based treatment, that is, one that has been proven to be effective in clinical trials. In the case of depression, this may be cognitive behavioural therapy. As you know, this approach has found some empirical support in carefully controlled experiments. Of course, in the overwhelming majority of cases the

evidence for this therapy was obtained in the most "stereotypical" samples of patients; in the case of depression that would be white, middle-class English-speaking women.

The adaptation of the evidence-based approach to a specific cultural context may be done on various levels, from relatively superficial (for example, a change in the approach to service delivery, changing the language, hiring bicultural support staff) to relatively deep (for example, a change in the nature of the relationship between the therapist and the client, a change in the focus of the treatment itself). Making relatively superficial changes to the treatment is known as **top-down adaptations** (because they take the existing treatment as the starting point and only change certain elements while keeping the overall approach and structure). On the contrary, making relatively deep changes is known as **bottom-up adaptations**, because culture is taken as a starting point. In bottom-up adaptations researchers usually use qualitative methods (interviews, focus groups) to generate a theory about the specificity of a culture and then build their treatment approach based on that information. The study of Naeem *et al* (2012) is a clear example of the bottom-up approach.

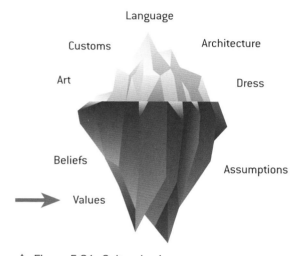

▲ Figure 5.21 Cultural values

One of the frameworks that has been used in designing culturally sensitive treatments is the so-called **Ecological Validity Framework** (Bernal, Bonilla and Bellido, 1995). It outlines eight areas that may be adapted. They are:

- language (for example, translation, specific jargon)

- persons (ethnic similarities between client and therapist)

- metaphors (expressing oneself in culturally relevant forms)

- content (cultural knowledge, client's values and traditions)

- concepts (beliefs about treatment in line with with the patient's culture)

- goals (using the beliefs about treatment goals from the country of origin)

- method (adaptation of culturally appropriate methods of treatment or accounting for cultural beliefs about treatment)

- context (accounting for the changing context such as acculturation, country of origin, social support).

Effectiveness of culturally sensitive treatments

Griner and Smith (2006) conducted a meta-analysis of 76 studies with a total sample of 25,000 participants to examine the benefit of culturally adapted treatments. They only used studies that included a quantitative indication of the effectiveness of therapy. The most frequently mentioned type of cultural adaptation was the inclusion of cultural values in the intervention. For example, in one of the research studies a treatment programme with children involved storytelling about cultural folk heroes. Other types of adaptations included consultations with individuals familiar with the client's culture, outreach efforts to recruit clients (especially when reporting bias was suspected), and cultural sensitivity training for staff. In the majority of cases, however, it was a combination of different adaptations.

They found a moderately strong benefit of culturally adapted interventions: the average effect size from pre- to post-intervention was 0.45. The format of the intervention (individual or group) did not influence the overall result. However, treatments for groups of same-race participants were four times more effective than treatments for mixed-race groups (effect size = 0.49 versus effect size = 0.14). From this, Griner and Smith concluded that cultural adaptations carried out for specific sub-populations may be more effective than just making treatments more culturally flexible in general.

Acculturation also proved to be an important factor in determining the effectiveness of culturally adapted treatment—older participants were more responsive to culturally adapted therapy than younger participants, presumably because older participants may be less acculturated.

When the therapist spoke the participant's native language, therapy was more effective than when the therapist spoke English (effect size = 0.49 versus effect size = 0.21).

Special attention was paid to eliminating the possibility of publication bias, a common threat in meta-analyses because studies with statistically significant findings are more likely to be published, therefore inflating the average effect size estimates. For this purpose, published studies were compared to unpublished studies (found in conference presentations, theses and dissertations), and it was shown that effect sizes of these two groups of studies did not differ.

This meta-analysis clearly shows that culturally sensitive therapy in general is effective, especially when it is targeted to specific groups of individuals based on their cultural background. However, which specific elements of the treatment are responsible for this increased effectiveness? Is it the language that the clinician speaks, the nature of patient-therapist relationship, or something else?

Kalibatseva and Leong (2014) conducted a meta-analysis to find this out. They used 16 published studies. This is fewer than Griner and Smith because the inclusion criteria were more stringent—Kalibatseva and Leong were looking for explicit identification of the cultural element that was changed in the culturally sensitive intervention programme. Most of the studies involved the use of CBT. Both individual and group approaches were utilized. In terms of the specific elements that prove to be most effective in the process of cultural adaptation of treatment, research findings pointed at **accommodating for culture-specific values** related to interpersonal relationships, family and spirituality. For example, among Latino patients culture-specific values included *respeto* (respect of hierarchical relationships), *familismo* (value of close relationships with family members) and *simpatia* (the importance of being polite and pleasant). Culturally sensitive treatments where the therapist was instructed to adhere to these values were particularly effective with Hispanic patients. Exploration of the client's illness beliefs and destigmatization of depression as an illness were also shown to be effective elements of cultural adaptation of treatments.

Discussion

What culture-specific values are there in your background culture? How do you think these values should be accommodated in a typical therapy session?

Topics:

Introduction

Health is more than the absence of illness or injury. Health has been defined as a positive state of physical, mental, and social well-being that moves over time along a continuum. At opposite ends of the continuum are illness and wellness (Sarafino, 2017). There remains plenty of active discussion and debate over where on the continuum wellness turns into illness, but it is a generally accepted model for human health.

The health continuum, sometimes called the illness/wellness continuum, is a model that is used specifically in health fields. It is designed to show how wellness and illness are two sides of the same coin. If you are more healthy, you are less ill and vice versa. It also makes the point that individuals all exist somewhere along the continuum; extremes of either wellness or illness are uncommon.

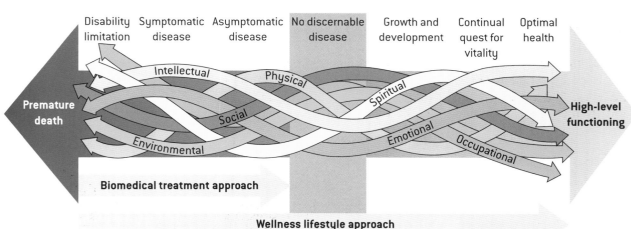

▲ Figure 6.1 Wellness continuum

Health psychology examines how biological, psychological, and social factors influence health and illness. Health psychologists use research to promote health, prevent illness and improve healthcare systems. Matarazzo

(1980) points out that health psychology has four main goals:

- the promotion and maintenance of health-related behaviour

- the improvement of healthcare systems policies
- the prevention and treatment of illness
- an understanding of the multifaceted causes of illness.

There are many areas of study in the field of health psychology, including addiction and substance abuse, obesity, chronic pain, sexual health and stress. In this unit we are going to learn more about how health-care professionals study, diagnose and attempt to prevent or treat behaviours that contribute to illness. Although this will be a general introduction to health psychology, we will be using health behaviour surrounding obesity and stress as examples to illustrate the main practices and models.

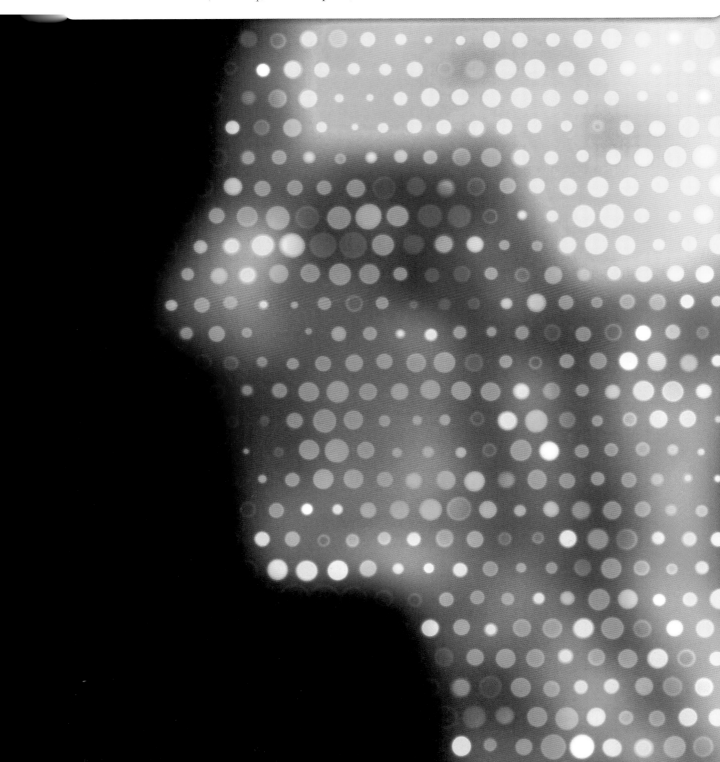

Inquiry questions

- What does it mean to be healthy?

- How can we measure health?

What you will learn in this section

- Models of health

  - The biomedical model concentrates on biological causes and treatments for illnesses

  - The biopsychosocial model is far more complex and takes into account biological, psychological, and social causes and treatments for illness

- Determinants of health

  - Social and personal determinants of health

  - Risk and protective factors: many factors affect our health, some in positive ways

and others negative; a risk factor is any attribute, characteristic or exposure of an individual that increases the likelihood of developing a condition, disease or injury while protective factors do the opposite

This section also links to:

- theory of knowledge—religious knowledge systems

- thinking and decision-making (cognitive approach to behaviour).

Models of health

In science, a model is a theoretical framework that helps people understand real-world complex systems. Models can be mathematical, visual or computational. Some very simple early models include a model of a flat Earth or Copernicus' heliocentric model of the solar system. They are often simplified and are created through the culmination of much research and theorizing and therefore evolve over time. Some examples of psychological models include the multi-store model of memory (Atkinson and Shiffrin) and the working memory model (Baddeley and Hitch). These models attempt to show visual representations of a complex process: memory. It is important to understand that models are not perfect; they contain the simplifications and biases of the theories used to create them. (For more on these models see Unit 3.)

TOK

Take a moment to decide if you agree with the following quotation: "The mind is what the brain does". In what ways is this statement true? Do you agree with it?

Biomedical model

If you agree with the quotation above, you may accept the biomedical model of health and wellness. The biomedical model represents an attempt to understand disease (and human behaviour) as a result of biological processes in the body. It leaves no room in the framework for social or cognitive influences (for example, the built environment, socio-economic status, appraisals and decision-making) on health or wellness. The main assumption made by the model is that illnesses can be attributed to somatic (physical) causes such as biochemical imbalances or neurological abnormalities. Hidden in this assumption is the belief that your brain is the only determinant of your psychology and your mental self; essentially the mind exists only as a result of the brain. It is therefore a **reductionist** model as it explains complex phenomena from a simple biological approach. Carl Sagan (1977) arguably supports this model with his claim that, "my fundamental premise about the brain is that its workings—what we sometimes call 'mind'—are a consequence of its anatomy and physiology, and nothing more" (Sagan, 1977, p 7).

As the field of medicine became more scientific and physicians were increasingly implementing the scientific method to understand physiological processes (and illness), the biomedical model gained support. Many common ailments could be explained and treated biologically. The biomedical model was very effective in treating physical illness and was therefore ascribed a power of explanation which may have overstretched its abilities. The dominant model for studying and treating illness until recently has been the biomedical approach. The use of the biomedical model had a tremendous impact on how illness was perceived and treated until the 1970s. Health campaigns and treatments were limited to biological treatments, ignoring sociocultural and psychological causes and treatments entirely.

Biopsychosocial model (BPS)

In the last quarter of the 20th century, theorists such as George L Engel began to publish works questioning the efficacy of the biomedical model's ability to accurately reflect the reality of health and wellness. His criticism centred around the reductionist nature of the biomedical model. The argument was that there is a lot more to health and wellness than simple biology. People's health depended on a number of things that would become known as determinants of health. These determinants have come to encompass everything including someone's social and physical environment, access to health services and individual behaviour as well as biology and genetics. So, as you can see, the biopsychosocial (BPS) model reaches far beyond the biomedical model and acknowledges the complexity of health-related behaviour and wellness.

Modern health-care professionals have largely adopted a much more holistic approach to understanding wellness and illness. According to Engel (1977), the BPS model was a "blueprint for research, a framework for teaching, and a design for action in the real world of health care". A reader might be forgiven for thinking that Engel had the answer to explaining health behaviour

finally and conclusively. The BPS model has proven a convincing and successful model for explaining health and well-being.

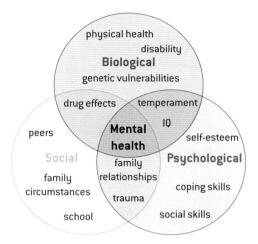

▲ Figure 6.2 The biopsychosocial model of health

The BPS model is less reductionist than the biomedical model and therefore accounts for more variables, allowing for more holistic explanations of behaviour. This is a strong argument for the merits of the BPS model and its successes should not be ignored. Despite its obvious benefits, criticisms have been raised by an increasing number of researchers.

Its holistic nature may imply that all three levels of analysis are always of interest when determining illness but the relative contributions of each level do not seem to be considered. Figure 6.3 illustrates how the three approaches may impact individuals to different extents. In fact, it is possible that some behaviours or health problems can be treated successfully with only one or two components of this model.

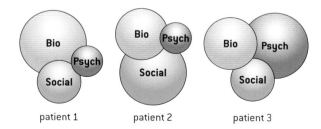

▲ Figure 6.3 Importance of approaches is relative

Whatever model we are considering, we must be cautious and avoid thinking that any of these is the best of all possible models. To paraphrase Francis Fukuyama (1992), we have not reached "the end of psychology". There is still a lot of learning to be done. The BPS model is the most commonly used model of health behaviour but history tells us this may change in the future. As critics voice their opinions, alternative models such as the method-based psychiatry model and the medical humanist model have already presented themselves as challengers to the status quo in explaining health behaviour.

Research in focus: Challenges to accepted truth

S Nassir Ghaemi (2009) has identified two alternatives to the BPS in an article in the *British Journal of Psychiatry*: the method-based psychiatry model and the medical humanist model. Jaspers' method-based psychiatry focuses, of course, on methodology. This model claims that we need to be aware of the methods we are using to identify and diagnose illness and use the best one for each particular case. In other words, sometimes the problem is biological, sometimes psychological and sometimes social; it is important to identify what combination is responsible and treat accordingly.

Osler's medical humanist model is similar but places stronger emphasis on the subjective human experience of an individual's illness.

Essentially, it states the following. Treat the body when disease is present with the intent to cure. When the disease is incurable, treat to ease suffering and attend to the needs of the sufferer. Where there is no disease but there is discomfort, the sufferer should still be treated (despite the lack of disease) with dignity and attended to as a person, not a patient. This represents a slight departure from the other models as it attempts to recognize the needs of the sufferer beyond their clinical needs. Indeed it captures the Hippocratic aim: cure sometimes, heal often, console always.

Do these models represent an improvement on the BPS model? Justify your answer, giving examples for specific health behaviours.

Determinants of health

The range of social, economic, environmental and personal factors that influence health and well-being are known as the determinants of health. These measures are used by governments and policy-makers to design interventions in areas where health inequalities are negatively impacting the health and wellness of a group of people. The determinants of health can be broken into two main categories: **social determinants of health** and **personal determinants of health**. The latter includes individual behaviour and genetics

while the former includes all other determinants of health such as the social and physical environment and access to health care.

Scientists generally recognize five determinants of health of a population, which are:

- social environment
- physical environment
- health services
- biology/genetics
- individual behaviour.

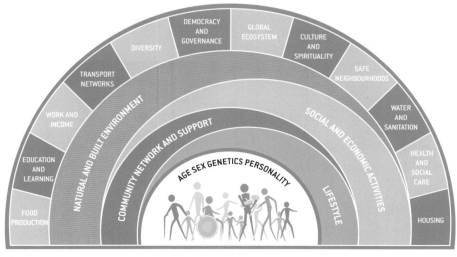

▲ Figure 6.4 Determinants of health diagram

Global challenges

In February 2017, Dr Margaret Chan, Director-General of the World Health Organization (WHO), outlined the **Grand Challenges** in global health that our world is facing over the next decade. To understand these challenges we need to take a look at the bigger picture.

The world is changing. Terrorist attacks targeting innocent civilians are becoming increasingly common. Armed conflicts such as the one in Syria are contributing to an increase in both physical and psychological harm with an estimated 3 million Syrian children experiencing post-traumatic stress disorder. Homelessness and hunger persist. Around 800 million people are starving, and yet in some of the world's richest countries more than 70% of the adult population has been classified as obese. Globalization has given us all access to a plethora of unhealthy products including junk food, cigarettes and pornography. Non-communicable diseases are more prevalent than infectious diseases and are now the biggest killers worldwide. The *World Health Statistics 2016* help paint a clearer picture of the challenges that we face.

Every year:

- 303,000 women die due to complications of pregnancy and childbirth
- 5.9 million children die before their fifth birthday
- 2 million people are newly infected with HIV, there are 9.6 million new TB cases and 214 million malaria cases

- more than 10 million people die before the age of 70 due to cardiovascular diseases and cancer
- 800,000 people commit suicide
- 1.25 million people die from road traffic injuries
- 4.3 million people die due to air pollution caused by cooking fuels.

In order to improve global health we must first address the risk factors contributing to disease. Around the world today:

- 1.1 billion people smoke tobacco
- 1.8 billion people drink contaminated water, and 946 million people defecate in the open
- 3.1 billion people rely primarily on polluting fuels for cooking
- an estimated 1 million people in the USA are absent from work every day due to work-related stress.

It is essential therefore that we prioritize reducing inequality, improve education, and continue to fund research into improving health around the world.

ATL skills: Thinking and communication

Write a headline for a newspaper article that you feel captures the main issues and topics raised in Dr Margaret Chan's WHO address.

Discuss your headlines with a partner. How are they different? What do they have in common?

Health risks and protective factors

Health-care professionals typically organize factors related to wellness and illness into two categories: risk factors or protective factors. A **risk factor** is any attribute, characteristic or exposure of an individual that increases the likelihood of developing a condition, disease or injury. For example, exposure to cheap, easily accessible junk food and a permissive environment may increase the likelihood of an individual becoming obese; this in turn will increase an individual's chances of developing type 2 diabetes, cardiovascular disease and other illnesses.

Some examples of the more important risk factors include obesity, being underweight, unsafe

sex, high blood pressure, tobacco and alcohol consumption, and unsafe water, sanitation and hygiene. Protective factors include regular exercise, a healthy diet and access to clean water.

ATL skills: Thinking

Use what you know to create a BPS analysis of the determinants for the following health behaviours: smoking tobacco, binge drinking, having unprotected sex and working in a stressful environment. You may lack the required information to do this thoroughly, but attempt to identify the risk and protective factors for each behaviour.

Health problem 1: obesity and being overweight

Inquiry questions

- Why do rational people make irrational health decisions?
- What is behind the current obesity pandemic?
- What are the dangers of obesity?
- What are the risk and protective factors of obesity?

What you will learn in this section

- Health problem—obesity
  - Obesity risk factors (inactivity, poor diet, genetics, family environment, socio-economic status) and protective factors (physical exercise, healthy eating)
  - Social determinants: poverty contributes to obesity (Beheshti, Igusa and Jones-Smith, 2016)
  - Biological determinants: sugar is argued to be the main culprit for the current obesity epidemic (Lustig, 2015)
  - Cognitive determinants: being overly optimistic can set up obese dieters for failure; an internal locus of control improves health behaviour

For the first time in human history, more people have health problems caused by being overweight than underweight. Obesity has become a **pandemic** over the past 50 years. Obesity, therefore, seems an appropriate lens through which to examine determinants of health and wellness and protective/risk factors. The following pages will look at the pandemic of obesity along with a biopsychosocial analysis of its **etiology**.

Key facts

These key facts are taken from the WHO 2016 Fact Sheet.

- Worldwide obesity has more than doubled since 1980.

- In 2014, more than 1.9 billion adults, 18 years and older, were overweight. Of these, over 600 million were obese.

- Most of the world's population lives in countries where being overweight kills more people than being underweight.

- 41 million children under the age of 5 were overweight or obese in 2014.

- Obesity is preventable.

Overweight and obesity have been defined as a state where an individual has accumulated excess body fat to the point that it affects health. The most commonly used metric for measuring overweight and obesity is the **body mass index (BMI)**. BMI was devised in the 19th century by Lambert Adolphe Jacques Quetelet. It is expressed as body mass divided by the square of the body height. Many criticize the index as an inadequate measure of overweight and obesity.

BMI is calculated using the formula:

$$\text{Metric: BMI} = \frac{weight\ (kg)}{height^2\ (m^2)}$$

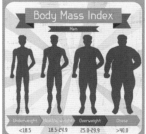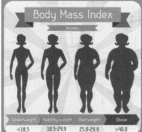

▲ Figure 6.5 BMI

Source: www.medicalnewstoday.com

Data collection on obesity rates can take several forms. Common collection techniques include surveys of populations, school-based assessments, data from public health services, and cohort studies. Data collection that is self-reporting may result in bias as respondents may not accurately report their weight or height. Longitudinal data, often gathered from cohort studies, provide insight into the long-term incidence and remission of obesity. It seems best then to collect proxy-reported, longitudinal data, in order to report bias while benefiting from long-term data collection.

Culture plays a role in obesity rates because food consumption, attitudes towards obesity, and definitions of desirable body shape and priorities placed on physical activity vary across cultures. Obesity rates vary greatly between nations. As of 2015, the USA had a 38.2% obesity rate, while OECD nations averaged 19.5% and Japan came in at 3.7% (OECD, 2017). For more on obesity prevalence, search online for the most recent OECD Obesity Update.

Despite these differences in obesity prevalence, worldwide globalization has been associated with fewer home-cooked meals, increased snacking and increased availability of fast foods (Bruss *et al*, 2005). Along with these changes in food consumption patterns, there has been an increase in patterns of physical activity linked to the risk of obesity including use of motorized transport, less recreational activity and increase in sedentary pastimes (Lobstein, Baur and Uauy, 2004). In short, although variety exists in prevalence, globally obesity prevalence is expected to increase in the years ahead.

ATL skills: Thinking

What are the pros and cons of using BMI as a measure of overweight or obesity? Do you think this affects validity of studies that use it as a measure? Why do you say that?

Risk factors and protective factors for obesity

There is no mystery surrounding what contributes to obesity and what protects against it. Eating a poor diet, high in fat and sugar, and following a sedentary lifestyle are risk factors for obesity, which is then a risk factor for type 2 diabetes and other non-communicable diseases (NCDs). Simply having these risk factors for obesity does not mean you will become overweight or obese. Many of the risk factors for obesity can be overcome with the protective factors of a healthy diet and exercise, or through a difference in personal dispositions.

Risk factors *for* obesity
• Inactivity, leading a sedentary lifestyle, can increase your chances of being obese.
• Eating an unhealthy diet high in salt and sugar has been linked to obesity.
• Your genes may affect the amount of body fat you store or determine your metabolism affecting obesity.
• Family environment—obesity tends to run in families; you develop eating and exercise patterns from your family.
• Socio-economic status, poverty and obesity appear to be linked. More nutritious foods are more expensive and access to safe areas for exercise requires time and money.

Risk factors *of* obesity
• Type 2 diabetes: a long-term metabolic disease that is characterized by high blood sugar, insulin resistance, and relative lack of insulin.
• Hypertension: abnormally high blood pressure.
• Some cancers: cancer of the breast (post-menopausal), uterus, pancreas, gallbladder, liver, esophagus, kidney, thyroid and ovaries. Risk is also increased for blood cell cancers, including myeloma, leukemia and non-Hodgkin lymphoma.
• Cardiovascular disease: a class of diseases that involve the heart or blood vessels such as angina and heart attack.

▲ Table 6.1 Risk factors *for* and *of* obesity

According to a 2013 report by the World Health Organization, NCDs account for 63% of annual deaths—that's 36 million deaths per year (WHO, 2013). As shown in the table above, obesity is a major risk factor for several NCDs. As these NCDs are largely preventable, it is important for public health researchers to examine the causes of the increasing worldwide obesity rates in order to arrive at effective prevention and treatment strategies for these life-threatening conditions.

Obesity is not new; there has been obesity since the earliest humans. From an evolutionary perspective, obesity can be argued to be a selective advantage as it aids survival in times of famine or shortage. Those individuals who were able to store energy (fat) effectively would have stores of energy when there was less to be gained from the environment. What is of concern to public health researchers today is the recent increase in cases of obesity and its related diseases worldwide. Much of the research used in this section is from the USA as the USA has robust and ongoing studies related to obesity. It would appear though that much of the developing world is on the same trajectory as the USA in terms of obesity prevalence.

ATL skills: Research and communication skills

Making a rich picture

A rich picture is an assembly of all of the elements that may be relevant to a complex situation. A rich picture is an excellent tool to use when studying topics in psychology. For example, in trying to understand the complex behavioural, social and biological determinants of obesity, a rich picture can be a great way to show the relationships between the variables.

These are the key points for making a rich picture.

- Use words only when you must; this is meant to be a visual representation.
- Use a whole sheet of paper and spread the concepts out in a way that makes sense to you; using sticky notes can be a good way to do this so you can move ideas around as you like.
- Include facts as well as concepts and ideas that you think of along the way.
- Draw the connections between the various elements of the rich picture. For example, in a causational relationship a bold line with an arrow in the direction of causation is useful; if the relationship is bidirectional, use a two-way arrow; if there is a weak connection use a dotted line. It is entirely up to you, this is a very personal activity.

Here are some hints to help you.

- Use key terms to get started but don't stop there.
- Look for relationships and processes.
- Try to illustrate relationships and elements with symbols that are meaningful to you. This is not meant to be an illustrated essay outline; it is a web of interrelated topics and concepts.
- If you are having trouble getting started, there are many examples of rich pictures online to give you some ideas, but remember this is a personal creation with personal meaning.

Exercise

Identify and research the prevalence of tobacco use, alcohol abuse, having unprotected sex or working in a stressful environment. Once you have identified the prevalence, try to identify and explain the risk and protective factors associated with those health behaviours.

Create a rich picture of the risk and protective factors for the one or more of above behaviours.

Social determinants of obesity

Two things that seem to play a role in the recent pandemic of obesity are a sedentary lifestyle and the type of foods we consume. These two components of health impact our health and our weight. First, we will examine a sedentary lifestyle. Very simply, we store energy and become obese when the amount of energy consumed is greater than the amount of energy used by our bodies. A sedentary lifestyle uses less energy than an active one. Sedentary behaviours include screen-time activities, commuting in a car, eating or working on a computer. People are spending more time in sedentary activities than their parents or grandparents did (Hill, Abraham and Wright, 2003). In April 2002, the WHO warned that physical inactivity was a leading cause of disability and disease (WHO, 2002).

The second major change that has taken place is the types of foods we eat and an increase in consumption of discretionary calories. Discretionary calories are defined as the difference between total energy requirements and the energy consumed to meet recommended nutrient intakes. **Discretionary calories** are allowable only "when the amount of calories used to meet recommended nutrient intakes is less than the total daily calorie expenditure" (USDA). So by eating nutrient-rich foods, you are getting the most caloric "bang for your nutritional buck" and will more likely have discretionary calories to "spend" as you like throughout the day. Thanks to the high amount of added sugars and solid fats in foods today, many people hit their daily caloric limit before their recommended daily nutrient needs are met, which results in excess fat storage.

It has not always been like this. Our food environment has changed dramatically in the past 40 years. One marker in particular stands out: soft drinks or sugar-sweetened beverages (SSBs). SSBs are the number one source of added sugars in Americans' diets (Johnson *et al*, 2009). An increase in the consumption of SSBs has been linked to the increase in obesity in the USA. The Center for Science in the Public Interest has reported that in 2013 American adults consumed an average of 144.5 litres of SSBs. The following information is from their 2015 report entitled "Carbonating the World".

- An extra 12-ounce sugary drink a day increases a child's risk of becoming obese by about 60%.
- Adults who drink one sugary drink or more per day are 27% more likely to be overweight or obese than non-drinkers.

- SSBs account for approximately 180,000 deaths around the world each year, comprising:
  - 133,000 to diabetes
  - 44,000 to cardiovascular disease
  - 6,000 to cancer.

The increase in consumption of sugary beverages cannot solely account for the increasing incidence of obesity worldwide. Our food environment is rife with packaged and processed foods that have added sugars. **Added sugars** are sugars or syrups that are mixed into foods to improve flavour. This not only happens in sweets and candies but in nearly all processed foodstuffs such as pasta sauces, potato chips and ketchup.

The term "added" is key because most foods already contain sugars that are healthy and natural like those found in milk and fruits. For example, 250 millilitres of chocolate milk has over 10 grams more sugar than white milk. Added sugars are often referred to as "empty calories". They are empty because there is no nutritive value to the sugars; they are simply energy to be used or stored. The average American consumes 88 grams of sugar each day but the American Heart Association recommends no more than 30 grams each day (Harvard, 2017). According to The Obesity Society, added sugar intake has increased in the USA by 30% between 1977–2010 (Turner, 2014). Recently there appears to have been a small reversal in this

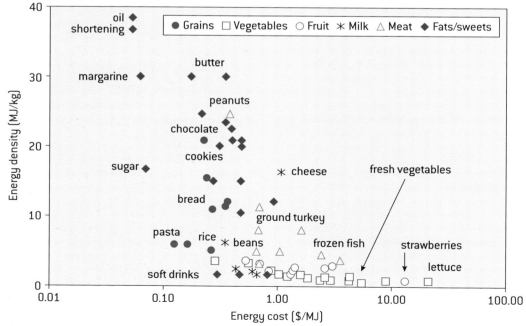

▲ Figure 6.6 Relationship between energy density of selected foods and energy cost.

Source: Drewnowski (2004)

trend but many Americans remain well above recommended daily levels of added sugar.

See video

Watch chef Jamie Oliver's TED Talk entitled "Teach every child about food" available at https://www.ted.com/talks/jamie_oliver

Access to SSBs and a landscape of foods filled with added sugars could be interpreted as a social determinant of obesity. However, people do not have to eat those foods. People should be able to make healthy choices and not choose to eat a lot of food with added sugars or drink SSBs. As it turns out, many people have no choice. Adam Drewnowski has pointed out that there is an inverse relationship between the energy density of a food and its cost. This means that diets based on refined grains and added sugars and fats are cheaper than diets based on lean meats, vegetables, fruits and fish (Drewnowski, 2004).

Often those living in poverty have no choice but to buy calorie-dense foods, even if those calories are empty and do not contain any nutritional value. Empty calories are cheap calories. The fact that low-income families tend to buy nutrient-deficient, high-sugar and fatty foods is reinforced by a 2016 article in the *Journal of Nutrition* which found that low-income consumers use a price/calorie model when deciding on food purchases (Beheshti, Igusa and Jones-Smith, 2016).

The cost of HEALTHY EATING

$3.00 =

312 calories

3,767 calories

▲ Figure 6.7 Calorie costs

Source: https://blogs.commons.georgetown.edu/cctp-638-mb1809/agricultural-policy/

While the WHO recommends no more than 25 grams of added sugar per day, the following figures seem to illustrate that where the USA goes, the world follows.

Rank	Country	Per capita sugar consumption (grams)
1	United States	126.4
2	Germany	102.9
3	Netherlands	102.5
4	Ireland	96.7
5	Australia	95.6
6	Belgium	95.0
7	United Kingdom	93.2
8	Mexico	92.5
9	Finland	91.5
10	Canada	89.1

▲ Table 6.2 Top sugar-consuming nations (2016)

Source: Pariona (2016); Euromonitor

On a positive note, recent research by **Wittekind and Walton (2014)** has pointed towards a levelling off or even a drop in the amount of added sugar being consumed globally. While they noted an increase in some countries, these were limited to certain subgroups within the population. It is too early to tell if this research represents the beginning of a reversal of the recent pandemic of obesity but it is, without doubt, good news.

ATL skills: Self-management

What kind of calories make up your diet? Do you think you are hitting your nutrient recommendations before your recommended daily caloric intake?

Biological determinants of obesity

In his 2014 book *Fat Chance, Beating the Odds Against Sugar, Processed Food, Obesity, and Disease*, **Robert H Lustig**, an American pediatric endocrinologist, points an accusing finger at added sugar as the main culprit for the current obesity pandemic. Lustig has been accused of exaggeration and alarmism by detractors but his research is certainly worth examination. He argues that there are two biological mechanisms that are driving the obesity pandemic: metabolism and addiction. In short, Lustig argues that fat in our diet is not the problem, sugar is. Lustig claims sugar is a chronic, dose-dependent hepato (liver) toxin. His research attempts to explain the biological processes behind a high-sugar diet and obesity in terms of appetite misregulation.

The **obesity metabolic syndrome** is the name given to the relationship between obesity and its related diseases, including type 2 diabetes, hypertension, heart disease and lipid problems. Obesity is simply a marker for those diseases. The cause of the diseases is the biological process that underlies our metabolic processes. In other words, some obese people may be obese due to genetic predispositions but they lead a healthy, active lifestyle. These people are not in any more danger of developing obesity-related diseases than a healthy person of normal weight. So, if it is not the obesity itself causing these diseases, what is?

According to Lustig, it is biochemistry and hormones that guide our eating behaviour. There are biochemical reasons why eating less and exercising may not work. **Leptin** is a hormone that travels from your fat cells to your brain to tell it that you have had enough food and that energy burning can happen at a normal rate. However, for some reason and despite the higher levels of fat and therefore leptin, obese individuals have developed a leptin resistance where they no longer receive the message that their body has had enough food.

This is where Lustig claims to be on the path to an answer. His claim is that the answer lies in the fact that **insulin** initiates a process to store sugar in fat cells in individuals who are already obese and live a sedentary lifestyle. When we consume sugar, insulin levels rise to metabolize the incoming glucose and fructose. Work done by Lustig and his team shows that higher levels of insulin block leptin from reaching the receptors in the brain. The higher the insulin levels, the more energy you store and the hungrier you feel (Lustig, 2014).

Discussion

Lustig's research is very controversial. He has been accused of alarmism and of attacking the sugar industry unfairly. Do you think Lustig's research is credible? What research or information helped you determine your answer?

Another argument for biochemical determination of eating behaviour is addiction. Addiction is related to a reward pathway in our brain that releases the pleasure hormone **dopamine** in response to certain behaviours. This system is connected to areas of the brain responsible for controlling behaviour and memory function. Food, and especially high-sugar and fatty food, causes the **mesolimbic dopamine reward system (MDRS)** to release dopamine in the **nucleus accumbens**. We are rewarded with a dopamine "hit" when we eat sugary or fatty foods that creates a feeling of pleasure. When we are constantly eating these foods and receiving the dopamine, it is possible to develop a tolerance for the dopamine, which will dampen its effect. In this case, after chronic stimulation of the MDRS, dopamine receptors begin to down regulate to accommodate for the higher levels of dopamine and tolerance is the result. To overcome the tolerance, more food is necessary to achieve the same dopamine effect. This leads to overconsumption of food.

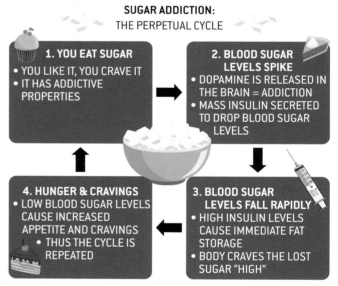

▲ Figure 6.8 The sugar addiction cycle

Following on from the concept of tolerance comes withdrawal. If the source of the increased dopamine (sugary, fatty foods) is removed, then there is a drop in the amount of dopamine coupled with fewer receptors. This results in the individual experiencing withdrawal symptoms. In some ways, it seems that food addiction among obese individuals can be similar to psychoactive drug dependence (Lustig, 2014). This is by no means a universally agreed-upon fact but evidence is growing that food may act on the MDRS in a similar way to a psychoactive drug.

The next big biological determinant that influences obesity is genetics. Our behaviour is more complex than simple genetic programming (although not even that is simple). Family members are likely to share many of the same genes. If certain genes are responsible for obesity, then it can be expected that families would share obese characteristics. One problem with this, as Robert Sapolsky (2009) points out is that, "not only do genes run in families, environments do too". Due to the close social and environmental experiences of family members, reasons for obesity are difficult to assign to genetics or environmental similarities. This is known as the **contamination effect**. In an attempt to avoid this, researchers have turned to twin studies.

Sorensen *et al* **(1989)** looked at adopted children and showed that the BMI of adopted children was positively correlated with the BMI of their birth parents (with whom they did not share an environment). Their BMI was also positively correlated with full siblings and, to a lesser extent, half siblings from whom they had also been separated. These findings seem to show a genetic relationship between biologically related siblings who did not share an environment.

In another twin study **Haworth** *et al* **(2008)** researchers selected just over 2,300 pairs of twins at 7 years old and 3,500 pairs at 10 years old. They found that BMI (not just obesity) was highly heritable (0.60–0.74) with only a relatively minor influence by environmental factors (0.12–0.22). This, of course, suggests that not only obesity but BMI more generally is genetically based. This is an important finding because it can inform clinicians of the genetic (and therefore non-behavioural) determinants of obesity and plan for the treatment of patients accordingly.

One last point on biological determinism comes from prenatal exposure to poor diets. Research on rats has shown that rat fetuses *in utero* of a mother with diabetes, overnutrition or obesity have a higher risk of becoming obese in their lifetimes. (Catalano and Ehrenberg, 2006). Additional research on rats has shown that exposure to a junk food diet *in utero* and while breastfeeding is associated with an increased preference for and intake of fat in early life. This suggests that the offspring of a snack-food-eating mother will have a predisposition to fattier foods and a heightened dopamine-related response in early life (Ong and Muhlhausler, 2011).

Discussion

1. Do you think that the findings of this research on obesity in rats is generalizable to humans? What makes you say that?

2. If you were sitting talking with a friend and your friend said that, "obese people are obese because they eat too much", what would you say?

Cognitive determinants of obesity

One of the main pillars of Lustig's research is based upon the **cognitive restraint theory**. When we are hungry, a hormone called **grehlin** is released from the gastrointestinal tract and binds to receptors on the hypothalamus. Grehlin essentially has the opposite effect of the hormone leptin; its message to the hypothalamus is: "you're hungry, consume something". People who are attempting to eat less are essentially trying to ignore these messages with cognitive restraint (similar to willpower). In other words, they are trying to tell themselves they are not hungry when their biological system is telling them they are. This sort of cognitive-biological infighting must be resolved, but the trouble is that you can't make yourself feel full just by thinking it. If your hypothalamus is binding with grehlin you will experience a biological drive to eat. This cannot be ignored or "restrained" by willpower for an extended period of time.

You may be tempted at this point to throw up your hands and surrender to what may seem like a fixed game on an uneven playing field. However, the types of food we eat are important and we can overcome the odds of becoming obese by simply adjusting our diets. Foods with high nutritive value and relatively low calories can stop grehlin and initiate the release of leptin, signalling that we are full. So perhaps instead of limiting the amount of food we eat, it would be best to limit the food we eat to certain healthy foods which are high in nutrient value and low in added sugar.

If we accept the cognitive restraint theory, it may help to explain why so many diets fail. Cognitive restraint theory when combined with **optimism bias** seems to set many obese dieters up for failure. Sharot (2011) points out that optimism bias is a common cognitive bias where we are less likely to believe that negative outcomes will happen to us. This false optimism could translate into many negative behaviours including overeating and "cheating" on a diet, as we exhibit a cognitive bias against unwanted outcomes and towards positive outcomes. For example, you might think, "I can have this soft drink and it won't affect my diet. After all, it's only one soft drink".

When repeated attempts at losing weight fail, obese dieters may develop **learned helplessness**. In 1972, Martin Seligman proposed that when an organism perceives a loss of control in a situation and faces repeated failures, that organism may abandon any future attempt to achieve related goals. In other words, organisms learn that they are helpless and give up. Seligman contextualized learned helplessness as a precursor to depression. In the case of dieting and obesity, it may explain why some obese people come to accept obesity, and the eventual related diseases, as unavoidable facts of life (and death).

Learned helplessness, in turn, is related to the concept of **locus of control**. Locus of control refers to the belief on the location (either internal or external) of an individual's control over a situation or behaviour. If individuals perceive the locus of control to be internal, they will have a stronger belief that they can change their behaviour for the better. Locus of control is very closely related to Bandura's concept of **self-efficacy**. A belief in an internal locus of control results in strong self-efficacy. Successes in meeting goals reinforces self-efficacy while failures erode it. A strong self-efficacy can result in persistence and perseverance in both improved food choices and exercise. Both of these have been shown to be protective factors against obesity.

ATL skills: Self-management

What is the link between self-efficacy or locus of control and self-management skills? What makes you say that?

Social cognitive explanations of health problems

Inquiry questions

- To what extent can we predict health decisions with models of behaviour?

- What can be done to change the health habits of populations?

- Do intentions determine behaviour?

What you will learn in this section

- Models of health behaviour—decision-making and health choices

  o Theory of planned behaviour (Ajzen, 1985); application of the theory of planned behaviour to health (Conner and Sparks, 2005)

- Health belief model (Hochbaum, Rosenstock and Kegels)

Have you ever found yourself lying on the sofa after a large meal thinking, "What was I thinking, why did I eat so much?" Sometimes we can't explain our own reasoning, so imagine how difficult it is for health officials. Trying to decipher what is happening in the mind of another person is a tricky thing. Health psychologists have developed tools called models of health behaviour to try to explain complex decision-making processes surrounding health behaviour.

The **theory of planned behaviour,** the **health belief model** and **protection motivation theory** are essentially models of decision-making. Each of these models represents an attempt to explain the thought process that occurs between an observable stimulus and a related behaviour (Abraham, 2008). In other words, these models try to explain what happens in an individual's mind when they are trying to decide how to act in a given situation. Why does a person smoke, drink alcohol or engage in risky sexual behaviour? Models of health behaviour attempt to predict and change negative health behaviour and decisions by first understanding how those decisions are made.

Any of the models mentioned above can be used to explain any health behaviour. We will be modelling the use of the health belief model and the theory of planned behaviour to attempt to explain behaviour surrounding the topic of obesity.

Health belief model

The health belief model (HBM) was developed and used in 1958 by **Hochbaum, Rosenstock and Kegels** at the US Public Health Service in an attempt to explain why people did not engage in disease prevention strategies, specifically for tuberculosis. They found that there are two main perceptions related to why people practise health behaviour: the perceived threat of the illness and the perceived effectiveness of the recommended health behaviour. The model has since been adapted by many researchers.

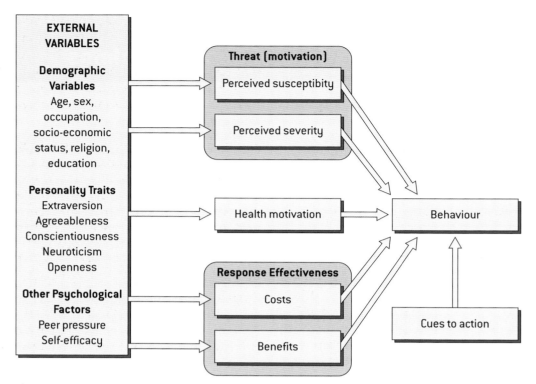

▲ Figure 6.9 Health belief model

Perceived threat is a combination of both perceived susceptibility and perceived severity. In other words, "how likely is it that I will get it?" and "if I get it, how bad will it be?" The assumption here is that if an individual perceives that he or she is likely to get sick with a serious illness, then that person is likely to act in a way that will prevent the outcome.

Effectiveness of health action is a combination of both potential benefits of a behaviour and perceived barriers (or costs) to action. Similarly the assumption is that if there appear to be great benefits to an action and few barriers, then an individual is likely to follow a given health action.

Another two components to the HBM featured in the diagram are cues to action and health motivation. **Cues to action** are triggers experienced by an individual that encourage the person to act. These cues can be internal such as noticing symptoms, or external such as a health campaign or advice from a friend or family member. Finally, **health motivation** refers to a dispositional attitude towards health. Some people attach

more importance to their health than others and are more likely to follow a given health action (Abraham, 2008).

In summary, the HBM suggests that people are likely to follow a given health action if the following apply.

- They think they are susceptible to an illness.
- They think the illness is serious.
- They believe the benefits of the action outweigh the costs.
- They are exposed to triggers for action.

We can use the HBM to predict behaviour related to exercise and dieting among obese individuals (O'Connell *et al*, 1985). It is important first of all to separate and be clear about exactly what we are examining. We could examine the risk factor of obesity and the outcome of an early death via a non-communicable disease (NCD). Alternatively, we could examine the risk factor of a poor diet or sedentary lifestyle on the outcome of obesity. These are related risk factors and outcomes but it is important to be clear that obesity is both a risk factor (for NCDs) and an outcome (from poor diet or lifestyle choices).

The likelihood of becoming obese due to poor diet and lack of exercise must be recognized. Related to this is the fact that the negative aspects of being obese are severe enough to influence decisions surrounding diet and exercise. This may or may not link to the ultimate outcomes of NCDs.

In this case, the perceived threat of the likelihood of developing any of several of the NCDs associated with obesity has to be recognized and considered severe enough that action needs to be taken to avoid this outcome, that is, by losing weight.

Education and **fear appeals** play important roles here. Often complicated research done by professionals in universities and research institutes needs to be simplified and spread to a population that is, or is in danger of becoming, obese. These messages have to be easy to understand and quickly communicated. They often use television, the internet, school and workplace advertising and, increasingly, social media.

Individuals need to believe that actions such as eating well and physical exercise will help avoid the outcome of obesity. This is the focus of many health campaigns that promote exercise as a way to lose weight.

Perceptions related to evaluation of threat and effectiveness of action can be accomplished with health and education campaigns such as the "Go4Life" initiative from the US Department of Health and Human Services or the "Obesity Action Campaign" in the UK. These campaigns and others like them also act as a cue to take action to avoid the negative consequences of an unhealthy diet or sedentary lifestyle which are the most important risk factors for obesity.

Effectiveness of the HBM

The HBM has been effective in tailored interventions designed to change the behaviour of a single person. These types of interventions are not part of the population health approach and a lot of time and resources are required to impact the behaviour of a single person. **Sohl and Moyer (2007)** conducted a meta-analysis of 28 studies between 1997 and 2005 designed to evaluate the effectiveness of the HBM in tailored interventions for promoting mammography use. They concluded that tailored interventions based on the HBM along with a recommendation from a physician were effective in promoting mammography screening.

Another study by **Downing-Matibag and Geisinger (2009)**, examined sexual risk-taking among university students. The researchers found that the HBM could be useful in understanding why students engaged in unprotected sex with friends, acquaintances and strangers. The qualitative study was based on 71 college students who reported experiences of "hooking up". The questionnaires were focused on discovering why participants did not use protection during "hook ups". It was found that students' perceived susceptibility to sexually transmitted infections (STIs) was misinformed, and this influenced their decision to engage in risky sexual behaviour because they did not believe they could get an STI.

Exercise

In this section, we have described and explained the HBM and modelled how it might explain health behaviour related to obesity. Now see if you can explain the decision-making process for engaging in (or not engaging in) other behaviours such as smoking tobacco, binge drinking, having unprotected sex or working in a stressful environment.

Theory of planned behaviour

The theory of planned behaviour (TPB) is an attempt to explain why people engage in or avoid certain behaviours. Ajzen developed the theory of planned behaviour in 1985. Conner and Sparks (2005) applied this theory to health behaviour. Similar to the HBM, the TPB attempts to explain what goes into a decision to engage (or not engage) in a particular behaviour.

We tend to assume that if people intend to do something, then they are likely to do it—but this isn't always the case. Someone may intend to start eating healthy, nutrient-rich foods but not be able to do so. Perhaps the food is inaccessible or too expensive. At best, it seems that if a person intends to do something, he or she will at least attempt to do it. The next question we need to ask is: what factors determine someone's intention to engage in a behaviour? The TPB argues it is a combination of attitude, social norms and the amount of control individuals believe they have over the intended behaviour.

Attitude: people tend to hold preconceived thoughts and feelings regarding a given behaviour. Individuals' attitude toward a behaviour is determined, in part, through how they evaluate how they would feel if they performed the behaviour and how they evaluate the consequences of performing the behaviour. The combination of how you think you will feel during and after engaging in the behaviour (for example, exercise) and your knowledge of its consequences are combined to determine your attitude toward that behaviour.

For example, changing your eating habits to eat more nutritiously may result in feelings of hunger and being unsated. Your physiological addiction to sugar may give you uncomfortable withdrawal symptoms. However, you may think that you will be healthier as a result of more nutritious food consumption. You will know that you are lowering your chances of acquiring type 2 diabetes, cancer and cardiovascular disease. An individual's attitude is determined through these often competing elements.

Norms: people are influenced by the attitudes and actions of those around them. Social norms and the actions of others play an important role in our behaviour. Our perception of whether a behaviour will generate approval or disapproval is determined by the norms of the society we live in. If a society values healthy eating and physical activity, then this healthy behaviour will probably be met with praise and other positive reinforcement. The individuals in that society will be therefore more likely to engage in that behaviour. This reinforcement is referred to as injunctive norms.

Additionally, it is important that other people are actually engaging in that behaviour as well. Perception of what others are doing plays an important role in determining behaviour (descriptive norms). When someone perceives that others are engaging in a health behaviour (and not simply talking about it), that person is more likely to engage in that behaviour as well. If an obese person is surrounded by people who are eating healthy, nutritious food and avoiding added sugars in their diets, that person is likely to perform that same behaviour.

Perceived behavioural control (similar to self-efficacy): People normally do not intend to do something they consider impossible or out of their control. This is the final section of the TPB and separates it from its predecessor, the theory of reasoned action. Perceived cognitive control is similar to the concept of self-efficacy. The idea breaks down into two parts.

- **Perceived control**: individuals tend to attempt changes in behaviour only when there is a belief that they can enact that change. People tend to avoid attempting change in situations where they feel they do not have control.

- **Perceived confidence**: people tend to avoid attempting change in situations where they expect to fail. This is important in dieting and physical exercise because without a strong self-efficacy message, many people will not attempt to change their behaviour.

If people feel that they have the time and the resources to eat more healthily or to go a gym and they are confident that they have the willpower to do so, they are more likely to attempt to eat healthily and go to the gym. In the case of those living in poverty or those working two or three jobs, they may feel that they do not have control; they cannot go to the gym more because they are working too much and they cannot afford to pay for more nutritious food. This will reinforce their negative behaviour and affect their confidence in their ability to get to the gym or to eat more nutritious foods.

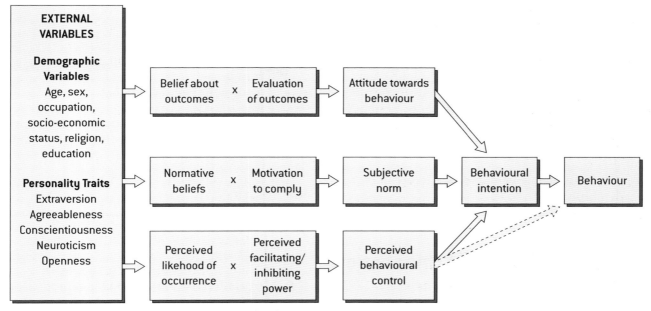

▲ Figure 6.10 Theory of planned behaviour (TPB)

ATL skills: Thinking

Can you see how religious belief or morality-based choices would fit into the theory of planned behaviour? If so, where would it fit? If not, do you consider this a weakness of the theory? What makes you say that?

Effectiveness of the TPB

The TPB has shown itself to be an effective predictor of health cognitions (Armitage and Connor, 2001). Interventions based on the TBP also appear to be effective, especially on the intention to promote physical exercise in school-aged children (Hill, Abraham and Wright, 2007).

Dunn *et al* (2011) examined the determinants of fast-food consumption using the TPB. This study sampled 404 Australians and interviewed them regarding the determinants of their consumption of fast food. The researchers used the TPB to examine these determinants and found that participants' food choices depended upon what others thought (injunctive norms), and their preference for tasty, satisfying and convenient foods (reflecting their attitude toward short-term satisfaction versus longer-term health). In short, the researchers concluded that the TPB successfully predicted fast-food consumption. Ajzen himself continues to defend his model against its opponents with vigour: "the TPB is alive and well and gainfully employed in the pursuit of a better understanding of human behaviour" (Ajzen, from *Health Psychology Review*, Vol. 9, Issue 2, published by Taylor & Francis, 2015).

ATL skills: Thinking

Research into the effectiveness of the TPB and other models of health behaviour often relies on self-reporting and assumes a connection between intention and behaviour. What might be the weaknesses of adopting a self-report study when researching health beliefs and behaviours?

Promoting health

What you will learn in this section

- Approaches to health promotion
  - Population health approach
  - Individual health approach

- How to make health promotions effective
  - Education and cognitive dissonance (Festinger, 1957): educating people of risk and protective factors can help improve health behaviour in a population; awareness of the dangers of an activity can lead to a feeling of discomfort (cognitive dissonance) if an individual both knows the activity can lead to harm and yet continues to engage in that activity
  - Fear appeals work best with strong self-efficacy messages (Witte and Allen, 2000): research has shown that instilling fear can strongly influence behaviour but that fear messages must be accompanied with a message of self-efficacy, that an individual's action can mitigate the danger

  - Legislation, subsidies, and taxation: informative food labelling serves to educate consumers of the risk factors associated with certain foods; the WHO points out that those most vulnerable (low-income consumers, young people and those at most risk of obesity) are most responsive to changes in food and beverage price so taxing unhealthy foods while subsidizing healthy ones can influence food choices

This section also links to:

- biases in thinking and decision-making, for example, cognitive dissonance and optimism bias

- the brain and behaviour (for example, neurotransmission)

- genetics

- the individual and the group (for example, self-efficacy).

The previous section demonstrated how the biopsychosocial model can be used to explain health-related behaviour related to obesity. The fact that we have a biological drive to eat, that we live in a permissive and often aggressive food culture, and that our cognitive choices are fairly predictable based on several models of cognition are all important considerations when we begin to look at health promotion. Ignoring any of these causes of being overweight or obese would be reductionist and ultimately may be ineffective in promoting healthy behaviour. Policy-makers need to tailor biopsychosocial solutions to this biopsychosocial problem.

Health promotion often uses a holistic **population health approach**. This approach focuses on improving health through policies that affect the health of an entire population, rather than individuals. Throughout the 20th century, states have been taking a larger and larger role in influencing the health of their populations. Over the past century, political leaders came to realize that a healthy working population was a necessity for a growing economy and so health promotion became a priority for developing and developed states.

There are a number of international agencies focused on health education and promotion.

Health organization	Based in:
World Health Organization	International
United States Public Health Services	USA
Public Health Agency of Canada	Canada
Public Health Europe	Europe
National Institute of Public Health	Japan
Centers for Disease Control and Prevention	USA/International
Public Health Association of Australia	Australia

▲ Table 6.3

Exercise

Do some research on the above institutions and identify their main goals. How are they similar? How are they different?

Health promotion can be defined as "the process of enabling people to increase control over, and to improve, their health" (WHO, 2017).

These are typically interventions that go beyond simple attempts to change people's opinions and decisions surrounding health. The most effective health promotion campaigns adopt an **ecological approach**. This means that the campaign is targeted at the environmental health determinants that surround individuals in a society. These include the individual, family and friends, organizations, the community and government policies.

Ecological approach	
Level	**Examples of action**
Individual	Education to change attitudes and beliefs, self-efficacy beliefs and subjective norms
Interpersonal	Social networking campaigns that encourage physical activity and healthy diets
Organizational	Healthy lunch initiatives at school or school-based non-profit breakfast programmes and workplace exercise facilities
Community	Mass media campaigns
Policy level	Legislation on food labelling and the implementation of taxes or incentives on business

▲ Table 6.4

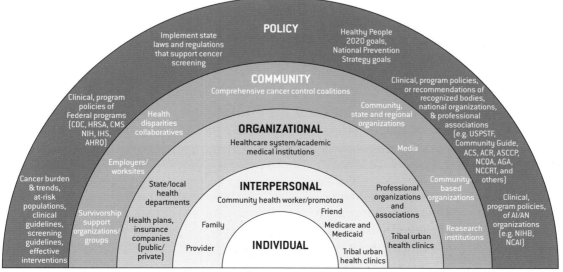

▲ Figure 6.11 The social ecological model of health promotion

Education and cognitive dissonance theory

Education is an important component in health campaigns because individuals must first understand the implications of a behaviour in order to understand a need for change. For example, changing attitudes and beliefs about smoking are dependent upon convincing individuals that smoking tobacco leads to a number of terminal cancers and cardiovascular diseases. The key idea behind education as a preventative factor is **cognitive dissonance theory**.

Cognitive dissonance theory was originally put forward by Leon Festinger in 1957. Cognitive dissonance theory is based on three basic tenets.

- People are aware when their beliefs and actions are inconsistent.

- People are uncomfortable with these inconsistencies.

- People will strive to align their beliefs and actions.

▲ Figure 6.12

They can do this in three ways: change their beliefs, change their actions or rationalize their irrational actions. One example of this kind of psychological inconsistency would be, "smoking tobacco will give me lung cancer and kill me" and "I smoke a pack of cigarettes every day". Holding these two ideas in your head at the same time causes discomfort. An individual can either stop smoking, change his belief that it is dangerous, or rationalize his decision to smoke tobacco. As it turns out, people are excellent at rationalizing irrational behaviour. Smokers often say that smoking calms them, that it helps them socialize, or keeps their weight down; these are all rationalizations that the risk is worth it.

See video

Elizabeth Pisani has examined the decision-making surrounding seemingly irrational and dangerous sexual activity among prostitutes in Indonesia. She discusses important examples that show how irrational actions can seem rational to the individuals involved.

Watch Elizabeth Pisani's TED Talk on rationality and sexual health available at https://www.ted.com/talks/elizabeth_pisani_sex_drugs_and_hiv_let_s_get_rational_1

The point of education in health promotion campaigns is to create cognitive dissonance by influencing an individual's beliefs about a certain behaviour. If an individual can be made to believe that a behaviour is unhealthy, rationalization becomes more difficult and it is more likely that an individual will need to change that behaviour in order to resolve the cognitive dissonance.

How might an individual rationalize the unhealthy behaviours of:

- working in a high-stress environment
- smoking tobacco
- binge drinking
- having unprotected sex?

Fear appeals

▲ Figure 6.13 Fear appeals have been effective in anti-smoking campaigns

Discussion

Is it ethical to use fear to change behaviour?

Fear appeals, along with education, are a key strategy of health promotions. Fear appeals "are persuasive messages that emphasize the potential danger and harm that will befall individuals if they do not adopt the messages' recommendations"(Albarracin, 2015). A meta-analysis of fear appeal campaigns undertaken by **Witte and Allen (2000)** found that fear could be a great motivator for health behaviour but that fear appeals had to be accompanied with strong messages of self-efficacy. In their words, "If fear appeals are disseminated without efficacy messages … they run the risk of backfiring, since they may produce defensive responses in people with low-efficacy perceptions". Self-efficacy is clearly an essential component of any fear appeal.

However, fear appeals do not always work. In another meta-analysis of 132 papers examining a wide range of actions, including dental hygiene, HIV/AIDS prevention and drug or alcohol abuse, **Tannenbaum *et al* (2015)** found that fear appeals worked better in some situations than in others.

Fear appeals worked differently on different samples. For example, they were more effective in samples made up of Asian participants and all female participants. Finally, Tannenbaum found that fear appeals were more effective with one-time-only behaviours such as health screenings than in ongoing behaviours such as dieting and exercise.

Discussion

How would you explain the role of education, fear appeals and the related concept of self-efficacy messages using either the HBM or the TPB?

Legislation and health promotion

Health behaviours are also often encouraged through government legislation. This goes beyond taxation or subsidies, for example, in the form of food labels, age limits on consumption and geographic limitations of sales. Food labelling is a growing area of intervention for many governments and agencies. The idea is that the concept of cognitive dissonance is brought to the product level. Consumers are reminded of the potentially negative health implications each time they look at a product. The effectiveness of nutrition and food labelling relies on the education and interest of the consumer. The US Food and Drug Administration (FDA) recently changed their policy on food labelling in an attempt to reflect recent scientific information, including the link between diet and chronic non-communicable diseases. This intervention is aimed at changing attitudes and thus influencing the cognitive determinant of obesity (see the TPB and HBM).

▲ Figure 6.14 Awareness campaign for added sugars

Nutrition Facts

8 servings per container

Serving size   2/3 cup (55g)

Amount per serving

Calories   **230**

	% Daily Value*
Total Fat 8g	**10%**
Saturated Fat 1g	**5%**
Trans Fat 0g	
Cholesterol 0mg	**0%**
Sodium 160mg	**7%**
Total Carbohydrate 37g	**13%**
Dietary Fiber 4g	**14%**
Total Sugars 12g	
Includes 10g Added Sugars	**20%**
Protein 3g	
Vitamin D 2mcg	10%
Calcium 260mg	20%
Iron 8mg	45%
Potassium 235mg	6%

* The % Daily Value (DV) tells you how much a nutrient in a serving of food contributes to a daily diet. 2,000 calories a day is used for general nutrition advice.

▲ Figure 6.15

Countries such as Chile and Mexico are catching up with US obesity rates and have acted to prevent obesity. Chile recently enacted some of the toughest food labelling laws on earth. It follows the WHO recommendations regarding food labelling identifying substances such as sugar, fats and salt (Press, 2016).

Do you think this type of food labelling will help fight obesity? What makes you say that?

Taxation and subsidies

Some risk factors require large-scale society-wide solutions. The World Health Organization recently published a report called *Fiscal Policies for Diet and Prevention of Noncommunicable Diseases* (WHO, 2016). This report calls on countries to introduce taxes and subsidies for food to encourage responsible and healthy eating habits. The report argues that increasing the price of sugar-sweetened beverages, subsidies on the price of fresh fruits and vegetables, and targeted taxation

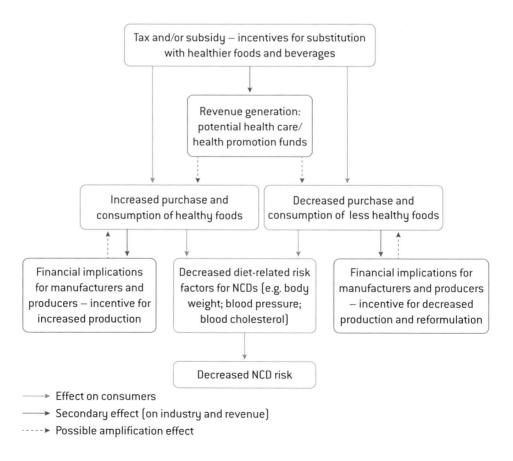

▲ Figure 6.16   Model of how taxes and subsidies affect consumption behaviour

Source: WHO (2015)–(draft of WHO, 2016)

on unhealthy foods will result in improved population health. Among the key conclusions of the report is that:

> "Vulnerable populations, including low-income consumers, young people, and those at most risk of obesity, are most responsive to changes in the relative prices of foods and beverages. It is beneficial to target non-core foods and foods for which good healthier alternatives are available". (WHO, 2016)

This report is a great example of how governments can promote healthy food choices through the targeted use of both taxation and subsidies. As one of the important risk factors for obesity is socio-economic status (or the inability to afford healthier foods), these recommendations seem like an effective way to counter the socio-economic risk factor of poverty.

An added bonus to this type of action is that the funds raised through taxation can be put toward the costs of implementing education programmes surrounding obesity or in helping to pay for the subsidizing of healthier food options.

Exercise

Search online for examples of successful use of taxation and/or subsidies to change health behaviour surrounding obesity. Hint: the "Fiscal policies for diet and prevention of noncommunicable diseases" (WHO, 2016) has lots of examples. Share your findings with others.

ATL skills: Thinking and research

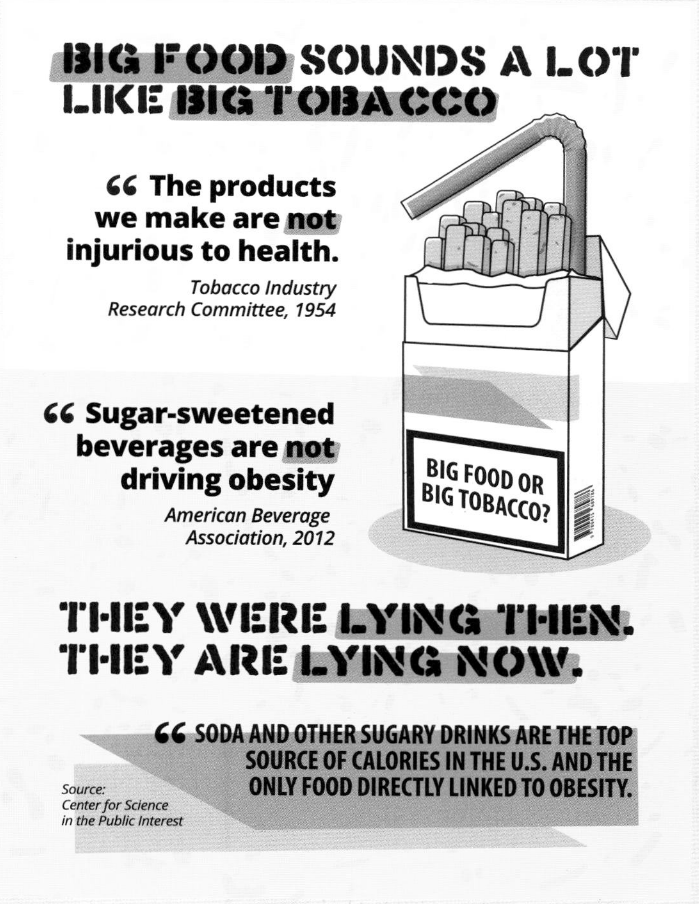

BIG FOOD SOUNDS A LOT LIKE BIG TOBACCO

" The products we make are **not** injurious to health.

Tobacco Industry Research Committee, 1954

" Sugar-sweetened beverages are **not** driving obesity

American Beverage Association, 2012

BIG FOOD OR BIG TOBACCO?

THEY WERE LYING THEN. THEY ARE LYING NOW.

" SODA AND OTHER SUGARY DRINKS ARE THE TOP SOURCE OF CALORIES IN THE U.S. AND THE ONLY FOOD DIRECTLY LINKED TO OBESITY.

Source: Center for Science in the Public Interest

▲ Figure 6.17

Conduct some research on how "Big Tobacco" responded to claims that smoking is bad for your health. Do you see any similarities? Do you think it is justified to make the comparison between the tobacco industry and the sugar industry?

Health problem 2: stress

Inquiry questions

- Are we working ourselves to death?
- How can we beat stress?
- Are women more stressed than men?
- Does being mindful improve health?

What you will learn in this section

- Definitions of stress
  - Acute physical stressors: short-term stressors that require your body to mobilize energy reserves to cope with the situation
  - Chronic intermittent stressors: long-term stressors that keep your body's stress response active over a long period of time
  - Homeostasis: the natural level of stability and balance occurring within the body as a result of physiological processes
  - Karoshi: a Japanese concept that means death from overwork but examples of karoshi death have been found all over the world

- Theories and models of stress
  - Stressful life events such as death of a spouse can have significant impact on our physical health (Holmes and Rahe, 1967)
  - Women consistently report higher levels of stress than men (The APA Stress in America Report, 2010–2017)
  - Small everyday occurrences may cause more serious symptoms of stress than more unusual stressful life events (Kannner *et al*, 1981)
  - Lazarus *et al* (1980) claim that stress is a transaction between the individual and their environment; in order for an event to be considered stressful, an individual must appraise it as such
  - Hofboll (1989) introduced the conservation of resources model which states that people feel threatened or stressed when their personal resources are threatened or taken; resources can include social support, self-esteem and employment
  - When an individual encounters a stressor their body must adapt to meet the demands of the stressor; prolonged exposure to a stressor may lead to a depletion of resources within the body resulting in stress-related illness, this is known as the general adaptation syndrome (Selye, 1951)
  - Karasek (1979) claims that jobs that are high in mental strain but low in control increase the likelihood of stress-related illness
  - Shan *et al* (2017) claim that a lack of available resources in the workplace has increased the likelihood of stress-related illness in Chinese doctors and this is in a contributing factor to karoshi in China
  - Lundberg and Hellström (2002) found elevated cortisol levels in women who regularly worked over 50 hours a week

- Stress and dispositional factors
  - The hardy personality may protect people from the effects of stress (Kobasa and Greenwald, 1979)
  - Individuals with type A personalities may be more likely to develop stress-related illness (Friedman and Rosenman, 1974)

- Health promotion and stress
  - Aitkens *et al* (2014) discovered that online mindfulness programs were effective in protecting people against stress

- ○ Yoga is successful in decreasing anxiety and depression in a range of populations (Pascoe and Bauer, 2015)

This section also links to:

- the role of animal research in understanding human behaviour (Sapolsky) (biological approach to behaviour)

- hormones and behaviour (cortisol) (biological approach to behaviour)

- cognitive processing in the digital world, for example, online social support (Nabi, Prestin and So, 2013) (cognitive approach to behaviour).

Definitions of stress

"If the problem can be solved why worry? If the problem cannot be solved worrying will do you no good." (Shantideva)

Research has shown that stress can be both a determinant of health and wellness, and a risk factor for obesity, substance abuse, as well as many non-communicable diseases. The relationship between stress, obesity and substance abuse is complicated and interrelated. These relationships and consistently increasing stress levels in the workplace mean there is a need for further examination of stress and wellness. The next section will focus on work-based stress as one of the most dangerous health problems of the 21st century.

Most of us will have at some point collapsed on the sofa at home after a long day at work, or a bad day at school and let out a big sigh. When a friend or relative asked, "What is the matter?" you may have uttered the words, "I'm just a bit stressed at the moment". What did you mean by this? Were you referring to a feeling of physical exhaustion, the emotional aftermath of an argument with a friend, a sense of being overwhelmed at having to complete multiple examinations, or frustration with the speed of the internet? The truth is "stress" is hard to define, because it means different things to different people. We tend to overgeneralize the term and apply it to any situation that causes us to feel angry, upset, agitated or helpless. It is important at this point to introduce and distinguish between some related concepts that we will refer to throughout this chapter. To help us, we will defer to **Robert Sapolsky**, considered one of the leading psychologists in the field of stress research and the author of the world-renowned book *Why Zebras Don't Get Ulcers.*

Sapolsky argues that it is important to distinguish between acute physical stressors, chronic physical

stressors (both of which are biological approaches to defining stressors), and psychological and social stressors in order to understand the nature of stress.

Acute physical stressors are those extremely demanding but short-lived events that require your body to mobilize its energy supplies to help you cope with the situation. If this situation was running away from an angry lion it is this **stress response (fight or flight response)** that will help to ensure that you survive. More common examples for humans may be a visit to the dentist or a wasp entering the car while you are driving (Elliott and Eisdorfer,1982; Hobfoll,1989). In these situations you may feel the stress response taking hold of your body (increased heart rate, sweaty palms and so on) but the stressor will soon pass and your system will return to its normal balance. We call this state of balance **homeostasis**. The concept of homeostasis refers to the notion that the body needs balance, and we have an ideal level of glucose, oxygen, temperature and so on that we need to maintain if our bodies are to function at their best.

Chronic physical stressors are not common in the western world, but you are likely to have seen examples in the news. These stressors require the body to prepare for a sustained physical challenge such as walking miles to find food or fighting a parasite. The stressor is having a long-term physical impact upon the body, but as humans we are quite good at dealing with these demands. Once these demands are met, our bodies can quite often return to a state of homeostasis.

Most importantly when looking at human stress, it is important to recognize **psychological** and **social stressors**. These stressors are common in our everyday lives and as human beings we are capable of creating or imagining stressful events that can invade our thoughts for days, weeks or months at a time. We can get stressed when we are stuck in traffic, worrying about an upcoming event or about a conversation that we had with our boss. These long-term psychological stressors keep the body's stress response activated. It is this prolonged activation of our body's stress response that can result in illness and injury.

Elliott and Eisdorfer (1982) include the **chronic intermittent stressors** in their explanation of the main kinds of stressor. These may include examinations and regular meetings with teachers who you don't like.

Putting it simply, a **stressor** is anything that knocks your body out of homeostatic balance (Sapolsky, 2009) and the psychological and physiological response to that stressor is called **strain** (Sarafino, 2017). It is worth noting that a stressor can be both positive and negative. We will therefore adopt the following definition from the beginning of the section: "stress is any uncomfortable emotional experience accompanied by predictable biochemical, physiological and behavioral changes" (Baum,1990).

ATL skills: Thinking

What are the limitations of the above definition of stress?

Life events and daily hassles: a sociocultural approach to stress

Our daily lives are full of stresses and strains. From the moment that our alarm clocks sound to wake us in the morning until the moment that we go to bed at night, our days are filled with events that we find psychologically and physiologically stressful.

In a classic study **Holmes and Rahe (1967)** recruited over 5,000 participants who generated a list of life events that they found stressful. These events were positive and negative, frequently occurring and unexpected. The researchers reduced the initial list down to 43 events that were common to all participants. Marriage was given an arbitrary value of 50 by the researchers, and they asked a new sample of participants to rate each event against marriage in terms of how much adjustment to their lives it would require (Morrison and Bennett, 2016). Events perceived as being twice as disruptive as marriage would be scored at 100. These events were then ranked and gained scores ranging from 11–100. This was known as a life-changing unit score (LCU). The highest level of adjustment was found to be to the death of a spouse. Holmes and Rahe hypothesized

that the more life events an individual had experienced within a one-year period, the more likely they would be to suffer from stress-related illness. Participants gaining a score below 150 were not reported as suffering from stress. Participants scoring over 200 were seen as suffering from severe stress and at risk of stress-related illness.

Social Readjustment Rating Scale (SRRS), examples	
Rank	*Life event (LCU)*
1	Death of a spouse (100)
2	Divorce (73)
6	Personal injury or illness (53)
7	Marriage (50)
10	Retirement (45)
12	Pregnancy (40)

▲ Table 6.5

In contrast to Holmes and Rahe's major life events theory, Kanner *et al* (1981) proposed that it was in fact the small, seemingly harmless, day-to-day occurrences which they termed "daily hassles" that were in fact causing us stress. They argue that daily hassles such as being stuck in a traffic jam or losing your phone could have a detrimental effect on our health if they are not experienced alongside an equal measure of positive occurrences. They termed these positive experiences "uplifts" and these include something as simple as getting a good night's sleep, receiving praise from a teacher or having an enjoyable first date. These uplifts have been studied in their own right by Lazarus and his colleagues and they found that positive experiences can indeed improve our overall sense of health and wellness.

Lazarus, Kanner and Folkman (1980) argue that positive events can act as a buffer to the negative events, providing some respite and therefore reducing the impact of the stressful daily hassles. McLean (1976) highlights the importance of investigating the occurrence of both negative and positive events together:

> "Perhaps because the unit of stress is relatively small and the stressors so familiar, these kinds of stressors have been taken for granted and considered to be less important than more dramatic stressors. Clinical and research data indicate that these 'microstressors', acting cumulatively, and in the relative absence of compensatory positive experience, can be potent sources of stress."

In their classic study, **Kanner** *et al* **(1981)** wanted to compare the impact of daily hassles and uplifts as predictors of psychological symptoms of stress with major life events as proposed by Holmes and Rahe. Over a period of 12 months, they studied 100 participants, primarily from California, USA, using both psychometric and self-report measures. Participants received the surveys one month before the start of the study to ensure all had received and understood the materials. They recorded their experiences using the following measures:

- the hassles and uplifts scale consisting of a possible 117 hassles and 135 uplifts which they rated for frequency of occurrence and intensity

- a life events scale

- the Hopkins Symptom Checklist

- the Bradburn Morale Scale (the last two test for psychological well-being in adults).

Results showed that daily hassles were in fact stronger predictors of psychological symptoms of stress than life events.

Furthermore, hassles caused symptoms of stress independent of life events. There were, however, some interesting differences in the findings between genders. It was found that life events and hassles were positively correlated with psychological symptoms in both men and women. Uplifts, however, were found only to be a predictor of symptoms in women, which may imply that women find both positive and negative change stressful. It was suggested that women may appraise or cope with daily hassles and uplifts differently, and adopt a more positive approach, or that the findings may reflect the level of daily activity in a person's life or the differences in daily situations that men and women find themselves in. (We will discuss the issue of sex differences below).

The table below contrasts the two approaches.

Life events approach

- The SRRS included a wide range of events and the impact of these was considered when ranking.
- Subsequent research has shown that stressful life events do indeed lead to illness.
- There is a contamination effect. Results of research have linked stressful life events to illness but causation cannot be inferred. Identifying the cause of an illness may not be possible.
- The survey has been accused of being vague. For example, changes in responsibility at work may be due to both promotion and demotion. As such items in the survey are not applicable to all individuals regardless of age, race and culture.
- Meanings attributed to each event are not considered. Ratings are retrospective and the causal link may be apparent in some cases and not in others.

Daily hassles approach

- Age, job and gender affected how hassles were perceived and appraised. This highlights that the same event can be experienced very differently by two people.
- Results indicated that participants may have lost interest in the task over time as fewer hassles and uplifts were recorded in the latter months.
- More active people may experience more daily hassles and as a result appraise these differently.
- The findings of studies of daily hassles allow us to identify stressors and particularly at-risk individuals and this can inform more effective coping strategies.
- Studies related to daily events can be longitudinal, assessing changes over time as opposed to life-event studies which tend to be snapshot studies.

▲ Table 6.6   A comparison of daily hassles and life events as explanations of stress and stress-related illness

Are there sex differences in stressful life events?

The American Psychological Association publishes a report annually entitled "APA Stress in America".

Below are examples of findings from reports published between 2010 and 2017.

- In the 2010 survey it was reported that men and women have very different physical and psychological responses to stress; they differ in their ability to manage stress. Women considered their stress levels to be increasing, and were much more likely to report symptoms of stress than men.

- In 2012, women continued to report experiencing more stress than men. Twenty-three per cent of women reported their stress level at an 8, 9 or 10 on a 10-point scale, compared to 16% of men. Top sources of stress included money, work and the economy and these were the same for men and women. This increase in perceived stress continued in 2013 and 2014, with women more likely to experience symptoms of stress and experience feelings of loneliness or isolation. Women were also more likely to recognize the importance of stress management and adopt successful strategies.

- In 2016, men reported higher stress levels than normal; women still continued to report higher levels of stress overall. Work, money and the economy continued to cause the most concern.

- In 2017, the gender gap remained but the overall reports of stress went down. Women reported higher levels of stress than men, and were more likely to report money and family responsibilities as a source of stress. Top sources of stress remained similar for all Americans, but when asked to cite three factors that had added to their stress levels over the last decade, Americans were likely to cite the economy, terrorism and mass shootings.

Discussion

Why do you think Americans were more likely to cite the economy, terrorism and mass shootings as their main sources of stress in 2017?

The APA surveys would indicate that American women experience more stress than men. It is important, however, not to oversimplify this issue and claim that one sex experiences more stress than another (Helgeson, 2010). Helgeson argues that we need to distinguish between traumatic life events, more common life events and daily hassles. **Tolin and Foa (2006)** conducted a meta-analysis and concluded that men, on average, experienced more trauma than women. The nature of the

trauma differed greatly between the sexes. Men were 3.5 times more likely to experience combat, war or terrorism, while women were 6 times as likely to report adult sexual assault.

It is possible, however, that men and women are exposed to different stressors due to their social roles. Men are more likely to experience undesired unemployment, the effects of which can lead to mental and physical health issues. Women may be more likely to experience chronic sources of strain such as sexual harassment and caregiving for the elderly. Evidence suggests that men are more susceptible to work-based stressors, with married men reporting greater stress than women in relation to work and finance-based stressors (Conger *et al*, 1993).

It has been found that in a meta-analytic review of studies on gender and stressful life events between 1960 and 1996, women are more likely to report more stressful events than men (Davis, Matthews and Twamley, 1999). It is worth noting, however, that the effect was extremely small. Helgeson (2010) argues that experiencing stressful life events is not the same as the effects of life events, and researchers should be careful not to confuse the two, as two people can experience the same life event but interpret and respond to it quite differently. One explanation for this discrepancy in reporting has been linked to encoding in memory. It is possible that both men and women experience the same number of stressful life events, but women are more likely to recall the stressful event. It has been argued by Seidlitz and Diener (1998) that this may be due to women encoding emotional events in more detail than men.

Much research has commented on the need to distinguish between reporting on sex and gender, as reporting on sex incorporates both status and gender roles (Helgeson, 2010). Women have reported experiencing more stressors than men. This could be linked to having a dual role as a mother or housewife and daily workloads associated with employment. This dual role has been linked to an increased likelihood of suffering from heart disease (D'Ovidio *et al*, 2015).

It has also been reported that men and women show differences in their reactivity to specific stressors. Men show greater reactivity to having their competence challenged than women, whereas women show greater reactivity when their friendship or love is challenged (Smith, Zautra and Stone, 2002).

ATL skills: Thinking and communication

It is clear from the above research on gender and stress that there are issues of definition and interpretation that should be considered when drawing conclusions on this topic. Cordelia Fine, a leading psychologist in the field of gender research, claims: "The sheer complexity of the brain, together with our assumptions about gender, lend themselves beautifully to over-interpretation and precipitous conclusions."

Write a short paragraph summarizing what you think she means by this statement. Do you agree with her? What makes you say that?

What should be clear by now is that no one event summons the same physical or emotional response in each individual—people see things differently and attach different meanings to events. This is a key aspect of stress. We call these varying interpretations **appraisals**. Understanding appraisal is critical to understanding why we find everyday events so stressful and why levels of stress can differ greatly between individuals in response to the same event. It may now be appropriate to adopt an alternative definition of stress. **Lazarus and Folkman (1984)** have defined stress as "a particular relationship between the person perceiving them as taxing or exceeding their resources and endangering well being". We will explore this definition further below.

Models of stress

Stress as a transaction: a cognitive approach to stress

Richard Lazarus and his colleagues in the 1970s argued that stress was the end result of a transaction between individuals and their environment. They argued that stressors are perceived in terms of potential threat, harm and challenges. Individuals also weigh their ability to cope with these stressors against the resources at their disposal. The **transactional stress model** claims that when confronted with a stressor, an individual will *simultaneously* engage in two types of appraisal: **primary appraisal** and **secondary appraisal**.

In primary appraisal we interpret the situation in terms of its potential to affect our well-being. We ask ourselves questions such as, "What does this mean for me?" and "Could this stressor hurt me?" Lazarus and Folkman suggest four ways to appraise such events:

- irrelevant (this does not concern me)
- benign and positive (this is good)
- harmful and a threat (an anticipated stressful situation where confidence to deal with the situation may be low)
- harmful and a challenge (an anticipated stressful situation where confidence to deal with the situation may be high).

Those situations that we do appraise as stressful undergo the process of **secondary appraisal** in which we consider our ability to cope with the situation by assessing our available resources. For example, individuals with low self-esteem may be more likely to appraise a situation as stressful as they believe they do not possess the resources needed. A final reappraisal of the situation is undertaken in light of our own responses to the stressor and the information available.

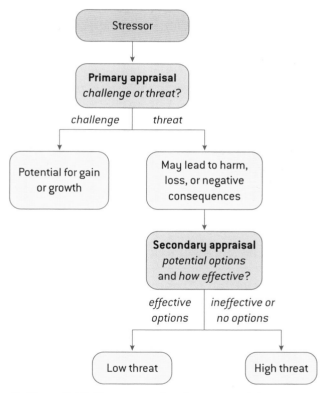

▲ Figure 6.18 The transactional stress model developed by Richard Lazarus

A classic study that appears to support the transactional model of stress was conducted by **Speisman *et al* (1964)**. Participants were boys who viewed a stressful film of a tribal genital mutilation ritual, while reporting on their own stress levels; their heart rate and skin conductance were measured by the researchers.

Participants were placed into one of four conditions:

1. no soundtrack, the **control condition**

2. a soundtrack that emphasized the pain and danger involved in the ritual, known as the **trauma condition**

3. a soundtrack that denied any pain was involved in the procedure and emphasized the boys' consent to be participants in the procedure, **the denial condition**

4. a soundtrack that was designed to give an objective, "scientific" account of events, **the science condition**.

Results showed that participants in condition 2 (the trauma condition) experienced more stress than participants in the other conditions, demonstrated by their self-reports, increased heart rates and skin conductance. The appraisal of the video as traumatic and painful influenced the participants' subsequent primary appraisal of events. The study highlights how it is our interpretation of an event that can cause an emotional response, that two people can perceive and appraise the same stressor differently, and that this will trigger differences in their stress response. It is therefore possible for purely psychological factors to increase or decrease the biological stress response.

Discussion

To what extent do you agree with the following statement that has been adapted from Stevan E Hobfoll's criticism of Lazarus' work?

"There is no stress without perception."

The conservation of resources model

Hobfoll (1989) introduced a new alternative model of stress, the conservation of resources model. The model's basic premise is that people strive to retain, protect and build **resources** and that stress is experienced when they feel that they may lose, or have lost these resources (Hobfoll, Briggs-Phillips and Stines, 1989). In order to make sense of this model we must once more adapt our definition of stress.

Hobfoll defines psychological stress as a reaction to the environment in which there is one of the following:

- the threat of a net loss of resources

- the net loss of resources

- a lack of resource gain following the investment of resources.

Perceived loss, actual loss or lack of gain in resources are sufficient to produce psychological stress. In order to understand this theory we must first understand what is meant by "resources". Resources are any object, characteristic or condition valued by the individual. These include social support, self-esteem and employment (Parry, 1986). An example of loss of resources may include a demotion at work, unemployment or divorce. These environmental resources are particularly important as not only are they functional—they provide financial support or security—but they also help people define their sense of self, and any loss would threaten their self-esteem.

Discussion

How has your understanding of stress changed as you have progressed through this section?

Which of the definitions of stress presented so far do you think is most accurate?

Stress at work: an integrated approach to studying stress

▲ Figure 6.19 Stress in the workplace

The average person will spend 39 hours per week at work. It is an important aspect of our daily lives and one in which we invest a lot of time and emotion. It is therefore essential that we are happy in our job. Patrick Lencioni (2015) claims that in order for us to be happy at work we must be truly engaged. He argues that misery at work can be caused by:

- anonymity (the feeling that you are invisible or that people do not know you)

- irrelevance (the feeling that your job doesn't matter)

- immeasurement (employees need to be able to assess how they are performing so that they can control their future).

Work engagement can be defined as a positive, fulfilling, work-related state of mind that is characterized by:

- vigour—a high level of energy and resilience in relation to your work

- dedication—a sense of significance, pride and enthusiasm

- absorption—being fully engaged and engrossed in one's work (Bakker *et al*, 2007).

See video

Watch Shawn Anchor's TED Talk "The happy secret to better work", available at https://www.ted.com/talks/shawn_achor_the_happy_secret_to_better_work.

▶ ❙❙ ■ ────────────

Situations at work that are not engaging could therefore cause stress. The Centre for Studies on Human Stress argue that there are four universal ingredients for stress.

- Novelty—something new, that you have not experienced before, happens.

- Unpredictability—something happens that you had no way of knowing would occur.

- Threat to the ego—your competence as a person is called into question.

- Sense of control—you feel you have little or no control over the situation.

Exercise

Make a list of work-or school-based examples for each one of these stressors.

Given that these ingredients for stress often appear during a typical working day, how prevalent is stress at work? Look at these statistics from the UK Labour Force Survey (LFS) 2016.

- The total number of cases of work-related stress, depression or anxiety in 2015/16 was 488,000 cases, a prevalence rate of 1,510 per 100,000 workers.

- The total number of working days lost due to this condition in 2015/16 was 11.7 million. This equated to an average of 23.9 days lost per case. Working days lost per worker showed a generally downward trend up to around 2009/10; since then the rate has been broadly flat.

- In 2015/16 stress accounted for 37% of all work-related ill health cases and 45% of all working days lost due to ill health.

- Stress is more prevalent in public service industries, such as education; health and social care; and in public administration and defence.

- The main work factors cited by respondents as causing work-related stress, depression or anxiety were workload pressures, including tight deadlines, too much responsibility and a lack of managerial support

ATL skills: Thinking

Why do you think stress is more prevalent in public service industries? Give reasons for your answer.

The National Institute for Occupational Safety and Health (NIOSH) in the USA reports a similar story, with 40% of Americans reporting being stressed at work and 25% reporting work as the number one stressor in their lives. This on-the-job stress has been strongly linked to physical health complaints and as a result it has been estimated that 1 million Americans are absent from work each day due to work-related stress.

The survey highlights that work stress is a result of interaction between employees and their working conditions. Both individual characteristics of an employee and the working conditions have the ability to cause stress. Job conditions associated with stress include:

- the design of tasks (boring and repetitive work, long hours, lack of control)

- management style (autocratic managers can reduce workers' feelings of worth)

- interpersonal relationships (friendships with colleagues, working in isolation)

- environmental conditions (noise pollution, poor lighting, crowding)

- career concerns (lack of job security).

Sir Michael Marmot led the now famous longitudinal **Whitehall studies** that investigated the relationship between working conditions and health in British civil servants from 1985–2015. The studies at Whitehall discovered that the level of stress that an individual experiences was directly correlated to that individual's position in the corporate hierarchy. Those lower down the hierarchy were more likely to experience stress-related disease. These health inequalities were attributed to lack of job control, job clarity and managerial support.

ATL skills: Research thinking and communication

It is often claimed that stress can make us sick and that one's position in the social hierarchy influences the stressors that we are exposed to. Supporters of this claim often refer to research that in part relies on the use of primates. Two studies in particular are commonly cited as being relevant. Robert Sapolsky's study of Serengeti baboons and Carol Shively's research on macaque monkeys highlight that a primate's social position can affect the level of stress hormones in the body and increase the likelihood of stress-related disease. In the National Geographic documentary *Stress: The Portrait of a Killer*, Sapolsky claims that the baboons in his study experience stress in a way that allows generalization of his findings to humans. As a result, his findings are often examined alongside the famous Whitehall studies that investigated stress in British civil servants. These generalizations and comparisons should, however, be treated with caution and the strength of the initial findings verified.

The research studies listed below are featured in the National Geographic documentary. Read them and answer the questions to investigate the accepted truth of these findings.

- Marmot, M *et al*. 1997. "Contribution of job control and other risk factors to social variations in coronary heart disease incidence".
- Sapolsky, RM. 2005. "The influence of social hierarchy on primate health".
- Sapolsky, R. 1999. "Hormonal correlates of personality and social contexts: from non-human to human primates".
- Shively, C and Clarkson, T. 1994. "Social status and coronary artery atherosclerosis in female monkeys".
- Epel, E *et al*. 2004. "Accelerated telomere shortening in response to life stress".
- Evans, R. 2002. Cited in Petticrew, M, Davey Smith, G and Gursky-Doyen, S. 2012. "The monkey puzzle: a systematic review of studies of stress, social hierarchies, and heart disease in monkeys (stress, dominance and heart disease in monkeys)".

Questions

1. Watch the documentary and make a list of the hypotheses that are being investigated by these researchers. To what extent are these presented as fact?

2. In groups, answer the following.
   a) What connections can you draw between the text, your own experiences and previous learning?
   b) What ideas, claims, or assumptions in these articles do you want to challenge or disagree with?
   c) What do you think are the key concepts that develop understanding of the topic?
   d) What changes in attitudes, thinking or action are suggested by the articles?

3. Using Google Scholar or a similar academic search engine, attempt to locate research that further supports the claims made in the human and non-human research cited in the documentary. To what extent have these findings received support from other researchers?

4. Read the article entitled "The monkey puzzle", which is a review of the primate research on stress. To what extent do you agree with the following claim: "Overall, non-human primate studies present only limited evidence for an association between social status and coronary artery disease"?

5. "The Whitehall and Serengeti studies are in a sense starting from opposite ends of a possible bridge. While the baboons show hierarchically associated variations in physiological responses to stress that are consistent with health effects, the civil servants show hierarchical variations in health outcomes that must emerge from some physiological pathway" (Evans, 2002).
   a) What do you think this statement is trying to say?
   b) To what extent do you agree with the claims made in this statement?

6. Using the research from the documentary, discuss the extent to which primate research can provide insight into human stress, hierarchy and illness.

Psychology in real life

Read the following article on the use of animal models in research: http://www.apa.org/science/about/psa/2012/04/animal-research.aspx. To what extent do you agree with the author's views on the values and ethics surrounding the use of animal models in psychological research?

Research in focus: Teaching

Bakker *et al* **(2007)** conducted a study to investigate the influence of job resources on employee engagement when demands of the job are high. The participants were 805 Finnish teachers recruited via postal questionnaire.

The researchers tested two hypotheses:

1. that job resources act as buffers and can reduce stress and disengagement when teachers are exposed to pupil misbehaviour (having more resources reduces stress caused by misbehaviour)

2. that when confronted with pupil misbehaviour job resources were increasingly important in influencing work engagement (resources were even more important when exposed to stressful situations).

Researchers measured work engagement using the Utrecht Work Engagement Scale (Finnish version) that measured engagement along three subscales: vigour, dedication and absorption. Participants were assessed on their responses to statements such as "When I wake up in the morning I feel like going to work" and "I am enthusiastic about my job".

Statements were rated on a 7-point scale (0 = never to 6 = always).

Pupil misbehaviour was measured on a 6-item scale adapted from Kyriacou and Sutcliffe (1978). Participants responded to a general opening question: "As a teacher, how great a source of stress are the following factors to you?" They were then asked to respond to six specific behaviours and situations such as noisy pupils and maintaining class discipline. Items were scored on a 5-point scale (1 = hardly ever to 5 = very often).

Job resources were assessed using the Health Organization Barometer. Each job resource was assessed with three items. Job resources included: job control, innovativeness, information, appreciation, organizational climate and supervisor support, and were measured by participants' responses to questions such as "Do your colleagues appreciate your work?" All resources were assessed on a 5-point scale (1 = hardly ever to 5 = very often).

The results were as follows.

- Pupil misbehaviour was not correlated or weakly correlated to the six job resources.

- All six job resources were positively correlated to vigour, dedication and absorption. Appreciation was the strongest predictor of work engagement.

- Five out of six job resources moderated the effects of pupil misbehaviour on vigour and absorption. Four resources interacted with pupil misbehaviour regarding dedication of work engagement.

Researchers concluded that supervisor support, organizational climate, innovativeness and appreciation had moderating effects on the relationship between pupil misbehaviour and work engagement and can therefore be considered important job resources. These resources acted as a buffer and reduced the negative impact of pupil misbehaviour. This study highlights that job resources are particularly relevant when under highly stressful conditions, lending support to the conservation of resources model of stress.

Questions

1. To what extent do you think it is possible to measure stress?

2. This research uses a variety of self-report measures. What practical and ethical considerations would the researchers need to consider before, during and after conducting this study?

3. How do you think Richard Lazarus and his colleagues would respond to the above findings?

These report findings therefore support elements of the theories of both Lazarus and Hobfoll. Work-based stress does seem to be related to appraisal and lack of resources.

Are we working ourselves to death?

"Karoshi" (death from overwork) was first reported in Japan in 1969. A 29-year-old man died having shown no signs of previous illness. Unfortunately, today cases of "karoshi" and "karojisatsu" (suicide from overwork) are increasingly common.

Uehata (1991) reported that five work patterns could result in karoshi. They are:

- extremely long working hours or working night shifts

- working continuously without a break

- high-pressure jobs

- extremely taxing physical work

- around-the-clock, high-pressure work.

Karasek (1979) suggested that jobs that are high in demand but low in control are often high in mental strain and can increase stress. Specific features cited as leading to stress included demand, controllability, predictability and ambiguity. The work of doctors often demonstrates such work pressures and as such research has investigated karoshi in the medical profession.

ATL skills: Research

Investigate the following models of stress as applied to the workplace:

- the demand-control support model (Karasek, 1979)

- job-demands-resources model (Demerouti *et al*, 2001).

1. Outline and explain the two models as they relate to work-related stress.

2. To what extent do they support the models and theories discussed earlier in this unit?

3. Conduct a literature search and locate studies that both support and refute the claims made by the models.

4. Evaluate the above models of work-based stress.

Shan *et al* (2017) reviewed 46 cases of karoshi among doctors in China between 2013 and 2015. The study found that the main medical causes of karoshi were heart attack and stroke ascribed to stress. More than half of these doctors had been found to be working continuously for 8–12 hours. Eleven of these doctors had worked continuously for 24 hours. When surveying Chinese doctors it was also found that they often sacrificed leisure time and worked 6–7 days a week. These long working hours often coincided with sleep deprivation. Lui *et al* (2002) reported that people sleeping less than five hours a night were two to three times more likely to suffer from cardiovascular illness.

Shan claims that the deaths of the Chinese doctors could be due to the fact that in China there is a scarcity of medical resources, despite accounting for 22% of the world's population. This supports the findings of Bakker *et al* (2007) who reported that high work demand and scarcity of resources leads to an increase in work-related stress. Low pay and conflicts at work were also reported to be a contributing factor to karoshi in China.

It is worth noting that karoshi is not unique to Asia. Cases have also been reported in Europe, the USA and Australia by **Kivimaki *et al* (2015)**. Long working hours were once again correlated with coronary heart disease and stroke. Kivimaki and colleagues claim that karoshi is most likely to be caused by a repetitive activation of the human stress response. Research on karoshi has found that work stress causes an increase in the secretion of stress hormones, which over time are associated with cardiovascular disease (Der-Shin Ke, 2012). **Lundberg and Hellstrom (2002)** found that cortisol levels were twice as high in women who regularly worked over 50 hours a week compared to those working a "normal" working week.

Karoshi research has highlighted that work-based stress is a serious issue. Cognitive strain, lack of sleep, and the pressure and long hours of a demanding job have the potential to make us sick or even kill us. It is essential therefore to put measures in place to prevent karoshi, improve work–life balance and reduce high-risk coping behaviours associated with high levels of stress such as overeating, smoking and alcohol consumption. Stress is therefore considered a determinant of health-related behaviour and a health problem.

Exercise

Karoshi is getting widespread news coverage and the Japanese government are attempting to promote healthy work-related behaviour by changing work legislation.

1. Research the initiatives that have been implemented by the Japanese government to date.

2. Evaluate the health promotion strategies adopted by governments to improve our work-life balance.

3. What assumptions are being made in relation to human health-related decision-making when implementing health promotions in the workplace?

See video

Watch this film on emotion, stress and health, available at https://www.youtube.com/watch?v=4KbSRXP0wik.

The physiology of stress: a biological approach to stress

These real-life examples of stress make it clear that our cognitions have the potential to alter our physiology, that is, our appraisal of events as stressful has the potential to activate a biological response. Walter Cannon (1932) termed this response the **"fight or flight" response**. When exposed to a stressor such as coming face to face with a bully, our body immediately attempts to deal with the threat by entering a higher state of arousal. Most of us will be familiar with this feeling: increased heart rate, pupils dilating and body shaking. Your body has prepared itself to deal with the threat by making use of all available resources allowing us to summon the energy to either fight or run away.

Stress and the autonomic nervous system

The nervous system acts as the body's communication centre, relaying information about internal and external conditions to our brain. The nervous system is divided into two parts: the **central nervous system** and the **peripheral nervous system**.

The central nervous system is composed of the brain and the spinal cord. The central and the peripheral nervous systems consist of neurons that are involved in the process of **neurotransmission**, sending chemical messages to various parts of the body. The peripheral nervous system has two parts.

- The somatic nervous system is responsible for sending messages from the skin and muscles to the brain and back.

- The autonomic nervous system is responsible for the stress response; during the stress response one half of the autonomic nervous system is activated while the other half is suppressed.

The **sympathetic nervous system** is activated during states of emergency, real or imagined. It helps ensure that we are equipped to deal with the challenge to our system by heightening arousal, vigilance and mobility. It means you have the strength and energy needed to deal with that bully—fight or flight. When this system is activated your adrenal glands secrete adrenaline (epinephrine) and noradrenaline (norepinephrine). It is the adrenaline rushing around your body that causes you to experience an increased heart rate or shaky hands.

While the sympathetic nervous system causes all hell to break loose, your **parasympathetic nervous system** calms things down. The parasympathetic nervous system mediates calmer

activities such as digestion and growth. The two systems work in opposition to each other. While you are preparing to fight, or more sensibly run away from that bully, activating your sympathetic nervous system, your reproductive systems shut down as they are not needed and the energy is mobilized elsewhere. The sympathetic and parasympathetic nervous systems cannot be switched on at the same time, so the functions of each are inhibited when their counterpart is active. As a result, our body does not respond well to prolonged exposure to the stress response as we neglect other essential functions such as fighting infection.

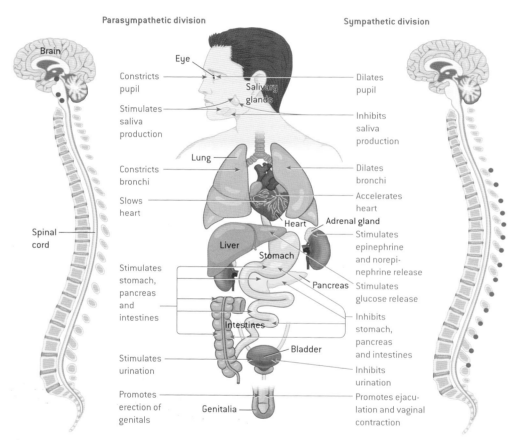

▲ Figure 6.20 The effects of the sympathetic and parasympathetic nervous systems

Stress and hormones

When you experience a stressful event, or even perceive an event as stressful, your body starts to secrete stress hormones: adrenaline and noradrenaline, released by the sympathetic nervous system, and glucocorticoids which are steroid hormones secreted by the adrenal glands. The most common glucocorticoid is **cortisol** and it

is often referred to as the stress hormone. It is the combination of glucocorticoids and the sympathetic nervous system secretions that create the stress response.

This process of hormone secretion starts in the brain when we appraise an event as stressful. The hypothalamus secretes corticotropin which tells the pituitary gland to produce the hormone ACTH. When ACTH reaches the adrenal glands it triggers the production of glucocorticoids and this results in the activation of the stress response. This system is often referred to as the **hypothalamic-pituitary-adrenal axis (HPA)**.

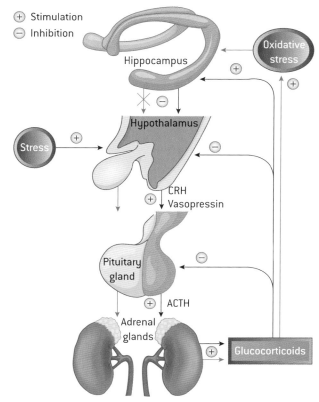

▲ Figure 6.21 The hypothalamus-pituitary-adrenal axis (HPA)

ATL skills: Research

Refer to the biological approach or search online to distinguish between:

- hormones and neurotransmitters
- adrenaline and noradrenaline.

The general adaptation syndrome

Hans Selye (1951) claimed that, "Anything that causes stress endangers life, unless it is met by adequate adaptive responses; conversely, anything that endangers life causes stress and adaptive responses." Adaptability and resistance to stress are therefore essential for survival. Selye claimed that in the biological sense stress is the interaction between damage and defence, and that all living organisms respond to stress in the same manner. He termed this adaptive response to stress the **general adaptation syndrome**.

Selye's research was the first to document the negative effects of stress on the human body. He concluded that prolonged exposure to stress will cause illness when he realized that the rats that he had been using in his research had developed stress-related illnesses regardless of the experimental conditions they had been placed in. Selye had been clumsily handling these rats and repeatedly injecting them with various substances. He concluded that it was the fear of being injected that caused the rats to repeatedly activate their stress response. This prolonged exposure to the fight or flight response flooded the rats' bodies with stress hormones which over time caused the rats to develop stress-related illnesses.

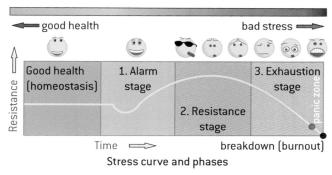

Stress curve and phases

▲ Figure 6.22 General adaptation syndrome

The general adaptation syndrome develops in three stages.

1. The alarm reaction—the body is exposed to a stressor and mobilizes the necessary resources in order to ensure survival, thereby turning on the fight or flight response.

2. The stage of resistance—the body actively defends itself against a persistent stressor, maintaining the stress response.

3. The stage of exhaustion—the body can no longer sustain the stress response and resources become depleted. This is the stage where we are most likely to get sick.

Selye's work highlighted that the human body will always respond to stress in similar ways, regardless of the stressor, and that prolonged exposure to the stress response could cause illness. It should be noted, however, that not all stress is bad stress. When we experience the right amount of stress humans can actually enjoy it. Selye termed positive stress, such as experiencing nerves before running a race, **eustress**. Negative stress is known as

distress. Selye believed the response to eustress and distress was the same and that eustress would eventually turn into distress if the intensity of the stressor increased. The Yerkes-Dodson law aimed to explain this relationship between arousal and performance. A certain degree of arousal would support performance but once arousal exceeded this optimum amount, performance would become impaired.

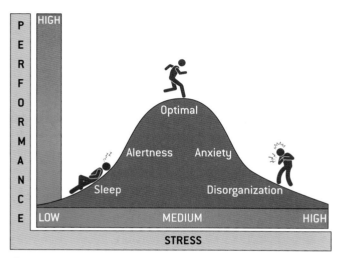

▲ Figure 6.23 Yerkes-Dodson law

See video

Watch Kelly McGonigal's TED Talk on how to make stress your friend, available at https://www.ted.com/talks/kelly_mcgonigal_how_to_make_stress_your_friend.

▶ ❚❚ ◼

Stress and illness

When we experience prolonged periods of stress our immune system functions differently. Stress hormones reduce the functioning of T-cells, cells that help fight infection. **Kiecolt-Glaser et al (1984)** investigated whether the stress of examinations would impair the functioning of the immune system in medical students. Blood was taken from participants one month before examinations when stress was low and during the examinations when stress was high. Participants also completed questionnaires examining life events and loneliness. The T-cell activity was reduced in the blood taken during the examination period, indicating that the immune system was suppressed at this time. Those students who reported stressful life events and loneliness had the most reduced T-cell activity.

Uchino, Cacioppo and Kiecolt-Glaser (1996) conducted further research on the immune function of elderly carers of people with Alzheimer's disease. It was discovered that wounds took significantly longer to heal than those of control participants and that when vaccinated against the flu virus their immune functioning was significantly more impaired. Findings in younger participants have not consistently supported these findings and as such more research needs to be conducted in this area (Vedhara *et al*, 2002).

Discussion

The IB Diploma Programme is academically rigorous and challenging: two years of in-depth and intense study culminating in a series of intense, high-stakes examinations. Examinations are well-known sources of stress and have been categorized as both acute and chronic intermittent stressors by researchers.

Reflect upon your experience as a student. To what extent do the research findings on examination stress and stress in the workplace apply to you?

Stress and dispositional factors
Hardiness

Certain personal characteristics have shown themselves to be effective protective factors against the effects of stress. Suzanne Kobasa and Greenwald (1979) describes the concept of **cognitive** or **personality hardiness** as "a stronger commitment to self, an attitude of vigorousness toward the environment, a sense of meaningfulness, and an internal locus of control". Having these characteristics as part of your personality protects against stress. Ouellette *et al* (1985) measured the relative effectiveness of hardiness, exercise and social support in a group of 85 male business executives. They found that the best way to avoid stress-related illness was by incorporating all three strategies but that hardiness was the most important of these resistance factors.

It is worth noting that an individual's hardiness is not fixed and can be improved with hardiness training (Maddi *et al*, 2009).

Personality

An individual's personality will affect his or her ability to engage in problem-focused coping, to develop coping strategies and seek effective support (Matthewman, Rose and Hetherington, 2009). Individuals with a type A personality tend to be competitive, self-critical and impatient. **Friedman and Rosenman (1974)** concluded that type A individuals are also more likely to develop coronary heart disease. Type A personalities can also increase stress in those around them with different personality traits; Type B personalities prefer to work at a slower pace and may find working with type A personalities challenging and stressful (Jamal, Baba and Carlson, 2003).

Health promotion and stress

Mindfulness is a cognitive practice similar to meditation, an attempt to focus an individual's attention on the present. Mindfulness can be defined as a mental state achieved by focusing one's awareness on the present moment, while calmly acknowledging and accepting one's feelings, thoughts and bodily sensations. It is the opposite of mindlessness which we experience every day. If you have ever reached for your drink only to find you have already finished it but didn't notice then you have experienced mindlessness. In our modern world of incessant notifications and computer-fuelled distractions, mindlessness seems to be on the rise and there is evidence this is not a healthy trend. When you are mindless you act like an automaton, relying not on active thoughts but an unconscious accessing of past experience.

Discussion

Has this ever happened to you? You grab your phone to check the time but you get a message from a friend with a link to a video of a kitten drinking a soda; this makes you think about how a kitten might react to a caffeinated energy drink. A few clicks later and you have your answer; now you start to wonder what is actually in those drinks. A few more clicks and a couple more messages later you have forgotten why you pulled your phone out in the first place.

Mindfulness seems directly at odds with the lifestyle of most young people today. Our digital connections mean we live every moment with limitless opportunities for distraction. Nicholas Carr, author of *The Shallows: What the Internet is Doing to Our Brains,* argues that we should be aware that constantly being online is eroding our ability to pay attention and build memories.

Do you think overuse of smartphones and the internet is undermining our ability to think deeply? What makes you say that?

Many still consider meditation or mindfulness to be "flakey" and without scientific support, something akin to quasi-scientific practices like phrenology. Jon Kabat-Zinn is credited with the recent resurgence and global awareness that mindfulness techniques have enjoyed in the past 20 years. Kabat-Zinn has been careful to avoid casting mindfulness as unscientific. In his words, "from the beginning of MBSR, I bent over backward to structure it and find ways to speak about it that avoided as much as possible the risk of it being seen as Buddhist, 'New Age', 'Eastern Mysticism' or just plain 'flakey'" (Kabat-Zinn, 2011).

He has specifically focused on the usefulness of mindfulness in stress reduction, what he calls **mindfulness-based stress reduction (MBSR)**. There is a growing body of evidence that misconceptions regarding the "flakiness" of MBSR are increasingly out of step with scientific investigation into the benefits of meditation.

See video

Watch Andy Puddicombe's TED Talk on mindfulness, available at https://www.ted.com/talks/andy_puddicombe_all_it_takes_is_10_mindful_minutes

▶ ❙❙ ■

365

MBSR interventions in the workplace have been successful in reducing stress and anxiety while improving concentration, vigour and overall health. **Aitkens *et al* (2014)**, in a study of Dow Chemical employees, aimed to determine whether an online mindfulness programme would be effective in reducing employee stress while enhancing resilience and well-being. Researchers recruited 89 Dow Chemical employees and randomly assigned 44 to the online MBSR intervention with 45 being placed on a waiting list (control). Participants completed self-reports on perceived stress, mindfulness, and resilience before and after the intervention, and again six months after. The MBSR intervention group had significantly decreased perceived levels of stress and increased mindfulness, resilience and vigour. According to this study, online MBSR interventions appear to be an effective protective factor against workplace stress and its related diseases.

In support of the research at Dow Chemical, a literature review of research on MBSR and nursing professionals found empirical evidence that using MBSR with nurses and other health-care professionals provides several benefits including decreased stress, burnout and anxiety while increasing empathy, focus, and mood (Smith, 2014).

Perhaps even more surprisingly, preliminary research by **Loucks *et al* (2015)** on a sample of 382 people in the state of Rhode Island in the USA has found that mindfulness is positively correlated with cardiovascular health. The study measured mindfulness using the Mindful Attention Awareness Scale (MAAS) while cardiovascular health was measured using American Heart Association criteria. Researchers found that mindfulness played a role in reducing risk factors related to smoking, overweight/obesity and lack of physical exercise.

It would appear that the modern workplace full of the latest gadgets and technology has some important lessons to learn from ancient practices a universe away from our digital work environment. Stepping away from technology and distractions may be part of the solution to solving the current pandemic of workplace stress.

Discussion

Look at the tips below on mindfulness. Would you find these useful in your everyday life?

You can find apps teaching mindfulness techniques at https://www.mindful.org/free-mindfulness-apps-worthy-of-your-attention/.

How to be mindful

- Stop multitasking: focus on one thing at a time and do only one thing at a time.

- Avoid distractions: practise being in the present moment.

- Limit your time on social media and online gaming.

- Practise, practise, practise: mindfulness has better results when it becomes a habit.

TOK

Religious knowledge systems

Mindfulness is based on the ancient Buddhist concept of dharma. There is no single accepted definition of dharma but it relates to the idea that all things are interconnected and inseparable parts of a united whole.

Mindfulness seems to have measurable, scientific support.

To what extent are religious knowledge systems such as Buddhism compatible with science and scientific inquiry? Are religious knowledge systems like Buddhism any more or less relevant today than they were centuries ago?

Promoting health

Physical activity can be an effective buffer against stress. This may seem paradoxical because exercise increases levels of circulating cortisol, the so-called stress hormone. Exercise improves your overall health and well-being and triggers the release of endorphins and noradrenaline. Endorphins are related to pain reduction and act similarly to drugs such as codeine and morphine. Despite the widely accepted belief that exercise reduces stress, the mechanisms through which exercise reduces stress are still not fully understood.

Yoga is also an effective buffer against stress. Yoga is a widely practised technique that uses breath control, simple meditation and specific postures for relaxation and well-being. Like mindfulness, it has its roots in ancient eastern practices. **Pascoe and Bauer (2015)** performed a systematic review of studies examining the effects of yoga on the sympathetic nervous system and hypothalamic-pituitary-adrenal axis (HPA). They reviewed 25 randomized control studies and found preliminary evidence that practising yoga leads to better regulation of the sympathetic nervous system and hypothalamic-pituitary-adrenal system. Both of these systems are key components of the biological stress response. They also found that yoga contributes to a decrease in anxiety and depressive symptoms in a range of populations. Yoga also happens to be particularly well suited to the office as it can be done in plain clothes, it is inexpensive and it need not take a long time.

Having someone to talk to and share hardship with can help with stress as well. **Social support** can act as a protective factor against stress. A study carried out by **Pow *et al* (2016)** examined the effect of social support on paramedics. Eighty-seven participants were asked to keep a diary describing their perceived stress, social support and sleep quality for one week. As workplace stress can have a negative effect on sleep quality, researchers were interested in finding out if social support could improve the quality of sleep among their sample. It was found that paramedics who reported more social support also reported better quality sleep over the week while those with lower levels of social support reported poor quality sleep.

It seems clear that interpersonal social support is important in reducing the effects of stress but recent research has illustrated that perceived support from online social networks may also play a role in stress reduction. **Nabi, Prestin and So (2013)** carried out a survey of 401 undergraduate students that revealed that a larger number of Facebook friends resulted in stronger perceptions of social support. This was then associated with reduced stress, less physical illness and greater well-being. This perhaps relates to the idea that it is the *perception* of social support that matters. If this is so, then a simple count of the number of Facebook friends a person has should suffice as a measurement of social support. This method does not seem to account for the quality or closeness of friendships.

Social support as a coping mechanism is culturally dependant. Research by **Kim, Sherman and Taylor (2008)** found that different cultures were more or less likely to use social support as a coping strategy. Researchers studied 603 adults.They found that Asians and Asian Americans were more reluctant to seek support from friends than European Americans because Asian Americans were concerned about possible negative consequences of their request. So it would seem that cultural differences in seeking help would impact the likelihood of using social support as a protective factor against stress.

In short, stress comes at us from many directions and coping with stress, whether it be through mindfulness, physical activity, yoga or social support, is an important skillset to master. Engaging in regular coping strategies such as these can be an effective protective factor that can provide a buffer against the risk factors associated with chronic stress.

Topics

Introduction

No explanation of human behaviour would be complete without a look at the psychology of human relationships. People derive meaning, identity and fulfilment through their relationships. In many ways, it is our relationships that define us. The field of social psychology looks at how individual behaviour is shaped by the societies we live in and the groups with which we choose to belong. The psychology of human relationships is closely related to and largely defined by social psychology.

The psychology of human relationships deals mainly with relationships between individuals in personal or group relations as opposed to the effect of the society or culture on behaviour. Reseacrh in this field aims to improve interpersonal relationships, promote prosocial behaviour, and to gain a better understanding of the complex world of human relationships.

The formation and maintenance of relationships is a complex process that requires an understanding of the biological roots of attraction, cognitive processes surrounding decision-making, and sociocultural explanations for interpersonal behaviour.

What you will learn in this section

- Introduction to the psychology of human relationships

- Formation of personal relationships

  - Biology and interpersonal relationships: evolution and mate selection; Helen Fisher—is love a physical addiction?; oxytocin and vasopressin; major histocompatibility (MHC) genes

  - Cognition and interpersonal relationships: reciprocity (we like those who like us); familiarity (we like those we meet often); similarity (we like those who are like us); matching (we tend to match with someone of similar attractiveness but often try for better)

  - Culture and interpersonal relationships: individualism/collectivism; arranged marriages

- The role of communication in personal relationships

  - Social penetration theory: self-disclosure increases liking

  - Attributional style: positive attributional patterns are a sign of a healthy relationship

  - Patterns of accommodation: constructive communication unites people

- Explanations for why relationships change or end

  - Gottman's Four Horsemen: criticism, contempt, defensiveness, stonewalling; Gottman claims to be able to predict relationship failure with over 90% success

  - Relationship frameworks: Knapp and Vangelisti's model for change in relationships; Rollie and Duck's five-stage model of relationship breakdown

This section also links to:

- hormones and behaviour—oxytocin (biological approach to behaviour)

- how technology has affected interpersonal relationships (cognitive approach to behaviour)

- how globalization has influenced attitudes, identities, and behaviour towards interracial dating and marriage (sociocultural approach to behaviour).

"The greatest thing you'll ever learn is just to love and be loved in return."

Eden Ahbez (songwriter)

It is perhaps the biggest of all understatements to say that love is an interesting and complex topic. Love is the central theme in countless paintings, sculptures, poems, movies and songs. It is the central motivating factor in much human behaviour. Despite being ubiquitous and nearly universally felt, it is one of the central mysteries of the human condition. What makes us fall in love? Why might love fade over time?

Formation of personal relationships

Biology and interpersonal relationships

Biologically, we can explain behaviour through evolutionary psychological explanations and biological processes such as the effects of hormones and genes. Some of the most fundamental explanations of relationship formation derive from evolutionary theories. These theories argue that many human behaviours have a basis in our distant past. The assumption is that behaviours that are beneficial in passing on our genes will be carried on through generations. One important component in this theory is **mate selection** and **relationship formation**.

There are certain universal traits that are considered physically attractive. Both sexes tend to be attracted to characteristics that signal health, youth and reproductive capacity. Traits such as smooth skin, good muscle tone, lustrous hair and full lips are considered universally attractive (Buss, 1989). Evolutionary arguments for mate selection should be universally applicable to all homo sapiens and transcend culture.

Evolutionary explanations

Gender plays a role in the determination of desirable characteristics in a mate. **Buss (1989)** completed a study to test for gender differences in mate selection. Researchers conducted a huge study of 37 samples including over 10,000 participants across 6 continents and 33 countries. Participants filled out questionnaires that contained three main sections. The first section asked for biographical information related to age,

religion, gender, and so on; a second section asked about their desired age of marriage as well as desired age differentials between spouses; a third section asked participants to rate 18 characteristics on how important they are in choosing a mate.

One limitation of many studies in the social sciences is the fact that studies often rely on self-reported data, that is, responses may not reflect actual, real-life outcomes but instead the perceptions of participants. In an attempt to check the credibility of the data, Buss checked age preferences in the second section of his 1989 questionnaire against actual marriage statistics of the countries in question. He found that the stated preferred age differences between spouses was reflected in actual age differences at marriage and that both preferred age of marriage and preferred age of mate corresponded closely to actual ages of grooms and brides (Buss, 1989).

Buss found that there were significant gender differences in the responses. Results showed that females valued the financial capacity of mates more than males. Women rated "financial capacity" higher in 36 of 37 samples and "ambition and industriousness" higher in 29 of 37. Women also preferred older males in all 37 samples. It was also found that males value physical attractiveness and youth more than females. These findings showed wide generalizability across cultures, suggesting something shared by all cultures and societies—common biological determinants.

These findings give support to an evolutionary theory of mate selection for both males and females. Males, in valuing youth and attractiveness, show a preference for females showing cues to high reproductive capacity. Females, in valuing financial capacity and age, show a preference for males that will be successful partners in raising children; additionally, age and success may also be cues to good genes.

These findings have been supported in many other studies including one on 402 Portuguese and Brazilian university students which found that men rated physical attractiveness more important than women did, while women identified "personality", "resources" and "abilities" as more important, (Neto, Da Conceição Pinto and Furnham, 2012). Shackelford et al (2005) likewise found in a cross-cultural study that women valued social status more than men and men valued physical attractiveness more than women.

See video

Watch the Discovery Channel documentary *The Science of Sex Appeal*.

https://www.discovery.com/playlists/science-of-sex-appeal-videos

A qualitative and quantitative research study conducted by **Boxer, Noonan and Whelan (2015)** found that over the past 20 years, both males and females have placed an increasingly higher value on a mate's financial prospects as well as a desire for a home and children. One strength of the qualitative method here is that emergent themes, not included in Buss' original 18 characteristics, were identified as humour, trust and loyalty. Similarly, **Buss *et al* (2001)** found that, over time, men and women are becoming more similar in mate selection preferences. "Chastity" and "domestic skill" both plummeted in importance in this research. Chastity was placed tenth (out of 18) for men in 1989 but dropped to last spot (eighteenth) in Buss' 1996 findings (cited in Buss *et al*, 2001). "Mutual attraction and love" climbed in importance for both sexes in the same period. These changes are too rapid to reflect biological change and instead point towards changing gender and social roles over the past century as an engine of change in mate preference. It is also worth noting that samples for these studies were taken from the USA, reflecting change in that one culture, not a global shift.

Attraction as addiction

Dr Helen Fisher makes the argument that intensely passionate romantic love is a neurobiological process similar to drug addiction. Fisher sampled ten women and seven men who reported being deeply in love. Participants filled out a questionnaire about their feelings toward their loved one, then were placed in an fMRI machine. Participants were shown a photograph of their loved one, then performed a distraction task, then shown a photograph of an acquaintance of theirs for whom they did not feel love. Each participant did this six times.

Results of the study using fMRI show that the same brain mechanism active in substance abuse, that is, the **mesolimbic dopamine reward pathway**, is also active when individuals think about a romantic partner. **Fisher *et al* (2016)** argued that the early state of intense, romantic love shares many symptoms with substance abuse (such as alcohol, nicotine or cocaine) and addictive behaviours (such as gambling)—for example, euphoria, craving, tolerance, dependence (emotional and physical), and withdrawal.

See video

Watch the Ted Talk "The brain in love" https://www.ted.com/talks/helen_fisher_studies_the_brain_in_love

This intense, passionate love will soon give way to longer-term, calm attachment. Fisher argues that this connection between relationships and drug addiction should be the basis for research into social support and bonding in the treatment of substance abuse and addictive behaviours (Fisher, Aron and Brown, 2016).

Related fMRI research has shown that physical pain and social exclusion activate the same part of the brain: **the anterior cingulate cortex**. Participants were scanned during a simulated (computer-generated) ball-tossing game from which they were eventually excluded. The fMRI scan results correlated with self-reported feelings of distress (**Eisenberger, Lieberman and Williams, 2003**). Findings suggest that the neurocognition of physical pain and social pain are comparable in certain respects. Pain is an alarm system alerting us to potential injury; it appears that we are similarly alerted to social injuries and loss. Science has caught up with poetry, as it turns out that loss of love really can hurt.

Hormones

The hormone **oxytocin** has also been found to play an important role in the first stages of animal and human bonding and in parent–infant bonding, suggesting a similar mechanism for many types of love and attachment. The field of **neuroendocrinology** studies the role of hormones and the brain and is a rich area of research concerning the role of oxytocin in bonding. Oxytocin in rats has been shown to play a role in mother–pup bonding. Removing oxytocin in a mother rat by either blocking the hormone or injecting receptor antagonists will result in neglect of the infant pup (**Strathearn, 2001**). (See also the section on hormones and behaviour in Unit 2 on the biological approach to behaviour.)

Human research also supports the theory of oxytocin's role in bonding. Schneiderman *et al* (2012) sampled 60 couples in new relationships (average of 2.4 months). A control group of 43 single individuals was also sampled. The individuals in relationships were interviewed independently and then as a couple and blood samples were taken to measure plasma oxytocin levels. Findings showed that higher levels of plasma oxytocin correlated with affectionate touching, a preoccupation with a partner, interpersonal focus, and dyadic states (that is, when both partners are engaged and interact equally). These findings echo findings of research previously conducted into parent–infant bonding and show that the same mechanism is in place for parent-child bonds as in enduring romantic bonds.

Other research has found evidence of this relationship, including a study by Ruth Feldman. Feldman (2013) suggests that oxytocin plays a role in all social interactions in humans. Feldman measured behaviour related to social bonding including gaze, touch, vocal, physical and facial (affective) expressions. Oxytocin was found to support the three major social bonds in humans: parental, pair and filial. It was also found that oxytocin supports bonding throughout life, not simply during parenting and romantic bonding.

Another hormone called **vasopressin** has been found to play a role in stable, long-term pair bonding in prairie voles. Prairie voles are rodents who actively select mates, are monogamous, share parenting and are characterized by long-term pair bonds. These shared social characteristics, along with similar brain structures and neurochemical make-up, seem to make them a perfect candidate to study social behaviour in humans. Researchers were able to show that vasopressin was necessary and sufficient for both aggression toward non-mates as well as mate preference formation (**Winslow *et al*, 1993**).

Major histocompatibility genes

One last example of a possible biological contributor to human relationships is related to body odour, genes and our immune system or our major histocompatibility complex (MHC). An interesting area of research is looking into how MHC may influence mate selection. The idea is that parents with differences in their MHC genes will pass on a stronger (more broadly defensive) immune system to their children because children inherit immune function from both parents. Evolutionary psychologists argue that we may have evolved ways to detect the level of MHC similarity between individuals. One line of research in this area is related to scent: we prefer the scent of those with more different MHC genes.

Psychology in real life

A pheromone is a chemical substance produced and released into the environment by an animal, especially a mammal or an insect, affecting the behaviour or physiology of others of its species. There is a growing industry in pheromones, and even dating sites that offer a scent-based match-making service. For an example go to: www.pheromoneparties.com.

Research into the role of MHC genes on mate selection has empirical support in both animal and human studies (Lee, 2010). However, the extent to which individual humans can identify dissimilarity in MHC genes through scent is controversial. The well-known "dirty shirt" study conducted by **Wedekind et al (1995)** claimed a correlation between attactiveness of men's scent to women and MHC dissimilarity, suggesting that, although they may not be able to express why, women prefer the scent of MHC dissimilar men.

Wedekind and his colleagues MHC typed 44 men and 49 women. The women were asked to rate the attractiveness of the odour of t-shirts worn by six men, three MHC similar and three dissimilar. The researchers found that women rated the odour of MHC dissimilar men as "more pleasant". Additionally, the scent of MHC dissimilar men was twice as likely to remind the women of their mate's scent. The researchers also found that women who were taking oral contraceptives reversed the findings: they preferred the scent of MHC similar men. The researchers hypothesized that because contraceptives mimic a state of pregnancy, the woman's biological response may have been to seek the support of kin and family as opposed to seeking a mate. Confusingly, further research by Wedekind and Furi two years later found that men were just as likely to prefer a man's scent to a woman's (**Wedekind and Furi, 1997**).

Research into the connection between MHC genes and mate selection has shown that women may prefer men with dissimilar MHC but findings are not consistent. In one review, researchers discovered that research was mixed: findings for MHC dissimilarity showed a bias towards similarity in one study, dissimilarity in two studies and a random distribution in several other studies. They also point to the fact that research into facial attractiveness has indicated a preference for MHC similar individuals, which would counter MHC dissimilarity theories (Havlicek and Roberts, 2009). However, a recent study points out potential reasons for the inconsistency of findings. Winternitz and Abate (2015) argue that in the 34 studies they reviewed, there was too much inconsistency in context (long-term or short-term relationships) and hormonal variations for findings to be valid. Future studies, they argue, should work to gain a better understanding of how these variables influence mate choice.

twin pairs. The researchers claim that genes predisposing a person to homosexuality confer an evolutionary advantage in heterosexuals which in turn helps to explain (through evolutionary psychology) the maintenance of homosexuality in human populations (Zeitsch *et al*, 2008).

Do you accept this evolutionary explanation of homosexuality? What makes you say that?

Cognition and interpersonal relationships

There are many cognitive determinants of attraction studied by social psychologists. **Reciprocity** is based on social exchange within a relationship. This simple theory argues that we like those who like us. This is related to self-esteem, self-enhancement and self-verification. People who like us are validating the choices we have made in constructing a self-image. They are also people who will likely be pleased to interact with us and help us in the future. Reciprocity is supported in empirical research. In a classic study, researchers found that when people feel welcomed and accepted in a group, they are more attracted to that group. When they feel poorly accepted they are not attracted. These findings were magnified with people who show low self-esteem (Dittes, 1959). Reciprocity also seems to increase over time so that an upward spiral of attraction will result from mutual feelings of likeability (Kenny and La Voie, 1982).

Familiarity is another cognitive determinant of interpersonal relationships. The familiarity hypothesis states that we like things that we see repetitively. The more we see an object or a face, the more we like it. This is true for both strangers' faces and acquaintances. This is a result of the **mere-exposure effect**; simply being exposed to something increases our liking of it (Zajonc and Mcguire, 1968). This theory has profound implications for advertising and political messages as well as on interpersonal relations. A study conducted on Facebook advertisements showed that among the 121 participants, those exposed to online adverts for beer (compared to water adverts) are more likely to select a bar gift card as an incentive for participation than one from a coffee shop (Alhabash *et al*, 2016).

The **attraction–similarity model** states that we are attracted to those we perceive to be similar to ourselves. This could be similarity in ethnicity, age, culture, social class, or any number of other areas. Perception is important here as actual similarity is not measured in most studies. Similarity has been shown in research to extend to physical traits as well as personality, attitudes and beliefs. Dr Marian Morry conducted a study that supported the attraction–similarity hypothesis; the more attracted we are to another individual the more we believe that this individual is similar to us (Morry, 2005). Similar research by Morry shows that friends not of the same sex perceived each other to be more similar to themselves, regardless of actual similarity, and that greater satisfaction in a friendship predicted similarity between friends (Morry, 2005).

A Dutch study of university undergraduate students supports Morry's findings. **Selfhout *et al* (2009)** discovered in a sample of approximately 400 participants that perceived similarity correlated with stronger liking scores. If participants recognized similarities, there was a greater chance they would like the person they perceived as similar. Underscoring the cognitive nature of this relationship is the fact that **perceived** similarity was more important than actual similarity in liking the other person.

The **matching hypothesis** predicts that individuals will assess their own attractiveness or social desirability and select partners who match their levels in these areas. **Berscheid *et al* (1971)** supports the matching hypothesis and presents reasons why previous studies may have failed to support the theory. They claim that the matching hypothesis may be a stronger predictor of the level of desirability of a person someone is willing to approach, more than how much another will be liked and pursued as a romantic partner. Overall, they found that members of the opposite sex will attempt interactions with people of similar levels of physical attractiveness.

In a real-world setting, however, different results were obtained. **Taylor *et al* (2011)** sampled 182 mostly Asian and European American undergraduates in an online experimental setting and again in an actual online dating scenario. In both samples, researchers found that both high self-worth and low self-worth participants were likely to contact more attractive participants

(Taylor *et al*, 2011). This may be the result of a common misappraisal of one's own attractiveness as a mate or simply that people are willing to face rejection for a shot at coupling with a more attractive partner. Either way, these findings seem to challenge the matching hypothesis.

Culture and interpersonal relationships

As the formation of relationships is, at its core, a social phenomenon, we must look to social origins of interpersonal relationships. Interestingly, **proximity** leads to frequency of meeting (mere-exposure effect) and so to familiarity but it seems to have an important role in human relationships on its own merit. It was once true that you had to meet someone face to face in order to establish a relationship but the internet has changed this. The internet and the rise of online dating sites, unrestricted by proximity, may be wearing away this social determinant of human relationships. We will revisit online social interactions later in this section.

Individualism and collectivism

Cultural factors play a strong role in interpersonal relationships. Specifically, **Dion and Dion (1993)** examined the influence of individualism/collectivism on romantic love and intimacy in marriage. They examined research done in two individualistic cultures (USA and Canada) and three collectivistic cultures (India, China and Japan). From the findings of multiple studies, researchers suggested ways in which individualism or collectivism could influence interpersonal relations.

- Romantic love is more likely to be the basis for marriage in individualistic cultures than in collectivistic cultures.

- Intimacy in marriage is more about satisfaction with marriage and personal wellness in individualistic cultures.

Dion and Dion pointed out that these findings may seem counterintuitive because individualism values romantic love and intimacy but a psychologically individual mindset should value independence rather than connection with others.

In later research, Dion and Dion argued that although culture plays a role in interpersonal relations, the process of acculturation is changing how. They argue that changes in cultural norms

related to romantic love are evident in collectivistic cultures and among immigrants from collectivistic cultures to individualistic ones. For example, it is no longer acceptable to assume that members of a Japanese (or Japanese American) sample will tend toward a collectivist mindset due to an increasing acculturation, especially among young and educated individuals.

Cultural differences are also evident in views on interracial dating, providing a link to social identity theory. For example, in response to a scenario describing conflict between a young adult and a parent regarding interracial dating, Chinese Canadian youths supported the parent's objections to the relationship more than European Canadian youths did. European Canadian males were also more favourable to interracial dating than Chinese Canadian males. However, Chinese Canadian acculturation with mainstream Canadian norms was suggested as higher endorsement of mainstream cultural identity was associated with greater support for the young adult in the scenario. Greater identification with mainstream Canadian culture also reflected more favourable attitudes and openness to interracial dating **(Uskul *et al*, 2007)**.

These findings were replicated in a similar study on South Asian Canadians. This study examined generational influences on attitudes to interracial dating. The method was similar to the above study using the conflict scenario between a young adult and a parent. Findings suggested that among South Asian Canadians, younger generations were more favourable to interracial dating and supported the young adult in the scenario. Canadian identity was again associated with more favourable views on interracial dating (Uskal, 2011).

Culture and marriage

Evidence, and intuition, tells us that love is a universal emotion experienced by most people across time and culture. It seems, though, that it manifests itself differently based on culture and it can have a profound influence on the way people behave, think and feel about romantic relationships (Karandashev, 2015). If romantic love is indeed universal but looks different in different cultures, it is important to examine its emic expression in a variety of cultures (Jankowiak and Fischer, 1992). One example of a difference in how love is expressed is its verbalization.

In many western cultures people do not consider it a big issue to express their love verbally with others; the words "I love you" tend to come easily. This is not the case in many other cultures around the world. Research by Nadal (cited in Karandashev, 2015) found that in Filipino families, verbal expressions of love are rare and saved for special events. Love is, instead, expressed through daily and indirect means such as sharing a laugh or working together on a problem of importance to one or both partners.

Cultural practices and traditions sometimes have a very direct and profound impact on relationships. Social norms vary on many issues, including taboos surrounding marrying outside the clan or ethnic group, appropriate marrying age, same-sex marriage, and arranged marriages. Culture is a key determinant of marriage and interpersonal relationships today.

Henrich, Heine and Norenzayan (2010) found that most psychology research focuses on western, educated, industrial, rich and democratic (WEIRD) societies which tend towards a tradition of marrying for love. This may skew conclusions towards a western bias. By many accounts, however, arranged marriages are still the most common form of marriage worldwide. A 2013 survey by IPSOS (a global market research and consulting firm) found that nearly 75% of Indians between 18 and 35 preferred arranged marriages to free-choice marriages (Dholakia, 2015). Generally speaking, collectivistic cultures consider the practice of arranged marriages more acceptable than individualistic cultures. Arranged marriages should not be confused with forced marriage as they are not necessarily the same thing.

▲ Figure 7.1 Shanghai's marriage market

Exercise

What is the difference between the following types of arranged marriage? Discuss the following types.

- Traditional
- Delegation (or assisted)
- Joint (or partnership)

Many studies have been conducted on the relative happiness of individuals in arranged and love marriages. **Regan, Lakhanpal and Anguiano (2012)** conducted a study to examine this comparison. They sampled 58 Indian couples living in the USA (28 arranged and 30 love marriages). Participants completed measures on marital satisfaction, commitment, companionate love and passionate love. No differences were found between participants in arranged and love marriages; high ratings of love, satisfaction and commitment were seen in both groups. Similar findings have been found in multiple studies (Gupta and Singh, 1982; Myers, Madathil and Tingle, 2005). Other studies have even found that arranged marriages resulted in happier, more satisfied couples (Xiaohe and Whyte, 1990).

These studies often rely on self-reporting questionnaires as "happiness" and "satisfaction" are both subjective states that cannot be accurately measured by a third party. This raises some potential problems as members of collectivistic cultures may be less likely to share negative feelings regarding their marriage because of the fear of upsetting the social harmony surrounding the collective nature of their mate choice.

Psychology in real life

Modernization and technology does not seem to be affecting the number of arranged marriages. Instead sites such as https://www.bharatmatrimony.com/ are increasing in number and represent a modern twist on delegation/assisted marriages.

Psychology in real life (continued)

The arranged marriage site http://www.hindur.com/ takes things one step further. It promises to find your perfect match by automating your profile creation using your Facebook profile. It has been described as Tinder for arranged marriages (Hirschlag, 2016).

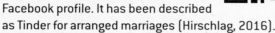

Putting this into context, technology may be replacing family input in arranged marriages.

For the purpose of clarity and simplification, we have separated this study of human relationships into convenient but arbitrary categories. It is important to remember that this type of categorical thinking is artificial and that attempting to explain any human behaviour in simplified terms is doomed to failure. Human social interactions are multifaceted and are always the result of very complex processes; millions of years of evolution, split-second neurochemical interactions and everything in between combine to influence our behaviours. Social situations are further complicated by the interplay between individuals, each with millions of years of genetic history and their own set of neurochemical balances.

See video

Watch the TED Talk "Alone together: why we expect more from technology and less from each other" available at https://www.ted.com/talks/sherry_turkle_alone_together.

Another interesting TED Talk on technology and love is available at https://www.ted.com/talks/helen_fisher_technology_hasn_t_changed_love_here_s_why

▶ ❚❚ ■

Discussion

Do you think online dating and social networking sites have improved our chances of finding true love?

The role of communication in interpersonal relationships

Every relationship is as unique as the individuals within it, however, when it comes to exploring why relationships change or end, there are some important patterns that emerge. These patterns can shed light on the reasons why connections that bond people are not always enduring.

Social penetration theory

Individuals don't share their deepest desires and concerns with just anyone; they choose very carefully who to share their innermost thoughts with. Social penetration theory argues that as relationships develop over time, exchanges between individuals move from a more shallow level to a more intimate level. Intimacy is characterized by greater discussion of emotions and feelings as well as self-doubt and concerns regarding identity and self-worth. This theory was originally put forward by **Altman and Taylor (1973)**.

In a meta-analysis of disclosure-liking studies, Collins, Miller and Steinberg (1994) confirmed three distinct disclosure-liking effects.

- Individuals who share at an intimate level tend to be more liked than those who share at a more shallow level.

- Individuals share more with those they initially like.

- Individuals like others as a result of having shared intimately with them.

These findings suggest that self-disclosure may be an important element in the formation as well as maintenance of relationships.

There also appear to be significant gender differences in self-disclosure. In a meta-analysis of 205 studies involving more than 23,000 participants, **Dindia, Allen and Steinberg (1992)** found that women disclosed more than men and that women tended to share more with other women than with men, especially when the target of the sharing was already a friend, relative or spouse.

In an online study of Facebook, Utz (2015) found that feelings of closeness and connection were enhanced on the site through intimate communication in private conversations (reinforcing classic social penetration theory), and entertaining and positive updates. Interestingly, the responsiveness of the communication partner had no significant impact on feelings of closeness.

Self-disclosure not only strengthens relationships but has been shown to be beneficial for the individuals doing the sharing. **Huang (2016)** examined the online self-disclosure habits of 333 Facebook users. Huang found that self-disclosure led to increased social support from other people on the social networking site, and also increased the reported happiness and satisfaction of their online experience. This suggests that communication and self-disclosure may strengthen individuals in a relationship as well as the strength of the bond between partners.

However, we must be cautious with the findings of online social penetration studies. **Callaghan, Graff and Davies (2013)** found that experimental evidence of self-disclosure may be skewed. Interviews conducted with 42 participants in laboratory and non-laboratory conditions found significantly higher self-disclosure in laboratory interviews, including longer and more intimate responses. These findings suggest that having a researcher present may influence the responses of the interviewee and stimulate more self-disclosure than in a more natural online setting where there is no researcher present.

Attribution style

Attribution theory is introduced in the unit on social psychology. This theory states that we understand the behaviours of ourselves and others by attributing behaviours to causes. Generally, these are either situational or dispositional. Attribution of behaviours in relationships is important because it is so tightly related to forgiveness and empathy among spouses.

Healthy relationships are characterized by an attributional style that has a positive bias toward one's partner. Individuals tend to assume best intent on the part of their significant other. Positive or helpful behaviours are attributed to personal disposition while negative or unhelpful

behaviours are attributed to situational factors. Universal statements including words such as "always" and "never" are used to describe their spouse in a positive light. For example, "he always works hard" or "he never hurts anyone's feelings". In contrast, negative attributional style can hurt a relationship. In this situation, universal statements are made that highlight personal attributes that are unsavoury. For example, "he's never on time" or "she loves to belittle people". Consistent negative attributions can lead to the end of a relationship and should not be underestimated.

This theoretical relationship has been found in research. Thirty-two marital couples (including both distressed and non-distressed couples) were sampled and each was given a hypothetical behaviour by their spouses. Participants were asked to rate the most likely cause for the behaviour, how the action would make them feel, and state what their response to the action would be. Research by **Fincham and O'Leary (1983)** found that for positive acts, the non-distressed couples assumed causes of the behaviour to be controllable (dispositional) while the distressed couples considered more negative behaviours to be controllable. This seems to imply that distressed couples considered positive acts as situational and non-distressed couples considered negative acts as uncontrollable.

Stratton (2003) has also shown that individuals in distressed family relationships make more global attributions about negative behaviour. In interviews, Stratton found that families averaged a surprising four attributions per minute during therapy. After coding the results he discovered that parents and children in distressed family relationships showed attribution patterns consistent with blaming others in the family for negative behaviour; in this case, children were most often the targets of blame for family conflict.

However, critics have raised concerns, arguing that distress within a marriage may cause a change in the attributional style, affecting the stability of the relationship. In other words, the direction of the relationship between marital satisfaction and attribution depends on whether researchers consider the pattern of attribution as a state of mind or an enduring trait of character. Those who claim attribution style determines marital satisfaction are also claiming that attributional style is largely a stable, unchanging trait. In this way, the causality of the relationship between attribution style and marital satisfaction is seen mostly as a one-way causality; critics argue this may not be the case.

In an attempt to decipher this tangle, **Karney and Bradbury (2000)** attempted a longitudinal analysis of attribution patterns in relationships to measure any difference between attribution style and satisfaction. They conducted a study measuring attributional style and marital satisfaction every 6 months for 8 years among 60 couples who had only recently married at the start of the study. Couples were offered cash to participate in the study and were recruited through a newspaper advert asking for couples interested in participating in a study of marriage.

Examining the 16 waves of longitudinal data, researchers found that rather than being constant for each individual, attributional style between spouses appeared to change as their satisfaction changed, suggesting attributional style is not a stable, unchanging trait. However, attributional style predicted change in marital satisfaction more than change in satisfaction predicted changes in attributions, suggesting there is a causal dominance of attributions. It turns out that the relationship is a complicated one but that even though both variables, attributional style and marital satisfaction, are dynamic, there remains a causal direction from attribution to marital satisfaction.

Attribution retraining is a cognitive treatment to change the way an individual tends to attribute behaviour. As a treatment it has been successfully applied to cases of bullying, depression, anxiety and eating disorders. However, researchers and relationship specialists have considered attribution training as a way to improve negative attribution style between individuals (both marital and family therapy). Karney and Bradbury's findings (2000) seem to suggest that attributional style is dynamic so cognitive therapy may be helpful in nudging it in a positive direction (Hilt, 2004). (See Unit 8 on developmental psychology for a discussion on cause-effect inferences.)

Patterns of accommodation

Whether or not therapy will be useful depends on the willingness of those in a relationship to deal constructively with conflict and to communicate openly. A relationship is not something that "happens" to someone; we are active agents in our lives and our decisions impact our behaviour and the behaviour of others. So, how individuals respond to conflict is very important. When positive, constructive strategies are used to maintain a relationship it is called **accommodation**.

Rusbult and Zembrodt (1983) conducted a series of studies to identify common responses to dissatisfaction in relationships among university undergraduates. Fifty students were asked to write an essay about a time in their life when they became dissatisfied in a relationship, describe their feelings and what they did about their unhappiness in the relationship. The researchers identified four main strategies that were either passive or active, and constructive or destructive: exit, voice, loyalty and neglect. Exit and voice are active responses while loyalty and neglect are passive strategies.

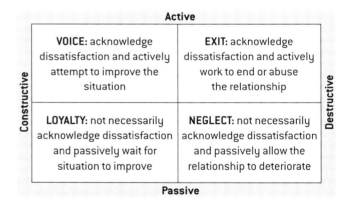

▲ Figure 7.2 Relationship conflict strategies

In addition to the conflict strategies identified by Rusbult and Zembrodt, earlier research identified probable reasons for the choice of the various strategies. In a 1982 study of 402 undergraduate students, researchers found that prior satisfaction and an individual's investment in the relationship predicted constructive strategies. The perception of more attractive relationship options also promoted exit and limited loyalty (Rusbult *et al*, 1982). These findings are supported in further research by Rusbult *et al* in 1991. The latter research also found that women were more likely to accommodate than men.

Explanations of why relationships change or end

Communication is very important for a stable and healthy relationship and its importance should never be underestimated. As a result, there is significant conceptual overlap between the above section on communication and this one. There are several communication styles and relationship frameworks that deal specifically with change and end.

Gottman's Four Horsemen

The Gottman Institute is headed by a husband and wife team who offer research-based relationship advice. John Gottman and Julie Schwartz Gottman have studied thousands of relationships in what they call the Love Lab. Over decades and through longitudinal analysis of thousands of couples, the Gottmans claim to be able to predict relationship outcomes after observation, questionnaires and scientific analysis of interviews.

▲ Figure 7.3 John Gottman and Julie Schwartz Gottman

John Gottman's predictions centre around communication style and focus specifically on what have become commonly known as the Four Horsemen of relationship apocalypse. Gottman claims these negative elements are helpful in predicting divorce and that they typically enter a marriage in the following order (Listisa, 2017).

1. **Criticism**: a statement that attacks the character of a person—is not a simple complaint about a single issue. For example, it could be attributing negative behaviour to character (disposition) not situation, in other words, a negative attributional bias.

2. **Contempt**: treating someone with disrespect or mocking sarcasm. Gottman considers this the worst of the Four Horsemen and it is the primary predictor of divorce. This is a truly mean activity and is normally the result of long-term negative thoughts about a partner. For example, it could include insulting the partner, eye rolling or mocking behaviour.

3. **Defensiveness**: a self-defence mechanism in the form of claimed innocent victimization where the target of criticism claims to be under attack for no reason. For example, this could be deflecting blame onto others in an attempt to conceal guilt or complicity.

4. **Stonewalling**: a listener withdraws from a conversation by refusing to acknowledge the other person; the listener shuts down and refuses to communicate with the partner. For example, there could be a one-way conversation where one person is tuning out or turning away or engaging in obsessive behaviours.

Gottman claims to be able to predict whether a couple would divorce with an average of 90% accuracy across his longitudinal studies (Gottman, 2017). A thorough behavioural observation method is used with couples. Two remote controlled video cameras and microphones are used to help record the interaction. Biometric data is also recorded. The video and audio are placed in a split screen so that both individuals are visible while their biometric data, including polygraphs and electrocardiograms, is matched. Further to these, Gottman also collects self-report measures of mood and relationship history through individual interviews and questionnaires. This represents an impressive combination of both quantitative and qualitative data collection (Gottman *et al*, 1998; Gottman and Levensen, 2002; Carrère *et al*, 2000).

Discussion

1. A 90% successful prediction rate of divorce is a remarkable claim. Do you think it is possible to predict human behaviour?

2. Do you see any potential ethical concerns with Gottman's work?

3. Evaluate his research methods. Do you think the use of both qualitative and quantitative research methods strengthens his claim? What makes you say that?

4. What criticisms do you have of his methods?

TOK

The natural sciences are commonly evaluated by their predictive validity, that is, their ability to predict future events given empirical analysis of the past. This is not the case for the human sciences, but Gottman's research seems to have amazingly accurate predictive powers for divorce.

Do you think theories in the human sciences should be evaluated according to their predictive validity?

Therapy for couples and families is often designed to reverse deterioration and re-establish positive relations. This is the focus of the Gottman Institute; strengthening relationships. Although originally interested in researching why relationships deteriorate, Gottman has shifted focus to improving relationships. The Gottman Institute uses research gained over decades to present workshops on how to establish, repair or otherwise improve marriages. The claim is that if you can predict divorce, you should be able to implement an intervention to prevent divorce.

ATL skills: Communication and thinking

Write a newspaper article explaining Gottman's findings. No research or studies are needed in this exercise; this is about linking concepts and ideas.

Start with a headline, followed by a one-sentence hook, then a short explanation of the concept, with the most important information coming first.

If you have any doubts about the claim, consider writing a follow-up "letter to the editor" to question the article.

Relationship frameworks

So far we have concentrated on the importance of communication in relationships. It is impossible to separate discussions on the importance of communication from concepts of relationship breakdown because they are intimately connected. We will now look at more general relationship frameworks that claim to provide some explanation of how relationships change and/or end.

Relationships have identifiable stages, most simply a beginning, a middle and an end. **Knapp and Vangelisti (1996)** have created a model of change in relationships that shows two main stages: growth and breakdown. This simple framework provides a decent outline of how relationships both grow and deteriorate. It can help us to understand how a relationship changes and may eventually end. In this model, each stage is characterized by a different type of communication.

Movement through the stages is generally sequential and systematic. Although stages can be skipped, it is risky as each stage provides information needed by individuals in the following stage. Couples can go through the same stage more than once, but relationships never revert to a previous stage. For example, bonding and integrating will be revisited by couples throughout a relationship, but the stage will never be experienced in the same way twice because as the relationship evolves so do the individuals within it.

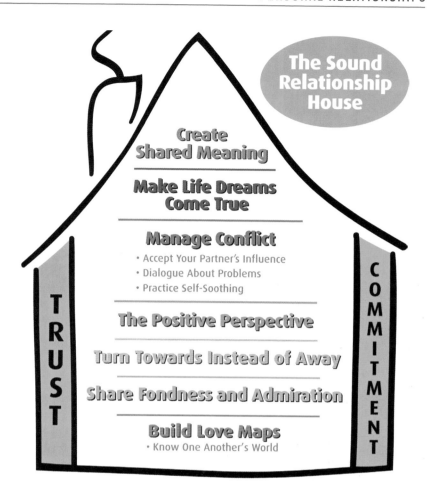

▲ Figure 7.4 The Gottman Method for Healthy Relationships

Relationship escalation

	Stage	Description
Growth	Initiation	This is a very short stage in which first impressions are made. Physical appearance is important and judgments are often inaccurate. We often "judge a book by its cover" and stereotypes play an important role at this stage.
	Experimenting	Each individual begins to explore the characteristics of the other. Many of the cognitive elements discussed above come into play here (attraction-similarity, reciprocity, and so on).
	Intensifying	This is where friendship begins and personal disclosure increases. Social penetration theory suggests that at this stage, intimacy begins to grow and relationships take root.
	Integrating	Intimacy continues to increase and close friendships or romantic associations begin.
	Bonding	This is often the first public stage of a relationship. Significant commitments are made that are mutually assured and recognized. Termination of the relationship normally requires formal dissolution.

▲ Table 7.1 Knapp and Vangelisti's stages of relational development

Relationship deterioration

	Stage	Description
Decline	Differentiating	This is where individuals may begin to grow apart and increasingly identify as individuals rather than a couple. This is often the result of external pressures or opportunities.
	Circumscribing	At this stage communication becomes problematic and Gottman's Four Horsemen may come into play in exchanges between partners.
	Stagnating	Communication is increasingly limited and couples recognize that the relationship is in serious danger of dissolution. At this stage it is normally external pressures such as family, cultural and social obligations or children that keep couples together.
	Avoiding	As the name of the stage implies, partners avoid contact and intimacy. This is evident physically, emotionally and communicatively. It is seen as the only option to avoid conflict.
	Terminating	This is the end of the relationship. It can be a formal, legal break such as a divorce or simply a mutual or one-sided decision to terminate the bond.

▲ Table 7.2 Knapp and Vangelisti's stages of relational development (continued)

In researching relationships, **Welch and Rubin (2002)** were frustrated with the subjective nature of relationship identification and looked for a more objective way of describing relationships. They wanted to be able to to quantify the way in which individuals spoke about their relationships. In short, how could researchers translate the subjective statements of individuals into measurable relationship stages? They turned to Knapp and Vangelisti's model and found it was a good way to quantify relationship stages, allowing for better definition of experimental findings. They found that the model provided a useful framework for standardizing subjective statements made by participants and encouraged future research in the area to use the model in an attempt to simplify comparison of findings across studies.

ATL skills: Thinking and communication

Play the role of a social psychology researcher. The following statements have been made by participants describing their relationships. From the statements below, identify what stage you believe their relationship is in. Defend your choice with a short explanation.

1. Communication between us is strained and difficult but we can still agree on many things.
2. I speak of our relationship in the past tense as it if were over.
3. I trust her completely; I am totally committed to her.
4. We share secrets and have in-depth discussions.
5. We don't talk to each other anymore.
6. So far I have only spoken briefly with this person.
7. Our friends refer to us as a couple.
8. Our conversations usually end in conflict.
9. I often make excuses to avoid him.

Rollie and Duck's five-stage model of relationship breakdown

Rollie and Duck (2006) have proposed a more specific model dealing with relationship breakdown which includes five stages and builds on their earlier four-stage model. The first three stages generally see a broadening acknowledgment of dissatisfaction. At first, individuals will pass through a cognitive stage where they wrestle with dissatisfaction but do not share their concerns with anyone. This stage is characterized by inner turmoil and cost-benefit analyses. The dyadic and social stages enter the social realm, as dissatisfaction is shared with others. It is at these stages that social influence begins to play a role on behaviour. The final two stages are post-relationship stages that focus on preservation of self-esteem, and understanding the reason for relationship failure. The last stage is also a largely cognitive stage but may manifest itself as a social transformation of the individual.

Phase	Description
Intrapsychic	This is an internal unhappiness with the relationship. Dissatisfaction is not communicated with the partner but may include withdrawal, resentment of the partner and an evaluation of alternatives to the relationship. This may be in the mind of one or both partners but no information is shared.
Dyadic	Dissatisfaction is now expressed to the partner. The couple may discuss the problems or dissatisfaction. They will adopt a pattern of accommodation and either actively or passively construct or deconstruct the relationship.
Social	This is the public phase where problems are shared with a wider community, perhaps in the search for social support. Normative social influence begins to play a larger role here as we are open to influence from members of a larger social community.
Grave dressing	This is about recovering from the relationship ending. It is characterized by defending the decision to break up and arguing that the break-up was justified. As always this can be argued by both partners or just one.
Resurrection	The resurrection phase was added later and involves recovery from the relationship. At this stage the "new person" who emerges from the end of the relationship and is characterized by a redefinition of the self in relation to the former partner and greater community.

▲ Table 7.3 Rollie and Duck's five-stage model of relationship breakdown

Exercise

Use a highlighter or coloured pencil to colour code concepts that you believe are related to each other (sometimes one concept or term will have multiple colours).

As mentioned in the introduction to this section, we have split up concepts in order to deliver information in a way that is orderly and structured. The trouble with this is, of course, that the categories used are not discrete but overlap and interrelate on every level. This exercise is meant to get you thinking about those interactions.

Try to bring in ideas from the core approaches as well; social psychology is particularly relevant to the psychology of human relationships.

This is a simple way to review and consolidate your learning. It can be done at any time and is very useful if done throughout your learning journey.

In a similar way, you can practise connecting ideas from this unit with images, arrows or symbols to show how your mind is interacting with the information. It is important to make this your own. Use images, colours and symbols that mean something to you and make it easy for you to see connections. This is a very subjective task and it is possible that someone with a different perspective from yours will not understand your work. The result of this activity is sometimes referred to as a pictogram or image-based concept map.

Group dynamics

Inquiry questions

- How does competition affect behaviour?

- How can we explain mob behaviour?

- How do stereotypes influence the way we perceive ourselves?

- How does isolation lead to extremism?

- How can psychology explain anti-immigration bias?

- How can we reduce conflict?

What you will learn in this section

- Definitions

  - A group consists of at least two individuals who perceive themselves to be a member of that group when the existence of the group is recognized by at least one other

  - Deindividuation refers to the sense of anonymity that individuals experience when they are acting as part of a group; this can result in group members engaging in extreme behaviours

- Competition between groups

  - Sherif's Robber's Cave (1953, 1955, 1961): group conflict can be created by simply introducing competition; these studies also highlighted that conflict can be resolved when groups are working towards a common goal

  - Blake and Mouton (1962): managerial staff favour ingroup solutions to organizational problems

  - British Social Attitudes Survey (2003–2011): 75% of the British public wanted to see the number of migrants entering the UK to be reduced

- Terror management theory

  - Green *et al* (1990) claim that when individuals become aware of their own mortality they create their own self-serving views of the world; when these views are challenged conflict is likely to occur

- The unified instrumental model of group conflict

  - Esses, Jackson and Armstrong (2010) combine previous models of inter-group competition to create a model they feel can explain contemporary social issues such as anti-immigration bias as a result of inter-group competition

This section also links to:

- cognitive approach to understanding behaviour

- sociocultural approach to understanding behaviour.

Discuss the following questions with a partner:

1. What groups do you belong to?

2. What attracted you to these groups?

3. What did you have to do (as initiation) to join these groups?

4. When do you think you were accepted as a member of the group?

5. How did membership to the group affect your self-concept and self-esteem?

6. Have you ever been tempted to leave the group? If so, what factors led to your loss of attraction to the group?

We interact or operate in groups a lot in our lives. Our families, friends and colleagues form significant groups with which we come into contact on a daily basis. The groups we belong to help shape our individual self and social identities and can have a significant impact on our happiness and self-esteem. This section will focus on an area of significant interest to psychologists: group dynamics. Group dynamics refers to the processes that occur within a group to which we belong, our **ingroup**, and also the processes or interactions that occur between the ingroup and an **outgroup**, known as **inter-group processes**.

Definitions of groups

Before discussing group processes, it is important to review some of the more common definitions of groups and explore their related implications. The eminent psychologist John Turner (1982) defined a group as "two or more individuals who perceive themselves to be members of the same social category". This definition emphasizes the importance of the individual recognizing his or her own group membership in relation to a common social category, that is, family, gender and ethnicity.

Brown (2000), however, extends this definition to acknowledge that the existence of any particular group is known to other people, and so he proposes the following: "a group exists when two or more people define themselves as members of it and when its existence is recognized by at least one

other". Defining groups in this way seems to make sense when we begin to explore the interaction between groups and what is often referred to as us (ingroup) and them (outgroup) thinking.

Johnson and Johnson's (1987) definition highlights some common features of groups, but also reflects the nature of much of the early work within social psychology conducted on group processes. According to them, "a group is two or more individuals in face to face interaction, each aware of his or her membership in the group, each aware of the others who belong to the group, and each aware of their positive interdependence as they strive to achieve mutual goals". Much of the emphases highlighted in this definition were tested by Tajfel in his work on the minimal group paradigms and inter-group conflict, so we can see that no definition is perfect and can account for all classifications of group in the modern world.

ATL skills: Thinking

- Make a list of all the types of group that you can think of in existence today that do not fulfill the criteria outlined in the above definitions of a group.

- In pairs, write your own definition of the term "group" that you feel reflects the myriad of groups present today.

The individual and the group

When studying group processes we need to acknowledge that a group's behaviour is directly influenced by the individuals within it. Floyd Henry Allport (1954) famously wrote that, "There is no psychology of groups which is not essentially and entirely a psychology of individuals". This means that despite being a collective, a group act can be considered large-scale interpersonal behaviour; behaviour no different from that occurring between two people.

There are those that adopt a different view. Some believe that when we are within a group our perception of ourselves changes as a result of the unique combination of individual and established group norms. Group behaviour is therefore the product of the relationships between group members and the importance they apply to the group's membership. Gustav Le Bon (1896) discusses the concept of a **group mind** which refers to the power of a group in its ability to shape individuals' behaviour and make them act totally out of character, performing acts that they would never have dreamed of on their own. This concept of a group mind is often cited in the literature and has influenced a lot of the research on **crowd behaviour** and **mob mentality**. The study of civil unrest or riots has been the focus of much of this research.

According to the early research, being part of a group causes the members to become anonymous and therefore free from social norms and the need to act in a socially desirable manner. Zimbardo's work on **deindividuation** develops upon the early work on a group mind and claims much of group behaviour regresses to the impulsive and unrestrained. His famous "learning experiments" conducted upon students supported his theory and demonstrated that when our identities are not known, we are more likely to engage in increasingly cruel behaviour (for example, administering longer electric shocks to another person). It is worth noting that when Zimbardo (1969) conducted a follow-up study on Belgian soldiers, the opposite was found! He claimed that the soldiers gave shorter shocks as they were used to being deindividuated and that anonymity reindividuated them.

Choosing your ingroup

When arriving at university, first-year students are filled with excitement about the opportunity and freedom that university life will offer. One of these opportunities is the ability to select a variety of new friends and social groups. New teams and clubs are all readily available. With such a range of choice on offer it seems reasonable to ask: how do we select the groups that we want to be a part of?

One explanation is provided by **social exchange theory** (Homans, 1950). People want to join a group that offers them the maximum reward. For example, if you are required to attend rugby training four times a week and play a match on Sunday you may want to ensure that you are rewarded for your efforts by being guaranteed a starting position every match or by being team captain. This cost-benefit analysis is obviously bidirectional, so rugby teams and fraternities will be conducting the same analysis when considering new recruits (Brown, 2000).

Prior experience with similar groups is another contributing factor when selecting potential group membership. Positive experiences with similar

groups in the past will encourage you to select a similar group in the future in the hope of yielding similar rewards (Pavelchak, Moreland and Levine, 1986).

Selecting the right group is clearly important to us. One reason for this is that the groups we belong to help to shape our identity, that is, they influence our self-concept and our self-esteem. **Moreland (1985)** illustrated this by conducting an experiment in which participants leading a group discussion were made to believe that they were new to a group. This was achieved by allowing them to believe that other participants had met before. This was, of course, not true. Moreland discovered that when participants believed that they were new to the group, they experienced more anxiety and were less optimistic about future meetings. As you would expect, participants experienced less anxiety over time.

Cooperation and competition

On 11 September 2001 the USA underwent a series of coordinated terrorist attacks perpetrated by the Islamic fundamentalist group al-Qaeda. The North and South Towers of the World Trade Center in New York City were hit by two commercial airline planes. Both towers collapsed, killing a total of 2,753 people. The attack rocked the USA and the rest of the world. The USA responded by launching the War on Terror and invading Afghanistan to overcome the Taliban, which eventually led to the killing of al-Qaeda leader Osama Bin Laden.

In the aftermath of the 9/11 attacks, support for President George Bush increased and he addressed the nation to outline the USA's response to the attacks. Hate crimes increased despite public appeals from the President outlining the valuable contributions of American Muslims to the country and calling for them to be "treated with respect". A clear outgroup had emerged. Sikhs were also targeted as they were often mistaken for Muslims. As a result of this incorrect religious categorization and stereotyping, a Sikh man in Arizona was tragically and fatally shot in 2001.

Discussion

What is the difference between competition and conflict? Use the internet to help you research the question.

This competition and conflict over religious ideologies has a long history. But like most of the conflicts that we have seen reported in the media, the conflicts can be perceived by some to be playing out the material interests of those involved (Brown, 2010). Regardless of whether the outcome is war, peace, tolerance or prejudice, it is often possible to trace the result back to the groups' economic and political goals. Psychologists have discovered that when goals are not shared by both groups, competition and conflict are likely to occur.

To this day, American citizens report that fear of terrorist attack is one of their main causes of daily stress (APA Stress in America Report, 2016). The events of 9/11 were tragic and significant to many as it indicated to the world that we can all become victims of terrorism. In 2015, a French satirical newspaper *Charlie Hebdo* was attacked by a gunman for allegedly publishing articles with anti-Muslim sentiment. In 2016 and 2017, Belgium, Germany and the UK all suffered devastating attacks at the hands of terrorists. These attacks have coincided with high levels of immigrant migration as a result of conflicts in Syria and Afghanistan.

Terrorism and immigrant migration were top of the political agenda in 2017 with both Donald Trump and the UK's Brexit campaign (the campaign for the UK to leave membership of the European Union) clearly utilising these issues for political leverage and to build a stronger sense of national identity. This resulted in some clear "us and them" thinking taking place and being explicitly reported in the media. Both campaigns clearly highlighted the pressures that countries face when there is competition for

resources such as land, jobs, prestige and religious or ideological dominance (Esses *et al*, 2010). In 2017, we clearly saw "psychology in real life" as countries and religious groups formed ingroups, and discriminated against outgroups as a result of long-held stereotypes, prejudices and conflicting goals.

Realistic group conflict theory

Campbell's (1965) realistic group conflict theory (RGCT), also known as realistic conflict theory (RCT), aims to explain inter-group conflict. The theory states that inter-group conflict can arise when groups have opposing goals and are competing for limited resources. Conflict often occurs because one group's goals are incompatible with the goals of the other, and one group's success in gaining these resources prevents the other group from doing so. Inter-group conflicts such as these often lead to groups developing ingroup norms, displaying overt acts of ingroup favouritism that encourage or reinforce negative stereotypes and discrimination towards the outgroup. Ingroup members who do not conform to these ingroup expectations can be punished or ostracized (Schofield, 2010).

RGCT also states that when groups are pursuing a **superordinate** (mutual) goal and success requires cooperation, this cooperation can help to reduce and overcome existing stereotypes, prejudice and conflict. This may be due to positive shared experiences among members developing over time. The most well-known demonstration of RGCT can be seen below in the classic research of Muzafer Sherif.

Research in focus: The Robber's Cave studies

Sherif and his colleagues conducted three famous field experiments known as the Robber's Cave or Summer Camp studies (1954, 1958, 1961) in order to demonstrate RGCT. These experiments are often considered together because of their contributions to the understanding of group dynamics and competition as they relate to RGCT, despite their subtle differences.

The field studies were longitudinal and lasted three weeks; this was sufficient time to observe the changes in group dynamics. The experiments included three stages: group

formation, inter-group conflict and conflict reduction. The context of the summer camp provided a very suitable and realistic setting in which to observe these processes. The boys participating in the experiments engaged in activities that were typical of a summer camp such as baseball, tug of war, football and even cabin inspections.

During the course of the three weeks, the researchers, posing as the camp leaders, made careful observations of all the boys' activities. It was, of course, important for the boys to feel that the camp was real, and that all events that took place occurred naturally. Parents paid a small fee to send the boys on the break and the researchers asked parents to stay away for the duration of the study.

The experiments were designed to test two hypotheses.

1. When individuals who have no prior relationships are brought together to interact in group activities with common goals, they produce a group structure with a clear hierarchy and roles.

2. If two existing groups are brought into contact with each other under conditions of competition and group frustration, each group will develop hostile attitudes and actions in relation to the outgroup and its members in relation to their existing ingroup norms.

Twenty-four white, lower middle-class boys from a Protestant background were brought to the campsite. The boys were not friends before the experiment and all were from stable home environments. This was to allow researchers to observe the formation of new friendships that would subsequently influence allocation to groups for the duration of the study.

In **stage 1** boys were placed into two groups in which they were matched as closely as possible to other boys in the group. The researchers observed who the boys related to and who became their best friends during the first few days. In two of the experiments, it was then arranged for the boys to be in different groups to the majority of their closest friends. So, their friends would be in the outgroup for the next phase of the experiment. In the third of the experiments the boys had no initial meeting and were placed directly into their groups. They were initially unaware of the other group's existence as they were camping at opposite ends of the site.

The groups, soon to become known as the Rattlers and the Eagles, developed ingroup norms, structure and rituals very quickly, and upon learning of the other group's existence the boys made comparisons between the groups in which "the edge was given to one's own group" (Sherif, 1966). It is interesting to note that this inter-group rivalry occurred before the boys were engaged in any real competition with each other.

In **stage 2** the boys were engaged in a series of competitions, for example, tug of war. The winners of the competition would receive a trophy and a much-desired new penknife. The losers would receive nothing. The groups were, therefore, working in opposition to each other and RGCT predicted conflict would be likely to occur. The groups were now **negatively interdependent**. The boys' behaviour changed dramatically as a result of this imposed competition, and these once peaceful boys became hostile and violent. The boys displayed clear **ingroup favouritism** and openly ridiculed and belittled the other group. Remember, the boys' best friends were in the outgroup!

Sherif highlighted that this was evidence for RGCT in that the introduction of group competition affected the group dynamics by developing the following.

- Ingroup favouritism: the boys became a tightknit group, focusing on their similarities and strengths; they stopped socializing with outgroup members. This ingroup favouritism and lack of contact with the outgroup is crucial to the maintenance of negative stereotypes and discrimination against an outgroup.

- Outgroup discrimination: the boys burnt the flags of the outgroup, ridiculed each other and traded insults. They even raided the cabins of the other team! This competition over resources created behaviours similar to what we see today in the media in relation to the migration crisis and the war in Syria.

For **stage 3**, after having successfully created conflict, the researchers acted to reduce it. They would reverse the groups from being negatively interdependent to being **positively interdependent**. The experimenters created

Research in focus (continued)

situations which would require the boys to cooperate with each other if they wanted to succeed. One such situation involved a heavy truck breaking down in the camp. This truck was used to drive the boys around the camp. It was too heavy for one group to "bump start" on their own, but if they worked together they could do it. The boys collaborated and fixed the truck. Over time, the positive inter-group contact, facilitated by the emergence of a superordinate goal, did succeed in reducing the inter-group conflict, providing support for RGCT.

Further research conducted by **Blake and Mouton (1962)** found that when groups worked in competition with each other they consistently over-evaluated their own ingroup value in comparison to the outgroup. In their experiment, 48 groups of managerial staff were asked to solve a problem. Groups were arranged into competing pairs. Each group then had to rate their own group's solution and that of the competition. Forty-six out of 48 groups favoured the ingroup solution. No group favoured the outgroup solution over their own.

In 2016 the voters in the UK voted in a referendum in which it was decided that the UK would leave the European Union. Immigration was an issue central to this campaign and resonated strongly with the British public. This was reflected in earlier statistics. The 2003–2011 British Social Attitudes Survey found that 75% of the British public believed that the number of immigrants entering Britain should be reduced. Why did they believe this? We need to look no further than the recent Brexit Leave campaign for a clearer picture.

The results of the Brexit campaign highlighted a perceived sense of competition between British residents and immigrants for scarce resources such as jobs, pensions and medical care. Quillian (1995) would argue that we should not be surprised. He claims that as the number of immigrants increases, so does the level of competition for resources and subsequent levels of prejudice and discrimination. Allport (1954) argues that in diverse societies such as the UK, there is a tendency for people to assume that their own individual needs link to that of the group as a whole. As a result, when there is a possibility of collective social mobility, as is the case with immigration, people are more sensitive and aware of changes to both groups' status. These concerns over social status lead to competition and conflict over material resources such as jobs and homes, and value dominance, that is, religion and patriotism. This competition can often act as the precursor to prejudice and discrimination.

Alternative theories on inter-group competition and conflict

While RGCT dominated much of the early literature on this topic, other theories have also made a contribution to our understanding of group dynamics and competition.

The theory of group position

Blumer (1958) claims that when members of an ingroup believe that they are entitled to, or have monopoly over certain resources and privileges, and they perceive an outgroup to be making claims to them, competition and conflict are likely to occur.

Social dominance theory

In most societies there is a social order. This order can often serve to legitimize the disproportionate allocation of resources (Sidanius and Pratto, 1999). There is a supporting ideology in place

See video

Watch the TED Talk "Don't feel sorry for refugees, believe in them" available at https://www.ted.com/talks/luma_mufleh_don_t_feel_sorry_for_refugees_believe_in_them.

that supports the maintenance of the system, a belief that for one group to succeed in society, then another group must fail. Esses *et al* (2003) found that individuals with high levels of social dominance view immigrants as directly competing with the host country for resources such as jobs and political power.

Terror management theory

Terror management theory (**Greenberg** *et al,* **1990**) proposes that humans fear their own meaninglessness in the world as we are very aware of our own mortality. In order to reduce the fear and give themselves meaning people create their own ideologies or cultural worldviews. These views cannot accommodate alternate views so conflicts arise. Much research supports the notion that when faced with death, humans increase their prejudice towards outgroups who threaten or challenge their religious or political views (Greenberg, Solomon and Pyszczynski, 1990). In support of this argument, Chenoweth (2010) argues that political ideologies and democracies are directly linked to an increase in terrorist activity due to inter-group competition.

Greenberg *et al* **(1990)** conducted a study in which they asked Christian participants to write down what they thought would happen to them after they died (mortality salience condition). The control group didn't write anything down. Participants were then asked to rate Christian and Jewish targets. Those in the mortality salience

condition rated Christian targets more positively and Jewish targets negatively, implying that a range of ideologies may inevitably lead to perceived competition and conflict.

The unified instrumental model of group conflict

Esses *et al* **(2010)** have integrated many theories of group competition and conflict to create the unified instrumental model of group conflict. They claim that both ideologies, such as religion or political view, and situational factors, such as instability and social mobility, can reinforce the perception of group competition and conflict by highlighting the outgroups' characteristics and the perception of competition. Attempts to reduce the perceived competitiveness of an outgroup can result in an ingroup displaying overt prejudice and discrimination towards an outgroup in order to avoid any changes to the status quo.

The researchers claim that this model can be applied to the inter-group relations experienced between immigrants and members of host countries as well as groups with differing religious views. In a relevant study, Esses *et al* asked participants to read an article that emphasized immigrant success in a highly competitive job market or an article that did not discuss immigration. Results demonstrated that those who read the article about immigrant employment success were likely to hold negative

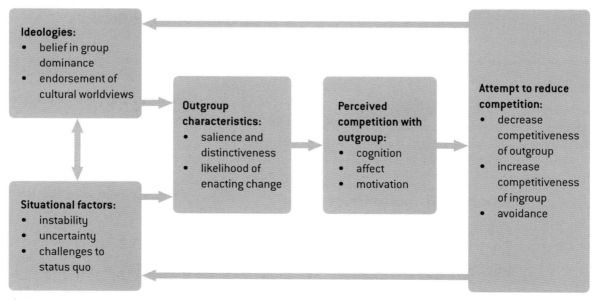

▲ Figure 7.5 The unified instrumental model of group conflict

views of immigrants new to the host country, and even support anti-immigration policy.

From an evolutionary standpoint, inter-group competition can increase ingroup cooperation, similar to that witnessed in the Robber's Cave experiments. **Burton-Chewell, Ross-Gillespie and West (2010)** tested if competition between groups leads to higher levels of cooperation. In their experiment, participants played a public goods game, an economics game where participants can allocate monetary units in the form of tokens to a public pot or claim the money themselves. When cooperation between groups of participants was introduced, participants were more likely to regard their group members as collaborators rather than competitors. Competition resulted in participants contributing more monetary units to the public pot despite earning less for themselves. This is significant as the benefits of contributing towards the group's success were actually cancelled out by the costs of contributing, implying that that it was the inter-group competition that encouraged ingroup cooperation. From an evolutionary perspective, this may have been an adaptive response. In the past, successful groups may have benefited from increased access to mates and scarce resources, and indirectly through increased fitness of their relatives.

ATL skills: Thinking

Social psychology aims to study participants in a realistic and natural environment. What ethical issues do you think researchers may face when studying topics such as group dynamics?

Jordan, Jordan and Rand (2017) have, however, criticized these studies and those using a similar design. They claim that there is no evidence of a unique effect of inter-group competition on cooperation. They claim that when creating ingroup competition, a new threshold is created (a prize that is shared among the group), offering a new incentive to collaborate. They conducted a series of four experiments controlling for these confounding effects of the new threshold. They concluded that there is no support for an evolutionary explanation for inter-group competition influencing cooperation, or for group selection shaping human evolution.

Discussion

1. Contrast RGCT with the unified instrumental model of group conflict.

2. To what extent do you agree with the authors that social issues such as anti-immigration and terrorism can be explained in terms of competition for limited resources? What makes you say that?

Prejudice and discrimination

Inquiry questions

- What is prejudice?
- Why do people discriminate against others?
- How can stereotyping influence decision-making?
- What factors influence discrimination?

What you will learn in this section

- Definitions
  - Prejudice is a pre-existing attitude towards an individual or group of people
  - Stereotypes are generalizations applied to groups of people used by individuals to help make sense of the world
  - Discrimination is the unfair treatment of another group based upon the group's membership
- Humans automatically categorize people and behaviour
- Modern prejudice is often implicit and psychologists need to use new methods for experimentation (Fiske, 2010)
- Levinson, Cai and Young (2010): implicit bias can affect legal proceedings, causing jurors and judges to misremember information
- Hartley and Phelps (2010): white participants presented with unfamiliar black faces experienced a heightened sense of fear as indicated by over-activation in the amygdala
- Cuddy, Fiske and Glick (2008): outgroups associated with competition perceived as cold by the ingroup
- Unkelbach, Forgas and Denson (2008): pre-existing stereotypes can influence the speed and nature of decision-making
- Savelkoul et al (2010): the size of an outgroup influences the level of perceived threat; increased contact with an outgroup can reduce outgroup bias

This section links to:

- biological approach to understanding behaviour.

This section will discuss issues and research surrounding three types of social bias: prejudice, stereotypes and discrimination. Each of these forms of bias has the potential to influence the way we view ourselves. It can affect the way we interact with people and how they interact with us. This may result in an individual avoiding contact with another or limiting job opportunities and living conditions. This behaviour is often grounded in a pre-existing incorrect and overgeneralized view of an individual or group of people. This section will discuss how the above forms of bias influence our daily lives as well as focusing on well-publicized forms of prejudice such as racism, sexism and anti-immigration bias. We will also discuss the development of prejudice in children.

Definitions

Allport (1954) defined **prejudice** as "an antipathy based on faulty and inflexible generalization. It may be felt or expressed. It may be directed toward a group as a whole, or toward an individual because [he] is member of that group". Most psychologists agree that prejudice is a negative attitude towards an individual or group of people.

As we saw in Unit 4, Lippmann referred to **stereotypes** as the little picture in our heads that comes to mind when we picture a specific social group. These are often inflexible, incorrect and overgeneralized. Cognitive psychologists have argued that stereotypes allow individuals to process large amounts of information more quickly by basing judgments on previous experiences with similar individuals. Stereotypes are essentially "schemas used by social perceivers to process information about others" (Hilton and von Hippel, 1996).

Discrimination is more than just an attitude or negative perception of people; it involves action. It often involves treating people in an unfair way based on their group membership, for example, gender, race and religion. Jones (1972) has defined discrimination as "those actions designed to maintain own-group characteristics and favored position at the expense of the comparison group". Again, it is commonly agreed that discrimination is a negative behaviour.

In Unit 4 we referred to the formation of stereotypes and the origins of prejudice in relation to classic psychological theory and experimental research. Social cognitive theory, social identity theory, and fundamental and ultimate attribution errors have all contributed to our understanding of how prejudice is formed. Claude Steele's research on stereotype threat has given us insight into the effects that this prejudice can have on academic performance. This chapter will focus on understanding prejudice and discrimination in relation to contemporary issues. Anti-immigration bias and racism are presented to the general public via the mass media on a daily basis and influence not only how a migrant or person of colour is perceived by an ingroup, but also how individuals perceive themselves. These perceptions have the potential to influence behaviour.

Racism

Racism is a form of discrimination that provides advantages to one's own ingroup and disadvantages or harms another group that is defined by racial characteristics. According to **Dovidio (2010)** racism can be defined by three characteristics.

- There is a culturally held belief that groups can be distinguished by race-specific characteristics that can be applied to all members.

- These racial characteristics render the outgroup inferior to the ingroup.

- Racism involves an element of social power in order to enable the negative attitude and behaviours directed towards the outgroup to result in real disadvantages relative to the ingroup.

Inter-group dynamics has long been influenced by race-related behaviour. History books record many accounts of one group attempting to gain an economic, political or social advantage on the basis of racial characteristics. Racism has the power to shape behaviour at the individual, group and institutional level and as such has the power to reshape social norms, a process that facilitates the maintenance of such prejudice, for example, through socialization and the media.

Classic psychology has sought to explain racism on the basis of it being a normal cognitive process. From as young as three years old children have an acute sense of **category awareness** and as such are able to identify male from female, black from white, and so on. **Clark and Clark (1947)** conducted a famous study that sought to test category awareness in children. The researchers presented a white doll with blonde hair and a brown doll with black hair to children and asked questions designed to test the child's ethnic awareness, for example, "which doll looks white?" By the age of five, over 90% were able to accurately identify the correct ethnicity of the doll.

Why is this significant? Categorization formed the basis of both **realistic group conflict theory (RGCT)** and social identity theory. Campbell (1958) argues that categorization occurs automatically and that factors such as proximity and similarity facilitate the process. We have a natural desire to belong so seeking out ingroup membership is inevitable as it raises our self-esteem. Both Sherif's Robber's Cave studies and Tajfel's research on minimal paradigms highlighted that we prioritize our ingroup over the outgroup. Ingroup favouritism and outgroup discrimination are therefore by-products of the categorization process and can result in very overt displays of prejudice and discrimination.

See video

James A White gives an emotional and thought-provoking TED Talk in which he describes attempting to rent a house in the USA in the 1960s. The talk is available at https://www.ted.com/talks/james_a_white_sr_the_little_problem_i_had_renting_a_house/transcript

► ▐▐ ■

Case study: Fictional scenario of renting an apartment

In his book *Prejudice: Its Social Psychology*, author Rupert Brown (2010) provides a fictional scenario of Geoff Small, a black man in his late twenties, attempting to rent an apartment in Bristol, a city in the west of England. After viewing the apartment Geoff Small asks the landlord what his criteria is for allocating the apartment to a tenant. The landlord replies that he is going to see all the applicants and give them a call afterwards.

Ten minutes later, another potential tenant, a white man, comes to view the same apartment. After viewing the apartment, he asks the landlord the same question: "How are you going to decide who will be your tenant in this apartment?" The landlord replies that it is on a first-come first-served basis providing he feels that the candidate is suitable. Before long the landlord declares that Geoff Small will not be getting the apartment as "he might create problems".

This is a fictional account designed to illustrate and help define the concept of prejudice. Unfortunately, this kind of overt prejudice and discrimination based upon skin colour takes place every day. Brown discusses how he experiences "everyday racism" and how this has shaped the life lessons that he would teach to his grandchildren.

On 14 October 2013, the BBC aired a documentary as part of their "Inside-out London" series where they observed London real estate agents refusing potential property tenants on the basis of their ethnicity. The documentary highlights an example of the "everyday racism" described by James A White illustrating that racism of this kind is very much part of real life.

The BBC article summarizing this can be found at: http://www.bbc.co.uk/news/uk-england-london-24372509

Contemporary research on racism, stereotyping and prejudice has had to evolve as societies' cultural norms have shifted. Overt displays of prejudice such as sexism and racism are considered taboo; there has been a decrease in displays of overt prejudice and social bias. Unfortunately, it has not been erased, it has merely gone underground. Stealth stereotyping, as coined by Fiske (2010), or implicit bias, refers to prejudice or social biases that may be operating at the unconscious level and may not be deliberate or within an individual's control. This has dramatic implications for research into racism as in order to negate the effects of this implicit bias and potential social desirability effects, new measures must be employed.

Implicit associations tests (**IATS**) have been well publicized and we looked at them in Unit 4. They are designed to assess our hidden biases by measuring whether we hold positive or negative associations towards social groups based upon ethnicity, gender, sexuality, and so on. These implicit associations often tend to favour the participant's ingroup and show negative associations towards an outgroup. Possessing a negative implicit bias can have disastrous consequences, as is highlighted in the following study.

Levinson (2007) claims that implicit bias can influence the memory and decision-making of judges and jurors in the legal system, causing them to misremember information that they had heard only seconds before. In his study, Levinson asked participants to recall facts from the stories that they had heard moments before. Results highlighted that participants held negative racial associations towards African American characters in the story. When reading about an African American character, participants were more likely to remember aggressive facts than those presented for a white Caucasian character.

This finding of implicit bias was further supported in a study conducted by **Levinson, Cai and Young (2010)** named "Guilty by implicit racial bias". Sixty-seven undergraduate students were asked to take part in the study for which they would gain extra course credit. The participants sat in a cubicle with a computer and completed several tests including: a (Black/White) Guilty/Not Guilty IAT, a (Black/White) Pleasant/Unpleasant IAT, the Modern Racism Scale, feeling thermometers, and a robbery evidence evaluation task. The Modern Racism Scale and the feeling thermometers were designed to assess explicit racial preferences. The findings found that participants held meaningful implicit associations between the words black and guilty, highlighting a strong implicit bias effect.

Interestingly, research using fMRI conducted by **Phelps** *et al* **(2000)** discovered that white participants presented with unfamiliar black faces show increased activation in the amygdala, highlighting a heightened fear response. This provides some support for the claims made by RGCT that prejudice and discrimination may be due to the fear and threat of loss of resources.

See video

This TED Talk specifically addresses the issue of implicit bias: https://www.ted.com/talks/verna_myers_how_to_overcome_our_biases_walk_boldly_toward_them/transcript

▶ ❚❚ ■

Anti-immigration bias

Migration is commonplace in today's world. Countries in western Europe, the USA and Canada are experiencing an increase in the number of migrants from different immigrant groups entering the country. This poses challenges for both the host country and for the migrants. Some of these have been discussed in other units in relation to acculturation and globalization. These challenges keep the issue firmly in the public eye. Unfortunately, media coverage, lack of contact and lack of understanding can feed negative stereotypes of migrants and result in discriminatory behaviour. This can lead to right-wing extremism in members of the host nation (Esses *et al*, 2001) and social isolation, resentment and in extreme cases, radicalization in the migrant population (Koomen and van der Plugt, 2016).

Much of the research history of anti-immigration bias echoes that of racism research. Sherif's RGCT emphasizes the importance of competition for resources in creating conflict. Competition, or at least perceived competition, for jobs, health care and other resources that arises when a

migrant group enters a host country can be enough to create negative attitudes towards the incoming population. Tajfel (1978) would argue that national identities become more salient, highlighting any differences between the two groups, including that of status and power. When members of a host country perceive a threat to their status and valued resources, they can begin to discriminate against the new migrant population. Esses *et al* (2010) argue that the potential stress placed upon resources can lead to fear and the need to compete. This may result in anti-immigration prejudice and discrimination.

Cuddy, Fiske and Glick (2008) claim that when groups are associated with competition they are perceived as cold rather than warm—a negative stereotype. The stereotype content model offers a new perspective in this arena as it looks not only at the influence of competition but also at the nature of the subsequent stereotypes.

It is hard to discuss the above theory and related research without introducing the concept of ethnocentrism. Ethnocentrism refers to the way that an ingroup views their group values, members and product at the centre of everything and this results in group members making a comparison with the outgroup. (See Unit 2 on the biological approach to behaviour 2 for a discussion on how oxytocin increases ethnocentrism.)

ATL skills: Research and thinking

Read the short article "Anti-immigration bias" by Wagner *et al* (2010) for a contemporary review of related literature on this topic.

1. What is the difference between nationalism and patriotism?

2. To what extent can social identity theory explain anti-immigration bias?

3. How does the article suggest that relationships between the host country and an immigrant population could be improved?

The concepts of stereotyping and categorization have been of great significance in the study of anti-immigration bias. This often takes place automatically and can be exacerbated by negative experiences with the outgroup and media coverage. Baron and Banjaji (2006) discovered that Japanese and American children already possess negative prejudice about the other group by the age of 10. The fact that stereotypes are often inaccurate and resistant to change only serves to exacerbate the problem of bias. These stereotypes can have a profound impact upon the way people process information (Koomen and van der Plugt, 2016).

In a variation of Levinson's race research, **Bodenhausen (1988)** asked participants to take part in a mock jury task in which they were to decide the guilt or innocence of a suspect accused of armed robbery. The suspect's name was manipulated and he was either introduced as Carlos Ramirez or Robert Johnson. Carlos Ramirez was more likely to be found guilty regardless of the information presented in the case. It was argued that this was due to the negative stereotypes of Latino males that had been evoked by the suspect's name. The manipulation of names has also been applied to job interview settings yielding similar results. The BBC documentary series "Inside-out London" recorded footage of this discrimination occurring in London in 2013.

Stereotypes can influence human behaviour. **Unkelbach, Forgas and Denson (2008)** conducted a laboratory experiment with Australian students in which they were asked to shoot armed people in a computer game. The researchers predicted and found that participants would shoot and kill more people wearing the Islamic headwear the hijab. The researchers strangely called this paper "The turban effect". The research findings seem to support the notion that pre-existing negative stereotypes of Muslims influenced their decision to shoot.

This result is particularly worrying as stereotypes can influence our behaviour at the subconscious level and under time pressure this may be enhanced. Stereotypes offer us a shortcut and help us make quick decisions such as deciding to shoot somebody wearing a hijab.

Case study: Jean Charles de Menezes

▲ Figure 7.6 Jean Charles de Menezes

Jean Charles de Menezes was a Brazilian man killed by London police officers two weeks after the London bombings in 2005. He was thought to be one of the men involved in the bombings as well as another failed bombing attempt.

Police had put de Menezes under surveillance after finding a gym membership card in a bag that had been used by the bombers in the attack. They followed him from his home on 22 July 2005 and watched him board a bus and attempt to get on the London underground. The trains were closed due to the earlier bombings so he was forced to re-board the bus. This behaviour was deemed strange by police officers.

Police officers also displayed some concern over de Menezes clothing which some claimed was a heavy coat and others a belt with wires coming out of it. He was wearing a denim jacket. It appears the existing stereotypes held by police officers were affecting their perceptions and behaviours.

De Menezes managed to board a train at a different station on which he was pinned to the ground by police officers and shot at close range. This tragic event allegedly took less than one minute to unfold. It was decided that the officers involved would not face disciplinary action by the Independent Police Complaints Commission.

One possible explanation for the terrible incident with Jean Charles de Menezes may be the influence of time, but when people feel threatened they tend to stereotype more frequently and in a more negative way (Fein and Spencer, 1997). Stereotypes can, however, also influence individuals' perception of themselves and their group. **Meta-stereotypes** refer to the opinions held by one group of the stereotypes of them held by another group. **Kamans *et al* (2009)** investigated the influence of meta-stereotypes in Moroccan teenagers who lived in the Netherlands. Researchers were interested in how they responded to the belief that they were regarded by the Dutch nationals as criminals or terrorists. It was discovered that these teenagers were harbouring strong resentment towards the Dutch population and were more motivated to engage in anti-social behaviours. Stereotyping combined with meta-stereotyping can therefore result in a very negative response; in this instance it was evidenced in a greater support for Muslim extremism. It is worth noting that these processes can result in a lack of contact between the host country and the migrant population. This can strengthen negative stereotyping and encourage discriminative behaviours.

Savelkoul *et al* (2010) investigated the nature of anti-Muslim attitudes in the Netherlands in relation to ethnic competition theory and inter-group contact theory. Ethnic competition theory claims that the larger the size of the outgroup, the greater the perceived threat will be to the ingroup, whereas inter-group contact theory claims that the larger the outgroup is, the more likely it is that the ingroup will meet members of this group and become friends. This links directly to the contact hypothesis. The findings highlighted that when the outgroup was perceived as bigger there was greater fear or perceived threat to the group and as a result stronger anti-Muslim sentiment. One exception should be noted. In areas that had higher proportions of outgroup members such as Amsterdam contact was inevitable. Fear and threat was found to decline over time and as such so would anti-Muslim attitudes. The research seems to provide support for Allport's contact hypothesis as a method of conflict resolution (see the next section for more on this).

ATL skills: Thinking

What might be some of the ethical implications of the above studies in relation to stereotyping, prejudice and discrimination?

Origins of conflict and conflict resolution

Inquiry questions

- What is conflict?

- Why are men more violent than women?

- How can contact reduce conflict?

What you will learn in this section

- McDonald, Navarrette and Van Vugt (2012): the male warrior hypothesis—men are evolutionarily predisposed to engage in inter-group conflict in order to acquire and protect reproductive partners

- Cikara, Botvinick and Fiske (2011): there is a cognitive explanation for inter-group conflict; they discovered a link between an individual's social identity, the value attached to this identity and their willingness to harm the outgroup

- De Dreu *et al* (2010): oxytocin may lead humans to engage in acts of defensive aggression

- Allport (1954): contact between groups has the ability to resolve conflict

- The jigsaw classroom (Aronson, 1997): a method for reducing conflict within the classroom by encouraging cooperation between students

- Al Ramaiah and Hewstone (2013): the contact hypothesis can be applied to contemporary issues such as war in the Middle East

This section also links to:

- genetics and behaviour—evolutionary explanations (biological approach to behaviour)

Inter-group conflict is widespread throughout human societies. War, discrimination, terrorism and conflict between gangs or political parties are all too common social phenomena. Psychologists have been fascinated by conflict, its origins and how to reduce it, partly because of its prevalence. Many cognitive psychologists have attributed the origins of inter-group conflict to the fact that we are cognitive misers, and at the most basic level have a need to categorize people into groups in order to make sense of the world.

As we have seen, Sherif's research highlighted the role that inter-group competition has upon the creation of conflict as two distinct groups are competing for the same scarce resources. **McDonald, Navarrette and Van Vugt (2012)** agree with Sherif in their observations that competition for resources such as food, water, land

and status may result in conflict, but attribute this to a more evolutionary explanation. In particular, they ask: why are men so often the aggressors and the victims involved in inter-group conflict?

ATL skills: Thinking and research

Aggression, violence and conflict are often used interchangeably.

Find the definition of each of the above concepts and consider the differences between them.

Consider the use of these terms and how their application may affect the understanding of related research.

Living in groups provides many benefits to humans. It offers protection and the ability to share resources with members of the ingroup in order to ensure survival. This is a clear evolutionary explanation for the benefits of living within groups; however, it does not explain discrimination and overt violence towards an outgroup. The **male warrior hypothesis** claims that men possess specific psychological mechanisms that predispose them to planning, initiating and executing acts of aggression with the specific goal of acquiring or protecting reproductive resources (women). (See Unit 2 on the biological approach to behaviour for a discussion on the limitations of evolutionary theories.)

ATL skills: Research and thinking

The research and figures listed below have been offered as support for the male warrior hypothesis.

- Men kill more: between 1980 and 2008, it was found that in the USA, men were responsible for 90% of murders.

- Men are killed more: in the same time period, men made up 77% of murder victims.

- Women are far more likely to be the victims of violent crime than the perpetrators (Hughes, 2015).

Locate the research abstracts for the studies below and assess their credibility as support for the male warrior hypothesis. To what extent do you agree with the claims made by the researchers in relation to the evolutionary origins of conflict? What makes you say that?

Navarrete, CD, McDonald, MM, Molina, LE and Sidanius, J. June 2010. "Prejudice at the nexus of race and gender: an outgroup male target hypothesis". *Journal of Personality and Social Psychology*. Vol 98, number 6. Pp 933–45.

Lee, IC, Pratto, F and Johnson, BT. 2011. "Intergroup consensus/disagreement in support of group-based hierarchy: An examination of socio-structural and psycho-cultural factors". *Psychological Bulletin*. Vol 137, number 6. Pp 1029–64.

Van Vugt, M, De Cremer, D and Janssen, DP. 2007. "Gender differences in cooperation and competition: The male-warrior hypothesis". *Psychological Science*. Vol 18, number 1. Pp 19–23.

Outgroup females are seen as being less of a threat than outgroup males so conflict is less likely to occur. This explains the high prevalence of male conflict. Furthermore, if a female does engage in inter-group conflict it is more likely that the conflict may result in sexual assault, encouraging females to avoid contact with outgroup males. The male warrior hypothesis, like all evolutionary theory, is controversial, but it does provide an explanation for the disproportionate levels of male violence in our society.

Research into inter-group competition has also highlighted that competition helps to define our social identities (Tajfel, 1982), and also affects the way an individual processes pleasure and pain of their respective ingroups and outgroups. For example, witnessing a member of your ingroup in pain may result in feelings of empathy (Batson, 1991), whereas an outgroup member in pain may result in feelings of pleasure. This explanation for the origins of inter-group conflict was explored by Cikara, Botvinick and Fiske (2011). They believed that attaching a positive value (happiness, cognitive reward) to an outgroup member's suffering may motivate an individual to inflict suffering and pain upon them. Under certain conditions, this may lead to large-scale conflict such as football hooliganism, riots and genocide.

The researchers investigated the link between an individual's social identity and aggression by examining the neural structures responsible for valuation of behaviour. They used self-report measure and fMRI scans. They measured the affective and neural responses of die-hard baseball fans (Red Sox or Yankees fans) while the fans were observing plays that were considered positive, negative and neutral for their team (comparing results against a third party). The researchers predicted that when observing a result positive to their team, fans would respond with positive affect (emotion), but when they experienced a result that was considered negative for their team they would experience negative affect and that this would also correlate with a willingness to cause an outgroup member harm.

As predicted, participants rated those plays that were favourable to their ingroup (ingroup win, outgroup failure) as significantly more pleasurable than those plays considered negative (ingroup failure, rival team win). According to self-reports, plays considered negative to an individual's ingroup were considered more angering and painful. Participants also reported that they would be more likely to heckle, insult and even hit a member of the outgroup than members of the control group (a neutral condition, observing a team for which they held no value). This corresponded with increased activation in the ventral striatum, a neural structure responsible for valuation (for example, pleasure at outgroup failure) and motivation (for example, urge to inflict pain). Researchers concluded that there is a link between an individual's social identity, the area of the brain used to encode ingoup and outgroup behaviour, and the willingness to harm.

Researchers at the University of Amsterdam have also provided a neurobiological explanation of intergroup conflict. **De Dreu et al (2010)** have discovered that oxytocin, often referred to as the love hormone, can lead humans to sacrifice themselves for the sake of the ingroup. More importantly, when there is a perceived level of threat from an outgroup, the likelihood of conflict is high as it may cause an individual to engage in acts of defensive aggression. (See Unit 2 on the biological approach to behaviour for a discussion of De Dreu et al's (2010) study.)

The above explanations are two of the lesser cited discussions around the origins of conflict. A classic explanation is provided by the **frustration-aggression hypothesis (Dollard et al, 1939)**. Dollard et al provide an explanation for conflict at the individual and group level. According to their hypothesis, aggressive behaviour is a result of frustration caused when something or someone obstructs us from fulfilling a need or a desired goal. This frustration must be released, and in the absence of a more productive release such as sport or consensual sexual contact, violence and therefore conflict may occur. In order to secure a successful release of the pent-up frustration, the researchers argue that weaker or minority groups are often targeted. This hypothesis was once held in high esteem and was applied to the effects of job loss on violence (Catalano, Novaco and McConnell, 1977).

Exercise

Social cognitive theory, social identity theory, culture of honour and deindividuation can all provide explanations for the origins of conflict.

1. In groups prepare an argument providing support for one of the above as an alternative explanation for the origins of conflict.

2. Hold a classroom discussion on the topic of conflict and debate the following argument: "Competition between groups is the primary cause of inter-group conflict".

3. Using the information you have gained from the debate, create a rich picture consisting of only pictures, arrows, single words or phrases to help create a causal map explaining the origins of conflict.

Conflict resolution

Throughout this unit we have been referring to Allport's (1954) work on "the nature of prejudice". Not only did he reflect on the origins of prejudice but he also provided some thought on how best to reduce conflict. The contact hypothesis is probably one of the most well-known theories, partly due to its simplicity: the best way to reduce conflict between groups is to bring them into contact with each other. This is easier said than done, however. There are plenty of examples where placing rival groups in contact with each other has produced even more hostility. Allport claimed that there were a number of conditions that needed to be satisfied if contact was to successfully reduce prejudice.

These conditions have been developed over the years by psychologists and include the following.

-   **Social and institutional support:** those with the power to enforce legislation and create the new social climate need to have a clear rationale and plan for implementation so that reducing prejudice is the common goal and they are all able to support the suggested policies.

- **High acquaintance potential:** the groups should meet on a frequent basis and for a long enough period for meaningful positive relationships to form.

- **Equal status between groups:** by providing a contact situation that offers equal status between the groups there is less chance that any pre-existing negative stereotype may be reinforced. This might be achieved by designing the group task in such a way that both parties are performing a similar role in the group.

- **Cooperation:** sherif's work and much of the research that followed it has highlighted the importance of cooperation in resolving conflict. It is worth noting that in order to ensure that prejudice is reduced, the groups must succeed at a task in which cooperation is required. Failure would provide groups with a negative contact experience and may serve to reinforce negative stereotypes and fuel conflict.

Cook (1978) applied these conditions to the cooperation experiments he conducted between prejudiced white participants and black confederates. Over the course of 20 days Cook asked participants to engage in a number of cooperative activities. Careful to employ the conditions required to ensure successful contact, Cook ensured that these tasks were frequent and allowed people to socialize during lunch breaks. Most importantly in this instance, participants were allocated roles equal in status to the black confederates. The experiments were monitored by an ethnically diverse staff to ensure that racial tolerance was the norm. At the end of the experiments, the white participants showed less prejudice towards the black confederates, as evidenced in their post-test prejudice scores.

The jigsaw classroom

While we would like schools to be safe havens for our children, schools can often be a source of fear and terror for those being bullied or ostracized. The jigsaw classroom technique for conflict reduction developed by Elliott Aronson (Aronson and Patnoe, 1997) has been successfully utilized in schools by encouraging the creation of cooperative learning groups in classrooms.

These tasks involve dividing the task equally among group members to ensure that success can only be achieved if students cooperate with each other. For example, on a psychology project concerning the origins of conflict, one student (or group) may research biological explanations, another may take cognitive explanations and another sociocultural explanations. At the end of the research phase students must collate their findings to create one product that requires them to work together.

Teachers are responsible for instilling the norms of cooperation and respect, and in some cases providing structure and allocating roles within a group to ensure equality. In doing so, the teacher has shown support for the process and can reinforce this through feedback and by rewarding the whole group product rather than individual contributions.

Slavin (1980) reviewed 14 studies of ethnically diverse classroom settings in which the jigsaw classroom technique had been employed. These jigsaw classrooms had been compared to a control classroom utilizing "normal" teaching methods. Eleven out of the 14 studies found significant evidence of improving attraction between social and racial groups, demonstrating support for the cooperative classroom and the principles of the contact hypothesis.

Al Ramaiah and Hewstone (2013) also applied the principles of contact hypothesis to reducing and resolving inter-group conflict. They refer to a number of successful interventions in their research, for example, in Rwanda, Sri Lanka and Israel. These interventions in these conflict zones encouraged the development of trust and forgiveness between group members. Al Ramaiah and Hewstone acknowledge that these conflicts have long histories and a new legislation or policy will not resolve the issue overnight, but that when those in authority foster a social norm of peace and cooperation then inter-group contact interventions can yield effective results.

Social responsibility

What you will learn in this section

- Social responsibility

  ○ Prosocial behaviour

  ○ Reciprocal altruism model: Trivers, 1971; Axelrod and Hamilton's use of the "Prisoner's dilemma" to illustrate reciprocity (1981)

  ○ Hamilton's kin selection theory (1964): helping relatives to pass on the genes you share

  ○ Empathy altruism hypothesis: people help out of genuine concern for another's wellness; social exchange theory; altruistic versus egoistic helping; Batson's empathy escape paradigm; Cialdini's challenge—negative-state relief model

  ○ Culture and prosocial behaviour: all cultures show helping behaviour but to different extents and in different ways; key researchers—Whiting and Whiting (1975), Levine (2001); role of individualism and collectivism

- Bystanderism

  ○ The bystander effect

  ○ Factors affecting bystanderism: Latane Darley and Mcguire (1968) on diffusion of responsibility and group inhibition: arousal—cost-reward model (Piliavin *et al* 1981) claims that people become physiologically aroused by a perceived emergency then perform an evaluation to determine whether net rewards outweigh net costs before acting

- Promoting prosocial behaviour

  ○ Legislation: a duty to rescue?; Good Samaritan legislation, does it work?

  ○ Socialization and early years education: mindfulness-based kindness curriculum; compassion training; prosocial modelling

This section also links to:

- prejudice and discrimination

- social networking and messaging to promote prosocial behaviour; cyberbystanderism (cognitive approach to behaviour)

- social cognitive models (health psychology)

- Bandura's social cognitive model; modelling prosocial behaviour (sociocultural approach to behaviour).

Prosocial behaviour

Behaviour can generally be broken down into either **prosocial** or **antisocial** behaviour. Examples of antisocial behaviour tend to get noticed in the media and by society at large because they shock us. They represent a rejection of the norms by which we have all agreed to live. Antisocial behaviour is any behaviour that causes (or will likely cause) harm to others including violent behaviour, abusive language, graffiti, vandalism or intimidation.

Conversely, prosocial behaviour is any behaviour that benefits others. This is considered supportive of social norms. It is commonplace and does not draw media attention except in the most pronounced examples. Examples of prosocial behaviour include lending a pen to a stranger, donating an organ to a sibling and everything in between.

Helping behaviour is any type of social assistance or interpersonal support. Prosocial behaviour is more focused; it is an action that is intended to help another but is not motivated by any professional obligation, where the recipient is an individual, not an organization. Altruism is the narrowest form of helping behaviour; it is behaviour that helps another person where the motivation for helping is entirely empathetic and characterized by a desire to benefit a person in need; no benefit to the helper is assumed. Note that there is philosophical debate to be had around the existence of true altruism but for the purposes of our discussion here, altruism is simply taken as a prosocial behaviour where the primary motivating factor is to benefit another person when there is no obligation to help or any anticipated reciprocation.

Prosocial behaviour and altruism can be difficult to differentiate from each other in experimental conditions; it is difficult to determine if helping is egoistic or altruistic and self-reporting is subject to **social desirability effects**. In experimental conditions, if you ask a participant why they performed a helping behaviour, they are likely to respond that they were acting altruistically rather than egoistically because the former is socially desirable while the latter is not.

Reciprocal altruism model

Robert Trivers explains altruism in terms of evolutionary psychology with his **reciprocal altruism theory**. **Trivers (1971)** defines altruism specifically to include prosocial behaviour between genetically distant or unrelated individuals that includes some detriment to the helper (in evolutionarily fitness), for example, someone diving into a rushing river to save a stranger. Trivers argues that helping a genetic relative is not altruism because the helper is simply contributing to the

survival of his own genes carried by the relative. In other words reciprocal altruism attempts to explain altruism where kin-selection can be ruled out. The basic tenet is that altruism between strangers (or even species) can be genetically beneficial because in the long run they benefit the helper.

Obviously, the benefit awarded to the helper would be a return of helping behaviour in their favour in the future. If a drowning man is saved by a helper today, he is likely to come to the aid of his helper in the future. The reciprocal altruism model claims that helping is genetically beneficial because helping when you can will translate into help when you need it, aiding in the propagation of your genes. The helping relationship is dependent on a cost-benefit ratio of the altruistic act where the benefit to the person in need is greater than the cost to the helper.

Exercise

Trivers (1971) gives several examples of reciprocal altruism from the animal world. Carry out research into examples of this such as bird and rodent warning calls and cleaning symbiosis in fish.

Cheating, as defined by Trivers, is when an altruistic act goes unreciprocated. In a social setting, generalized altruism can take root. Given that people learn from others and that cheaters may be noticed and denied reciprocation by the group, altruism between members of an ingroup can flourish. In this way, altruism can become socialized to a group where altruistic acts are performed freely with anticipation of reciprocity. This could be a mechanism of **group selection** where natural selection acts at the group level, favouring groups with norms such as reciprocal altruism because of the benefits they provide to its members. This makes even more sense from an evolutionary perspective where in ancient times individuals of an ingroup would be likely to share significant genetic relationships, reinforcing the reciprocal altruism model with kin selection theory (see below) in terms of prosocial behaviour.

Axelrod and Hamilton (1981) used the "Prisoner's dilemma" (a thought experiment introduced in Unit 2) to describe reciprocal altruism. Two "prisoners" are caught at a crime

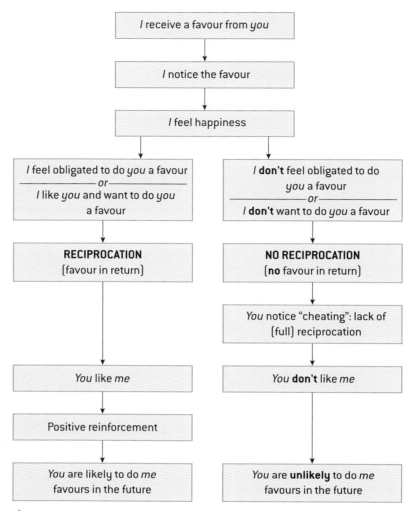

▲ Figure 7.7 Reciprocal altruism model

scene and brought in for police questioning. They are presented with a situation where they may cooperate with each other or cheat. The individuals are rational and do not know what the other is doing. Each person can cheat on the other or remain loyal, so there are four possible outcomes. The best communal outcome requires both individuals to cooperate but the best individual outcome requires individuals to cheat. When repeating this game over and over, individuals are given the opportunity to learn the patterns of the other so cheating behaviour may result in retaliation while loyalty may result in loyalty. If this is a single occurrence and no future relationship between the individuals is assumed, the likelihood of cheating is higher. However, if they are given the opportunity to learn over time, cooperation is more likely to be the option of choice because reciprocal altruism will have been learned.

		Person 1	
		Cooperate (reward)	Cheat (reward)
Person 2	Cooperate (reward)	Person 1 (3)	Person 1 (6)
		Person 2 (3)	Person 2 (0)
	Cheat (reward)	Person 1 (0)	Person 1 (0)
		Person 2 (6)	Person 2 (0)

▲ Table 7.4 The "Prisoner's dilemma"

Kin selection theory

Kin selection theory **(Hamilton, 1964)** is another evolutionary explanation of prosocial behaviour. In short, it proposes that prosocial behaviour can be explained through the concept of indirect fitness or inclusive fitness. The idea here is that it is evolutionarily beneficial to help those with similar genes to you so helping behaviour can be explained through an evolutionary perspective. Helping an identical twin will help that twin pass on his or her (and your) genes to the next generation. Similarly, helping a brother or sister means you are helping to pass on half of your genes. This would imply that helping behaviour is more likely to be targeted at younger, healthy kin who are likely to have more children.

There are problems with this theory that must be addressed. It seems limited to helping only those members of society who share your genes, and preferentially helping those with whom you share more genes. There are two problems here: first, helping (altruistic) behaviour takes place between strangers, and second, there is an assumption that we are able to identify kin from strangers. Both of these problems can be explained with evolutionary explanations.

When humans were still grouped in small, hunter-gatherer tribes neither of these things would be a problem. Hunter-gatherer bands were made up largely of interrelated individuals so nearly everyone you saw everyday was somehow genetically related to you. You would simply help universally as all members shared some genetic information. One factor found in animal research that seems to counter this effect is competition between kin. Competition between kin can not only decrease helping behaviour but increase aggression.

Kin relationships are also defined by much more than a genetic similarity. Individuals living in close proximity share environments (and related challenges) and have bonded to each other. Kajanus (2016) points out that this **nurture kinship** may influence helping behaviour and help extend Hamilton's theory from biological to sociocultural applications of kinship. It would also explain adoption kinship as a nurture kinship.

Empirical support for Hamilton's kin selection theory can be found in several studies. In **Essock-Vitale and Maguire's (1985)** study 300 Caucasian, middle-class women in Los Angeles were randomly sampled in a random-digit telephone dialling procedure to solicit participation. Once selected, participants completed the social relationships questionnaire. Results supported the hypothesis predicted by both kin selection theory and the reciprocal altruism model. These were some of the findings.

- Helping among friends was more likely to be reciprocal than between kin.

- Closer kin were more reliable sources of help than more distant kin.

- Reproductive potential increased helping among kin.

- More substantial instances of helping were more likely to be offered by kin.

The social relationship questionnaire has been shown to be a reliable measure but it is still reliant on self-reporting and could be subject to bias and the social desirability effect. The researchers acknowledge that participants reported giving more help than they got and paying back more often than they were paid back.

Further support can be found in **Stewart-Williams (2007)**. In a study of undergraduate students researchers supported the Essock-Vitale and Maguire study and found that with a higher cost of helping, kin received more of the help and non-kin less. Friends received more help than kin in the low-cost helping condition, medium-cost help was equal between friends and kin, and high-cost help was preferentially given to kin. They also noted high levels of reciprocal exchange between kin and non-kin. Another area of interest for researchers is how individuals differentiate between kin when helping. **Webster (2003)** found that scarcer resources resulted in more evolutionarily conservative actions, for example, favouring closer kin who were more likely to reproduce successfully. So, the effects of kin selection seem to be exaggerated when resources are scarce. Webster (2003) found that when resources are scarce, behaviour predicted by kin selection theory is magnified, for example, more closely related kin is favoured over more distant relatives and younger relatives are favoured over older relatives.

Empathy-altruism hypothesis

The empathy-altruism hypothesis was proposed by C Daniel Batson who, refreshingly, believed that people act to help others out of empathetic feelings and genuine concern for the well-being of other people. In contrast to social exchange theory (people only help others when benefits outweigh costs), Batson argues that empathetic concern for others will predict helping behaviour regardless of what they will gain.

This is a comforting theory and it implies some wonderful things about human nature if it is true. However, in experimentation, Batson was faced with a methodological problem: the social desirability effect. He had to distinguish between altruistic helping and egoistic helping but people will tend to self-report in a way that makes their actions seem socially desirable—that is, altruistic not egoistic.

Exercise

Research August Comte, the man who coined the term "altruism". Helping a crying child because the sound of a crying child is distressing to you is an example of egoistic helping. Helping a crying child because you feel empathy and concern for the distressed child is an example of altruistic helping. What other examples can you find of altruistic helping and egoistic helping?

Batson designed an experimental model called the **empathy escape paradigm** to solve the tricky problem of differentiating between the two types of helping motivation. This experimental design rests on an assumption that empathy for a sufferer can be evoked. Batson often relies on perceived similarity between observer and victim to evoke empathy. If we accept that similarity leads to empathy then it is possible to set up a condition of high empathy (perceived similarity) and low empathy (perceived dissimilarity). A second variable, ease of escape, is controlled so that some participants are allowed an easy escape from a condition while others are not. (See Unit 1 on research methodology for a discussion of the 2 × 2 experimental design that Batson uses here.)

Batson hypothesized that those in high empathy conditions will help in both "difficult escape" and "easy escape" conditions, while those in low empathy conditions will offer help mainly in difficult escape conditions and simply choose to escape in easy escape conditions. Since escape solves personal distress it was hypothesized that those motivated by distress would simply leave the situation. Batson's empathy-altruism hypothesis

has been supported in more than 25 experiments that share the empathy escape design.

Research shows that individuals who are told to imagine another person's distress experience more intense physiological arousal than those told simply to observe movements (Stotland, 1969, cited in **Toi, Batson and Steiner (1982)**. The researchers manipulated empathy levels in female introductory psychology students by asking one group to imagine the feelings of a victim while the second group was asked to simply focus on movements of the victim. Both the high and low empathy groups were further broken down into easy and difficult escape conditions. Results showed that participants in the low empathy condition helped less when escape was easy than when it was difficult, suggesting that their helping was egoistic (reducing their own distress). Participants in the high empathy condition displayed a high rate of helping no matter the escape condition. A further study tested whether helping could be explained by two alternative egoistic explanations: expectation of reward (praise or honour) or avoiding punishment (guilt or shame). Findings showed support for the empathy-altruism hypothesis while neither of the egoistic explanations was supported (Batson *et al*, 1988).

Possibly one of the strongest alternatives to Batson's hypothesis is the **negative state relief model** argued by **Cialdini *et al* (1987)**. They argue that increased empathy for a victim brings increased sadness for the observer and that it is the egoistic relief of this sadness rather than altruistic motivation to relieve suffering in the victim that motivates helping. To test their suggestion, Cialdini *et al* claim to have separated empathy and sadness in their experimental design. They found that sadness predicted helping behaviour but empathy did not, suggesting empirical evidence against the empathy-altruism hypothesis as participants were acting primarily to diminish personal levels of sadness. In a second experiment, Cialdini *et al* found that participants who were led to believe that their moods could not be altered (as a result of a temporary "mood-fixing" placebo drug) did not help despite high levels of empathy. These results suggest support for a helping model based on egoistic helping, even in high empathy conditions.

In one of the great debates of psychology, Batson and colleagues fired back with another study testing Cialdini *et al*'s claims. In a clever experiment,

Batson's team was able to separate participants into two groups: one expecting mood improvement and one not expecting mood improvement. They then further separated the groups into high and low empathy conditions. Batson *et al* found that the rate of helping among high empathy participants did not change between the group expecting improved mood and the one that did not. Regardless of anticipated mood change, high empathy participants helped more than low empathy participants. **Batson *et al* (1989)** claim further support for the empathy-altruism model from these findings.

Culture and prosocial behaviour

If helping behaviour is affected by culture, we should expect to see significantly different findings in cross-cultural research. As we have seen, many explanations of helping behaviour are based on evolutionary psychology and should therefore transcend cultures. There seems no doubt that helping behaviour is evident in all cultures; what remains to be examined is what motivates helping across cultures and how culture affects the extent and the type of help offered. Researching a complex social phenomenon such as helping behaviour can be challenging but there is a growing body of research focused on identifying differences in helping behaviour across cultures.

Psychology in real life

The World Giving Index is a publication of the Charities Aid Foundation and claims to be the world's leading study of global generosity, exploring how countries donate money, volunteer and help strangers. It can be viewed at https://www.cafonline.org/about-us/publications/2016-publications/caf-world-giving-index-2016.

In their book *Children of Six Cultures*, **Whiting and Whiting (1975)** suggested that differences in prosocial behaviour may be caused by differing socialization and child-rearing practices. Research for the book included naturalistic observations of children between the ages of 3 and 11 in six

different cultures: India, Mexico, Kenya, Japan, the Philippines and the USA. Results showed that children in Kenya displayed the most prosocial behaviour followed by those in Mexico and the Philippines. Those from Japan, India and the USA showed the lowest levels of prosocial behaviour. Whiting and Whiting suggested traditional cultures socialize children to be more prosocial. They also suggested a link between Hofstede's concept of cultural collectivism and prosocial behaviour.

Johnson *et al* (1989) conducted research on university students across six cultures (Australia, Egypt, South Korea, Taiwan, the USA and Yugoslavia) to test cultural differences in giving help, receiving help, and the rated importance of helping behaviour. After analysis of the self-reported data, the researchers found that helping behaviour between the samples showed substantial consistency. The frequency of giving, receiving and the importance of helping was also consistent across samples. Johnson *et al* did acknowledge that their self-reported findings are subject to social desirability but that because reports of giving and receiving help roughly balanced, social desirability did not play a significant role.

Levine *et al* (2001) ran an international field experiment spanning 23 cities examining helping behaviour across cultures. Previous research showed that helping behaviour does vary across communities, particularly illustrating that as the population size and density of a city increases, helping behaviour decreases (Levine *et al*, 1994; Amato, 1983).

Levine's team measured three types of non-emergency helping behaviours: alerting a person who dropped a pen, offering to help a person with an injured leg trying to reach magazines, and helping a blind person cross the street. Helping rates across the three measures were stable, however, between cultures there was large variation in helping behaviour, suggesting cultural influences. Overall, helping behaviour was inversely related to economic productivity (GDP), perhaps due to the more traditional value systems associated with less developed cultures. Another cultural measure that was discussed by Levine was the concept of *simpatia*—*simpatia* cultures are characterized by an emphasis on socio-emotional awareness and concern with the well-being of others. Countries with a tradition of *simpatia* were more helpful, on average, than countries without this tradition. Despite these findings, there are still outliers such as Vienna ranking very high despite a high GDP and Kuala Lumpur rating low.

The table below shows the top five and bottom five scores from the study.

City, country	Ranking by helping behaviour	Overall helping index (%)
Rio de Janeiro, Brazil	1	100
San Jose, Costa Rica	2	100
Lilongwe, Malawi	3	100
Calcutta, India	4	92
Vienna, Austria	5	75
Sofia, Bulgaria	19	57
Amsterdam, The Netherlands	20	53.7
Singapore, Singapore	21	48
New York, USA	22	44.7
Kuala Lumpur, Malaysia	23	40.3

▲ Table 7.5

Source: Levine *et al*, 2001.

Recent cross-cultural research by **Chopik *et al* (2017)** looking at the role of culture and its influence on dispositional empathy, agreeableness, conscientiousness and perspective taking was conducted with a massive online sample of over 104,000 participants in 63 different cultures. Participants completed an online questionnaire. Internet sampling is considered a strength as it is often more diverse in terms of age, ethnicity and income than traditional undergraduate samples (Gosling *et al*, 2004). Remember that it is assumed that empathy is associated with prosocial behaviour. The researchers found the following.

- Collectivism is positively related with higher empathetic concern.

- Empathetic concern was not related to any of Hofstede's other dimensions of culture.

- Volunteerism and helping were positively related to empathetic concern, perspective taking and total empathy.

- Charitable giving was unrelated to any of the empathy measures. However, this is not a

reliable measure of prosocial behaviour as it may be related to wealth more than empathetic concern.

In summary, it appears from empirical research that prosocial behaviour is indeed influenced by culture and that collectivism and an emphasis on traditionalism play a role in promoting prosocial behaviour while population density and the degree of modernization limit it.

Discussion

Altruism has many definitions. Let's use a strict definition: altruism is an act to help another person at a cost to the helper. We have spent time discussing whether helping behaviour is altruistic (Batson) or egoistic (Cialdini). Without a doubt, both types of helping are present all around us. Consider the example of anonymous kidney donation.

Would you donate one of your kidneys anonymously? Why do you think some people are willing to do so? Do you think anonymous kidney donation is a purely selfless act to help another person?

Bystanderism

In October 2011, Wang Yue, a two-year-old in Foshan, China, was tragically struck by a van after she wandered into an alleyway behind her father's hardware store. The driver initially stopped but continued running over the young girl. That is tragic but what offended tens of millions of Chinese citizens, and led to the story of this tragedy reaching millions more around the world, was that no fewer than 18 passers-by ignored the bleeding, crying toddler as she lay dying in the street. She was run over by another truck before being dragged to the side by a rubbish collector and taken to hospital where she died eight days later.

In September 2016, a 22-year-old woman was stabbed to death on a busy street in Delhi as people walked past without intervening. Just two days before, a 28-year-old woman in Burari, India was stabbed to death in front of her house in full view of her neighbours, but no one offered help.

The normal response to the above situations is revulsion and condemnation of those who did not intervene. Questions inevitably asked include, "what are they thinking, why didn't someone help?" or "how could they be so uncaring and heartless?" These questions are often followed with self-righteous indignation declaring that, "I would have done something if I had been there!"

The bystanders who witnessed these acts are not heartless animals; they simply succumbed to something psychologists call the **bystander effect**.

We like to believe we are good people; that we are the kind of person someone can count on in an emergency. Decades of psychological research into something called the bystander effect raises doubts about that. The bystander effect refers to the phenomenon where a person's likelihood of helping decreases when passive bystanders are present in a critical situation. There are countless examples like the ones given above describing tragedies that could have been avoided if only someone had intervened to help someone in need.

A similar murder to the ones mentioned above happened in New York in 1964. Kitty Genovese was stabbed to death in two attacks that spanned 30 minutes. The *New York Times* published an article stating that 38 people had witnessed the murder and did nothing. This turned out to be an exaggeration but it was enough to spark public outrage. The story of her murder has been turned into a movie entitled *37*. Acting on the story, two young social psychologists, Bibb Latane and John Darley, set out to understand the behaviour that would become known as the bystander effect.

Factors affecting bystanderism

Latane and Darley spent most of their careers looking at social inhibition and continually built upon theories of social psychology related to bystanderism. Their first two studies are still classics in social psychology.

Research in focus: Bystander intervention in emergencies—diffusion of responsibility

This study is a classic in social psychology by **Latane, Darley and Mcguire (1968)**. In this study, undergraduate students at a New York university took part for partial course credit.

Participants were told they would be asked questions and have a discussion over an intercom about the personal problems of being a university student under stress. Participants were kept in separate rooms and communicated by intercom, supposedly to allow for anonymity but in reality it allowed for the necessary deception to take place. At a designated point in the "discussion" a confederate posing as a participant faked

a seizure over the intercom so that the real participant could hear it.

The independent variable in this experiment was the number of people (bystanders) that the participant thought were listening to the seizure on the intercom.

The dependent variable was the time it took for the participant to react, from the start of the confederate's seizure until the participant contacted the experimenter.

The number of witnesses had a significant impact on the participant's reaction time as shown in the chart below.

Group size	N	% responding by the end of seizure	Time in seconds to contact experimenter
Participant and victim	13	85	52
Participant, victim and one other	26	62	93
Participant, victim and four others	13	31	166

The findings concluded that the ambiguity of the situation (being unsure that something serious was wrong) and the belief that others would do something (diffusion of responsibility) prevented participants from reacting. The researchers

reported that the participants' reactions revealed that they believed the seizure to be genuine and those who intervened or asked the experimenter at the termination of the study if the person was all right were relieved to find out all was well.

Research in focus (continued)

The researchers were able to conclude that inaction (bystanderism) in the face of emergency or recognition that others are in need of help is the result of two factors: diffusion of responsibility and fear of possibly misreading a situation. This is in contrast to what many claimed at the time of Kitty Genovese's murder: "alienation by industrialization", "dehumanization by industrialization", or "psychopaths" as the cause of inaction.

Perhaps the most important conclusion to be taken from this study, in the words of the researchers, is that, "If people understand the situational forces that can make them hesitate to intervene, they may better overcome them."

Research in focus: Group inhibition of bystander intervention in emergencies

This study, also by **Latane, Darley and Mcguire (1968)** is commonly referred to as the "smoke-filled room study". This experiment is different from the one above in an important way. Whereas participants in the above study were alone (isolated in their own private interview room communicating over intercom), this study put confederates into the same room as participants. Given that responding to emergencies could be considered a social norm, one might assume that individuals would be more likely to react in the presence of other people. If this is true, then groups in direct communication with each other should respond to emergencies better than those not in communication.

In order to take action, an individual must first perceive an emergency is taking place. In the presence of others, they may take cues from others. If others do not interpret an emergency, this may play a role in an individual's choice to intervene.

In this study, participants (male Columbia University students) were directed to a waiting area for the experiment to begin and were asked to fill out a questionnaire while they waited. In the first condition, participants witnessed an ambiguous but potentially dangerous situation where smoke began entering the room from an air vent. The second condition had the participant sit with two confederates who did not respond to the smoke and were instructed to limit conversation with the participant. A third condition had three participants in the room without confederates. All participants were observed through a one-way mirror and timed on their reaction to the smoke entering the room. If

Condition	% responding before termination	Notes
Alone	75	Short hesitation then left room to inform experimenter that, "something strange going on in there, there seems to be some sort of smoke coming through the wall ..." Mean reaction time was 2 minutes.
Two passive confederates	10	Nine of ten participants kept working while waving smoke from their faces, coughing and rubbing their eyes and even opening a window for air for the duration of the six-minute time period.
Three naive participants	38	Given that three participants are now able to respond, mathematical analysis claims that response rate should be near 98%. Only 1 of 24 reported within four minutes. Only 3 of 24 reported within six minutes.

Research in focus (continued)

participants did not report the smoke within six minutes, the experiment was terminated.

The independent variable in this experiment was the number of witnesses to the smoke in the room.

The dependent variable was the reaction time of the participants in reporting the smoke to experimenters.

Again, the number of witnesses had a very significant effect on the reaction time of participants, with the "alone" participants reacting the most quickly.

Researchers concluded that if an individual is to intervene the person must first notice an event, then label it an emergency, and then take responsibility. Each of these steps represents an opportunity for inaction. This experiment primarily examined the second step. People look to those around them for cues to action or inaction. The reaction of others exerts a strong influence on behaviour. We look to others to guide our behaviour; when the group is inhibited, so are we.

These research studies show that the following are important factors in a person's decision to act or not to act.

- **Diffusion of responsibility**: the perception that others are witnessing an event will significantly decrease the likelihood that an individual will intervene in an emergency. This may be because they believe someone else will act but also because they are more comfortable sharing blame than taking all the blame personally.

- **Ambiguity of the situation**: if individuals are unsure whether there is indeed an emergency, they may be less likely to react for fear that they have misread the situation and acted in a way that breaks social norms of decorum.

- **Group inhibition**: we look to others in order to help us interpret situations, especially in ambiguous situations. If others are not acting, we are likely not to act either. A social norm of not acting has been established and acting while others are not would break that norm. As we are social animals, we choose not to break the norm and appear foolish or as if we are overreacting.

Another way to explain bystanderism is through conformity and social influence. Conformity is social influence defined as adherence to social norms or group behaviour. Conformity can help us understand bystanderism if we interpret bystanders as a social group who have implicitly agreed to a norm of non-action. Bystanderism could be viewed as a type of conformity governed by informational and normative social influence.

- **Informative social influence (social proof)**: acting in accordance with group behaviour in an attempt to act "correctly". Individuals are convinced the group is acting in the correct manner and adjust behaviour to act correctly. For example, individuals are convinced by the inaction of others that a situation they initially identified as an emergency is, in reality, not one and so, like those around them, they don't act.

- **Normative social influence**: acting in accordance with group norms in order to "fit in" and be seen as a member of the group. Individuals may not be convinced of the truth of the group belief but adjust behaviour to maintain the group norms and membership within the group. For example, an individual is worried about being judged and excluded from the group if he or she acts. Fear of embarrassment, overreaction, or ridicule may be motivating factors here.

In a follow-up study called "A lady in distress", Latane and Rodin (1969) examined how a witness's relationship to other witnesses could affect behaviour in an ambiguous situation. They submitted 120 male undergraduates to one of three conditions: waiting alone, waiting with a stranger, or with a friend when a woman appeared to cry out in pain in a room nearby. The "waiting alone" condition resulted in the quickest response while the paired friends responded faster than paired strangers, suggesting that the relationship with other bystanders may act as a factor in bystanderism. A non-reacting confederate resulted in the most inhibition, a stranger moderately inhibits and then a friend results in the least inhibition of the three. Early research on bystanderism suggests that the old maxim that "there's safety in numbers" might be false and that if you find yourself in need of help, it is safest to have only one bystander nearby.

Research also suggests that social inhibition will occur in a field experiment as readily as it did in the above laboratory experiments. An analysis of a decade's worth of work and 50 studies both in the field and in the laboratory suggests that social inhibition (bystanderism) is a remarkably consistent phenomenon (Latane and Nida, 1981). The next meta-analysis of bystanderism studies was not published until 2011. Fischer *et al* (2011) examined data from studies on over 7,700 participants and identified several factors that weakened bystander inhibition. The bystander effect was reduced in the following conditions.

- Dangerous situations: these are more quickly and definitely identified as emergencies, and a higher cost for refusing help increases the accepted costs for helping (Fischer *et al*, 2006). This is especially true when more than one bystander is present (Harari, Harari and White, 1985).

- Bystander's perceived competency: a belief in the ability to intervene successfully on the part of a witness can weaken the bystander effect (Van den Bos, Müller and Van Bussel, 2009).

In addition to these, we know from conformity research that once unanimity within a group is broken, conformity weakens and more bystanders are likely to intervene. Bystanders are not always inhibitory. Sometimes there is strength in numbers; bystanders can act in a supportive role that encourages rather than inhibits helping behaviour.

Link to prejudice and discrimination

Finally, social identity seems to play a role, suggesting that people are more likely to come to the aid of ingroup members than those considered members of an outgroup. Researchers in Gdansk, Poland found that prosocial behaviour was directed to ingroup religious members, but not towards religious outsiders. In a field experiment completed on public transport, researchers set up three conditions: a disabled researcher boarded a train in the habit of a Christian nun (ingroup member), as a Muslim woman in a hijab, or as an atheist wearing a T-shirt with the word "God" crossed out. Ninety trials were run (30 in each condition). Researchers found that the ingroup member was consistently offered a seat in shorter time than the two other conditions (Różycka-Tran, 2017).

Cyberbystanderism, the bystander effect on the internet

Several studies have illustrated that the bystander effect transfers to the online world. Online chat rooms were explored in one study. Results showed that the higher the number of people in an online chat group, the longer it took for a request for help to be answered. They also found that the bystander effect was virtually eliminated when help was requested while specifying one bystander's name (Markey, 2000).

Other research on cyberbystanderism and cyberbullying also supported the concept of online bystander effects. A study by Brody and Vangelisti (2015) found that a higher number of bystanders and perceived anonymity were both negatively related to helping. These findings add the disturbing effect of anonymity as a reinforcing component of bystanderism.

As online environments are sometimes anonymous, researchers tested helping behaviour in two studies examining the role of anonymity. In two conditions where public self-awareness was higher, one in which participants' usernames were visible online and another where a webcam was used, more helping behaviour was in evidence. Researchers concluded that increased public self-awareness weakened the bystander effect online (Van Bommel *et al*, 2012).

Arousal: cost-reward model

Another way to look at helping behaviour and bystanderism is the arousal: cost-reward model (Piliavin *et al*, 1981). This model is based on social exchange theory: the idea that people engage in social interactions that maximize benefits to themselves, sometimes referred to as the resource theory of social exchange. The premise is that people exchange social goods such as smiles, a friendly "hello", love, reproachful glances, angry stares and so on in the same way they exchange commercial goods and services. A strength of this model is that it takes both physiological arousal and cognition into consideration.

This is an interpretation of helping as an egoistic behaviour. According to this model, people experience an unpleasant emotional/physiological arousal when they witness others in distress. Arousal acts as a motivator for action. Witnesses perform a cost-reward appraisal to determine if they should act to help or remain a bystander. There are costs and rewards to both acting and not acting; witnesses are evaluating if there will be a net cost or a net reward for action. If there is a net reward, a bystander will become a helper.

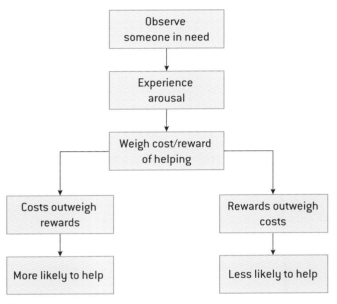

▲ Figure 7.8 Arousal: cost-reward model

The bystander effect is consistently, and too often tragically, seen in real-life situations as well as in experimental research. We have explained prosocial behaviour and the bystander effect separately but they are, of course, inextricably linked to each other. In a way, bystander research is simply a way to observe a group's influence on prosocial behaviour. It is important to remember that categorical thinking is **reductionist**. Human behaviour is complex, and infinitely more so in social situations. Categorical thinking is harmful to full explanations; you can use everything you know about human psychology to explain human behaviour. In short, any lines drawn between different behaviour such as bystanderism and prosocial behaviour are entirely arbitrary and should be erased when it makes for a better explanation of behaviour.

ATL skills: Research

Search the internet to find an example of a real-life situation where the bystander effect has been observed. These situations are tragically common and should be easy to find on reliable news sites. Then do a similar search for a more uplifting story of witness intervention where someone intervened to help an individual in need of help.

Research in focus: "Good Samaritanism: An underground phenomenon"

In a now famous field experiment called "Good Samaritanism: An underground phenomenon", Piliavin and fellow researchers (1981) set up an emergency situation and explained the findings using the arousal: cost-reward model.

The experiment was staged on a short subway ride in New York. Escape was impossible as the train was in motion. In each trial four researchers (two male and two female) entered the train as a team. One male played the victim while the other was a model; the female researchers sat, observed and took notes discreetly. The model was to help if no one intervened after 70 seconds. In 38 trials, the victim appeared drunk while in 65 trials he had a cane and appeared sober.

The independent variable was the condition of the victim, either drunk or sober.

The dependent variables included the frequency of help, the time it took for help to come, and the gender of the helper.

Findings showed that 93% of the time help was offered before the model had to act (70 seconds). The "cane/sober" condition received help 100% of the time with a mean response time of only 5 seconds. The "drunk" condition received help 81% of the time but with a much slower mean time of 109 seconds. Interestingly, diffusion of responsibility was not found in this study. The fact that this was a public field study with little ambiguity may explain why this was so. Piliavin's team explained the findings in terms of the arousal: cost-reward model.

- The drunk is helped less because costs for helping are higher (potential danger) and

Research in focus: (continued)

costs for not helping are lower (less negative judgments from others because he is a victim of his own alcohol consumption).

- Females helped less because costs for helping are higher in this situation (potential for harm) and costs for not helping are lower (less negative judgment from others as at

the time, it was not considered a woman's role).

Helping others of the same race can be explained by different costs for not helping (less censure if one is of opposite race) and in the drunk condition, different costs for helping (fear of other race based upon negative stereotypes).

Discussion

With a partner, try to analyse the situations identified above. Can you use the models and theories of prosocial behaviour and the bystander effect to explain why the two situations resulted in different behaviours?

Promoting prosocial behaviour

Prosocial behaviour is desirable in a population because everyone benefits when those around them are concerned and act in a way that promotes their well-being. However, we have seen evidence that reasonable people do not always respond to situations in a way that supports others in need. Are there ways to encourage individuals to overcome the bystander effect and act prosocially?

Legislation: A duty to rescue?

Individuals often decide not to help in situations where they fear there may be legal consequences for helping. For example, a young man came to the aid of an elderly woman and took her to the hospital. He was then accused by the woman of knocking her over. He was forced to pay 40,000RMB (US$6,000) in medical expenses for his good deed (Ye, 2011).

Many countries around the world have a **Good Samaritan law**. These laws are designed to protect from blame any person who tries to help someone in need. In legal speak, many of these laws protect rescuers from legal liability if they provide help but end up failing in their rescue or even cause harm in the attempt. Many go even

further and require punishment for bystanders in both criminal and civil law if they directly witness a dangerous incident but do not intervene in situations that pose no risk to the helper or another person.

Examples of these laws appear below.

- **Australia:** "Any person who, being able to provide rescue, resuscitation, medical treatment, first aid or succor of any kind to a person urgently in need of it and whose life may be endangered if it is not provided, callously fails to do so is guilty of a crime and is liable to imprisonment for 7 years" (cited in Pardun, 1998).

- **Argentina:** "A person who endangers the life or health of another, either by putting a person in jeopardy or abandoning to their fate a person unable to cope alone who must be cared for ... will be imprisoned for between 2 and 6 years" (Germán Hassel, n.d.).

- **Quebec, Canada:** "Every human being whose life is in peril has a right to assistance. Every person must come to the aid of anyone whose life is in peril, either personally or calling for aid, by giving him the necessary and immediate physical assistance, unless it involves danger to himself or a third person, or he has another valid reason" (Gouvernement de Quebec, n.d.).

These laws are based on social exchange theory. The costs of acting when you might face legal liability is a very strong deterrent. The point of these laws is to reverse that deterrent so that inaction becomes punishable while helpers are protected from punishment (liability) in the event that they attempt to help.

Psychology in real life

One area of research for Good Samaritan laws has been in the area of drug overdoses and immunity from prosecution. The Good Samaritan Drug Overdose Act in Canada protects individuals from prosecution if they call a rescue line to help a person who has overdosed on an illegal substance. The theory is that worries about police involvement at an overdose incident may decrease calls to emergency lines for medical care, increasing the chances of death. This fundamentally changes the cost-reward analysis of helping a victim of a drug overdose by calling emergency services.

Read the article below for more information on how this works.

https://sooke.pocketnews.ca/good-samaritan-drug-overdose-act-becomes-law-in-canada/

These bills are relatively new and there is little research on their effectiveness. Nevertheless they are theoretically sound and have widespread support. The bill in Canada was passed in the legislative branch unanimously and has support from the British Columbia provincial health officer, chief coroner, and the major municipal unions of firefighters and police. Time will tell whether this manipulation of human cost-reward appraisal will save lives.

Socialization and early years education

Perhaps the best way to promote prosocial behaviour is to enculturate or socialize young people into a culture of caring. The question then shifts from a focus on changing people's behaviour to instilling values through education and socialization. If children are taught that social norms include expectations of helping those in need, perhaps normative and informational social influence can play a larger role in promoting prosocial behaviour and weakening the bystander effect.

Early education is important for two reasons: young children are still learning social norms and will conform more readily and the plasticity at this age of development leads to more effective,

long-term behavioural change. Patterns of empathy and prosocial action remain plastic throughout life but plasticity is pronounced in early childhood (Davidson *et al*, 2012).

Research into a **mindfulness-based kindness curriculum (KC)** has shown that promoting prosocial dispositions (empathy and compassion) and self-regulation in pre-school children may be an effective way to build a culture of caring. The KC aims to cultivate attention and emotional regulation and promote empathy, gratitude and sharing.

Researchers investigated the effects of a four-month KC on prosocial behaviours and self-regulation in 68 pre-schoolers. Participants were either assigned to the KC (30) or a wait list (38). Those in the KC condition spent two lessons of 20 to 30 minutes each week for 12 weeks in the trial. Participants were assessed on relevant measures before and after the trial. Results showed that students in the KC condition showed larger gains in teacher-reported social skills and that the control group acted more selfishly over time. Researchers also found that those with the lowest prosocial scores before the training ended up benefiting the most (Flook *et al*, 2015).

In related research, it was found that short-term **compassion training** can increase prosocial behaviour (and improvements in mood and health) in adults. Researchers used the Zurich Prosocial Game, a measure of prosocial behaviour that claims to be sensitive to the influence of reciprocity, helping costs and distress cues. Researchers concluded that those who had received compassion training in the form of short, guided compassion meditation showed more prosocial behaviour in the post-training prosocial game (Leiberg *et al*, 2011).

Similarly, a study by Hutcherson, Seppala and Gross (2008) examined whether short loving-kindness meditation increased feelings of social connection and positivity towards strangers. Results showed that loving-kindness meditation did increase feelings of connection and positivity towards unknown others. The interesting thing is that this was found at both explicit and implicit levels, meaning that the active, conscious practice of meditation seems to affect automatic, implicit behaviours. Given that prosocial behaviour is more likely towards those we feel close with, this is another area that could help to promote prosocial behaviour.

ATL skills: Self-management

Meditation has been shown in a wide variety of research to have benefits on stress reduction, self-regulation and prosocial behaviour as well as physical benefits related to cardiovascular health and other stress-related non-communicable disease. Given the growing amount of evidence, it is something we should all be willing to try.

When learning about meditation, there are many mobile apps that can help guide you through the process. Some popular free apps include: The Mindfulness App, Headspace, Calm, MINDBODY, buddhify.

If you have never tried meditating in the past, now is your chance to try it out. Download one of the apps suggested above or search to find one that appeals to you. Find yourself a comfortable and quiet place to sit and try out one of the shorter guided meditations in one of the apps. When you are done, record your thoughts about the experience, noting the date. Keep up with the practice two or three times a week and record your thoughts after each meditation. You should notice it getting easier to concentrate and stay in the present as you progress. Remember, as you practise, you are physically rewiring your brain to reach relaxation, compassion and concentration on command.

Modelling behaviour (as discussed in Unit 4 on sociocultural behaviour) can be a powerful method to promote prosocial behaviour. As Bandura's social cognitive theory argues (and his research shows) individuals learn from observing the behaviour of others. Changing behaviour can be as simple as exposing individuals to the type of behaviour you hope them to adopt. Prosocial modelling is defined as the way that individuals model prosocial values and behaviours in their interactions with learners or clients (Trotter, 2009). As shown by Bandura, positive and negative reinforcement can aid in the learning process.

Prosocial modelling is an effective way to promote prosocial behaviour among offenders. Prosocial modelling on the part of social workers, probation officers and corrections officers has been shown to reduce rates of recidivism (repeat offending). Andrews *et al* (1979) found from tape-recorded interviews that Canadian probation officers who modelled and reinforced prosocial behaviour had clients with lower recidivism rates compared to officers who did not model prosocial behaviours. Two studies by Trotter (1990 and 1996) backed up these findings by showing that volunteer officers who scored above average on socialization scales also had clients with lower recidivism. These findings suggest that modelling prosocial behaviour may decrease antisocial behaviour and therefore reduce recidivism. It seems from this research that something as simple as how we treat offenders may help prevent them from engaging in antisocial behaviours.

DEVELOPMENTAL PSYCHOLOGY

Topics

- Developing as a learner
  - Brain development
  - Cognitive development
- Developing an identity
  - Development of empathy and theory of mind
  - Gender identity and social roles
  - Attachment

- Influences on cognitive and social development
  - Role of peers and play
  - Childhood trauma and resilience
  - Effects of poverty on development

Introduction

Developmental psychology is a study of changes as they occur over the human lifespan. These changes are driven by two interacting processes: maturation and learning. **Maturation** refers to the gradual unfolding of the genetic programme. We develop certain abilities at a certain age because that is how our genes work. **Learning** refers to changes in response to environmental stimuli. Maturation and learning interact. On the one hand, maturation creates a "predisposition" to learning, which manifests itself in the form of "critical periods". For example, there's a critical period for the development of language abilities, and if language is not developed at that time there's a high chance that the brain will never be able to learn language at all (this is evidenced, for example, by the case studies of feral children). On the other hand, learning is often a necessary condition of development: learning is essential to bring the genetic plan to life. The relative contributions of maturation and learning to human development have been the focus of "**nature versus nurture** debate", which remains one of the most fundamental debates in psychology.

As you know, there are three important dimensions of human behaviour: biological, cognitive and sociocultural. Human development is studied through the lens of these three broad aspects. They are not isolated. For example, the genetically programmed development of certain areas of the brain at a certain age makes it possible for a person to develop certain cognitive abilities. Cognitive abilities will influence the way we interpret social interactions and so lead to a formation of **identity**, a representation of one's self in a larger social group. Identity will determine a lot about our interactions with people and these will influence both our cognitive and brain development. This complex process of interaction between the various dimensions of human development is the focus of developmental psychology.

It is essential to understand the major factors that influence cognitive and social development. This research has a lot of practical implications. For example, what is the role of peers and play in a child's development? This has practical implications for home schooling and the design of pre-school curricula. What is the role of childhood trauma in a child's cognitive and social development? This will influence how we approach treatment and education. What is the role of poverty and socio-economic status? This is important for various enrichment programmes.

From the standpoint of theory of knowledge, it seems logical today that our understanding of something might be enhanced by our knowledge of how it has developed. For example, the nature-nurture debate can benefit a lot from the knowledge of how maturation and learning interact in the growing child. This has not always been understood. The first philosopher who emphasized the idea of change and its importance was Heraclitus in Ancient Greece, who said "Everything flows" and "No man ever steps in the same river twice". For a long time after that, however, the idea of change was not given too much attention and much of the discussion focused on things and phenomena as they are (in their current state). The ideas of change and development were later reintroduced by a German philosopher Georg Hegel (1770–1831). Think about this: the genius of Charles Darwin largely depended on his idea to trace the existing species back to their ancestors, and to look at the species in their development rather than the current state. Before Darwin, there were numerous attempts to classify and explain existing species (for example, by the French naturalist Lamarck).

These were largely unsuccessful because they ignored evolution. Darwin did his research shortly after the publication of Hegel's influential philosophical ideas.

Similarly, it seems natural today to look at childhood and adolescence as special periods in human development, but this was not always so. The concept of childhood only emerged in the 17th century when the new advances of society required prolonged education and protection. Previously, children had mostly been viewed as little versions of adults and it was expected they would have similar behaviour, similar experiences and similar responsibilities. The idea that people go through certain "stages" in their psychological development is a relatively recent one.

Psychology in real life

Children can grow up to be very different from what we expect. Think of child soldiers. One of the organizations that was notorious for recruiting children in military operations was Liberation Tigers of Tamil Eelam (LTTE)—a militant organization (recognized as a terrorist group in 32 countries) based in north-eastern Sri Lanka. It was founded in 1976 and suppressed by the Srilankan military forces in 2009. Its goal was to create an independent state for Tamil people in the north and east of Sri Lanka. It was estimated that at least 40% of LTTE fighters were boys and girls aged 9–18. Until 1986 the LTTE had sufficient adult forces so child units went through a standard four-month military training. After 1990, when the LTTE suffered huge losses and, as a result, decided to use child units more extensively, the training was intensified. Apart from the typical physical training in the jungle and reading LTTE literature, the child units were shown lots of Rambo-style videos and carried out "practice" attacks on unprotected border villages. They were trained to be reckless. Many witnesses claimed that LTTE child units were more fanatic, ferocious and dangerous than adult fighters. Children were also used as suicide bombers. At age 13 a girl would be offered the "opportunity" to sacrifice her life and the life of innocent people for the ideas of her military leaders, and she would frantically grab this opportunity because she believed she was doing the right thing.

Why and how does a person become what he or she becomes? What are the contributions of genetics and environmental influences? What is the role of culture? How do people develop their values, attitudes, relationships and abilities?

At some point in history, children were viewed as "small adults", and once they became physically capable they were used as apprentices in their parents' workshops or engaged in other manual labour activities.

Children are not "small adults", though. They are qualitatively different. They do not perceive the world in the same way as adults do. Also, there's no way that a child can understand adult reasoning, so it is the responsibility of adults to understand how children's minds work.

Child-rearing practices have also changed dramatically in the history of mankind. In Medieval Europe, for example, children were often restricted in their cribs so that they could stay motionless and "humble".

It is probably too early for you to have children, but imagine you have. If you have experience in taking care of younger siblings, it will be easier for you to imagine what it is like. If you were responsible for these small people's lives, would you:

- have talked to them while they were still in the womb
- raise them in a bilingual environment assuming that this will boost their cognitive development
- impose a strict set of rules that they have to follow
- punish them when they break the rules
- shout at them if they have done something potentially dangerous for their health?

8 Brain development

Inquiry questions

- What structural change does the brain go through as it is growing?

- How does this change of structure reflect in a change of function?

- Does a young brain function differently from a mature brain?

- When and how do brain cells die, and what are the consequences?

- What methods can be used to study the growing brain?

- How does deprivation affect brain development?

What you will learn in this section

- Structural changes of the brain

  - Neurogenesis

  - Migration

  - Differentiation

  - Pruning

- The study of structure–function relationships

  - Structure–function relationships cannot be studied by one method: using a combination of methods and studies enables us to make generalizations based on sound theory

  - Kolb and Fantie (1989): used triangulation of evidence on the performance of children and adults on the Chicago Word Fluency Test

- Empirical studies of brain development

  - Chugani (1999): PET scans to investigate glucose metabolism in the brains of children aged 0–1

  - Chugani *et al* (2001): the effects of early deprivation on brain development in Romanian orphans

  - Giedd (2004): MRI scans to study white matter and grey matter volume during adolescence

- The limitations of developmental neuroscience

  - Selection of samples

  - Ability/strategy controversy—for example, Hale, Bronik and Fry (1997) on the development of working memory in early childhood

  - Maturation/learning controversy

  - Changing functions

  - Correlational nature of research

This section also links to:

- the nature-nurture debate

- using brain scanning technology, neuroplasticity, localization of function and brain structure (biological approach to behaviour)

- the working memory model (cognitive approach to behaviour)

- Piagetian stages of cognitive development

- methods of research in psychology (experiment, case study, correlation, longitudinal study).

We know that humans go through a process of development. We may look at this process using the three approaches to behaviour: biological (structural brain changes), cognitive (changes in the cognitive functions) and sociocultural (development of the interactions with other people). In developmental psychology it is even more difficult to use these three approaches in isolation: all the aspects of the ongoing development constantly interact with each other. At the same time, to maintain focus of research one has to concentrate on one of the aspects. As a result, studies of brain development (developmental neuroscience) often look at how changes in the brain structure coincide with changes in certain cognitive functions—the so-called **structure–function relationships**. If they do coincide, we may infer that there's a link between structure and function. Whether or not one causes the other is another question.

First, we will look at what is known about the structural changes of the brain, then discuss evidence linking these structural changes to changes in cognitive functioning.

ATL skills: Research

What are the ways to study structure–function relationships? What research methods can be used and to what extent would they be useful for furthering our understanding of the role of maturation in human development?

Discuss the relative advantages and disadvantages of:

- experiments (intentionally manipulating brain structure variables and observing the effects on animal and human development)

- case studies (observing the development of animal and human children with brain damage)

- longitudinal correlational studies (observing the natural course of human development and establishing correlations between brain structure variables and cognitive functioning)

- brain scanning technology (observing brain scans as participants are performing cognitive tasks)

- interviews

- the experience sampling method. (See the section "Role of peers and play" for an explanation.)

ATL skills: Thinking and communication

Suppose you have conducted a longitudinal correlational study where you systematically observed two variables: a biological variable A (for example, density of grey matter in the hippocampus) and a cognitive variable B (for example, the capacity of short-term memory). You registered these two variables every month for two years in a sample of 5 year olds as they grew to 7 years old. Data analysis showed that there was a significant correlation between A and B.

Discuss several alternative explanations of this finding. To what extent are these explanations plausible? Are there reasons to prefer one explanation to the others? Consider, for example, the following explanations.

- A causes B directly. A changes and this causes B to change.

- A causes B with a delay. A changes, and this creates certain conditions that cause a change in B. However, B does not change immediately after A changes.

- A creates a predisposition to B. As A changes, it creates a basis (favourable conditions) for the development of B. B may or may not develop in response to that, depending on other conditions such as environmental variables.

- A and B do not influence each other. The fact that they have similar rates of development is a coincidence.

- B influences A. Short-term memory develops in response to increasing environmental demands and this causes grey matter density to increase due to neuroplasticity.

- Both A and B influence each other in turn.

- There is a third variable—C—that causes both A and B. As C is developing, it causes both A and B to change in similar ways, so we observe correlations between them. However, A and B are not directly related.

Structural changes of the brain

The brain is a complex system of highly interrelated elements, and the successful development of this system requires that each component be formed timely, fully and integrated correctly with other components. Broadly, this process can be viewed in terms of four stages:

1. neurogenesis (the birth of neurons)

2. the migration of neurons to their correct location

3. differentiation (development of connections between neurons)

4. pruning (elimination of these connections as well as neurons themselves).

Neurogenesis is the production of new nerve cells. Mostly, the formation of all the cells in the cortex is finished in the period of gestation; that is, the neurons your brain consists of are all produced by the time you leave your mother's womb. Curiously, the cortex actually overproduces neurons to account for the future normal cell death. This means you have fewer neurons now than when you were just born.

Migration—at about the age of 9 weeks from conception, simultaneously with the production of new cells, neurons start to migrate to their "correct" positions. They travel along special glial fibres that form very early in the fetal brain and extend from the brain's inward structures to the cortical layers.

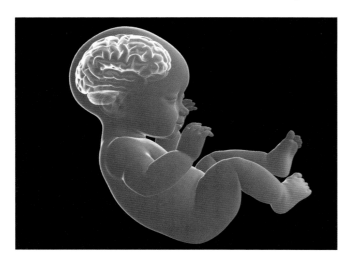

As the brain grows in size, these fibres stretch and curve. Each fibre will subsequently serve as a neuron's pathway to its correct position in the brain. The neuron "climbs" along the fibre like a snake on a tree trunk. After the cell reaches its final position,

dendritic growth starts. It should be noted that neuronal growth in the brain cortex happens layer after layer "inside out"; that is, new neurons are formed below the previously formed layers and then travel outside, passing the existing layers of neurons on their way. Knowing this, it would be logical to assume that whatever stages one can observe in human cognitive development do not substitute, but rather subsume, each other. New patterns of behaviour or abilities are added to the old ones in a complementary manner. This seems to be supported by numerous studies. For example, Piagetian stages of cognitive development (discussed in "Cognitive development") follow the same pattern.

TOK

Development is not always a smooth, linear process. Think about various patterns of development that may be observed in different areas of knowledge. How are these patterns different? Here are some examples to give you a general direction.

- Evolution of species: combinations of genes occur randomly; however, as certain genotypes die out because they are less adapted to environmental demands, more successful genotypes are gradually consolidated.

- Revolution in the development of political systems: governments are overthrown and replaced, which sometimes causes dramatic changes in society.

- Paradigm shifts in sciences: a critical mass of new evidence triggers the process of rethinking the very foundations of science.

Which of these examples do you think is most similar to the development of a human child?

Differentiation is the growth of neural connections (synapses) and **pruning** is the elimination of these connections. Differentiation and pruning occur as follows. Synapses start growing shortly after conception. After some critical point this growth becomes rapid (40,000 synapses per second) and continues rapidly until nearly two years of age in humans. This is followed by a plateau and then rapid reduction in the number of synapses. Elimination of synapses continues at a rate of up to 100,000 synapses per second and lasts until the end of puberty. (No wonder adolescents can be so moody!). Around 50% of initially formed synapses are eliminated during this period. This is followed by another plateau, and then there's another drop in the number of synapses in old age. Interestingly, synaptic density in infants is higher than that of adults. You might have heard the idea that a larger number of connections in the brain means better cognitive abilities. So are infants smarter than adults? It is not that simple, it turns out. The process of pruning and elimination of synapses that are not used might be connected to some qualitative refinement of a developing ability (Kolb and Fantie, 1989).

Pruning and death of neurons are perhaps among the most intriguing findings of developmental neuroscience. Both are linked to environmental stimulation: a lack of such stimulation at a certain critical period may lead to a loss of neurons and/ or connections between them (the "use it or lose it" principle). It would therefore be an understatement to say that knowledge of such critical periods for every function would come in handy. Pruning has been demonstrated in a variety of research studies. One example is **Werker and Tees (1992)** who studied the ability of infants to discriminate between phonemes from English and Hindi. It was shown that infants could discriminate between speech sounds of both languages, but this ability became largely confined to one language only (the one their parents spoke) by the time these infants reached 1 year old.

Exercise

Go online and find out more about pruning and the death of neurons.

For example, review these three short articles with intriguing headings:

"Your brain has a 'delete' button—here's how to use it": https://tinyurl.com/mjnja2w

"Teen brains clear out childhood thoughts": https://tinyurl.com/4yydpuw

"Pruning synapses improves brain connections": https://tinyurl.com/pgyr72u

There is a popular belief that the number of neurons (and the number of inter-neuron connections) directly corresponds to ability. To what extent do you think this belief is substantiated? Write a paragraph either supporting or debunking this belief.

Discussion

The "use it or lose it" principle states that brain connections will be lost if they are not used. Given that infants have the largest number of connections, does this mean that infants must be constantly stimulated with enriched environments (films, toys, flashcards and languages) to ensure future cognitive development as an adult?

The study of structure–function relationships

The knowledge of structural changes in the developing brain alone does not give us much understanding about the psychology of human maturation. A structure–function relationship is too complex and intricate to make inferences such as "area X has grown in size, so function Y has developed".

Moreover, as you know, localization of function is not absolute. Some functions are distributed over large areas of the brain and for some functions it is impossible to establish the exact area that is responsible for it (see "Localization of function" in Unit 2 on the biological approach to behaviour).

All this means that knowledge of structural brain changes should be coupled with knowledge of structure–function relationships in the adult brain. This includes:

- behavioural changes in adults with brain lesions
- neuroimaging evidence for brain areas responsible for performing certain tasks.

Frontal lobes of the cortex have been known to be responsible for performing tasks that involve categorization based on linguistic features (of course, this is not the only function of frontal lobes, but one among many others). One popular measure of this ability is the Chicago Word Fluency Test. In this test participants are required to write as many words as they can think of beginning with the letter "S" in five minutes. After this, the task changes and requires them to write as many four-letter words beginning with the letter "C" in another four minutes. **Kolb and Fantie (1989)** summarize some observations that have involved participants' performance on the Word Fluency Test.

- Frontal lobe regions are active when healthy adult subjects are performing the test.

- Patients with confined frontal lobe lesions do very poorly on the test.

- At the same time, the same patients perform normally on a modification of the test that requires categorization based on non-linguistic features (for example, when asked to write the names of as many objects or animals as they can think of).

- Children perform poorly on the Chicago Word Fluency Test when very young and gradually improve performance as they age.

- In contrast, even very young children perform well on an adult level on the modification of the test (categorization based on non-linguistic features).

Taken together, these observations seem to imply that categorization based on linguistic features depends on the function of frontal lobes, and frontal lobes in a developing brain mature more slowly (and later) than other cortical lobes.

Therefore, it always requires a combination of methods and research studies to arrive at inferences about structure–function relationships in a developing brain. Data triangulation has to be used to eliminate competing explanations. Due to the lack of a more straightforward method of establishing structure–function relationships in a growing brain, it may be said that developmental psychology and neuroscience remain to be segregated. However, the bridges between the two areas of research that have been built so far—and with so much difficulty—look very promising.

Empirical studies of brain development

Before the advent of developmental neuroscience, knowledge of brain development was mostly based on **post-mortem studies**.

Not surprisingly, studies were also focused on the most obvious characteristic—brain size. It was established that the brain increases in size until the age of 9–10 years. However, we know that the size of the brain does not determine cognitive ability linearly. The pattern of connections between neurons is more important than the bulk of neurons as such.

The invention of **brain imaging technology** allowed researchers to get an insight into the physiology of the living brain—first its structure and then even its processes—in almost real time. For a discussion of merits and otherwise of different brain imaging methods, see "Brain imaging technology" in Unit 2 on the biological approach to behaviour.

Chugani (1999) used PET scans extensively to investigate glucose metabolism in newborn babies (aged 0–1 month) to see when brain areas reach the adult level of functioning. This research demonstrated that glucose metabolism in newborn human babies was most prominent in primary sensory and motor cortex, thalamus and brainstem. Other regions were not active.

Note that behaviour of newborn babies is as limited as the number of brain regions displaying metabolic activity—this converging evidence from neuroimaging and from observation may support the idea that brain development is the basis of, or at least in some way linked to, cognitive development. Further studies showed that at the age of 2–4 months glucose metabolism increases in parietal, temporal and primary visual cortex. Behaviourally, children of this age also demonstrate an improvement in a number of tasks such as those requiring integration of visual and spatial information. At the age of 8–12 months there is a rise in glucose metabolism in the frontal cortex. This coincides with the appearance of some cognitively complex behaviours (Chugani and Juhasz, 2006).

Chugani *et al* (2001) studied the effects of early deprivation (environmental factors) on brain development. PET scans were used with 10 children (mean age 8.8 years) adopted by US families from Romanian orphanages. Political and economic problems in Romania in the 1980s resulted in a large number of children being placed in orphanages. Eighty-five per cent of these children were placed in orphanages within the first month of their life, and child–caregiver ratio was low: infants spent up to 20 hours per day in their cribs unattended (Ames and Carter, 1992; cited in Chugani *et al*, 2001). Earlier research had revealed some common patterns in the development of children adopted from orphanages: they show poor cognitive performance at the time of adoption, but considerably recover by the age of 4. Also, some longitudinal studies had shown that those deficits that are still present at the age of 4 persist until at least 6 years of age. This explains Chugani *et al*'s selection of age group: with the mean age of 8.8 years the focus is only on the impairments that have been enduring and were not compensated by the new family environment. The researchers used two control groups.

- One group consisted of 17 normal adults (mean age 27.6 years).

- The other group contained seven age-matched children with focal epilepsy (epileptic symptoms confined to one hemisphere).

In terms of the cognitive and behavioural profile, all orphans showed significant deviations from the norm at the time of adoption. At one year in the adoptive home, however, substantial "catch-up" was reported in all 10 children. At the time of the PET scans parents described their children as having largely caught up with their peers. At the same time there were continued concerns, mostly with regard to attentional difficulties (for example, staying on task), behavioural and academic achievement difficulties.

As compared to normal adults or the non-epileptic hemisphere of children with epilepsy, the orphans in this study showed decreased glucose metabolism in some brain areas; in particular, the prefrontal cortex, amygdala, hippocampus and the lateral temporal cortex. It is also interesting that the brain areas with significantly decreased glucose metabolism in the Romanian orphans are known to be strongly interconnected and vulnerable to prolonged periods of stress. Researchers conclude that dysfunction of these brain regions may result from the stress of early deprivation and may be involved in the long-term cognitive and behavioural disturbances observed in some orphans (Chugani *et al*, 2001).

Discussion

Chugani *et al* (2001) bring together several pieces of evidence, some of them from prior studies, to arrive at conclusions about structure–function interaction in brain development. Note that in this study decreased glucose metabolism in certain brain areas is the "structure", and attentional and other difficulties experienced by the children is the "function".

- Why did the researchers use two control groups?
- What is the role of knowledge from prior research in this study?

How does your knowledge of Chugani *et al*'s (2001) study match with findings from the adoption studies with twins reared apart? If you do not remember these studies, go back and review "Genetics and behaviour" in Unit 2 on the biological approach to behaviour.

Giedd (2004) used MRI scans to study the changing anatomy of the brain during adolescence. Data for this study were derived from an ongoing longitudinal brain MRI study conducted by the National Institute of Mental Health (NIMH). It contained a total of 161 participants who went through MRI scans and neuropsychological testing repeatedly at two-year intervals. Results of the study showed that the healthy adolescent brain cortex goes through a series of changes.

- White matter increases linearly, and the rate of growth is practically the same in the four major lobes (frontal, parietal, temporal and occipital).

- Grey matter shows an inverted U-shape pattern: first it grows, then it reduces in size due to pruning.

- Grey matter also has greater regional variation than white matter.

    ○ For example, frontal grey matter volume peaks at about the age of 11.5 and temporal grey matter volume peaks at about 16.5 years.

    ○ One of the latest brain regions to mature is the prefrontal cortex (responsible for controlling impulses). It does not reach its adult level until the early 20s.

Converging evidence is very valuable in this field of research. It is also important to evaluate research findings in light of the existing theoretical explanations of human development. It is even better if the research process itself is guided by sound theory. If this is the case, we will know what to look for and how to interpret it. A good theory is what we need in order to make sense of the wealth of data.

TOK

A topic for a TOK essay was: "Facts are needed to establish theories, but theories are needed to make sense of facts. Discuss this statement with reference to two areas of knowledge."

Does this statement apply to developmental neuroscience and the role of psychological theories in designing and interpreting research studies in this area?

For example, in his theory of developmental stages Piaget suggested that a child cannot reach a new stage without mastering the previous one. Similarly, evidence from developmental neuroscience suggests that grey matter develops at different rates for different brain regions, and a change in grey matter in a higher-order brain region will not have any effect on cognition if grey matter changes in a supporting brain region have not been completed (Casey *et al*, 2005).

Limitations of developmental neuroscience

Developmental neuroscience has its limitations, some of them not obvious at first sight. Let's consider several of them: selection of samples, the ability/strategy controversy, maturation/learning controversy, changing functions and correlational nature of research.

Crone and Ridderinkhof (2011) argue that the **selection of samples** in developmental neuroscience should be rigorously guided by developmental theories. They give the following example. Although information-processing theories argue that the most prominent changes in working memory occur between the ages of 7 and 12, almost all developmental neuroimaging studies have collapsed these participants in one group, comparing this larger group to adults. As a result, we know that "children and adults are different", but we do not get sufficient insight into the nature of development.

To understand the **ability/strategy controversy**, refer to evidence from dual-task studies of working memory in adults— see Unit 3 on the cognitive approach to behaviour, "Working memory model" (for example, the study of articulatory suppression effects by Baddeley, Lewis and Vallar, 1984). This evidence suggests that distracting verbal information impairs verbal working memory capacity, but not spatial working memory capacity (we used this evidence to support the working memory model in that the "inner ear" and the "inner eye" are two separate components). However, **Hale, Bronik and Fry (1997)** demonstrated that this effect was not seen in 8-year-old children: distracting spatial information also impaired these children's verbal memory and distracting verbal information also impaired their spatial memory. Do we conclude that 8-year-old children have a weaker working memory capacity? Or do we conclude that 8 year olds simply use a different memory strategy, where working memory is less modality-specific? Generally, if we observe a weaker performance on a test in children, this might be due to two reasons, which are:

- having an underdeveloped ability
- using a different strategy for information processing.

It is very difficult to separate these two explanations.

Maturation/learning controversy lies in the fact that the emergence of specific behaviours may be due either to maturation of brain structure or learning. It is hard to separate these two processes because they are constantly interacting.

Developmental neuroscience largely rests on the assumptions of the theory of brain localization (specific brain areas are responsible for specific cognitive functions), but there is limited opportunity to apply these assumptions in the case of the developing brain. The function of a specific brain area may **change over time**. It may happen either due to natural maturation (certain brain areas may naturally re-specialize in a different function) or due to neuroplasticity compensating for brain damage, especially at an early age. (You can refer to other parts of this course for more on this; for example, see "Neuroplasticity" in Unit 2 on the biological approach to behaviour.)

Finally, hypotheses about brain development are hard to test since the human brain cannot be manipulated during growth (or it would be extremely unethical to do so). The overwhelming majority of research studies in developmental neuroscience are therefore **correlational** in nature, which limits cause-effect inferences about structure–function relationships.

Cognitive development

What you will learn in this section

- Piaget's theory of cognitive development

  ○ Cognitive development as a form of adaptation

  ○ Two processes: assimilation and accommodation

  ○ The idea that intelligence develops progressively in a series of stages

    ◆ Sensorimotor stage (birth to 2 years)

      ◇ Object permanence

      ◇ Egocentrism

    ◆ Pre-operational stage (age 2–7 years)

      ◇ Conservation tasks

      ◇ Egocentrism: Piaget and Inhelder (1956) the three-mountains task and research study

      ◇ Borke (1975): criticism of the original study and contrasting evidence

    ◆ Concrete operational stage (age 7–11 years)

    ◆ Formal operational stage (age 11–16 years)

  ○ Evaluation of Piaget's theory of cognitive development

    ◆ The concept of clear-cut stages

    ◆ Maturation as the driving force of development

    ◆ Individual differences

    ◆ Confounding variables in the methods

    ◆ Strengths of the theory

- Lev Vygotsky's sociocultural theory

  ○ The role of culture

    ◆ Higher-order functions

    ◆ Culture provides the tools, the child internalizes them: "every function appears twice"

  ○ The zone of proximal development (ZPD)

    ◆ Teaching should follow maturation (Piaget) versus teaching should be ahead of maturation (Vygotsky)

    ◆ Scaffolding

  ○ Using tools

    ◆ The interpersonal becomes intrapersonal through the use of tools (signs and symbols)

    ◆ The most important system of symbols is language

    ◆ Culture is therefore internalized gradually through language

    ◆ Speech is a tool of thinking

    ◆ Evidence: egocentric speech gradually turns into silent inner speech

○ Evaluation of the theory

♦ Pedagogical experiments

♦ Leontyiev's study of the ability of children to use signs as a tool of memory

This section also links to:

● schema theory and models of memory (cognitive approach to behaviour)

● social learning (sociocultural approach to behaviour)

● role of peers and play in cognitive and social development.

Jean Piaget's theory of cognitive development

Jean Piaget (1896–1980), a Swiss clinical psychologist, is famous for his theory of cognitive development and ground-breaking work in discovering the natural stages through which a human child progresses in the process of cognitive development. His ideas are sometimes referred to as "**genetic epistemology**" (epistemology means theory of knowledge). Early in his career, part of Piaget's work was to mark intelligence tests done by children of various ages. He noticed that certain types of task were almost always done incorrectly when attempted by children of a certain age. This led him to believe that children's cognitive processes are different from those of adults and that children go through a number of relatively clear-cut stages in their development. Much of Piaget's extensive research was done on his own three children.

▲ Figure 8.1 Jean Piaget

Piaget believed that intellectual development is a form of **adaptation**. There are two processes involved: **assimilation** and **accommodation**.

Assimilation occurs when a child reacts to a new object or idea in a way that is consistent with the child's existing mental representations (schemas). Accommodation occurs when after encountering a new object or idea the child modifies the existing mental representation. Think about it as fitting the world into your schema (assimilation) versus fitting your schemas better to the world (accommodation). Both are processes of adaptation.

ATL skills: Self-management

What is a schema? Give a definition. Name five key words (concepts) most closely linked with schema. Then check Unit 3 on the cognitive approach to behaviour to see if you are correct.

Another assumption of Piaget's theory is that intelligence develops progressively in a series of stages that are related to age. "Progressive" development means that for the next stage to occur the previous stage had to be fully formed, because one stage is a prerequisite of another. At the same time each new stage is a better, more adapted version of mental structure: the old structures are modified and superseded. This is somewhat like successive versions of software or hardware: iPhone 6 works pretty well, but iPhone 7 might be even better because certain functions (or structures) are modified in an attempt to be more adaptive to users' needs. The question is, how often does the developing human mind produce "new iPhone versions", and what model is the latest?

Piaget has distinguished four stages of cognitive development.

At the **sensorimotor stage (birth to 2 years)** children's reasoning is subordinate to movement and sensation; that is, they "think" with their hands (and mouth) trying different things, achieving sensory results by accident and then repeating the actions that produced those results (for example, shaking a rattle produces an amusing sound, so they repeat the action). Two important experimentally observed phenomena characterize intellectual development at this stage: **object permanence** (understanding that objects exist even when they are outside your perceptual field; this is formed by the age of 1 year) and **egocentrism** (the belief that the world revolves around you and the inability to understand other people's viewpoints).

Psychology in real life

You might have seen how amused young children are when adults play "peekaboo" with them. The adults hide their face with their hands, then pop back into the view of the child and say "Peekaboo, I see you!". Why is this so much fun? Well, because until object permanence is formed, the child actually thinks that the adult's face disappears and pops back into existence! When you cover your face with your hands, you do not exist anymore. When you remove your hands, you exist again. Spooky, isn't it? That's how an infant's mind works, though.

Similarly, you might have witnessed how young children, when they play hide-and-seek, hide by simply covering their eyes. This is explained by cognitive egocentrism—if they don't see you, they actually believe that you don't see them either.

You'll find more on this in this short article: "Why do children hide by covering their eyes?"

https://tinyurl.com/mk7baeb

The **pre-operational stage (age 2–7 years)** is when children engage a lot in playing and pretending, which means that they are mastering the world of symbols. Manipulating symbols may take the form of pretending that a stick is a spoon, a box is a house, and so on. Unlike during the previous stage, children at this stage are not manipulating the objects as such, instead they play with the meanings associated (sometimes loosely) with those objects. However, the child is still not capable of operations; that is, performing a task mentally in the absence of a physical object or at least a symbol (for example, a drawing). Characteristic of this stage are such phenomena as centration, lack of conservation and irreversibility. Egocentrism still characterizes thinking as well.

Centration is a tendency to focus all attention on one aspect of the situation while ignoring all other

aspects. **Irreversibility** is when the child is unable to mentally reverse the sequence of events. The concept of **conservation** means that physically an object remains the same even when its appearance changes.

Centration, irreversibility and conservation are connected. These phenomena are demonstrated in a number of famous **conservation tasks** that Piaget used in his research. An example is when the child is shown two equal glasses (or beakers) of water and asked which glass has more water in it (the child correctly says that the amount of water is the same). Then the experimenter pours water from one of the glasses into another glass, narrower but taller. The child sees this. When asked which of the glasses now has more water in it, the child points to the tall glass. Piaget's interpretation is that the child is not yet able to mentally reverse the action (irreversibility), so there is lack of conservation in the child's reasoning about the properties of physical objects. Centration is a part of this process because the child only concentrates on one aspect of the situation (how tall the glass is), ignoring the other aspects.

Conservation tasks have been subject to some criticism, especially on the basis of how the questions were formulated. Arguably, the question itself might suggest an answer to young children, and there might be a difference in results depending on whether you are asking "Which of these glasses has more water?" or "Are these equal?". However, most research studies converge in their claim that inability to understand conservation is characteristic of this (pre-operational) age.

▲ Figure 8.2 Piaget's conservation task involving the amount of water in different-shaped glasses

Exercise

There are many videos on YouTube of children being given a conservation task. Watch five or six of those videos. Do you think the results of these studies depend on the way the instruction is worded?

Egocentrism was demonstrated in an experiment by **Piaget and Inhelder (1956)** known as the three mountains task. In this task the child is shown a three-dimensional model of three mountains. There are some features (a cross, a house and snow, for example) that are visible from certain angles and not visible from others. After the child has spent some time exploring the model the researcher introduces a doll. The doll is positioned facing the mountains from a viewpoint different from the child's, and the child is asked to describe what the doll can see. The child gives an answer by choosing one from a range of pictures. Piaget and Inhelder (1956) found that the ability to choose the picture corresponding to the doll's viewpoint dramatically varied with age: 4-year-old children almost always chose the picture that corresponded to their own viewpoint (without realizing that the doll's perception might be different), and only by 7–8 years of age did they begin to pick the correct picture consistently.

▲ Figure 8.3 The three mountains task (Piaget and Inhelder, 1956)

The three mountains task has been criticized on the grounds of its cognitive complexity (possibly being inaccessible to 4-year-old children).

Borke (1975) replicated the study keeping the basic design, but changing the content of the task, avoiding the use of pictures and giving children some initial practice. Grover, a character from popular children's television show *Sesame Street*, was used in this study instead of Piaget's doll. There were two identical objects of the display: one for the child and Grover to look at, and another one on a turntable next to the child. The display itself showed a farm area with details such as people, trees, animals, a lake and a house. Results showed that children as young as 3 years old were able to use the turntable to match Grover's viewpoint, and in 4-year-olds this ability was quite obvious. The

researcher concluded that results of the original study (Piaget and Inhelder, 1956) might have been biased due to the nature of the task, which was cognitively complex and unfamiliar to the children.

At the **concrete operational stage (age 7–11 years)** children are no longer egocentric, they understand conservation and reversibility. Children start solving problems logically. However, they can only solve problems that apply to concrete events or objects. Inductive reasoning (drawing inferences from observations) is developed thoroughly, but children still find it difficult to reason deductively. However, children at this stage acquire mental reversibility, which means that they can understand relationships between mental categories (for example, if a dog is an animal, some animals are dogs). Conservation tasks are passed successfully.

The **formal operational stage (age 11–16 years)** is when children develop abstract thought. Another new formation of this stage is metacognition ("thinking about thinking"). Adolescents become capable of deductive reasoning.

> ### TOK
>
> Piaget's theory of cognitive development is sometimes referred to as "genetic epistemology". In fact, it was Piaget's intention to use systematic observation of children's cognitive development to tackle much wider issues of epistemology (theory of knowledge).
>
> - Can you name examples from different areas of knowledge that illustrate such phenomena as egocentrism, irreversibility and centration?
> - Can you name TOK concepts that are related to these phenomena? (Hint: for example, consider confirmation bias and selectivity of perception).
> - Does the history of scientific views (from antiquity to the modern era) resemble the stages of maturation in a child's cognitive development? For example, think about the parallel between children's performance on the conservation task and the law of conservation of matter.

Evaluation of Piaget's theory of cognitive development

Consider these key points.

- The concept of **clear-cut stages** in human development has been challenged. Initially, Piaget proposed that development progresses in a smooth manner from stage to stage due to biological maturation. However, some observations have shown that children might be capable of solving some tasks from a higher stage with relative ease. This might depend on a number of variables, such as learning.

- **Biological maturation** as the driving force of cognitive development has been brought into question. Piaget seems to have neglected the potential role played by sociocultural variables. Social interaction as a driving force of human development was especially stressed in the theory of Vygotsky (see below).

- The theory does not take into account **individual differences**. The assumption is that all children develop along the same trajectory and approximately at the same rate, as dictated by biological factors.

- **Methods** used by Piaget and his colleagues have also been criticized. First, since most of Piagetian tasks involve one-on-one interaction with the child in a play-like scenario, there are some potentially confounding variables that may skew the results. An example would be the wording of the question in the conservation task. Second, Piaget and his team mainly used a combination of qualitative and quantitative techniques. They devised rigorous replicable tasks where the number of successful trials could serve as a quantitative measure of performance. At the same time, they relied on observation and interviews (for example, asking children why they thought there was more water in the taller glass or beaker) to interpret the reasons behind children's behaviour on a task.

Finally, for many of the studies that Piaget performed, especially in the initial stages of developing the theory, the participants were his own three children. This opens the door to additional objections such as limited generalizability, potential researcher bias and potential participant bias.

However, Piaget has made an important contribution to the field of developmental psychology and beyond. His research prompted systematic collection of data regarding the intellectual development of children. He changed the way scholars think about growing children, drawing attention both to the qualitative differences between children and adults and to the systematic, gradual nature of the cognitive changes that children undergo in their development. Most of the points of criticism, including the ones outlined above, target some limitations of the theory in terms of the areas that need additional research. However, they do not challenge the core idea. Some of the elements of the theory may sound simplistic (for example, lack of attention to possible individual differences) or reductionist (for example, the belief that biological maturation is the main driving force of development), but this is always necessary when someone designs a theory to investigate something that has never been investigated before. Piaget himself never meant his theoretical generalizations to be rigorous. He encouraged his followers to treat them as a starting point, continue systematic observation and experimentation with children, and refine the theory constantly.

Lev Vygotsky's sociocultural theory
The role of culture

This theory stresses that the development of a child cannot be viewed separately from the child's **culture**. As a consequence, the theory emphasizes the role of social interaction, language and a wider historical context (how culture itself was developed throughout the history of humankind).

Vygotsky was born in 1896 (the same year as Piaget) in western Russia, in a town now belonging to Belarus. He died in 1934. His ideas were controversial for the Soviet ideology. On the one hand, the idea that social and cultural factors play a major role in human development went well with the socialist philosophy. On the other hand, the way these ideas were developed (theoretically and empirically) did not always coincide with the preferred viewpoints of the official ideology. This is why it took some time for Vygotsky's work to be recognized as a game-changing contribution to developmental psychology.

Vygotsky was particularly interested in cognitive processes he called "**higher-order functions**". These include voluntary attention, semantic memory and conceptual thinking. The difference between lower and higher cognitive functions is in how voluntary or conscious they are. Lower cognitive functions are not voluntary, so the leading factor in their development is biological maturation. Higher cognitive functions, on the other hand, are subject to voluntary control, and the leading factor of their development is culture.

Vygotsky believed that every function in the child's development "**appears twice**": first it appears on the social level as a characteristic of interaction between people, and then it gets internalized and appears on the individual level as a child's cognitive function. While Vygotsky recognized basic biological constraints dictating what children are and are not able to do, he was mostly interested in the tools that the culture provides—and children internalize—because these tools are what enables children to use their biological potential.

▲ Figure 8.4 Lev Vygotsky

The zone of proximal development

An important part of the theory is the concept of the "**zone of proximal development**" (ZPD). The ZPD is broadly defined through the comparison of three areas: what the child can do by herself or himself, what the child can do with the help of an adult, and what the child cannot do even with a helping adult. The ZPD is the second zone. This also relates to the role of learning in a child's development. For Vygotsky, learning is (and should be) the driving force of development, it is always one step ahead of the natural maturation process. In Vygotsky's interpretation, Piaget's theory suggested that learning should follow "behind" maturation: material should be taught to children at a level that is suited to their current stage of intellectual development. Vygotsky did not agree with that and thought that education should be built in the ZPD: too challenging for children to accomplish by themselves, but perfectly manageable in communication with a helping knowledgeable adult. An example is the role of **scaffolding** in education.

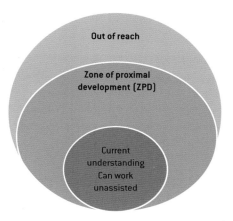

▲ Figure 8.5 The zone of proximal development (ZPD)

Using tools

If culture (which for a child takes the form of interpersonal interaction) is the leading factor of the development of higher cognitive functions, how exactly does the internalization process occur? How does the interpersonal become intrapersonal? Vygotsky stated that reasoning is mediated by **signs and symbols**. Just as we use a physical tool to transform physical reality around us, we use signs to transform ourselves and others.

The most important and culturally universal system of signs is **language**. Vygotsky stressed the importance of language in internalizing the cultural content.

There's a difference between language (the formal system of communicative units) and **speech** (the act of speaking). Language is universal and interpersonal, whereas speech is individual. Vygotsky focused his research on the development of speech as a tool of thinking. The title of his last book was *Thinking and Speech*. Vygotsky claimed that silent inner speech was different from verbal external speech.

Young children, according to his observations, can only think out loud—they accompany all their activities by a running commentary. This is what Piaget called "egocentric speech". It is later that they learn to "compress" their speech gradually; external speech is **"internalized"** and becomes a tool of thinking. This is a step-by-step process. It is evidenced, for example, by recordings of electrical activity in speech muscles. As it turns out, even when you are using your inner speech while you are doing something (for example, solving a mathematics problem), your brain sends motor signals to your speech muscles, but these signals get inhibited along the way. It's as if by default we are programmed to speak out loud to accompany whatever we are doing, but this "default" option is later suppressed.

Evaluation of Vygotsky's sociocultural theory

A common criticism of Vygotsky's theory is that it's too heavily theoretical with a lack of empirical supporting studies. However, it is worth considering these points.

- Vygotsky was aiming at creating a new paradigm in psychology that would incorporate cultural factors into the understanding of an individual subject. This required a lot of theoretical work at the start.

- He died at the age of 37, leaving much of his work unfinished. Experimentally testing his major theoretical claims became his followers' task.

- Vygotsky was against artificial experimental conditions as the basis of experimental psychology, and much of the research that followed was based on a combination of experiments, observations, clinical interviews and the so-called "**pedagogical experiments**" (experiments incorporated into the natural process of teaching). As a result, there are no "outstanding" experiments in this field. Instead, the empirical basis of Vygotsky's sociocultural theory is a vast number of smaller-scale studies.

One example of a typical experimental study to support Vygotsky's claims is a study of memory as a higher cognitive function in the works of **AN Leontyiev**, another important Russian psychologist (1903–1979). In this study subjects of varying age were required to memorize 15 words read out by the experimenter (for example, "hand", "book" and "bread"). In one condition subjects could use 30 cards with pictures as a tool to help them memorize words. The experimenter would say: "When I say the word, look at the cards and put aside one that will help you remember this word later". In the other condition there were no cards. The study compared memory performance in both conditions for participants in three age groups: pre-school children, school children and adults.

The results showed that in pre-school children memory was not aided by the cards: memory performance in both conditions was the same, and often children started playing with the cards instead of using them as a memory tool. Memory performance in adults was the same in both the conditions as well, but the reason for that was different. Adults did not need cards; they had already internalized memorization strategies. In school children, however, memory performance in the condition with the cards was about the same as in the adult group, but memory performance in the condition without the cards was the same as in pre-school children. School-age children are able to use signs as a tool of memory, and adult level of memory performance is in their ZPD.

Development of empathy and theory of mind

Inquiry questions

- Can children, adults and animals feel what others feel?
- Can they understand what others understand?
- Can they take the perspective of others?
- When do these abilities develop?
- How can these abilities be studied?
- Where are they localized?

What you will learn in this section

- Empathy and theory of mind
  - As a concept, theory of mind is simultaneously broader and narrower than empathy
  - Manifestations of emotional empathy develop first; fully fledged theory of mind develops starting at age 4–5 years

- Early manifestations of emotional empathy
  - Young children are capable of a variety of empathy-related behaviours; Simner (1971): newborns cry when exposed to the sound of another infant crying
  - Young infants are not able to differentiate the self from others; self-other differentiation and perspective-taking is only developed during the second year of life
  - The variety of empathy-related behaviours increases between 1–3 years (Zahn-Waxler et al, 1992)
  - Pre-school age (4–5 years) is when the development of theory of mind is most obvious

- Theory of mind in higher primates
  - Why are animal studies important in this research area?
    - Animal studies may inform our understanding of human behaviour due to our common ancestors and similar brain structure

    - Ontogeny broadly repeats phylogeny
  - Does the chimpanzee have theory of mind?
    - Premack and Woodruff (1978): yes, the chimpanzee understood the actor's purpose and chose alternatives in accordance with that purpose
    - Povinelli and Eddy (1996): no, chimpanzees can predict the actions of others based on past experiences, but cannot understand the psychological states (intentions) of others
    - Buttelmann et al (2007): yes, chimpanzees can understand the psychological states of others (such as intentions). Rational imitation paradigm studies
    - Call and Tomasello (2008): review and clarifications—chimpanzees have some components of theory of mind (such as understanding intentions) but lack others (such as understanding of false beliefs)

- Theory of mind in human children
  - Understanding intentions of others: Meltzoff (1995), children as young as 18 months old can read the intentions behind the actions of another human (but not a machine)

○ Understanding false beliefs: Baron-Cohen, Leslie and Frith (1985), the Sally-Anne task—performance on the false-belief test is a critical milestone in the development of theory of mind, and human (non-autistic) children normally acquire this ability by age 4–5 years

- Recent research with the use of modern technology

  ○ There is always a chance that conclusions are contaminated by confounding variables inherent in the method

  ○ Krupenye *et al* (2016): eye-tracking technology with chimpanzees shows that they do have an ability to understand false beliefs

  ○ Ruffman, Garnham and Rideout (2001): the Sally-Anne task, coupled with eye-tracking, lends support and clarifications to the study of Baron-Cohen, Leslie and Frith (1985)

- Localization of theory of mind

  ○ Saxe and Kanwisher (2003) conducted an fMRI study that showed that the tempo-parietal junction (TPJ) is involved in understanding false beliefs

  ○ Iacoboni *et al* (2005) investigated the role of mirror neurons in coding the intentions of other people

This section also links to:

- psychological theories of altruism (psychology of human relationships)

- the role of technology in investigating human behaviour

- the role of animal studies in investigating human behaviour

- localization of function (biological approach to behaviour).

Empathy and theory of mind

Empathy and theory of mind are important dimensions of the development of social interactions. Many researchers claim that these two phenomena are what makes people social. There is considerable overlap between the two.

Empathy is the capacity to understand what another person is experiencing. Empathy has two components: cognitive (the ability to cognitively place yourself in another person's shoes) and emotional (feeling what the other person is feeling). Traditionally, when people use the concept "empathy" they emphasize two things: the emotional component (feelings) and negative experiences (for example, a response to another person's pain). This emphasis is not implied in the concept itself, but it has driven empathy research for many decades. This is why the typical empathy study in published research involves a degree of suffering of one subject and an emotional response observed in another.

Theory of mind is the ability to attribute mental states (beliefs, intentions, knowledge) to others. In other words, it is the ability to understand another person's beliefs, intentions and perspectives. Theory of mind is therefore a cognitive phenomenon. Theory of mind is a "theory" simply because you cannot see directly into another person's mind, so whatever ideas you have about that other person's beliefs, intentions or knowledge are your (theoretical) inferences. Theory of mind guides our expectations from other people and our prediction of their behaviour.

As a concept, theory of mind is simultaneously broader than empathy (in the sense that it is not confined by understanding of other people's negative emotional experiences) and narrower than empathy (in the sense that it is only cognitive). However, due to the considerable overlap in meaning, the two terms are sometimes used interchangeably.

Available evidence suggests that emotional components of empathy develop earlier than the cognitive components (and theory of mind). We will first briefly review evidence for early manifestations of emotional empathy (age 0–4) and then consider the development of theory of mind (age 4 and older) in more detail.

Early manifestations of emotional empathy

The ability to empathize is an important part of development affecting the quality of social relationships. It is difficult to study empathic abilities in very young pre-verbal children because they cannot directly express what they are feeling. When studying young children, however, researchers do not have to worry about some confounding variables such as demand characteristics.

There is some evidence demonstrating that young children are capable of a variety of **empathy-related behaviours**. **Simner (1971)** found that newborns (as young as 18–72 hours of age) who were exposed to the sound of another infant crying often displayed distress reactions—they started crying as well. This response was stronger than responses to white noise, synthetic cry sounds or non-human cry sounds. We can conclude that this distress reaction is not simply a response to the aversive noise. It may be an early precursor to empathy.

In fact, young infants are not able to differentiate the self from others. Others' negative emotions may be perceived by them as their own distress. This is supported by observations of young infants engaging in self-comforting behaviours in response to someone else's aversive reactions. It is only with the development of self-other differentiation during the second year of life that concern for the self is transformed into concern for the other (Knafo *et al*, 2008). This links to psychological theories of altruism (see Unit 7 on the psychology of human relationships) and the two competing explanations, the empathy-altruism model (Batson, 1991) and the negative-state-relief model (Cialdini *et al*, 1987). Apparently, up to a certain young age at least, it's all about relieving your own negative emotional states.

Zahn-Waxler *et al* (1992) studied the further development of empathy-related behaviours in children between the ages of 14 and 36 months. They found that such behaviours underwent significant development in the second year of

life: children demonstrate empathic concern (for example, with a sad look), hypothesis testing (for example, saying "What happened?"), and prosocial behaviour (for example, offering hugs or saying "Are you okay?"). The variety of empathy-related behaviours also increases in the third year of life.

ATL skills: Self-management

Make a timeline of the development of theory of mind in human children. As you read on, add important milestones on this timeline. You may want to use one of the many infographic tools available online.

Theory of mind

Cognitive empathy starts its development in pre-school and primary school years. A significant prerequisite of cognitive empathy is **language** because it allows us to abstractly understand feelings and take perspectives. Pre-school age, specifically 4–5 years, is when the development of theory of mind is most obvious.

Animal studies can come in handy in this area of research, because the formation of a theory of mind in higher primates may be more easily observable. If apes do have a theory of mind and we learn how to register it, we may then apply these methods to study the formation of theory of mind in human children.

Theory of mind in higher primates

Premack and Woodruff (1978) in their seminal paper "Does the chimpanzee have a theory of mind?" argued that the answer was positive.

ATL skills: Communication

Can you invent an experimental procedure that will allow you to see whether primates have a theory of mind? How will you test it? Come up with ideas in small groups and discuss in class.

As you read on, you will come across several theory of mind studies with animals. Check whether the researchers used approaches similar to what you have suggested.

An adult female chimpanzee was shown videotaped scenes of a human actor struggling with a variety of problems. The problems ranged from simple to complex. They included trying to reach a bundle of bananas, trying to get out of a locked cage, shivering because of a malfunctioning heater, or being unable to play a phonograph because it was unplugged. With each videotape the chimpanzee was given several photographs, one of which represented a solution to the problem (a stick for the inaccessible bananas, a key for the lock, a lit wick for the malfunctioning heater). The chimpanzee consistently chose the correct photograph, which led the authors to believe that she recognized the videotape as representing a problem, understood the actor's purpose and chose alternatives in accordance with that purpose.

▲ Figure 8.6 One of the problems presented in the study: a key needed to open a lock

Source: Premack and Woodruff (1978)

However, 30 years later **Call and Tomasello (2008)** reviewed new evidence and provided some clarifications. There had been contradictory findings that brought into question the ability of chimpanzees to understand human goals and perception. For example, **Povinelli and Eddy (1996)** showed that chimpanzees begged with equal probability from humans facing them and humans with buckets over their heads. This led some scientists to claim that chimpanzees could **predict the actions** of others based on past experiences, but could not **understand the psychological states** of others (that is, chimpanzees did not have a theory of mind).

Can we design a research study to differentiate between reading overt behaviours and reading goals or intentions? Call and Tomasello (2008) proposed measures involving **unsuccessful** attempts of the actor in **novel** situations. In this case the chimpanzee would have neither any memory of past behaviour nor any representation of a successfully completed action. Their review of 10 studies brought them to the conclusion that chimpanzees, like humans, understand the goals and intentions involved in the action of others.

For example, in one of the studies (**Buttelmann et al, 2007**) six chimpanzees were tested in the so-called **rational imitation paradigm**. In this paradigm there is an "interesting" apparatus that produces light or sound when turned on. The human first demonstrates how to operate the apparatus and then the chimpanzee is given a turn. The human never uses his hands, though, and switches the apparatus on with an unusual body part such as his leg or head. In some cases the human has to do so (due to a constraint, for example, he is holding a heavy bucket with both hands), but in some cases the human chooses to do so (there are no constraints). Results showed that chimpanzees use their hands when the role model's behaviour is constrained (which means that they understand the intention behind the action and simply perform the same action in a more accessible way). When there was no rational explanation why, for example, the human turned on the switch with his leg, chimpanzees would probably imitate the behaviour and use their leg, too.

▲ Figure 8.7 The experimenter turning on the light with his foot because his hands were full, then because he chose to

Source: Call and Tomasello (2008, p 188)

On the other hand, there is currently no experimental evidence that chimpanzees understand **false beliefs**. In other words, when chimpanzees know that an experimenter has a false belief, they seem to be unable to predict the experimenter's actions based on that false belief. They seem to think the experimenter has to act based on what is true, not on what the person **believes to be** true. This is where human children perform much better. Call and Tomasello

(2008) conclude that chimpanzees do have a theory of mind, but it is not quite as developed as that of human children, mainly due to a lack of understanding of false beliefs.

Why is a study of theory of mind in primates important to us? At least for two reasons. First, animal studies may inform our understanding of human behaviour due to our common ancestors and similar brain structure. (See Unit 2 on the biological approach to behaviour, for more information.) If we assume that theory of mind has a special neural basis, it would be plausible to expect to see it in animals, too, at least in some form. Second, biologically **ontogeny** (the development of an individual) has been known to broadly repeat **phylogeny** (the evolutionary history of the species). In this sense we might expect the development of theory of mind in a human child to share some features or patterns with the development of theory of mind in the animal kingdom.

So how—and when—does theory of mind develop in human children?

ATL skills: Communication

Does the chimpanzee have a theory of mind? Write an answer to this question, using no more than 100 words.

To help you, here is the overview of the main arguments mentioned so far.

- Can the chimpanzee understand intentions of others? Premack and Woodruff (1978) said yes, Povinelli and Eddy (1996) doubted it, but Buttelmann *et al* (2007) refuted the doubt—so the answer is yes.

- Can the chimpanzee understand false beliefs of others? Call and Tomasello (2008), based on their review of existing evidence, say no.

Theory of mind in human children

Research with chimpanzees and pre-verbal human children is similar in the way it's organized—and it yields similar results.

To establish the earliest pre-verbal age when the ability to understand the intentions of others is formed **Meltzoff (1995)** investigated whether children would re-enact what an adult actually did or what the adult intended to do—much like

Buttelmann *et al* (2007) in their chimpanzee study. Children in the experimental group were shown an adult who tried but failed to perform certain target acts, whereas children in the control group were exposed to completed target acts. Results showed that children as young as 18 months old could infer the adult's intended act. For example, adults in the control group demonstrated how they used a small rectangular block of wood to push a slightly recessed rectangular button in a wooden box. Pushing the button activated a buzzer.

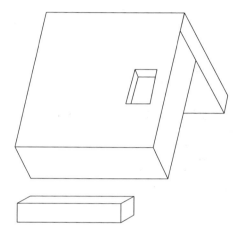

▲ Figure 8.8 The equipment used in the experiment

Source: Meltzoff, 1995

In the experimental condition all movements and actions would be exactly the same, with the exception that the experimenter would try to push the button but miss, and there would be no activation of the buzzer. Strikingly, there was no difference in the number of successfully accomplished imitation acts between the two groups. Infants in the experimental group did not go through a period of trial and error with the test objects but directly produced the target act, just as those who observed the complete act. This shows that infants were able to "read" the adult's intentions. Here is an interesting question that arises from this: is this a response to the physics of the situation (pattern of movements) or is there a psychological interpretation involved?

The experiment was replicated, but this time the same movements were produced by an inanimate device. The device closely mimicked the movements of the actor—both the completed action and the failed action condition. Results showed that infants do **not** read an intention behind the movements of a mechanical device: they were six times more likely to produce the target act after seeing the human attempt than after seeing the same demonstration by a machine.

As we have seen, understanding intentions is also accessible to chimpanzees. It is in understanding **false beliefs** that humans outperform their animal ancestors. When do human children acquire this ability? One of the most commonly used tasks designed for false-belief experiments is the so-called **Sally-Anne task**. The child is shown two dolls, Sally and Anne. Sally has a basket and Anne has a box. Sally takes a marble, places it in her basket and leaves the room. Anne takes the marble from the basket and puts it in her box. When Sally returns, the child is asked where Sally will be looking for her marble. To pass the task, it is necessary to understand that another person can have beliefs different from your own, that the person will base his or her behaviour on those beliefs, and that those beliefs might be false. So we conclude that the false-belief task is passed if the child says that Sally will be looking for her marble in the basket, and we conclude that the task is failed if the child points to the box.

Baron-Cohen, Leslie and Frith (1985) were the first researchers to use this procedure. Their study involved clinically normal pre-school children (mean age 4.5 years) as well as children with Down syndrome and autistic children. In the Sally-Anne task 85% of Down syndrome children and 86% of clinically normal children passed the test, whereas 80% of autistic children failed it. The researchers explain the result in terms of autistic children's inability to represent mental states, which is a disadvantage in trying to predict behaviour of other people. This makes the 20% of children clinically diagnosed with autism who nevertheless passed the false-belief test an interesting group of subjects that requires further research. However, it is clear that performance on the false-belief test is a critical milestone in the development of a theory of mind, and human children normally acquire this ability by the age of 4–5 years.

TOK

What is the significance of theory of mind skills in various areas of knowledge? Is it important in:

- the arts
- religious knowledge systems
- natural sciences?

Psychology in real life

As Baron-Cohen, Leslie and Frith (1985) demonstrated, children with autism have difficulty understanding other people's beliefs and intentions. As they do not fully understand that other people's perceptions and thoughts are different from their own, autistic individuals experience problems with social relationships and communication. For example, they may not be able to predict correctly what others will say or do in a particular situation. From the practical viewpoint, the important questions are: how can we teach autistic children theory of mind skills? Is it even possible?

One of the methods used in this area is "Social stories", developed by Carol Gray. "Social stories" are scenarios that allow autistic people to understand others better and motivate autistic people to start asking questions about others.

To find out more, explore Carol Gray's website. In particular, watch her introductory presentation: http://carolgraysocialstories.com/social-stories/what-is-it/

This is Sally.   This is Anne.

Sally has a basket.   Anne has a box.

Sally has a marble. She puts the marble into her basket.

Sally goes out for a walk.

Anne takes the marble out of her basket and puts it into the box.

Now Sally comes back.   She wants to play with her marble.

Where will Sally look for her marble?

▲ Figure 8.9 The Sally-Anne task

Source: Baron-Cohen, Leslie and Frith (1985)

Recent research with the use of modern technology

We should always remember that research findings are inseparable from the methods used to obtain them, and there's always a chance that conclusions are contaminated by confounding variables inherent in the method. This is especially true when our repertoire of methods is limited, as is the case with young pre-verbal children and primates.

Recently, as new technology or experimental approaches started to make their way slowly to the study of theory of mind, conflicting findings emerged. For example, **Krupenye *et al* (2016)** obtained evidence that seems to suggest that great apes do understand false beliefs, after all. In this study apes were shown videos of an actor dressed in a King Kong suit. This was to increase the ecological validity of the experiment by making the procedure more interesting or engaging for the apes. In the video the King Kong actor hits a man and then darts under one of two haystacks while the man is looking. The human then disappears behind a door and the ape either switches haystacks or stays under the same haystack (depending on the experimental condition). When the man returns holding a long pole, he smacks the haystack he thinks his opponent is under. Using **eye-tracking technology**, researchers showed that apes anticipated the human's behaviour based on his beliefs.

See video

You can watch a video of this study at: https://tinyurl.com/lsrc7ez

▶ ❙❙ ■

Similarly, **Ruffman, Garnham and Rideout (2001)** used the Sally-Anne task coupled with a measure of eye gaze (where children looked when anticipating the return of Sally) as well as a traditional verbal measure (a direct question). They found that eye gaze was better than verbal performance at differentiating children with autism from other children. Children with autism did not look to the correct location in anticipation of the story character's return, even if they answered the false-belief question correctly verbally. This clarifies the unexplained 20% of autistic children who passed the false-belief test in the study by Baron-Cohen, Leslie and Frith (1985). The occasional correct responses to the false-belief question have something to do with general linguistic ability, whereas eye tracking taps into more fundamental abilities implicated in theory of mind.

Exercise

Make a mind map or any other visual representation of the "dialogue" between the following researchers:

Premack and Woodruff (1978)

Povinelli and Eddy (1996)

Buttelmann *et al* (2007)

Call and Tomasello (2008)

Meltzoff (1995)

Baron-Cohen, Leslie and Frith (1985)

Krupenye *et al* (2016)

Ruffman, Garnham and Rideout (2001).

Make sure you represent the main claim put forward by each research team. There could be claims that contradict each other. Other claims may be complementary. Represent all such cases differently. Be brief and precise.

Localization of theory of mind

Now we will look at whether theory of mind is localized and, if so, where. As we know, many cognitive processes and abilities are localized in specific brain areas, some more obviously than others. Being a highly specific ability, theory of mind could be expected to reside in a well-defined area of the cortex.

To find out whether this was true, **Saxe and Kanwisher (2003)** used false-belief stories to compare reasoning about true and false beliefs to reasoning about non-social control situations. Participants had to read short stories, some of which involved false beliefs and some did not.

The researchers carried out fMRI scans and these revealed that one particular region in the tempo-parietal junction (TPJ) was involved specifically in reasoning about the contents of another person's mind. The researchers concluded that TPJ was responsible for theory of mind at least in terms of one of its components—understanding beliefs of others. There is some controversy around this interpretation, though, as later studies revealed that the same region was activated during visuospatial reorienting. One of the possible explanations is that TPJ serves a more general function that is involved in both spatial reorienting of visual stimuli and understanding false belief.

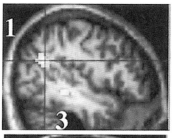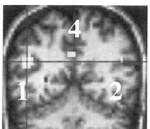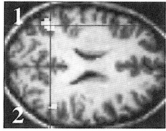

▲ Figure 8.10 Example fMRI scan from the study

Source: Saxe and Kanwisher (2003)

Empathy and theory of mind have also been explained with reference to **mirror neurons**. Mirror neurons were originally discovered in the motor cortex. These are neurons that are activated both when you perform an action and when you watch someone else perform the same action.

See video

V Ramachandran, a famous neuroscientist, claimed that the existence of mirror neurons means that all humans are fundamentally connected. To learn more, watch his TED Talk "The neurons that shaped civilization": https://www.ted.com/talks/vs_ramachandran_the_neurons_that_shaped_civilization

▶ ❚❚ ■

Mirror neurons were discovered by Giacomo Rizzolatti with his colleagues at the University of Parma (Italy) in the 1980s. Later **Iacoboni** *et al*

(2005) investigated the role of mirror neurons in performing tasks that involve a theory of mind.

They found that observing grasping actions embedded in contexts yielded greater activity in mirror neuron areas in the inferior frontal cortex than observing grasping actions in the absence of contexts or while observing contexts only. Subjects in this study viewed video clips referred to as Context, Action and Intention. The Context condition consisted of two scenes with objects arranged before and after having tea. The Action condition consisted of a hand grasping a cup in the absence of a context in an objectless background. There were two types of grasping movements. In the Intention condition the same two types of grasping movements were embedded in a context—either drinking tea or cleaning. The drinking context suggested that the hand was grasping the cup to drink, whereas the cleaning context suggested that the hand was grasping the cup to clean up. The critical question was whether there were significant differences between Action and Intention conditions in brain areas known to have mirror neurons. The researchers found that there was increased activity in the right inferior frontal cortex in the Intention condition as compared to both the Action and the Context conditions. In other words, a small extra part of a participant's brain "lights up" when Context and Action are combined. This suggests that mirror neurons play a role in coding the intentions of other people.

▲ Figure 8.11 Six images taken from the Context, Action and Intention conditions

Source: Iacoboni *et al* (2005, p 530)

Gender identity and social roles

Inquiry questions

- Is gender biological, cognitive or social?

- Can someone who was born a boy be brought up as a girl (and vice versa)?

- When and how do children acquire gender identity?

- How do children understand what is gender-appropriate behaviour?

- Is the concept of gender-appropriate behaviour even justified?

What you will learn in this section

- Gender identity

  - Biological sex and gender

  - The debate about the origins of gender identity

- Biological approaches

  - Sex-determining hormones (for example, testosterone)

    - Animal studies

    - Studies of individuals with congenital adrenal hyperplasia (CAH)

  - Chromosomes

    - Turner's syndrome

    - Kleinfelter's syndrome

  - Evolutionary explanations

- Cognitive approaches

  - Cognitive developmental theory (Kohlberg, 1966)

    - Gender constancy, internal and external rewards for behaving in a gender-consistent way

    - Contrasting evidence: gender-related preferences in behaviour are displayed before the formation of gender constancy (for example, Marcus and Overton, 1978); children prefer to model the behaviour of same-sex models (for example, Bandura, 1977)

  - Gender schema theory (Bem, 1981)

    - Martin and Halverson (1981): the ability of children to label themselves as males or females (which develops around the age of 3) is sufficient for gender schema development to begin

    - Contrasting evidence: Fagot and Leinbach (1989): both gender labelling and sex-typed behaviour may be products of parental influence rather than cognitive schemas

- Social approaches

  - Gender socialization by parents

    - Social learning theory (Bandura, 1977): gender roles are learned both through direct tuition and modelling

    - The "baby X" studies (Smith and Lloyd, 1978): parents react differently to babies on the basis of their perceived sex

  - Gender socialization by peers

    - Maccoby (1990): differences in behaviour between girls and boys are most obvious when children are playing in sex-segregated groups

    - Draper and Cashdan (1988): among the !Kung bushmen, foraging groups and farming groups differ significantly in child behaviour

- Cultural approaches

  ○ Mead (1935): anthropological research with three tribes from Papua New Guinea

  ○ Williams and Best (1982): a "pancultural gender stereotype"

  ○ Whiting and Edwards (1973): research showing that gender roles are more clearly defined in traditional cultures where children have more assigned tasks (chores)

This section also links to:

- Tajfel's social identity theory (sociocultural approach to behaviour)

- cognitive dissonance, cognitive schemas, principles of the cognitive approach (cognitive approach to behaviour)

- evolutionary explanations of behaviour (biological approach to behaviour)

- social learning theory (sociocultural approach to behaviour).

In the process of socialization and cognitive development children inevitably face the task of defining themselves. Who are they? What role do they play in the bigger group? Answering these questions leads to the formation of **social identity**. To learn more about this concept refer to Tajfel's social identity theory (see Unit 4 on the sociocultural approach to behaviour).

Note that the words "identity" and "identification" have a common root. Your identity is determined by which group you identify yourself with (for example, "I am a student", "I am a teenager", "I am a girl"). In this way, gender identity is a type of social identity. Below we will focus our discussion of social identity on the example of gender identity.

Social identity is linked to the concept of **social roles**. Social roles are sets of expectations of one's own and others' behaviours based on belonging to certain social groups. Roles may be achieved (roles that a person assumes voluntarily or strives for, such as doctor, scientist, sportsperson). Other roles are ascribed or forced upon a person (for example, citizen of a particular country as a child).

Gender identity

Although these words are sometimes used interchangeably in everyday language, **gender** is different from **sex**: sex is biological whereas gender is social. Gender is a set of societal expectations about your gender-appropriate behaviour, and it starts from the moment you are given a name and everyone around starts treating you as a boy or a girl. Gender identity refers to "one's sense of oneself as male, female or something else" (APA, 2015). Gender identity does not necessarily correlate with the sex assigned at birth. Some societies have **third gender categories** (for example, transgender is officially recognized as the third gender in India). Although some scholars claim that gender identity is formed as early as at 18 months of age, many researchers agree that core gender identity is established by the age of 3 years, and it is difficult to change gender identity afterwards (any attempts to do that may result in gender identity disorders). Core gender identity is further refined until early adulthood.

There is ongoing debate about the **origins** of gender identity. Some scientists claim that biological factors, such as genetic set-up or hormones, are the main factors determining gender identity. Remember that gender is not the same as sex; gender identity refers to one's self-identification; that is, a psychological rather than biological phenomenon. However, the claim is that gender identity, being a psychological phenomenon, originates from biological factors.

Other scientists claim that the major role in the development of gender identity is played by society and culture. They stress the importance of such factors as vicarious learning, societal expectations and assigned social roles, as well as cross-cultural differences in gender-related expectations and behaviours. They also view gender as malleable—it is not something you are "stuck with" from the moment of your birth. A third group of scientists brings forward the cognitive dimension. According to them, once children develop a cognitive gender schema, they start perceiving information through that schema and so reinforce their initial ideas. Since gender schema is learned early, information processing becomes, in a sense, biased in a gender-specific way.

ATL skills: Self-management

Reflect on your own gender identity. How strong is it? Do you think it was mainly influenced by biological variables, by the way you interpret the world, or by environmental factors? Did you grow up in an environment that strictly imposed gender roles?

Discussion

Currently approximately 20% of the world's population are able to identify themselves as "something else"—neither male nor female. In 2008, Nepal became the first country to introduce a third gender category into the constitution. In 2011, the people of Australia were allowed to have an "X" in their passport rather than an "M" or "F" to describe their gender.

In a historic ruling of the Supreme Court of India in 2014, a third gender category was created for transgenders ("Hijras") and transgenders were legally allowed admission in educational institutions and employment on the official basis of belonging to the third gender. If you travel to India today and fill out a visa application form, it will have three options for "gender". Here is the full story:

https://tinyurl.com/lxnjshg

Is there a third gender category in your country? What is the legal status of third-gender people?

Biological approaches

One of the biological factors that may be linked to the formation of gender identity is **sex-determining hormones**. They are produced in the prenatal period and affect how the hypothalamus will regulate hormonal secretion later in life. If hormone secretion in the fetus is disrupted or changed, it may affect hormonal regulation irreversibly and, as a result, the brain may not be predisposed to the same gender as the one dictated by the child's sexual organs.

For example, **testosterone** is a sex hormone that is more present in males than females. When released in the womb, it affects development of the brain, influencing the appearance of some stereotypically male characteristics, such as aggression, competitiveness and better visuospatial abilities (possibly due to the evolutionary need to hunt and forage). Some studies have demonstrated that exposure to testosterone during prenatal development can have an effect on gender-related behaviour later in life.

It has been discovered in a number of animal studies that exposing developing female animals prenatally to high levels of testosterone (by injecting them or their mothers with the hormone) increases the incidence of male-typical behaviour when they are born. For example, in rats it took a single injection of testosterone on the day of birth to irreversibly change behaviour of females, leading them to demonstrate higher levels of rough-and-tumble play, which is a typically male behaviour. Increased incidence of male-typical sexual behaviour in females was also registered (for example, females tried to mount other females). Removing testosterone from developing male rats (for example, by castration) has been shown to have the opposite effects (Goy and McEwan, 1980).

ATL skills: Thinking

What are the ethical considerations involved in the study of effects of prenatal exposure to hormones on subsequent development? What are the costs and benefits of conducting these studies with animal and human subjects?

The critical period for the influence of testosterone on brain development in humans appears to be before birth, from weeks 8–24 of gestation. Of course, prenatal administration of testosterone to human fetuses is unethical, so research in this area has used other sources of information, namely:

- studying individuals who have genetic disorders causing them to have abnormalities in prenatal testosterone levels

- studying children whose mothers were prescribed hormones during pregnancy.

In the first group the focus has been on **congenital adrenal hyperplasia (CAH)**, a genetic disorder causing an increased level of testosterone beginning in the prenatal period. When such children are born, the disorder is noticed and corrective hormonal therapy is started. Arguably, though, the influence of increased levels of testosterone in the prenatal period may have some irreversible consequences for behaviour. It has been shown that girls with CAH show increased male-typical behaviour (choosing toys traditionally associated with boys, choosing boys as playmates and engaging in rough-and-tumble play). These findings have been replicated cross-culturally (Hines, Brook and Conway, 2004). However, the researchers noted that transition to male-typical behaviour was never complete: behaviour of girls with CAH was more male-typical than expected, but not completely male-typical. This suggests the influence of a number of other factors.

Another biological factor linked with the development of gender identity is **chromosomes**. Evidence for this comes from the study of people with atypical chromosomes: either **Turner's syndrome,** occurring when females lack the second X chromosome (XO) or **Kleinfelter's syndrome,** when males have an extra X chromosome (XXY). In both cases it has been demonstrated that people with atypical chromosomes demonstrate some behaviours that are typical of the opposite sex. However, research into gender identity of people with atypical chromosomes is limited.

Finally, **evolutionary explanations** of gender identity have been proposed. These claim that gender role division is a consequence of the long history of adaptation where males typically were hunters and breadwinners whereas females typically were staying at home and looking after the children. These explanations, however plausible, have all the limitations inherent in evolutionary explanations in general—including using ad hoc reasoning and being impossible to test experimentally.

ATL skills: Social

What are the typical limitations of evolutionary explanations in psychology?

In small groups, recall evolutionary explanations you studied in other parts of the course and identify their common weaknesses. Bring them together in one list of limitations. Compare the lists between groups to see how much they overlap.

Cognitive approaches

There have been two major theories to explain the cognitive mechanism behind the formation of gender identity: cognitive developmental theory (Kohlberg, 1966) and gender schema theory (Bem, 1981).

According to the **cognitive developmental theory (Kohlberg, 1966)** children develop socially stereotypical perceptions of gender after they process gender-related information around them. Once they achieve **gender constancy**—that is, the belief that their gender is fixed and irreversible, which happens at around the age of 5—they start being biased towards behaving and thinking in a way that is consistent with this perception. (See the discussion on cognitive dissonance in Unit 3 on the cognitive approach to behaviour.)

Cognitive dissonance is a psychologically uncomfortable discrepancy between one's belief and one's behaviour, and people try to avoid this discrepancy by making their beliefs more consistent with their behaviour. In line with this reasoning, cognitive developmental theory states that once the child has developed an initial belief (for example, "I am a boy") the child starts demonstrating a preference for belief-consistent behaviour ("I should play with boys' toys"), and this behaviour in turn strengthens the child's initial belief. This reciprocal process leads to a stable gender identity. In this theory the driving force of the formation of gender identity is the fact that an individual **feels rewarded** for behaving in a gender-consistent way (both internally because of less discrepancy between beliefs and behaviour and externally because gender-consistent behaviour is reinforced by adults).

However, some empirical evidence **contradicted** the theory, especially the idea that a stable gender identity can only be developed after the formation of gender constancy. Research showed that gender-related preferences in behaviour are displayed long before the formation of gender constancy. For example, children prefer to play with toys traditionally associated with their gender (Marcus and Overton, 1978). Children prefer to model the behaviour of same-sex models; this links to Bandura's research of social learning: in Bobo doll experiments children aged 3–5 years more often imitated the behaviour of a same-sex model—see Unit 4 on the sociocultural approach to behaviour).

Bem (1981) introduced **gender schema theory** in an attempt to provide a cognitive explanation of how people start to identify themselves with a particular gender in society. In Unit 3 we saw that cognitive schemas are defined as mental representations that organize our knowledge, beliefs and expectations. Gender schemas are a special type of schema—they are mental representations related to gender roles.

Martin and Halverson (1981) have focused on the developmental aspects of gender schemas. According to them—and unlike Kohlberg's cognitive developmental theory—the ability of children to **label themselves** as males or females (which develops around the age of 3 years) is sufficient for gender schema development to begin. Attainment of gender constancy is not necessary. The driving force in the formation of gender identity is schema processing—the way new information gets "sifted" through the existing schema and integrated with it (remember that schemas have been demonstrated to affect information processing at all stages).

One limitation of this theory is that it is difficult to establish a cause–effect link between gender labelling and sex-typed behaviour. For example, both might be products of social influences. **Fagot and Leinbach (1989)** found that children of parents who react evaluatively to children's sex-typed behaviour develop gender labels earlier. This may mean that both gender labelling and sex-typed behaviour are in fact products of parental influence rather than cognitive schemas.

However, research supports the gender-schema theory of gender identity more than Kohlberg's theory. It has been demonstrated that gender labelling is enough to produce a number of sex-typed behaviours, including preferences for certain toys and activities.

Since the focus of this theory is on how individuals process gender-related information, it leads us to explore **individual differences**. Some children (and

adults) are more "gender-schematic" than others, and some are "multischematic". Bem (1981) distinguishes and defines the following four categories of people.

- Sex-typed people process information in line with their biological sex.
- Cross-sex-typed people process information in line with the sex opposite to theirs.
- Androgynous people process information in a way that relates to both genders.
- Undifferentiated individuals find it difficult to process any sex-typed information.

Psychology in real life

Watch the short TED Talk by McKenna Pope, who at the age of 13 petitioned Hasbro to market its Easy-Bake Oven to boys as well as girls, and to make it available in gender-neutral colours, "Want to be an activist? Start with your toys", (November 2013): https://www.ted.com/talks/mckenna pope want to be an activist start with your toys

What psychological and social issues are raised by producing toys that are not gender-neutral? What ethical considerations should be tackled by the toy industry? Would you personally advocate gender-neutral marketing of toys?

Social approaches

Social approaches to the research of gender identity development focus on the "nurture" side of the debate and claim that socialization processes are what influences gender identity the most. Other approaches (biological and cognitive) do not deny the role of social factors (such as reinforcement of certain behaviours by parents or modelling of adults and peers), but they differ in the **degree** to which they emphasize the influence of these factors.

Social influences can be broadly divided into two parts: influence by adults and influence by peers.

Gender socialization by parents and other adults was emphasized in social learning theory (Bandura, 1977, 1986). **Bandura (1977)** claimed that gender roles are learned both through direct tuition (adults reinforce stereotypically acceptable gender behaviour and discourage stereotypically inconsistent gender behaviour) and through modelling (vicarious learning).

A series of Bandura's experiments demonstrated that just observing the behaviour of an adult model leads to imitating and learning new behaviours. This applies to sex-typed behaviours such as the modelling of aggressive behaviour investigated in Bandura's most commonly cited Bobo doll experiments (see details in Unit 4 on the sociocultural approach to behaviour, "The individual and the group—social cognitive theory"). In this research, several factors were shown to influence the probability that certain behaviour would be imitated. One of these factors was the sex of the model: children were more inclined to copy the behaviour of same-sex adult models (Bandura, 1977).

For gender socialization by parents to occur, parents should **react differently** to babies on the basis of their perceived sex. This has been investigated in a series of "**baby X studies**"—studies in which one and the same baby was presented to adults either as a boy or as a girl. In one of these studies **Smith and Lloyd (1978)** found that adults' responses to an infant's perceived sex were indeed somewhat stereotyped. In this study mothers of 5–10-month-old infants were invited to play with a 6-month-old baby who was dressed as either a girl or a boy (depending on the experimental condition). The only variable that was manipulated was the colour of the baby's snowsuit (either blue or pink). The actual sex of the child was also varied, so that in some cases it was a boy in a pink snowsuit and in some cases it was a girl in a pink snowsuit (and the same for the blue snowsuit). The room where participants were playing had an abundance of toys traditionally viewed as appropriate for one or the other sex. It was shown that in playing with the infants the adults preferred gender-stereotyped toys.

One **limitation** of the social learning theory in the context of gender identity development is that it doesn't explain individual differences in conforming to gender role stereotypes. Even in similar environments with similar adult models, different children will have a different response in terms of their gender identity. This can only be explained by taking into account "internal" factors that mediate the social influences the child is exposed to. That is why the majority of modern approaches and research studies adopt an **interactionist approach** and study biological, cognitive and social factors in interaction, although it makes research designs far more complex.

Discussion

Your child—a boy—prefers playing with dolls to playing with toy cars and action figures.

What do you do as a parent?

Gender socialization by peers can also be considerable in the development of gender identity and gender roles. There is some evidence that peer socialization plays an important part in the development of gender identity.

For example, **Maccoby (1990)** observed that differences in behaviour between girls and boys are most obvious when children are playing in sex-segregated groups. If children are observed individually the differences in behaviour are much less pronounced.

This might explain some cultural differences, for example, the contrast between foragers and farmers. **Draper and Cashdan (1988)** observed the !Kung Bushmen of western Botswana. Among the !Kung, foraging groups and farming groups differ significantly in terms of children's behaviour. Children from families that are settled down show more sex-differentiated behaviour and interact more with peers. This is because the number of potential playmates is greater and children are more likely to form sex-segregated groups. In contrast, in foraging families the number of potential playmates is smaller, boys and girls play together, and so sex-related behavioural differences are less obvious.

Case study: David Reimer

▲ Figure 8.12 David Reimer

David Reimer (1965–2004) was originally named Bruce. His identical twin brother was named Brian. Due to a medical condition (phimosis, inability of the foreskin to be pulled back) they both had to undergo circumcision at the age of 7 months. The routine operation involved using heat. However, it did not go as planned for Bruce, and his penis was burnt off. In 1967 the parents consulted John Money, a psychologist famous for his work with intersex patients and a proponent of the idea that gender identity is a result of social influences. Money believed that gender identity could be changed depending on how the child is brought up. He had never had an opportunity to test the theory though, because experimentation in this field would have been completely unethical.

Based on his beliefs, observations and research Money suggested that Bruce should be raised as a girl. Physicians at that time could not replace a penis but could construct a functional vagina. Another factor was that two identical twins, one of whom is raised as a boy and the other as a girl, presented themselves as a unique case study to test Money's theories. At 22 months old Bruce underwent sex reassignment surgery (his testes were removed and a vulva was constructed) and given the name Brenda. To assess and support success of the procedure, Money saw the Reimers annually for a decade. Money reported that the procedure had been successful and Brenda was growing up with an identity and behaviour of a girl. Reimer received oestrogen treatment to induce breast growth and was forced to dress as a girl.

In 1997, when Reimer went public with his story, it became clear that the follow-up visits to Money had been experienced by the family as traumatic rather than supporting. Reports revealed that Reimer had not developed a female gender identity. He was bullied by peers and developed depression. He also had suicidal thoughts as early as at the age of 13. At the age of 14 Reimer was told the truth about his gender reassignment. Reimer decided to switch back and change his name to David. He underwent reverse surgery and testosterone treatment.

Both the brothers ended up having a tragic life. Brian developed schizophrenia and in 2002 died from an overdose of antidepressants. David committed suicide in 2004 shortly after his wife announced her decision to separate from him.

Although there were various factors influencing the outcome, as well as alternative explanations, this case seems to contradict the theory that sex can be reassigned and gender identity can be socially constructed.

Cultural approaches

Cultural approaches to gender identity do not contradict the other approaches, but they draw attention to important cross-cultural differences in gender behaviour. The existence of such differences suggests that many dimensions of gender are social constructs rather than biological phenomena.

The traditional, and to some extent intuitively appealing, approach to the cultural determinants of gender roles has been based on the division of labour between men and women: traditionally they perform different tasks (for example, hunting and looking after the children), so they are bound to have different roles and internalize those roles.

However, this idea was challenged by Margaret Mead's seminal anthropological research where she investigated gender roles in three geographically close New Guinean tribes (Mead, 1935).

Research in focus: Margaret Mead (1935)

Margaret Mead (1901–1978), a cultural anthropologist from the USA, is most famous for her research into gender roles in traditional societies. This research, together with her numerous appearances in mass media, influenced the sexual revolution in the 1960s.

In one of the influential books she wrote, *Sex and Temperament in Three Primitive Societies* (1935), she described her field observations of three tribes from Papua New Guinea. She stayed with each of the tribes for six months.

The **Arapesh** people were pacifists. Both men and women were peaceful, gentle, responsive and cooperative. Both demonstrated sensitive behaviour and feminine personalities.

In the **Mundugumor** (now Biwat) tribe both men and women were violent and aggressive and sought power and dominance. Both could be described as ruthless, dominant and masculine.

Among the **Tchambuli** (now Chambri) people male and female temperaments were different, with women being dominant and managerial and men being less responsible and more emotionally dependent. Men were also more concerned about their personal appearance.

Mead concluded that temperamental differences between the sexes are culturally determined rather than innate.

TOK

The existence of cross-cultural differences in what is considered sex-appropriate behaviour, especially in three tribes located so close to each other and living in such similar conditions, suggests that gender is a social construct rather than a biological "fact". This is a somewhat counter-intuitive idea.

Can you think of other social constructs that can be often mistaken for "facts"? How about "authority", "evidence", "science" and "knowledge"?

Some cross-cultural studies conducted later emphasize cultural similarities in gender stereotypes, while other studies bring forward cultural differences. Apparently, both apply: **core similarities** in gender stereotypes do exist cross-culturally, but there are some important differences as well, and the differences can potentially be explained by **economic or cultural variables**.

For example, in a study that emphasized cross-cultural similarities **Williams and Best (1982)** asked participants to characterize a list of 300 adjectives as male versus female characteristics. Men were generally viewed as active, strong, critical, dominant, aggressive and achieving. Women were viewed as passive, weak, nurturing and adaptive. The study involved participants from 25 countries from

Europe, Asia, Africa, Oceania and the Americas, approximately 100 male and female university students from each country. The authors concluded that a "**pancultural gender stereotype**" exists.

Conversely, in a study that emphasized cross-cultural differences as a result of economic variables, **Whiting and Edwards (1973)** investigated non-western societies and looked at behaviour of children aged 3–11 years. Data was gathered by field teams who lived in communities located in Kenya, Okinawa, India, the Philippines, Mexico and New England.

The children were observed in natural settings, usually in the house or yard, on an average of 17 different times over a period of 6–14 months. Observers first wrote down their observations in a free form, and the paragraphs were subsequently analysed. Results of the study were interpreted to suggest that gender differences in a particular culture are determined to a large extent by the nature of tasks (chores) assigned to children by the parents. For example, girls were usually given tasks that required more frequent interaction with infants and adults, and the nature of the tasks themselves involved taking care of others. On the other hand, boys were given tasks such as feeding and herding cattle (that is, tasks outside of home). Gender roles varied across cultures in terms of how pronounced they were. Gender roles were more clearly defined in traditional cultures where children have more assigned tasks, for example in Kenya. Conversely, American children did little work around the house so gender roles were less defined.

We can conclude that gender roles, while sharing a common core cross-culturally, do differ in terms of how sharply they are expressed in society. These differences might depend on the economic parameters characterizing the traditional household. They are also subject to changes as long as the economic environment of a society undergoes development and/or westernization.

Attachment

Inquiry questions

- What is the nature of children's attachment to their parents? Is it purely biological or instinctive?

- Do problems with attachment cause problems in cognitive development?

- Is attachment to caretakers vital for further development?

- What happens if the parents do not reciprocate a child's attachment?

- What are the individual differences in attachment?

- What are the cultural differences in attachment?

What you will learn in this section

- Biological basis of attachment

  - Research by Konrad Lorenz: imprinting as a form of learning

  - Harlow's research

    - Experiment 1: contact comfort versus satisfaction of basic needs

    - Experiment 2: secure base—properly formed attachment may serve as the basis of exploration of the environment and cognitive growth

    - Applicability to humans and ethical considerations

- Psychological theories of attachment

  - Bowlby (1960)

    - The attachment behavioural system

    - The internal working model

  - Ainsworth *et al* (1978): attachment styles

    - The "Strange situation paradigm"

    - Confirmation of the secure base theory

  - Individual differences: the "strange situation" classification

- Cultural variations in attachment

  - Van Ijzendoorn and Kroonenberg (1988): cross-cultural meta-analysis of studies using the "Strange situation paradigm" in eight countries

  - Tronick, Morelli and Winn (1987): caretaking practices among the Efe people

- Attachment in later life

  - Shaver and Hazan (1988): adult patterns of attachment closely resemble those they had with their caregivers in the past

This section also links to:

- neuroplasticity, animal studies, evolutionary explanations of behaviour (biological approach to behaviour)

- mental representations, schema theory (cognitive approach to behaviour).

Attachment as a concept refers to an emotional connection between individuals that is most clearly seen in one individual's reaction to separation from the other (**separation distress**). Studies on animals and on humans suggest that attachment of infants to their caregivers is an important stage that provides a basis for further development. This means that if attachment is disrupted, this has negative long-term consequences in terms of child development.

Biological basis of attachment

Patterns of attachment behaviour seem to be shared between humans and many animals. This has led many psychologists to believe that attachment has an evolutionary basis.

Konrad Lorenz: imprinting

Konrad Lorenz (1935) conducted extensive research of **imprinting**—rapid instinctive learning that occurs at a particular critical life period. An obvious example of imprinting is that of birds (for example, chickens) that imprint on their parents and follow them around, instinctively copying the behaviour of the adult.

Lorenz experimented with a moving stimulus that incubator-hatched geese saw in the critical period shortly (13–16 hours) after hatching. He proved that the goslings would imprint on multiple moving stimuli, for example, Lorenz himself—they imprinted on his wading boots and followed him around. This suggests that attachment is based on a genetic programme: at a certain critical period the organism perceives a certain environmental cue, and this triggers a complex instinctive behaviour. In this case the environmental cue was Lorenz's boots and the instinctive behaviour was to follow Lorenz around. Lorenz believed that the effects of imprinting are irreversible; that is, the organism cannot imprint on anything else, and that the short critical period within which imprinting occurs is highly important. If this period is missed, imprinting as a genetically pre-programmed behavioural sequence will not occur.

Discussion

As Lorenz's goslings spent the first few hours of their lives with him rather than their mother, they imprinted on Lorenz (his boots, actually) and followed him around because they were mistaking him for their mother. When they grew up, they preferred the company of humans to that of other birds of their species. This shows how important those first few hours of their lives were.

Does this occur in human infants? Do you know anything about birth practices in your culture? Usually the first person an infant sees is the mother, but there are variations. In some cultures it is customary for the extended family to gather together and pass the baby around from hands to hands for several hours immediately after the birth. What significance do you think this might have?

However, imprinting only explains attachment as **a form of learning.** It does not explain all the other complexities of attachment, such as the emotional bond between the caregiver and the child, separation distress, sense of security, and so on. Attachment is certainly more complex than just a chain of instinctive behaviours triggered by a specific environmental cue.

An attempt to shed some light on these dimensions of attachment using animal studies was made by Harry Harlow.

ATL skills: Self-management

Before moving on, make sure that you remember these concepts and can clearly explain their meaning: environment, behaviourism, learning.

Harry Harlow: contact comfort and secure base

In his article "The nature of love" (1958) Harlow set out to explore effects of early childhood experiences with one's mother (or a primary caregiver) on later development. At that time it was widely believed that attachment was secondary to satisfaction of **basic needs** such as thirst and hunger. This went well together with the behaviourist stance: since the mother is the source of food, attachment is just a behavioural response to anticipation of food. Harlow criticized this belief, saying that it was simplistic and did not explain the persistence of infant–maternal ties. Why does a person stay attached to the caregiver when the caregiver no longer satisfies the primary needs? Hunger and thirst satisfaction are probably not the main factors in attachment.

In his research Harlow used rhesus monkeys. Compared to human babies, they are more mature at birth and grow more rapidly, but the basic behaviours such as nursing and clinging, as well as basic cognitive phenomena such as perception, memory and learning capability, are very similar in rhesus monkeys and human children.

An artificial surrogate monkey mother was built from a block of wood and cotton cloth. A light bulb that radiated heat was placed behind her, and a milk-dispensing mechanism was installed in the breast area. This meant that this surrogate mother provided food, warmth and comfort whenever the baby needed it, a mother with limitless patience that never scolded her infant. In Harlow's opinion, they "engineered a very superior monkey mother, although this position is not held universally by the monkey fathers" (Harlow, 1958).

The second type of surrogate mother that he constructed was much less comforting. She had the same milk-dispensing device and a heat radiator, but she was made of wire—in other words, similar to the first condition in every way except for "contact comfort". She could satisfy all the basic needs, but an infant monkey could not cling to her. Harlow called this surrogate mother monkey "biologically adequate, but psychologically inept" (Harlow, 1958). Harlow conducted a number of experiments with eight infant rhesus monkeys and these two surrogate mothers —"the cloth mother" and "the wire mother".

In the first experiment infant rhesus monkeys were placed in a cage adjacent to both the cloth and the wire mother. They could freely choose who they wanted to "spend time with". For four infant monkeys the cloth mother lactated and the wire mother did not, for the other four monkeys the reverse was true. Results showed that baby monkeys preferred to spend time with the cloth mother (maximizing **contact comfort** rather than satisfaction of basic needs). Even in the condition where the wire mother was the one providing food, by the age of 20 days monkeys learned to use the wire mother only to get milk and spent increasing amounts of time with the cloth mother. This was completely contrary to the traditional belief that attachment was contingent on hunger and thirst reduction.

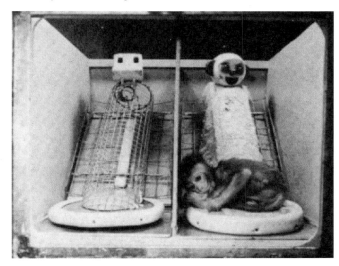

▲ Figure 8.13 Wire and cloth mother surrogates

Source: Harlow (1958)

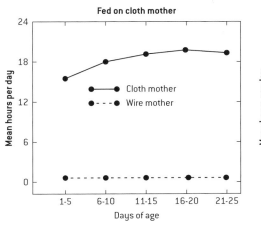

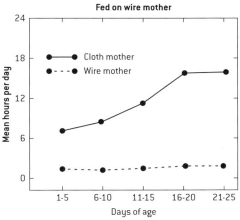

▲ Figure 8.14 Time spent on the cloth and wire mother surrogates

Source: Harlow (1958)

In another experiment with the same subjects Harlow also tested the "**secure base**" hypothesis. This is the idea that infants need a sense of security and comfort from their mother in order to be willing enough to take risks to explore the environment and so grow cognitively. Harlow placed the monkeys in a small room containing multiple stimuli that monkeys usually like to play with (for example wooden blocks and blankets). This was called the "**open-field test**". On some trials monkeys were in the room alone, on other trials either a wire or a cloth mother was placed with them. Results showed that baby rhesus monkeys did indeed use the cloth mother as a secure base: when the cloth mother was present, they would rush to her, clutching her and manipulating her body and face. After a while they would leave her to explore and manipulate one of the toys, then rush back to her again, and so on. In contrast, in the conditions with a wire mother, and no mother at all, monkeys' behaviour was much more anxious: frequently they would freeze and stay motionless in the corner in a crouching position, sometimes screaming or crying, and nothing could calm them down. It should be noted that the infant always sought the cloth mother regardless of the nursing condition (which mother—cloth or wire—was the one providing food).

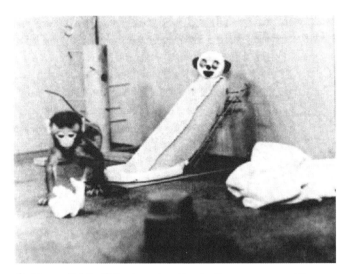

▲ Figure 8.16 Object exploration in the presence of the cloth mother

Source: Harlow (1958)

▲ Figure 8.17 Response in the open-field test in the absence of the mother surrogate

Source: Harlow (1958)

Given what we know about **neuroplasticity** and the effects of environment on the brain, results of the open-field test suggest that properly formed attachment may serve as the basis of exploration of the environment and so cognitive growth.

An obvious point of criticism for this study is its **applicability to humans**. It has been noted that, despite all the similarities between rhesus monkeys and human babies, attachment processes develop much more slowly in humans. **Ethical considerations** of the study are also standing out: infant monkeys were intentionally raised

▲ Figure 8.15 Response to the cloth mother in the open-field test

Source: Harlow (1958)

in conditions that deprived them of appropriate mother–infant contact and potentially disrupted their cognitive development. At the same time, one needs to take into consideration the potential benefits of such studies to people and society: the study certainly contributed a lot to our understanding of the nature of attachment. These findings are related to such important areas as adoption and institutionalized care. For example, it has changed the way we understand "basic care" provided at an orphanage: it has been acknowledged that human contact in infancy is an essential component of successful development. Another implication of the study is that, since contact comfort takes priority over nursing, adoptive parents may be as effective in raising children as biological parents.

Whether or not the study can be generalized to human beings, findings of Harlow's research (especially the ideas of contact comfort and secure base) influenced other scientists significantly. They started to look for a theory that would fully explain attachment in human infants. John Bowlby was the first prominent figure among these scientists.

Psychological theories of attachment

John Bowlby: the attachment behavioural system and the internal working model

In a series of publications in **1958–1960, Bowlby** proposed a theory of attachment that combined biological factors (biologically determined drive for attachment) and cognitive factors (mental representations about attachment and relationships in general that can be changed in the course of life). Attachment in this theory includes two aspects: the attachment behavioural system and the internal working model.

The attachment behavioural system is an instinctive sequence of behaviours triggered by certain environmental cues. Therefore, it is biologically based. When an individual senses danger, the corresponding activation of the attachment behavioural system is called "alarm". When an individual experiences an anticipation of fear or discomfort, it triggers another mode of the system: "anxiety". Both alarm and anxiety are characterized by the infant's seeking and maintaining physical proximity with the caregiver.

The internal working model includes beliefs about attachment figures, beliefs about the self and

beliefs about one's relationships with others (that is, various mental representations). It comprises the cognitive aspect of Bowlby's theory. It underlies a person's relationship with other people, including the ones to be met in the future, which is why the formation of a healthy internal working model is a prerequisite for successful interpersonal interaction. What can go wrong? Suppose a child is being neglected and denied attention, even when she seeks proximity and expresses distress. If this neglect is consistent, she may develop an internal working model in which she is not "worthy" of attention. On the other hand, excessive attention and catering to the child's needs (when parents anticipate her distress even before she expresses it) may lead to an internal working model of relationships that includes unrealistic expectations about other people's responsiveness.

According to Bowlby, attachment has a critical period between the ages of 6 months and 3 years, which means that if attachment is not formed during this period, it will never be formed. Bowlby also claimed that the effects of attachment were irreversible. However, these views were somewhat revised in the research that followed his original theory.

Mary Ainsworth: attachment styles

Bowlby did not conduct any experimental studies of his own. He relied heavily on his clinical experience, theoretical analysis and published research (for example, Harlow's work). Further research into attachment required a special systematic method.

Ainsworth, a student of Bowlby, developed a method for assessing attachment in infants known as the **"Strange situation paradigm"** and used it in her research first in Uganda and later in the USA. In this laboratory procedure the mother and the infant are placed in an unfamiliar playroom with toys. What follows is a scripted interaction of the infant with the mother as well as a stranger (unfamiliar person). This interaction is observed by the researchers through a one-way mirror. The script usually includes eight steps lasting three minutes each.

1. Mother, baby and the experimenter. The experimenter gives all necessary instructions.

2. Experimenter leaves. Mother with baby.

3. Mother, baby and a stranger. The stranger enters the room, talks to the mother and approaches the baby.

4. Mother leaves. Stranger and baby (first separation).

5. Stranger leaves. Mother and baby (first reunion).

6. Mother leaves. Baby alone (second separation).

7. Stranger enters. Stranger and baby.

8. Stranger leaves. Mother enters (second reunion).

See video

There are several videos on YouTube that you can watch to get a better understanding of the procedures used in Ainsworth's "Strange situation paradigm", some of them documenting classical studies, some more modern re-enactments.

Here is just one of them: https://www.youtube.com/watch?v=W5IjfcK3a_Y

Ainsworth observed that children were much more active in the exploration of the environment (the playroom) when their mother was around, as compared to when she left or when there was a stranger in the room. This behaviour was common for all the infants.

However, differences were also observed. The main differences were the behaviour patterns that the infant exhibited on key stages of the "strange situation" procedure, especially separation anxiety (reaction of the infant when the mother walked out of the playroom), stranger anxiety (reaction of the infant to a stranger in the playroom) and reunion behaviours (reaction to the mother when she returned to the playroom after a while). Analysis of these behaviour patterns resulted in the identification of three attachment styles: insecure avoidant (type A), secure (type B) and insecure ambivalent/resistant (type C) (Ainsworth *et al*, 1978).

In **type A (avoidant attachment)**, observed in 20% of infants, the infant did not show any signs of distress when the mother left the playroom.

Neither did the infant show any anxiety in the presence of the stranger—the child would continue playing as usual. These children's reunion behaviour could be characterized as indifferent.

In **type B (secure attachment)**, observed in 70% of infants, the infant showed separation anxiety every time the mother left. The infant avoided the stranger when alone, but acted in a friendly way towards the stranger when the mother was in close proximity. The infant showed a clear positive reaction to the reunion when the mother returned after a short absence.

In **type C (ambivalent/resistant attachment)**, observed in 10% of infants, the infant showed very intense separation anxiety, but at the same time when the mother returned the infant would resist contact and even push her away. The stranger was avoided at all times, whether the mother was in close proximity or not.

Discussion

Do these three types of attachment match with your real-life observations? What consequences do you think having one of these three types of attachment may have in later life, both behaviourally and cognitively?

According to your childhood memories, what attachment patterns did you demonstrate when you were very young? Do you think it has influenced you?

ATL skills: Thinking

If you were to replicate a study using the "Strange situation paradigm", what would you do to ensure that the study was conducted ethically? Think about the fact that you are creating distress in very young children—first by separating them from their mothers and then by exposing them to a stranger.

How would you share the results of the study with the parents? For example, if the study showed their child to have an ambivalent/resistant attachment, would you tell the parents? We know that resistant attachment in early childhood may create certain difficulties with relationships in later life, but will revealing this information only make matters worse?

Cultural variations in attachment

Although attachment is to a large extent biologically based, cultural variations in attachment patterns are observed in multiple studies. Cultural variations are especially interesting because they allow us to understand whether attachment is a predominantly biological or predominantly social phenomenon (which links back to the nature-nurture debate).

Van Ijzendoorn and Kroonenberg (1988) carried out a cross-cultural meta-analysis of studies using the "Strange situation paradigm" in eight countries. The key focus of the study was the "strange situation" classifications; that is, what percentage of children in this or that country tend to be classified as having secure, avoidant or ambivalent attachment.

The researchers carefully selected studies to be included in their analysis, making sure that the comparisons were meaningful and reliable.

Thirty-two studies from 8 countries were selected, with a total of 1,990 participants. Of those samples, 18 were from the USA; other samples were from Germany, Great Britain, Sweden, Japan, the Netherlands, China and Israel.

An aggregated average across all 18 US samples did broadly match Ainsworth's findings (A = 20%, B = 70%, C = 10%), but this was only true for aggregated data. There was considerable variation between the samples even within the same country. The most striking finding of the study was that **intracultural variation** (that is, differences in "strange situation" classifications in different samples in the same country) was nearly 1.5 times as large as **cross-cultural variation** (the difference between countries). This variation could possibly be attributed to the socio-economic status of the family. For example, middle-class professional families seemed to have higher rates of secure attachment as compared to lower-class families where avoidant and especially ambivalent attachment styles were registered.

Although intracultural differences were larger, cross-cultural differences were also significant. Most notably, B (secure attachment) was the most predominant style in all cultures but, within that, A classifications (avoidant attachment) were relatively more frequent in western European countries, while C classifications (ambivalent attachment) were relatively more frequent in Israel and Japan. Potential interpretations of this finding are numerous. For example, it has been suggested that a relatively higher incidence of avoidant attachment in western Europe may be attributed to a cultural predisposition to push infants to more independence. A relatively higher incidence of ambivalent attachment styles in Israel and Japan has been attributed to rare contact with strangers in childhood (Bretherton, 1992).

Discussion

Based on the studies reviewed so far, would you say that attachment is predominantly biological, psychological or sociocultural? What are your arguments?

While most cultures demonstrate similarities rather than differences in terms of attachment styles, some cultures show striking deviations from the average "standards". Anthropological research of such cultures sheds light on the role of social factors in the development of attachment behaviour. The case study below gives an example.

Case study: Caretaking practices among the Efe

Tronick, Morelli and Winn (1987) studied caretaking practices among the Efe (pronounced as Ef-fay) people of the Democratic Republic of Congo. They inhabit part of the Ituri Forest. They found that the Efe engage in a system of multiple care until a child reaches the age of at least 18 weeks. Multiple care in this society involves being suckled by lactating and non-lactating women. This study challenges the idea that caretaking practices are shaped evolutionarily (if that were the case, these practices would be similar across cultures).

The Efe are a society of hunters and gatherers. They are semi-nomadic, changing location once a month. It is not likely to see an Efe engaged in a solitary task: most of their activities are shared because of their way of life. When the camp is moved to a new place, they clear a small area in the forest and build huts. Due to the temporary nature of the dwelling, as well as limited space when it comes to food storage or protection from rain, there are practically no physical barriers for this group of (usually) 6–50 residents, so they lead very public lives. Efe values and survival goals require that the interests of the group always take priority over personal interests, and conflicts are minimized. Tronick, Morelli and Winn (1987) collected information using interviews and observation. In particular, four behaviours interested the researchers. These behaviours were:

- time in physical contact with individuals other than mother
- transfer rate (the number of times the infant is passed from one person to another)
- number of caretakers (people who hold and care for the infant)
- latency of response to an infant fuss or cry (time between the onset of the fuss or cry and the first response of a caretaker).

Rich data collected in the course of this study revealed a lot of interesting facts, some of which are summarized as follows.

- Most female camp members attend the birth.
- Immediately after birth the infant is passed among the group of women and sometimes suckled by them whether or not they are lactating.
- The first contact between the mother and the infant does not occur until several hours later.
- The Efe believe that a mother's milk lacks nutritional value. This is why other women suckle the baby. If no female in the camp is lactating, a woman from another camp is recruited to suckle the baby.
- The percentage of time the baby spends in physical contact with people other than the mother gradually increases and reaches 60% by the time the baby is 18 weeks old.
- At 18 weeks old, infants are transferred on average 8 times per hour.
- Each infant is cared for by an average of 14 people.
- The Efe are sensitive to their infants and quickly respond to fussing or crying. Observations showed that infants were usually comforted within 10 seconds from the onset of the fuss.

All these findings suggest that caretaking practices are culturally variable and so attachment behaviour is at least to some extent culturally shaped.

Attachment in later life

The internal working model of attachment relationships continues to develop in childhood and adolescence, becoming more diverse and detailed. Attachment behaviours also become more complex. For example, children can delay their automatic separation distress reactions if they have negotiated a plan for a reunion with their caregiver. It is possible, for instance, to reassure a 4 year old that you will see him again in the evening so that he does not cry or exhibit separation distress when you leave for work. In the following years the child becomes increasingly independent, and the internal working model of relationships becomes more consciously self-regulated.

Attachment in adults manifests itself in the form of romantic relationships. **Shaver and Hazan (1988)** found that adult patterns of attachment (for example, to romantic partners) closely resemble those that they had with their caregivers in the past. In a self-report measure, adults who described their attachment style in romantic relationships as secure also reported a secure style of attachment to their parents in childhood. The same correspondence between adult and child attachment patterns was established for avoidant and ambivalent styles. This shows how attachment in early childhood may have an influence on patterns of adult romantic relationships.

Discussion

Do you think a relationship with a romantic partner is determined to a large extent by the patterns of interaction with your primary caregiver in infancy? Can you change these patterns of attachment later in life through conscious effort?

TOK

This section has been organized historically: we gradually reviewed arguments about human attachment behaviours that were voiced as evidence was building up. The initial theories and hypotheses put forward by such researchers as Lorenz or Bowlby were rejected in some aspects and had to be supplemented in other aspects.

One of the components of the knowledge framework that is applied in TOK to the analysis of an area of knowledge is its "historical development". Does the development of ideas in the field of infant attachment that we reviewed in this section resemble the development of ideas in any other area of knowledge?

If you had to represent this development graphically, what would it be—a straight line, a sine function, a spiral or chaotic fluctuations?

Think about it in connection with such concepts as paradigm, paradigm shift, scientific revolution, replication, refutation and reductionism.

Role of peers and play

Inquiry questions

- How does play change as a child is growing up?

- What is the significance of play for development?

- Does lack of interaction with peers in childhood lead to long-term consequences?

- Do you need to have friends in childhood in order to grow up socially adjusted?

What you will learn in this section

- Development of play and peer interaction from birth to adolescence

  ○ Infancy

    ◆ Object manipulation, joint attention, inhibitory control

    ◆ Individual differences in complexity of peer interaction: Howes and Phillipsen(1998)

  ○ Pre-school age

    ◆ Development of pretend play: Howes (1992)

    ◆ Group structures: friendship, peer acceptance and rejection; bullying

  ○ Middle to late childhood

    ◆ Play with rules; elaboration of group structures

  ○ Adolescence

    ◆ Increased role of peers: Csikszentmihalyi and Larson (1984)

    ◆ Cliques: Shrum and Cheek (1987)

- Methods to study peer experiences

  ○ Experience sampling method

  ○ Sociometry

- Significance of peers and play for cognitive development

  ○ Interaction with peers influences the development of a child as a learner:

    ◆ Piaget (1932): peers are more important than adults; perspective-taking and overcoming the emerging discrepancies in perspectives is emphasized

    ◆ Vygotsky (1978): adults are more important than peers; the role of interaction with a more knowledgeable partner is emphasized

  ○ Evidence

    ◆ Damon and Killen (1982): comparing moral perspectives may speed up the development of moral reasoning

    ◆ Nedospasova (1985): children who played with a more knowledgeable other performed better on the three mountains task

    ◆ Sylva, Bruner and Genova (1976): object manipulation in the process of play helps children to understand more deeply the properties of the objects

    ◆ Andersen and Kekelis (1986): language in blind children was developing more successfully in their interaction with siblings rather than parents

- Significance of peers and play for social development

  ○ Basic skills that are known to be prerequisites to more complex social skills

    ◆ Perspective-taking

- ◆ Self-regulation while performing a social role (Manuilenko, 1948)
  - ○ Long-term effects of lack of interaction with peers
    - ◆ Animal studies: Suomi and Harlow (1975)
    - ◆ Studies with human subjects
      - ◇ Children who grew up without same-age peers (Hollos and Cowan, 1973)

- ◇ Retrospective analysis of peer adjustment in early childhood for socially disordered adults (Roff, 1963)

This section also links to:

- ● experience sampling method, Moreno *et al* (2012) (cognitive processing in the digital world).

Development of play and peer interaction from birth to adolescence

Most developmental psychologists have argued that peer relationships are an important factor of development, both cognitive and social. Relationships with peers evolve over the course of life. Arguably, peers play a different role for the growing individual in different stages of development.

Infancy (0–2 years)

The first form of peer interaction is **contagious crying**: after they are born, many children in well-developed societies spend some time in a hospital nursery ward, and it has been documented that one infant may influence the others to cry. At age 6–12 months infants can smile at other infants and reach out to them with the intention to touch. Between the ages of 1 year and 2 years peer interaction becomes **mediated by objects**: children can offer objects to peers and direct their attention to toys by pointing at them, for example.

In terms of social development, prosocial behaviours such as sharing, helping and comforting have been observed in 1 year olds. However, children of this age also engage in the first forms of conflict with peers. Most conflicts revolve around the possession of toys.

It should be noted that adult behaviours usually interfere with peer interaction patterns at this age. For example, parents can inhibit conflicts with peers as well as some forms of positive peer interactions (Hay, Payne and Chadwick, 2004).

Successful social interaction with peers depends on the child having certain abilities or skills developed at a certain time. First, the ability to interact depends on **joint attention**. Coordination of attention with another partner first develops in interaction with adults during the first year of life. Coordination of attention is important for the subsequent development of theory of mind skills (Hay, Payne and Chadwick, 2004). Second, the child has to develop **inhibitory control**. Infants must inhibit impulses to explore other infants in the same way they explore objects, as this would provoke conflict. The same concerns the impulse to grab toys from other children.

Play at this age takes the form of joint object manipulation. It can be said that, even if two children are playing with the same toy, they are not playing together—that is, they are not coordinating their actions.

Play goes through a number of stages of development. The overall logic of this process is as follows.

1.	Play starts as simple object manipulation (age 1–2 years). The focus of attention is the object and its properties, and the child is not concerned about the meaning behind the object. For example, a spoon is just a nice shiny thing. The child does not see the social function of the spoon.
2.	Pretend play starts (age 3–5 years). Objects are no longer the focus of attention here, but social roles are. Children can play doctor and patient and use a stick instead of a syringe. This is because they are modelling social interactions; they are much less concerned about the properties of objects, as long as the objects can be used as symbols and these symbols are mutually understood by the players.

▲ Table 8.1

3.	Play with rules then develops (age 6–7 years). As cognitive structures become more complex, both object properties and social roles are moved to the background and the focus is on rules. Children engage in complex play that revolves around imitating the real world and mutually following regulations. If the child is playing a sentry, he can stand motionless, as required, for a long time—something that younger children are not able to do.

▲ Table 8.1 (continued)

Naturally, there are **individual differences**— some children interact with peers deeper and more frequently than others. This is called **complexity of peer interaction**. Reasons for these individual differences have been studied and evidence suggests that the more experience children have with siblings and caregivers, the more complex their interaction with peers is at this age. Interpersonal interaction within the family seems to prepare children for interpersonal interaction with non-relatives. An interesting question is whether or not these early individual differences in interaction with peers are consequential for the subsequent development of children (both cognitive and social). Evidence suggests a positive answer. For example, **Howes and Phillipsen (1998)**, in an eight-year longitudinal study, showed that toddlers who engage in more complex play with peers become more prosocial and less likely to demonstrate either aggressive or withdrawn behaviour by the age of 9 years.

Pre-school age (2–6 years)

Later in pre-school age, children consolidate their social skills and spend more time in groups. The nature of play changes: there's a gradual transition from manipulation with objects to **pretend play**.

Howes (1992) describes how pretend play gradually unfolds in the period from 16 months to 3 years, going through a sequence of stages. First, pretend play is built on familiar routines with little meaning (for example, games involving running and chasing). It is the action itself that is the centre of the child's attention. Note, however, how attention is shifted from objects (toys) to actions. From when children are 16–20 months of

age, pretend play becomes gradually more abstract, revealing the non-literal meaning behind actions. For example, children match the pretend acts of other children. This is the age when children genuinely start to play together, so it becomes important to coordinate actions. By the time children are 25–30 months old, scripted joint play emerges. This places joint action into a broader context and shifts the focus from the actions themselves to the meaning behind those actions. The next stage in the development of pretend play is the ability to assign social roles in play (such as the role of teacher or doctor). As complexity of play increases, the skills required to communicate meaning in social contexts become stronger.

Pre-school children engage in pretend play a lot, and this becomes a driving force for the formation of **friendship**. Interaction gradually becomes group-based rather than dyadic (that is, in pairs), which opens the door to preferences. As a result, simple **group structures** emerge. The early patterns in group structure include friendships, gender segregation (pre-school children prefer interaction with same-sex peers), peer acceptance and rejection.

Peer rejection has been shown to be a risk factor in the development of a number of disorders later in life. Not surprisingly, it has been studied extensively. Among the factors that affect peer acceptance in pre-school age are prosocial behaviour (pre-school children report that they like their prosocial peers) and aggressiveness (aggressive peers tend to be rejected).

Middle to late childhood (6–12 years)

The next stage in the development of interaction with peers is middle to late childhood (6–12 years). Formal schooling transforms peer experiences by dramatically increasing their diversity. Play in its pre-school form (which included a lot of spontaneity and fantasy with very little structure) declines. What emerges instead is cooperative play in **games with rules**. Rules may be formal (as in dodgeball, board games and football) or informal (as in hide-and-seek and tag). In any case, games with rules are more complex and require greater collaboration and teamwork.

Friendship transforms. It is no longer joint actions, objects or play that keep friends together, but rather mutual thoughts and feelings. At this age children are very vulnerable to rejection. Social structure becomes more complex and leaders emerge, and leaders can invite some children and exclude others, so children of this age spend a good deal of time maintaining their social status and guarding against rejection. This links to a child's self-esteem. Social rejection may be damaging to it.

Adolescence (12–18 years)

In adolescence, some trends continue and others reverse. The amount of time spent with peers continues to increase.

Csikszentmihalyi and Larson (1984) used the **experience sampling method** to establish that high school students typically spend 29% of their waking time with peers, not counting time spent in classroom instruction. This is significantly more than the amount of time spent with parents and other adults (13%). More emphasis in friendship is placed on intimacy and self-disclosure.

Adolescents recognize an obligation to give friends a certain degree of independence (Parker *et al*, 2006). As a result, jealousy over friends declines.

An important role is played by **cliques**. A clique is a group of people who interact with each other and share similar interests. Clique membership helps adolescents at a time when the number of interactions with strangers increases, giving them a sense of stability. **Shrum and Cheek (1987)** used **sociometry** to analyse the clique structure of a large school. They found a decline from 11–18 years of age in the proportion of students who were definitely clique members. At the same time there was an increase in the proportion of students who were tied to more than one clique. This indicates that the importance of belonging to a clique is counterbalanced by more openness to other peer groups. At this stage cliques also become increasingly heterosexual. Romantic relationships evolve.

ATL skills: Research methods

Experience sampling method

If you are an HL student, you have been introduced to the experience sampling method in Unit 3 HL extension "Cognitive processing in the digital world". Look at the study by Moreno *et al* (2012) of media multi-tasking in university students.

The experience sampling method was designed by Csikszentmihalyi and Larson (1984) to study everyday experiences of adolescents. In this method participants are usually given a journal with many identical pages and they are required to stop at points of time throughout a day and fill out one page of the journal. The moment when this has to be done is determined randomly and can be signalled by an SMS message or an alarm tone from a specially pre-programmed watch. In their first studies Csikszentmihalyi and his colleagues used pagers. Participants can receive several (or sometimes several dozen) messages each day, and the study continues for several days. The journal page can include a short survey or open-ended questions asking participants to describe, for example, what they are doing at that particular moment, what they are feeling and what they are thinking about. When averaged across all the random moments and all days, this technique allows researchers to get a statistical "snapshot" of participants' everyday experiences.

Sociometry

Sociometry is a method for revealing the structure of social relationships in a group. Suppose you want to look at the structure of social relationships in a class of fifth-grade students. You might give each of them a list of the names of all members of the class and ask questions such as: "Who would you invite to your birthday party?", "Who would you ask for important advice?" For each of the questions students are required to indicate their first, second and third choice. After all information is collected, the researcher typically draws a sociogram (see Figure 8.18) where each student is a node and the choices are lines that connect the nodes. The choices might be mutual or not. It is also easy to see subgroups such as "stars" and rejected students.

ATL skills (continued)

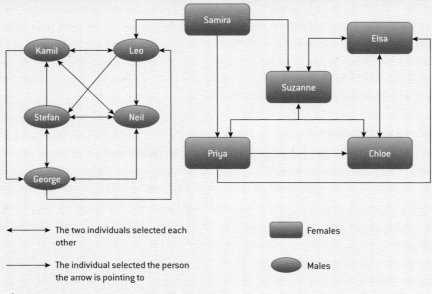

▲ Figure 8.18 Example of a sociogram

A more recent development of this method with the use of modern technology is social network analysis. In this, you apply statistical techniques to analyse patterns of friendship on social networks such as Facebook.

Exercise

Make a timeline of the development of play and peer interaction from infancy to adolescence. Mark the most important milestones.

Compare your timeline with those of your classmates. Did you mark the same milestones?

Discussion

Review the timeline of the development of play and peer interaction. Discuss when children are most vulnerable in terms of their cognitive and social development.

What can go wrong? At what time can it go wrong? What consequences can it have?

As you read on, check your answers against the ideas in this unit.

See video

This powerful TED Talk is a personal exploration of rejection and isolation felt by many Muslim children growing up in the west.

Deeyah Khan: "What we don't know about Europe's Muslim kids" (2016), https://www.ted.com/talks/deeyah_khan_what_we_don_t_know_about_europe_s_muslim_kids

Significance of peers and play for cognitive development

So what exactly is the significance of play and interaction with peers for the cognitive development of a child? There are multiple perspectives, differing mostly in how they distribute importance between peer interaction and other factors such as the influence of parents, teachers, school and community.

For example, **Piaget (1932)** proposed that in the process of interaction peers develop a **perspective-taking** approach. If perspectives on a particular problem differ, children try to resolve the **discrepancy**, which becomes a driving force of their cognitive development. In this way discrepancies in perspectives push children to higher levels of reasoning. Does it mean that children have an innate desire to understand the perspectives of others? According to Piaget, the answer is no. It is the understanding that their current strategies may be incorrect that drives children to abandon old cognitive strategies and develop new ones. Why don't they question their old strategies in interaction with adults? They do, but not to the same extent, because children are likely to accept the reasoning of higher-status individuals without questioning. Peers, on the other hand, are more relatable. The cognitive interaction between peers in Piaget's view is symmetrical—neither of the peers assumes a leading role.

In contrast, **Vygotsky (1978)** emphasized the importance of hierarchical interactions where one of the partners assumes a leading role. Examples are a parent and a child, or an expert child and a novice child. In other words, it is interaction with a **more knowledgeable partner** that is important, be it a child or an adult.

You are familiar already with Piaget's and Vygotsky's approaches to children's development. This difference in focus (any peer versus more knowledgeable peer) may be easily attributed to these researchers' general views on the nature of learning and development. Piaget believed that learning should be fitted to the natural process of development, whereas Vygotsky believed that learning always has to be one step ahead, in the ZPD. However, both these perspectives share the same implicit claim: in interaction with peers children can achieve more in terms of their cognitive development. Is there empirical support for this assertion?

Empirical studies have demonstrated that children working together can indeed solve problems that neither of them can solve alone. Along the same lines, it has been shown that if two children do not have conflicting perspectives on a problem, the cognitive advance is slower. This highlights the importance of alternative viewpoints. Having a partner who has better understanding of a problem has been shown to lead to greater cognitive advances in some studies (for example, Parker *et al*, 2006).

TOK

To what extent is it more difficult to study interaction between individuals as compared to individuals on their own?

Is it reductionist to study individuals outside the context of their interaction with others?

Given that experiments (as a method) model influence of one (independent) variable on another (dependent) variable, to what extent can experiments be used to study interaction, which is bidirectional?

An example of a study that showed constructive discussion with peers to be a factor of cognitive development is **Damon and Killen (1982)**. The authors studied moral development. Note that according to Piaget moral development is a cognitive process—judgment and decision-making in ethically ambiguous situations. Moral development, as well as cognitive development in general, was shown to go through a set of stages, developing from very primitive moral reasoning based on one's own benefit to higher levels of moral reasoning based on values of humanity. The level of moral reasoning in a child is established through a structured interview using a set of ethical dilemmas. Children need to make a choice and justify it, and researchers analyse their responses. Damon and Killen (1982) found that children who engaged in peer discussions of a justice problem were more likely to advance in their moral reasoning than children who discussed the same problem with an adult. It can be concluded that comparing moral perspectives may speed up a child's moral development.

If the role of peers is to provide (a possibility of) an alternative viewpoint that results in the necessity to develop perspective-taking, what exactly is the role of play? Play that involves interaction with a more knowledgeable partner such as a parent enables children to overcome cognitive egocentrism.

According to Piaget, overcoming cognitive egocentrism is a milestone in children's development. It is also a good indicator of the rate of cognitive development and can be easily tested. Remember that one of the widely used tests for cognitive egocentrism is the three mountains task. Another observation that highlights cognitive egocentrism is the way children answer questions about their siblings. If a child has a sibling (say a brother), then at the egocentric age the child will claim that he or she has a brother, but that the brother has no siblings. The child is unable to decentralize cognitively and acquire the perspective of his or her brother.

Nedospasova (1985) aimed to investigate whether play can speed up the process of overcoming cognitive egocentrism in pre-school children. She measured cognitive egocentrism (the dependent variable) with a variety of tests including the three mountains task. In the experiment the child (let's say a boy for this example) was presented with three dolls and told they were all brothers. The dolls were given names, and the child was asked to identify with one of the dolls with a prompt such as "This is going to be you, your name is …". Next he was asked to say how many brothers one of the other dolls had. If the child said one, mistakenly, he was prompted with the dolls, and then he gave the correct answer. After this happened, the same procedure was repeated with graphical representations (with an introduction such as "These three circles are three brothers, and this circle is you …"). When the child was successful in this trial, the experimenters repeated the procedure verbally ("There are three brothers …"). This three-step procedure was meant to overcome cognitive egocentrism in play. Indeed, results showed that children who participated in this formative experiment were much more likely to solve the three mountains task correctly with little or no help from the experimenter.

Even the most primitive forms of play (object manipulation) have been shown to facilitate cognitive development. Manipulating an object, a child explores its various properties. Randomly combining objects and separating them, the child engages in the first primitive forms of analysis and synthesis.

Sylva, Bruner and Genova (1976) demonstrated the role of object manipulation in the process of play. They gave pre-school children problem-solving tasks. An example is the task to retrieve food that is positioned out of reach when presented with two sticks, neither of them long enough individually to reach the food. The solution to the problem is to join the two sticks with a clamp (also given) and then use this longer stick to retrieve the reward. Children were split into five groups.

- Group 1 watched an adult join two sticks with a clamp.

- Group 2 made attempts to attach the clamp to a stick.

- Group 3 watched an adult solve the problem in its entirety (join the sticks and use the longer stick to retrieve the food).

- Group 4 could play with the objects outside the problem-solving context (they could freely manipulate the sticks and the clamp).

- Group 5 was simply presented with the problem-solving task without any preparation.

Results showed that group 4 (the play group) did as well as group 3 (the vicarious learning group) and much better than the other three groups. This shows how in the process of unconstrained play with objects children may deeply learn the properties of these objects and their combinations; that is, play performs a cognitive function.

Finally, for some cognitive skills peer influence can even be more favourable than the influence of parents. **Andersen and Kekelis (1986)** conducted a study involving blind children who had older siblings. They found that language in blind children was developing more successfully in their interaction with siblings rather than parents. Parents did not seem to adapt properly to the child's situation and they spent a lot of time in the role of teachers and testers, for example, requiring children to label things. Siblings, on the other hand, engaged in more interaction. For example, they described things that could be observed around, initiated conversations and resolved conflicts. They also acted as cooperative communicators in joint play, actively involving the blind children.

ATL skills: Thinking and research

Review evidence from these studies:

Damon and Killen (1982)

Nedospasova (1985)

Sylva, Bruner and Genova (1976)

Andersen and Kekelis (1986).

Does the evidence support Piaget's theory or Vygotsky's theory, or both? To what extent do the theories overlap in terms of their views on the role of peers in cognitive development? Can these theories be viewed as complementary?

Significance of peers and play for social development

Cognitive and social development are **interrelated**. Perspective-taking (which later forms the basis of theory of mind) is the most basic cognitive skill that underlies successful social interaction. However, social skills cannot be **reduced** to cognitive skills. Social skills are patterns of behaviour that enable efficient interaction with other people in a variety of situations. How can we understand the role of peer interaction in the development of social skills?

First, we can look at the development of more basic skills that we know to be prerequisites to the formation of more complex social competencies. Apart from perspective-taking and theory of mind (discussed above), one such basic prerequisite skill is **self-regulation while performing a social role**. It is important for social interaction because it allows people to assume full responsibility for the social role and perform the role as long as society requires them to.

Manuilenko (1948) studied the role of play in the development of self-regulation by comparing three conditions.

- Condition 1: the child played the role of a sentry in a game where the other children played in the same room.

- Condition 2: the child played the role of a sentry in the same game, but was required to stay in a different room alone.

- Condition 3: the child was directly given the task to stand still in the presence of the peer group.

The amount of time spent standing still in condition 1 was much higher, especially in 4–6-year-old children. It was somewhat lower in condition 2 and the lowest in condition 3. Observations also showed that other children, when present in the same room and playing the same game, often verbally enforced the child's behaviour (by saying "You should not move"). So the presence of other children strengthened control over the child's behaviour. Gradually, this sort of control gets internalized and becomes what we know as self-regulation.

Second, we can study long-term effects of poor peer interaction in childhood. For obvious ethical reasons, this cannot be done experimentally.

However, we can turn to animal studies. In continuation of Harlow's famous study of attachment in rhesus monkeys, **Suomi and Harlow (1975)** observed that if a rhesus monkey is raised with enough adult contact but limited exposure to peers, it grows up displaying inappropriate sexual and aggressive behaviour. Of course, animal studies are very limited in terms of their generalizability to humans, especially when it comes to complex forms of behaviour such as social interactions.

One way to conduct a similar study with humans is to have a sample of participants who are known to have had poor peer interaction in the past—for example, children who grew up without same-age peers. **Hollos and Cowan (1973)** studied children who grew up in isolated farms in Norway. Naturally, these children had rare encounters with same-age peers. When they were compared to controls, it was observed that social skills were impaired but cognitive skills (logical operations) were not. This suggests that the role of peer interaction in childhood has detrimental effects on social development, but not so much on cognitive development. However, such research is based on limited and quite unique samples of individuals, which in turn brings generalizability into question.

Another approach is to conduct a retrospective analysis of peer adjustment in early childhood for socially disordered versus non-disordered adults. **Roff (1963)** looked at military service records in search of servicemen who had been referred to a guidance clinic in their mid-childhood. The clinical records were analysed for signs of peer maladjustment, such as inability to keep friends or being regarded as odd by teachers. The sample was split in two groups: those who received a dishonorable discharge from service for anti-social conduct and those who had exemplary military service records. Results showed that 54% of servicemen discharged from service had experienced poor peer adjustment in childhood, as compared to only 24% of exemplary servicemen. However, one has to be aware of the major limitation inherent in retrospective designs. Such studies can suggest a possible link between two variables but they do not directly establish causation.

ATL skills: Communication

Write four sentences that explain the significance of peers in social interaction. Each sentence should express the perspective taken by one of these researchers, in turn.

1. Manuilenko (1948)
2. Suomi and Harlow (1975)
3. Hollos and Cowan (1973)
4. Roff (1963)

Make sure that every new sentence clearly contributes to what has already been said. Keep your sentences as brief as possible.

When you have written your four sentences, print them out and display them in the class.

The overwhelming majority of research studies suggest a link between peer interaction in

childhood and social development in later life. Whether or not this link is causal is very difficult to establish due to the impossibility of experimental research in this area. However, existing evidence suggests that interaction with peers in childhood does correlate with social skills in adults: lack of peer interaction may link to lack of social skills.

Psychology in real life

You find out that your child is being rejected by peers in school. He is not being bullied, but he is being left out of things, and his opinions are largely ignored by classmates during class discussions. Usually he has lunch alone or with a friend, who is also rejected.

What do you do as a parent? What does your intuition say?

You may want to review some papers with advice from experienced practitioners:

How to help teens deal with rejection: https://tinyurl. com/lhh4x8s

Is your child inviting rejection? https://tinyurl.com/ mplbgkc

How to help children deal with peer rejection: https:// tinyurl.com/l87a6xb

Childhood trauma and resilience

Inquiry questions

- What makes children capable or incapable of overcoming adverse life circumstances?

- Are the effects of trauma on cognitive and social development irreversible?

- What should be done to enable children to "bounce back" from traumatic events such as family abuse, wars or natural disasters?

- Are there cultural differences in how children react to traumatic experiences?

What you will learn in this section

- Trauma and deprivation

  - Two approaches to study the effects of traumatic experiences

- Effects of deprivation in critical periods

  - The case of Genie (Curtiss *et al*, 1974)

  - The case of Anna (Davis, 1947)

  - The case of Isabelle (Mason, 1942)

- PTSD as a consequence of trauma

  - Feldman and Vengrober (2011): PTSD in children living near the Gaza strip; resilient children have parents who are more often physically and emotionally available

  - Luo *et al* (2012): cortisol in adolescents who experienced Wenchuan earthquake in China; stress responses to trauma can be measured by registering the concentration of cortisol in hair as it grows

- Resilience

  - Resilience of children depends on resilience of parents

    - McFarlane (1987): a study of Australian households in the aftermath of the bushfires in 1983

  - All children are resilient in some way

    - Betancourt *et al* (2013): a six-year longitudinal study in Sierra Leone with war-affected youth

- Resilience is culturally specific

  - Determining factors of resilience: deVries (1984), a field study of family stress and Maasai children overcoming a natural disaster

  - Overcoming consequences of trauma: Burbank (1994), anthropological study of aggression in Aboriginal women in Australia

- Sources of resilience: Schoon and Bartley (2008)

  - Maintaining academic competence

  - A stable and supportive family environment

  - The wider social context

  - Employment

This section also links to:

- qualitative research methodology— interview, observation, case study

- generalization from qualitative research

- ethical considerations in qualitative research

- cultural dimensions of behaviour (sociocultural approach to behaviour).

Trauma and deprivation

The National Institute of Mental Health (NIMH) in the USA defines childhood **trauma** as "an emotionally painful, shocking, stressful, and sometimes life threatening experience. It may or may not involve physical injuries, and can result from witnessing distressing events" (NIMH, 2015). Many events may be potentially traumatic, from something as obvious as a devastating natural disaster or physical abuse to something as simple as overhearing an argument between parents. Whether or not the event becomes traumatic (produces trauma) depends on the individual's reaction to it. To study the effects of traumatic experiences on later development **two research approaches** may be used. On the one hand, we can broaden the scope of potential adversities included in the research study. In this case we will have to rely on retrospective self-report methods, as it will be necessary to ask individuals how strongly they reacted to a certain event. On the other hand, we may study populations that experience obvious adversities that surely were traumatizing (such as loss of family members, physical abuse and natural disasters). Note that in this case ethical considerations become especially sensitive.

When trauma is not a one-time event, but continuous exposure to adverse circumstances, it links closely to **deprivation**. This may take many forms, including extreme poverty, malnutrition or language deprivation (growing up in an environment where you are hardly exposed to any language).

ATL skills: Research

Regardless of the approach you take, research into the effects of trauma requires you to deal with sensitive issues and ask your participants sensitive questions.

What are the ethical considerations associated with sensitive research? If you were conducting a sensitive interview, what would you do to ensure that participants are protected from harm?

Effects of deprivation in critical periods

Studying effects of trauma and deprivation in early childhood allows researchers to understand the role of **critical periods** in the development of an individual.

The idea is that if the function is not developed at the critical period, it will never be developed at all. Of course, for ethical reasons the only way to study this phenomenon is through case studies of individuals who suffered from severe deprivation in their childhood. Matters are complicated by the fact that, when such children are discovered, they can be so cognitively underdeveloped that they cannot consciously give their informed consent. A well-known example studied by Curtiss *et al* (1974), the case of Genie, is given in the case study below.

ATL skills: Thinking

What ethical procedures need to be followed if the participant is not physically or mentally capable of giving fully informed consent?

Case study: Genie

Genie is a pseudonym. Since her birth Genie was severely abused, neglected and isolated. Her father believed that she was mentally retarded. He decided to keep her as socially isolated as possible, and until the age of 13 years and 7 months she was locked alone in her room. He barely gave her enough food and at all times kept her immobilized (tied to her seat). She was not exposed to any interpersonal interaction and so she did not acquire language in the critical period.

Her abuse was discovered by child welfare authorities in 1970 and then she was extensively studied by scientists. After being discovered and given proper care, Genie started to make considerable progress in her mental development. She developed good non-verbal communication skills, but she was never able to fully acquire a language. While doctors and researchers were working with her, they noted her curiosity, but it was mainly directed at objects and sounds, and to a much lesser extent focused on people. Sounds interested her especially and she was keen on finding out their source. It was later established that her father had been extremely intolerant to noise so he kept the whole house as quiet as possible, even making his wife always ask permission before she could say anything.

Case study (continued)

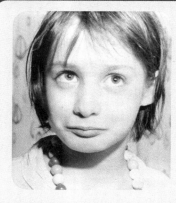

▲ Figure 8.19 "Genie"

Socially, Genie did not show any signs of attachment and could approach and walk with complete strangers. Her behaviour was highly antisocial and difficult to control, for example she constantly salivated and spat everywhere. When upset, she would attack herself without changing her facial expression or vocalizing (crying).

Initially being placed in a children's hospital, she was later placed with the family of the scientist who studied her. However, when she was 18 years old Genie returned to live with her mother. After several months her mother decided that she could not take proper care of her, and authorities placed Genie in an institution for disabled adults, where she was abused again, and many of the skills she had acquired were lost. In 1978 Genie's mother discontinued her consent for scientific research, and Genie's track was lost (Curtiss *et al*, 1974; James, 2008).

Interestingly, early childhood deprivation does not inevitably imply impossibility to restore the lost rates of cognitive growth. Cases such as that of Genie cannot be completely conclusive because Genie suffered from a lot of abuse factors at the same time (it was not only lack of exposure to language). This can be compared to two other well-known case studies (see below).

Case studies: Anna and Isabelle

The case of Anna

The case of Anna is a study of an illegitimate child born in 1932. Anna's mother tried giving her up for several months, all attempts being unsuccessful due to the financial problems in the USA at the time of the Great Depression. The child was then kept in a store room for five and a half years, tied to a broken chair that was too small for her to sit on. She suffered from malnutrition, she was never bathed and never attended to.

When Anna was taken away and placed in a foster home, she gradually became "more human" and was said to be similar to a 1 year old in mentality. However, there were over 300 inmates in the foster home and only one nurse; Anna was often taken care of by other inmates. At the age of 9 she started to conform to social norms and to develop some speech, for example, she had a comprehension for instructions, but she never developed speech properly. Unfortunately, she died in 1942 (Davis, 1940, 1947).

The case of Isabelle

Mason (1942) describes a similar case—that of a girl called Isabelle, who was confined to a room with a deaf and mute mother. Isabelle spent six and a half years in silence. When she was discovered and sent to a hospital, she began language training and developed a rich vocabulary (up to 2,500 words) as well as the ability to produce complex sentence structures. Mason (1942) believes that the crucial success factor might have been the fact that Isabelle had communicated with her deaf mother through hand gestures.

Given the similarity of the cases of Anna and Isabelle, however, it is especially interesting how one girl seemed to overcome the adverse circumstances while the other did not. Are some children more "resistant" to trauma and deprivation than others? Or does the deciding factor lie somewhere in the environment (for example, better connection with the mother in Isabelle's case)? As usual, causality is very difficult to establish through case studies.

PTSD as a consequence of trauma

Although deprivation is a prolonged period of living in a state of various forms of neglect, even trauma (a powerful shock experienced in response to a one-off event) may be very similar in its effects. This means that it is mostly impossible to distinguish between the psychological effects of deprivation and trauma, and they are often studied together. Another reason for this is that deprivation itself often causes a psychological trauma.

Research studies that focused on the effects of trauma (rather than deprivation) have highlighted **post-traumatic stress disorder** (**PTSD**) as the most common consequence of experiencing trauma in childhood.

Feldman and Vengrober (2011) in a qualitative research study examined PTSD symptoms in children aged 1.5–5 years who were living near the Gaza strip and therefore exposed to war-related trauma. Children and their mothers were interviewed and videotaped. Children's traumatic experiences and PTSD symptoms were rated by their mothers. PTSD was diagnosed in 38% of children exposed to war-related trauma. PTSD symptoms include disturbing thoughts, feelings and dreams, excessive reactions to anything related to the trauma, constant emotional arousal and spontaneous traumatic memories reproduced in play.

PTSD is not studied in children as thoroughly as in adults, because it is rare for young populations to have it, but arguably untreated PTSD symptoms in children can last for years and keep affecting a child's development in a variety of areas. It is clear that 38% is a very disturbing finding given that the regular rates of PTSD in populations of children not exposed to war-related traumatic events are less than 1%.

However, some children in this study were exposed to trauma but did not fully meet criteria for PTSD. These children were labelled **resilient**. What distinguished them from the other children in the sample? Their mothers had more social support (for example, from friends and family) and more sensitivity to their children (including being attentive and responsive to the child's needs). Resilient children themselves actively sought maternal support, for example, seeking their advice or opinion during the interview itself. Feldman and Vengrober (2011) concluded that resilient children often have **resilient parents** with strong social support networks. Another conclusion was that parents of resilient children are more often **physically and emotionally available** for their children and respond sensitively when their children are in distress.

ATL skills (continued)

Hair cortisol concentrations were measured in each 3-centimetre segment of hair sample from the scalp. This allowed the researchers to see back in time and "observe" how the levels of cortisol in the organism had been changing for the past seven months. Research showed that hair cortisol can indeed be a biomarker of stress reactions in traumatic experiences.

Psychology in real life

It is estimated that the Rwandan Genocide, which took place in 1994 in the context of the Rwandan Civil War, took the lives of more than 800,000 Rwandans. Another 2 million people were misplaced and became refugees. The core of the conflict was a mass slaughter of the Tutsi by members of the Hutu majority government. Civilians were killed rapidly (within three months) and mostly by hand-to-hand combat, primarily with machetes. The horrors of this genocide are well documented online.

The genocide gave rise to a PTSD epidemic. A survey carried out shortly after those events estimated that 22% of the country's population met the diagnostic criteria for depression and another 20% for PTSD. Many of these were children.

In one of its outreach programs the United Nations (UN) has collected first-hand testimonies of survivors of the Rwandan genocide. These can be accessed on the UN website: https://tinyurl.com/ntsrrbl

Resilience

Resilience can be defined as the capacity to adapt to stressful situations and "bounce back" from harmful effects of severe adversity. It comes from the Latin word *resilire*, which means "to rebound".

A difficulty that usually accompanies any study of resilience in children is the fact that both the experienced adversity (how strong the adversity was) and the success of re-adjustment (the extent to which the individual was able to rebound) are **hard to quantify**. For example, the success of re-adjustment in some studies was defined by the absence of mental disorders and in other studies by performance on age-appropriate developmental tasks.

Researchers have also distinguished between "**resources**" of resilience and "**protective factors**". Resources are factors that help overcome adversities, however big or small they are. Protective factors, on the other hand, reduce the risk of developing severe trauma in response to severe adversities: protective factors moderate risk.

An important consideration that influences long-term consequences of trauma is when exactly in the course of a person's development the trauma occurred (that is, its **timing**). Generally speaking, the earlier the series of traumatic events is experienced, the deeper and more long-lasting the effects. Timing may also be important for protective factors: if a protective factor is not present at a critical period, this may prove more detrimental for the subsequent development (Masten, 2014).

Resilience of children depends on resilience of parents

Research into resilience was mainly started shortly after the Second World War. Systematic research at that time was limited, as most attention was given to actually providing care. However, initial observations revealed several important findings: children rarely showed traumatic shock when the parents were present, and children's reactions depended on those of their caregivers (Masten, 2014).

One of the studies that demonstrated this dependence of children on the behaviour of their caregivers when traumatic events are experienced is a study of Australian households in the aftermath of the bushfires in 1983 (**McFarlane, 1987**).

On 16 February 1983 a series of bushfires in Australia resulted in a loss of 75 lives and destruction of more than 3,000 buildings. In the 26 months after the fire McFarlane (1987) studied 808 children. The study relied on reports from parents and teachers; no children were directly interviewed. It is worth considering how that characterizes the ethics of the study.

The children and parents were scored for symptoms of PTSD. Results showed that there was a correlation between the parents' and children's PTSD symptoms. There were some counter-intuitive findings—and in psychology they are the most valuable ones. For example, it was found that the most powerful predictors of post-traumatic phenomena experienced 26 months after the fire were separation from parents in the days immediately after the fire, continuing maternal preoccupation with the disaster and changed family functioning. These factors predicted post-traumatic phenomena even more strongly than degree of exposure to fire and losses suffered by the family (McFarlane, 1987). Therefore, the initial, most immediate reaction of the parents after the traumatic event seems to make a huge difference, and so does modelling positive behaviour in the following period.

ATL skills: Thinking and research

When psychologists use the term "predictor" they usually mean a correlation between two variables measured at different points of time. Suppose you measured variable A two years ago and variable B just recently. When you calculate the correlation between A and B, you find out that it is sufficiently large and statistically significant. In this case you will be able to claim that A is a predictor of B, or that A predicts B. You will also be able to quantify the predictive power (that would be the size of the correlation).

Now suppose that two years ago you also measured C, D and F. You will be able to compare correlations between A and B, C and B, D and B, F and B. You will make inferences, for example: "A predicts B better than D".

Given what you know about correlations, does the fact that "A is a predictor of B" imply that "A causes B"?

All children are resilient in some way

It has been observed in a large number of studies that the majority of children can show resilience in some form even after a very severe trauma. For example, **Betancourt et al (2013)** conducted a six-year longitudinal study in Sierra Leone with war-affected youth (ages 10–17 years at baseline). The study included three interviews at three different points in time. For the most part the sample consisted of former child soldiers, so the participants had been all exposed to severely traumatizing experiences. Researchers identified four common trajectories in the development of internalizing problems (for example, anxiety and depression). The four categories were:

- maintaining a low level of internalizing problems (depression and anxiety) over time: 41%
- significantly improving over time despite very limited access to care: 48%

- stable reporting of severe difficulties: 5%
- experiencing worsening symptoms: 6%.

A closer investigation into factors that triggered continued internalizing problems (anxiety and depression) revealed the following major causes: loss of a caregiver, family abuse and neglect, and community stigma related to the person's previous association with fighting forces. As we see, all these causes are linked to lack of support from the surrounding people after the trauma.

One of the limitations of the study is that no information was available on pre-war levels of internalizing problems or life difficulties. The study was conducted in a highly specific sample of participants. This means that generalization of results should be treated with caution and findings should be corroborated by other research. Another limitation of the study is its reliance on self-report data. However, the study does lend support to the idea that, given appropriate care, many children can overcome negative effects of even the most severe traumatic experiences.

Discussion

Recall what you know about interviews as a qualitative research method. If you were part of Betancourt's team of researchers and you were asked to interview a former child soldier, how would you plan the interview?

Resilience is culturally specific

Both resources and protective factors, as well as the adverse circumstances themselves, should be studied in context, because the same factors in different contexts might lead to different outcomes. For example, **deVries (1984)** reviewed a number of western studies to conclude that infants with a "difficult" temperament (who were difficult to raise, intense, inflexible and irregular) cause more family stress, which results in them being more likely to experience abuse and developmental problems, as compared to infants who are more docile.

With this in mind, deVries (1984) conducted a field study to investigate if the same would be true for Maasai children overcoming a natural disaster. The sub-Saharan droughts in 1974 disrupted the life of the Maasai people of east Africa and resulted in higher rates of infant mortality. After analysing questionnaire responses from mothers of 45 infants, the researcher selected 10 infants who were identified as easy to manage and 10 who were identified as difficult to manage. They were scheduled for follow-up two or three months later to assess and compare the level of nutrition. Unfortunately, during these months the drought worsened and many families were forced to relocate to distant areas. Researchers were able to find 13 of those 20 families anyway (7 "easy" and 6 "difficult" infants). Although the number of cases was small, observation showed, to the investigator's surprise, that more demanding infants were more likely to get nutrition and survive during periods of severe ecological stress. During the research period itself five of the "easy" infants and two of the "difficult" infants died. It was concluded that infants who are more aggressive and demanding are more likely to be fed and have their needs satisfied. This indicates that the cultural context may be important for determining **factors of resilience** (deVries, 1984).

▲ Figure 8.20 Maasai people

ATL skills: Research

Reflexivity is an important part of qualitative research. How can reflexivity be used in interviews and observations?

What is the scope of using reflexivity in deVries's (1984) study?

Are there any special ethical considerations involved in the study of Maasai children undergoing a very harsh period of life where survival is at stake?

Systems of social support—an essential factor in **overcoming consequences of trauma**—may also differ from society to society. An interesting example of a culturally specific social-support system that helps overcome consequences of adverse situations is the **rituals** in indigenous societies. Some rituals apparently have the purpose of "healing" and support a person in readjusting to the society. For example, in an anthropological study, **Burbank (1994)** describes how Aboriginal women in Australia experience aggression and domestic violence. Of interest in the context of resilience is how aggression is controlled. In this population while revenge is the first natural reaction when a family member is murdered, there exists a mechanism to prevent escalation of aggression and overcome "grief" (*wungari*) in another way. Burbank describes a situation where a man from the community that she was studying was killed by another during a visit to a nearby settlement. Before the attacker was taken away to jail by Australian authorities, people from the community went to that nearby settlement to engage in a "highly structured form of aggressive retribution", *mana magaranganyji*. This is how the indigenous people explained it:

> "In olden days there was a big *wungari* called *mana magaranganyji* that happened after one man killed another man …
>
> In olden times when a man killed another man he would have to stand up for the dead man's relations. At that time, old women could stand there with poles and knock the spears out of the air. But if people said, "No, you can't stop the spears, he has to get a mark," they wouldn't. A man might jump spears from early morning until dinnertime. If he jumped them all, finally a relation of the murdered man would walk up to him and stab him with a spear in the leg or the shoulder. Then the trouble would be finished, that man would be free…
>
> After they throw the spears they are satisfied; no more *wungari*."

(Burbank, 1994, p 90)

In other words, the existence of a structured ritual where relatives of the dead man imitate retribution (without seriously hurting the murderer) served as a powerful cultural buffer against aggression. It also served as a resilience factor that helped relatives overcome the trauma associated with a loss of a family member.

Sources of resilience

Schoon and Bartley (2008) stressed that resilience should not be reduced to an individual's trait of personality, because the belief that resilience is a personal matter is an obsolete illusion. Instead, Schoon and Bartley (2008) suggest singling out factors (social, cultural, interpersonal and others) that support individuals in overcoming the adverse effects of trauma. Such an approach, in their view, would allow us to avoid blaming sufferers for their own problems and concentrate instead on the ways that the society can help them explore opportunities to overcome the effects of adversities.

Based on their extensive review of research studies, Schoon and Bartley (2008) identified the following **sources of resilience**.

- Maintaining academic competence: it was shown that individuals who were engaged in the school context—who believed in their abilities, participated in extracurricular activities and were otherwise active participants in school life—were more likely to overcome the effects of adversities. The implication of this is that by changing the school context (as well as changing policies regarding accessibility of schools for all children) we may improve the life

of many children, regardless of whether or not they possess resilience as an "individual trait".

- A stable and supportive family environment: research shows that some children effectively overcome adversities in their life and become well adjusted even though their family finds itself in extremely adverse circumstances (economically and otherwise). In such cases, however, the family environment could be characterized as supportive: for example, parents read to their children, take an interest in their children's education and career planning, and engage in joint activities with them. All this was shown to create secure attachment, which in turn was associated with greater life success despite all misfortunes.

- The wider social context (such as school, neighbourhood, childcare): this relates to finding support in people outside the immediate family circle. For example, a positive interaction with peers in a school setting may support a child's self-esteem and provide the necessary sense of belonging. This is different from academic competence in the sense that it goes beyond academics.

- Employment that includes opportunities for fair pay and working conditions that stimulate feelings of autonomy is a source of resilience.

Schoon and Bartley (2008) therefore highlight that in order to support individuals and families who experience difficult circumstances, larger-scale economic and social interventions are necessary.

Effects of poverty on development

481

Inquiry questions

- Does growing up in poverty influence the cognitive development of a child?

- How can we separate the effects of poverty from other related effects (such as parenting, neighbourhood or substance abuse)?

- Are the effects of poverty irreversible?

- Will children from poor families catch up with children in better circumstances, once placed in an enriched environment?

What you will learn in this section

- Interacting factors and confounding variables
  - Multiple interacting factors associated with poverty; the importance of separating the factors
  - Irreversibility of effects; the importance of longitudinal studies
- Effects of poverty
  - Range of outcomes
    - Physical health (factors such as stunting, lead poisoning)
    - Cognitive ability
    - School achievement: Duncan (1998), the only variable that predicted high school graduation was parental income in early childhood; timing of poverty episodes is important
    - Emotional and behavioural outcomes
    - In early childhood: internalizing problems (Barajas, Philipsen and Brooks-Gunn, 2007)
    - In adolescence: externalizing problems (Great Smoky Mountains Study)
- Pathways of poverty (Brooks-Gunn and Duncan, 1997)
  - Health and nutrition: (Korenman, Miller and Sjaastad, 1995), effects of stunting on short-term memory
  - The home environment
  - Parental interaction with children

- Parental mental health
- Neighbourhood conditions
- Two broad approaches: the family stress theory and the investment model (Barajas, Philipsen and Brooks-Gunn, 2007)

- Disentangling confounding variables
  - Statistical separation of effects
    - Dickerson and Popli (2016): the UK Millennium Cohort Study—poverty has both direct and indirect effects on cognitive development; the indirect effect of poverty is through parental investment
  - Natural longitudinal experiments
    - Costello *et al* (2003): Great Smoky Mountains study—poverty has an effect on the child's development over and above relatively stable family characteristics, at least for some disorders (conduct disorder, oppositional defiant disorder)

This section also links to:

- methods of research in psychology—correlational research, longitudinal study
- social learning theory (sociocultural approach to behaviour)
- attachment
- adoption studies of heritability of intelligence, behavioural epigenetics (biological approach to behaviour).

Interacting factors and confounding variables

What do you think is the influence of poverty on cognitive and social development of a child? The answer seems to be intuitively obvious: poverty negatively affects development because of more difficult access to quality education and enriching learning environments. However, we should be careful about accepting the intuitively obvious answer as the truth.

First, there are multiple **interacting factors** that are associated with poverty. One example is the quality of parenting (the attention given to the child and supportive parent–child relationships). The quality of parenting tends to be lower in families experiencing poverty. This in turn might be associated with higher rates of crime, more substance abuse in the family and other detrimental situations. Therefore, simply comparing cognitive achievements of children from poor families with those of children from financially well-off families will not lead to any definitive conclusions. Even if the scores of children from poor families turn out to be lower, is this caused by financial variables or by quality of parenting? How do we separate these two potential causes?

At the same time, they need to be separated, as there are different implications depending on which of the two factors is the determining cause of weaker cognitive skills. If the cause is the quality of parenting, then the risks for cognitive

development of children can probably be mitigated by the provision of parenting support services, special early education programmes, and so on. However, if it is purely income poverty that is the cause of slower cognitive development, prevention strategies will have to be purely economic.

In this way, in research these interacting factors become **confounding variables**: we want to separate the effects of the factors from each other to understand the problem of poverty more deeply.

Second, it is not enough to demonstrate that children from poor environments have lower scores on standard tests of cognitive development. Would they get back on track and catch up with the other children once placed in a more financially stable family environment? Or are the effects of poverty on cognitive (and social) development irreversible? To find out, we need to look at children who were shifted from one environment to another, and we need to look at their development rate **longitudinally**.

All this means that the answer to the question about what influence poverty has on children's cognitive and social development is not as obvious as it seems. In any case, scientific understanding of the impact of poverty or socio-economic status on development requires carefully planned research studies that would consider alternative explanations and try to separate effects of poverty from effects of other (confounding) variables.

ATL skills: Self-management

What is the role of confounding variables in research? When you think about this question, consider comparing qualitative and quantitative research. For example, when we are conducting an experiment we try to minimize the effect of potentially confounding variables by keeping them constant (controlling them) so as to avoid bias. However, it may be argued that because in a qualitative research study it is, in principle, impossible to avoid researcher bias, the role of confounding variables is different. We do not necessarily try to get rid of them. What do we do instead? Review Unit 1 on research methodology if you find it difficult to answer this question.

Effects of poverty

Poverty is not a rare occurrence. For example, according to statistics from the US Census Bureau in 2004, the percentage of US residents living in poverty was 12.7. The definition of poverty depends on the method of establishing the **threshold** of poverty in a particular country.

For example, the so-called Federal Poverty Threshold is used in the USA. It represents the minimum standard of economic well-being for a family and is defined on the basis of anticipated food expenditures, cost of living and the consumer price index (Barajas, Philipsen and Brooks-Gunn, 2007). Some countries use a percentage of median income. One of the criticisms of such federal-defined thresholds of poverty is that they provide a "black-and-white" poor versus non-poor measure, but underestimate the various degrees of poverty below the threshold. At the same time, the **degree** of poverty may be a decisive factor in the way poverty is experienced by a family and so in the effects it has on the children. The most dramatic losses in terms of cognitive development have been reported for children living in deep poverty.

Poverty has a range of effects on children's development. Whether or not these effects are direct and immediate or associated with some other variable linked to poverty rather than poverty itself is a separate question requiring investigation. First, let's look at the range of influences that this intertwined combination of poverty-related variables may have on children's development.

Brooks-Gunn and Duncan (1997) list the following groups of outcomes of poverty.

- Physical health—this includes such factors as low birth weight, growth stunting and lead poisoning. Stunting is defined as considerably reduced growth rate, and it has been shown to be a measure of nutritional status. Lead poisoning may have a detrimental effect on children's development. Its leading cause in US households has been reported to be deteriorating lead-based house paint. In poorer families infants who live in old housing are exposed to lead-based paint to a greater extent, for example, they can breathe dust from the paint. A negative correlation has been reported between family income and levels of lead in children's blood.

- Cognitive ability—this includes developmental delays and scores on standardized cognitive and developmental tests such as IQ tests.

- School achievement—for example, **Duncan (1988)** conducted an analysis of predictors of completed schooling (that is, whether or not the child will complete the standard number of years of school education). Three measures of income were used: average parental income between ages 0–5, 6–10 and 11–15 years. Results showed that the only variable that significantly predicted high-school graduation was parental income in early childhood (ages 0–5 years). This shows that the **timing** of poverty episodes is an extremely important factor to be considered in research.

- Emotional and behavioural outcomes—this includes externalizing behaviours (such as aggression, fighting or acting out) and internalizing behaviours (such as anxiety, withdrawal or depression). Behavioural outcomes of poverty in **early childhood** are not as obvious as cognitive outcomes, but existing research suggests that young children living in poverty are more likely to display emotional or behavioural problems. The most common way to measure social development of young children is through self-report measures given to parents. Such surveys indicate that emotional and behavioural problems associated with poverty in early childhood (at the age of 3 years) mainly revolve around internalizing problems. Externalizing problems do not seem to be affected (Barajas, Philipsen and Brooks-Gunn, 2007).

In contrast, behavioural outcomes of poverty in **adolescents** are more visible. It has been demonstrated repeatedly that teenagers from poor families tend to have more externalizing problems (such as aggression and fighting) and be more criminalized. However, it is unclear whether these problems are a direct consequence of poverty at this age or a by-product of the developmental trajectory triggered much earlier in life. As shown by the Great Smoky Mountains study (see below), externalizing behaviours tend to alleviate when the financial situation in the family improves, so poverty must be responsible for at least a part of social development in adolescence, whether directly or indirectly.

Exercise

Work in a small group to make a poster with a visual representation of various effects of poverty on cognitive and social development. Collect the posters from the other groups in your class and make an exhibition.

Pathways of poverty

Establishing that poverty has a long-lasting effect on human development is only one part of the scientific inquiry. We have to know the **mechanism** of this influence: how exactly, or through what pathway, poverty influences development.

According to Brooks-Gunn and Duncan (1997), the pathways through which poverty operates include the following.

- Health and nutrition—although health is in itself an outcome of poverty, it can also serve as a pathway to other problems such as deficits in cognitive development. For example, **Korenman, Miller and Sjaastad (1995)** found that the effect of stunting on short-term memory was equivalent to being raised in a family that had experienced poverty for 13 years.

- The home environment—this includes opportunities for learning, parent–child interaction (for example the amount of time spent with the children) and the physical condition of the home.

- Parental interactions with children—this is similar to home environment; however, while home environment variables include explicit objectively measured characteristics, researchers who stress parental interactions with children attempt to go further and tap into the "quality" of such interactions. This may include positive versus negative behaviours towards children, punishment practices, communication strategies and parenting styles.

- Parental mental health—parents who are poor are more likely to exhibit a wider range of mental health symptoms compared to non-poor parents. This may be manifested in their behaviour towards the children. In turn, through vicarious reinforcement or otherwise, children may start developing similar behaviours.

- Neighbourhood conditions—low-income residential areas may come with a number of "side effects" contributing negatively to children's development: examples are high levels of crime and unemployment, few child-care facilities and poor schooling.

Exercise

Draw a flowchart or any other visual representation of pathways of poverty.

Since it is impossible to account for all pathways in one particular study, different researchers have stressed the importance of different **clusters of variables** that they thought were major **mediators** between poverty and delayed cognitive and social development. Two main approaches emerged.

One approach—**the family stress theory**—claims that the deciding factors in the influence of economic deprivation on a child's outcomes are the home environment, parent–child interaction, the amount of time spent with the child, and similar factors. In other words, this theory emphasizes the detrimental effects poverty might have on within-family interpersonal interactions, and how these effects lead to deficits in cognitive and social development.

The other approach—**the investment model**—stresses the fact that lower income means less ability to provide the child with material goods, services and experiences. This approach emphasizes the role of home environment (Barajas, Philipsen and Brooks-Gunn, 2007). Another facet of the investment model is malnutrition: children in the state of persistent poverty may suffer the effects of poor nutrition that might have physiological consequences for the brain, especially if experienced for a prolonged period of time and early in childhood.

Both the family stress model and the investment model have found support in empirical studies, which highlights once again the many pathways through which poverty and variables associated with it may influence children's development.

TOK

Given this complexity of interacting variables in human sciences, to what extent is it even possible to single out identifiable causes? Is reductionism the only way to identify such causes?

How are human sciences different from natural sciences in terms of:

- the complexity of interacting variables
- the possibility of separating one variable from the others?

Disentangling confounding variables

We will discuss two methods that can be used to separate the effects of poverty from the effects of accompanying variables. These methods are statistical separation of effects and longitudinal natural experiments.

Statistical separation of effects involves using complex statistical methods to analyse correlations between multiple variables and calculate correlations between A and B after the correlations of C (confounding variables) are statistically "removed". This idea is illustrated in the Venn diagram below: if three variables (A, B and C) all correlate with each other, it is possible to mathematically "remove" area 1 and estimate the "pure" correlation between A and B—area 2 in Figure 8.21. This correlation between A and B is now "unaffected" by the confounding variable, C.

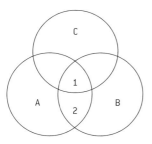

▲ Figure 8.21 Venn diagram illustrating the statistical separation of effects

Dickerson and Popli (2016) used data from the UK Millennium Cohort Study, a sample of 19,000 children born in the UK in 2000–2001, and traced their cognitive development up until the age of 7 years. The researchers especially stress the difference between **episodic poverty** (temporary periods of poverty) versus **persistent poverty**, and analyse the effects of these types of poverty separately. The UK Millennium Cohort Study is conducted in "sweeps", which means that all participants are tested periodically all at the same time. Dickerson and Popli (2016) used four such sweeps: data from when participants were 9 months old, 3 years old, 5 years old and 7 years old. Information in all the sweeps was gathered in face-to-face interviews and included a wide range of characteristics about the child, the family, parenting activities and cognitive assessments.

Results showed that children who experienced poverty in early years had lower cognitive development test scores (various age-appropriate cognitive tests were used including those for verbal, mathematical, spatial and other abilities). The **timing** of poverty episodes was also demonstrated to be important. The rule was that the most recent episode of poverty had the least impact. Being born into poverty had the biggest impact on the child's subsequent cognitive development. Even a single episode of poverty (preceded and followed by non-poverty periods) was shown to influence test scores significantly.

In line with our discussion above, this still doesn't imply the influence of poverty by itself. Maybe the real influence was exerted by other characteristics associated with poverty, such as parental investment (how much time the mother spends reading to the child, and so on), parental style (positive versus negative communication, for example) or such background characteristics as parents' education or level of distress. To separate these effects from poverty as such Dickerson and Popli (2016) made use of statistical techniques that analyse patterns of correlations among multiple variables at once. This makes it possible to separate the effects statistically. Application of these techniques showed that poverty does have a negative effect on cognitive test scores over and above what is explained by other associated variables. However, parental investment was also particularly important. It was concluded that poverty has **both direct and indirect effects** on cognitive development. The indirect effect of poverty is through parental investment: poverty leads to lower parental investment, which in turn leads to lower scores on cognitive tests.

All this evidence combined suggests that any policy aimed at reduction of negative developmental consequences of poverty should particularly target poverty at the child's very early years.

ATL skills: Thinking

Recall what you know from Unit 2 on the biological approach to behaviour, and say how the effects of poverty on cognitive development link to the following ideas and research studies.

- Adoption studies of heritability of intelligence (Kendler *et al*, 2015; Scarr and Weinberg, 1983): adopting into a higher-income family increases the IQ of the child, but by the age of 18 the correlation of IQ with that of biological parents is stronger.

- Behavioural epigenetics (Weaver *et al*, 2004): less nurturing in early childhood is associated with greater methylation of the glucocorticoid receptor gene, which results in fewer glucocorticoid receptors in the brain and higher stress levels later in life.

Another way to disentangle the complex mix of factors influencing children's development and see whether or not poverty has an impact over and above other factors is through **natural longitudinal experiments. Costello *et al* (2003)** in their Great Smoky Mountains study gave a sample of 1,500 rural children aged 9–13 years annual psychiatric assessments. This continued for eight years (1993–2000). One quarter of the sample were Native American, the rest were predominantly white. The naturally occurring variable was a casino that opened on the Indian reservation. This happened halfway through the study and it gave every Native American an income supplement that increased annually. Incomes of non-Indian families were unaffected. The increase of income changed the poverty status of some of the Native American families: 14% of the study's families moved out of poverty (the "ex-poor" group), 53% remained poor ("persistently poor"), while the remaining 32% were the "never poor" group. Psychiatric symptoms (assessed against DSM-IV) were compared in the never poor, persistently poor and ex-poor children in the four years before and after the casino opened.

Results showed that for the four years before the casino opened the persistently poor and ex-poor children had more psychiatric symptoms than never poor children. However, in the four years after the casino opened the psychiatric symptoms among the ex-poor children dropped to the level of never poor children. At the same time, levels of psychiatric symptoms among persistently poor children remained high.

This decrease of symptoms for ex-poor children was not universal: externalizing behaviours (such as conduct disorder and aggression) were affected, but internalizing behaviours such as anxiety and depression were not.

Similar patterns were observed in non-Native American families that moved out of poverty due to reasons other than the casino opening.

How does this natural experiment further our understanding of poverty as a factor that may or may not influence children's development by itself, putting aside the influence of other associated variables? There are two competing hypotheses as to what may cause symptoms of psychiatric disorders in children: poverty or family characteristics. Family characteristics (such as psychiatric symptoms found in parents and parents' education) remained constant throughout the course of the study. **Financial status** of the family was the variable that changed. Therefore, we may conclude that poverty has an effect on the child's development over and above relatively stable family characteristics, at least for some disorders (such as conduct disorder and aggression).

Discussion

To what extent do these two studies— Dickerson and Popli (2016) and Costello *et al* (2003)—solve the problem of separating effects of poverty on cognitive and social development from all other associated effects?

Of course, it is not possible to isolate all accompanying effects completely. For example, changing financial circumstances may lead to increased time interacting with children in the family or to better access to quality educational materials. However, the research findings allow us to come closer to pinpointing the exact developmental outcomes that depend on the exact isolated factors. This knowledge can potentially enable us to implement better intervention programmes that would mitigate the negative effects of poverty on children's development.

Psychology in real life

Now we know that poverty, together with poverty-related factors, can influence a child's cognitive and social development. Moreover, we know that the timing of poverty episodes plays a huge role (the earlier these episodes occur, the more risky they are). The question is, what can we do about it? Given that we cannot just help all affected families financially, can we use whatever limited resources are available to reduce the risks associated with poverty experienced in early childhood? This is the task for non-government organizations so they need to be smart, they need to target resources to areas that are most crucial for child development, and the interventions need to be evidence-based.

An example of a programme that aims to reduce the effects of poverty on the development of children on a national level is Head Start. Currently Head Start is a programme of the US Department of Health and Human Services. It was launched in 1965, originally as a summer school programme that taught low-income children in a few weeks the basics so that they could successfully start elementary school. Now it provides comprehensive early education, health, nutrition and parent involvement services.

Review the website of Head Start programme. Explore the range of services it offers.

http://www.nhsa.org/

Can you suggest any additional services that you think might have a positive impact?

INTERNAL ASSESSMENT

Internal assessment is an integral part of the IB psychology course. It is responsible for 25% of your marks at SL and 20% at HL. This component is internally assessed by your teacher and externally moderated by the IB at the end of the course.

The aim of the internal assessment component is for you to demonstrate the application of the skills and knowledge that you have acquired by studying psychology, with sufficient time to plan and implement your project without the stress and time constraints associated with a regular examination situation.

You need to select a published piece of psychological research and replicate it with the aim of investigating the underlying psychological model or theory. There are certain limitations, both methodological and ethical, to what studies you can replicate. The result of your work will be a written report documenting all stages of the investigation. You will be required to conduct the experiment, collect data, analyse data in line with your aim and hypothesis, and report and discuss the findings.

The internal assessment component relies heavily on your knowledge of the experiment as a method of research in psychology. The skills that you used when evaluating experimental studies discussed throughout the book will come in handy as you carry out your own investigation and analyse the findings. The discussion of the experiment in Unit 1 on research methodology is also useful.

To analyse the findings in your experiment you will need to apply some simple statistical tests. You are free to use software to do that, but you need to understand which statistical tests to choose, what output values to look at and how to interpret the results. To make this process more transparent, we are walking you through manual calculations of the most popular statistical tests. If you understand how to calculate manually, you will have no difficulty with using software properly.

What you will learn in this unit

- Overview of the requirements for internal assessment
- Planning the investigation
  - Choosing the study
  - Simplification and modification
  - Examples: Bransford and Johnson (1972); Loftus and Palmer (1974)
- Writing the introduction
- Writing the exploration
- Conducting the analysis
  - Descriptive statistics: levels of measurement; measures of central tendency; measures of dispersion; graphing the results
  - Inferential statistics: overview; unrelated t-test; related t-test; Mann–Whitney U test; Wilcoxon signed-rank test
- Writing the evaluation
- References and appendices

Internal assessment in psychology is compulsory for students at both SL and HL with the same requirements for both levels. You have to carry out a replication of an experiment and report the results.

Choice of topic

The topic of your investigation can be taken from any area of psychology as long as it meets the methodological, ethical and other requirements outlined below.

- The theory, model or the research study upon which the investigation is based must appear in a peer-reviewed journal.

- This must be an experiment. As you know, that means that at least one independent variable (IV) must be manipulated, at least one dependent variable (DV) must be accurately measured and the potential confounding variables must be controlled.

- Quasi-experiments are not suitable for internal assessment. In quasi-experiments the IV is not manipulated by the researcher but occurs naturally. Examples include:
  - gender
  - age
  - native language
  - culture
  - socio-economic status
  - left- or right-handedness.

- You cannot conduct experiments involving the following elements:
  - placebos
  - ingestion or inhalation (for example, food, drink, smoking)
  - deprivation (for example, sleep, food).

- Only one IV must be used in the experiment.

- In the study that your investigation is based on, the IV will have two or more levels (conditions). You may use all the levels used in the original study or limit the number of conditions. However, it is strongly recommended to simplify the original study and only use two levels of the IV, otherwise it becomes increasingly difficult to present a strong analysis within the permitted word count.

- Only one DV must be used. Operationalization of this variable may be based on the original study or adapted to better suit your context (for example, you may alter the type of measurement taken). You can even use a different DV altogether, but the link between the original study and your experiment must then be clearly justified.

Word count

The word count for the report is between 1,800 and 2,200 words. The report includes the following components:

- Introduction
- Exploration
- Analysis
- Evaluation
- References
- Appendices

Ethical guidelines

Ethical guidelines must be adhered to throughout the process. These include, but are not limited to, the following.

- It is not permitted to carry out a study that creates anxiety, pain, stress or discomfort in the participants. This is why you should rule out experiments involving, for example, unjustified deception, conformity or obedience.

- Partial deception may be allowed on these conditions.

  - Participants' knowledge of the real aim of the experiment would fundamentally affect the outcome.

  - Deception results in no harm to the participants.

  - At the end of the experiment participants are fully debriefed.

  - At the end participants are given the right to withdraw their data.

- Studies involving involuntary participation or invasion of privacy are not allowed. All participants must be informed before the experiment that they have the right to withdraw at any time.

- Informed consent must be gained from all participants in writing.

- Children younger than 12 years old must not be used as participants. For participants aged 12 to 16 years informed consent must be obtained from parents or guardians.

- Non-human animals must not be used.

Choosing the study

The starting point of your investigation is to select a research study that you want to replicate. Apart from the study meeting all the requirements outlined above, these points are essential.

- You have found the original article in a peer-reviewed journal (or a secondary source which gives sufficient information about the study, including its procedural details and numerical findings).

- You have identified the theory or the model upon which the study is based. Very often this theory or model will be discussed in the article itself as the authors provide theoretical justification for the research.

Simplification and modification

The original study will usually have to be simplified for the purposes of your internal assessment. You may also make a small modification to the procedure.

The simplification of the original study will usually involve one or several of:

- reducing the number of IVs (you must have only one)

- reducing the number of DVs (only one is necessary)

- reducing the number of levels of the IV, that is, the groups or conditions

- simplifying the sampling procedure—you will not have access to the same resources that the original researchers did. (IB students often use other students from the same school as their participants.)

The modification of the original study must be a minor change so that it is still a replication, not a different study, and a direct comparison is possible with the original findings. This means that your replication must test the same hypothesis and link to the background theory, model or study in the same way. Consequently, the nature of

the IV cannot be changed either. Examples of modifications that would be acceptable are:

- the way you measure the DV

- a completely changed DV, as long as the link to the background theory or model is retained

- small details of the procedure such as an additional control variable

- the nature of the sample.

Examples

Let's use two examples of studies discussed in this book: Bransford and Johnson (1972) and Loftus and Palmer (1974) (see Unit 3 on the cognitive approach to behaviour). Both of them are popular choices among IB students, so you are encouraged to look for other studies that would be more in line with your interests.

Psychology in real life

Below you will find the details of the original studies published in peer-reviewed journals. Both papers are available online for free and you can find them using Google Scholar or similar search engines. Look through them one more time before reading on.

- Example A: Bransford, JD and Johnson, MK. 1972. "Contextual prerequisites for understanding: Some investigations of comprehension and recall". *Journal of Verbal Learning and Verbal Behavior*. Vol 11. Pp 716–726. https://tinyurl.com/kp479dh

- Example B: Loftus, EF and Palmer, JC. 1974. "Reconstruction of automobile destruction: An example of the interaction between language and memory". *Journal of Verbal Learning and Verbal Behavior*. Vol 13. Pp 585–589. https://tinyurl.com/y772kup4

Example A

Reading the original Bransford and Johnson paper (1972), we find the following details.

Theory or model upon which the study is based

In the introduction to their paper, Bransford and Johnson discuss how prior knowledge is necessary for the meaningful processing of information. This links to the role of schema in memory at the stage of information encoding. The theory upon which the study is based is schema theory, but more specifically a model that postulates the influence of prior knowledge on comprehension and memory of linguistic material.

Variables

There are four separate experiments reported in this paper. We will be using the first one because it is the one discussed in detail in this book (see Unit 3).

The IV in this experiment is the availability of prior knowledge. This is operationalized as a picture giving the context of the text passage.

The IV has five levels:

1. no context
2. no context, passage read twice
3. full context before
4. partial context before
5. full context after.

There are two DVs:

1. comprehension (subjects were asked to rate how difficult the passage was for comprehension, on a scale from 1 to 7)
2. recall (subjects were given seven minutes to recall all the details they could; researchers later counted the number of correctly recalled details).

Sample and design

This experiment uses an independent measures design, with different groups of participants randomly assigned to different levels of the IV. The sample consists of 50 male and female high school students who volunteered to participate in the experiment (no further information about the sample is given in the paper).

What can be simplified and modified for IA purposes

Consider the following.

- First, you must choose one of the DVs. You are allowed to use a different DV altogether, but in this context it is hard to think of something that links to the background theory or model in the same way. Suppose you have chosen recall.

- You are also allowed to change the way the DV is measured. In the original experiment, participants were given a blank sheet of paper and asked to recall the passage as closely as they could in seven minutes. Fourteen idea units were designated beforehand, and the recall protocols were scored by two independent judges against this list of idea units. Any differences were resolved by the third judge. Paraphrases were allowed. However, the list of idea units themselves is not given in the paper. So you would probably be justified in making the following modifications: use one judge only for the sake of simplicity, and design your own list of idea units based on the original text passage.

- Five levels of the IV is also too many, so you might want to reduce the number of levels to two, for example, "no context" and "full context before".

Example B

Reading the original Loftus and Palmer paper (1974) we find the following details.

Theory or model upon which the study is based

This study is based on the theory of reconstructive memory: post-event information may change one's memory of the event. The significance of this theory is in its link to real-life situations of eyewitness testimony (see Unit 3).

Variables

Two experiments are reported in the paper. We will focus on the first one. There is one IV and one DV. Post-event information (the IV) is operationalized as the emotional intensity of the key verb in the question ("smashed", "collided", "bumped", "hit", "contacted"). Memory of the event (the DV) is operationalized as the estimate of the speed with which the cars were moving, the answer to the question, "About how fast were the cars moving when they hit (smashed into, collided with, etc.) each other?"

Sample and design

There are five groups of participants in the experiments (independent measures design). The total sample consisted of 45 students (no further information about the sample is given in the paper).

What can be simplified or modified for IA purposes

Consider the following.

- You should reduce the number of levels of the IV (and the number of groups). For example, you could use only the conditions "smashed" and "hit".

- Since it is a replication, for the purposes of comparing your results with the original study it makes sense to use the same DV measured in the same way (you may have a different opinion and that is fine as long as you justify it).

- You may need to modify the procedure, however, because the original videos used in the experiment are not available.

Writing the introduction

The *Psychology guide* provides the assessment criteria against which your work will be assessed. For the introduction (assessed against criterion A), the top markband for 5–6 marks states:

"The aim of the investigation is stated and its relevance is explained.

The theory or model upon which the student's investigation is based is described and the link to the student's investigation is explained.

The independent and dependent variables are stated and operationalized in the null or research hypotheses."

Aim and relevance of the investigation

As we can see above, the first part of the markband descriptor relates to the aim of the investigation and its relevance.

The way the aim is formulated sets the focus for the whole investigation, so choose your wording carefully. In many published research papers the aim is stated explicitly, and since this is a replication you would only need to adapt it to the context of your investigation.

With rare exceptions the aim is a sentence that brings together three elements:

- the IV
- the DV
- a statement of cause-effect relationship.

Note that the IV and the DV in the aim should be presented as constructs, not operationalizations. For example, the IV in Loftus and Palmer (1974) was "post-event information", and it was operationalized through the emotional intensity of the verb in the leading question. Similarly, the DV was "memory", operationalized as a speed estimate. The aim will usually connect the two constructs in a statement of causal relationship, for example, "To investigate the effect of post-event information on memory of the event in an eyewitness situation".

Now that you have stated the aim, you should explain its relevance. This is a brief explanation as to why this research is worth doing.

Theory or model that the investigation is based upon

The second part of the markband descriptor focuses on a description of the theory or model upon which the investigation is based and an explanation of the link to the investigation.

This requires a clear description of the background theory or model and the replicated experiment. Reading the original paper will help you greatly in understanding the connections to the background theory because authors will typically make links to theory when they formulate their hypothesis as well as later when they discuss their findings. In Loftus and Palmer (1974) you will probably focus on the theory of reconstructive memory, and in Bransford and Johnson (1972) on schema theory and the idea that prior knowledge affects comprehension and memory of new information.

You will also need to describe relevant details of the original experiment. Relevance is determined by the aim of your investigation. To make a comparison of your findings with the original findings more effective, you will need to include information about the sample, experimental design, essential details of the procedure, controls, and also ideally state the numerical results from the original study, both descriptive and inferential statistics. Use whatever information is available in the paper, but only mention what is absolutely relevant to your hypothesis.

After providing details of the original study you will also explain the nature of your simplification and modification (if any). If modification has been done, this needs to be justified briefly.

Stating the variables and formulating the hypothesis

The third part of the markband descriptor requires that both the IV and DV are stated (as constructs) and operationalized. The research hypothesis is a prediction that you are making about the cause–effect relationship between the two variables.

It is recommended to have a set of three statements.

Theoretical prediction

This is the prediction using theoretical terms (constructs) rather than operationalizations. It is linked directly to the background theory or model, for example, "Post-event information will influence memory of an event", or "Presence of contextual information will enhance comprehension and memory of a text". The theoretical prediction is similar to the aim.

Operationalized research hypothesis

This is the theoretical prediction "translated" in operationalized terms. The research hypothesis should be formulated in a way that makes the following points clear:

- what research design is used—comparing different groups of participants or comparing different conditions in the same group

- how the variables are measured

- what is the direction of relationship.

Regarding the last point, hypotheses can be **directional** or **non-directional**. The former predicts the direction, for example, "X will be higher than Y". The latter postulates a relationship, but does not specify its direction, for example, "X will be different from Y".

Using the Loftus and Palmer (1974) example, the operationalized research hypothesis may be something like, "Participants who are asked a question with a verb of higher emotional intensity ('smashed') will report higher speed estimates than participants who are asked a question with a verb of lower emotional intensity ('contacted')". Note that this statement uses operationalized variables; it is easy to tell that different groups of participants will be allocated to different conditions, and the hypothesis is directional.

Null hypothesis

A **null hypothesis** is a statement that is opposite to the operationalized research hypothesis. Usually it expresses the idea that "X will not be different from Y". For "X is independent of Y", for example, "Speed estimates reported by participants who were asked a question with a verb of higher emotional intensity ('smashed') will not be different from speed estimates reported by participants who were asked a question with a verb of lower emotional intensity ('contacted')".

Why do we even need a null hypothesis? In accordance with the principles of falsification of Karl Popper (remember your TOK classes), the proper scientific way to test theories is to try to refute them. If you try to refute a theory but fail, it increases your trust in a theory. Accordingly, we test the null hypothesis. If it gets rejected, we accept the research hypothesis.

Writing the exploration

Looking again at the *Psychology guide* and the assessment criteria against which your work will be assessed, for the exploration (assessed against criterion B), the top markband for 3–4 marks states:

- The research design is explained.
- The sampling technique is explained.
- The choice of participants is explained.
- Controlled variables are explained.
- The choice of materials is explained.

Explaining the research design

As you saw in Unit 1 on research methodology, experiments have three types of design: independent measures, dependent measures and matched pairs. You need to correctly identify the type of design you are using and explain it. Both Loftus and Palmer (1974) and Bransford and Johnson (1972) used independent measures design where participants were randomly allocated into groups.

Note the following points.

- When you use the independent measures design, allocation into groups must be random. You need to think of a procedure that ensures sufficient randomness of allocation, otherwise there would be incorrect implementation of the experimental design. For example, let's say that for a particular male participant you toss a coin and this determines that he has to be allocated to the experimental group. Then you decide to allocate him to the control group anyway to make the male/female ratio in the two groups more equal. This defeats the purpose of the independent measures design.

- When you use the repeated measures design, order effects are inevitable, so you must use counterbalancing. This means that you will end up having two groups of participants anyway, differing in the order of the experimental conditions they are exposed to (AB and BA). Note that when it comes to result analysis, you will still be comparing conditions, not groups. You will compare A from the first group and A

from the second group (collated together) to B from the first group and B from the second group (also collated together).

So, what does the markband descriptor mean when it says you need to explain the research design?

First, explain what features of your experimental design allow you to identify it as a particular type. For example, you might say that two separate groups of participants were used with random allocation into the groups, therefore the design was independent measures.

Second, explain why you have chosen this design over the alternatives. Depending on the aim and the context of your investigation, there can be various reasons that could potentially drive this choice. Here are just a few of them.

- Repeated measures design may be preferred because it minimizes the effect of participant variability (initially existing differences between participants). However, order effects are an issue.

- Independent measures design may be preferred because it is not susceptible to order effects: participants only take part in one experimental condition, so they cannot practise, do not get too tired, and it is harder for them to work out the real aim of the study if you have used deception. However, participant variability could be an issue.

- You may choose the experimental design that was used in the original study because it is important for you to compare your findings to the original findings as precisely as possible.

Explaining the sampling technique and the choice of participants

As you will remember, several sampling techniques may be used in experiments: random, stratified, self-selected and opportunity sampling. Start with identifying your target population—this is the group of people you will generalize your findings to. If there are reasons to believe that the phenomenon you are studying is universal and does not differ with age, education, culture or other demographic variables, your target population may be quite broad. In this case some sampling techniques such as random or stratified will probably be inaccessible to you for logistical reasons, and your choice of sampling method will be driven by accessibility of participants. If there are reasons to believe that the phenomenon is highly variable, you will probably narrow down your target population (for example, to students from your school) and will not claim that your results can be generalized beyond that. In this case the range of accessible sampling techniques is wider.

Once you have recruited the sample, make sure you identify its essential characteristics, such as age, gender distribution, education and whatever else is important to the aim of your investigation. For example, in a replication of Loftus and Palmer (1974) you might want to mention language proficiency because there are reasons to believe that participants will behave differently if the leading question is asked in a language that is not their mother tongue.

How do you explain the procedure of the experiment?

Explaining the procedure of your experiment involves the following elements: explaining the controlled variables, outlining the step-by-step procedure of the experiment, and explaining the choice of materials.

Explaining the controlled variables

Remember that you only need to control variables that can potentially be confounding for your experiment. This means that such variables first need to be identified. Think about what can affect the results of your study. Come up with a list of

factors. For each of the factors explain how it can potentially interfere with the results. Range the factors and look at the most important ones. For each of them, decide which of the following you are going to do about them:

- do nothing and acknowledge they might be influencing your results

- use random allocation into groups and expect that these factors will influence all experimental conditions equally, so will not affect the comparison

- eliminate the confounding factors.

Outlining the step-by-step procedure of the experiment

The main characteristic of this section of your report is its replicability. Write it in a way that will allow an independent researcher to take the description and replicate the whole procedure step by step. In the process you will make references to materials. For example, if at a certain stage of the procedure standardized instructions were given to participants, you are expected to include the full text of the standardized instructions in an appendix and make a reference to it in the text. The same applies to the standard debriefing notes, informed consent form, stimulus materials that you used in the experiment, and so on.

Explaining the choice of materials

Some of the materials will need to be explained. For example, in a replication of Loftus and Palmer (1974), why did you use this particular video of a car accident? How many videos did you use and why? In a replication of Bransford and Johnson (1972), why did you choose to use this text? All the explanations you suggest should be supported by what works best to test your hypothesis and achieve the aim of your investigation.

Conducting the analysis

Let's go again to the *Psychology guide* and the assessment criteria against which your work will be assessed. For analysis (assessed against criterion C), the top markband for 5–6 marks states:

- Descriptive and inferential statistics are appropriately and accurately applied.

- The graph is correctly presented and addresses the hypothesis.

- The statistical findings are interpreted with regard to the data and linked to the hypothesis.

Let's suppose you followed our suggestion and conducted a simple experimental study with one IV, two conditions (or groups, depending on the experimental design) and one DV. Now you need to analyse the data and report the results. For this you will need to choose descriptive and inferential statistical tests. In this section we explain the rationale behind the choice of the tests that you are most likely to use in internal assessment, the calculations associated with the tests how to report them.

Descriptive statistics

As the name suggests, the purpose of descriptive statistics is to describe variables. You will need to determine the level of measurement of the DV, normality of its distribution, and calculate a measure of central tendency and a measure of dispersion.

Levels of measurement

There are four levels of measurement, or types of variable.

Nominal-level variables cannot be quantified. They represent a set of labels that cannot be placed in either descending or ascending order. Examples of nominal variables are: car brands, zodiac signs, gender, nationality and music genre preferences. Some people prefer jazz and some listen to rock, but you cannot rank people by their music preferences from the lowest to the highest. Answers to yes/no questions and other **dichotomous variables** (that is, variables that can only take one of two values) are also usually

treated as nominal data. Since nominal variables cannot be quantified; procedures such as addition, subtraction or multiplication cannot be applied to them. This affects the range of statistical tests that is possible.

Ordinal-level variables can be ranked from the lowest to the highest, but the intervals between ranks may be unequal. An example would be the results of a car race: competitors come first, second, third and so on, but the difference between the person who comes first and the one who finishes second is not necessarily the same as the difference between the second and the third finishers.

Interval-level variables are like ordinal variables, but the intervals are assumed to be equal. Importantly, these variables may have a zero value, but zero does not mean an "absence" of the parameter. An example would be an ordinary thermometer that measures temperature in Centigrade. You can say that the difference between 35°C and 37°C is the same as the difference between 31°C and 33°C. You also know that 0°C does not mean an "absence of temperature", it is just an arbitrary point on the scale. Due to these properties of interval variables, addition and subtraction can be used with them but multiplication and division cannot. For example, it is correct to say that 12°C + 5°C = 17°C, but it is incorrect to say that 20°C is twice as much as 10°C because if you move the zero point, that would no longer be true.

Finally, **ratio-level variables** are like interval variables, but the zero is fixed and meaningful—it means the absence of something. For example, the number of words correctly recalled from a list may be considered ratio data because if you recalled no words it simply means that you have not recalled anything! Annual salary, age and weight are all examples of ratio-level data. Building on our example above, if you measure temperature in Kelvin (where 0 degrees corresponds to minus 273°C and is known as the "absolute zero", the lowest temperature possible), then your data is measured on the ratio level. The full range of mathematical operations can be applied to ratio-level data including division and multiplication.

Normality of distribution of the dependent variable

Normality of distribution as a concept is only applicable to interval and ratio data. **Distribution** is the range of values of a variable according to their frequency. Let's use an example to clarify this.

Suppose you gave people a list of words under two conditions, quiet and noisy, and asked them to recall the words later, registering the number of words that they recalled correctly. These could be the numeric results of the investigation.

| Experimental condition (noisy) | | Control condition (quiet) | |
Participant	Number of words recalled	Participant	Number of words recalled
1	5	1	14
2	4	2	5
3	6	3	9
4	3	4	4
5	4	5	6
6	5	6	5
7	5	7	6
8	6	8	5
9	4	9	6
10	6	10	7
11	7	11	8
12	5	12	6
13	3	13	7
14	7	14	6
15	8		
16	2		

If we plot the frequency distribution of the data from the experimental group, noisy, this is what we get:

For the control group, quiet, we get the following distribution:

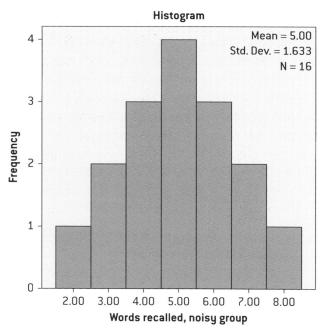

▲ Figure 9.1 Distribution of words recalled correctly, noisy condition

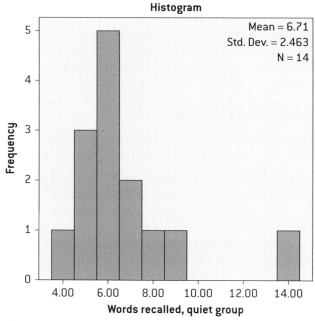

▲ Figure 9.2 Distribution of words recalled correctly, quiet condition

Normal distribution is a special type of distribution that visually looks like a bell. This is why it is sometimes called the "bell curve". Here is a visual representation of an ideal normal distribution:

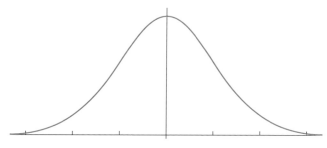

▲ Figure 9.3 Normal distribution

Normal distribution occurs naturally in many situations. For example, IQ scores, height of people, age, blood pressure would all be normally distributed. Most people would be "average", and when the scores are more extreme, fewer people in the population would have these extreme scores.

In reality most data sets will deviate to some extent from the ideal normal distribution. How large is this deviation, however, and can we still assume that data are normally distributed even if minor deviations take place? Rigorous tests exist to compare the empirical distribution (the one you obtained in a study) to the ideal normal distribution and conclude whether the deviation is small enough to assume normality. However, these tests fall outside the scope of the internal assessment requirements; you just need to know the concept of normality of distribution and use the following general principles.

- Scan the raw data for outliers. An outlier is an observation that is extremely different from most or all other observations. For example, in the distribution plot for the control group in our fictitious data set, the participant who scored 14 (participant 1) may be called an outlier because the score is so different from all other scores. If severe outliers are present, the distribution is probably not normal, especially with small sample sizes.

- Optionally, use software to build the distribution of your data (current versions of MS Excel have this function, for example) and visually assess it. If its shape resembles a bell approximately (with average values being most frequent and extreme values less frequent), you may assume normality.

You must include your raw data table in an appendix in your report. It is not necessary to include the distribution plot, but your decision regarding normality of distribution will affect your choice of descriptive and inferential tests.

First, let's look at descriptive statistics: measures of central tendency and measures of dispersion. These measures help us summarize data to make sense of it.

Measures of central tendency

There are three measures of central tendency: the mean, the median and the mode.

The mean is simply the average of all scores. Add all the data points and divide them by the number of observations (participants in the group). The mean is the most common measure of central tendency, but it may be biased if there are some extreme outliers in the sample. The problem with outliers is that they can skew the mean so that it is no longer a meaningful indicator of central tendency, so you need to be careful in applying the mean to data sets with extreme outliers and maybe use the median or the mode instead.

The median is the "middle" of a sorted list of numbers. To find the median, place the numbers in value order. For example, suppose we have the following values:

3, 5, 7, 12, 13, 14, 21, 23, 23, 23, 23, 29, 40, 56

There are fourteen values so the "middle" should be between the seventh and the eighth value: we just find the average. $\frac{(21 + 23)}{2} = 22$. The median of this data set is 22.

The median is used when there are strong deviations from normality of distribution making the mean misleading.

The mode is the value that appears most often in the data set. In our hypothetical experiment with the quiet and the noisy condition, the mode in both groups is 6. There are cases when a data set has more than one mode, for example, here is a binomial data set (the modes are 3 and 6):

1, 3, 3, 3, 4, 4, 6, 6, 6, 9

In an ideally normal distribution the mean, the median and the mode will coincide. As the distribution deviates from normality, especially if there are outliers, they may move apart. So when the level of measurement is interval or ratio, your choice of the measure of central tendency should be guided by your assumptions about the normality of distribution in the data sets. When the level of measurement is ordinal, the mean cannot be used. When the level of measurement is nominal, you can only use the mode.

Measures of dispersion

To make sense of data, measures of central tendency are not enough because some data sets are more spread out around the centre than others. Two measures of dispersion are commonly used: the standard deviation and the semi-interquartile range.

Standard deviation is calculated using the following formula:

$$SD = \sqrt{\frac{\sum(x_i - \overline{X})^2}{N - 1}}$$

Let's decipher the formula step by step. First you calculate the mean of the dataset ($\overline{X}$), then for each individual value (x_i) you calculate its deviation from the mean ($x_i - \overline{X}$). After this you square the deviation, obtaining squared deviations (($x_i - \overline{X}$)²). This eliminates the signs (positive and negative). You calculate the sum of all squared deviations and divide it by the number of observations (participants) minus one. This gives you the "average squared deviation". Finally, you calculate the square root of that value.

Standard deviation is an accurate measure of dispersion that takes into account all individual values and uses all information available in the data set, making it the preferred choice when possible. A low standard deviation indicates that the data points tend to be closely grouped around the mean whereas a high standard deviation indicates that the data points are further spread out around the mean.

However, since the formula uses the mean, the standard deviation cannot be used with nominal or ordinal data, or with data sets that severely violate normality of distribution. So, even if your level of measurement is interval or ratio, you might prefer other methods if there are outliers.

Semi-interquartile range, unlike standard deviation, does not assume normality of distribution and can be used with ordinal-level data.

When you sort a list of numbers, you can find the so-called **quartiles**:

Q2 (the middle quartile) is the median

Q1 (the lower quartile) is the median of the numbers to the left of Q2

Q3 (the upper quartile) is the median of the numbers to the right of Q3

Taking our example from before:

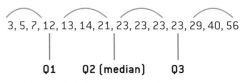

▲ Figure 9.4 Finding quartiles

Q1 is the median of the dataset 3, 5, 7, 12, 13, 14, 21, that is, Q2 = 12

Q2 = the median = 22

Q3 is the median of the dataset 23, 23, 23, 23, 29, 40, 56, that is, Q3 = 23.

The semi-interquartile range is calculated simply as:

$$SIR = \frac{Q3 - Q1}{2}$$

In this example the semi-interquartile range is equal to $\frac{(23 - 12)}{2} = 5.5$

Similarly to the standard deviation, the higher the semi-interquartile range, the more the individual data points are spread out around the centre of the distribution.

Graphing the results

Whatever measures of central tendency and dispersion you have chosen, you need to clearly show this information graphically. In the most typical scenario where you compare two conditions, a **bar chart with error bars** would be the most appropriate choice. Once you know your measures of central tendency and dispersion, it is easy to produce such charts in widely available software, for example, MS Excel.

Psychology in real life

If you use MS Excel to generate error bars, you will need to use the "custom values" option for your error bars and indicate the range of cells where your dispersion values are stored. You can find many tutorials online, such as this one: https://www.youtube.com/watch?v=s3_hcCQGc50.

An example of a bar chart is shown below.

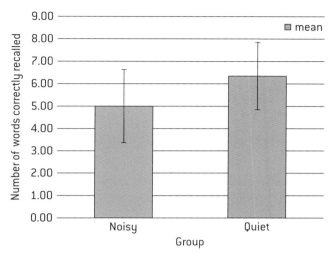

▲ Figure 9.5 Means and standard deviations of the number of words correctly recalled in the "noisy" and "quiet" conditions (note that error bars denote one standard deviation)

When making the bar chart, follow these guidelines.

- The bar chart should be clearly linked to the hypothesis. Do not include information that is not essential for the testing of your hypothesis.

- Do not forget to include clear and meaningful labels for both the axes. Avoid vague labels like "Group 1" and "Group 2".

- Mention the units of measurement for the DV if necessary.

- Include a clear title that is self-explanatory.

- The y-axis should start with the lowest possible value, not with the lowest value observed in your data. Note how the y-axis in our example starts with a zero.

Inferential statistics

While descriptive statistics are used to describe the DV, inferential statistics are used to test hypotheses about its relationship with the IV.

Your choice of the inferential test will depend on:

- the experimental design

- the level of measurement

- your assumptions regarding normality of distribution of the DV.

Below you will find an overview of some of the appropriate inferential tests. Note that all these tests are only suitable for situations when the IV has two levels (that is, you are comparing either two groups or two conditions).

		Experimental design			
		Independent measures		**Repeated measures (or matched pairs)**	
Level of measurement	**Nominal**	Chi-squared (χ^2) test		McNemar's test (for dichotomous data)	
	Ordinal	Mann–Whitney U test		Wilcoxon signed-rank test	
	Interval	Mann–Whitney U test	Unrelated t-test	Wilcoxon signed-rank test	Related t-test
	Ratio				

Each inferential test has some assumptions and can only be used if these assumptions are met.

First, some tests assume normality of distribution. Such tests are called **parametric** because they use "parameters" (mean and standard deviation) in their formula, and, as you know, neither the mean nor the standard deviation are meaningful under severe violations of normality of distribution. The related t-test and unrelated t-test are parametric. All the other tests in the table above are **non-parametric**: they do not assume normality of distribution because they do

not use the mean or the standard deviation in the calculations.

Second, tests assume a certain level of measurement. As you know, the level of measurement determines what mathematical operations can be performed with a variable, which is why there are restrictions. For example, the Mann–Whitney U test assumes at least the ordinal level of measurement. It means the test cannot be used with data below that level. It can be used with interval and ratio data but such data will be first reduced to the ordinal level of measurement.

Third, inferential tests are specific to the experimental design. For example, there are two types of t-test, one for unrelated samples (independent measures design) and one for related samples (repeated measures or matched pairs design). You need to take care in applying the appropriate inferential test.

Exam tip

It is helpful to know the calculation procedure and to be able to compute your chosen test manually, and you are encouraged to learn how to do that. However, manual calculations are not required for internal assessment purposes, you can use software. Below we will focus on the four most commonly used tests (unrelated t-test, related t-test, Mann–Whitney U test and Wilcoxon signed-rank test), looking at the calculation process and reporting the results of these tests. Although you can use software, understanding of the calculations will help you greatly in terms of knowing which option to choose and how to interpret the output.

Should I choose a parametric or a non-parametric test?

On the one hand, parametric tests have greater power, that is, they are more capable of detecting existing differences. Non-parametric tests reduce the level of measurement to ordinal, ignoring the information about the intervals between data points, and therefore lose some power. It is more likely that they will not detect an existing difference. The difference in power is not great: under normal distribution non-parametric tests will detect the existing difference as well as parametric tests in 95% of cases. However, parametric tests can still be considered to be more sensitive.

On the other hand, parametric tests depend on a number of assumptions, most importantly, normality of distribution. With small sample sizes there is no rigorous way to assess normality of distribution, so we can only rely on the visual analysis of the data for obvious outliers. When we are not too sure that the distribution is normal, it might be safer to prefer non-parametric methods.

Unrelated t-test

The unrelated t-test is used to test the difference between two independent samples. It is also known as independent t-test, independent sample t-test and Student's t-test for independent samples.

The unrelated t-test relies on the following assumptions.

- The level of measurement is either interval or ratio.

- You are using an independent measures design with two groups of participants.

- The DV should be approximately normally distributed for each group of the IV. We say "approximately" because the t-test has been shown to be quite robust to moderate violations of normality. This means that it is still valid even if data somewhat deviates from normality. However, severe deviations may compromise the validity of the test. If there are doubts, the safest option is to choose a non-parametric test instead. When looking at outliers and normality of distribution, remember to look separately at the two groups.

- There is homogeneity of variances in the two groups. This means that the standard deviations in the two groups should be approximately equal or at least comparable. However, there is a modification of the unrelated t-test that can handle data when homogeneity of variances is not met. As a general rule, we suggest that you always use this modification, especially when the sample size is small.

The formula of the unrelated t-test is:

$$t = \frac{M_1 - M_2}{\sqrt{\dfrac{SD_1^2}{n_1} + \dfrac{SD_2^2}{n_2}}}$$

where M, SD and n are the means, standard deviations and sample sizes in the two compared groups respectively. Note that equal variances are not assumed in this formula, so it is robust to the violation of the fourth assumption outlined above.

Let's go back to our example, but change the value for the first participant in the control group to get rid of the outlier.

Experimental condition (noisy)		Control condition (quiet)	
Participant	Number of words recalled	Participant	Number of words recalled
1	5	1	9
2	4	2	5
3	6	3	9
4	3	4	4
5	4	5	6
6	5	6	5
7	5	7	6
8	6	8	5
9	4	9	6
10	6	10	7
11	7	11	8
12	5	12	6
13	3	13	7
14	7	14	6
15	8		
16	2		
Mean	5.0		6.36
SD	1.63		1.50

Plugging the values into the formula, we get:

$$t = \frac{5 - 6.36}{\sqrt{\dfrac{1.63^2}{16} + \dfrac{1.50^2}{14}}} = -2.38$$

So the test statistic for the unrelated t-test is -2.38. To find out its statistical significance, we compare this value to the table of critical values easily found on the internet (just search for "t-test critical values table").

Here is a part of that table:

	Critical values for the t-test:						
	one-tailed	.05	.025	.01	.005	.001	.0005
df	two-tailed	.1	.05	.02	.01	.002	.001
1		6.314	12.706	31.821	63.657	318.31	636.62
2		2.920	4.303	6.965	9.925	22.327	31.598
3		2.353	3.182	4.541	5.841	10.214	12.924
4		2.132	2.776	3.747	4.604	7.173	8.610
13		1.771	2.160	2.650	3.012	3.852	4.221
26		1.706	2.056	2.479	2.779	3.435	3.707
27		1.703	2.052	2.473	2.771	3.421	3.690
28		1.701	2.048	2.467	2.763	3.408	3.674
29		1.699	2.045	2.462	2.756	3.396	3.659
120		1.658	1.980	2.358	2.6117	3.160	3.373

First, we choose whether the test is one-tailed or two-tailed. It depends on your hypothesis. If it predicted the direction of the relationship between variables (for example, "A will be higher than B"), then the test is directional. Supposing we had predicted that recall in the "quiet" group would be higher, we would need to look at levels of significance for a one-tailed test.

The next piece of information we need is degrees of freedom (df). For the unrelated t-test degrees of freedom are simply N (the total number of participants) minus 2. So for our example df = 30 − 2 = 28.

The sign of the t statistic can be ignored for now, because it only shows which of the groups has a higher mean. In line with our hypothesis, we see that the mean for the "quiet" group (6.36) is higher than the mean for the "noisy" group (5.0).

The cut-off level of significance, as you know, is p < 0.05. According to the table, the critical value for a one-tailed t test at p = 0.05 and 28 degrees of freedom is 1.701. Our value (2.38) is greater than that, so we need to conclude that the result is statistically significant. We should reject the null hypothesis and accept the experimental hypothesis.

Results of the test will be reported like this: recall in the "quiet" condition (M = 6.36, SD = 1.50) was significantly better than recall in the "noisy" condition (M = 5.0, SD = 1.63); t(28) = −2.38, p < 0.05, one-tailed.

Should I choose the unrelated t-test or the Mann–Whitney U test?

Reviewing all considerations in the context of a typical internal assessment project in IB psychology, our recommendation would be to choose the unrelated t-test in the following situations.

- Your sample size is sufficient, for example, no fewer than 15 participants in each group so that you can visually detect outliers.

- Group sizes are approximately equal, that is, the ratio of the largest to the smallest group size is not larger than 1.5.

- There are no apparent outliers in any of the two groups and the distributions do not seem to deviate severely from normality.

If one or more of these criteria are not met, we suggest it would be safer to use the non-parametric test instead.

Related t-test

The related t-test is used to compare means in two related (dependent) samples.

It relies on the following assumptions.

- The level of measurement is either interval or ratio.

- You are using either a repeated measures or matched pairs design.

- The distribution of the differences in the DV between the two related groups should be approximately normal. We will explain this in the example below.

The formula for the test is:

$$t = \frac{M_{diff}}{\frac{SD_{diff}}{\sqrt{n}}}$$

Where M_{diff} is the mean of the differences, SD_{diff} is the standard deviation of the differences and n is the sample size.

Suppose that you have conducted the same "quiet versus noisy" experiment, but this time you have used a repeated measures design (the same participants were tested twice under different conditions). You make a raw data table and for each participant calculate the difference score (quiet minus noisy).

Participant	Control condition (quiet)	Experimental condition (noisy)	Difference (quiet minus noisy)
1	9	5	4
2	5	4	1
3	9	6	3
4	4	3	1
5	6	4	2

Participant	Control condition (quiet)	Experimental condition (noisy)	Difference (quiet minus noisy)
6	5	5	0
7	6	5	1
8	5	6	−1
9	6	4	2
10	7	6	1
11	8	7	1
12	6	5	1
13	7	3	4
14	6	7	−1
Mean	6.36	5.0	1.36
SD	1.50	1.30	1.55

The third assumption of the related t-test tells you that the distribution of difference scores (the values in the last column of the table) should be approximately normal. There are no obvious outliers, so let us assume it is so.

Plugging the values into the formula, we get:

$$t = \frac{1.36}{\frac{1.55}{\sqrt{14}}} = 3.28$$

The number of degrees of freedom for this test is n−1. The critical values table for the related and the unrelated t-test is the same, so for our example the critical value for a one-tailed test at the p = 0.05 level of significance for 13 degrees of freedom is 1.771. Our value is greater than that, so we can report: there was a significant difference in the scores for the quiet condition (M = 6.36, SD = 2.25) and the noisy condition (M = 5.0, SD = 1.69), with the quiet condition resulting in better recall; t(13) = 3.28, p < 0.05, one-tailed.

Should I choose the related t-test or the Wilcoxon signed-rank test?

Reviewing all considerations in the context of a typical internal assessment project in IB psychology, our recommendation would be to choose the related t-test in the following situations.

- Your sample size is sufficient, for example, no less than 15 participants so that you can visually detect outliers.

- There are no apparent outliers in the difference scores and the distribution of the difference scores does not seem to deviate severely from normality.

If one or more of these criteria are not met, we suggest it would be safer to use the non-parametric test instead.

Mann–Whitney U test

The Mann–Whitney U test is a non-parametric equivalent of the unrelated t-test.

It has the following assumptions.

- The level of measurement is at least ordinal.

- You have used an independent measures design.

The Mann–Whitney U test does not rely on any assumptions regarding the distribution of the DV, making it non-parametric, so the test uses neither the mean nor the standard deviation in the formula. Instead it reduces the level of measurement to ordinal and uses ranks.

Importantly, the test can only be interpreted as comparing two medians if some additional assumptions are met. Without these assumptions the test is still valid, but should be interpreted as a test of difference in mean ranks. That is exactly what we will do.

Let's take the same data as we used in the example for the unrelated t-test:

Experimental condition (noisy)		Control condition (quiet)	
Participant	Number of words recalled	Participant	Number of words recalled
1	5	1	9
2	4	2	5
3	6	3	9
4	3	4	4
5	4	5	6
6	5	6	5
7	5	7	6
8	6	8	5
9	4	9	6
10	6	10	7
11	7	11	8
12	5	12	6
13	3	13	7
14	7	14	6
15	8		
16	2		

First we need to rank the data, so as to reduce the level of measurement to ordinal and avoid the need to use the mean and the standard deviation. There are four steps.

1. Grouping—we order all values, regardless of the group, from the smallest to the largest, placing all "ties" in the same lines.

2. Ordering—we assign these values ranks, from the lowest to the highest, ignoring the ties.

3. Ranking—we replace the ranks for the ties with their respective means, so that equal values get the same ranks.

4. We calculate the mean rank and the sum of ranks in each group.

Step 1 (grouping)		Step 2 (ordering)		Step 3 (ranking)	
Control condition (quiet)	Experimental condition (noisy)	Control condition (quiet)	Experimental condition (noisy)	Control condition (quiet)	Experimental condition (noisy)
	2		1		1
	3		2		2.5
	3		3		2.5
4	4	4	5	5.5	5.5
	4		6		5.5
	4		7		5.5
5	5	8	9	11	11
5	5	10	11	11	11
5	5	12	13	11	11
	5		14		11
6	6	15	16	18.5	18.5
6	6	17	18	18.5	18.5
6	6	19	20	18.5	18.5
6		21		18.5	
6		22		18.5	
7	7	23	24	24.5	24.5
7	7	25	26	24.5	24.5
8	8	27	28	27.5	27.5
9		29		29.5	
9		30		29.5	
			Mean rank	19.04	12.41
			Sum of ranks	266.5	198.5

Now we plug these values into the formulas:

$$U_1 = n_1 n_2 + \frac{n_1(n_1 + 1)}{2} - R_1$$

$$U_2 = n_1 n_2 + \frac{n_1(n_1 + 1)}{2} - R_2$$

where R_1 and R_2 are sums of ranks for the two groups respectively, and n_1 and n_2 are the group sizes.

For our example we get:

$$U_1 = 14 \times 16 + \frac{14 \times (14 + 1)}{2} - 266.5 = 62.5$$

$$U_2 = 14 \times 16 + \frac{14 \times (14 + 1)}{2} - 198.5 = 130.5$$

As the resulting test statistic for Mann–Whitney, we simply choose the smallest of U_1 and U_2, so for our example the test statistic U = 62.5.

To find the critical value, you just need to know the group sizes. The table critical value for a one-tailed U test at p = 0.05 for n_1 = 14 and n_2 = 16 is 71. To be significant, the empirical value must be equal to or smaller than the table value, so for our example, since 62.5 < 71, we may conclude that the result is statistically significant and report: a Mann–Whitney U test indicated that recall in the quiet condition (mean rank = 19.04) was significantly higher than recall in the noisy condition (mean rank = 12.41); U(14,16) = 62.5, p < 0.05, one-tailed.

Wilcoxon signed-rank test

The Wilcoxon signed-rank test is a non-parametric equivalent of the related t-test.

It has the following assumptions.

- The level of measurement is at least ordinal.

- You are using a repeated measures or matched pairs design.

Participant	Control condition (quiet)	Experimental condition (noisy)	Difference (quiet minus noisy)
1	9	5	4
2	5	4	1
3	9	6	3
4	4	3	1
5	6	4	2
6	5	5	0
7	6	5	1
8	5	6	−1
9	6	4	2
10	7	6	1
11	8	7	1
12	6	5	1
13	7	3	4
14	6	7	−1

Just like the Mann–Whitney U test, the Wilcoxon signed-rank test reduces the level of measurement to ordinal, and just like the related t-test, it deals with differences between pairs of values.

Let's take the same example we used for the related t-test (table at the top of the page).

After calculating the difference scores (the last column of the table), we need to do some transformations with the obtained differences. There are four steps.

1. We order them by their absolute value (ignoring the sign).

2. We assign ranks while still ignoring the signs. At this point we eliminate data points where the difference is zero, thus "reducing" the sample size. Remember to observe the ties.

3. We return the signs to the ranks.

4. We calculate the sum of positive ranks (W+) and the sum of negative ranks (W−).

Step 1	Step 2	Step 3
Difference (quiet minus noisy), ordered (sign ignored)	**Ranked difference (sign ignored)**	**Sign returned**
0	---	---
1	4.5	+ 4.5
1	4.5	+ 4.5
1	4.5	+ 4.5
−1	4.5	− 4.5
1	4.5	+ 4.5
1	4.5	+ 4.5
1	4.5	+ 4.5
−1	4.5	− 4.5
2	9.5	+ 9.5
2	9.5	+ 9.5
3	11	+ 11
4	12.5	+ 12.5
4	12.5	+ 12.5
	W+ (the sum of positive ranks)	82
	W− (the sum of negative ranks)	9

W+ in this example is larger, and this tells you that recall in the quiet condition was generally better than recall in the noisy condition (because we subtracted noisy from quiet). However, we still need to test this difference for statistical significance.

The test statistic for Wilcoxon signed-rank test is denoted by the letter T and is simply the smallest of W+ and W–. In this case T = 9.

The table of critical values for Wilcoxon signed-rank test gives 21, 12 and 4 as the values for a one-tailed test with n = 13 (remember we "reduced" the sample by one!) and at p = 0.05, p = 0.01 and p = 0.001 respectively. The result is significant if the obtained value is equal to or smaller than the critical value. In our case 9 is smaller than 12 so we can conclude that the result is significant at p < 0 .01. We should reject the null hypothesis and accept the experimental hypothesis. We can report: a Wilcoxon signed-rank test indicated that recall in the quiet condition was significantly better than recall in the noisy condition: T = 11, p < 0.01, one-tailed.

Note that if you do calculations by hand and compare the obtained value to the value of critical tables, you will be using the T statistic because it is easier and tables of critical values are made for it. However, if you use a statistical package it may report the Z statistic instead. Do not be confused by that; both T and Z are statistics related to the Wilcoxon test. The software will calculate the level of significance automatically, so all you need to do is to report the Z value (and the corresponding level of significance) instead of T.

Useful resources

You will find the following resources helpful.

Tables of critical values:

- t-tests: https://tinyurl.com/5wtxc9h

- Mann–Whitney U test: https://tinyurl.com/y8j2xrhm

- Wilcoxon signed-rank test: https://tinyurl.com/yctlm2av

Online statistical software:

- GraphPad allows you to calculate descriptive statistics and t-tests; it also has a feature to run tests to detect outliers in your data: http://graphpad.com/quickcalcs/contMenu/

- VassarStats has a variety of statistical tests that can be run online: http://vassarstats.net

Writing the evaluation

Let's go back again to the *Psychology guide* and the assessment criteria against which your work will be assessed. For evaluation (assessed against criterion D) the top markband for 5–6 marks states:

- The findings of the student's investigation are discussed with reference to the background theory or model.

- Strengths and limitations of the design, sample and procedure are stated and explained and relevant to the investigation.

- Modifications are explicitly linked to the limitations of the student's investigation and fully justified.

The final step of your investigation and the last section of your report is evaluation. This should include three major elements: linking the findings to the background theory or model, analysing strengths and limitations, and suggesting modifications.

When you link the findings to the background theory or model, the main question to answer is whether or not your findings support the background theory and why. Aspects of this discussion may include the comparison between your findings and those of the original experiment. You can also reiterate the modifications you have made to the original procedure and discuss how this might have influenced the discrepancy (if any). But most importantly, this is where you switch from the operationalized language of hypothesis testing to the language of constructs again. If you were replicating Loftus and Palmer, you should discuss what your findings mean in the context of the theory of reconstructive memory: do your findings support the idea that post-event information may influence memory of the event? If you were replicating Bransford and Johnson, you should discuss your findings in the context of schema and prior contextual information influencing comprehension and recall of verbal material.

When you analyse the strengths and limitations of your study, keep in mind the following considerations.

- Your analysis should be comprehensive. Take into account construct validity, internal validity and external validity of your experiment. Consider how the constructs were operationalized, what variables were controlled, how the sample was selected, what the target population was, and to what extent various forms of bias might have taken place.

- Your analysis should be directly relevant to your investigation. Avoid general statements that are applicable to almost any experimental study. A typical mistake that students make is to say that since the study was a laboratory experiment, it lacked ecological validity, and to say nothing else. This might be a valid point, but why is this an issue particularly in your experiment as compared to other research?

- Talk about both strengths and limitations.

- Draw a line between methodological limitations of your experiment and limitations in the quality of its implementation. For example, suppose in a replication of Bransford and Johnson (1972) you decided to use a filler task between listening to the text and reproducing it. This decision was justified: you said that the filler task is necessary to avoid mechanical repetition and only measure information retained in the long-term memory. Later you said that using a filler task is a limitation of the experimental design because it extends the duration of the study and makes possible such threats to internal validity as history effect. This is reasonable: you made a choice, justified it, but recognized the limitations of this choice in terms of potential threats to internal validity. This counts as a methodological limitation of the experiment. In contrast, suppose participants in your Bransford and Johnson replication were tested as a group. They listened to the text and then engaged in the filler activity. While doing that, they occasionally talked to each other or distracted each other. You cannot say that this is a methodological limitation of your experiment: it is just bad implementation!

Methodological and other limitations of the study you have identified will be closely linked to suggested modifications. Continuing our example with the filler task activity in a replication of Bransford and Johnson, you might suggest, for example, that future studies vary the duration of the filler activity and assess its impact on the results. All potential confounding variables cannot be possibly eliminated in a single research study, so it is perfectly fine to suggest modifications for future research endeavours. However, avoid generic suggestions such as increasing the sample size or conducting the study in more naturalistic settings. The modifications you suggest should target your hypothesis and be potentially informative in the context of the background theory or model.

References and appendices

References

Remember that a failure to acknowledge the ideas of others is a breach of academic honesty. It is important to reference properly to acknowledge all ideas that are not yours in an academically acceptable manner. We are not going to outline the basic principles of academic honesty here because it is expected that you will already be familiar with them, but here are some guidelines for formatting your in-text citations and list of references, to avoid some common mistakes.

- For every in-text citation in the report there must be a corresponding entry in the list of references. Similarly, you should not include in the list of references anything that does not appear as a citation in the text.

- Your references must include all necessary information required by the citation style. For example, for a journal article you need to include the surnames and initials of the authors, year of publication, full name of the article and the journal, the number of journal or issue, and page numbers. It is good practice to make full references as you are doing the theoretical research so that you will not have to look for all these details again later.

- Your references must consistently follow one citation style, for example, APA, MLA or Chicago. Strictly stick to the rules of your citation style and follow it throughout your report.

One useful resource is the Purdue Online Writing Lab. It provides guidance for formatting your papers in accordance with a variety of styles. Just choose your preferred citation style and explore the links: https://owl.english.purdue.edu/owl/section/2.

Appendices

The appendices should include:

- any standardized instructions used in the experiment

- briefing and debriefing notes

- a copy of the consent form

- standardized stimulus materials used in the experiment

- a raw data table

- calculations for both descriptive and inferential statistics—it is not a requirement to do calculations manually, but if you are using software you must include a print-out of the output with a clear indication of the options you have chosen (for example, one-tailed or two-tailed) and the values you are using as your results

- any other materials necessary for your investigation.

Introduction

The aim of the IB psychology course is to provide students with a holistic understanding of the subject of psychology. This is achieved by exploring human behaviour through the biological, cognitive and sociocultural approaches to understanding behaviour (the core) in paper 1. Looking through these individual lenses in isolation may not, however, be the best way to understand human behaviour. Our behaviours are often impacted by biological, cognitive and social factors in combination. In fact Robert Sapolsky (2017) argues in his latest book *Behave* that it makes no sense to distinguish between aspects of behaviour that are biological, psychological or cultural as they are "utterly intertwined". He does claim, however, that putting facts into demarcated buckets (the approaches to understanding behaviour) has some advantages as it can help you remember facts better. Nevertheless it is important to note that by examining a behaviour in isolation we can actually think about the behaviour differently and neglect the importance of the other perspectives.

Paper 2 offers an opportunity to examine the interdependence of these factors via the biopsychosocial model. The model states that all behaviour is a result of an interaction between any number of interrelated factors. One thing we can be certain of is that human behaviour can rarely, if ever, be attributed solely to a single biological, cognitive or sociocultural factor. In order to understand human behaviour it is essential to consider the relationships between all the contributing factors. Developing a strong understanding of the topic and related concepts is, therefore, essential to succeeding in the final examinations.

This section will explain the key ingredients for developing understanding, provide some suggested individual and group revision strategies and interpret the rubrics that will be used to assess your final examinations.

The IB psychology curriculum adopts a conceptual model to teaching and learning. Teachers encourage students to develop a holistic understanding of psychology in order to gain a deeper understanding of the discipline and avoid learning or teaching merely to pass examinations. Revising from an essay plan written by somebody else limits understanding and does not facilitate effective recall. Students who try to rote learn essay plans often display limited scope and understanding in their responses.

By focusing on key concepts students learn about broad and abstract concepts they can apply to a wide variety of topics that have been relevant throughout the ages. Studying concepts and big ideas allows students to make their own links between research and topics, which helps to improve recall of information. A single concept can be applied to multiple topics or arguments so links can be readily made. For example, prejudice, conflict and cooperation have been studied by psychologists for decades and there is a wide body of research on these topics. Not all this research in these areas has focused on the same aspects, or reached a consensus about human behaviour. Students should therefore acknowledge that psychology is cumulative, which means the body of knowledge is constantly growing, and our understanding of behaviour developing. It is appropriate therefore to avoid discussing psychological research in absolutes and refrain from using the word "prove" when writing assessments.

The core elements of the IB psychology curriculum

To be successful, IB students are required to adopt an inquisitive mindset, a strong set of self-management skills, a detailed knowledge and understanding of the subject, and of its assessment criteria. The IB learner profile attributes and ATL skills must be put into practice if a student is to succeed in psychology.

In order to maximize the learning experience that you receive in psychology and demonstrate the highest levels of thinking, you must **get your DUKS in a row**.

Dispositions (IB learner profile attributes): it is hoped that by following the Diploma Programme and using ATL skills you will be developing in skill *and* character.

Understanding: broadly speaking, this is when you understand a topic or issue and are able to write a response on it. You need to be able to filter out the irrelevant material and tell the examiner why this information is important to know. When writing a response, it is good practice to conduct the "so what?" test. Ask yourself, "Why should anyone care about what I have written? Why is it important to psychology?" If you have selected the appropriate material, placed it in context and explained why it is important information in relation to the topic, then you have demonstrated understanding.

Knowledge: this refers to the things you need to know before you can understand. This includes dates, concepts, facts, terminology and definitions. Merely including these details in a response does not, however, display understanding. It is common for students to try to remember essays or answers from study guides but they are insufficient. Essays must include both understanding and critical thinking. Therefore, it is essential to include knowledge, but also to interpret it in relation to the question on the examination paper to demonstrate understanding.

Skills (ATL): ATL skills are taught throughout the Diploma Programme. In order to reach a point when you can demonstrate mastery in the subject you will have already exercised some research, self-management, communication and social skills as you have progressed through your classes. In the examination you have to demonstrate your knowledge and understanding to the examiner. This is achieved in part through critical thinking. Challenging the claims made by researchers, providing alternative explanations for research findings or highlighting strengths and limitations of theories and studies all demonstrate that you are able to analyse the material within the context of the assessment question.

See video

Watch Robert Sapolsky's TED Talk "The biology of our best and worst selves", available at https://www.ted.com/talks/robert_sapolsky_the_biology_of_our_best_and_worst_selves.

The examination papers are designed to assess a student's knowledge and understanding of psychology. Students are expected to be able to recall facts, apply them to a specific topic or issue, critically analyse content and express the relevance of their work explicitly to the examiner.

It is essential therefore that you have a strong knowledge of the examination structure and expectations, including a working knowledge of the command terms and assessment rubrics.

Papers 1 and 2

Paper 1 is a two-hour examination with two sections. Section A consists of three short-answer questions (SAQs) and section B consists of three essay questions (often called extended response questions or ERQs).

- In section A, students must answer all of the SAQs. These questions use AO1 and AO2 command terms that focus on knowledge, understanding and application.

- In section B, students must select and write only one of the three essays. The essays use AO3 command terms that require synthesis and evaluation.

Students should aim to complete each SAQ within 20 minutes (60 minutes total for section A), leaving one hour for the essay (section B).

There are different papers for standard level (SL) and higher level (HL) students. The structure is the same but the content is different. HL students can expect one, two or all of the essays on paper 1 to make reference to the HL extension topics.

Paper 2 will present students with questions from each of the four possible options: abnormal psychology, health psychology, the psychology of human relationships and developmental psychology. SL students study one option only while HL students study two of the options.

It is important that students only attempt questions that are from the options they have studied with their teacher.

SL students answer one of the possible three essay questions from their chosen option. HL students must answer one question from each of their two options.

In order to demonstrate the highest levels of thinking in an IB psychology examination, students must understand the demands of the examination. To do this, you must understand the requirements of all command terms as their definitions and therefore the associated rubrics are explicitly different from each other. An essay that asks you to "evaluate" requires a very different response from a question that asks you to "discuss" the topic. Applying a "one size fits all" response may highlight to the examiner that you do not understand the question and are unable to select appropriate material. Fortunately, there are strategies you can adopt to help you structure your thinking and answers appropriately.

Exercise

Flashcards are often used by students when they want to remember facts (knowledge). Students have a habit, however, of revising their favourite topics. Anki is a program that will allow you make your own flashcards using a spaced repetition system. This means that the system knows which information you are finding hard to remember and tests you on these cards more often. You can download this program from https://apps.ankiweb.net/.

When making the flashcards it is important to use images and key concepts only and do not try to fit as much information as possible onto each card. Less is definitely more when trying to commit information to memory. You can make flashcards that help remember individual studies, theories or even essay plans. A flashcard with the word "PREJUDICE" on one side and four images on the reverse that correspond to related studies, concepts or arguments will really challenge the memory and facilitate learning.

Try making flashcards for a topic that you find challenging.

Paper 1 section A: SAQs

The SAQs in this section focus on application of knowledge to the examination question. These questions do not require synthesis and evaluation, so they provide students with an easy opportunity to demonstrate their understanding of the approaches to the examiner. Showing that you know something is not the same as showing that you understand it. To successfully answer an SAQ you should remember the following steps.

- Read and reread the question. Rewrite the question in your own words making reference to the command term and relevant concepts.

- Write in a clear and succinct manner. This is not an essay and should be direct. Ensure that each point links back to the SAQ.

- Remember to conclude using key words from the question. This will help ensure that the information contained in the answer is relevant and has been applied explicitly. For example, in a question that uses the command term "explain" you should use the words "reason" and/or "cause/causing" in your answer. Using signposts, or marker words, to signal to the examiner that you are making a relevant point is also good technique. Words such as "therefore", "indicating", "highlighting" and "supporting" all force you to make a conclusion.

- Stop writing each SAQ after 20 minutes. There are only 9 marks available for each question.

The best answers will focus only on information relevant to the question and meet the demands of the command term. They will be written in sufficient depth to demonstrate understanding and be explicitly applied to the issue addressed in the question.

Discussion

When answering an SAQ it is important to apply the "so what?" test. This is because the questions are designed to get students to write about the facts they can recall and apply them to the question to show their understanding. The "so what?" test will encourage you to display your understanding by forcing you to explain why your writing is relevant to the question.

In groups look at some questions that may appear on examination papers and practise using the "so what?" test. Discuss how it prompts you to explain your thinking.

The top markband of the rubric for section A states that you need to demonstrate the following.

- The response is fully focused on the question and meets the command term requirements.

- Knowledge and understanding is accurate and addresses the main topics/problems identified in the question.

- The response is supported by appropriate research which is described and explicitly linked to the question.

Paper 1 section B and paper 2: essay questions

For these questions students must write a critical essay that includes knowledge and understanding; however, students must also evaluate and synthesize the material they have included in relation to the question.

It is important that you take the time to consider the question, command terms and key issues before you put pen to paper. This valuable thinking time may stop you misinterpreting a question or, even worse, attempting the wrong one.

Create a plan, mind map or causal map that includes key arguments and researchers to help structure your thinking and your essay. This is an important step as the pressure of the examination can sometimes cause students to forget key information halfway through a sentence.

There are many ways to structure an essay so we will focus only on the key ingredients before interpreting the essay rubric. A well-written essay will include:

- a specific focus on the command term

- a clear introduction that outlines the question and the main issues and topics to be explored

- a series of paragraphs that explicitly explain the relevance of the theory or evidence included in the essay

- a strong conclusion that links back to the essay title to help ensure the relevance of all the material contained within the essay.

A body paragraph may have a structure like this.

Point: the opening of the paragraph outlines the issue to be discussed. It should not be limited to one sentence as you want to ensure it is clear and explicitly related to the title. In a "discuss" question this would be an

517

argument, factor or hypothesis that would be stated and explained. In an "evaluate" question this may be a strength or limitation that is provided with clearly stated reasons why it is indeed a strength or limitation in this context.

Evidence (first piece): this may be a specific fact from a study or theory that applies explicitly to the question.

Comparison/contrasting point: present a similar or alternative explanation or piece of evidence to facilitate critical thinking and explain its relevance. Key words such as "however" are often used.

Evidence (second piece): support your comparison/contrasting point with a second piece of evidence. This could be a different part of the previous study or a new piece of research. There is no specified number of studies that you need to include in an essay.

Conclusion: you need to reach a conclusion in relation to the evidence and the essay question. A good conclusion will make a clear interpretation of the facts presented in this paragraph and provide a link to the next body paragraph. Remember that it is also important to evaluate and challenge concepts as well as the methodology of studies. Challenging methodology can be an element of the paper but should not be the main focus.

Interpreting the essay rubric

The top markband for criterion A, focus on the question, reads as follows.

- Explains the problem/issue raised in the question.

In order to write a good essay you must demonstrate to the examiner that you understand the question. This is often achieved by merely restating or rewording the question in order to highlight the causal relationships, issues or problems identified in the question. This is a very important part of your essay. Stating the question or briefly outlining the factors that you will discuss in relation to the question shows that you have understood the question being asked of you.

The top markband for criterion B, knowledge and understanding, reads as follows.

- The response demonstrates relevant, detailed knowledge and understanding.

- Psychological terminology is used appropriately.

You are rewarded for including relevant content in your response. It is important to select the research and theory that you feel applies most directly to the question. Including absolutely everything that you know on a given topic does not demonstrate understanding; you must filter your response to form a valid argument or point. It is essential, therefore, that you plan your answer and select three or four main points, arguments or hypotheses that you would like to debate, discuss or evaluate. These will form the foundation of your paragraphs and allow you to bring in appropriate psychology to support or refute the claims they make. The purpose or contribution of each point you make in your essay must be clear to the examiner. The "so what?" test will help you to check that you have written in sufficient detail and made the material's relevance clear to the reader.

The top markband for criterion C, use of research to support your answer, reads as follows.

- Relevant psychological research is used in support of the response and is thoroughly explained.

- Research selected is effectively used to develop the argument.

When writing your response it is important to support all claims with evidence. Psychology is a research-based subject and as such you should not make any point that cannot be supported by evidence. You can apply the "who says?" test here: when making a point ask yourself, "Who says this?" or "Is this psychology or common sense?"

It is very important, however, that you do not adopt a shopping list approach to your essay; listing lots of researchers' names without making each one explicitly relevant can damage the strength of your response. Select a smaller number of studies and learn them well.

The top markband for criterion D, critical thinking, reads as follows.

- The response consistently demonstrates well-developed critical thinking.

- Evaluation or discussion of relevant areas is consistently well developed.

In this section students are rewarded for asking well-considered questions, challenging the theory and evidence, discussing the underlying assumptions and biases within the theory and research, and including alternative explanations to accepted findings in their response. Demonstrating explicit critical thinking exemplifies the characteristics and dispositions of the IB learner profile. Using words and phrases such as "however, one alternative explanation is" will help draw attention to your use of critical thinking.

The top markband for criterion E, clarity and organization, reads as follows.

- The answer demonstrates organization and clarity throughout the response.

Students are rewarded in this section for writing a clear and well-organized response. The answer should be well structured and allow the reader to follow the writer's arguments and train of thought. For example, some answers that refer to a lot of theory may be well suited to a chronological approach if we assume that each new theory has built upon the limitations of the last. Finally, don't forget to write a strong conclusion. This will help to provide closure to the essay and signals to the examiner that you have made all the information in your essay relevant to the essay question.

Applying the command terms to the essays

The essay command terms require students to think critically about the issue or topic raised in the question. There are four command terms that may appear in the essay titles:

- evaluate
- contrast
- to what extent
- discuss

Each command term requires a different response so it is important to review and think about topics in relation to the above command terms before writing an essay. "Evaluate" and "contrast" questions can be considered and planned in a table as this can help students to visualize and organize their thinking. Look at the example below.

Question: Evaluate schema theory.

Strengths	Limitations
One strength is …	One limitation is …
"Says who?"	"Says who?"
"So what?"	"So what?"

It is important to consider the "says who?" and "so what?" tests to make this relevant to the question and engage in the highest level of thinking. Failure to take this step will often result in a student producing a response that looks as if it has been lifted from a study guide without demonstrating any understanding.

"To what extent" questions are often viewed as a debate. Debates typically consist of well-prepared and informed arguments that can be supported by evidence. It is suggested that students include between two and four clear arguments that can be discussed within the body of the essay. As would occur in a verbal debate, alternative explanations and challenges to the research should be included. Working in pairs or study groups can make preparation for this command term more fun and can be beneficial as you can challenge your memory by having a mini-debate.

"Discuss" questions require students to engage in a well-balanced review of the topic or issue under discussion, making reference to clear factors, arguments or hypotheses. All claims should be supported by relevant psychological evidence. When planning these questions it may help you to write between two and four arguments or hypotheses you can use as the opening sentence in a paragraph. This will then encourage discussion around the truth or validity of the claims made. By placing the statement first you are ensuring that the discussion is the most important thing and that you bring in evidence only to support the claims that you have made.

Paper 3: research methods (HL only)

Paper 3 is a one-hour examination paper that assesses a student's knowledge of approaches to research methods. The paper contains stimulus material in the form of a research scenario and three questions. **All three questions must be answered.** There are a total of 24 marks available.

In order to succeed on this paper you will need to ensure that you highlight and consider relevant methodological issues that you read in the stimulus material. Underline or highlight information such as the research aim, participants, research design, research method, potential issues and/or ethical considerations. When attempting to answer the questions that follow, it is essential that you consider the specific context outlined in the stimulus material. The examiner does not want a generic response, but one that considers the issues faced by the researchers who conducted the research outlined in the paper. It may help you to place yourself in their shoes and consider what decisions they may have had to make when conducting the research.

The three examination questions are drawn from a bank of six static questions, each focusing on approaches to research.

Question 1 is a three-part question. Each part is worth 3 marks, so question 1 is worth 9 marks in total. The three parts will be as follows.

- Identify the research method used and outline two characteristics of the method.

- Describe the sampling method used in the study.

- Suggest an alternative or additional research method giving one reason for your choice.

Question 2 is worth 6 marks. The question will be one of the following two options.

- Describe the ethical considerations that were applied in the study and explain if further ethical considerations could be applied.

- Describe the ethical considerations in reporting the results and explain additonal ethical considerations that could be taken into account when applying the findings of the study.

Question 3 is worth a total of 9 marks and will be one of these three options.

- Discuss the possibility of generalizing the findings of the study.

- Discuss how a researcher could ensure that the results of the study are credible.

- Discuss how the researcher in the study could avoid bias.

Questions 1 and 2 will be assessed using an analytical markscheme that is unique to each examination. Question 3 will be assessed using a rubric. The top level descriptor reads as follows.

- The question is understood and answered in a focused and effective manner with an accurate argument that addresses the requirements of the question.

- The response contains accurate references to approaches to research with regard to the question, describing their strengths and limitations.

- The response makes effective use of the stimulus material.

As you work through the questions, the command terms change in order to meet different assessment objectives. Question 1 is testing knowledge. Question 2 is testing knowledge, understanding and application. Question 3 is testing all of the above, as well as the ability to think critically about the research scenario in relation to the examination question.

It is important to note that you do not need to be an expert in the field of research outlined in the stimulus material. The assessment focuses on the research methodology. It may help you, however, to consider the practical and ethical considerations that a psychologist may have been faced with before, during and after conducting the research cited in the stimulus material. This will help you to ensure that your answers are contextual and not a generic discussion of research methodology. This will help you to meet the demands of the rubric.

A strong answer will clearly address the issues highlighted in the question, using examples from or issues raised in the text. It is important, however, not to reproduce long passages from the stimulus material. This is often a sign that the student doesn't understand the question and uses the stimulus material to fill space on their answer sheet.

Strong answers to questions on paper 3 will define the terminology stated in both the question and the research scenario to demonstrate understanding. The answer will also be well structured and consist of clear interrelated parts. For example, if the question was, "Discuss the possibility of generalizing the findings of the study", the answer should start by explaining what is meant by the term "generalization". As there are multiple forms of generalization to consider, there may be one section dedicated to a discussion on inferential generalizations and one focusing on theoretical generalizations. Each paragraph would clearly consider the specific context of the research scenario in the stimulus material.

Exercise

Create your own glossary of key terms. Start with the words in each of the paper 3 examination questions. You cannot answer the question effectively if you do not understand the term or concept referred to in the question.

Choosing a topic and refining your research question

Getting started can be the toughest part of any job. An extended essay is challenging in any subject; there are no easier or harder options. Choose based on interest and you will find the process easier and more enjoyable. It is recommended that only students studying psychology should write an extended essay in psychology as it requires a sound understanding of the subject and its methods of inquiry.

You are free to research topics discussed in class but your research should go beyond what you learned in class. In other words, independent work is needed to meet the requirements of the essay. An extended essay in psychology is a research-based, independent work of up to 4,000 words. It is important to note that no primary research is allowed; you can use only secondary sources so no experimentation or primary research should be carried out. The extended essay is an excellent opportunity for you to further explore human behaviour beyond the scope of the course material.

Now that you have selected psychology as your subject, you need to choose a topic. Start by identifying the field of psychology that you would like to explore. As the study of human behaviour continues to expand, more and more fields are available for study. It is dangerous to compartmentalize subjects in psychology as it risks reductionist explanations; nonetheless, choosing a field is important to limit the scope of your paper.

Examples of fields of study in psychology

Biological	Sport
Cognitive	Criminal
Social/cultural	Organizational
Developmental	School/educational
Abnormal	Consumer
Health	Forensic
Human relationships	Personality
Business	Clinical

Now that you know what you are looking for and where to start looking, it is time to start conducting proper research. At this stage you are looking for veins of research that interest you. In other words, what is it about developmental, health or abnormal psychology that interested you in particular? Within each field of psychology there are countless topics and within each topic, countless questions and debates.

Examples of some notable debates in psychology

Human relationships: Is helping behaviour fuelled by empathy (Batson) or egoism (Cialdini)?

Health: Why do we eat too much and exercise too little?

Cognitive: Why do some people seek danger and take risks for fun?

Abnormal: Diagnosing disorders—how do we define normal behaviour?

Avoid popular (pop) psychology. Pop psychology is defined as concepts or ideas about human behaviour that claim to be based in psychology and have a significant following among non-psychologists but have no basis in psychological research or scientific evidence. The assessment criteria of the extended essay require the topic under investigation to be "appropriate"; pop psychology topics are not considered appropriate. Examples of pop psychology topics include things such as self-help books, psychics, astrology and palm reading. These topics have no basis in modern psychology and are not testable concepts.

Hints for researching and writing

The research question needs to be an answerable, open-ended question related to a specific topic in psychology. It should be clear, concise, complex and debatable. Your research question is the most important single aspect of your whole essay—without a really good research question you cannot have a really good essay. Your essay must be critical and analytical, which means that your research question must lend itself to that kind of study. Once you have selected your topic and have done some preliminary research, you should start asking yourself questions starting "how", "to what extent" and "why". One of these may end up becoming your question.

Ask yourself whether your question meets the following criteria.

Clear	Is your research question easy to understand?
Complex	Is your research question open-ended and does it require explanation and evidence? Avoid questions with simple answers.
Concise	Is your research question as simple as possible? Avoid anything extra that may confuse the question.
Debatable	Is there more than one possible answer to your question? Can this question be debated soundly from more than one perspective?

The process

The research process can be tedious but it doesn't have to be. Start big and go small. You do not need to start reading academic, peer-reviewed journals about your topic right away. Start with your textbook or other resources in your classroom to get an idea of the vocabulary and the general topic. Move on to an internet search of some key terms. Read entries in encyclopedias and see where others have sourced their information. An online source such as Wikipedia does not belong in your bibliography but contributors often use reliable sources that may be useful to you. For each source, ask: "Is this reliable? Why/why not?" Look for the reliable sources independently and dig deeper. Google Scholar is a great way to harness the power of a great search engine to help with this task. You will find yourself reading academic journals and electronic resources that are considered reliable, relevant and applicable. Make sure you dig through the pop psychology and baseless claims until you find sources that you consider rigorous and reliable. If you are unsure, ask your teacher or librarian.

Don't be afraid to refocus, reword or abandon your research question for something new. Your research question does not have to be perfect from the beginning. The process of creating your research question, along with selecting your topic and the content of your paper itself, is fluid and will change as your learning deepens.

Outlining

Organization is an important first step to good writing. Make sure you take the time to write a clear and detailed outline of your argument and an idea of the support that you have for those arguments. You should have some idea of the evidence that can be included. However, more research will be needed as your argument advances.

By the end of your outlining stage, you should be able to share your ideas with your supervisor or other students so that they can feedback to you on the merit of your argument. Since your outline should contain your main points and the order in which they are presented, your argument and support should be clear. This is more than just a plan of what you will do; it should reflect the initial research you have already done.

Writing is a messy process. Few writers are able to start and work through an argument without changing directions, deleting sections, restarting several times and sometimes even having two "competing" essays on the go at the same time. All of this is normal. Be honest but easy with yourself. Having a plan is important. A plan will keep you on track and should give you a place to refocus if you find yourself getting frustrated or lost in ideas.

Writing

When deciding where to start, the first question you should ask yourself is, "What is the context readers need?" At each step along the way, you should be asking yourself, "What do they need to know next?" It is a good idea to break your essay into sections and concentrate on each section sequentially. This makes writing far more manageable. For example, if your essay has three main supporting points, separate these with subheadings and write each one in such a way that is has an introduction, a middle and a conclusion. These subsections should directly support the overall conclusion of your essay. This guarantees that you have analysis throughout your essay and you are not spending too much of your essay setting up or describing your argument.

By the time you start your writing, you should have a good portion of your research completed. You will probably find yourself doing more research, but at this stage research should be very focused.

What to do when you have finished

Did you answer the research question? Did you go beyond simple description? Does your argument make sense? Is there irrelevant material that needs to be removed? There are many questions that are difficult to answer on your own. **Bring someone else you trust into the proofreading process.**

When you think you are finished you are probably not. Rereading your own work for clarity and accuracy requires immense levels of self-discipline and self-management. It is always a good idea to reread your work once it is complete but it is an even better idea to have others read it. They will read it with a dispassionate and attentive eye. Take their criticism seriously and be honest with yourself regarding their criticisms. Conversely, it is a great idea to read someone else's extended essay. This will give you an insight into how others wrestled with similar challenges to your own and may give you some ideas of how to improve your work. Refer to the assessment criteria during this process and give each other feedback that will help improve clarity as well as achievement as measured against the assessment criteria.

Knowing the assessment criteria

Criterion	Title	Includes	Marks
Criterion A	Focus and method	Topic Research question Methodology	6
Criterion B	Knowledge and understanding	Context Subject-specific terminology and concepts	6
Criterion C	Critical thinking	Research Analysis Discussion and evaluation	12
Criterion D	Presentation	Structure Layout	4
Criterion E	Engagement	Process Research process	6

Criterion A, focus and method

This criterion is used to assess your choice of topic, the research question, and the method of examination. Make sure you include some sort of justification for the study: why is this topic important and what do you hope to achieve in researching this material? Along with an

explanation of the topic choice, there must be a clear and focused research question that accurately addresses the topic under investigation. Vocabulary is particularly important; effectively explaining the topic requires precise and correct use of vocabulary specific to psychology. Methodology refers to the type and amount of research undertaken.

Topic	Research question	Methodology
Best practice	**Best practice**	**Best practice**
Clearly identify the research topic under investigation.	Clearly state the research question.	Research is planned; appropriate methods of data collection are evident and are described.
Give context for your topic, where it fits in relation to the field of study and other related topics.	Write a focused research question that is not too broad and is appropriately and consistently connected to the discussion in the essay.	A broad range of sources must be used. You should use only reliable sources and explain the reasoning behind the research method.
Justify or explain the purpose of an appropriate research topic.	Ensure that your research question is narrow enough to be fully explored within the scope of a 4,000-word essay.	An explanation of method should include some description and explanation of how data collection has been narrowed down from initial research.
Identify what this topic can tell us about human behaviour and why that is important.	Ensure that your research question requires analysis, not simply description.	Sources and methods must be relevant to psychology.
Be specific and use appropriate vocabulary.		Peer-reviewed journals and reliable websites and publications would be considered appropriate sources.
Ensure that you explain any concepts that your reader needs to fully understand for this topic.		
Questions examiners ask themselves	**Questions examiners ask themselves**	**Questions examiners ask themselves**
How well is the topic explained, identified, justified and communicated to the reader?	Is the research question clear and easily understandable?	How did the student find this research and why did he or she choose this method?
	Can the research question be answered in 4,000 words or less?	How did using this method improve the quality of information used to answer the research question?
	Is the essay focused on the research question throughout?	

Criterion B, knowledge and understanding

This criterion assesses the relevance of the knowledge used to answer the research question. It should be clear that students have read about and understood relevant topics and concepts related to their area of study. Sources must be used effectively to support claims and relevant vocabulary must be accurately used throughout the essay to improve the explanation of complex concepts and relationships in psychology. Showing that you know something is not the same as showing that you understand it. Knowing something is simply a matter of repeating a fact when asked, for example, what is the capital of Brazil. Understanding something requires more. You need to be able to explain why something is what it is, and why it is not something else, for example, why isn't Rio de Janeiro the capital of Brazil? You need to show that you understand the topic you are writing about, and show you understand the relationship between the variables and the behaviour you are examining.

Context	Use of terminology and concepts
Best practice The research question is contextualized in the appropriate field of study and in a broader understanding of human behaviour. Appropriate and relevant sources have been selected.	**Best practice** Psychology-specific vocabulary is accurately used throughout the essay to illustrate understanding and improve communication.
Questions examiners ask themselves Is it clear where this research fits in a wider understanding of human behaviour? Are the sources used appropriate to the topic under investigation?	**Questions examiners ask themselves** Does this sound like a psychology student? Is communication confusing because of inaccurate or unspecific vocabulary?

Criterion C, critical thinking

This criterion assesses critical thinking, the heart of your essay. Critical thinking opportunities can come from: examination of research design and methodologies; triangulation; uncovering assumptions and biases; examining alternative explanations and/or theories; and exposing and explaining areas of uncertainty. Critical thinking shows that you have engaged with the content beyond simply describing concepts. You must show that you can critically analyse and evaluate published research regarding your topic.

Students too often do not give themselves enough credit and believe that they do not have the authority or experience to question published researchers. Do not fall into that trap. Use your reason and curiosity to challenge assumptions and claims. If you are a thoughtful person with an interest in your topic, you are capable and qualified to challenge published research.

Critical thinking needs to be independent and original. If you have taken an idea or criticism from someone else, it is not your critical thinking and must be cited. Ensure that you include your own ideas in your essay and that you are not simply rewriting the analyses or evaluations of others.

Research	Analysis	Discussion and evaluation
Best practice Include only research that is relevant to your argument. Do not simply add research to pad out a bibliography. Use relevant research throughout the essay, not just in certain parts.	**Best practice** Ensure that subsections of your essay have complete arguments and that these points support an overall argument. Do not get distracted by irrelevant research.	**Best practice** There is a clear argument that is directly based on the evidence presented. A well-reasoned argument is evident throughout the essay; supporting points are sequential and well structured.
Questions examiners ask themselves Does the writer wander off course or include information irrelevant to his or her argument? Are the sources reliable? Is there a range of sources or is the writer too dependent on too few sources?	**Questions examiners ask themselves** Does the essay go beyond description and provide evidence of critical thinking? Are relevant conclusions to relevant points made throughout the essay? Does the essay come to a supported conclusion that answers the research question?	**Questions examiners ask themselves** Is the argument clear? Can I easily identify supporting points for the main argument? Has the writer evaluated choices made in his or her research? Have alternative explanations from the thesis been examined or evaluated?

Criterion D, presentation

This criterion focuses on how well the writer followed the standard format for academic writing in psychology and the extent to which this aids communication of concepts and ideas. Examiners will not read beyond the 4,000-word limit. All relevant information should be included in the body of the essay. If material needs to be placed into the appendices it should be selected carefully and used sparingly. Given the holistic nature of assessment of the extended essay, students who exceed the 4,000-word limit will be penalized across all criteria. Anything beyond the 4,000-word limit will be treated as if it were not present so the examiner may not read paragraphs that include evidence of your knowledge or critical thinking, affecting the level awarded.

Charts, graphs and tables should be used sparingly. These elements of essays are meant to enhance understanding of what is written in the text. Tables should not include large amounts of text. If they do, they will be included in the word count. Charts and graphs should only be used to enhance understanding of the main argument of the essay. Too many charts, graphs and tables distract from the message of the essay and can really hinder communication of ideas.

Material must be appropriately and consistently cited. It does not matter what referencing method is used (MLA, APA, and so on) but it must be consistently and accurately applied. Use websites such as Easybib to write your bibliography as you go and keep track of material you refer to. In other words, the day you start your essay should also be the day you start your bibliography.

Structure and layout

Best practice

Ensure that all required elements are included and in the correct order: title page; table of contents; body; bibliography; appendices (if applicable).

Ensure that page numbers are correct. Pagination should begin on the first page of your essay (do not include the title page or table of contents).

If you are using subheadings, apply them consistently.

All tables, graphs and charts should be labelled and used only when needed.

In-text citations are required and should follow the same citation format chosen for the bibliography.

Questions examiners ask themselves

Are all required elements included and labelled correctly?

Are in-text citations and bibliography entries consistent with a single citation style?

Are the tables, charts and graphs appropriately labelled and used with good judgment?

Criterion E, engagement

Assessment against this criterion is based only on the student's reflections on the *Reflections on planning and progress form* (RPPF), with the supervisor's comments and the extended essay used as context for the reflections. Students are expected to reflect on how they arrived at the topic they chose as well as on the decisions they made in terms of method and approach. This criterion assesses how well students have thought about the decisions they made throughout both the research and writing processes.

The reflection process is a formal one where you are required to enter three reflections throughout the research and writing process. The first reflection should focus on your initial thoughts and ideas about how to plan your research. The interim reflection is completed once a significant amount of work has been done and should explain alterations and challenges. The final reflection (viva voce) is completed after you have finished writing and handed in your extended essay. Taken together, these three reflections should not exceed 500 words.

Process

Best practice

Think about the choices you have made from the beginning of the process to the end. It is a good idea to keep a diary or journal of the process. It can be a helpful resource when it is time to fill out the RPPF near the end of the extended essay process.

Stay in touch with your extended essay supervisor; he or she will be eager to help you. This is the person who will be asked to comment on how he or she thought you progressed through the research and writing.

Be honest in your reflections. You are not assessed on being right; you are assessed on how well you provide evidence for your rationale and your decisions.

Frame your reflections around the ATL skills, that is, thinking, communication, social, self-management and research skills. These will give you a narrative for your thoughts to help ground your reflections on the important elements of the extended essay process.

Explain any challenges you faced but do not make excuses for shortcomings. How did you overcome challenges and show resilience?

Questions examiners ask themselves

Did the student think about the choices he or she made?

Can the student explain the reasons he or she made the choices he or she did?

Is there evidence of learning about the process of writing, not just about the topic of study?

Is there more than just a description of the process?

Are there enough "because" statements that show the student is attempting to explain his or her choices?

This short chapter has given you a brief introduction to the assessments you will be expected to complete in IB psychology. Psychology requires a unique style of writing that is direct and to the point. With practice and guidance from your teacher improvement can come quickly.

Much of the factual information in this section has been taken from the following official IB

publications, all of which your teacher has access to:

Extended essay guide

Extended essay teacher support material

Psychology guide.

Bibliography

Unit 1: Research methodology

American Psychological Association. 2012. "Guidelines for ethical conduct in the care and use of nonhuman animals in research". Washington DC. Retrieved from http://www.apa.org/science/leadership/care/guidelines.aspx

Campbell, DT. 1969. "Reforms as experiments". *American Psychologist*. Vol 24. Pp 409–429.

Cohen, J. 1988. *Statistical Power Analysis for the Behavioral Sciences*. London, UK. Routledge.

Elo, E and Kungäs, H. 2008. "The qualitative content analysis process. *Journal of Advanced Nursing*". Vol 62, number 1. Pp 107–115.

Firestone, WA. 1993. "Alternative arguments for generalizing from data as applied to qualitative research". *Educational Researcher*. Vol 22. Pp 16–23.

Goodwin, CJ. 2010. *Research in Psychology: Methods and Design* (Sixth edition). New York, USA. Wiley.

Haney, C, Banks, WC and Zimbardo, PG. 1973. "A study of prisoners and guards in a simulated prison". *Naval Research Review*. Vol 30. Pp 4–17.

Piliavin, IM, Rodin, JA and Piliavin, J. 1969. "Good Samaritanism: An underground phenomenon?" *Journal of Personality and Social Psychology*. Vol 13. Pp 289–299.

Polit, DF and Beck, CT. 2010. "Generalization in quantitative and qualitative research: Myths and strategies". *International Journal of Nursing Studies*. Vol 47. Pp 1451–1458.

Rosen, LD, Carrier, ML and Cheever, NA. 2013. "Facebook and texting made me do it: Media induced task-switching while studying". *Computers in Human Behaviour*. Vol 29. Pp 948–958.

Rosenthal, R and Fode, K. 1963. "The effect of experimenter bias on performance of the albino rat". *Behavioral Science*. Vol 8. Pp 183–189.

Watson, JB and Rayner, R. 1920. "Conditioned emotional reaction". *Journal of Experimental Psychology*. Vol 2. Pp 1–14.

Unit 2: Biological approach to behaviour

American Psychological Association. 2012. "Guidelines for ethical conduct in the care and use of nonhuman animals in research". Washington DC. Retrieved from http://www.apa.org/science/leadership/care/guidelines.aspx

Bach-y-Rita, P, Collins, CC, Saunders, FA, White, B, and Scadden, L. 1969. "Vision substitution by tactile image projection". *Nature*. Vol 221. Pp 963–964.

Bailey, J. 2008. "An assessment of the role of chimpanzees in AIDS vaccine research". *Alternatives to Laboratory Animals*. Vol 36, number 4. Pp 381–428.

Bennett, CM, Baird, AA, Miller, MB, and Wolford, GL. 2009. "Neural correlates of interspecies perspective taking in the post-mortem Atlantic salmon: an argument for multiple comparisons correction". Retrieved from http://prefrontal.org/files/posters/Bennett-Salmon-2009.pdf

Bouchard, TJ and McGue, M. 1981. "Familial studies of intelligence: A review". *Science*. Vol 212. Pp 1055–1059.

Bouchard, TJ, Lykken, DT, McGue, M, Segal, NL and Tellegen, A. 1990. "Sources of human psychological differences: The Minnesota study of twins reared apart". *Science*. Vol 250. Pp 223–228.

Call, J and Tomasello, M. 2008. "Does the chimpanzee have theory of mind? 30 years later". *Trends in Cognitive Sciences*. Vol 12, number 5. Pp 187–192.

Caspi, A, Hariri, AR, Holmes, A, Uher, R and Moffitt, TE. 2010. "Genetic sensitivity to the environment: The case of the serotonin transporter gene and its implications for studying complex diseases and traits". *American Journal of Psychiatry*. Vol 167, number 5. Pp 509–527.

Chiao, JY and Blizinsky, KD. 2010. "Culture-gene co-evolution of individualism-collectivism and the serotonin transporter gene". *Proceedings of the Royal Society B: Biological Sciences*. Vol 277, number 1681. Pp 529–537.

Crockett, MJ, Clark, L, Hauser, MD and Robbins, TW. 2010. "Serotonin selectively influences moral judgment and behaviour through effects in harm aversion". *Proceedings of the National Academy of Sciences*. Vol 107, number 40. Pp 17433–17438.

Curtis, V, Aunger, A and Rabie, T. 2004. "Evidence that disgust evolved to protect from risk of disease". *Proceedings of Royal Society of London B*. Vol 271. Pp 131–133.

Cutler, WB, Friedmann, E and McCoy, NL. 1998. "Pheromonal influences on sociosexual behavior in men". *Archives of Sexual Behavior*. Vol 21, number 1. Pp 1–13.

De Dreu, CKW, Greer, LL, Van Kleef, GA, Shalvi, S and Handgraaf, MJJ. 2011. "Oxytocin promotes human ethnocentrism". *Proceedings of National Academy of Sciences*. Vol 108. Pp 1262–1266.

De Dreu, CKW, Shalvi, S, Greer, LL, Van Kleef, GA and Handgraaf, MJJ. 2012. "Oxytocin motivates non-cooperation in intergroup conflict to protect vulnerable in-group members". *Public Library of Science*. Vol 7, number 11. Retrieved from https://www.ncbi.nlm.nih.gov/pmc/articles/PMC3492361/pdf/pone.0046751.pdf

Doidge, N. 2007. *The Brain that Changes Itself: Stories of Personal Triumph from Frontiers of Brain Science*. New York, USA. Penguin Books.

Draganski, B, Gaser, C, Busch, V and May, A. 2004. "Neuroplasticity: Changes in grey matter induced by training". *Nature*. Vol 427. Pp 311–312.

Draganski, B, Gaser, C, Kempermann, G, Kuhn, HG, Winkler, J, Buchel, C and May, A. 2006. "Temporal and spatial dynamics of brain structure during extensive learning". *Journal of Neuroscience*. Vol 26, number 23. Pp 6314–6317.

Fisher, H, Aron, A and Brown, LL. 2005. "Romantic love: An fMRI study of a neural mechanism for mate choice". *The Journal of Comparative Neurology*. Vol 493. Pp 58–62.

Freed, CR, Greene, PE, Breeze, RE, Wei-Yann Tsai, DuMouchel, W, Kao, R and Dillon, S. 2001. "Transplantation of embryonic dopamine neurons for severe Parkinson's disease". *The New England Journal of Medicine*. Vol 344, number 10. Pp 710–719.

Gazzaniga, MS. 1967. "The split brain in man". *Scientific American*. Vol 217, number 2. Pp 24–29.

Gazzaniga, MS. 2005. "Forty-five years of split-brain research and still going strong". *Nature Reviews: Neuroscience*. Vol 6. Pp 653–659.

Gould, SJ and Lewontin, RC. 1979. "The spandrels of San Marco and the Panglossian Paradigm: A critique of the adaptationist programme". *Proceedings of the Royal Society of London. Series B, Biological Sciences*. Vol 205, number 1161. Pp 581–598.

Hamilton, W. 1964. "The genetical evolution of social behaviour I". *Journal of Theoretical Biology*. Vol 7, number 1. Pp 1–16.

Hare, RM, Schlatter, S, Rhodes, G and Simmons, LW. 2017. "Putative sex-specific human pheromones do not affect gender perception, attractiveness ratings or unfaithfulness judgments of opposite sex faces". *Royal Society Open Science*. Vol 4. doi: 160831. http://dx.doi.org/10.1098/rsos.160831

Hays, WST. 2003. "Human pheromones: Have they been demonstrated?" *Behavioral Ecology and Sociobiology*. Vol 54, number 2. Pp 97–98.

Herz, R. 2009. "The truth about pheromones". *Psychology Today*. Retrieved from https://www.psychologytoday.com/blog/smell-life/200905/the-truth-about-pheromones-part-1

Joseph, J. 2015. *The Trouble with Twin Studies: A Reassessment of Twin Research in Social and Behavioural Sciences*. New York, USA. Routledge.

Kaminsky, Z, Petronis, A, Wang, S-C, Levine, B, Ghaffar, O, Floden, D and Feinstein, A. 2008. "Epigenetics of personality traits: An illustrative study of identical twins discordant for risk-taking behavior". *Twin Research and Human Genetics*. Vol 11, number 1. Pp 1–11.

Kendler, KS, Turkheimer, E, Ohlsson, E, Sundquist, J and Sundquist, K. 2015. "Family environment and the malleability of cognitive ability: A Swedish national home-reared and adopted-away cosibling control study". *Proceedings of National Academy of Sciences*. Vol 112, number 15. Pp 4612–4617.

Konnikova, M. 2013. "The man who couldn't speak and how he revolutionized psychology". *Scientific American*. Retrieved from https://blogs.scientificamerican.com/literally-psyched/the-man-who-couldnt-speakand-how-he-revolutionized-psychology/

Kosfeld, M, Heinrichs, M, Zak, PJ, Fischbacher, U and Fehr, E. 2005. "Oxytocin increases trust in humans". *Nature*. Vol 435. Pp 673–676.

Lashley, KS. 1929. *Brain Mechanisms and Intelligence: A Quantitative Study of Injuries to the Brain*. Chicago, Illinois, USA. University of Chicago Press.

Le, QV, Isbell, A, Matsumoto, J, Nguyen, M, Hori, E, Maior, RS, Tomaz, C, Tran, AH, Ono, T and Nishijo, H. 2013. "Pulvinar neurons reveal neurobiological evidence of past selection for rapid detection of snakes". *Proceedings of National Academy of Sciences*. Vol 110. Pp 19000–19005.

LeDoux, JE. 1996. *The Emotional Brain*. New York, USA. Simon & Schuster.

Lundstrom, JN and Olsson, MJ. 2005. "Subthreshold amounts of a social odorant affect mood, but not behavior, in heterosexual women when tested by a male, but not a female experimenter". *Biological Psychology*. Vol 60. Pp 197–204.

Ma, X, Luo, L, Geng, Y, Zhao, W, Zhang, Q and Kendrick, KM. 2014. "Oxytocin increases liking for a country's people and national flag, but not for other cultural symbols or consumer products". *Frontiers in Behavioural Neuroscience*. Vol 8, number 266. doi:10.3389/fnbeh.2014.00266.

MacLean, PD. 1990. *"The Triune Brain in Evolution: Role in Paleocerebral Functions"*. New York, USA. Plenum Press.

Madsen, EA, Tunney, RJ, Fieldman, G, Plotkin, HC, Dunbar, RI, Richardson, JM and McFarland, D. 2007. "Kinship and altruism: a cross-cultural experimental study". *British Journal of Psychology*. Vol 98, number 2. Pp 339–359.

Maguire, EA, Gadian, DG, Johnsrude, IS, Good, CD, Ashburner, J, Frackowiak, RSJ and Frith, CD. 2000. "Navigation-related structural change in the hippocampi of taxi drivers". *Proceedings of the National Academy of Sciences*. Vol 97, number 8. Pp 4398–4403.

McCoy, NL and Pitino, L. 2002. "Pheromonal influences on sociosexual behaviour in young women". *Physiology & Behaviour*. Vol 75. Pp 367–375.

McGowan, PO, Sasaki, A, D'Alessio, AC, Dymov, S, Labonté, B, Szyf, M, Turecki, G and Meaney, MJ. 2009. "Epigenetic regulation of the glucocorticoid receptor in human brain associates with childhood abuse". *Nature Neuroscience*. Vol 12, number 3. Pp 342–348.

Merzenich, MM, Nelson, RJ, Stryker, MP, Cynader, MS, Schoppmann, A and Zook, JM. 1984. "Somatosensory cortical map changes following digit amputation in adult monkeys". *The Journal of Comparative Neurology*. Vol 224. Pp 591–605.

Miller, G. 2010. "The seductive allure of behavioral epigenetics". *Science*. Vol 329. Pp 24–27.

Miller, GE, Chen, E, Fok, AK, Walker, H, Lim, A, Nicholls, EF, Cole, S and Kobor, MS. 2009. "Low early-life social class leaves a biological residue manifested by decreased glucocorticoid and increased proinflammatory signaling". *Proceedings of National Academy of Sciences,* Vol 106, number 34. Pp 14716–14721.

Premack, D. 2007. "Human and animal cognition: continuity and discontinuity". *Proceedings of National Academy of Sciences*. Vol 104, number 35. Pp 13861–13867.

Ramachandran, VS, Rogers-Ramachandran, DC and Cobb, S. 1995. "Touching the phantom". *Nature*. Vol 377. Pp 489–490.

Romero, T, Nagasawa, M, Mogi, K, Hasegawa, T and Kikusui, T. 2014. "Oxytocin promotes social bonding in dogs". *Proceedings of National Academy of Sciences*. Vol 111, number 25. Pp 9085–9090.

Samuels, R. 1998. "Evolutionary psychology and the massive modularity hypothesis". *British Journal for the Philosophy of Science*. Vol 49, number 4. Pp 575–602.

Saxe, R and Kanwisher, N. 2003. "People thinking about thinking people: The role of the temporo-parietal junction in 'theory of mind'". *NeuroImage*. Vol 19, number 4. Pp 1835–1842.

Scarr, S and Weinberg, RA. 1976. "IQ test performance of black children adopted by white families". *American Psychologist*. Vol 31. Pp 726–739.

Scarr, S and Weinberg, RA. 1983. "The Minnesota adoption studies: genetic differences and malleability". *Child Development*. Vol 54, number 2. Pp 260–267.

Scheele, D, Striepens, N, Gunturkun, O, Deutschlander, S, Maier, W, Kendrick, KM and

Hurlemann, R. 2012. "Oxytocin modulates social distance between males and females". *The Journal of Neuroscience.* Vol 32, number 46. Pp 16074–16079.

Schulz, D, Southekal, S, Junnarkar, SS, Pratte, JF, Purschke, ML, Stoll, SP, Ravindranath, B, Maramraju, SH, Krishnamoorthy, S, Henn, FA, O'Connor, P, Woody, CL, Schlyer, DJ and Vaska, P. 2011. "Simultaneous assessment of rodent behavior and neurochemistry using a miniature positron emission tomograph". *Nature Methods.* Vol 8. Pp 347–352.

Shapiro, KJ. 1998. "Psychology's use of animals: current practices and attitudes". In Shapiro, KJ. *Animal Models of Human Psychology: A Critique of Science, Ethics, and Policy.* Seattle, Washington, USA. Hogrefe & Huber.

Sharot, T, Martorella, EA, Delgado, MR and Phelps, EA. 2007. "How personal experience modulates the neural circuitry of memories of September 11". *Proceedings of the National Academy of Sciences.* Vol 104, number 4. Pp 389–394.

Sperry, R. 1968. "Hemisphere disconnection and unity in conscious awareness". *American Psychologist.* Vol 23, number 10. Pp 723–733.

Stevens, A and Price, J. 2000. *Evolutionary Psychiatry: A New Beginning* (Second edition). London, UK. Routledge.

Taupin, P. 2006. "Neurogenesis and the effect of antidepressants". *Drug Target Insights.* Vol 1. Pp 13–17.

Thaler, L, Arnot, SR and Goodale, MA. 2011. "Neural correlates of natural human echolocation in early and late blind echolocation experts". *Public Library of Science.* Vol 6. doi:10.1371/journal.pone.0020162

US National Library of Medicine. 2017. https://ghr.nlm.nih.gov/primer/basics/dna

Verhaeghe, J, Gheysen, R and Enzlin, P. 2013. "Pheromones and their effect on women's mood and sexuality". *Facts, Views and Vision in ObGyn.* Vol 5, number 3. Pp 189–195.

Weaver, ICG, Cervoni, N, Champagne, FA, D'Alessio, AC, Sharma, S, Seck, JR, Dymov, S, Szyf, M and Meaney, MJ. 2004. "Epigenetic programming by maternal behavior". *Nature Neuroscience,* Vol 7. Pp 847–854.

Wedekind, C, Seebeck, T, Bettens, F and Paepke, AJ. 1995. "MHC-dependent mate preference in humans". *Proceedings of the Royal Society of London.* Vol 260. Pp 245–249.

Wysocki, CJ and Preti, G. 2004. "Facts, fallacies, fears, and frustrations with human pheromones". *The Anatomical Record.* Vol 281A, number 1. Pp 1201–1211.

Unit 3: Cognitive approach to behaviour

Ajzen, I and Fishbein, M. 1973. "Attitudinal and normative variables as predictors of specific behaviours". *Journal of Personality and Social Psychology.* Vol 27. Pp 41–57.

Albarracin, D, Johnson, BT, Fishbein, M and Muellerleile, PA. 2001. "Theories of reasoned action and planned behaviour as models of condom use: A meta-analysis". *Psychological Bulletin.* Vol 127, number 1. Pp 142–161.

Baddeley, A. 1996. "Exploring the central executive". *The Quarterly Journal of Experimental Psychology.* Vol. 49A, number 1. Pp 5–28.

Baddeley, AD, Lewis, V and Vallar, G. 1984. "Exploring the articulatory loop". *Quarterly Journal of Experimental Psychology.* Vol 36A. Pp 233–252.

Baron, J. 2008. *Thinking and Deciding* (Fourth edition). New York, USA. Cambridge University Press.

Bohannon, JN. 1988. "Flashbulb memories for the space shuttle disaster: A tale of two theories". *Cognition.* Vol 29, number 2. Pp 179–196.

Bower, GH, Black, JB and Turner, TJ. 1979. "Scripts in memory for text". *Cognitive Psychology.* Vol 11. Pp 177–220.

Brown, R and Kulik, J. 1977. "Flashbulb memories". *Cognition.* Vol 5, number 1. Pp 73–99.

Bruner, J. 1957. "Going beyond the information given". In Gruber, H (ed). *Contemporary approaches to cognition.* Cambridge, Massachusetts, USA. Harvard University Press.

Bugelski, BR and Alampay, DA. 1961. "The role of frequency in developing perceptual sets". *Canadian Journal of Psychology.* Vol 15. Pp 205–211.

Cannon, WB and Bard, P. 1927. "The James-Lange theory of emotion: A critical examination and an alternative theory". *The American Journal of Psychology.* Vol 39. Pp 106–124.

Carrier, LM, Spradlin, A, Bunce, JP and Rosen, LR. 2015. "Virtual empathy: Positive and negative impacts of going online upon empathy in young adults". *Computers in Human Behaviour*. Vol 52. Pp 39–48.

Chapman, LJ and Chapman, JP. 1969. "Illusory correlation as an obstacle to the use of valid psychodiagnostic signs". *Journal of Abnormal Psychology*. Vol 74. Pp 271–280.

Craik, F and Tulving, E. 1975. "Depth of processing and the retention of words in episodic memory". *Journal of Experimental Psychology: General*. Vol 104, number 3. Pp 268–294.

Darley, JM and Gross, PH. 1983. "A hypothesis-confirming bias in labeling effects". *Journal of Personality and Social Psychology*. Vol 44, number 1. Pp 20–33.

Darwin, C. 1872. *The Expression of Emotions in Man and Animals*.

Dokoupil, T. 2012. "Is the internet making us crazy? What the new research says". http://europe.newsweek.com/internet-making-us-crazy-what-new-research-says-65593?rm=eu

Fery, YA and Ponserre, S. 2001. "Enhancing the control of force in putting by video game training". *Ergonomics*. Vol 44. Pp 1025–1037.

Festinger, L, Riecken, HW and Schachter, S. 1957. *When Prophecy Fails: A Social and Psychological Study of a Modern Group that Predicted the Destruction of the World*. Minneapolis, Minnesota, USA. University of Minnesota Press.

Fishbein, M. 1967. "Attitude and predicting behaviour". In Fishbein, M (ed). *Readings in Attitude Theory and Measurement*. Pp 477–492. New York, USA. Wiley.

Freedman, JL and Fraser, SC. 1966. "Compliance without pressure: The foot-in-the-door technique". *Journal of Personality and Social Psychology*. Vol 4, number 2. Pp 195–202.

Galotti, KM. 2008. *Cognitive Psychology: Perception, Attention and Memory*. New Delhi, India. Cengage Learning Ltd.

Howard-Jones, P. 2011. "The impact of digital technologies on human wellbeing. Evidence from the sciences of mind and brain". www.nominettrust.org.uk

Huber, J, Payne, JW and Puto, C. 1982. "Adding asymmetrically dominated alternatives: Violations of regularity and the similarity hypothesis". *Journal of Consumer Research*. Vol 9. Pp 90–98.

James, W. 1884. "What is an emotion?" *Mind*. Vol 9, number 34. Pp 188–205.

Lazarus, RS. 1982. "Thoughts on the relations between emotion and cognition". *American Psychologist*. Vol 37. Pp 1019–1024.

LeDoux, JE. 1996. *The Emotional Brain*. New York, USA. Simon & Schuster.

Loftus, EF and Palmer, JC. 1974. "Reconstruction of automobile destruction: An example of the interaction between language and memory". *Journal of Verbal Learning and Verbal Behavior*. Vol 13. Pp 585–589.

Loftus, EF, Miller, DG and Burns, HJ. 1978. "Semantic integration of verbal information into a visual memory". *Journal of Experimental Psychology: Human Learning and Memory*. Vol 4, number 1. Pp 19–31.

Loh, KK and Kanai, R. 2014. "Higher media multi-tasking activity is associated with smaller gray-matter density in the anterior cingulate cortex". *PLoS ONE*. Vol 9, number 9. doi:10.1371/journal.pone.0106698

Luce, MF, Bettman, JR and Payne, JW. 1997. "Choice processing in emotionally difficult decisions". *Journal of Experimental Psychology: Learning, Memory, and Cognition*. Vol 23, number 2. Pp 384–405.

McCloskey, M and Zaragoza, M. 1985. "Misleading post-event information and memory for events: Arguments and evidence against memory impairment hypothesis". *Journal of Experimental Psychology: General*. Vol 114, number 1. Pp 1–16.

Merikle, PM and Skanes, HE. 1992. "Subliminal self-help audiotapes: A search for placebo effects". *The Journal of Applied Psychology*. Vol 77, number 5. Pp 772–776.

Moreno, MA, Jelenchick, L, Koff, R, Eikoff, J, Diermyer, C and Christakis, DA. 2012. "Internet use and multitasking among older adolescents: An experience sampling approach". *Computers in Human Behavior*. Vol 28. Pp 1097–1102.

Neisser, U and Harsh, N. 1992. "Phantom flashbulbs: False recollections of hearing the news about Challenger". In Winograd, E and Neidder, U (eds). *Affect and Accuracy in Recall: Studies of flashbulb memories*. New York, USA. Cambridge University Press.

Neisser, U, Winograd, E, Bergman, ET, Schreiber, CA, Palmer, SE and Weldon, MS. 1996. "Remembering the earthquake: Direct experience vs. hearing the news". *Memory*. Vol 4, number 4. Pp 337–357.

Newell, A and Simon, HA. 1972. *Human Problem Solving*. Englewood Cliffs, New Jersey, USA. Prentice Hall.

Nie, NH. 2001. "Sociability, interpersonal relations, and the Internet—Reconciling conflicting findings". *American Behavioral Scientist*. Vol 45. Pp 420–435.

Payne, DG, Toglia, MP and Anastasi, JS. 1994. "Recognition performance level and the magnitude of the misinformation effect in eyewitness testimony". *Psychonomic Bulletin & Review*. Vol 1, number 3. Pp 376–382.

Payne, JW and Bettman, JR. 2004. "Walking with the scarecrow: The information-processing approach to decision research". In Koehler, DJ and Harvey, N (eds). *Blackwell Handbook of Judgment and Decision Making*. Pp 110–132. Oxford, UK. Blackwell. Publishing Ltd.

Payne, JW, Bettman, JR and Johnson, EJ. 1993. *The Adaptive Decision Maker*. Cambridge, UK. Cambridge University Press.

Pichert, JW and Anderson, RC. 1977. "Taking different perspectives on a story". *Journal of Educational Psychology*. Vol 69. Pp 309–315.

Popper, K. 1959. *The Logic of Scientific Discovery*. London, UK. Hutchinson & Co.

Rosen, LD. 2012. *iDisorder: Understanding our Dependency on Technology and Overcoming its Hold on Us*. New York, USA. Palgrave Macmillan.

Rosen, LD, Lim, AF, Carrier, LM and Cheever, NA. 2011. "An examination of the educational impact of text message-induced task switching in the classroom: Educational implications and strategies to enhance learning". *Psicologia Educative (Spanish Journal of Educational Psychology)*. Vol 17, number 2. Pp 163–177.

Rosen, LD, Carrier, ML and Cheever, NA. 2013. "Facebook and texting made me do it: Media-induced task-switching while studying". *Computers in Human Behaviour*. Vol 29. Pp 948–958.

Rosser, JC, Lynch, JP, Cuddihy, L, Gentile D and Klonsky, J. 2007. "The impact of video games on training surgeons in the 21st century". *Archives of Surgery*. Vol 142. Pp 181–186.

Sanchez, CA. 2012. "Enhancing visuospatial performance through video game training to increase learning in visuospatial science domains". *Psychonomic Bulletin Review*. Vol 19. Pp 58–65.

Schachter, S and Singer, J. 1962. "Cognitive, social and physiological determinants of emotional state". *Psychological Review*. Vol 69. Pp 379–399.

Sharot, T, Delgado, MR and Phelps, EA. 2004. "How emotion enhances the feeling of remembering". *Nature Neuroscience*. Vol 7, number 12. Pp 1376–1380.

Sharot, T, Martorella, EA, Delgado, MR and Phelps, EA. 2007. "How personal experience modulates the neural circuitry of memories of September 11". *Proceedings of the National Academy of Sciences*. Vol 104, number 1. Pp 389–394.

Siegel, D. 17 September 2011. "The brain, mindfulness, and youth: Supporting well-being and connection in young people". Paper presented at The Wisdom 2.0 Youth Conference. Computer Science Museum. Mountain View, California, USA.

Skinner, BF. "Superstition in the pigeon". http://psychclassics.yorku.ca/Skinner/Pigeon/

Sperling, G. 1960. "The information available in brief visual presentations". *Psychological Monographs: General and Applied*. Vol 74, number 11. Pp 1–29.

Swing, EL, Gentile, DA, Anderson, CA and Walsh, DA. 2010. "Television and video game exposure and the development of attention problems". *Pediatrics*. Vol 126. Pp 214–221.

Talarico, JM and Rubin, DC. 2003. "Confidence, not consistency, characterizes flashbulb memories". *Psychological Science*. Vol 14, number 5. Pp 455–461.

Tschirgi, JE. 1980. "Sensible reasoning: A hypothesis about hypotheses". *Child Development*. Vol 51. Pp 1–10.

Turkle, S. 2011. *Alone Together*. New York, USA Basic Books.

Tversky, A and Kahneman, D. 1981. "The framing of decisions and the psychology of choice". *Science*. Vol 211. Pp 453–458.

Wason, PC. 1960. "On the failure to eliminate hypotheses in a conceptual task". *Quarterly Journal of Experimental Psychology*. Vol 12. Pp 129–140.

Wason, PC. 1968. "Reasoning about a rule". *Quarterly Journal of Experimental Psychology*. Vol 20. Pp 273–281.

Yuille, JC and Cutshall, JL. 1986. "A case study of eyewitness memory of a crime". *Journal of Applied Psychology*. Vol 71, number 2. Pp 291–301.

Unit 4: Sociocultural approach to behaviour

Abrams, D. "The migration crisis – psychological perspectives". 31 May 2017. https://thepsychologist.bps.org.uk/migration-crisis-psychological-perspectives

Allport, GW. 1954. *The Nature of Prejudice*. Reading, Massachusetts, USA. Addison-Wesley.

Aronson, E. 2008. *The Social Animal*. (Tenth Edition). New York, USA. Worth/Freeman.

Asch, SE. 1946. "Forming impressions of personality". *Journal of Abnormal & Social Psychology*. Vol 41. Pp 258–290.

Bains, G. 2015. *Cultural DNA: The Psychology of Globalization*. Hoboken, New Jersey, USA. Wiley.

Bandura, A. 1965. "Influence of model's reinforcement contingencies on the acquisition of imitative responses". *Journal of Personality and Social Psychology*. Vol 1. Pp 589–595.

Bandura, A. 1977. *Social Learning Theory*. Englewood Cliffs, New Jersey, USA. Prentice-Hall.

Bandura, A. 1986. *Social Foundations of Thought and Action: A Social Cognitive Theory*. Englewood Cliffs, New Jersey, USA. Prentice-Hall.

Bandura, A. 1994. "Self-efficacy". In Ramachaudran, VS (ed). *Encyclopedia of Human Behavior*. Vol 4. Pp 71–81. New York, USA. Academic Press. Reprinted in Friedman, H (ed). 1998. *Encyclopedia of Mental Health*. San Diego, California, USA. Academic Press.

Bandura, A. 2001. "Social cognitive theory of mass communication". *Media Psychology*. Vol 3, number 3. Pp 265–299.

Bandura, A. 2001. "Social cognitive theory: An agentic perspective". *Annual Review of Psychology*. Vol 52, number 11. Pp 1–26.

Bandura, A. 2005. "Evolution of social cognitive theory". In Smith, KG and Hitt, MA (eds). *Great Minds in Management*. Pp 9–35. Oxford, UK. Oxford University Press.

Bandura, A. 2012. *Self-efficacy: The Exercise of Control*. New York, USA. W.H. Freeman.

Bandura, A, Ross, D and Ross, SA. 1961. "Transmission of aggression through imitation of aggressive models". *Journal of Abnormal and Social Psychology*. Vol 63, number 3. Pp 575–582.

Bandura, A, Ross, D and Ross, SA. 1963. "Imitation of film-mediated aggressive models". *Journal of Abnormal and Social Psychology*. Vol 66. Pp 3–11.

Bar-on, M, Broughton, D, Buttross, S and Corrigan, S. 2001. "Media violence". *Pediatrics*. Vol 108, number 5. Pp 1222–1226.

Baron, RA and Byrne, D. 1997. *Social Psychology*. (Eighth edition). Boston, Massachusetts, USA. Allyn and Bacon.

Batista-Pinto Wiese, E. 2010. "Culture and migration: Psychological trauma in children and adolescents". *Traumatology*. Vol 16, number 4. Pp 142–152.

Bem, D and Cofer, CN. 1967. "Self-perception: An alternative interpretation of cognitive dissonance phenomena". *Psychological Review*. Vol 74, number 3. Pp 183–200.

Berry, J. 2005. "Acculturation: Living successfully in two cultures". *International Journal of Intercultural Relations*. Vol 29, number 6. Pp 697–712.

Berry, J. 2008. "Globalisation and acculturation". *International Journal of Intercultural Relations*. Vol 32, number 4. Pp 328–336.

Berry, J. 2009. "A critique of critical acculturation". *International Journal of Intercultural Relations*. Vol 33, number 5. Pp 361–371.

Berry, J and Katz, D. 1967. "Independence and conformity in subsistence-level societies". *Journal of Personality and Social Psychology*. Vol 7, number 4. Pp 415–418.

Brockner, J, Ackerman, G, Greenberg, J, Gelfand, MJ, Francesco, AM, Chen, ZX, Leung, K, Bierbrauer, G, Gomez, C, Kirkman, BL, Shapiro, D. 2001. "Culture and procedural justice: The influence of power distance on reactions to voice". *Journal of Experimental Social Psychology*. Vol 37, number 4. Pp 300–315.

Brophy, JE. 1983. "Research on the self-fulfilling prophecy and teacher expectations". *Journal of Educational Psychology*. Vol 75. Pp 631–661.

Brown, R. 2000. "Social identity theory: Past achievements, current problems and future challenges". *European Journal of Social Psychology*. Vol 30, number 6. Pp 745–778.

Brown, RP, Osterman, LL and Barnes, CD. 2009. "School violence and the culture of honor (report)". *Psychological Science*. Vol 20, number 11. Pp 1400–1405.

Buchan, N, Brewer, M, Grimalda, G, Wilson, R, Fatas, E and Foddy, M. 2011. "Global social identity and global cooperation". *Psychological Science*. Vol 22, number 6. Pp 821–828.

Carr, N. 21 April 2017. "How technology created a global village—and put us at each other's throats". *The Boston Globe*. https://www.bostonglobe.com/ideas/2017/04/21/how-technology-created-global-village-and-put-each-other-throats/pu7MyoAkdyVComb9aKyu6K/story.html

Carr, NG. 2011. *The Shallows: What the Internet is Doing to our Brains*. New York, USA. WW Norton.

Chatterjee, I. 2012. "How are they othered? Globalisation, identity and violence in an Indian city". *Geographical Journal*. Vol 178, number 2. Pp 134–146.

Cohen, D, Nisbett, R, Bowdle, B, Schwarz, N and Miller, N. 1996. "Insult, aggression, and the Southern culture of honor: An 'experimental ethnography'". *Journal of Personality and Social Psychology*. Vol 70, number 5. Pp 945–960.

CNN. 31 May 2017. "Alternative facts: Why the Trump team is 'planting a flag' in war on media". From http://money.cnn.com/2017/01/22/media/alternativefacts-donald-trump/index.html

Da Costa, L, Dias, S and Martins, M. 2017. "Association between length of residence and overweight among adult immigrants in Portugal: A nationwide cross-sectional study". *BMC Public Health*. Vol 17.

Davidson, J. 26 May 2016. "3.2 billion people now using internet worldwide". *Money*. http://time.com/money/3896219/internet-users-worldwide/

Dawkins, R. 2006. *The Selfish Gene: 30th Anniversary Edition*. Oxford, UK. Oxford University Press.

Delavari, M, Sønderlund, A, Swinburn, B, Mellor, D and Renzaho, A. 2013. "Acculturation and obesity among migrant populations in high income countries—A systematic review". *BMC Public Health*. Vol 13. Pp 458.

Digman, J. 1990. "Personality structure—emergence of the five-factor model". *Annual Review of Psychology*. Vol 41. Pp 417–440.

Duncan, BL. 1976. "Differential social perception and attribution of intergroup violence: Testing the lower limits of stereotyping blacks". *Journal of Personality and Social Psychology*. Vol 34. Pp 590–598.

Dunham, Y, Chen, E and Banaji, M. 2013. "Two signatures of implicit intergroup attitudes". *Psychological Science*. Vol 24, number 6. Pp 860–868.

Esteban-Gonzalo, L, Veiga, OL, Regidor, E, Martínez, D, Marcos, A and Calle, MA. 2015. "Immigrant status, acculturation and risk of overweight and obesity in adolescents living in Madrid (Spain): The AFINOS Study". *Journal of Immigrant and Minority Health*. Vol 17, number 2. Pp 367–374.

Eylon, D and Au, KY. 1999. "Exploring empowerment cross-cultural differences along the power distance dimension". *International Journal of Intercultural Relations*. Vol 23, number 3. Pp, 373–385.

Farr, R. 1991. "The long past and the short history of social psychology". *European Journal of Social Psychology*. Vol 21, number 5. Pp 371–380.

Festinger, L. 1975. *A Theory of Cognitive Dissonance*. Palo Alto, California, USA. Stanford University Press.

Finkelstein, MA. 2010. "Individualism/collectivism: Implications for the volunteer process (report)". *Social Behavior and Personality: An International Journal*. Vol 38, number 4. Pp 445–452.

Fischer, R and Schwartz, S. 2011. "Whence differences in value priorities?" *Journal of Cross-Cultural Psychology*. Vol 42, number 7. Pp 1127–1144.

Fiske, S and Taylor, S. 1991. *Social Cognition*. (Second edition). New York, USA. McGraw-Hill.

Fletcher, GJO and Ward, C. 1988. "Attribution theory and processes: A cross cultural perspective". In Bond, MH (ed) *The Cross Cultural Challenge to Social Psychology*. Newbury Park, California, USA. Sage.

Freedom House. 11 May 2017. "Freedom of the Press 2017". https://freedomhouse.org/report/freedom-press/freedom-press-2017

Friscolanti, M. 17 March 2017. "Inside the Shafia killings that shocked a nation". http://www.macleans.ca/news/canada/inside-the-shafia-killings-that-shocked-a-nation/

Friscolanti, M. 2012. "The honour killing trial: Shafia family". *Maclean's*. Vol 125, number 5. P 38.

Garcia, S. 1999. "Primary socialization theory: Comments on racism, sexism, generational neglect, abuse, and abandonment". *Substance Use & Misuse*. Vol 34, number 7. Pp 1005–1011.

Geert Hofstede (n.d.). Retrieved 25 May 2017 from https://www.geert-hofstede.com/national-culture.html

Giddens, A. 1991. *Modernity and Self-Identity: Self and Society in the Late Modern Age*. Cambridge, UK. Polity Press.

Gladwell, M. 2008. *Outliers: The Story of Success*. New York, USA. Back Bay Books, Little, Brown and Company.

Goldstein, A and McGinnis, E. 13 May 2017. "Skillstreaming". http://www.skillstreaming.com/

Government of Canada, Department of Justice, Electronic Communications. "Preliminary examination of so-called 'honour killings' in Canada". 30 December 2016. http://www.justice.gc.ca/eng/rp-pr/cj-jp/fv-vf/hk-ch/p1.html

Gross, R. 2001. *Psychology: The Science of Mind and Behaviour*. (Fourth edition). London, UK. Hodder Education.

Hamburger Kolleg, K and Centre for Global Cooperation Research. 8 June 2017. "Global Cooperation Research Papers". https://www.gcr21.org/publications/research-papers/2198-0411-gcrp-10/

Hamilton, DL and Gifford, RK. 1976. "Illusory correlation in interpersonal perception: A cognitive basis of stereotypic judgments". *Journal of Experimental Social Psychology*. Vol 12. Pp 392–407.

Heider, F. 1958. *The Psychology of Interpersonal Relations*. New York, USA. Wiley.

Heppner, PP, Kivlighan, DM and Wampold, BE. 2007. *Research Design in Counseling*. Belmont, California, USA. Thomson.

Hewstone, M. 1990. "The 'ultimate attribution error'? A review of the literature on intergroup causal attribution". *European Journal of Social Psychology*. Vol 20. Pp 311–335.

Hofstede, G. (n.d.). Cited in https://geerthofstede.com/tl_files/art%20organisational%20culture%20perspective.pdf.

Hofstede, G. 1980. *Culture's Consequences*. Beverly Hills, California, USA. Sage.

Hofstede, G. 1991. *Cultures and Organizations: Software of the mind*. London, UK. McGraw-Hill.

Hofstede, G. 2011. *Culture's Consequences: Comparing values, behaviors, institutions, and organizations across nations*. Thousand Oaks, California, USA. Sage.

Hofstede, G and McCrae, R. 2004. "Personality and culture revisited: Linking traits and dimensions of culture". *Cross-Cultural Research*. Vol 38, number 1. Pp 52–88.

Hogg, MA and Vaughan, GM. 2014. *Social Psychology*. (Seventh edition). Harlow, UK. Pearson Education Limited.

Hsu, SY and Barker, GG. 2013. "Individualism and collectivism in Chinese and American television advertising". *International Communication Gazette*. Vol 75, number 8. Pp 695–714.

Hur, Y. 2012. "J.P. Rushton's contributions to the study of altruism. *Personality and Individual Differences*. Vol 55, number 3. Pp 247–250.

Ishizawa, H and Jones, A. 2016. "Immigrant neighborhood concentration, acculturation and obesity among young adults". *Journal of Urban Affairs*. Vol 38, number 2. Pp 298–311.

Iyengar, SS, Lepper, MR and Ross, L. 1999. "Independence from whom? Interdependence with whom? Cultural perspectives on ingroups versus outgroups". In Prentice, DA and Miller, DT (eds). *Cultural divides: Understanding and overcoming group conflict*. Pp 273–301. New York, USA. Russell Sage.

Jones, EE and Davis, KE. 1965. "From actors to dispositions: the attribution process in person perception". In Berkowitz, L (ed). *Advances in Experimental Psychology (Vol 10)*. New York, USA. Academic Press.

Jones, EE and Harris, VA. 1967. "The attribution of attitudes". *Journal of Experimental Social Psychology*. Vol 3, number 1. Pp 1–24.

Jones, EE and Nisbett, RE. 1971. *The Actor and the Observer: Divergent Perceptions of the Causes of Behavior*. Morristown, New Jersey, USA. General Learning Press.

Jones, MV, Bray, SR, Mace, RD, MacRae, AW and Stockbridge, C. 2002. "The impact of motivational imagery on the emotional state and self-efficacy levels of novice climbers". *Journal of Sport Behavior*. Vol 25, number 1. P 57.

Kantorovich, A. 2014. "An evolutionary view of science: Imitation and memetics". *Social Science Information*. Vol 53, number 3. Pp 363–373.

Kelley, HH. 1950. "The warm-cold variable in first impressions of people". *Journal of Personality*. Vol 18. Pp 431–439.

Kelley, HH. 1967. "Attribution theory in social pychology". In Levine, D (ed). *Nebraska Symposiumon on Motivation (Vol 15)*. Lincoln, Nebraska, USA. Nebraska University Press.

Kelley, HH. 1972. "Causal schemata and the attribution process". In Jones, EE and Kanhouse, DE, Kelley, HH, Valins, S and Weiner, B (eds). *Attribution: Perceiving the Causes of Behaviour*. Morristown, New Jersey, USA. General Learning Press.

Kemmelmeier, M, Jambor, EE and Letner, J. 2006. "Individualism and good works: Cultural variation in giving and volunteering across the United States". *Journal of Cross-Cultural Psychology*. Vol 37, number 3. Pp 327–344.

Lakey, PN. 2003. "Acculturation: A review of the literature". *Intercultural Communication Studies*. Vol 12, number 2.

Lin, C. 2001. "Cultural values reflected in Chinese and American television advertising". *Journal of Advertising*. Vol 30, number 4. Pp 83–94.

Lippmann, W. 1922. *Public Opinion*. New York, USA. Harcourt, Brace and Company.

Luchin, AS. 1957. "Primacy-recency in impression formation". In Hovland, C (ed). *The Order of Presentation in Persuasion*. New Haven, Connecticut, USA. Yale University Press.

Marsella, A. 2012. "Psychology and globalization: Understanding a complex relationship". *Journal of Social Issues*. Vol 68, number 3. Pp 454–472.

Matsumoto, D. 2007. "Culture, context, and behavior". *Journal of Personality*. Vol 75, number 6. Pp 1285–1320.

McCrae, R and John, O. 1992. "An introduction to the five-factor model and its applications". *Journal of Personality*. Vol 60, number 2. Pp 175–215.

McKeown, S, Haji, R, Ferguson, N. 2016. *Understanding Peace and Conflict Through Social Identity Theory (Peace Psychology Book Series)*. Cham, Switzerland. Springer International Publishing.

McLuhan, M. 1964. *Understanding Media: The Extensions of Man*. New York, USA. McGraw Hill.

Mead, M. 1963. "Melville J. Herskovits Festschrift: Socialization and enculturation". *Current Anthropology*. Vol 4, number 2. P 184.

Meeuwesen, L, van den Brink-Muinen, A and Hofstede, G. 2009. "Can dimensions of national culture predict cross-national differences in medical communication?" *Patient Education and Counseling*. Vol 75, number 1. Pp 58–66.

Merritt, A. 2000. "Culture in the cockpit: Do Hofstede's dimensions replicate?" *Journal of Cross-Cultural Psychology*. Vol 31, number 3. P 283.

Meyer, E. 2015. *The Culture Map: Decoding how People Think, Lead, and Get Things Done Across Cultures*. New York, USA. Public Affairs.

Mihalic, S and Elliott, W. 1997. "A social learning theory model of marital violence". *Journal of Family Violence*. Vol 12, number 1. Pp 21–47.

Miller, JG. 1984. "Culture and the development of everyday social explanation". *Journal of Personality and Social Psychology*. Vol 46. Pp 961–978.

National Transportation Safety Board. 6 August 1997. "Aircraft Accident Report: Controlled flight into terrain; Korean Air flight 801, Boeing 747-300, HL7468". http://www.ntsb.gov/investigations/AccidentReports/Reports/AAR0001.pdf

Nisbett, RE and Ross, L. 1980. *Human Inference: Strategies and Shortcomings in Social Judgement*. New York, USA. Prentice Hall.

Nisbett, RE and Ross, L. 1991. *The Person and the Situation*. London, UK. Pinter and Martin Publishers.

Oakes, PJ, Haslam, SA and Turner, JC. 1994. *Stereotyping and Social Reality*. Oxford, UK. Blackwell.

Oetting, ER. 1999. "Primary socialization theory. Developmental stages, spirituality, government institutions, sensation seeking, and theoretical implications". *Substance Use & Misuse*. Vol 34, number 7. Pp 947–982.

Oh, SHD. 2013. "Do collectivists conform more than individualists? Cross-cultural differences in compliance and internalization". *Social Behavior and Personality: An International Journal*. Vol 41, number 6. Pp 981–994.

Osterman, L and Brown, R. 2011. "Culture of honor and violence against the self". *Personality and Social Psychology Bulletin*. Vol 37, number 12. Pp 1611–1623.

Parboteeah, KP, Cullen, JB and Lim, L. 2004. "Formal volunteering: A cross-national test". *Journal of World Business*. Vol 39, number 4. Pp 431–441.

Perry, DG, Perry, LC and Rasmussen, P. 1986. "Cognitive social learning mediators of aggression". *Child Development*. Vol 57, number 3. Pp, 700–711.

Pettigrew, TF. 1979. "The ultimate attribution error: Extending Allport's cognitive analysis of prejudice". *Personality and Social Psychology Bulletin*. Vol 5, number 4. Pp 461–476.

Pinker, S. 2016. *The Blank Slate: The Modern Denial of Human Nature*. New York, USA. Penguin Books.

Rosenmann, A, Reese, G and Cameron, J. 2016. "Social identities in a globalized world". *Perspectives on Psychological Science*. Vol 11, number 2. Pp 202–221.

Rosenthal, R and Jacobson, L. 1968. *Pygmalion in the Classroom: Teacher Expectations and Pupils' Intellectual Development*. New York, USA. Holt, Rinehart and Winston.

Ross, L. 1977. "The intuitive psychology and his shortcomings: Distortions in the attribution process". In Berkowitz, L (ed). *Advances in Experimental Social Psychology*. Vol 10. New York, USA. Academic Press.

Ross, L, Amabile, TM and Steinmetz, JL. 1977. "Social roles, social control, and biases in social-perception processes. *Journal of Personality and Social Psychology*. Vol 33, number 7. Pp 485–494.

Schaller, M. 1991. "Social categorization and the formation of group stereotypes: Further evidence for biased information processing in the perception of group-behavior correlations". *European Journal of Social Psychology*. Vol 21, number 1. Pp 25–35.

Scholte, J. 2005. *Globalisation: A Critical Introduction*. New York, USA. Palgrave.

Schwartz, S. 2006. "Basic human values: Theory, measurement, and applications". *Revue Française de Sociologie*. Vol 47, number 4. Pp 929–968.

Schwartz, SH. (Online) *Basic Human Values: An Overview*. The Hebrew University of Jerusalem. http://segr-did2.fmag.unict.it/Allegati/convegno%207-8-10-05/Schwartzpaper.pdf

Schwartz, SH. 1990. "Individualism-collectivism: Critique and proposed refinements". *Journal of Cross-Cultural Psychology*. Vol 21, number 2. Pp 139–155.

Shah, S, Loney, T, Al Dhaheri, S, Vatanparast, H, Elbarazi, I, Agarwal, M, Blair, I and Ali, R. 2015. "Association between acculturation, obesity and cardiovascular risk factors among male South Asian migrants in the United Arab Emirates—A cross-sectional study". *BMC Public Health*. Vol 15, number 1.

Sheridan, B, Macdonald, D, Donlon, M, Kuhn, B, McGovern, K and Friedman, H. 2011. "Evaluation of a social skills program based on social learning theory, implemented in a school setting". *Psychological Reports*. Vol 108, number 2. Pp 420–436.

Sherif, M. 1954. "Experimental study of positive and negative intergroup attitudes between experimentally produced groups: Robbers cave study". Norman, Oklahoma, USA. University of Oklahoma.

Skorinko, J, Lun, J, Sinclair, S, Marotta, S, Calanchini, J and Paris, M. 2015. "Reducing prejudice across cultures via social tuning". *Social Psychological and Personality Science*. Vol 6, number 4. Pp 363–372.

Skowronski, J, Carlston, D and Masters, JC. 1989. "Negativity and extremity biases in impression formation: A review of explanations". *Psychological Bulletin*. Vol 105, number 1. Pp 131–142.

Snyder, M. 1984. "When belief creates reality". In Berkowitz, L (ed). *Advances in Experimental Social Psychology*. Vol 18. Orlando, Florida, USA. Academic Press.

Spencer, SJ, Steele, CM and Quinn, D. 1999. "Stereotype threat and women's math performance". *Journal of Experimental Social Psychology*. Vol 35. Pp 4–28.

Steele, CM. 2010. *Whistling Vivaldi: How Stereotypes Affect Us and What We Can Do*. New York, USA. WW Norton.

Steele, CM and Aronson, J. 1995. "Stereotype threat and the intellectual test performance of African Americans". *Journal of Personality and Social Psychology*. Vol 69. Pp 797–811.

Steele, CM, Spencer, SJ and Aronson, J. 2002. "Contending with group image: The psychology of stereotype and social identity threat". *Advances in Experimental Social Psychology*. Vol 34. Pp 379–440.

Stevenson, C, Dixon, J, Hopkins, N and Luyt, R. 2015. "The social psychology of citizenship, participation and social exclusion: Introduction to the special thematic section". *Journal of Social and Political Psychology*. Vol 3, number 2. Pp 1–19.

Stone, J, Lynch, C, Sjomeling, M, Darley, J and Insko, CA. 1999. "Stereotype threat effects on black and white athletic performance". *Journal of Personality and Social Psychology*. Vol 77, number 6. Pp 1213–1227.

Sullivan, L. 2009. *The SAGE Glossary of the Social and Behavioral Sciences*. Thousand Oaks, California, USA. Sage.

Tajfel, H. 1969. "Cognitive aspects of prejudice". *Journal of Social Issues*. Vol 25. Pp 79–97.

Tajfel, H. 1970. "Experiment in intergroup discrimination". *Scientific American*. Vol 223. Pp 96–102.

Tajfel, H and Turner, JC. 1979. "An integrative theory of intergroup conflict". In Austin, WG and Worchel, S (eds). *The Social Psychology of Intergroup Relations*. Monterey, California, USA. Books/Cole.

Tajfel, H, Flament, C, Billig, MG and Bundy, RF. 1971. "Social categorization and intergroup behaviour". *European Journal of Social Psychology*. Vol 1. Pp 149–177.

Taylor, DM and Jaggi, V. 1974. "Ethnocentrism and causal attribution in a South Indian context". *Journal of Cross-Cultural Psychology*. Vol 119. Pp 187–198.

Triandis, H. 2001. "Individualism-collectivism and personality". *Journal of Personality*. Vol 69, number 6. Pp 907–924.

Trudeau, J. "Diversity is Canada's strength". 24 October 2016. http://pm.gc.ca/eng/news/2015/11/26/diversity-canadas-strength.

Tsai, W and Lee, W. 2006. "Between and within culture variations of cultural value orientations reflected in television commercials: An exploratory study of China and the United States". *American Academy of Advertising Conference Proceedings*. Pp 93–102.

Türken, S and Rudman, FW. 2013. "On psychological effects of globalization: Development of a scale of global identity". *Psychology & Society*. Vol 5, number 2. Pp 63–89.

United Nations. 12 January 2016. "Number of international migrants reached 244 million in 2015". http://www.un.org/sustainabledevelopment/blog/2016/01/244-million-international-migrants-living-abroad-worldwide-new-un-statistics-reveal/

Van de Waal, E, Renevey, N, Favre, C and Bshary, R. 2010. "Selective attention to philopatric models causes directed social learning in wild vervet monkeys". *Proceedings of the Royal Society B*. Vol 277, number 1691. Pp 2105–2111.

Ward, C. 2008. "Thinking outside the Berry boxes: New perspectives on identity, acculturation and intercultural relations". *International Journal of Intercultural Relations*. Vol 32, number 2. Pp 105–114.

Yi, W. 2007. "Globalization and cultural identity". *Intercultural Communication Studies*. Vol XVI, number 1. Pp 83–88.

Unit 5: Abnormal psychology

Alarcon, RD. 2009. "Culture, cultural factors and psychiatric diagnosis: review and projections". *World Psychiatry*. Vol 8. Pp 131–139.

Alloy, LB, Abramson, LY and Francis, EL. 1999. "Do negative cognitive styles confer vulnerability to depression?" *Current Directions in Psychological Science*. Vol 8, number 4. Pp 128–132.

Andrews, PW, Thomson Jr, JA, Amstadter, A and Neale, MC. 2012. "Primum non nocere: an evolutionary analysis of whether antidepressants do more harm than good". *Frontiers in Psychology*. Vol 3, article 117.

Beck, AT. 1967. *Depression: Clinical, Experimental, and Theoretical Aspects*. New York, USA. Harper and Row.

Beck, AT, Ward, CH, Mendelson, M, Mock, JE and Erbaugh, JK. 1962. "Reliability of psychiatric diagnoses: 2. A study of consistency of clinical judgments and rating". *The American Journal of Psychiatry*. Vol 119, number 4. Pp 351–357.

Bernal, G, Bonilla, J and Bellido, C. 1995. "Ecological validity and cultural sensitivity for outcome research: Issues for the cultural adaptation and development of psychosocial treatments with Hispanics". *Journal of Abnormal Child Psychology*. Vol 23. Pp 67–82.

Bockting, CLH, ten Doesschate, MC, Spijker, J, Spinhoven, P, Koeter, MWJ and Schene, AH. 2008. "Continuation and maintenance use of antidepressants in recurrent depression".

Psychotherapy and Psychosomatics. Vol 77, number 1. Pp 17–26.

Bolton, P, Bass, J, Neugebauer, R, Verdeli, H, Clougherty, KF, Wickramaratne, P, Speelman, L, Ndogoni, L and Weissman, M. 2003. "Group interpersonal psychotherapy for depression in rural Uganda: A randomized controlled trial". *JAMA*. Vol 289, number 23. Pp 3117–3124.

Brown, GW and Harris, TO. 1978. *Social Origins of Depression A Study of Psychiatric Disorder in Women*. London, UK. Tavistock Publications.

Caseras, X, Garner, M, Bradley, BP and Mogg, K. 2007. "Biases in visual orienting to negative and positive scenes in dysphoria: An eye movement study". *Journal of Abnormal Psychology*. Vol 116, number 3. Vol 491–497.

Caspi, A, Hariri, AR, Holmes, A, Uher, R and Moffitt, TE. 2010. "Genetic sensitivity to the environment: the case of the serotonin transporter gene and its implications for studying complex diseases and traits". *American Journal of Psychiatry*. Vol 167, number 5. Pp 509–527.

Chapman, LJ and Chapman, JP. 1969. "Illusory correlation as an obstacle to the use of valid psychodiagnostic signs". *Journal of Abnormal Psychology*. Vol 74. Pp 271–280.

Chiao, JY and Blizinsky, KD. 2010. "Culture-gene co-evolution of individualism-collectivism and the serotonin transporter gene". *Proceedings of the Royal Society B: Biological Sciences*. Vol 277, number 1681. Pp 529–537.

Chmielewski, M, Clark, LA, Bagby, RM and Watson, D. 2015. "Method matters: Understanding diagnostic reliability in DSM-IV and DSM-5". *Journal of Abnormal Psychology*. Vol 24, number 3. Pp 764–769.

Cohen, J. 1960. "A coefficient of agreement for nominal scales". *Educational and Psychological Measurement*. Vol 20. Pp 37–46.

Cooper, JE. 1972. "Concepts of schizophrenia in the United States of America and in Great Britain; a summary of some studies by the U.S-U.K. Diagnostic Project". In Lader, MH (ed). *Studies of Schizophrenia*. P 1924. London, UK. Headley Brothers.

Cowen, PJ and Browning, M. 2015. "What has serotonin to do with depression?" *World Psychiatry*. Vol 14, number 2. Pp 158–160.

DelBello, MP, Lopez-Larson, M, SoutuUo, CA and Strakowski, SM. 2001. "Effects of race on psychiatric diagnosis of hospitalized adolescents: A retrospective chart review". *Journal of Child and Adolescent Psychopharmacology*. Vol 11. Pp 95–103.

DeRubeis, RJ, Hollon, SD, Amsterdam, JD, Shelton, RC, Young, PR, Salomon, RM, O'Reardon, JP, Lovett, ML, Gladis, MM, Brown, LL and Gallop, R. 2005. "Cognitive therapy vs medications in the treatment of moderate to severe depression". *Archives of General Psychiatry*. Vol 62. Pp 409–416.

Di Nardo, P, Moras, K, Barlow, DH, Rapee, RM and Brown, TA. 1993. "Reliability of DSM-III-R anxiety disorder categories. Using the Anxiety Disorders Interview Schedule-Revised (ADIS-R)". *Archives of General Psychiatry*. Vol 50, number 4. Pp 251–256.

Dick, DM. 2011. "Gene-environment interaction in psychological traits and disorders". *Annual Review of Clinical Psychology*. Vol 7. Pp 383–409.

Elkin, I, Shea, MT, Watkins, JT, Imber, SD, Sotsky, SM, Collins, JF, Glass, DR, Pilkonis, PA, Leber, WR, Dicherty, JP, Fiester, SJ and Parloff, MB. 1989. "National Institute of Mental Health Treatment of Depression Collaborative Research Program: General effectiveness of treatments". *Archives of General Psychiatry*. Vol 46. Pp 971–982.

Eysenck, HJ. 1952. "The effects of psychotherapy: An evaluation". *Journal of Consulting Psychology*. Vol 16. Pp 319–324.

Fournier, JC, DeRubeis, RJ, Hollon, SD, Gallop, R, Shelton, RC and Amsterdam, JD. 2013. "Differential change in specific depressive symptoms during antidepressant medication or cognitive therapy". *Behavioural Research and Therapy*. Vol 51, number 7. Pp 392–398.

Furnham, A and Malik, R. 1994. "Cross-cultural beliefs about 'depression'". *The International Journal of Social Psychiatry*. Vol 40, number 2. Vol 106–123.

Goldapple, K, Segal, Z, Garson, C, Lau, M, Bieling, P, Kennedy, S and Mayberg, H. 2004. "Modulation of cortical-limbic pathways in major depression: Treatment-specific effects of cognitive behavioural therapy". *Archives of General Psychiatry*. Vol 61. Pp 34–41.

Griner, D and Smith, TB. 2006. "Culturally adapted mental health intervention: A meta-analytic review". *Psychotherapy: Theory, Research, Practice, Training*. Vol 43. Pp 531–548.

Hammen, CL and Krantz, S. 1976. "Effect of success and failure on depressive cognitions". *Journal of Abnormal Psychology*. Vol 85, number 6. Pp 577–586.

Harmer, CJ, Goodwin, GM and Cowen, PJ. 2009. "Why do antidepressants take so long to work? A cognitive neuropsychological model of antidepressant drug action". *British Journal of Psychiatry*. Vol 195. Pp 102–108.

Hodges, J and Oei, TP. 2007. "Would Confucius benefit from psychotherapy? The compatibility of cognitive behaviour therapy and Chinese values". *Behaviour Research and Therapy*. Vol 45, number 5. Pp 901–914.

Hollon, SD, DeRubeis, RJ, Evans, MD, Wiemer, MJ, Garvey, MJ, Grove, WM and Tuason, VB. 1992. "Cognitive therapy and pharmacotherapy for depression: Singly and in combination". *Archives of General Psychiatry*. Vol 49. Pp 774–781.

Hollon, SD, DeRubeis, RJ, Shelton, RC, Amsterdam, JD, Salomon, RM, O'Reardon, JP, Lovett, ML, Young, PR, Haman, KL, Freeman, BB and Gallop, R. 2005. "Prevention of relapse following cognitive therapy vs modifications in moderate to severe depression". *Archives of General Psychiatry*. Vol 62, number 4. Pp 417–422.

Hunsley, J and Lee, CM. 2007. "Research-informed benchmarks for psychological treatments: Efficacy studies, effectiveness studies, and beyond". *Professional Psychology: Research and Practice*. Vol 38. Pp 21–33.

Hyman, SE. 2010. "The diagnosis of mental disorders: The problem of reification". *Annual Review of Clinical Psychology*. Vol 6. Pp 155–179.

Jacobson, NS, Dobson, KS, Truax, PA, Addis, ME, Koerner, K, Gollan, JK, Gortner, E and Prince, SE. 1996. "A component analysis of cognitive–behavioral treatment for depression". *Journal of Consulting and Clinical Psychology*. Vol 64. Pp 295–304.

Jahoda, Marie. 1958. *Current Concepts of Positive Mental Health. Joint Commission on Mental Health and Illness Monograph Series. Vol 1*. New York, USA. Basic Books.

Kalibatseva, Z and Leong, FTL. 2014. "A critical review of culturally sensitive treatments for depression: Recommendations for interventions

and research". *Psychological Services*. Vol 11, number 4. Pp 433–450.

Kendler, KS, Gatz, M, Gardner, CO and Pedersen, NL. 2006. "A Swedish national twin study of lifetime major depression". *American Journal of Psychiatry*. Vol 163, number 1. Pp 109–114.

Kessler, RC and Bromet, EJ. 2013. "The epidemiology of depression across cultures". *Annual Review of Public Health*. Vol 34. Pp 119–138.

Kinzie, JD, Leung, P, Boehnlein, JK and Fleck, J. 1987. "Antidepressant blood levels in Southeast Asians: clinical and cultural implications". *Journal of Nervous and Mental Disorders*. Vol 175. Pp 480–485.

Kirmayer, LJ. 2001. "Cultural variations in the clinical presentation of depression and anxiety: Implications for diagnosis and treatment". *Journal of Clinical Psychiatry*. Vol 62. Pp 22–30.

Kirsch, I. 2014. "Antidepressants and the placebo effect". *Zeitschrift Fur Psychologie*. Vol 222, number 3. Pp 128–134.

Kirsch, I and Sapirstein, G. 1998. "Listening to Prozac but hearing placebo: A meta-analysis of antidepressant medication". *Prevention and Treatment*. Vol 1, number 2. P 2a.

Kirsch, I, Moore, TJ, Scoboria, A and Nicholls, SS. 2002. "The emperor's new drugs: An analysis of antidepressant medication data submitted to the U.S. Food and Drug Administration. Prevention and Treatment". *PLOS Medicine*. Vol 5, number 2. Pp 260–268.

Kleinman, A. 1977. "Depression, somatisation and the new 'cross-cultural psychiatry'". *Social Science and Medicine*. Vol 11. Pp 3–10.

Kleinman, AK. 1982. "Neurasthenia and depression: A study of somatization and culture in China". *Culture, Medicine and Psychiatry*. Vol 6. Pp 177–190.

Lambert, MJ. 2013. "Outcome in psychotherapy: The past and important advances". *Psychotherapy*. Vol 50, number 1. Pp 42–51.

Langwieler, G and Linden, M. 1993. "Therapist individuality in the diagnosis and treatment of depression". *Journal of Affective Disorders*. Vol 27, number 1. Pp 1–11.

Lin, EHB, Carter, WB and Kleinman, AM. 1985. "An exploration of somatization among Asian refugees and immigrants in primary care".

American Journal of Public Health. Vol 75, number 9. Pp 1080–1084.

Lohoff, FW. 2011. "Overview of the genetics of major depressive disorder". *Current Psychiatry Reports.* Vol 12, number 6. Pp 539–546.

March, JS, Silva, S, Petrycki, S, Curry, J, Wells, K, Fairbank, J, Burns, B, Domino, M, McNulty, S, Vitiello, B and Severe, J. 2007. "The Treatment of Adolescents with Depression Study (TADS): Long-term effectiveness and safety outcomes". *Archives of General Psychiatry.* Vol 64, number 10. Pp 1132–1143.

McHugh, ML. 2012. "Interrater reliability: the kappa statistic". *Biochemia Medica.* Vol 22, number 3. Pp 276–282.

McRoberts, C, Burlingame, GM and Hoag, MJ. 1998. "Comparative efficacy of individual and group psychotherapy: A meta-analytic perspective". *Group Dynamics: Theory, Research, and Practice.* Vol 2, number 2. Pp 101–117.

Naeem, F, Ayub, M, Kingdon, D and Gobbi, M. 2012. "Views of depressed patients in Pakistan concerning their illness, its causes, and treatments". *Qualitative Health Research.* Vol 22, number 8. Pp 1083–1093.

Nevid, JS, Rathus, SA and Greene, BS. 2014. *Abnormal Psychology in a Changing World* (Ninth edition). Upper Saddle River, New Jersey, USA. Pearson Education.

NIMH. 2015. Retrieved from https://www.nimh.nih.gov/health/statistics/prevalence/major-depression-among-adults.shtml

Pande, S. 1968. "The mystique of Western psychotherapy: An Eastern interpretation". *Journal of Nervous and Mental Disease.* Vol 146. Pp 425–432.

Patten, SB. 1991. "Are Brown and Harris 'vulnerability factors' risk factors for depression?" *Journal of Psychiatric Neuroscience.* Vol 16, number 5. Pp 267–271.

Payne, JS. 2012. "Influence of race and symptom expression on clinicians' depressive disorder identification in African American men". *Journal of the Society for Social Work and Research.* Vol 3, number 3. Pp 162–177.

Plomin, R, DeFries, JC and Loehlin, JC. 1977. "Genotype-environment interaction and correlation in the analysis of human behavior". *Psychological Bulletin.* Vol 84. Pp 309–322.

Poland, J and Caplan, PJ. 2004. "The deep structure of bias in psychiatric diagnosis". In Caplan, PJ and Colgrove, S (eds). *Bias in psychiatric diagnosis.* Pp 9–24. Lanham, Maryland, USA. Jason Aronson.

Ramsden, P. 2013. *Understanding Abnormal Psychology. Clinical and Biological Perspectives.* London, UK. Sage.

Regier, DA, Narrow, WE, Clarke, DE, Kraemer, HC, Kuramoto, SJ, Kuhl, EA and Kupfer, DJ. 2013. "DSM-5 field trials in the United States and Canada, part II: Test-retest reliability of selected categorical diagnoses". *The American Journal of Psychiatry.* Vol 170, issue 1. Pp 59–70.

Robins, E and Guze, SB. 1970. "Establishment of diagnostic validity in psychiatric illness: Its application to schizophrenia". *American Journal of Psychiatry.* Vol 126. Pp 983–987.

Rosenhan, DL. 1973. "On being sane in insane places". *Science.* Vol 179. Pp 250–258.

Rosenhan, DL and Seligman, MEP. 1989. *Abnormal Psychology.* New York, USA. WW Norton.

Rosenquist, JN, Fowler, JH and Christakis, NA. 2011. "Social network determinants of depression". *Molecular Psychiatry.* Vol 16. Pp 273–281.

Silberg, J, Pickles, A, Rutter, M, Hewitt, J, Simonoff, E, Maes, H, Carbonneau, R, Murrelle, L, Foley, D and Eaves, L. 1999. "The influence of genetic factors and life stress on depression among adolescent girls". *Archives of Genetic Psychiatry.* Vol 56. Pp 225–232.

Skinner, LJ, Berry, KK, Griffith, SE and Byers, B. 1995. "Generalizability and specificity of the stigma associated with the mental illness label: A reconsideration twenty-five years later". *Journal of Community Psychology.* Vol 23. Pp 3–17.

Smith, ML and Glass, GV. 1977. "Meta-analysis of psychotherapy outcome studies". *American Psychologist.* Vol 32. Pp 752–760.

Spitzer, RL. 1976. "More on pseudoscience in science and the case of the psychiatric diagnosis: A critique of D. L. Rosenhan's 'On being sane in insane places' and 'The contextual nature of psychiatric diagnosis'". *Archives of General Psychiatry.* Vol 33. Pp 459–470.

Steele, CM and Aronson, J. 1995. "Stereotype threat and the intellectual test performance of African Americans". *Journal of Personality and Social Psychology*. Vol 69, number 5. Pp 797–811.

Steinberg, M. 1990. "Transcultural issues in psychiatry: The Ataque and multiple personality disorder". *Dissociation*. Vol 3, number 1. Pp 31–33.

Sullivan, PF, Neale, MC and Kendler, KS. 2000. "Genetic epidemiology of major depression: Review and meta-analysis". *American Journal of Psychiatry*. Vol 157, number 10. Pp 1552–1562.

Taupin, P. 2006. "Neurogenesis and the effect of antidepressants". *Drug Target Insights*. Vol 1. Pp 13–17.

Toseland, RW and Siporin, M. 1986. "When to recommend group treatment: A review of the clinical and the research literature". *International Journal of Group Psychotherapy*. Vol 36, number 2. Pp 171–201.

Turner, EH, Matthews, AM, Linardatos, E, Tell, RA and Rosenthal, R. 2008. "Selective publication of antidepressant trials and its influence on apparent efficacy". *New England Journal of Medicine*. Vol 358. Pp 252–260.

Wampold, BE. 2007. "Psychotherapy: The humanistic (and effective) treatment". *American Psychologist*. Vol 62. Pp 857–873.

Williams, JBW, Gibbon, M, First, MB, Spitzer, RL, Davis, M, Borus, J, Howes, MJ, Kane, J, Pope, HG, Rounsaville, B and Wittchen, H. 1992. "The Structured Clinical Interview for DSM-III-R (SCID) II. Multi-site test-retest reliability". *Archives of General Psychiatry*. Vol 49. Pp 630–636.

Zanarini, MC and Frankenburg, FR. 2001. "Attainment and maintenance of reliability of axis I and axis II disorders over the course of a longitudinal study". *Comprehensive Psychiatry*. Vol 42, number 5. Pp 369–374.

Unit 6: Health psychology

Abraham, C. 2008. *Health psychology: Topics in applied psychology*. London, UK. Hodder Arnold.

Ahmad, MH, Shahar, S, Teng, NIMF, Manaf, ZA, Sakian, NIM and Omar, B. 2014. "Applying theory of planned behavior to predict exercise maintenance in sarcopenic elderly". *Clinical Interventions in Aging*. Vol 9. Pp 1551–1561.

Aikens, KA, Astin, J, Pelletier, KR, Levanovich, K, Baase, CM, Park, YY and Bodnar, CM. 2014. "Mindfulness goes to work: Impact of an online workplace intervention". *Journal of Occupational and Environmental Medicine*. Vol 56, number 7. Pp 721–731.

Ajzen, I. 2015. "The theory of planned behaviour is alive and well, and not ready to retire: A commentary on Sniehotta, Presseau, and Araújo-Soares". *Health Psychology Review*. Vol 9, number 2. Pp 131–137.

Albarracin, D. 22 October 2015. "Fear-based appeals effective at changing attitudes, behaviors after all". Retrieved 24 April 2017 from http://www.apa.org/news/press/releases/2015/10/fear-based-appeals.aspx

American Psychological Association. 9 November 2010. "APA stress in America findings". Retrieved 8 May 2017 from APA website: http://www.apa.org/news/press/releases/stress/2010/national-report.pdf

American Psychological Association. 8 May 2017. "Stress in America press room". http://www.apa.org/news/press/releases/stress/index.aspx

Armitage, C and Conner, M. 2001. "Efficacy of the theory of planned behaviour: A meta-analytic review". *British Journal of Social Psychology*. Vol 40, number 4. Pp 471–499.

Baer, JC, Kim, M and Wilkenfeld, B. 2012. "Is it generalized anxiety disorder or poverty? An examination of poor mothers and their children". *Child and Adolescent Social Work Journal*. Vol 29, number 4. Pp 345–355.

Bakker, AB, Hakanen, JJ, Demerouti, E and Xanthopoulou, D. 2007. "Job resources boost work engagement, particularly when job demands are high". *Journal of Educational Psychology*. Vol 99, number 2.

Baum, A. 1990. "Stress, intrusive imagery, and chronic distress". *Health Psychology*. Vol 6. Pp 653–675.

Beheshti, R, Igusa, T and Jones-Smith, J. 2016. "Simulated models suggest that price per calorie is the dominant price metric that low-income individuals use for food decision making". *The Journal of Nutrition*. Vol 146, number 11. Pp 2304–2312.

Benning, TB. 2015. "Limitations of the biopsychosocial model in psychiatry". *Advances in Medical Education and Practice.* Vol 6. Retrieved from http://go.galegroup.com.uml.idm.oclc.org/ps/i.do?p=HRCA&sw=w&u=univmanitoba&v=2.1&it=r&id=GALE%7CA445751567&asid=5a1cb4f6c3a6888136fb9b8aa898a820

Boswell, R. 2012. "Sugar: There's more to the obesity crisis". *Nature.* Vol 482, number 7386. doi:10.1038/482470d.

Bratman, GN, Hamilton, JP and Daily, GC. 2012. "The impacts of nature experience on human cognitive function and mental health". *Annals Of The New York Academy Of Sciences.* Vol 1249, number 1. Pp 118–136.

Bruss, MB, Morris, JR, Dannison, LL, Orbe, MP, Quitugua, JA and Palacios, RT. 2005. "Food, culture, and family: Exploring the coordinated management of meaning regarding childhood obesity". *Health Communication.* Vol 18. Pp 155–175.

Cannon, WB. 1932. *The Wisdom of the Body* (Second edition). New York, USA. WW Norton.

Catalano, P and Ehrenberg, H. 2006. "The short- and long-term implications of maternal obesity on the mother and her offspring". *BJOG: An International Journal of Obstetrics & Gynaecology.* Vol 113. Pp 1126–1133.

Center for Food Safety and Applied Nutrition. 25 April 2017. "Labeling and nutrition—changes to the nutrition facts label". Retrieved 26 April 2017 from https://www.fda.gov/Food/GuidanceRegulation/GuidanceDocumentsRegulatoryInformation/LabelingNutrition/ucm385663.htm

Centers for Disease Control. 6 June 2014. "Stress at work". Retrieved 8 May 2017 from https://www.cdc.gov/niosh/docs/99-101/

Centre for Science in the Public Interest. 9 February 2016. "Carbonating the world". Retrieved 1 May 2017 from https://cspinet.org/resource/carbonating-world

Conger, RD, Lorenz, FO, Elder, JR, Simons, RL and Ge, X. March 1993. "Husband and wife differences in response to undesirable life events". Retrieved 8 May 2017 from https://www.ncbi.nlm.nih.gov/pubmed/8463637

Conner, M and Sparks, P. 2005. "The theory of planned behavior". In Conner, P and Norman, P (eds). *Predicting Health Behaviour: Research and Practice with Social Cognition Models.* Pp 121–162. Buckingham, UK. Open University Press.

CSDH. 2008. "Closing the gap in a generation: health equity through action on the social determinants of health. Final Report of the Commission on Social Determinants of Health". Geneva. World Health Organization.

Dannenberg, AL, Frumkin, H and Jackson, RJ (eds). 2011. *Making Healthy Places: Designing and Building for Health, Well-being, and Sustainability.* Island Press. doi: 10.5822/978-1-61091-036-1_1

Davis, MC and Matthews KA. 1996. In Twamley, EW. 1999. "Is life more difficult on Mars or Venus? A meta-analytic review of sex differences in major and minor life events". *Annals of Behavioral Medicine,* Vol 21. Pp 83–97.

"Definitions". 21 March 2014. Retrieved from https://www.cdc.gov/nchhstp/socialdeterminants/definitions.html

Demerouti, E, Evangelia, E, Nachreiner, F, Bakker, AB and Schaufeli, WB. 2001. "The job demands-resources model of burnout". *Journal of Applied Psychology.* Vol 86, number 3. Pp 499–9010.

Dodson, J and Yerkes, RM. 1915. "The relation of strength of stimulus to rapidity of habit-formation in the kitten". *Journal of Animal Behavior.* Vol 5, number 4. Pp 330–336.

D'Ovidio, F, d'Errico, A, Scarinzi, C and Costa, G. 2015. "Increased incidence of coronary heart disease associated with 'double burden' in a cohort of Italian women". *Social Science & Medicine.* Vol 135, number 40–46.

Downing-Matibag, T and Geisinger, B. 2009. "Hooking up and sexual risk taking among college students: A health belief model perspective". *Qualitative Health Research.* Vol 19, number 9. Pp 1196–1209.

Drewnowski, A. 2004. "Obesity and the food environment dietary energy density and diet costs". *American Journal of Preventive Medicine.* Vol 27, number 3s. Pp 154–162.

Dunn, KI, Mohr, P, Wilson, CJ and Wittert, GA. 2011. "Determinants of fast-food consumption. An application of the theory of planned behaviour". *Appetite.* Vol 57, number 2. Pp 349–357.

Eguchi, HR, Wada, K and Smith, D. 2016. "Recognition, compensation, and prevention of karoshi, or death due to overwork". *Journal of Occupational and Environmental Medicine.* Vol 58, number 8. Pp E313–E314.

Elliott, G, Eisdorfer, C and Institute of Medicine. 1982. *Stress and Human Health: Analysis and Implications of Research: A Study (Springer Series on Psychiatry; 1)*. New York, USA. Springer Publications.

Engel, G. 1977. "The need for a new medical model: A challenge for biomedicine". *Science*. Vol 196, number 4286. Pp 129–136. Retrieved from http://www.jstor.org/stable/1743658

Engel, GL. 1981. "The clinical application of the biopsychosocial model". *Journal of Medicine and Philosophy*. Vol 6, number 2. Pp 101–124.

Epel, E, Blackburn, E, Lin, J, Dhabhar, F, Adler, N, Morrow, J and Cawthon, R. 2004. "Accelerated telomere shortening in response to life stress". *Proceedings of the National Academy of Sciences of the United States of America*. Vol 101, number 49. Pp 17312–17315.

Evans, R (2002). Cited in Pettigrew, M, Davey Smith, G and Gursky-Doyen, S. 2012. "The monkey puzzle: A systematic review of studies of stress, social hierarchies, and heart disease in monkeys (stress, dominance and heart disease in monkeys)". *PLoS ONE*. Vol 7, number 3.

Evans, WD, Christoffel, KK, Necheles, JW and Becker, AB. 2010. "Social marketing as a childhood obesity prevention strategy". *Obesity*. Vol 18, number S1. Pp S23–S26.

Festinger, L. 1957. *A Theory of Cognitive Dissonance*. Evanston, Illinois, USA. Row & Peterson.

Fiksenbaum, LM, Greenglass, ER and Eaton, J. 2006. "Perceived social support, hassles, and coping in the elderly". *Journal of Applied Gerontology*. Vol 25, number 10. Pp 17–30.

Finkelstein, DM, Capitaman, J and Goodman, E. 2007. "Socioeconomic differences in adolescent stress: The role of psychological resources". *Journal of adolescent health*. Vol 40, number 2. Pp 127–134.

Folkman, S. 1997. "Positive psychological states and coping with severe stress". *Social Science and Medicine*. Vol 45, number 8. Pp 1207–1221.

Folkman, S. "Stress, health, and coping". Cited in Folkman, S. 2011. *The Oxford Handbook of Stress, Health, and Coping (Oxford Library of Psychology)*. Oxford and New York. Oxford University Press.

Folkman, S and Hogan, R. 1984. "Personal control and stress and coping processes: A theoretical analysis". *Journal of Personality and Social Psychology*. Vol 46, number 4. Pp 839–852.

Friedman, M and Rosenman, RH. 1974. *Type A Behaviour and Your Heart*. London, UK. Wildwood House.

Fukuyama, F. 1992. *The End of History and the Last Man*. New York, USA. Free Press.

Galea, S, Ahern, J, Rudenstine, S, Wallace, Z and Vlahov, D. 15 September 2005. "Urban built environment and depression: A multilevel analysis". *Journal of Epdiemiology and Community Health*. Vol 59, number 10. P 822.

Gallo, LC and Matthews, KA. 2003. "Understanding the association between socioeconomic status and physical health: Do negative emotions play a role?" *Psychological Bulletin*. Vol 129, number 1. Pp 10–51.

Ghaemi, SN. 2009. "The rise and fall of the biopsychosocial model". *The British Journal of Psychiatry: The Journal of Mental Science*. Vol 195, number 1. Pp 3–4.

Grandey, AA and Cropanzano, R. 1999. "The conservation of resources model applied to work-family conflict and strain". *Journal of Vocational Behavior*. Vol 54. Pp 350–370.

Harvard, TH and Chan School of Public Health. 3 March 2017. "Added sugar in the diet". Retrieved 19 April 2017 from https://www.hsph.harvard.edu/nutritionsource/carbohydrates/added-sugar-in-the-diet/#ref27

Haworth, CM, Plomin, R, Carnell, S and Wardle, J. 1 July 2008. "Childhood obesity: Genetic and environmental overlap with normal-range BMI". *Obesity*. Vol 16, number 7. Pp 1585–1590.

Health and Safety Executive. 2016. "Work related stress, anxiety and depression statistics in Great Britain 2016". Retrieved 8 May 2017 from http://www.hse.gov.uk/statistics/causdis/stress/

Helgeson, VS. "Gender, Stress, and Coping". Cited in Folkman, S. 2011. *The Oxford Handbook of Stress, Health, and Coping (Oxford Library of Psychology)*. Oxford and New York. Oxford University Press.

Hill, C, Abraham, C and Wright, DB. 2007. "Can theory-based messages in combination with cognitive prompts promote exercise in classroom settings?" *Social Science & Medicine*. Vol 65, number 5. Pp 1049–1058.

Hill, J, Wyatt, H, Reed, G and Peters, J. 2003. "Obesity and the environment: Where do we go from here?" *Science*. Vol 299, number 5608.

Pp 853–855. Retrieved from http://www.jstor.org/stable/3833601

Hobfoll, SE. 1989. "Conservation of resources: A new attempt at conceptualizing stress". *American Psychologist*. Vol 44, number 3. Pp 513–524.

Hobfoll, SE. "Conservation of resources theory". Cited in Folkman, S. 2011. *The Oxford Handbook of Stress, Health, and Coping (Oxford Library of Psychology)*. Oxford, UK and New York, USA. Oxford University Press.

Hobfoll, SE, Briggs-Phillips, M and Stines, LR. 2003. "Fact and artifact: The relationship of hope to a caravan of resources". In Jacoby, R and Keinana, G (eds). *Between Stress and Hope: From a Disease-centered to a Health-centered Perspective*. Westport, Connecticut, USA. Praeger Publishers/Greenwood Publishing Group.

Holmes, TH and Rahe, RH. 1967. "The social readjustment rating scale". *Journal of Psychosomatic Research*. Vol 11, number 2. Pp 213–218.

Honjo, K. 2004. "Social epidemiology: Definition, history, and research examples". *Environmental Health and Preventive Medicine*. Vol 9, number 5. Pp 193–199.

Jamal, M, Baba, V and Carlson, JG. 2003. "Type A behavior, components, and outcomes: A study of canadian employees". *International Journal of Stress Management*. Vol 10, number 1. Pp 39–50.

Johnson, RK, Appel, LJ, Brands, M, Howard, BV, Lefevre, M, Lustig, RH and Wylie-Rosett, J. 14 September 2009. "Dietary sugars intake and cardiovascular health". *Circulation*. Vol 120, number 11. doi:10.1161/CIRCULATIONAHA.109.192627.

Jull, G. 2017. "Biopsychosocial model of disease: 40 years on. Which way is the pendulum swinging?" *British Journal of Sports Medicine* Vol 51, number 16. Pp 1187–1188.

Kabat-Zinn, J. 2011. "Some reflections on the origins of MBSR, skillful means, and the trouble with maps". *Contemporary Buddhism*. Vol 12, number 1. Pp 281–306.

Kanner, A, Coyne, D, Schaefer, J and Lazarus, C. 1981. "Comparison of two modes of stress measurement: Daily hassles and uplifts versus major life events". *Journal of Behavioral Medicine*. Vol 4, number 1. Pp 1–39.

Kaplan, S. 1995. "The restorative benefits of nature: Toward an integrative framework". *Journal of Environmental Psychology*. Vol 15, number 3. Pp 169–182.

Karasek, R. 1979. "Job demands, job decision latitude, and mental strain: Implications for job redesign". *Administrative Science Quarterly*. Vol 24, number 2. Pp 285–308.

Ke, DS. June 2012. "Overwork, stroke, and karoshi-death from overwork". Retrieved from https://www.ncbi.nlm.nih.gov/pubmed/22879113

Kiecolt-Glaser, J, Garner, W, Speicher, C, Penn, G, Holliday, J and Glaser, R. 1984. "Psychosocial modifiers of immunocompetence in medical students". *Psychosomatic Medicine*. Vol 46, number 1. Pp 7–14.

Kim, HS, Sherman, DK and Taylor, SE. 2008. "Culture and social support". *American Psychologist*. Vol 63, number 6. Pp 518–526.

Kivimaki, M, Jokela, M, Nyberg, ST, Singh-Manoux, A, Fransson, EI, and Alfredsson, L. 2015. "Long working hours and risk of coronary heart disease and stroke: A systematic review and meta-analysis of published and unpublished data for 603 838 individuals". *Lancet*. Vol 386. Pp 1739–1746.

Kobasa, S and Greenwald, AG. 1979. "Stressful life events, personality, and health: An inquiry into hardiness". *Journal of Personality and Social Psychology*. Vol 37, number 1. Pp 1–11.

Kyriacou, C and Sutcliffe, J. 1978. "Teacher stress: Prevalence, sources, and symptoms. *British Journal of Educational Psychology*. Vol 48. Pp 159–167.

Lazarus, R. 1993. "From psychological stress to the emotions: A history of changing outlooks". *Annual Review of Psychology*. Vol 44. Pp 1–21.

Lazarus, RS and Folkman, S. 1984. *Stress, Appraisal and Coping*. New York, USA. Springer.

Lazarus, RS, Kanner, A and Folkman, S. 1980. "Emotions: A cognitive phenomenological analysis". In Plutchik, R and Kellerman, H. *Theories of Emotion (Emotion, Theory, Research, and Experience; Vol 1)*. New York, USA. Academic Press.

Lencioni, P. 2015. *The Truth about Employee Engagement: A Fable about Addressing the Three Root Causes of Job Misery*. San Francisco, California, USA. Jossey-Bass, Wiley.

Li, J. 2016. "Karoshi: An international work-related hazard?" *International Journal of Cardiology*. Vol 206. Pp 139–140.

Liu Y, Tanaka H. 2002. "The Fukuoka Heart Study Group. Overtime work, insufficient sleep, and risk of non-fatal acute myocardial infarction in Japanese men". *Occupational and Environmental Medicine*. Vol 59. Pp 447–51.

Lobstein, T, Baur, L, Uauy, R. 2004. "Obesity in children and young people: A crisis in public health". *Obesity*. Rev 5 (Supplement 1). Pp 4–104.

Loucks, E, Britton, B, Howe, W, Eaton, C and Buka, J. 2015. "Positive associations of dispositional mindfulness with cardiovascular health: The New England family study". *International Journal of Behavioral Medicine*. Vol 22, number 4. Pp 540–550.

Lundberg, U, Hellström, B. 2002. "Workload and morning salivary cortisol in women". *Work & Stress*. Vol 16. Pp 356–363.

Lustig, R. 11 March 2014. "The complete skinny on obesity". Retrieved 19 April 2017 from http://www.uctv.tv/skinny-on-obesity/

Lustig, RH, Mulligan, K, Noworolski, SM, Tai, VW, Wen, MJ, Erkin-Cakmak, A and Schwarz, J. 2016. "Isocaloric fructose restriction and metabolic improvement in children with obesity and metabolic syndrome". *Obesity*. Vol 24, number 2. Pp 453–460.

Lustig, RH, Schmidt, LA and Brindis, CD. 2012. "Public health: The toxic truth about sugar". *Nature*. Vol 482, number 7383. Pp 27–29.

Lustig, RH. 2014. *Fat Chance: Beating the Odds Against Sugar, Processed Food, Obesity and Disease*. New York, USA. Plume.

Maddi, S, Harvey, R, Khoshaba, D, Fazel, M and Resurreccion, N. 2009. "Hardiness training facilitates performance in college". *The Journal of Positive Psychology*. Vol 4, number 6. Pp 566–577.

Mani, A, Mullainathan, S, Shafir, E and Zhao, J. 2013. "Poverty impedes cognitive function". *Science*. Vol 341, number 6149. P 976.

Marmot, M, Bosma, H, Hemingway, H, Brunner, E and Stansfeld, S. 1997. "Contribution of job control and other risk factors to social variations in coronary heart disease incidence". *Lancet*. Vol 350. Pp 235–239.

Matarazzo, J. 1980. "Behavioral health and behavioral medicine—Frontiers for a new health psychology". *American Psychologist*. Vol 35, number 9. Pp 807–817.

Matthewman, L, Rose, A and Hetherington, A. 2009. *Work Psychology: An Introduction to Human Behaviour in the Workplace*. New York, USA. Oxford University Press.

McLaren, N. 2006. "Interactive dualism as a partial solution to the mind–brain problem for psychiatry". *Medical Hypotheses*. Vol 66, number 6. Pp 1165–1173.

McLean, P. 1976. Cited in Spielberger, C and Sarason, IG (eds). *Stress and Anxiety*. Vol 3. Pp 297–323. New York, USA. Wiley.

Mikkonen, J, Raphael, D, York University: School of Health Policy Management and Canadian Electronic Library. 2010. *Social Determinants of Health: The Canadian Facts (Canadian Electronic Library. Documents Collection)*. Toronto. York University School of Health Policy and Management.

Morrison, V and Bennett, P. 2016. *An Introduction to Health Psychology*. Harlow, UK. Pearson.

Mulainathan, S and Shafir, E. 2013. *Scarcity: Why Having Too Little Means So Much*. New York, USA. Henry Holt.

Muntaner, C, Eaton, WW, Miech, R and O'Campo, P. 1 July 2004. "Socioeconomic position and major mental disorders". *Epidemiologic Reviews*. Vol 26, number 1. Pp 53–62.

Muratsubaki, T, Hattori, T, Li, J, Fukudo, S and Munakata, M. 2016. "Relationship between job stress and hypo-high-density lipoproteinemia of Chinese workers in Shanghai: The rosai karoshi study". *Chinese Medical Journal*. Vol 129, number 20. P 2409. Retrieved from http://go.galegroup.com.uml.idm.oclc.org/ps/i.do?p=HRCA&sw=w&u=univmanitoba&v=2.1&it=r&id=GALE%7CA467928796&asid=56e272ea6a5d3ba553487d8537128eda

Nabi, R, Prestin, A and So, J. 2013. "Facebook friends with (health) benefits? Exploring social network site use and perceptions of social support, stress, and well-being". *Cyberpsychology, Behavior and Social Networking*. Vol 16, number 10. Pp 721–727.

Nicol, M and World Economic Forum. 28 October 2015. "Which countries consume the most added sugar?" Retrieved 19 April 2017 from https://www.weforum.org/agenda/2015/10/which-countries-consume-the-most-added-sugar/

Norris, FH. 1999. "Stability and change in stress, resources, and psychological distress following natural disaster: findings from Hurricane Andrew". *Anxiety, Stress and Coping: An International Journal*. Vol 12, number 4. Pp 363–396.

O'Connell, J, Price, J, Roberts, S, Jurs, S and Mckinley, R. 1985. "Utilizing the health belief model to predict dieting and exercising behavior of obese and nonobese adolescents". *Health Education Quarterly*. Vol 12, number 4. Pp 343–351.

OECD. (2017). "Health, obesity update". Retrieved 9 September 2017 from http://www.oecd.org/health/obesity-update.htm

Ong, ZY and Muhlhausler, BS. 2011. "Maternal 'junk-food' feeding of rat dams alters food choices and development of the mesolimbic reward pathway in the offspring". *The FASEB Journal*. Vol 25, number 7. Pp 2167–2179.

Ouellette, SCO, Kobasa, SC, Maddi, SR, Puccetti, MC and Zola MA. 1985. "Effectiveness of hardiness, exercise and social support as resources against illness". *Journal of Psychosomatic Research*. Vol 29, number 5. Pp 525–533.

Pariona, A. 2016. "Top sugar consuming nations in the world". Retrieved 5 July 2017 from http://www.worldatlas.com/articles/top-sugar-consuming-nations-in-the-world.html.

Park, A. 27 October 2015. "How sugar affects the body: New study looks beyond calories". Retrieved 19 April 2017 from http://time.com/4087775/sugar-is-definitely-toxic-a-new-study-says/

Parry, G. 1986. "Paid employment, life events, social support, and mental health in working-class mothers". *Journal of Health and Social Behavior*. Vol 27, number 2. Pp 193–208.

Pascoe, M and Bauer, I. 2015. "A systematic review of randomised control trials on the effects of yoga on stress measures and mood". *Journal of Psychiatric Research*. Vol 68, number 270.

Pow, J, King, D, Stephenson, E and DeLongis, A. 2016. "Does social support buffer the effects of occupational stress on sleep quality among paramedics? A daily diary study". *Journal of Occupational Health Psychology*. Vol 22, number 1. Pp 71–85.

Press, A. 28 June 2016. "Chile seeks to fight obesity with new food labeling law". Retrieved 26 April 2017 from http://www.voanews.com/a/chile-seeks-to-fight-obesity-with-new-food-labeling-law/3395681.html

Queensland Country Life. 16 February 2012. "A spirited defence of Australia's sugar". *Queensland Country Life*. Ormiston, Australia. P 19. Retrieved from http://link.galegroup.com/apps/doc/A280108325/GIC?u=idjisedu&xid=d2716540

Sagan, C. 1977. *The Dragons of Eden: Speculations on the Evolution of Human Intelligence*. New York, USA. Ballantine.

Sapolsky, R. 1999. "Hormonal correlates of personality and social contexts: from non-human to human primates". In Panter-Brick, C and Worthman, C (eds). *Hormones, Health and Behaviour*. New York, USA. Cambridge University Press.

Sapolsky, RM. 2005. "The influence of social hierarchy on primate health". *Science*. Vol 308, number 5722. Pp 648–652.

Sapolsky, RM. 2009. *Why Zebras Don't Get Ulcers*. New York. Times Books.

Sarafino, EP and Smith, TW. 2017. *Health Psychology: Biopsychosocial Interactions*. (Ninth edition.) Hoboken, New Jersey, USA. John Wiley & Sons.

Seidlitz, L and Diener, E. January 1998. "Sex differences in the recall of affective experiences". Retrieved from https://www.ncbi.nlm.nih.gov/pubmed/9457787

Seligman, ME. 1 February 1972. "Learned helplessness". *Annual Review of Medicine*. Vol 23, number 1. Pp 407–412.

Selye, H. 1951. "The general-adaptation-syndrome". *Annual Review of Medicine*. Vol 2. Pp 327–342.

Shan, H, Yang, X, Zhan, X, Feng, C, Li, Y, Guo, L and Jin, H. June 2017. "Overwork is a silent killer of Chinese doctors: A review of karoshi in China 2013–2015". *Public Health*. Vol 147. Pp 98–100.

Sharot, T. 6 December 2011. "The optimism bias". *Current Biology*. Vol 21, number 23. R941–R945.

Shively, C and Clarkson, T 1994. "Social status and coronary artery atherosclerosis in female monkeys". *Arterioscler Thromb*. Vol 14. Pp 721–726.

Slaunwhite, AK. 2015. "The role of gender and income in predicting barriers to mental health care in Canada". *Community Mental Health*

Journal. Vol 51, number 621. doi:10.1007/s10597-014-9814-8.

Smith, S. 2014. "Mindfulness-based stress reduction: An intervention to enhance the effectiveness of nurses coping with work-related stress". *International Journal of Nursing Knowledge*. Vol 25, number 2. Pp 119–130.

Smith, B, Zautra, A and Stone, AA. 2002. "The role of personality in exposure and reactivity to interpersonal stress in relation to arthritis disease activity and negative affect in women". *Health Psychology*. Vol 21, number 1. Pp 81–88.

Sohl, SJ and Moyer, A. 2007. "Tailored interventions to promote mammography screening: A meta-analytic review". *Preventive Medicine*. Vol 45, number 4. Pp 252–261.

Sørensen, TI, Price, RA, Stunkard, AJ and Schulsinger, F. 14 January 1989. "Genetics of obesity in adult adoptees and their biological siblings". *BMJ*. Vol 298, number 6666. P 87.

Speisman, JC, Lazarus, RS, Mordkoff, A and Davison, L. 1964. "Experimental reduction of stress based on ego-defense theory". *Journal of Abnormal and Social Psychology*. Vol 68, number 4. Pp 367–380.

Steffen, PR, Smith, TB, Larson, M and Butler, L. 2006. "Acculturation to western societies as a risk factor for high blood pressure. A meta-analytic review". *Psychosomatic medicine*. Vol 68. Pp 386–97.

Sutton, J. 2010. "The battle of the sex differences". Retrieved 8 May 2017 from https://thepsychologist.bps.org.uk/volume-23/edition-11/battle-sex-differences

Tannenbaum, M, Hepler, J, Zimmerman, R, Saul, L, Jacobs, S, Wilson, K and Albarracín, D. 2015. "Appealing to fear: A meta-analysis of fear appeal effectiveness and theories". *Psychological Bulletin*. Vol 141, number 6. Pp 1178–1204.

Taubes, G. 16 April 2011. "Is sugar toxic?" Retrieved from http://www.nytimes.com/2011/04/17/magazine/mag-17Sugar-t.html

Thomee, S, Harenstam, A and Hagberg, M. 2011. "Mobile phone use and stress, sleep disturbances, and symptoms of depression among young adults—A prospective cohort study". *BMC Public Health*. Vol 11, number 66. Retrieved from http://go.galegroup.com.uml.idm.oclc.org/ps/i.do?p=HRCA&sw=w&u=univm

anitoba&v=2.1&it=r&id=GALE%7CA249717225&asid=27dd67c17199075c5bbfd0e6450fa234

Tolin, DF and Foa, E. 2006. "Sex differences in trauma and posttraumatic stress disorder: A quantitative review of 25 years of research". *Psychological Bulletin*. Vol 132, number 6. Pp 959–992.

Tonello, L, Rodrigues, F, Souza, J, Campbell, C, Leicht, A and Boullosa, D. 2014. "The role of physical activity and heart rate variability for the control of work related stress". *Frontiers in Physiology*. Vol 5.

Turner, M. 3 November 2014. "U.S. adult consumption of added sugars increased by more than 30% over three decades". Retrieved 19 April 2017 from http://www.obesity.org/news/press-releases/us-adult

Uchino, B, Cacioppo, JT and Kiecolt-Glaser, JK. 1996. "The relationship between social support and physiological processes: A review with emphasis on underlying mechanisms and implications for health". *Psychological Bulletin*. Vol 119, number 3. Pp 488–531.

Uehata, T. "Long working hours and stress-related cardiovascular attacks among middle aged workers in Japan". Cited in Shan, H, Yang, X, Zhan, X, Feng, C, Li, Y, Guo, L and Jin, H. June 2017. "Overwork is a silent killer of Chinese doctors: A review of karoshi in China 2013–2015". *Public Health*. Vol 147. Pp 98–100.

USDA. (n.d.). "Nutrition and your health: Dietary guidelines for Americans". Retrieved 19 April 2017 from https://health.gov/dietaryguidelines/dga2005/report/HTML/D3_DiscCalories.htm

Vedhara, K, McDermott, MP, Evans, TG, Treanor, JJ, Plummer, S, Tallon, D and Schifitto, G. 2002. "Chronic stress in nonelderly caregivers: Psychological, endocrine and immune implications". *Journal of Psychosomatic Research*. Vol 53, number 6. Pp 1153–1161.

Webber, L, Kilpi, F, Marsh, T, Rtveladze, K, Brown, M and Mcpherson, K. 2012. "High rates of obesity and non-communicable diseases predicted across Latin America". *PLoS One*. Vol 7, number 8. P E39589.

Weiss, J. June 1972. "Psychological factors in stress and disease". *Scientific American*. Vol 226.

Weissman, J, Pratt, LA, Miller, EA and Parker, JD. 2 June 2015. "Serious psychological distress among adults: United States, 2009–2013". Retrieved 16 April 2017 from https://www.cdc. gov/nchs/data/databriefs/db203.htm

WHO. 2002. "Physical inactivity a leading cause of disease and disability, warns WHO". Retrieved 19 April 2017 from http://www.who.int/ mediacentre/news/releases/release23/en/

WHO. 2011. "Rio political declaration on social determinants of health (declaration)". Retrieved 1 May 2017 from http://www.who. int/sdhconference/declaration/Rio_political_ declaration.pdf

WHO. 2013. "10 facts on noncommunicable diseases". Retrieved 19 April 2017 from http://www.who.int/features/factfiles/ noncommunicable_diseases/en/

WHO. 2016. "Dietary guidelines for Americans 2015–2020 (Eighth edition)". Retrieved 16 April 2017 from https://health.gov/ dietaryguidelines/2015/guidelines/

WHO. 2016. "Fiscal policies for diet and the prevention of noncommunicable diseases". Retrieved 24 April 2017 from http://www. who.int/dietphysicalactivity/publications/fiscal- policies-diet-prevention/en/

WHO. 2016. "Grand challenges for the next decade in global health policy and programmes". Retrieved from http://www. who.int/dg/speeches/2017/address-university- washington/en/

WHO. 2017. "Health promotion". Retrieved 24 April 24 from http://www.who.int/topics/ health_promotion/en/

Witte, K and Allen, M. 1 October 2000. "A meta-analysis of fear appeals: Implications for effective public health campaigns". *Health Education & Behavior*. Vol 27, number 5. Pp 591–615.

Wittekind, A and Walton, J. 2014. "Worldwide trends in dietary sugars intake". *Nutrition Research Reviews*. Vol 27, number 2. Pp 330–345.

World Health Report. 2013. "Research for universal health coverage". (n.d.). Retrieved from http:// www.who.int/whr/en/

Wu, JT, Boat, TF, National Academies of Sciences (US) and Institute of Medicine, (US). 2015. *Mental Disorders and Disabilities Among Low-Income Children*. Washington DC, USA. National Academies Press.

Unit 7: Human relationships

Adler, LL and Gielen, UP. 2003. *Migration: Immigration and Emigration in International Perspective*. Westport, Connecticut, USA. Praeger.

Al Ramiah, A and Hewstone, M. 2013. "Intergroup contact as a tool for reducing, resolving, and preventing intergroup conflict". *American Psychologist*. Vol 68. Pp 527–542.

Alhabash, S, Mcalister, A, Kim, W, Lou, C, Cunningham, C, Quilliam, E and Richards, J. 2016. "Saw it on Facebook, drank it at the bar! Effects of exposure to Facebook alcohol ads on alcohol-related behaviors". *Journal of Interactive Advertising*. Vol 16, number 1. Pp 44–58.

Allport, GW. 1954. *The Nature of Prejudice*. Reading, Massachusetts, USA. Addison-Wesley.

Altman, I and Taylor, DA. 1973. *Social Penetration: The Development of Interpersonal Relationships*. New York, USA. Holt, Rinehart and Winston.

Amato, PR. 1983. "Helping behavior in urban and rural environments: Field studies based on a taxonomic organization of helping episodes".

Journal of Personality and Social Psychology. Vol 45, number 3. Pp 571–586.

American Psychological Association. 2017. "Stress in America: Coping with change". Stress in America Survey.

Andrews, DA, Keissling JJ, Russell RJ and Grant BA. 1979. "Volunteers and the one to one supervision of adult probationers". Ontario Ministry of Correctional Services, Toronto.

Aronson, E and Patnoe, S. 1997. *The Jigsaw Classroom: Building Cooperation in the Classroom* (Second edition). New York, USA. Addison Wesley Longman.

Aronson, E and Patnoe, S. 2011. *Cooperation in the Classroom: The Jigsaw Method* (Third edition). London, UK. Pinter & Martin, Ltd.

Axelrod, R and Hamilton, W. 1981. "The evolution of cooperation". *Science*. Vol 211, number 4489. Pp 1390–1396.

Baron, AS and Banaji, MR. 2006. "The development of implicit attitudes". *Psychological Science*. Vol 17, number. Pp 53–58.

Batson, CD. 1991. *The Altruism Question: Towards a Social-Psychological Answer*. Hillsdale, New Jersey, USA. Lawrence Erlbaum.

Batson, CD and Shaw, LL. 1991. "Evidence for altruism: Toward a pluralism of prosocial motives". *Psychological Inquiry*. Vol 2. Pp107–122.

Batson, CD, Batson, JG, Griffitt, CA, Barrientos, S, Brandt, JR, Sprengelmeyer, P, Reis, HT. 1989. "Negative-state relief and the empathy–altruism hypothesis". *Journal of Personality and Social Psychology*. Vol 56, number 6. Pp 922–933.

Batson, CD, Dyck, JL, Brandt, JR, Batson, JG, Powell, AL, Mcmaster, MR, Reis, HT. 1988. "Five studies testing two new egoistic alternatives to the empathy—altruism hypothesis". *Journal of Personality and Social Psychology*. Vol 55, number 1. Pp 52–77.

BBC News. 20 September 2016. "India stabbing: Bystanders watch as Delhi woman killed". Retrieved 22 June 2017 from http://www.bbc.com/news/world-asia-india-37415843

Berscheid, E, Dion, K, Walster, E and Walster, GW. 1971. "Physical attractiveness and dating choice: A test of the matching hypothesis". *Journal of Experimental Social Psychology*. Vol 7, number 2. Pp 173–189.

Bierhoff, HW. 2009. *Prosocial Behaviour*. Hove, UK. Psychology Press.

Blake, RR and Mouton, JS. 1962. "Overevaluation of own group's product in intergroup competition". *Journal of Abnormal and Social Psychology*. Vol 64. Pp 237–238.

Bleske-Rechek, A, Vanden Heuvel, B and Vander Wyst, M. (n.d.). "Age variation in mating strategies and mate preferences: Beliefs versus reality". *Evolutionary Psychology*. Vol 7, number 2.

Blumer, H. 1958. "Race prejudice as a sense of group position". *Pacific Sociological Review*. Vol 1. Pp 3–7.

Bodenhausen, GV. 1988. "Stereotypic biases in social decision making and memory: Testing process models of stereotype use". *Journal of Personality and Social Psychology*. Vol 55. Pp 726–737.

Boxer, C, Noonan, M and Whelan, C. 2015. "Mate preferences". *Journal of Family Issues*. Vol 36, number 2. Pp 163–187.

British Social Attitude Survey. Accessed on bsa.natcen.ac.uk on 1 July 2017.

Brody, N and Vangelisti, A. 2015. "Bystander intervention in cyberbullying". *Communication Monographs*. Pp 1–26.

Brown, R. 2000. *Group Processes: Dynamics Within and Between Groups* (Second edition). Oxford. UK. Blackwell Publishing.

Buehlman, K, Gottman, JM and Katz, L. 1992. "How a couple views their past predicts their future: predicting divorce from an oral history interview". *Journal of Family Psychology*. Vol 5, numbers 3–4. Pp 295–318.

Burton-Chellew, MN, Ross-Gillespie, A and West, SA. 2010. "Cooperation in humans: competition between groups and proximate emotion". *Evolution and Human Behavior*. Vol 31, number 2. Pp 104–108.

Buss, D. 1989. "Sex differences in human mate preferences: Evolutionary hypotheses tested in 37 cultures". *Behavioral and Brain Sciences*. Vol 12, number 1. Pp 1–14.

Buss, D, Shackelford, T, Kirkpatrick, L and Larsen, R. 2001. "A half century of mate preferences: the cultural evolution of values". *Journal of Marriage and Family*. Vol 63, number 2. Pp 491–503.

Callaghan, D, Graff, M and Davies, J. 2013. "Revealing all: Misleading self-disclosure rates in laboratory-based online research". *Cyberpsychology, Behavior and Social Networking*. Vol 16, number 9. Pp 690–694.

Campbell, DT. 1958. "Common fate, similarity, and other indices of the status of aggregates of persons as social entities". *Systems Research and Behavioural Science*. Vol 3. Pp 14–25.

Campbell, DT. 1965. "Ethnocentric and other altruistic motives". In Levine, D (ed). *Nebraska Symposium on Motivation*. Vol 13. Pp 283–311. Lincoln, Nebraska, USA. University of Nebraska Press.

Carrère, S, Buehlman, K, Gottman, J, Coan, J, Ruckstuhl, L and Parke, D. 2000. "Predicting marital stability and divorce in newlywed couples". *Journal of Family Psychology*. Vol 14, number 1. Pp 42–58.

Catalano, R, Novaco, R and McConnell, W. 1997. "A model of the net effect of job loss on violence". *Journal of Personality and Social Psychology*. Vol 72, number 6. Pp 1440–1447.

CBC News. 22 October 2011. "The bystander effect". Retrieved 22 June 2017 from http://

www.cbc.ca/news/canada/the-bystander-effect-1.1059522

Chenoweth, E. 2010. "Democratic competition and terrorist activity". *The Journal of Politics*. Vol 72, number 1. Pp 16–30.

Chopik, W, O'Brien, E and Konrath, S. 2017. "Differences in empathic concern and perspective taking across 63 Countries". *Journal of Cross-Cultural Psychology*. Vol 48, number 1. Pp 23–38.

Cialdini, R, Schaller, M, Houlihan, D, Arps, K, Fultz, J, Beaman, A and Reis, HT. 1987. "Empathy-based helping: Is it selflessly or selfishly motivated?" *Journal of Personality and Social Psychology*. Vol 52, number 4. Pp 749–758.

Cikara, M, Botvinick, M and Fiske, S. 2011. "Us versus them: Social identity shapes neural responses to intergroup competition and harm". *Psychological Science*. Vol 22, number 3. Pp 306–313.

Clark, KB and Clark, MP. 1947. "Racial Identification and racial preference in Negro children". In Newcomb, TM and Hartley, EL (eds). *Readings in Social Psychology*. New York, USA. Holt, Rinehart and Winston.

Collins, N, Miller, L and Steinberg, RJ. 1994. "Self-disclosure and liking: A meta-analytic review". *Psychological Bulletin*. Vol 116, number 3. Pp 457–475.

Cook, SW. 1978. "Interpersonal and attitudinal outcomes in cooperating and interracial groups". *Journal of Research and Development in Education*. Vol 12. Pp 97–113.

Cuddy, A JC, Fiske, ST and Glick, P. 2008. "Warmth and competence as universal dimensions of social perception: the stereotype content model and the BIAS map". *Advances in Experimental Social Psychology*. Vol 40. Pp 61–149.

Darley, J, Latane, B and Mcguire, WJ. 1968. "Bystander intervention in emergencies: Diffusion of responsibility". *Journal of Personality and Social Psychology*. Vol 8, number 4. Pp 377–383.

Davidson, R, Dunne, J, Eccles, JS, Engle, A, Greenberg, M, Jennings, P, Jha, A, Jinpa, T, Lantieri, L, Meyer, D, Roeser, RW and Vago, D. 2012. "Contemplative practices and mental training: Prospects for American education". *Child Development Perspectives*. Vol 6, number 2. Pp 146–153.

De Dreu, CK, Greer, LL, Handgraaf, MJ, Shalvi, S, Van Kleef, GA, Baas, M, Ten Velden, FS, Van Dikj, E and Feith, SW. 2010. "The neuropeptide oxytocin regulates parochial altruism in intergroup conflict among humans". *Science*. Vol 328. Pp 1408–1411.

Dholakia, UM. 24 November 2015. "Why are so many Indian arranged marriages successful?" Retrieved 14 June 2017 from https://www.psychologytoday.com/blog/the-science-behind-behavior/201511/why-are-so-many-indian-arranged-marriages-successful

Dindia, K, Allen, M and Steinberg, R J. 1992. "Sex differences in self-disclosure: A Meta-analysis". *Psychological Bulletin*. Vol 112, number 1. Pp 106–124.

Dion, KK and Dion, KL. 1993. "Individualistic and collectivistic perspectives on gender and the cultural context of love and intimacy". *Journal of Social Issues*. Vol 49. Pp 53–69.

Dion, KK and Dion, KL. 1996. "Cultural perspectives on romantic love". *Personal Relationships*. Vol 3, number 1. Pp 5–17.

Dittes, J. 1959. "Attractiveness of group as function of self-esteem and acceptance by group". *Journal of Abnormal and Social Psychology*. Vol 59, number 1. Pp 77–82.

Dollard, J, Doob, L, Miller, NE, Mowrer, OH and Sears, RR. 1939. *Frustration and Aggression*. New Haven, Connecticut, USA. Yale University Press.

Dovidio, JF. 2010. Cited in *The Sage Handbook of Prejudice, Stereotyping and Discrimination*. London, UK. Sage.

Eisenberger, N, Lieberman, M and Williams, K. 2003. "Does rejection hurt? An fMRI study of social exclusion". *Science*. Vol 302, number 5643. Pp 290–292.

Esses, VM, Dovidio, JF, Jackson LM and Armstrong, TL. 2001. "The immigration dillemma: The role of perceived group competition, ethnic prejudice, and national identity". *Journal of Social Issues*. Vol 57. Pp 389–412.

Esses, VM, Hodson G and Dovidio, JF. 2003. "Public attitudes towards immigrants and immigration: Determinants and policy implications". In Beach, CM, Green, AG and Reitz, JG (eds). *Canadian Immigration Policy for the 21st Century*. Montreal, Canada. McGill Queen's Press.

Esses, VM, Jackson, L and Armstrong, T. 1998. "Intergroup competition and attitudes toward immigrants and immigration: An instrumental model of group conflict". *Journal of Social Issues*. Vol 54, number 4. Pp 699–724.

Esses, VM, Jackson, LM, Bennett-Abu, C and Ayyash, C. 2010. "Intergroup competition". In Dovidio, J, Hewstone, M, Glick, P and Esses, F. 2013. *The Sage Handbook of Prejudice, Stereotyping and Discrimination*. London, UK. Sage.

Essock-Vitale, SM and McGuire, MT. 1985. "Women's lives viewed from an evolutionary perspective: II. Patterns of helping". *Ethology and Sociobiology*. Vol 6. Pp 155–173.

Fein, S and Spencer, SJ. 1997. "Prejudice as self-image maintenance: Affirming the self through derogating others". *Journal of Personality and Social Psychology*. Vol 73. Pp 31–44.

Feldman, R, Gordon, I, Influs, M, Gutbir, T and Ebstein, RP. 2013. "Parental oxytocin and early caregiving jointly shape children's oxytocin response and social reciprocity". *Neuropsychopharmacology*. Vol 38, number 7. Pp 1154–1162.

Fine, MA and Harvey, JH. 2006. *Handbook of Divorce and Relationship Dissolution*. Mahwah, New Jersey, USA. Lawrence Erlbaum.

Fisher, H, Xu, X, Aron, A and Brown, L. 2016. "Intense, passionate, romantic love: A natural addiction? How the fields that investigate romance and substance abuse can inform each other". *Frontiers in Psychology*. Vol 7, number 687.

Fischer, P, Greitemeyer, T, Pollozek, F and Frey, D. 2006. "The unresponsive bystander: Are bystanders more responsive in dangerous emergencies?" *European Journal of Social Psychology*. Vol 36, number 2. Pp 267–278.

Fischer, P, Krueger, JI, Greitemeyer, T, Vogrincic, C, Kastenmuller, A, Frey, D and Kainbacher, M. 2011. "The bystander-effect: A meta-analytic review on bystander intervention in dangerous and non-dangerous emergencies". *Psychological Bulletin*. Vol 137, number 4. Pp 517–537.

Fiske, ST. 2010. *Social Beings: Core Motives in Social Psychology*. New York, USA. Wiley.

Flook, L, Goldberg, SB, Pinger, L and Davidson, RJ. 2015. "Promoting prosocial behavior and self-regulatory skills in preschool children through a mindfulness-based kindness curriculum". *Developmental Psychology*. Vol 51, number 1. Pp 44–51.

Fincham, F and O'Leary, KD. 1983. "Causal inferences for spouse behavior in maritally distressed and nondistressed couples". *Journal of Social and Clinical Psychology*. Vol 1, number 1. Pp 42–57.

Germán Hassel, GE. (n.d.). Penal especial (página 2). Retrieved from http://www.monografias.com/trabajos52/penal-especial/penal-especial2.shtml

Gosling, SD, Vazire, S, Srivastava, S and John, OP. 2004. "Should we trust web-based studies? A comparative analysis of six preconceptions about Internet questionnaires". *The American Psychologist*. Vol 59, number 2. Vol 93–104.

Gottman, PJ. 13 March 2017. "The empirical basis for Gottman Method couples therapy". Retrieved 17 June 2017 from https://www.gottman.com/blog/the-empirical-basis-for-gottman-method-couples-therapy/

Gottman, J and Levenson, R. 2002. "A two-factor model for predicting when a couple will divorce: Exploratory analyses using 14-year longitudinal data". *Family Process*. Vol 41, number 1. Pp 83–96.

Gottman, J, Coan, J, Carrere, S and Swanson, C. 1998. "Predicting marital happiness and stability from newlywed interactions". *Journal of Marriage and the Family*. Vol 60, number 1. Pp 5–22.

Gouvernement de Quebec. (n.d.). C-12 Charter of Human Rights and Freedoms. Retrieved 24 June 2017 from http://legisquebec.gouv.qc.ca/en/showdoc/cs/C-12

Greenberg, J, Pyszczynski, T, Solomon, S, Rosenblatt, A, Veeder, M, Kirkland, S and Lyon, D. 1990. "Evidence for terror management theory II: The effects of mortality salience on reactions to those who threaten or bolster the cultural worldview". *Journal of Personality and Social Psychology*. Vol 58, number 2. Pp 308–318.

Gupta, U and Singh, P. 1982. "An exploratory study of love and liking and type of marriages". *Indian Journal of Applied Psychology*. Vol 19, number 2. Pp 92–97.

Hamilton, W. 1964. "The genetical evolution of social behaviour". *Journal of Theoretical Biology*. Vol 7. Pp 1–16.

Harari, H, Harari, O and White, RV. 1985. "The reaction to rape by American male bystanders". *Journal of Social Psychology*. Vol 125, number 5. Pp 653–658.

Hartley, CA and Phelps, EA. 2010. "Changing fear: The neurocircuitry of emotion regulation". *Neuropsychopharmacology*. Vol 35, number 1. Pp 136–146.

Havlicek, J and Roberts, SC. 2009. "MHC-correlated mate choice in humans: A review". *Psychoneuroendocrinology*. Vol 34, number 4. Pp 497–512.

Henrich, J, Heine, S and Norenzayan, A. 2010. "The weirdest people in the world?" *Behavioral and Brain Sciences*. Vol 33, numbers 2–3. Pp 61–83.

Hilt, L. 2004. "Attribution retraining for therapeutic change: Theory, practice, and future directions". *Imagination, Cognition and Personality*. Vol 23, number 4. Pp 289–307.

Hilton, JL and von Hippel, W. 1996. "Stereotypes". *Annual Review of Psychology*. Vol 47, number 1. Pp 237–271.

Hirschlag, A. 25 March 2016. "Arranged marriage dating app claims to find your perfect match based on your Facebook page". Retrieved 14 June 2017 from http://www.sheknows.com/love-and-sex/articles/1116971/arranged-marriage-dating-app

Homans, GC. 1950. *The Human Group*. New York, USA. Harcourt, Brace and World.

Huang, H. 2016. "Examining the beneficial effects of individual's self-disclosure on the social network site". *Computers in Human Behavior*. Vol 57. Pp 122–132.

Hughes, I. 26 February 2015. "Why are men more likely to be violent than women?" Retrieved 25 June 2017 from http://www.thejournal.ie/readme/violence-against-women-1959171-Feb2015/

Hutcherson, C, Seppala, E, Gross, J and Phelps, EA. 2008. "Loving-kindness meditation increases social connectedness". *Emotion*. Vol 8, number 5. Pp 720–724.

Jankowiak, W and Fischer, E. 1992. "A cross-cultural perspective on romantic love". *Ethnology*. Vol 31, number 2. Pp 149–155.

Johnson, DW and Johnson, FP. 1987. *Joining Together: Group Theory and Group Skills*. (Third edition). Englewood Cliffs, NJ. Prentice Hall.

Johnson, RC, Danko, GP, Darvill, TJ, Bochner, S, Bowers, JK, Huang, YH, Park, JY, Pecjak, V, Rahim, ARA and Pennington, D. 1989. "Cross-cultural assessment of altruism and its correlates". *Personality and Individual Differences*. Vol 10, number 8. Pp 855–868.

Jones, JM. 1972. *Prejudice and Racism*. Reading, Massachusetts, USA. Addison-Wesley.

Jordan, MR, Jordan, JJ and Rand, DG. 2017. "No unique effect of intergroup competition on cooperation: Non-competitive thresholds are as effective as competitions between groups for increasing human cooperative behaviour". *Evolution and Human Behavior*. Vol 38, number 1. Pp 102–108.

Kajanus, A. 2016. "Social bonding and nurture kinship: Compatibility between cultural and biological approaches". *Social Analysis*. Vol 60, number 3. Pp 132–134.

Kamans, E, Gordijn, EH, Oldenhuis, H and Otten, S. 2009. "What I think you see is what you get: Influence of prejudice on assimilation to negative meta-stereotypes among Dutch Moroccan teenagers". *European Journal of Social Psychology*. Vol 39. Pp 842–851.

Karandashev, V. 2015. "A cultural perspective on romantic love". *Online Readings in Psychology and Culture*. Vol 5, number 4. http://dx.doi.org/10.9707/2307-0919.1135

Karney, BR and Bradbury, TN. 2000. "Attributions in marriage: State or trait? A growth curve analysis". *Journal of Personality and Social Psychology*. Vol 78, number 2. Pp 295–309.

Kenny, D and La Voie, L. 1982. "Reciprocity of interpersonal attraction: A confirmed hypothesis". *Social Psychology Quarterly*. Vol 45, number 1. Pp 54–58.

Knapp, ML, Caughlin, JP and Vangelisti, AL. 2014. *Interpersonal Communication and Human Relationships*. Boston, Massachusetts, USA. Pearson.

Knapp, ML and Vangelisti, AL. 1996. *Interpersonal Communication and Human Relationships*. (Third edition). Boston, Massachusetts, USA. Allyn and Bacon.

Koomen, W and van der Plugt, J. 2016. *The Psychology of Radicalization and Terrorism*. New York, USA. Routledge.

Latane, B and Rodin, J. 1969. "A lady in distress: Inhibiting effects of friends and strangers on bystander intervention". *Journal of Experimental Social Psychology*. Vol 5, number 2. Pp 189–202.

Latane, B, Darley, J and Mcguire, WJ. 1968. "Group inhibition of bystander intervention in emergencies". *Journal of Personality and Social Psychology*. Vol 10, number 3. Pp 215–221.

Latane, B and Nida, S. 1981. "Ten years of research on group size and helping". *Psychological Bulletin*. Vol 89, number 2. Pp 308–324.

Lavner, J, Karney, B, Williamson, H and Bradbury, T. 2016. "Bidirectional associations between newlyweds' marital satisfaction and marital problems over time". *Family Process*.

Le Bon, G. 1896. *The Crowd: A Study of the Popular Mind*. London, UK. T Fisher Unwin.

Leiberg, S, Klimecki, O, Singer, T and Verdejo García, A. 2011. "Short-term compassion training increases prosocial behavior in a newly developed prosocial game (compassion training increases prosocial behavior)". *PLoS ONE*. Vol 6, number 3. P E17798.

Levine, R, Martinez, T, Brase, G and Sorenson, K. 1994. "Helping in 36 U.S. cities". Journal of *Personality and Social Psychology*. Vol 67. Pp 69–81.

Levine, RV, Norenzayan, A and Philbrick, K. 2001. "Cross-cultural differences in helping strangers". *Journal of Cross-Cultural Psychology*. Vol 32, number 5. Pp 543–560.

Levinson, JD, Cai, H and Young, D. 2010. "Guilty by implicit racial bias: The guilty/not guilty implicit association test". *Ohio State Journal of Criminal Law*. Vol 8. Pp 1–21.

Levinson, J. 2007. "Forgotten racial equality: Implicit bias, decision making, and misremembering". *Duke Law Journal*. Vol 57, number 2. Pp 345–424. Retrieved from http://www.jstor.org/stable/40040596

Lisitsa, E. 12 June 2017. The Four Horsemen: Criticism, contempt, defensiveness, and stonewalling. Retrieved 17 June 2017 from https://www.gottman.com/blog/the-four-horsemen-recognizing-criticism-contempt-defensiveness-and-stonewalling/

Markey, P. 2000. "Bystander intervention in computer-mediated communication". *Computers in Human Behavior*. Vol 16, number 2. Pp 183–188.

McDonald, MM, Navarrette, CD and Van Vugt, M. 2012. "Evolution and the psychology of intergroup conflict: the male warrior hypothesis". *Philosophical Transactions of the Royal Society B*. Vol 367 Pp 670–679.

McWilliams, S and Barrett, A. 2014. "Online dating in middle and later life". *Journal of Family Issues*. Vol 35, number 3. Pp 411–436.

Miller, E. 2000. "Homosexuality, birth order, and evolution: Toward an equilibrium reproductive economics of homosexuality". *Archives of Sexual Behavior*. Vol 29, number 1. Pp 1–34.

Moreland, RL. 1985. "Social categorisation and the assimilation of 'new' group members". *Journal of Personality and Social Psychology*. Vol 48. Pp 1173–1190.

Morry, M. 2005. "Relationship satisfaction as a predictor of similarity ratings: A test of the attraction-similarity hypothesis". *Journal of Social and Personal Relationships*. Vol 22, number 4. Pp 561–584.

Myers, J, Madathil, J and Tingle, L. 2005. "Marriage satisfaction and wellness in India and the United States: A preliminary comparison of arranged marriages and marriages of choice". *Journal of Counseling and Development*. Vol 83, number 2. Pp 183–190.

Nadal, KL. 2012. "Mahal: Expressing love in Filipino and Filipino American families". In Paludi, MA (ed.), *The psychology of love (Vol 3)*. Santa Barbara, CA. Praeger

Neto, F, Da Conceição Pinto, M and Furnham, A. 2012. "Sex and culture similarities and differences in long-term partner preferences". *Journal of Relationships Research*. Vol 3. Pp 57–66.

Pardun, J. 1998. "Good Samaritan laws: A global perspective". *Loyola of Los Angeles International and Comparative Law Journal*. Vol 20, number 3. Pp 591–613.

Pavelchak, MA, Moreland, RL and Levine, JM. 1986. "Effects of prior group memberships on subsequent reconnaissance activities". *Journal of Personality and Social Psychology*. Vol 50. Pp 56–66.

Pettigrew, TF. 1998. "Intergroup contact theory". *Annual Review of Psychology*. Vol 49. Pp 65–85.

Phelps, EA, O'Connor, KJ, Cunningham, WA, Funayama, ES, Gatenby, JC, Gore, JC and Banaji, MR. 2000. "Performance on indirect measures of race evaluation predicts amygdala activation". *Journal of Cognitive Neuroscience*. Vol 12, number 5. Pp 729–738.

Piliavin, JA, Dovidio, JF, Gaertner, SL and Clark, RD. 1981. *Emergency Intervention*. New York, USA. Academic Press.

Post, SG. 2002. *Altruism and Altruistic Love: Science, Philosophy, and Religion in Dialogue*. New York, USA, Oxford University Press.

Quillian, L. 1995. "Prejudice as a response to perceived group threat: Population composition and anti-immigrant and racial prejudice in Europe". *American Sociological Review*. Vol 60. Pp 586–611.

Regan, P, Lakhanpal, S and Anguiano, C. 2012. "Relationship outcomes in Indian-American love-based and arranged marriages". *Psychological Reports*. Vol 110, number 3. Pp 915–924.

Reicher, SD and Stott, C. 2011. *Mad Mobs and Englishmen: Myths and Realities of the 2011 Riots*. London, UK. Robinson.

Rollie, SS and Duck, SW. 2006. "Stage theories of marital breakdown". In Harvey, JH and Fine, MA (eds). *Handbook of Divorce and Dissolution of Romantic Relationships*. Pp 176–193. Mahwah, New Jersey, USA. Lawrence Erlbaum Associates.

Rosenfeld, M and Thomas, R. 2012. "Searching for a Mate". *American Sociological Review*. Vol 77, number 4. Pp 523–547.

Różycka-Tran, J. 2017. "Love thy neighbor? The effects of religious in/out-group identity on social behaviour". *Personality and Individual Differences*. Vol 115. Pp 7–12.

Rusbult, C and Zembrodt, I. 1983. "Responses to dissatisfaction in romantic involvements: A multidimensional scaling analysis". *Journal of Experimental Social Psychology*. Vol 19, number 3. Pp 274–293.

Rusbult, C, Zembrodt, I, Gunn, L and Steiner, ID. 1982. "Exit, voice, loyalty, and neglect: Responses to dissatisfaction in romantic involvements". *Journal of Personality and Social Psychology*. Vol 43, number 6. Pp 1230–1242.

Rusbult, CE, Verette, J, Whitney, GA, Slovik, LF and Lipkus, I. 1991. "Accommodation processes in close relationships: Theory and preliminary empirical evidence (interpersonal relations and group processes)". *Journal of Personality and Social Psychology*. Vol 60, number 1. P 53.

Savelkoul, M, Scheepers, P, Tolsma, J and Hagendoorn, L. 2010. "Anti-muslim attitudes in the Netherlands: Tests of contradictory hypotheses derived from ethnic competition theory and intergroup contact theory". *European Sociological Review*. Vol 27, number 6. Pp 741–758.

Schneider, S. 2008. "Anti-immigrant attitudes in Europe: Outgroup size and perceived ethnic threat". *European Sociological Review*. Vol 24, number 1. Pp 53–67.

Schneiderman, I, Zagoory-Sharon, O, Leckman, JF and Feldman, R. 2012. "Oxytocin during the initial stages of romantic attachment: Relations to couples' interactive reciprocity". *Psychoneuroendocrinology*. Vol 37, number 8. Pp 1277–1285.

Schofield, J. 2010. "Realistic group conflict theory". In Levine, JM and Hogg, MA (eds). *Encyclopedia of Group Processes and Intergroup Relations*. Thousand Oaks, California USA. Sage.

Selfhout, M, Denissen, J, Branje, S, Meeus, W and Simpson, J. 2009. "In the eye of the beholder: Perceived, actual, and peer-rated similarity in personality, communication, and friendship intensity during the acquaintanceship process". *Journal of Personality and Social Psychology*. Vol 96, number 6. Pp 1152–1165.

Shackelford, T, Goetz, A, Buss, D, Euler, H and Hoier, S. 2005. "When we hurt the ones we love: Predicting violence against women from men's mate retention". *Personal Relationships*. Vol 12, number 4. Pp 447–463.

Sherif, M. 1966. *Group Conflict and Cooperation: Their Social Psychology*. London, UK. Routledge and Kegan Paul.

Sherif, M. 1977. "Crisis in social psychology: Some remarks towards breaking through the crisis". *Personality and Social Psychology Bulletin*. Vol 3. P 368.

Sherif, M and Sherif, CW. 1969. *Social Psychology*. New York, USA. Harper & Row.

Sidanius, J and Pratto, F. 1999. *Social Dominance: An Intergroup Theory of Social Hierachy and Oppression*. New York, USA. Harper & Row.

Slavin, RE. 1980. "Cooperative learning in teams: State of the art". *Educational Psychologist*. Vol 15. Pp 93–111.

Slavin, RE. 1985. "Cooperative learning: applying contact theory in desegregated schools". *Journal of Social Issues*. Vol 41. Pp 45–62.

Stewart-Williams, S. 2007. "Altruism among kin vs. nonkin: Effects of cost of help and reciprocal exchange". *Evolution and Human Behavior*. Vol 28, number 3. Pp 193–198.

Strathearn, L. 2011. "Maternal neglect: Oxytocin, dopamine and the neurobiology of attachment". *Journal of Neuroendocrinology*. Vol 23, number 11. Pp 1054–1065.

Stratton, P. 2003. "Causal attributions during therapy I: Responsibility and blame". *Journal of Family Therapy*. Vol 25, number 2. Pp 136–160.

Tajfel, H. 1978. "Social categorisation, social identity and social comparison". In Tajfel, H (ed). *Differentiation between social groups: Studies in the Social Psychology of Intergroup Relations*. London, UK. Academic Press.

Tajfel, H. 1982. "Social psychology of intergroup relations". *Annual Review of Psychology*. Vol 33, number 1. Pp 1–39.

Tajfel, H and Turner, JC. 1979. "An integrative theory of intergroup conflict". *The Social Psychology of Intergroup Relations*. Vol 33. P 47.

Taylor, L, Fiore, A, Mendelsohn, G and Cheshire, C. 2011. "'Out of my league': A real-world test of the matching hypothesis". *Personality and Social Psychology Bulletin*. Vol 37, number 7. Pp 942–954.

Toi, M, Batson, C and Steiner, ID. 1982. "More evidence that empathy is a source of altruistic motivation". *Journal of Personality and Social Psychology*. Vol 43, number 2. Pp 281–292.

Trivers, R. 1971. "The evolution of reciprocal altruism". *The Quarterly Review of Biology*. Vol 46, number 1. Pp 35–57.

Trotter CJ. 1990. "Probation can work, A research study using volunteers". *Australian Journal of Social Work*. Vol 43, number 2. Pp 13–18.

Trotter C. 1996. "The impact of different supervision practices in community corrections". *Australian and New Zealand Journal of Criminology*. Vol 29, number 1. Pp 29–46.

Trotter, C. 2009. "Pro-social modelling". *European Journal of Probation*. Vol 1, number 2. Pp 142–152.

Turner, JC. 1982. "Towards a cognitive redefinition of the social group". In Tajel, H (ed), *Social Identity and Intergroup Relations*. Cambridge, UK. Cambridge University Press.

Universiteit van Amsterdam (UVA). 15 June 2010. "Neurobiological cause of intergroup conflict: 'Bonding hormone' drives aggression towards competing out-groups". *Science Daily*. Retrieved 24 June 2017 from www.sciencedaily.com/releases/2010/06/100614114445.htm

Unkelbach, C, Forgas, JP and Denson, TF. 2008. "The turban effect: The influence of Muslim headgear and induced effect on aggressive responses in the shooter bias. *Journal of Experimental Social Psychology*. Vol 47. Pp 667–685.

Uskul, A, Lalonde, R and Cheng, L. 2007. "Views on interracial dating among Chinese and European Canadians: The roles of culture, gender, and mainstream cultural identity". *Journal of Social and Personal Relationships*. Vol 24, number 6. Pp 891–911.

Uskul, A, Lalonde, R and Konanur, S. 2011. "The role of culture in intergenerational value discrepancies regarding intergroup dating". *Journal of Cross-Cultural Psychology*. Vol 42, number 7. Pp 1165–1178.

Utz, S. 2015. "The function of self-disclosure on social network sites: Not only intimate, but also positive and entertaining self-disclosures increase the feeling of connection". *Computers in Human Behavior*. Vol 45. Pp 1–10.

Van Bommel, M, Van Prooijen, J, Effers, H and Van Lange, PM. 2012. "Be aware to care: Public self-awareness leads to a reversal of the bystander effect". *Journal of Experimental Social Psychology*. Vol 48, number 4. Pp 926–930.

Van Den Bos, Müller and Van Bussel. 2009. "Helping to overcome intervention inertia in bystander's dilemmas: Behavioral disinhibition can improve the greater good". *Journal of Experimental Social Psychology*. Vol 45, number 4. Pp 873–878.

Wagner, U, Christ, O and Heitmeyer, W. 2010. "Anti-immigration bias". In Dovidio, JF, Hewstone, M and Glick, P. *The SAGE Handbook of Prejudice, Stereotyping and Discrimination*. Pp 361–376. London, UK. Sage.

Webster, G. 2003. "Prosocial behavior in families: Moderators of resource sharing". *Journal of Experimental Social Psychology*. Vol 39, number 6. Pp 644–652.

Wedekind, C and Füri, S. 1997. "Body odour preferences in men and women: Do they aim for specific MHC combinations or simply heterozygosity?" *Proceedings, Biological Sciences.* Vol 264, number 138. Pp 1471–1479.

Wedekind, C, Seebeck, T, Bettens, F and Paepke, A. 1995. "MHC-dependent mate preferences in humans". *Proceedings of the Royal Society B: Biological Sciences.* Vol 260, number 1359. Pp 245–249.

Welch, S and Rubin, R. 2002. "Development of relationship stage measures". *Communication Quarterly.* Vol 50, number 1. Pp 24–40.

Whiting, B and Whiting, JW. 1975. *Children of Six Cultures.* Cambridge, Massachusetts, USA. Harvard University Press.

Winslow, JT, Hastings, N, Carter, SC, Harbaugh, CR and Insel, TR. 1993. "A role for central vasopressin in pair bonding in monogamous prairie voles". *Nature.* Vol 365, number 6446. Pp 545–548.

Winternitz JC and Abbate JL. 2015. "Examining the evidence for major histocompatibility complex-dependent mate selection in humans and nonhuman primates". *Research and Reports in Biology.* Vol 2015. Pp 73–88.

Xiaohe, X and King Whyte, M. 1990. "Love matches and arranged marriages: A Chinese replication". *Journal of Marriage and the Family.* Vol 52, number 3. Pp 709–722.

Ye, A. 30 November 2011. "China's first Good Samaritan law drafted in Shenzhen". Retrieved 24 June 2017 from http://shanghaiist. com/2011/11/30/chinas_first_good_samaritan_law.php

Zajonc, R and Mcguire, WJ. 1968. "Attitudinal effects of mere exposure". *Journal of Personality and Social Psychology.* Vol 9, number 2. Pp 1–27.

Zietsch, Morley, Shekar, Verweij, Keller, Macgregor and Martin. 2008. "Genetic factors predisposing to homosexuality may increase mating success in heterosexuals". *Evolution and Human Behavior.* Vol 29, number 6. Pp 424–433.

Zimbardo, P. 1969. "The human choice: individuation, reason and order versus deindividuation, impulse and chaos". In Arnold, WJ and Levine, D (eds). *Nebraska Symposium on Motivation.* Vol 17. Lincoln, Nebraska, USA. University of Nebraska Press.

Unit 8: Developmental psychology

Ainsworth, M, Blehar, M, Waters, E and Wall, S. 1978. *Patterns of Attachment: A Psychological Study of the Strange Situation.* Hillsdale, New Jersey, USA. Lawrence Erlbaum.

American Psychological Association and National Association of School Psychologists. 2015. "Resolution on gender and sexual orientation diversity in children and adolescents in schools". http://www.apa.org/about/policy/orientation-diversity.aspx

Andersen, ES and Kekelis, L.1986. "The role of sibling input in the language socialization of younger blind children". In Connor-Linton, J, Hall, C and McGinnes, M (eds). *Southern California Occasional Papers in Linguistics 11: Social and Cognitive Perspectives on Language.* Pp 141–156. Los Angeles, California, USA. University of Southern California Press.

Baddeley, AD, Lewis, V and Vallar, G. 1984. "Exploring the articulatory loop". *Quarterly Journal of Experimental Psychology.* Vol 36A. Pp 233–252.

Bandura, A. 1977. *Social Learning Theory.* Englewood Cliffs, New Jersey, USA. Prentice-Hall.

Bandura, A. 1986. *Social Foundations of Thought and Action: A Social Cognitive Theory.* Englewood Cliffs, New Jersey, USA. Prentice-Hall.

Barajas, GR, Philipsen, N and Brooks-Gunn, J. 2007. "Cognitive and emotional outcomes for children in poverty". In Crane, DR and Heaton, T (eds). *Handbook of Families and Poverty.* Pp 311–333. New York, USA. Sage.

Baron-Cohen, S, Leslie, AM and Frith, U. 1985. "Does the autistic child have a 'theory of mind'?" *Cognition.* Vol 21, number 1. Pp 37–46.

Batson, CD. 1991. *The Altruism Question: Toward a Social-Psychological Answer.* Hillsdale, New Jersey, USA. Lawrence Erlbaum.

Bem, SL. 1981. "Gender schema theory: A cognitive account of sex typing". *Psychological Review.* Vol 88. Pp 354–364.

Betancourt, TS, McBain, R, Newnham, EA and Brennan, RT. 2013. "Trajectories of internalizing problems in war-affected Sierra Leonean youth: Examining conflict and post conflict factors". *Child Development.* Vol 84. Pp 455–470.

Borke, H. 1975. "Piaget's mountains revisited: Changes in the egocentric landscape". *Developmental Psychology.* Vol 11, number 2. Pp 240–243.

Bowlby, J. 1958. "The nature of the child's tie to his mother". *International Journal of Psycho-Analysis,* Vol XXXIX. Pp 1–23.

Bowlby, J. 1959. "Separation anxiety". *International Journal of Psycho-Analysts.* Vol XLI. Pp 1–25.

Bowlby, J. 1960. "Grief and mourning in infancy and early childhood". *The Psychoanalytic Study of the Child.* Vol VX. Pp 3–39.

Bretherton, I. 1992. "The origins of attachment theory: John Bowlby and Mary Ainsworth". *Developmental Psychology.* Vol 28. Pp 759–775.

Brooks-Gunn, J and Duncan, GJ. 1997. "The effects of poverty on children". *The Future of Children: Children and Poverty.* Vol 7, number 2. Pp 55–71.

Burbank, V. 1994. *Fighting Women. Anger and Aggression in Aboriginal Australia.* Berkeley, California, USA. University of California Press.

Buttelmann, D, Carpenter, M, Call, J and Tomasello, M. 2007. "Enculturated chimpanzees imitate rationally". *Developmental Science.* Vol 10. F31–F38.

Call, J and Tomasello, M. 2008. "Does the chimpanzee have a theory of mind? 30 years later". *Trends in Cognitive Sciences.* Vol 12, number 5. Pp 187–192.

Casey, BJ, Tottenham, N, Liston, C and Durston, S. 2005. "Imaging the developing brain: what have we learned about cognitive development?" *Trends in Cognitive Sciences.* Vol 9, number 3. Pp 104–110.

Chugani, HT. 1999. "Metabolic imaging: A window on brain development and plasticity". *Neuroscientist.* Vol 5. Pp 29–40.

Chugani, HT, Behen, ME, Muzic, O, Juhasz, C, Nagy, F and Chugani, DC. 2001. "Local brain functional activity following early deprivation: A study of postinstitutionalized Romanian orphans". *Neuroimage.* Vol 14. Pp 1290–1301.

Chugani, HT and Juhasz, T. 2006. "Functional imaging of the developing human brain". In Coffey, CE and Brumback, RA (eds). *Pediatric Neuropsychiatry.* Philadelphia, Pennsylvania, USA. Lippincott Williams and Wilkins.

Cialdini, RB, Schaller, M, Houlihan, D, Arps, K, Fultz, J and Beaman, AL. 1987. "Empathy-based helping: is it selflessly or selfishly motivated?" *Journal of Personality and Social Psychology.* Vol 52, number 4. Pp 749–758.

Colapinto, J. 2001. *As Nature Made Him: The Boy Who Was Raised as a Girl.* New York, USA. Harper Perennial.

Costello, EJ, Compton, SN, Keeler, G and Angold, A. 2003. "Relationships between poverty and psychopathology: A natural experiment". *Journal of the American Medical Association.* Vol 290. Pp 2023–2029.

Crone, EA and Ridderinkhof, KR. 2011. "The developing brain: From theory to neuroimaging and back". *Developmental Cognitive Neuroscience.* Vol 1, number 2. Pp 101–109.

Csikszentmihalyi, M and Larson, R. 1984. *Being Adolescent.* New York, USA. Basic Books.

Curtiss, S, Fromkin, VA, Krashen, SD, Rigler, D and Rigler, M. 1974. "The development of language in Genie: A case of language acquisition beyond the 'critical period'". *Brain and Language.* Vol 1, number 1. Pp 81–107.

Damon, W and Killen, M. 1982. "Peer interaction and the process of change in children's moral reasoning". *Merrill-Palmer Quarterly.* Vol 28. Pp 347–378.

Davis, K. 1940. "Extreme social isolation of a child". *American Journal of Sociology.* Vol 45, number 4. Pp 554–565.

Davis, K. 1947. "Final note on a case of extreme isolation". *American Journal of Sociology.* Vol 52, number 5. Pp 432–447.

deVries, MW. 1984. "Temperament and infant mortality among the Masai of East Africa". *American Journal of Psychiatry.* Vol 141. Pp 1189–1194.

Dickerson, A and Popli, GK. 2016. "Persistent poverty and children's cognitive development: Evidence from the UK Millennium Cohort Study". *Journal of the Royal Statistical Society.* Series A, number 179. Pp 535–558.

Draper, P and Cashdan, E. 1988. "Technological change and child behaviour among the !Kung". *Ethnology.* Vol 27. Pp 339–365.

Duncan, GJ. 1988. "Volatility of family income over the life course". In Baltes, P, Featherman, D and Lerner, RM (eds). *Life-span Development and Behavior. Vol. 9*. Hillsdale, New Jersey, USA. Erlbaum.

Fagot, BI and Leinbach, MD. 1989. "The young child's gender schema: Environmental input, internal organization". *Child Development*. Vol 60. Pp 663–672.

Feder, HH, Phoenix, CH, and Young, WC. 1966. "Suppression of feminine behaviour by administration of testosterone propionate to neonatal rats". *Journal of Endocrinology*. Vol 34, number 1. Pp 131–132.

Feldman, R and Vengrober, A. 2011. "Posttraumatic stress disorder in infants and young children exposed to war-related trauma". *Journal of the American Academy of Child Adolescent Psychiatry*. Vol 50, number 7. Pp 645–658.

Giedd, JN. 2004. "Structural magnetic resonance imaging of the adolescent brain". *Annals of the New York Academy of Sciences*. Vol 1021. Pp 77–85.

Goy, RW and McEwen, BS. 1980. *Sexual Differentiation of the Brain*. Cambridge, Massachusetts, USA. MIT Press.

Hale, S, Bronik, MD and Fry, AF. 1997. "Verbal and spatial working memory in school-age children: Developmental differences in susceptibility to interference". *Developmental Psychology*. Vol 33. Pp 364–371.

Harlow, HF. 1958. "The nature of love". *American Psychologist*. Vol 13. Pp 673–685.

Harris, JR. 1995. "Where is the child's environment? A group socialization theory of development". *Psychological Review*. Vol 102. Pp 458–489.

Hay, DF, Payne, A and Chadwick, A. 2004. "Peer relations in childhood". *Journal of Child Psychology and Psychiatry*. Vol 45, number 1. Pp 84–108.

Hines, M. 2004. *Brain Gender*. New York, USA. Oxford University Press.

Hines, M, Brook, C and Conway, GS. 2004. "Androgen and psychosexual development: core gender identity, sexual orientation and recalled childhood gender role behavior in women and men with congenital adrenal hyperplasia (CAH)". *Journal of Sex Research*. Vol 41. Pp 1–7.

Hollos, M and Cowan, PA. 1973. "Social isolation and cognitive development: Logical operations and role-taking abilities in three Norwegian social settings". *Child Development*. Vol 44. Pp 630–641.

Howes, C. 1992. *The Collaborative Construction of Pretend*. New York, USA. SUNY Press.

Howes, C and Phillipsen, L. 1998. "Continuity in children's relationships with peers". *Social Development*. Vol 7. Pp 340–349. https://www.theguardian.com/science/2016/oct/06/apes-can-guess-what-others-are-thinking-just-like-humans

Iacoboni, M, Molnar-Szakacs, I, Gallese, V, Buccino, G, Mazziotta, JC and Rizzolatti, G. 2005. "Grasping the intentions of others with one's own mirror neuron system". *PLoS Biology*. Vol 3, number 3. e79.

James, SD. 2008. "Wild child 'Genie': A tortured life". ABC News. Archived from the original on 23 April 2013. Retrieved 4 March 2013.

Knafo, A, Zahn-Waxler, C, Van Hulle, J, Robinson, L and Rhee, SH. 2008. "The developmental origins of a disposition toward empathy: Genetic and environmental contributions". *Emotion*. Vol 8. Pp 737–752.

Kohlberg, L. 1966. "A cognitive-developmental analysis of children's sex-role concepts and attitudes". In Maccody, EE (ed). *The Development of Sex Differences*. Stanford, California, USA. Stanford University Press.

Kolb, B and Fantie, B. 1997. "Development of the child's brain and behavior". In Reynolds, CR and Fletcher-Janzen, E (eds). 2009. *Handbook of Clinical Child Neuropsychology*. New York, USA. Plenum Press.

Korenman, S, Miller, JE and Sjaastad, JE. 1995. "Long-term poverty and child development in the United States: Results from the National Longitudinal Survey of Youth". *Children and Youth Services Review*. Vol 17, number 1/2. Pp 127–151.

Krupenye, C, Kano, F, Hirata, S, Call, J and Tomasello, M. 2016. "Great apes anticipate that other individuals will act according to false beliefs". *Science*. Vol 354. Pp 110–114.

Leontyev, AA, Leontyev, DA, Sokolova, EE (eds). 2003. *Stanovleniye psihologii deyatel'nosti: Rannie raboti (Development of Psychology of Activity: Early works)*. Moscow. Smisl. (In Russian.)

Lorenz, KZ. 1935. "Der Kumpan in der Umwelt des Vogels" ("The companion in the bird's world"). *Journal fur Ornithologie*. Vol 83. Pp 137–213. (Abbreviated English translation published 1937 in *Auk*. Vol 54. Pp 245–273.)

Luo, H, Hu, X, Liu, X, Ma, X, Guo, W, Qiu, C and Li, T. 2012. "Hair cortisol level as a biomarker for altered hypothalamic-pituitary-adrenal activity in female adolescents with posttraumatic stress disorder after the 2008 Wenchuan earthquake". *Biological Psychiatry*. Vol 72. Pp 65–69.

Maccoby, EE. 1990. "Gender and relationships: A developmental account". *American Psychologist*. Vol 45. Pp 513–520.

Manuilenko, ZV. 1948. "Development of self-regulated behaviour in pre-school children". *Izvestiya APN RSFSR (Proceedings of Academy of Pedagogical Sciences of RSFSR)* Vol 14. Pp 89–125. (In Russian.)

Marcus, DE and Overton, WF. 1978. "The development of cognitive gender constancy and sex role preferences". *Child Development*. Vol 49. Pp 434–444.

Martin, CL and Halverson, CF. 1981. "A schematic processing model of sex typing and stereotyping in children". *Child Development*. Vol 52. Pp 1119–1134.

Mason, MK. 1942. "Learning to speak after six and one-half years of silence". *Journal of Speech Disorders*. Vol 7. Pp 295–304.

Masten, AS. 2014. "Global perspectives on resilience in children and youth". *Child Development*. Vol 85, number 1. Pp 6–20.

McDonald, N and Messinger, DS. 2011. "The development of empathy: How, when, and why". In Acerbi, A, Lombo, JA and Sanguineti, JJ (eds). *Free Will, Emotions and Moral Actions: Philosophy and Neuroscience in Dialogue*. IF-Press. http://www.psy.miami.edu/faculty/dmessinger/c_c/rsrcs/rdgs/emot/McDonald-Messinger_Empathy%20Development.pdf.

McFarlane, AC. 1987. "Posttraumatic phenomena in a longitudinal study of children following a natural disaster". *Journal of the American Academy of Child and Adolescent Psychiatry*. Vol 26. Pp 764–769.

Mead, M. 1935. *Sex and Temperament in Three Primitive Societies*. New York, USA. William Morrow.

Mead, M. 2003. *Sex and Temperament in Three Primitive Societies*. (First Perennial Edition). New York, USA. Harper Perennial.

Meltzoff, A. 1995. "Understanding the intentions of others: Re-enactment of intended acts by 18-month-old children". *Developmental Psychology*. Vol 31, number 5. Pp 838–850.

Miller-Johnson, S, Coie, JD, Maumary-Gremaud, A and Bierman, K. 2002. "Peer rejection and aggression and early starter models of conduct disorder". *Journal of Abnormal Child Psychology*. Vol 30, number 3. Pp 217–230.

Moreno, MA, Jelenchick, L, Koff, R, Eikoff, J, Diermyer, C and Christakis, DA. 2012. "Internet use and multitasking among older adolescents: An experience sampling approach". *Computers in Human Behavior*. Vol 28. Pp 1097–1102.

National Institute of Mental Health. 2015. "Helping children and adolescents cope with violence and disasters: what parents can do". Retrieved from www.nimh.nih.gov/health/publications/helping-children-and-adolescents-cope-with-violence-and-disasters-parents/index.shtml

Nedospasova, VA. 1985. "The role of perspective in the development of logical thinking". In Poddyakov, NN and Govorkova, AF (eds). *Razvitiye Mishleniya i umstvennoe vospitaniye shkol'nikov (Development of thinking and intellectual upbringing of pre-school children)*. Moscow. Pedagogika. (In Russian.)

Parker, JG, Rubin, KH, Erath, SA, Wojslawowicz, JC and Buskirk, AA. 2006. "Peer relationships, child development, and adjustment: A developmental psychopathology perspective". In Cicchetti, D and Cohen, DJ (eds). *Developmental Psychopathology: Theory and Method. Vol. 1*. (Second edition). Pp 419–493. Hoboken, New Jersey, USA. John Wiley and Sons Inc.

Peterson, CC and Siegal, M. 2002. "Mindreading and moral awareness in popular and rejected preschoolers". *British Journal of Developmental Psychology*. Vol 20. Pp 205–224.

Piaget, J. 1932. *The Moral Judgment of the Child*. Glencoe, Illinois, USA. Free Press.

Piaget, J and Inhelder, B. 1956. *The Child's Conception of Space*. London, UK. Routledge.

Povinelli, DJ and Eddy, TJ. 1996. "What young chimpanzees know about seeing". *Monograph of the Society for Research in Child Development*. Vol 61. Pp 1–152.

Premack, D and Woodruff, G. 1978. "Does the chimpanzee have a theory of mind?" *Behavioral and Brain Sciences*. Vol 1, number 4. Pp 515–526.

Prinstein, MJ and La Greca, AM. 2004. "Childhood peer rejection and aggression as predictors of adolescent girls' externalizing and health risk behaviors: A 6-year longitudinal study". *Journal of Consulting and Clinical Psychology*. Vol 72, number 1. Pp 103–112.

Roff, M. 1963. "Childhood social interactions and young adult psychosis". *Journal of Clinical Psychology*. Vol 19. Pp 152–157.

Rubin, KH, Burgess, KB and Hastings, PD. 2002. "Stability and social-behavioral consequences of toddlers' inhibited temperament and parenting behaviors". *Child Development*. Vol 73. Pp 483–495.

Ruffman, T, Garnham, W and Rideout, P. 2001. "Social understanding in autism: Eye gaze as a measure of core insights". *Journal of Child Psychology and Psychiatry*. Vol 42, number 8. Pp 1083–1094.

Saxe, R and Kanwisher, N. 2003. "People thinking about thinking people: The role of the temporo-parietal junction in 'theory of mind'". *NeuroImage*. Vol 19, number 4. Pp 1835–1842.

Schoon, I and Bartley, M. 2008. "The role of human capability and resilience". *Psychologist*. Vol 24, number 1. Pp 24–27.

Shaver, PR and Hazan, C. 1988. "A biased overview of the study of love". *Journal of Social and Personality Relationships*. Vol 5. Pp 473–501.

Shrum, W and Cheek, NH. 1987. "Social structure during the school years: Onset of the degrouping process". *American Sociological Review*. Vol 52. Pp 218–223.

Simner, ML. 1971. "Newborn's response to the cry of another infant". *Developmental Psychology*. Vol 5. Pp 136–150.

Smith, C and Lloyd, B. 1978. "Maternal behavior and perceived sex of infant: Revisited". *Child Development*. Vol 49. Pp 1263–1265.

Suomi, SJ and Harlow, HF. 1975. "The role and reason of peer relationships in rhesus monkeys". In Lewis, M and Rosenblum, LA (eds). *Friendship and Peer Relations*. New York, USA. Wiley.

Sylva, K, Bruner, JS and Genova, P. 1976. "The role of play in the problem solving of children 3+ –5 years old". In Jerome, S, Bruner, JS, Jolly, A and Sylva, K (eds). *Play: Its Role in Development and Evolution*. New York, USA. Basic Books.

Tronick, EZ, Morelli, GA and Winn, S. 1987. "Multiple caretaking of Efe (Pygmy) infants". *American Anthropologist*. Vol, 89, number 1. Pp 96–106.

Van Ijzendoorn, MH and Kroonenberg, PM. 1988. "Cross-cultural patterns of attachment; A meta-analysis of the Strange Situation". *Child Development*. Vol 59. Pp 147–156.

Vygotsky, LS. 1978. *Mind in Society: The Development of Higher Psychological Processes*. Translated by Cole M, John-Steiner, V, Scribner, S and Souberman, E (eds). Cambridge, Massachusetts, USA. Harvard University Press.

Werker, JF and Tees, RC. 1992. "The organization and reorganization of human speech perception". *Annual Review of Neuroscience*. Vol 15. Pp 377–402.

Whiting, B and Edwards, CP. 1973. "A cross-cultural analysis of sex differences in the behaviour of children aged three through 11". *Journal of Social Psychology*. Vol 91, number 2. Pp 171–188.

Williams, JE and Best, DL. 1982. *Measuring Sex Stereotypes: A Thirty Nation Study*. Newbury Park, California, USA. Sage.

Zahn-Waxler, C, Radke-Yarrow, M, Wagner, E and Chapman, M. 1992. "Development of concern for others". *Developmental Psychology*. Vol 28. Pp 126–136.

Unit 9: Internal assessment

Bransford, JD and Johnson, MK. 1972. "Contextual prerequisites for understanding: Some investigations of comprehension and recall". *Journal of Verbal Learning and Verbal Behavior*. Vol 11. Pp 717–726.

Loftus, EF and Palmer, JC. 1974. "Reconstruction of automobile destruction: An example of the interaction between language and memory". *Journal of Verbal Learning and Verbal Behavior*. Vol 13, number 5. Pp 585–589.

Unit 10: External assessment

Sapolsky, RM. 2017. *Behave: The Biology of Humans at Our Best and Worst*. New York, USA. Penguin Random House.

INDEX

Acknowledgements

The publisher and authors would like to thank the following for permission to use photographs and other copyright material:

Cover: PASIEKA/Getty Images; **p3:** Mary Evans Picture Library/Alamy Stock Photo; **p42:** Wikimedia Commons/Public Domain; **p43:** Jbarta/Wikimedia Commons/Public Domain; **p49:** Reprinted from N. F. Dronkers, O. Plaisant, M. T. Iba-Zizen, E. A. Cabanis; Paul Broca's historic cases: high resolution MR imaging of the brains of Leborgne and Lelong. Brain 2007; 130 (5): 1432-1441. doi: 10.1093/brain/awm042/© 2017 Oxford University Press; **p51(t):** Rice University/CC BY 4.0/http://cnx.org/contents/14fb4ad7-39a1-4eee-ab6e-3ef2482e3e22@8.81; **p51(m):** The Original Homunculus Company/Wikimedia Commons/CC BY-SA 4.0; **p51(b):** Special Collections Research Center, University of Chicago Library; **p53(l):** Scientific American/Michael Gazzinga/Eric Mose; **p53(r):** Scientific American/Michael Gazzinga; **p57(t):** Joel Sartore, National Geographic Photo Ark/Getty Images; **p57(b):** Reprinted from Merzenich, M. M., Nelson, R. J., Stryker, M. P., Cynader, M. S., Schoppmann, A. and Zook, J. M. (1984), Somatosensory cortical map changes following digit amputation in adult monkeys. J. Comp. Neurol., 224: 591–605. doi: 10.1002/cne.902240408; **p60:** Reprinted from Temporal and Spatial Dynamics of Brain Structure Changes during Extensive Learning/Journal of Neuroscience 7 June 2006, 26 (23) 6314-6317; DOI: 10.1523/JNEUROSCI.4628-05.2006; **p61:** Reprinted from Maguire EA, Gadian DG, Johnsrude IS, et al. Navigation-related structural change in the hippocampi of taxi drivers. Proceedings of the National Academy of Sciences of the United States of America. 2000;97(8):4398-4403., Copyright (2000) National Academy of Sciences, U.S.A; **p69:** Reprinted from Fisher, H., Aron, A. and Brown, L. L. (2005), Romantic love: An fMRI study of a neural mechanism for mate choice. J. Comp. Neurol., 493: 58–62. doi:10.1002/cne.20772; **p71:** Reprinted from Curt R. Freed, M.D., Paul E. Greene, M.D., Robert E. Breeze, M.D., Wei-Yann Tsai, Ph.D., William DuMouchel, Ph.D., Richard Kao, Sandra Dillon, R.N., Howard Winfield, R.N., Sharon Culver, N.P., John Q. Trojanowski, M.D., Ph.D., David Eidelberg, M.D., and Stanley Fahn, M.D., Transplantation of Embryonic Dopamine Neurons for Severe Parkinson's Disease, N Engl J Med 2001; 344:710-719, March 8, 2001, DOI: 10.1056/NEJM200103083441002; **p73:** Getty Images; **p75:** PHILIPPE PSAILA/SCIENCE PHOTO LIBRARY; **p76:** Reprinted from Woody, C & Kriplani, A & O'Connor, P & Pratte, Jean-Francois & Radeka, Veljko & Rescia, Sergio & Schlyer, David & Shokouhi, Sepi & Stoll, S & Vaska, Paul & Villanueva, A & Volkow, Nora. (2004). RatCAP: A small, head-mounted PET tomograph for imaging the brain of an awake RAT. Nuclear Instruments & Methods in Physics Research Section A-accelerators Spectrometers Detectors and Associated Equipment - NUCL INSTRUM METH PHYS RES A. 527. 166-170. 10.1016/j.nima.2004.03.114.; **p89:** 123rf; **p90:** Robin M. Hare, Sophie Schlatter, Gillian Rhodes, Leigh W. Simmons, R. Soc. open sci. 2017 4 160831; DOI: 10.1098/rsos.160831. Published 8 March 2017/CC BY 4.0; **p91:** David Cooney/CartoonStock; **p101:** Shutterstock; **p105:** Courtesy of Ed Himelblau; **p112:** Reprinted from Curtis, Val, Robert Aunger, and Tamer Rabie. "Evidence That Disgust Evolved to Protect from Risk of Disease." Proceedings of the Royal Society B: Biological Sciences 271.Suppl 4 (2004): S131–S133.; **p117:** Shutterstock; **p124:** Wikimedia Commons/Public Domain; **p125:** SAM FALK/SCIENCE PHOTO LIBRARY; **p143:** Reprinted from Journal of Verbal Learning and Verbal Behaviour, 11, John D. Bransford and Marcia K. Johnson, Contextual Prerequisites for Understanding: Some Investigations of Comprehension and Recall, 717-726, 1972, with permission from Elsevier.; **p143:** Reprinted from Journal of Verbal Learning and Verbal Behaviour, 11, John D. Bransford and Marcia K. Johnson, Contextual Prerequisites for Understanding: Some Investigations of Comprehension and Recall, 717-726, 1972, with permission from Elsevier.; **p147:** © 2011 Kietzmann et al/Kietzmann TC, Geuter S, König P (2011) Overt Visual Attention as a Causal Factor of Perceptual Awareness. PLoS ONE 6(7): e22614. doi:10.1371/journal.pone.0022614; **p148:** NASA; **p163:** Reprinted from Learning & Memory. 2005. 12: 1-2, Cold Spring Harbor Laboratory Press; **p166(t):** Shuttertsock; **p176(t, b):** iStockphoto;

p177: iStockphoto; **p190:** OUP; **p192:** Shuttertsock; **p200(t):** Lefteris Pitarakis/AP/REX/Shutterstock; **p200(b):** Nilufer Demir/Getty Images; **p201(tl):** David Ryder/Reuters; **p201(tr):** Jstone/Shutterstock; **p201(m):** Robert Hoetink/Shutterstock; **p201(b):** Peter MacDiarmid/REX/Shutterstock; **p203(t):** iStockphoto; **p203(bl):** Cultural DNA: The Psychology of Globalization, Gurnek Bains, 2015/Reproduced by permission of John Wiley & Sons, Inc.; **p203(br):** The Culture Map: Breaking Through the Invisible Boundaries of Global Business, Erin Meyer, 2014, Little, Brown; **p205(t):** IFLA; **p205(b):** The Selfish Gene, Richard Dawkins, 1976/2006, Oxford University Press; **p206:** Shutterstock; **p213:** Crazy Like Us: The Globalization of the American Psyche, Ethan Watters, 2010, Simon & Schuster; **p215:** KAZUHIRO NOGI/Getty Images; **p216:** United States Marine Corps/Lanc Cpl. Pedro Cardenas; **p217:** Wikimedia Commons/Public Domain; **p235(t):** Yang Liu Design; **p235(b):** Shutterstock; **p236(l-r):** Joel Parés Photography; **p238:** Courtesy of Project Implicit; **p239:** JOSE F. MORENO/REX/Shutterstock; **p240:** Whistling Vivaldi: How Stereotypes Affect Us and What We Can Do, Claude M. Steele, 2011, W. W. Norton & Company; **p241:** Courtesy of Concord Media; **p253:** 123rf/OUP; **p263:** Barbara Alper/Getty Images; **p265:** Chinese Classification of Mental Disorders, 3rd ed. Shandong, China: Shandong Science and Technology Press Co., Ltd.; 2001. Used with permisison.; **p277:** Bettmann/Getty Images; **p283:** David Cooney/CartoonStock; **p285:** Jennifer Shepard Payne, "Influence of Race and Symptom Expression on Clinicians' Depressive Disorder Identification in African American Men," Journal of the Society for Social Work and Research 3, no. 3 (2012): 162-177.; **p292:** Culture–gene coevolution of individualism–collectivism and the serotonin transporter gene, Joan Y. Chiao, Katherine D. Blizinsky, Proc. R. Soc. B 2010 277 529-537; DOI: 10.1098/rspb.2009.1650., Published 11 January 2010, Figure 2/CC-BY version 4.0; **p296:** Leif Skoogfors/Getty Images; **p331:** Shutterstock; **p334:** Reprinted from American Journal of Preventive Medicine, Volume 27, Issue 3, Adam Drewnowski, Obesity and the food environment Dietary energy density and diet costs, 154-162, Copyright 2004, with permission from Elsevier; **p336:** Shutterstock 123rf, OUP; **p346:** DILBERT © 1996 Scott Adams. Used By permission of ANDREWS MCMEEL SYNDICATION. All rights reserved.; **p347(t):** Sean Kilpatrick/The Canadian Press/PA Images; **p347(b):** helovi/iStockphoto; **p348(t):** © FDA; **p349:** OUP; **p356:** Carol Simpson Cartoons; **p359:** Bigstock; **p373:** Shutterstock; **p377:** Gwoeii/Shutterstock; **p381, 383:** Courtesy of The Gottman Institute www.gottman.com; **p398:** REX/Shutterstock; **p420, 424:** Shutterstock; **p431:** AFP/Getty Images; **p435:** Heritage Image Partnership Ltd/Alamy Stock Photo; **p440(l):** Premack, D. and Woodruff, G. (1978), "Chimpanzee problem-solving: A test for comprehension," Science 3, vol 202(4367), pp. 532-535; **p440(r):** Reprinted from Trends in Cognitive Sciences, Volume 12 , Issue 5, Call, Josep et al., Does the chimpanzee have a theory of mind? 30 years later / 187 - 192, Copyright 2008, with permission from Elsevier.; **p445(t):** Reprinted from NeuroImage 19 (2003) 1835–1842 , Saxe R, Kanwisher N, People thinking about thinking people. The role of the temporo-parietal junction in "theory of mind," Copyright 2003, with permission from Elsevier.; **p445(b):** Iacobon© 2005 Iacoboni et al/i M, Molnar-Szakacs I, Gallese V, Buccino G, Mazziotta JC, Rizzolatti G (2005) Grasping the Intentions of Others with One's Own Mirror Neuron System. PLoS Biol 3(3): e79. doi:10.1371/journal.pbio.0030079; **p451:** Shuttertsock; **p452:** Sipa Press/REX/Shutterstock; **p457-458:** The nature of love. Harlow, Harry F. American Psychologist, Vol 13(12), Dec 1958, 673-685/Public Domain; **p461:** Steve Winn/Anthrophoto; **p470:** Shutterstock; **p475:** Bettmann/Getty Images; **p479:** Ariadne Van Zandbergen/Alamy Stock Photo; **p491-528:** Shutterstock.

Artwork by Thomson.

Every effort has been made to contact copyright holders of material reproduced in this book. Any omissions will be rectified in subsequent printings if notice is given to the publisher.